BY THE EDITORS OF CO

MOVIE TRIVIA MANIA

BEEKMAN HOUSE
New York

Louis Weber, President
Publications International, Ltd.
3841 West Oakton Street
Skokie, Illinois 60076

Manufactured in the United States of America
10 9 8 7 6 5 4 3 2 1

Library of Congress Catalog Card Number: 84-61082

ISBN: 0-517-45251-0

This edition published by:
Beekman House
Distributed by Crown Publishers, Inc.
One Park Avenue
New York, New York 10016

Contributors: Steve Dale; Matthew Daniels; Philip Kaplan; John Kobal; Leon Michelson; P. Gregory Springer; Midge Stocker; Ian D. Toll; Bonny O. Van Orman.

Photographs: The Kobal Collection; The Museum of Modern Art, Film Stills Archive, New York.

Design: Phyllis Ritthaler

CONTENTS

ABOUT THIS BOOK

Movie Trivia Mania, crammed with thousands of facts, figures, quotes, behind-the-scenes stories, and quiz questions, is a source of endless fascination for everyone who loves movies. Something for everyone—that's what this book offers. Just consider what's here: illuminating and little-known facts about the making of some of the world's most famous movies; detailed biographies of nearly three hundred of the actors and actresses who have made —and continue to make— the movies great; profiles of fifty directors, past and present, who have made a distinctive contribution of the art of filmmaking.

There are pages of quotes by and about people in the film industry— quotes from performers on themselves and others, quotes from filmmakers on how they approach their work, quotes from the movies themselves. There are lists of the actors and actresses who have been the top box office draws over the years (and you'll find some surprising names there), and lists of the top moneymaking films—again, there are some surprises.

There's a special chapter on 'significant tens'— like ten of the most famous star teams in movie history, and ten teams for whom the chemistry just didn't work. And then, of course, there are the quizzes—question-and-answer quizzes and picture quizzes that add up to literally hundreds of mind-benders for movie lovers of all persuasions, from beginners to those who think they know it all.

To the movie trivia enthusiast, all this information is a source of endless fascination, building up an increasingly complete understanding of movies, the people who make them, and how the magic that finally appears on the screen comes about.

Movie trivia mania means not just knowing who played a certain role but who was originally slated for the part and why he or she didn't get it. It means knowing not only how Vivien Leigh came to play Scarlett O'Hara in *Gone With the Wind*, but also which actresses were in the running for the role before Leigh came along. It means being able to recognize the distinctive quality a certain director imparts to a film—and who influenced him. It means knowing not just the faces but the names of the great and valuable army of character actors who never became stars but spent their whole careers just beyond the spotlight.

Movie trivia mania means being able to name every film that Spencer Tracy and Katharine Hepburn—or Fred Astaire and Ginger Rogers, or Richard Burton and Elizabeth Taylor—ever made together; knowing which new film is a remake of a classic *and* when the original was made and who starred in it; knowing who won the best actor Oscar in a certain year and who he was competing against for the honor.

Movie trivia mania means being able to quote *exactly* what Humphrey Bogart said to the piano player in *Casablanca* (he did *not* say, "Play it again, Sam"). It means knowing which classic popular song was introduced in which movie—and who sang it. It means knowing which films made it big at the box office, which were the biggest bombs of all time, which films *should* have made it big but bombed anyway. And all this information is in this book.

So here it is: a compendium of challenging, compelling movie trivia for everyone who loves movies and is interested in what brings the magic to the screen.

In *Movie Trivia Mania* we've tried to provide something for everyone. But we had to stop somewhere. It's possible that your favorite movie of all time does not appear in the anecdote chapter; or a cherished performer is left out of one of the chapters on actors and actresses; or you can't understand how even so tight a list of di-rectors could possibly exclude someone whose work you particularly admire. In such a case, attribute the omission not to neglect, but to lack of space. Even in a movie trivia book as comprehensive as this one, it's impossible to include everybody's personal favorites. Deciding who (and what) to put in or leave out was a major challenge for everyone who contributed to this book.

Another point: movie trivia is, almost by definition, sometimes extremely difficult to pin down. Much of the history of the movies is already the stuff of legend. There comes a time when fact and fiction merge and it's very hard to separate the two. Trying to do so, though, is one of the challenges the true trivia enthusiast accepts with pleasure. There's also information which simply isn't available, and this is sometimes the case with biographical details about performers who are unwilling to expose their private lives to public scrutiny. The information in this book is as complete as we can get it; some details are just not to be found.

All in all, *Movie Trivia Mania* is a treasure trove for anyone who loves movies and is fascinated by the people who make them. It's a book to have fun with and to learn from. We hope you do both.

4

THE STORIES BEHIND
THE MAKING
OF THE MOVIES

*How did Marlon Brando transform himself
into the 70-year-old Don Corleone in* The
Godfather? *How did Linda Blair's head do
that terrifying 360-degree turn in* The Exorcist? *Why did the special effects people on*
E.T. *have so much trouble getting the little
extra-terrestrial's heart to glow? Why didn't
Richard Burton want to play opposite
Elizabeth Taylor in* Who's Afraid of Virginia
Woolf? *Find the answers in these fascinating stories behind the movies and learn why
what appears on the screen is only half the
story: the other half is what went on behind
the scenes. Here we take you behind the
scenes of some movies that have become,
or are on the way to becoming, classics.*

THE ADVENTURES OF ROBIN HOOD

1938
Directors, Michael Curtiz and William Keighley
Producer, Hal B. Wallis

The Adventures of Robin Hood was originally developed by Warner Brothers as a James Cagney vehicle. Cagney, who could do gangster films as well as musicals, was always interested in expanding his repertoire. However, Cagney left Warners in 1935 over a contract dispute, and by the time he came back there was a new star at the studio.

Errol Flynn was a relatively obscure Australian actor until 1935 when he was given the lead in the swashbuckling film *Captain Blood*. The role was originally intended for Robert Donat, but he walked out of the film because of an argument with the studio. Flynn was screen-tested with the then unknown Olivia de Havilland; they both got the parts, which turned them into instant stars. The film was such a success that a follow-up teaming seemed in order, so both Flynn and de Havilland were cast in *Robin Hood*, along with Basil Rathbone who had also played in *Captain Blood*, and Alan Hale who played Little John, repeating the role he played in the silent Douglas Fairbanks version of the Robin Hood story.

The forest locations for the film were shot in Bid-

The Adventures of Robin Hood

well Park in Chico, California, 350 miles from Los Angeles. There the film proceeded normally, and there Errol Flynn behaved like Errol Flynn. He had a habit of taking joyrides in private airplanes. He was a professional pilot, but even so the studio was worried about the occasional updraft which might put an end to both their star and their multimillion-dollar film. Flynn was given direct orders not to fly so he did the next best thing, he drank. Whenever he started a film, Flynn would conspire with his makeup men to replace their bottles of cologne and skin freshener with colored gin and vodka, which he would drink surreptitiously. There was little the studio could do about this; besides, it was better than flying.

Another problem was that the film's budget kept mounting and mounting with no sign of an end in sight. When the crew came back from Chico director

William Keighley was taken off the film and Michael Curtiz, who had directed *Captain Blood*, was brought in to replace him. Flynn disliked Curtiz but had little choice in the matter. Curtiz was a workmanlike director, and the film was finished at a much faster pace.

The score was written by Erich Wolfgang Korngold, a serious composer of operas and symphonies. He was called in from his home in Vienna to screen the film and decide whether or not he would accept the assignment. He didn't like the film, and said no. However, he soon changed his mind when he heard about Hitler's meeting with the Chancellor of Austria. Korngold decided it would be safer to stay in America—a wise choice. Shortly after he started work, the Nazis invaded Austria, and Korngold's property was confiscated. Moreover, Korngold won an Oscar for *The Adventures of Robin Hood*.

AN AFFAIR TO REMEMBER

1957
Director, Leo McCarey
Producer, Jerry Wald

An Affair to Remember was made because Leo McCarey's fortunes were low. Although he had once been one of Hollywood's most successful directors—he directed such films as *The Awful Truth* (1937) and *Going My Way* (1944), as well as some of Laurel and Hardy's greatest movies—he was now ill and hadn't had a hit in several years. Faced with the need for a surefire project he was drawn back to one of his older films, *Love Affair* (1939). *Love Affair* was a romantic film, starring Charles Boyer and Irene Dunne, concerning two people who meet on an ocean liner, fall in love, and arrange a rendezvous on land. However, Irene Dunne never makes the rendezvous because she is hit by a car and is paralyzed. McCarey replaced the winning combination of Dunne and Boyer with the even more fetching Deborah Kerr and Cary Grant.

Grant had always wanted to play the male lead in this film. Years earlier he had visited the set of *Love Affair* and been enthralled with the script. He was, therefore, overjoyed at the opportunity to remake the film. McCarey was a little more cautious. He had worked with Grant on the classic *The Awful Truth* (winning an Academy Award in the process) and found Grant difficult to work with. In McCarey's opinion, Grant was too tense, unsure, and uneasy.

An Affair to Remember

THE AFRICAN QUEEN

1951
Director, John Huston
Producer, Sam Spiegel

The African Queen was originally planned as a vehicle for Elsa Lanchester and her husband, Charles Laughton. Then Bette Davis had hopes of doing it with James Mason. When director John Huston teamed up with producer Sam Spiegel, Spiegel thought Humphrey Bogart and Katharine Hepburn, who had never worked together, would make an exciting team as the boozing Charlie Allnut and the missionary Rosie. It was an inspired combination.

Huston not only directed the film; he helped write the screenplay adaptation of C. S. Forester's novel, and he requested that James Agee co-write. He had never met Agee but greatly admired him, and when the two men went off to a Santa Barbara resort to work in peace and quiet they became good friends. It was Huston's idea that they take the opportunity, away from temptation, to live the clean life—tennis twice a day and early to bed. When the writing was nearly finished Agee had a heart attack, and it was then Huston learned that Agee had slipped back into the habit of writing all night. That schedule, combined with the tennis, had done him in. Agee left the job to recuperate and, with the help of writer Peter Viertel, Huston finished the script.

When *An Affair to Remember* started shooting, however, McCarey discovered a changed Grant—the actor was now completely relaxed and calm. What McCarey didn't know was that Grant had just started a new type of psychoanalysis. In this experimental program the patients were told to relax on a bed with their eyes and ears covered, and were then given doses of the new drug LSD. No wonder Grant was relaxed.

Although Deborah Kerr plays a nightclub singer and sings several songs during the course of the film, it is not her voice we hear on the screen. Instead we hear the voice of Marni Nixon. Nixon dubbed several non-singing actresses, including Deborah Kerr again in *The King and I* (1956) and Audrey Hepburn in *My Fair Lady* (1964). The songs that Kerr (or Nixon) sings in *An Affair to Remember* are notable because they are by songwriter Harry Warren, one of the most prolific of Hollywood tunesmiths, who had written dozens of standards including "Chattanooga Choo Choo," "Lullaby of Broadway," and "42nd Street." Warren stopped writing for films because he was squeezed out when, during the '50s, soundtrack composers such as Max Steiner became more demanding, wanting not only to compose the soundtrack but to write the songs as well. Since Warren would not compose soundtracks he had nothing to do, except live off his residuals.

The African Queen

Then it was off to Africa for location scouting. Huston had never been to Africa and he began spending time in the bush playing great white hunter. Sam Spiegel learned of Huston's big game activities and wondered if the director would settle down long enough to shoot the movie. A wrecked boat was restored to serve as the *African Queen*, but it sank just about the time Spiegel called to see how work was progressing. The boat was floated and patched, and things got back to normal. Huston set up camp and built a restaurant and bar almost as good as the studio canteen. A local native was hired to supply the company with fresh meat, which he called "long pig." But one day the fellow was arrested, suspected of having something to do with the mysterious disappearance of nearby villagers. It was then that Huston realized what long pig was.

What with the soldier ants, the black mamba snakes, the wasps, the heat, and the diarrhea, filming *The African Queen* was hardly a walk in the woods. Some days while the crew was shooting on the mock-up of the *Queen*, a family of baboons would take front row seats and provide an audience.

Katharine Hepburn took to Africa like an old hand, pitching in wherever needed, but Bogie would just as soon have been home. He was not happy with his portrayal of Charlie Allnut until Huston defined the character for him. As soon as Bogie began to understand Charlie, he put his heart into his performance, and his acting won him an Academy Award for best actor.

All About Eve

ALL ABOUT EVE

1950
Director, Joseph L. Mankiewicz
Producer, Darryl F. Zanuck

Bette Davis was born to play Margo Channing, the woman whose career Eve (Anne Baxter) sets her sights on in *All About Eve*. Some believe it was Davis' greatest achievement as an actress, and she won two critics' awards for it. Davis, at 42, was at the peak of her career, a star who had earned her stripes through various studio battles.

The part of Margo Channing had been written for Gertrude Lawrence, but when Lawrence insisted on singing along with the piano on "Liebestraum" during her drunk scene, director Joseph Mankiewicz resisted, and Lawrence walked out. Claudette Colbert was then considered for the part, but a skiing accident delayed her and Bette Davis was signed. Mankiewicz was warned that he would have trouble with Davis, that she would rewrite every line and end up directing the movie herself, but he found that just the opposite was true. She was early to the set, knew her lines, and performed well with the entire company, which included newcomer Marilyn Monroe.

Designer Edith Head was borrowed from Paramount just to design Davis' clothing. One day, during a fitting, Davis suddenly fell to the floor. Head was horrified, thinking there must be something wrong with the dress, but Davis explained she was merely testing it for a scene. That scene never did get shot, but one that did was of Davis and Celeste Holm stranded in a car on a wintry night. Bundled in their warmest mink coats, they were actually sitting on a studio sound stage in 90-degree Hollywood heat.

Although *All About Eve* received fourteen Academy Award nominations (a record) and garnered six Oscars (one for best picture), Bette Davis did not win the prize. In a move characteristic of Eve, Anne Baxter hinted that she should be placed in the best actress rather than the best supporting actress category, and—with the votes split between her and Bette Davis—neither woman won.

ALL QUIET ON THE WESTERN FRONT

1930
Director, Lewis Milestone
Producer, Carl Laemmle, Jr.

After the success of such anti-war spectaculars as *Wings* (1927) and *The Big Parade* (1925), Universal decided to film Erich Maria Remarque's best-seller *All Quiet on the Western Front*. The film was begun as a silent, but after a few weeks shooting production was halted and it was redone as a talkie. After it was finished it was sent back for more reshooting, this time because in previews it was shown with a comedy short starring Zasu Pitts, who also played the mother of hero Paul Baumer (Lew Ayres) in *All Quiet*. Consequently audiences laughed at her even though her part was serious, so her scenes were reshot with Beryl Mercer.

Lew Ayres, who became a star after the success of *All Quiet*, had been a musician in the Coconut Grove orchestra when he decided to become an actor. After a few bit roles he acted opposite Greta Garbo in *The Kiss* in 1929. *All Quiet* was to affect him deeply—he was a conscientious objector during the Second World War, a fact which almost destroyed his reputation until it was learned that he had served with distinction in the Medical Corps.

The film was shot on a ranch in Southern California where 28 acres were turned into a replica of the Western Front and two thousand ex-servicemen were hired as extras. In an ironic bit of casting, the French soldier with whom Baumer shares a foxhole, not realizing at first that the soldier is dead, was played by Raymond Griffith, the brilliant silent comedian whose career was cut short because his low voice would not record. Even though the battle scenes were worked out with military precision,

director Lewis Milestone had trouble coming up with a suitable ending. The one that was used—Baumer being shot by a sniper as he reaches out for a butterfly—was a bit of eleventh-hour improvisation. The reason only Baumer's hands were shown was because Ayres had long finished his part in the production—the hands belonged to Milestone.

Although the film was a critical and commercial success in the United States, it did not go over too well in Germany. The Nazis picketed the movie theatres and disrupted screenings by loosing rats and snakes in the theatres. Ultimately the Berlin censors banned it for its "demoralizing effect on youth." All this was to catch up with Remarque himself. The Nazis burned his book, confiscated his bank account, and revoked his citizenship. He went into exile, eventually settling in Hollywood where he later married noted leading lady Paulette Goddard.

AMERICAN GRAFFITI

1973
Director, George Lucas
Producer, Francis Ford Coppola

When George Lucas proposed the script for *American Graffiti* he was a talent who could, at best, be termed promising. He had turned his senior film project into a feature-length film, *THX-1138* (1971), which was stylish and intelligent but also dull and unpopular; that was the extent of his credits. Universal Studios gave a thumbs-down to the project because they didn't like the script and because it would have a cast of unknowns. They didn't close the door completely, though, and said they would make the film if Lucas could get a big name connected to the project. Since Lucas specifically didn't want a "star" in the cast, he decided to look for an important producer.

While Francis Ford Coppola was making *Finian's Rainbow* (1967), Lucas—who had won a scholarship to observe the filming—became a protégé of Coppola. And when Coppola agreed to produce the film Universal snapped to attention. Coppola had just finished *The Godfather* (1972) and could do no wrong. Coppola, however, did more than just donate his name and leave. He proved helpful on more than one occasion. Lucas was director of photography for the film as well as director. He knew exactly what sort of look the film should have and thought that only he

All Quiet on the Western Front

American Graffiti

AN AMERICAN IN PARIS

1951
Director, Vincente Minnelli
Producer, Arthur Freed

The idea of *An American in Paris* came up one night when musical producer Arthur Freed was playing pool over at the home of his friend Ira Gershwin. Freed asked Ira what he thought about the idea of MGM making a movie based on George Gershwin's symphonic tone poem "An American in Paris." Gershwin said it would be fine as long as the 17-minute piece was performed in its entirety in the film. With a handshake and a title, the film was put in motion.

Once Vincente Minnelli was chosen as director and Alan Jay Lerner had written the screenplay (one of the few of his musicals where he did not write the songs as well), casting began. Gene Kelly was an obvious choice for Jerry Mulligan, the American in Paris, and Oscar Levant for Adam Cook, Mulligan's friend who is described in the film as the world's oldest child prodigy. However, when it came to casting Lise, the French girl with whom Mulligan falls in love, the filmmakers' plans went awry. Cyd Charisse was the number one choice, and she was greatly excited because she knew this film could make her a star. But she was prevented from doing the picture because she became pregnant, and she had to wait another year before getting her first important screen role in *Singin' in the Rain* (1952). Stuck for someone to replace Charisse, Gene Kelly remembered a girl who had been featured in a Roland Petit ballet two years before. Kelly went to France, located Leslie Caron, and made the 20-

could achieve it. However, when Coppola dropped by the set one day he was confronted by an exhausted Lucas. Coppola convinced Lucas that he needed help and that he knew someone who wouldn't give the film a "slick" look, and cameraman Haskell Wexler came onto the scene. To keep things right with the studio, Wexler worked in his spare time for nothing. In gratitude, Lucas gave him a share in the film, which resulted in a phenomenally high salary.

When the film was completed, it was premiered before an enthusiastic audience. The Universal executives, however, were not pleased with the movie and demanded cuts and rephotography. After listening to these negative reactions for a while Coppola blew up and said that if they didn't like the film

he would buy it from them and release it himself. Universal, much to their later gain, backed down.

Still, the studio did alter the film slightly. They made about ten minutes worth of cuts, allowing Lucas to re-release the film years later in an expanded edition (which gave the world the opportunity to hear Harrison Ford sing "Some Enchanted Evening" in one of his few solos). The most damaging change they made concerned the soundtrack. The film had been recorded in stereo and designed for stereo. Universal released the film in mono.

Eventually the film made stars of virtually all of its unknown actors, including Suzanne Somers who, playing the "Girl in the T-Bird," doesn't say a word during the course of the film.

An American in Paris

year-old dancer into a star.

The role of the French entertainer was written for Maurice Chevalier, but he was unavailable and another French performer, Georges Guetary, was chosen. His big number was "I'll Build a Stairway to Paradise," where he walks up a giant set of steps which light up. His accent was so thick that there was a problem getting him to sing the song so he could be understood. But after exhausting rehearsals and many retakes, an intelligible recording was produced.

The ballet at the end of the film proved the most controversial aspect of the production. Minnelli had finished the entire movie except for this ballet, and hadn't even done any choreography for it. Worse, the film had gone over budget. A rough cut of the film was screened and people like screenwriter and lyricist Betty Comden, who was working for MGM but not on this movie, upset Minnelli by saying the film was good enough to release as it was. Irving Berlin also sounded his note of gloom, claiming that movie audiences weren't ready for ballet. However, MGM head Dore Schary thought the ballet sounded charming, and that was enough for him.

The most striking thing about the ballet is the cartoon-like sets, which are drawn in the style of French painters. The original concept was to shoot the ballet on location in Paris, but this would have cost too much money. The ballet took so long to prepare that Minnelli directed *Father's Little Dividend* (1951) while waiting.

ANNIE HALL

1977
Director, Woody Allen
Producer, Charles H. Joffe

What better name than *Annie Hall* for a film about a neurotic Jewish comedian's love affair with a flighty Midwestern WASP named Annie Hall? Well, how about *Anhedonia*? The word means an inability to experience pleasure, and to Woody Allen it seemed a perfect title for a movie about a 40-year-old New Yorker looking back on his life, his aspirations, his relationships with women, and his feelings about the banality of life.

But that, you may say, is not what the film is about. But that's what it was about originally. As with most of Woody Allen's films, a lot of material never made it to the screen. It was only when the film was cut that Allen and his editor, Ralph Rosenblum, decided to concentrate on one major aspect of the story: the romance between Alvy and Annie.

In order to maintain this focus, many scenes had to be eliminated. These included a nightmare sequence in which Alvy is captured by the Nazis and refuses to talk until threatened with execution, whereupon he pulls out a hand puppet and gives the information ventriloquially; a fantasy scene in which Alvy's trip to Los Angeles turns into a parody of *Invasion of the Body Snatchers* (Alvy and Annie are in danger of turning into Californians overnight); and a scene in which Alvy imagines his parents behaving with the Halls' WASP reserve—

Annie Hall

Father: "Make me a martini." Mother: "Of course, sweetheart, how would you like it, dear?" Father: "On white bread with mayonnaise." Also cut were trips to Hell and the Garden of Eden and assorted childhood reminiscences.

The scenes that *did* make it into the final print deserve further comment. The first is when Alvy, waiting to go into a movie theatre, is annoyed by the pretentious blather about Federico Fellini and Marshall McLuhan spouted by a pompous Columbia professor standing behind him; Alvy pulls McLuhan from behind a nearby sign in order to prove that the professor does not know what he is talking about. At first, Allen wanted the Spanish surrealist filmmaker Luis Buñuel (whose credits include *Viridiana* in 1961, and *The Discreet Charm of the Bourgeoisie* in 1972) to be the man Alvy produces. Buñuel was willing to do the

scene, but a change in plans made it impossible for him to be in New York when the scene was shot.

The other notable scene is the one which never fails to get the film's single biggest laugh: here Alvy talks about his forthcoming trip to Los Angeles, while a friend ostentatiously cuts up a couple of thousand dollars worth of cocaine—only to have Alvy sneeze and blow it all over the room. This scene was an afterthought, added to set up the California scenes after an earlier introductory scene had been cut. So great was the laughter at previews, however, that Rosenblum found himself having to add more and more dead film to the end of the shot so that audiences would not miss the next scene altogether—thus proving that even audiences who appreciate wit and sophistication will fall for a good pie-in-the-face gag (or its equivalent) every time.

APOCALYPSE NOW

1979
Director/Producer, Francis Ford Coppola

Although it has become a cliché to talk about how the shooting of *Apocalypse Now* came to mirror the story of the film to an uncomfortable degree, the analogy is still valid. There's certainly a parallel between the fictional Captain Willard in his quest for the renegade Colonel Kurtz, and director Francis Ford Coppola in his long slog through endless production difficulties in search of his script: both ultimately found themselves up the creek without a paddle.

Apocalypse Now had its origins in a 1969 script by right-wing surfing enthusiast John Milius (who directed *Big Wednesday* in 1978 and *Conan the Barbarian* in 1982). Milius' script attempted to set Joseph Conrad's novella *Heart of Darkness* in the context of the Vietnam War. At one point George Lucas was set to direct the project, but that was before the pressures of *Star Wars* (1977) and its ancillary merchandise intervened. Coppola then decided to rewrite the right-wing script into something less politically Neanderthal and direct it himself.

Shooting began in the Philippines on March 20, 1976, and almost immediately Coppola ran into trouble. Coppola's original Willard, Harvey Keitel, quit after he was accidentally marooned in the jungle because of a logistical foul-up (he was

Apocalypse Now

found screaming, "You wouldn't do this to Brando!" into his walkie-talkie). Keitel was replaced by Martin Sheen, who later had a heart attack, further delaying the production. And the problems were not confined to the casting. Sets were destroyed by typhoons; and equipment and ammunition had to be guarded against Moslem rebels. Originally the film was to be shot for $12,000,000 in 16 weeks. In fact, the budget ballooned to $31,500,000 and shooting dragged on for over a year.

Ultimately more than 1,100,000 feet of film were exposed. For the "Ride of the Valkyries" air attack, 1200 gallons of gasoline were burnt in 90 seconds to simulate a napalm drop. The 90-second climax to the Do Lung Bridge scene consumed over 500 smoke bombs, 100 phosphorous sticks, another 1200 gallons of gas, 1750 sticks of dynamite, 5000 feet of detonating cord, and 2000 rockets, flares, and tracers. The production company enlisted a tribe of 264 Philippine Ifuagao aborigines to play Kurtz's Montagnard followers. Coppola's wife Eleanor remembers asking a prop man about rumors

that real bodies were being used on the Kurtz Compound set and being told "the script says 'a pile of burning bodies,' not 'a pile of burning dummies.'"

Brando arrived on the set on September 3, 1976, immensely overweight. The actor wanted to disguise this excess weight in some way, but Coppola suggested he play up that aspect of the character and stuff himself continually. He and Brando then argued for weeks about how Kurtz should be played, until one day Brando announced that he wanted to play the character closer to Conrad's original. Coppola pointed out that he had been asking for exactly that interpretation all along; didn't Brando remember discussing that point when they first talked about the film? Brando agreed that he did indeed remember, but had been bluffing: he had not gotten around to reading the book until the previous night.

Finally, on May 21, 1977, the 238th shooting day, Coppola wrapped the production, announcing to the crew, "I bet there have never been so many people so happy to be unemployed!"

THE BEST YEARS OF OUR LIVES

1946
Director, William Wyler
Producer, Samuel Goldwyn

Producer Samuel Goldwyn's wife is the reason *The Best Years of Our Lives* was made. She had read a magazine article about the trauma experienced by returning World War II veterans and showed it to Sam, who became intrigued with the idea of portraying another side of the war. He asked MacKinlay Kantor to write a screenplay based on the idea, and Kantor ended up writing a short novel, *Glory For Me*, which in the hands of writer Robert Sherwood and director William Wyler became *The Best Years of Our Lives*.

It was fortunate that Wyler was chosen to direct, because he had just come home from the war and knew how it felt to return to civilian life after years overseas. Wyler remembered seeing a training film in which a young soldier was being fitted for artificial hands. He tracked down the soldier, Harold Russell, and put him in the movie along with Dana Andrews and Fredric March. Producer Goldwyn had once made the mistake of not grabbing Clark Gable when he had the chance, but he scored a hit by taking a chance on Harold Russell. Russell proved to be right for the part not only physically but in every way, and he won an Academy Award for best supporting actor for his role as

Homer. Fredric March signed to do the movie because he had been denied the part he wanted in *Life With Father* (1947), and he too won an Oscar. Goldwyn wanted Myrna Loy to play March's wife, and when she refused he invited her to dinner to find out why. She told Goldwyn that she was afraid of director William Wyler. She had heard that he was a tyrant on the set. Goldwyn put her fears to rest: "That isn't true. He's just a very mean fellow." She took the part anyway.

Wyler paid close attention to every detail, particularly the look of the movie. He hired renowned cinematographer Gregg Toland to film the story in black and white, even though color was more popular. He also brought in award-winning designer Irene Sharaff, not to create the elegant gowns for which she was known but to shop for off-the-rack clothes, which the actors then wore around the set to achieve just the right rumpled look.

The dedicated crew, poignant story, and fine cast brought the movie seven Oscars. And although *The Best Years of Our Lives* received mixed reviews at the time, it has become known for its portrayal of what some people look back on as the best years of their lives.

The Best Years of Our Lives

THE BIRTH OF A NATION

1915
Director/Producer, D. W. Griffith

Since its inception the cinema has always raised strong emotions. It seems only fitting, then, that the medium's first acknowledged masterpiece should continue to be a topic of controversy to this day. The charges of racism that have haunted *The Birth of a Nation* and its creator, D. W. Griffith, while not exactly groundless, have so overshadowed the film's considerable achievements that it has become almost impossible to discuss the movie without either condemning it or apologizing for it.

In order to understand *The Birth of a Nation* it is necessary to look at it in the context of Griffith's other work. Between 1907 and 1931 he made well over four hundred films (mostly one- and two-reelers), many of them dealing with a wide variety of social problems from religious bigotry to alcoholism. Although his viewpoint was certainly shaped by the naive sentimentality of his Victorian upbringing, his faith in the cinema's ability to elevate public morality was unshakeable. People who think of him as a racist would be surprised to find that when he deals with racial issues in his films he almost always sides with the oppressed. His treatment of American Indians in such films as *Ramona* (1910), while tending towards romanticism on "noble savage" lines, is actually quite

sympathetic. And one of the most memorable characters of his later films is that of the Chinaman (played by Richard Barthelmess), who rescues slum child Lillian Gish from her tyrannical father in *Broken Blossoms* (1919).

When depicting blacks Griffith was often condescending and paternalistic. He was, after all, born in Kentucky in 1875, the son of a Confederate officer— so it's a wonder he was not *more* of a racist. But by and large his films tend to avoid the eye-rolling, stereotypical black caricatures for which Hollywood became notorious. Some of his films even had black heroes; in the two-part *His Trust* (1911) and *His Trust Fulfilled* (1911) a black retainer saves a rich white family after their fortunes fail; and in the World War I drama *The Greatest Thing in Life* (1918)—now unfortunately lost—a white bigot is converted after a black soldier saves his life. Even in *The Birth of a Nation* the blacks are, for the most part, shown to be tools of unscrupulous whites.

Griffith believed the commonly-held Southern notion that after the Civil War the newly enfranchised blacks were manipulated by Northern carpetbaggers who wanted to break the political and economic power of the Old South. The Ku Klux Klan, according to Griffith, was formed solely to correct this "injustice," and having done so was disbanded. (Griffith was horrified by subsequent revivals of the Klan, and he was genuinely mortified when Klan chapters began showing *The Birth of a Nation* in order to raise money.) While this view is

The Birth of a Nation

BLADE RUNNER

1982
Director, Ridley Scott
Producers, Michael
Deeley and Ridley Scott

When director Ridley Scott, along with production designer Laurence Paull, special effects supervisors Douglas Trumbull and Richard Yurevich, and "visual futurist" Syd Mead began to work on building a believable version of Los Angeles in 2019, they tried to get as far away as possible from the jumpsuit and monorail look of most science fiction films. Instead they envisaged a society more or less like our own—only worse. In the world of *Blade Runner*, pollution and overpopulation are out of control and space and raw materials are at a premium; it is no longer feasible to tear down old buildings and put up new ones; instead, old ones are "retrofitted" to suit climatic changes, and new ones are built on top of them.

To build this imagined city, Scott and his crew took over the old Warner Brothers "New York" street set, where literally hundreds of movies had been shot—from *The Maltese Falcon* (1941) and *The Big Sleep* (1946) to *Hello, Dolly!* (1969) and *Annie* (1982). Then they "retrofitted" this set, adding air conditioning ducts, electrical cables, heavy machinery, and $100,000 worth of neon signs (all they could afford, plus all they could salvage from the 1982 film *One From the Heart*), turning the enormous, 50-year-old set into the punk/*noir*/deco urban nightmare the film crew was to nickname "Ridleyville."

In order to give the film its dense, lived-in look, Scott and his collaborators

not entirely groundless, it is certainly far from correct. Unfortunately, however, although Griffith's command of film technique was as modern as the medium itself, his approach to storytelling was hopelessly Victorian.

The Birth of a Nation was Griffith's first major feature, and he poured into it everything he had learned. He used crosscutting to build suspense, and close-ups and insert shots to build detail. Cutting on action and coherent screen direction created a constant sense of motion, and dynamic compositions made full use of both the foreground and the background of the frame. He also employed tracking shots and backlighting. Griffith was not the first to use most of these devices, but he *was* the first to bring them all together.

The Birth of a Nation ran over two hours, cost a then astronomical $600,000, and grossed well over a hundred million dollars; it was the cin-

ema's first blockbuster popular and critical success. Never before had a film moved audiences so powerfully. But it is here that Griffith's sense of narrative, wedded as it was to the Victorian stage, tripped him up. He used all the new techniques of the cinema to draw the strongest possible reaction from his audience, and in an attempt to achieve the same reaction he tended to make his characters either strictly good or thoroughly evil. This approach may work in a barnstorming melodrama like *Way Down East* (1920), or a "problem picture" whose issues are clear cut, but it can't be applied to the moral ambiguities of actual history without coming up with a hopelessly biased final product. This is what makes *The Birth of a Nation* so controversial even now; its power to move and its power to offend are inseparable. All the same, its very power created a new art form.

Blade Runner

added layers and layers of background detail to the sets and props, much of it unnoticeable on screen unless you're actually looking for it. Mead, a noted industrial designer who had helped build the Concorde, actually invented a unique hydraulic steering system for the flying "spinner" cars he created for the film. He also contributed other futuristic vehicles, weapons, telephones—even parking meters. These last carried official-looking notices—the work of illustrator Tom Southwell—warning vandals that tampering with them would result in electrocution. Southwell also designed the film's Oriental neon signs (chosen not only to reflect the increased ethnic diversity of Los Angeles in 2019, but because the Japanese graphics added visual clutter without being distracting), as well as magazines for Ridleyville's newsstands (including *Krotch*, which sold for $29 a copy; and *Moni*, which featured a story on illegal aliens by R. Scott).

The *Blade Runner* team sometimes resorted to extreme measures to get an appropriately dense look. When building the model cityscape used for aerial views of Ridleyville, Douglas Trumbull's Entertainment Effects Group borrowed miniature skyscrapers left over from *Escape From New York* (1981). So desperate were they to get more buildings that a model of the *Star Wars* spaceship *Millennium Falcon* was balanced on end, turning it into an instant skyscraper, and stuck into several shots—perhaps the ultimate test of "retrofitting."

Butch Cassidy and the Sundance Kid

BUTCH CASSIDY AND THE SUNDANCE KID

1969
Director, George Roy Hill
Producer, John Foreman

William Goldman, screenwriter for *Butch Cassidy and the Sundance Kid*, researched the movie for eight years before writing a word. He was particularly taken with the character of Butch Cassidy, a man who, next to Jesse James, was one of America's most famous outlaws. In the course of his research Goldman was amazed to learn that most cowboys could not swim, and he wanted somehow to include that fact in the movie. Goldman had

always admired the jump scene in *Gunga Din* (1939), and he built the 27-minute super-posse sequence in *Butch Cassidy* just to be able to include the scene where Sundance admits—before he jumps off the cliff—that he can't swim.

The first studio executive to read Goldman's screenplay objected to the part where Butch and Sundance flee to Bolivia rather than face the super-posse—John Wayne would never have turned tail and run. That executive found out later that he had let a box office hit get away.

One scene that never got into the movie was the account of how Butch went straight. The Governor of Wyoming, whose jail Butch was occupying at the time, offered to set Butch free if he would reform. Butch said he was sorry, he couldn't do that, but he could promise never to commit another crime in Wyoming. Butch

walked and, true to his word, he never again broke the law in Wyoming.

Butch and Sundance had shared their life of crime with a woman named Etta, who was either a school teacher or a prostitute—there were few other jobs for single women in the West. Because Butch enjoyed posing for the camera, many photographs exist of the trio and in them Etta looks like a school teacher. Whatever her occupation in real life, for *Butch Cassidy and the Sundance Kid* Etta became a school teacher.

Before *Butch Cassidy and the Sundance Kid* debuted in 1969, Robert Redford was considered just another tow-headed kid with a Malibu mentality. Eight years later, he had gained sufficient stature to warrant a role in *A Bridge Too Far* at a reported half a million dollars a week.

THE CAINE MUTINY

1954
Director, Edward Dmytryk
Producer, Stanley Kramer

The Caine Mutiny, a novel by Herman Wouk, had already been turned into a successful Broadway play. Stanley Kramer thought it was a natural subject for a film and bought the property for Columbia Pictures.

Since *The Caine Mutiny* dealt with the Navy and it would be necessary to borrow some ships, Kramer showed the script to several people in the armed forces. He was not received warmly. The Navy objected on several counts. They felt the film was un-American; they didn't like the way the character of Captain Queeg was portrayed and felt that it reflected poorly on the Navy; and they objected to the word "mutiny" in the title. Kramer argued that since the book was already so popular it would be ridiculous to change it. He gave in to one demand and toned down the character of Queeg slightly, making him more sympathetic than in the book. The Navy, however, still had problems, but finally a compromise which satisfied everyone was reached. The film opens with the title "There has never been a mutiny in the U.S. Navy." That line was worth two destroyers.

Humphrey Bogart played Captain Queeg, and many feel that it was his best acting job in the cinema. As soon as he heard about the role, Bogart wanted it. Colum-bia was more than de-lighted to oblige him, but Bogart overplayed his hand. Columbia, sensing that Bogart wanted the role, offered him the part at a good salary—but not as good as a star of his magnitude should have been offered. Bogart was furious, but faced with a take it or leave it offer he took it.

Although Kramer produced the film and had much to do with its casting and writing, the direction was actually in the hands of Edward Dmytryk. Dmytryk was the director of such films as *Murder My Sweet* (1944) and *Crossfire* (1947), but he was also notorious as a member of the Hollywood Ten—the Hollywood professionals who refused to testify before the House Un-American Activities Committee about communism in Hollywood. All of the Ten, who included such notables as screen-writers Ring Lardner, Jr. and Dalton Trumbo, went to prison, and all were blacklisted on their release. Only Dmytryk changed his mind, how-ever, and decided to tes-tify after all. He was rewarded for this by being removed from the blacklist and after he got out of prison he did some of his best films, among them *The Caine Mutiny* and *The Young Lions* (1958).

The Caine Mutiny

CASABLANCA

1943
Director, Michael Curtiz
Producer, Hal B. Wallis

Casablanca, the enduring Hollywood classic, began life as a play called *Everybody Comes to Rick's*, written by Murray Burnett and Joan Alison. For his vacation in 1938 Burnett went to Europe and managed to witness Hitler's invasion of Vienna. He then travelled to France, where he visited a small nightclub frequented by Frenchmen, Nazis, and refugees. He turned these experiences into the play which formed the rough schema for the final film *Casablanca*.

There are a number of differences between the play and the movie. For one thing, in the play Rick Blaine was a married lawyer before he came to Casablanca; in the film he follows the more exotic occupation of freedom fighter. Another change concerns the Ingrid Bergman character, Ilsa Lund; in the play, Ilsa was an American named Lois Meredith. The plot, though, is by and large similar in both the play and the film. Among those who worked on adapting the play (which was never produced) for the screen were Julius and Philip Epstein, and Howard Koch who had written the "War of the Worlds" radio broadcast for Orson Welles.

Humphrey Bogart was always the first choice to portray Rick, but the movie might have looked quite different if the producers had gone with their first choices for the other roles. For example, imagine Ronald Reagan playing

Casablanca

CHARIOTS OF FIRE

1981
Director, Hugh Hudson
Producer, David Puttnam

Producer David Puttnam had difficulty selling the screenplay of *Chariots of Fire* because the plot, based on the 1924 Olympics in Paris, was considered too outdated and not sufficiently interesting to American audiences. When the $6 million financing was finally found, half of it came from 20th Century-Fox's European operation and half from an Egyptian shipping conglomerate. "Believe me," Puttnam sighed, "you've been fairly well around the track before you get to Egyptian shipping lines."

In 1978 Puttnam had produced *Midnight Express*, a synthesizer-scored movie for which composer Giorgio Moroder won an Academy Award, and he thought synthesizer music would work equally well in *Chariots of Fire*. Puttnam hired Vangelis to do the scoring and brought him in at the beginning of the film, rather than at the end as is customary. What with the composing, orchestrating, and performing being done by just one man, the extra time was needed to bring it all together.

Hoping for some help with the story line, scriptwriter Colin Welland advertised in the British papers for anyone who had reminiscences of the 1924 Olympics. His ad brought a response from runner Aubrey Montague's son, who had saved his father's letters and sent

Victor Laszlo, played in the film by Paul Henreid. Further imagine Ann Sheridan, the "oomph" girl, as Ilsa. Actually, Sheridan was considered when the character was still the American Lois, but when they decided to Europeanize her and change her to Ilsa, Bergman became the top contender. For a time, even though the part was written for a man, they were considering Hazel Scott for the role of Rick's piano-playing friend. Eventually the role went to Dooley Wilson, whose piano playing was dubbed in the film. It is to his character that the most often misquoted line in movie history is assumed to have been addressed, but at no point in the film does Bogart actually say "Play it again, Sam."

Casablanca started without a completed script. Howard Koch would deliver scenes in the morning as he wrote them, and in the afternoon they would be filmed. Thus Ingrid Bergman never

knew which of the two main characters she would end up with, Laszlo or Rick. This was fortuitous because she had to play the part as if she were in love with both of them, which is what was intended.

After the film was finished Max Steiner was brought in to write the music. He had only one objection: he didn't like the song "As Time Goes By," which was written by Herman Hupfeld. The thing he didn't like about it was that it wasn't written by Max Steiner. He set about writing his own song and everything was set in motion to substitute it in the film. However, one scene with Ingrid Bergman would have had to be refilmed, and this proved impossible because Bergman had started filming *For Whom the Bell Tolls* (1943) and had cut her hair. It would be too jolting to have Bergman change hair length for that one scene so Hupfeld's song stayed.

Chariots of Fire

them to Welland. The letters proved to be invaluable, for they became the basis of the movie's narration, which was told through Aubrey's character (played by Nigel Havers). For the movie, a slight alteration was performed on the very first of Aubrey's letters—from "Dear Mummy," which sounded a bit too childish, to "Dear Mum."

In the movie, Jennie, Scottish runner Eric Liddell's sister, is depicted as having stood in the way of his running, when in truth she had no such objections. Nor did she attend the 1924 Olympics to see her brother win. Those incidents were created for the benefit of the plot.

There were many firsts on *Chariots of Fire*. It was director Hugh Hudson's first movie—he had produced documentaries and commercials up until then—and the first movie for the two principal actors, Ben Cross, who played Harold Abrahams, and Ian Charleson, who played Eric Liddell. Once Cross got the part, he hired a coach to help him with his running, and he studied the character of Abrahams so thoroughly that his wife complained, "I thought I married a crazy Irish actor. Why am I living with a crazy Jewish athlete?" Charleson's approach was different. To familiarize himself with devout runner Eric Liddell, he read the Bible from cover to cover.

Chariots of Fire fared very well at the Academy Awards ceremony, winning for best picture, best writing, and best original music score—quite an achievement for a first-time director directing first-time movie actors.

Citizen Kane

CITIZEN KANE

1941
Director/Producer, Orson Welles

Before Orson Welles' first film, *Citizen Kane*, even appeared on a movie screen, efforts were made to subvert the whole project. MGM's Louis B. Mayer offered RKO president George J. Schaefer $842,000 to destroy the picture. It seems word had got out that the film was a thinly disguised and highly unflattering portrait of publishing magnate William Randolph Hearst. And Mayer, who was a friend of Hearst's, was afraid that the publisher might strike back at the film industry in his newspapers. By accepting Mayer's offer Schaefer would have come out ahead financially—the film had cost only $686,000 to make. Schaefer turned down the offer, however,

because he thought he had a blockbuster.

He was wrong. Although advance word on the film was nothing short of ecstatic, audiences never really got the chance to judge for themselves. Most theatres would not touch the movie. The Hearst papers refused to carry ads either for *Citizen Kane* or for any other RKO picture (Hearst's papers also magnified a minor contract dispute involving Schaefer and RKO into a front page scandal). The film's premiere at Radio City Music Hall was cancelled after Louella Parsons of the Hearst publication *American Weekly* called up the directors of the Rockefeller-owned theatre and asked them if they would like to see an uncomplimentary two-page spread on John D. Rockefeller in that paper's magazine section. When the film finally made it into a few theatres it did poorly

and sank after a few weeks.

Although Welles has said in interviews that *Citizen Kane* was not based specifically on Hearst's life, the similarities are obvious. Welles' co-writer, Herman J. Mankiewicz, knew Hearst and incorporated many actual incidents into the screenplay. Hearst really did get into publishing after inheriting a fortune in mining stock. He actually was instrumental in involving the United States in the Spanish-American War through his inflammatory newspaper articles. And he did indeed live in an enormous mansion filled with "the loot of the world." Many of Hearst's own words ended up in Kane's mouth.

Ironically, there's one part of the film that was *not* true, but that was immediately taken as confirmation that the film was about Hearst—this was the character of Kane's mistress (and later wife), Susan Alexander, whom most people identified with actress Marion Davies. Although Hearst did bankroll Davies' movies (and she was, in fact, his mistress), Davies was by no means as lacking in talent as the hapless Susan. Given the limitations of the material, Davies comes off quite well in the overstuffed period pieces in which Hearst liked to see her. But in contemporary comedies like King Vidor's delightful *Show People* (1928), Davies is revealed as a gifted comedienne and an actress of considerable charm.

There is, however, one characteristic she shared with Susan—they both liked jigsaw puzzles.

CITY LIGHTS

1931
Director/Producer,
Charles Chaplin

The silent era ended officially in 1927 when *The Jazz Singer* premiered. From 1927 to 1929 silent films were still being made, although in diminishing numbers, because many theatres still didn't have sound equipment. Some films were released in both silent and sound versions. By 1930, silent films had vanished. This took its toll on many actors who were trained in pantomime but not in elocution, but one man decided not to let the silent movie die. He had been one of the most popular stars of the silent era, and the silence was crucial to his success. That man was Charles Chaplin, and in 1931 he defied conventional wisdom and released *City Lights*, a silent movie. Chaplin was vindicated, because the film was a critical and financial success. He was to make one more silent film, *Modern Times* (1936); then, with *The Great Dictator* (1940), Chaplin too went over to the talkies.

Chaplin made *City Lights* in exactly the same way that he made his earlier silent films. He wrote the movie on film. Someone would bring a prop out and Chaplin would film himself playing with it; then, as he watched the clip, he would get another idea and reshoot it as many times as necessary until it satisfied him. This was fine with a crew consisting of only a few low-paid people, but it was a different matter with the

City Lights

crew required for a feature-length film. This situation especially worried United Artists, since they had put up the money for the film. (Chaplin was one of the founders of UA, along with Mary Pickford, Douglas Fairbanks, and D. W. Griffith.) A lot of people were convinced that Chaplin was never going to finish the film at all. The scene where Chaplin first meets the blind girl, played by Virginia Cherrill, troubled him the most. He felt that the success or failure of the film depended on making this meeting convincing. It took Chaplin over two months to achieve the

ideal blend of humor and poignancy. Once that was done the rest of the shooting was plain sailing.

Although *City Lights* was a silent, Chaplin did make use of the soundtrack. When they were released, most silent films had musical accompaniment of some sort (often a full orchestra in major cities), and *City Lights* also had its music. This was composed by Chaplin, who, in addition to all of his other talents, considered himself a musician. One melody which Chaplin composed for *Modern Times* became quite popular when lyrics were added. The song was "Smile."

CLOSE ENCOUNTERS OF THE THIRD KIND

1977
Director, Steven Spielberg
Producers, Michael and Julia Philips

After the overwhelming success of *Jaws* in 1975, Steven Spielberg was pretty much free to write his own ticket for his next picture. When Spielberg was 16 he had made a two-and-a-half hour home movie called *Firefight* about hostile aliens; now he wanted to do a movie about benign aliens, so he went back to an old idea entitled *Night Skies* which was a story about an average Middle American meeting creatures from outer space.

Paul Schrader wrote the first script, but he was leaning toward making the central character a heroic figure, so Spielberg ended up writing the script himself with the protagonist once more an average Joe. About this time the title was changed to *Close Encounters of the Third Kind*, a phrase coined by UFOlogist Allen Hynek and meaning actual contact with extra-terrestrials. (Close encounters of the first kind are simple UFO sightings; those of the second kind are sightings that leave behind physical evidence.)

Close Encounters began shooting in total secrecy and without a finished script. Spielberg could not locate a soundstage large enough to accommodate the film's climax and was forced to shoot in an

Close Encounters of the Third Kind

DIRTY HARRY

1971
Director/Producer, Don Siegel

Paul Newman was the first actor to be offered the role of police inspector Harry Callahan, but he considered the character too tough—he would have preferred to produce *Dirty Harry*. Universal sold the screenplay to Warners because they couldn't find anyone to make the movie,

and at Warners it was suggested that Frank Sinatra play Harry. When that did not pan out, Clint Eastwood agreed to do it if he could get his friend Don Siegel at Universal to produce and direct. The two men had worked together before. Siegel had not only directed Eastwood before, but had made his only movie appearance—as Murphy the bartender—in the Eastwood-directed movie *Play Misty For Me* (1971). The deal went through and Siegel, after a

abandoned dirigible hangar in Mobile, Alabama. The noted French filmmaker François Truffaut was hired to play the part of the leading UFO researcher, but professed himself completely baffled as to what the movie was all about, commenting, "All I can say is that, like Greta Garbo, I had an overwhelming sensation of waiting."

Spielberg did manage to pull off this tricky movie, but not without some difficulty. One of the major problems was creating a believable alien to appear at the movie's conclusion. He tried clothing the creatures in rubber suits but the effect was not sufficiently convincing. He hired muppeteer Jim Henson to create a puppet alien, but was dissatisfied with the result. Finally he brought in Carlo Rambaldi, who had designed mechanical versions of King Kong for Dino de Laurentiis' 1976 film, and through Rambaldi, Spielberg got the alien he was looking for. (Rambaldi would create other extra-terrestrials for Ridley Scott's *Alien* in 1979 and Spielberg's own *E.T. The Extra-Terrestrial* in 1982.) However, the alien chil-

dren in *Close Encounters* were real children in rubber suits (at first Spielberg put them on roller skates so they would glide rather than walk—but the children kept falling over instead).

The spaceships were built by Douglas Trumbull, who performed similar chores on *2001: A Space Odyssey* (1968) and *Blade Runner* (1982), and who gave the Mothership its unique "chandelier" look by studding the surface with tiny light bulbs and bits from model kits (including kits for a Volkswagen, a mailbox, a toy shark, and a model of R2D2).

Although Spielberg was never satisfied with it, *Close Encounters* was a resounding success. Two years later he recut it, adding an earlier scene in which an ocean liner is discovered in the Gobi Desert, and deleting some of the family material. Spielberg also added a new ending in which a now-thinner Richard Dreyfuss actually enters the Mothership. This recut version, he proclaimed, was the film he wanted to make all along. Both versions are still available to viewers.

Dirty Harry

22-year absence, was back on the Warner lot.

Dirty Harry was shot not at Warners, but at Universal and in San Francisco, where Siegel would be up at 3:00 a.m. shooting at Kezar Stadium, and until midnight filming on top of a moving bus, on the Golden Gate Bridge, and on San Francisco rooftops.

Audie Murphy was Siegel's first choice for the killer, Scorpio, but Murphy died and Siegel had to look elsewhere. He found Andy Robinson, who had never acted in movies before. When Robinson tested for the part, Siegel thought he had too gentle a face to play Scorpio. Robinson patterned his characterization of Scorpio on Richard Widmark's Tommy Udo in *Kiss of Death* (1947), and in the scene where Scorpio slaps the kids in the bus, Siegel worked Robinson to such a pitch that he was overtaken by his character and lost control. Siegel added to Robinson's characterization the peace symbol belt buckle, to create without words the idea of a pacifist killer.

Dirty Harry did well at the box office and is generally considered the best of the Harry Callahan movies, but it received widespread criticism for its portrayal of Callahan as rogue cop. Siegel claims no political or social moral for the film—he only wanted to make an exciting movie. And Warner Brothers was happy enough with the result to ask if Siegel would be interested in a percentage of the profits. The director was overwhelmed, considering his usual adversary relationship with studio brass, but he didn't say no.

Dr. Strangelove

DR. STRANGELOVE,
OR HOW I LEARNED TO STOP WORRYING AND LOVE THE BOMB

1963
Director/Producer, Stanley Kubrick

Almost twenty years after its release, *Dr. Strangelove* remains the ultimate black comedy. Certainly the film's depiction of the world's military and political leaders as a pack of self-serving buffoons ready, willing, and able to destroy the world out of incompetence and mendacity is just as true today as it was when the film was made. In spite of the rather stuffy disclaimer (added at Air Force insistence) stating that such a thing could never happen, no one has ever seriously contested the strategic premise on which the story is based.

Director Stanley Kubrick's passion for detail contributed enormously to the film's authenticity. He originally set out to do a serious film based on Peter George's novel *Red Alert*, a straightforward account of how a nuclear war could be triggered accidentally. However, as he and George were writing the screenplay they found themselves having to throw out a great deal of factual material simply because it *seemed* absurd. It was then that they had a sudden inspiration—put all the absurd-sounding facts back in and make the picture a comedy. (Later on humorist Terry Southern, author of *Candy* and *The Magic Christian*, was brought in to work on the script.) Consequently, no matter how farfetched or surreal the film may get, it is nonetheless firmly grounded in reality. Even the evasive action procedure used by the B-52 crew after their plane is struck by a missile was taken directly from a TWA pilot's manual.

In spite of the meticulous plotting, many of the film's best moments were actually improvised. Peter Sellers played three roles: the Adlai Stevenson-like President Merkin Muffley; the Herman Kahn/Edward Teller/Werner von Braun-inspired Strangelove; and Flight Lieutenant Lionel Mandrake, the British aide-de-camp to the insane General Jack D. Ripper. Sellers was to have played yet another character, Major T. J. "King" Kong, the redneck bomber pilot. However, a hip injury prevented him from taking on this fourth role and Slim Pickens did it instead. In his triple role, Sellers contributed much of his own business, including Strangelove's problems with his mechanical hand and his last-minute resurrection from his wheelchair. In fact, the reason for Sterling Hayden's continual expression of ox-like bafflement during the Ripper/Mandrake scenes is that Hayden, strictly a by-the-script actor, was constantly having to keep up with Sellers' ever-changing line readings—thus greatly increasing his character's sense of psychotic detachment.

One scene which was ultimately cut yet remains notorious is the original ending. The film was to have ended with a huge pie-fight in the war room, and although the scene was actually shot, it was dropped for two reasons: its slapstick nature was out of step with the rest of the film; and one of George C. Scott's lines— "Gentlemen, our beloved president has been struck down in the prime of life by a pie!"—seemed a trifle tasteless, coming as it did so soon after John Kennedy's assassination. Similarly, a change was made in Pickens' exclamation after reading the contents of the B-52 survival kit, "Shoot! A feller could have a pretty good time in Dallas with all of that stuff!" The line was redubbed, substituting Vegas for Dallas. Even bad taste has its limits.

Easter Parade

EASTER PARADE

1948
Director, Charles Walters
Producer, Arthur Freed

Easter Parade was bedevilled by so many pre-production problems that it's a wonder the final movie emerged so light and breezy. Vincente Minnelli was set to direct the film because it starred his wife, Judy Garland. He had directed Garland in several films, including *Meet Me in St. Louis* (1944), *The Clock* (1945), and *Till the Clouds Roll By* (1947)—although in the latter film he directed only the sequences with Garland—and was certainly her most flattering director. However, Garland's psychiatrist concluded that it would not help the star's emotional well-being to be directed by Minnelli at this time. The psychiatrist may have been right; their marriage was under stress and they divorced three years later.

In any event, Minnelli was replaced by Charles Walters, who had done choreography for such films as *Meet Me in St. Louis* before becoming a director.

The second casualty was co-star Gene Kelly. Kelly had made his movie debut opposite Garland in *For Me and My Gal* (1942), and had recently co-starred with Garland in Minnelli's delightful *The Pirate* (1948). All was set for another teaming when the worst thing that can happen to a dancer happened to Kelly; he broke his ankle. Kelly told the studio that he broke the ankle while rehearsing a dance; in fact, he broke it while playing touch football outside his house.

The producer, Arthur Freed, decided that the only one who could replace Kelly was Fred Astaire. Freed and Astaire had ties that went way back; they had appeared in vaudeville together, once on the same bill, when Freed was fourteen and Astaire was nine. Freed

was able to coax Astaire out of retirement, and Astaire accepted because he wanted to work with Garland.

The final casualty was Cyd Charisse. Charisse was an MGM contract player whose movie career so far had offered her nothing but bit parts. She was also an accomplished dancer. This was to be her first featured role, but it was not in the stars. Before shooting started she broke her leg and was replaced by Ann Miller.

For *Easter Parade* Irving Berlin wrote one of his most delightful scores, including such classics as "It Only Happens When I Dance With You" and "Steppin' Out With My Baby." At one point Freed asked Berlin for a fun song, one which could be sung as a duet between Astaire and Garland. Berlin brought in "Let's Take an Old Fashioned Walk," but Freed didn't like it. Discouraged, Berlin walked out, only to return an hour later with "We're a Couple of Swells," which he had written in that short time. The song became the high point of the picture.

After the film was finished it was decided to cut Garland's rendition of "Mr. Monotony." Everyone agreed that the song was a show-stopper; however, it was also a film-stopper. The song broke up the flow of the picture, and no matter how good it was it had to go. Later, Berlin put the song in *Miss Liberty* on Broadway, where it again stopped the show so thoroughly that it had to be yanked out. The same thing happened when he tried to put it in *Call Me Madam*. The song, apparently, was too good for its own good.

E.T. THE EXTRA-TERRESTRIAL

1982
Director, Steven Spielberg
Producers, Steven Spielberg and Kathleen Kennedy

E.T. originally came to life as part of a different project. Steven Spielberg had come up with an idea for a movie called *Night Skies* about man's first contact with aliens. In this film the aliens were anything but friendly and were to come to Earth and terrorize a small community. Spielberg described it as a science fiction version of *Straw Dogs* (1971). However, in the middle of directing *Raiders of the Lost Ark* (1981), he decided that for his next film he needed to do something a little more tranquil, so he changed the concept to involve a friendly alien and drafted an outline. He then told the story to Melissa Mathison, a screenwriter, who happened to be on the set of *Raiders* because she was going out with Harrison Ford. She loved the idea and quickly set about writing a screenplay.

Without doubt, the star of the film was E.T. the extra-terrestrial himself. E.T. was kept a well-guarded secret to preserve the element of surprise in the movie. No visitors were allowed on the set and no stills were released. Spielberg didn't even let the publicity department see E.T., so the publicists were faced with the problem of designing a poster for a film they knew nothing

E.T. The Extra-Terrestrial

about. They came up with a poster which showed a misshapen finger wrapping itself around the edge of a door. Of course, after the film became a blockbuster, E.T. dolls flooded the market and the little alien became one of the most recognizable film stars in movie history.

Creating a believable alien required the cooperation of several make-up men. Carlo Rambaldi was responsible for coming up with the general design of the body and for making E.T. move. He created several E.T.s for different activities, and depending on the scene E.T. moved through radio-controlled devices, hand puppets, or midgets in E.T. suits. Rambaldi was facing an immovable deadline, though, and he had to enlist the help of Craig Reardon to finish E.T. Reardon was responsible for painting E.T. and for creating the creature's eyes.

The effect which caused the most difficulty was E.T.'s glowing heart. E.T. was made out of a heavy latex and it was found that anything bright enough to show through it would also be hot enough to set the little extra-terrestrial on fire. As a result, a separate E.T. chest was designed and fabricated out of transparent plastic.

Inside this plastic chest were several organs, which moved when air was pumped into them, and a bright light. The chest was then painted out with a translucent paint and on command the chest lit up and the organs moved. A separate suit with a light was designed for the midget.

Getting E.T.'s voice right was also a lot of work. To achieve the desired alien effect, 18 different animals were recorded and the sounds synthesized. The animals included raccoons, cats, and horses. Once E.T. learned to speak English, however, distorted human voices were used; actress Debra Winger read much of his dialogue.

Elliott's use of Reese's® Pieces (made by the Hershey Foods Corp.) to tempt E.T. out of hiding was not a matter of chance. The company paid good money to have their product featured in the film. M&M/Mars were the first to be approached about having "M&M's"® featured in the movie, but they balked at the modest price that they'd have to pay for this exposure, and the studio went with Hershey. This proved to be a major coup for the candy manufacturer; after the film was released the sale of Reese's® Pieces shot up.

THE EXORCIST

1973
Director, William Friedkin
Producer, William Peter Blatty

Mike Oldfield's theme for *The Exorcist*, the haunting "Tubular Bells," ushered in a whole new style of horror film music. The influence of Oldfield's intense, repetitive rhythms can be heard in the scores to such films as *Halloween* (1978), *Dawn of the Dead* (1979), and Paul Schrader's 1982 remake of *Cat People*. Trend setting, however, was the furthest thing from director William Friedkin's mind when he first set out to hire a composer. His first choice was Bernard Herrmann, who had written the soundtracks for some of Hitchcock's greatest films, including *Psycho* (1960), *Vertigo* (1958), and *North by Northwest* (1959), as well as the scores for *Citizen Kane* (1941), *The Magnificent Ambersons* (1942), and *All That Money Can Buy* (1941). Full symphonic scores were currently out of style, however, and Herrmann was now living in England in semi-retirement. Friedkin flew him out to California especially to show him a rough cut of *The Exorcist* and when the lights went up told him, "I want you to write me a better score than the one you wrote for *Citizen Kane*."

"Then you should have made a better movie than *Citizen Kane*," replied Herrmann.

Fortunately Friedkin had better luck turning young Linda Blair into a creature possessed by the Devil. To effect the transformation he hired make-up expert Dick Smith, but even Smith's skills faced a tremendous challenge: all the usual means of suggesting evil—gauntness, sunken eyes, thin lips, pronounced bone structure—were completely incompatible with Blair's chubby wholesomeness. He settled instead on a series of scratches that grew progressively worse as the story progressed, deepening the effect with

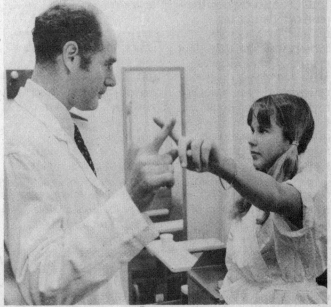

The Exorcist

matted hair, yellow contact lenses, and an overall greyish skin tone that made the scratches look even more livid and repulsive.

For some of the more elaborate evidences of the child's possession by the Devil, Smith had to construct whole body parts. He designed concealed tubes that could spray "vomit" and ooze "bile"; a false chest on which the words "help me" could be spelt out in welts; and a full-scale dummy that could make it appear that Blair's head was rotating 360 degrees—this last producing one of the most horrific effects in a movie already replete with shock value. Smith even concocted fake spittle when Blair proved incapable of producing a sufficient quantity naturally. Much of the heavy-duty effects work was done on a specially refrigerated set, so that the actors' breath would be visible. These scenes were actually shot in temperatures between 0°F and 10°F, causing much discomfort to the cast and crew.

Smith also created the more subtle old age makeup for Max von Sydow, who was only 44 at the time the movie was made. Von Sydow was the cause of a major script revision—in the book and the original script it is the priest he plays who performs the exorcism, but in the movie the character dies before the exorcism takes place and the ritual is performed by Jason Miller instead. The reason for this plot change was simple: Von Sydow was an atheist, and he could not bring the necessary conviction to the priest's lines he was required to speak.

Frankenstein

FRANKENSTEIN

1931
Director, James Whale
Producer, Carl Laemmle, Jr.

After the phenomenal success of *Dracula* earlier in 1931, Universal began looking for a follow-up vehicle for its star Bela Lugosi. Director Robert Florey suggested Mary Shelley's novel *Frankenstein* and began work on a script. The script, however, didn't please production head Carl Laemmle,

Jr., who turned the project over to James Whale—a new director who was just beginning to make a name for himself in Hollywood.

A true eccentric (and an acknowledged gay at a time when homosexuality was much less widely accepted than it is today), Whale was a former cartoonist, set designer, and stage director. He had made his reputation in his native England with his production of R. C. Sherriff's play *Journey's End*. He had come to America to direct the film version, and stayed to serve as dia-

logue director on Howard Hughes' *Hell's Angels* (1930) and then to direct the first film version of *Waterloo Bridge* (1931). Reluctant to be typecast as a war-movie director, Whale jumped at the chance to direct *Frankenstein*. He also realized that the project would give him an opportunity to indulge a penchant for black humor which he'd never before been able to express.

Whale's first directorial power play on *Frankenstein* was to get rid of Lugosi, instead allotting the role of the monster to Boris Karloff, a character actor who had been specializing in gangster roles. Whale felt that Karloff's gaunt features were perfectly suited to the monster created by Frankenstein. The embodiment of the monster was the work of Jack Pierce, who painstakingly built up Karloff's forehead to give the impression that Frankenstein had simply sawed off the top of his creature's head in order to insert the brain. Pierce then increased the monster's bulk with padding and his height with the thick-soled, weighted boots that also caused his stiff, forward-leaning walk. This transformation of man into monster took four hours, plus another couple of hours to reverse the process. This time-consuming make-up routine, combined with Universal's desire to keep the monster's appearance secret until the film's premiere, meant that Karloff got very little opportunity to socialize with anyone else on the set of the movie.

One of *Frankenstein's* most infamous scenes occurs when the monster meets a little girl who, feeling no fear despite his grotesque appearance, invites him to join her in throwing flowers into a stream and watching them float away. When all the flowers are gone, the monster picks up the little girl and throws her in the stream, expecting her to float like a flower. But the child drowns.

The 1931 preview audiences, less accustomed to graphic violence than filmgoers of the '80s, found this incident so disturbing that the scene was cut. Secretly, Whale was delighted that the scene had been removed because he had never been happy with it. Karloff's cumbersome costume made it difficult for him to lift the child, let alone throw her, so Whale had a couple of stagehands actually throw the child into the stream, cutting from a shot of Karloff picking up the child to a shot of her in the water. Whale never considered that the scene looked sufficiently convincing. And to add to his discomfort he also had to contend with an unusually obnoxious stage mother who kept yelling "Farther! Farther!" each time her daughter was tossed into the water.

The success of *Frankenstein* made it possible for Whale to direct *The Old Dark House* (1932), *The Invisible Man* (1933), and—his most extreme excursion into the bizarre—*The Bride of Frankenstein* (1935). Then wearying of being tagged as a horror film director, he made a film totally out of character with his earlier standards, the 1936 version of the Jerome Kern musical *Showboat*.

FREAKS

1932
Director/Producer, Tod Browning

MGM got more than they bargained for when they tried, with Tod Browning's *Freaks*, to climb on the horror film bandwagon set in motion by Universal with *Dracula* (1931), *Frankenstein* (1931), and *Murders in the Rue Morgue* (1932). The finished version of *Freaks* was cut. The ending, in which the avenging freaks punish the two "normals" who have attempted to murder one of their number, was toned down somewhat, and a totally incongruous happy ending added (this ending still survives in some prints). The studio also appended a ludicrous disclaimer assuring audiences that medical science was making obsolete the sort of deformities on display in the picture. And the MGM name was taken off the film.

Part of the reason that the film shocks so deeply is that all the freaks are real people, not just actors made up or masked to fit their roles. Browning employed real circus

Freaks

freak-show performers to portray his carnival denizens, among them dwarfs Harry and Daisy Earles; Siamese twins Daisy and Violet Hilton; Prince Randian the Living Torso; Josephine-Joseph, the half-man/half-woman; pinheads Elvira and Jenny Lee Snow; Martha the Armless Wonder; "Lady Olga" Barnell, the bearded lady (who was later to denounce the film as "an insult to all freaks"); and Koo-Koo the Bird Girl. Some of these performers had moderately successful film careers. Harry Earles appeared in Browning's *The Unholy Three* (1925) playing a burglar who gets into houses by disguising himself as a baby; and the Hilton sisters were later to star in *Chained for Life*, a musical (inappropriate as that might seem in view of its subject) which posed the question of how to punish a Siamese twin who commits a murder of which the other twin is innocent. It is not just that the freaks are real people, however, that makes the film so disturbing, but the fact that they are shown to be far more likeable and sympathetic than the "normal" people.

Browning's sympathy for the freaks and their

world was predictable—it was a world he knew at first hand. At the age of 16 he had run away from home to join the circus and had toured in carnivals and vaudeville as a barker, contortionist, and blackface comedian. Eventually D. W. Griffith hired him as a bit-part actor and stuntman, and later Browning became an assistant director on *Intolerance* (1916). Once set on a career as a director he became successful with a string of exotic melodramas made with Lon Chaney (whom he had discovered), in which his penchant for bizarre and obsessional black humor and Chaney's for extreme make-up and costuming effects could be exploited to their fullest. Chaney was to have starred in Browning's 1931 production of *Dracula*, but the actor died before he could make the picture.

After *Freaks*, MGM never quite trusted Browning again; they refused to let him do his dream project, a film based on the novel *They Shoot Horses, Don't They?* by Horace McCoy (which was finally filmed in 1969 and starred Jane Fonda). After directing only five films of varying quality between 1932 and 1939 (including the hilariously perverse *The Devil Doll* in 1936, which Browning wrote with Erich von Stroheim), he retired into obscurity. *Variety* mistakenly published his obituary in 1944, but in fact Browning lived until 1962, drinking heavily and staying up all night watching old movies on TV. He outlived his wife, his pet mynah bird, and his dog; and he left his 1941 Chrysler to his mailman.

From Here to Eternity

FROM HERE TO ETERNITY

1953
Director, Fred Zinnemann
Producer, Buddy Adler

From Here to Eternity was the film they said couldn't be made; after all, in the 1950s how could you condense a 1000-page book with obscene language and frank sex into a Hollywood movie? As it happened, it could be done by focusing on the love interest and changing the prostitutes in the book into hostesses at a "conversation club" on an army base. Through this and other not so subtle changes the film was able to make it past the censor and onto the screen.

Frank Sinatra learned of the role of Angelo Maggio when he was in Africa. He had accompanied his wife, Ava Gardner, when she went to film *Mogambo* (1953) with Clark Gable. Gable suggested that Sinatra would be perfect for the role and even paid his airfare back to the States. However, it was not that easy to walk into Columbia pictures and claim the part. For one thing, Harry Cohn, the head of Columbia, had already announced that he wanted Eli Wallach for the role. For another, Sinatra was thought to be washed up. His last few pictures had been duds, and whatever allure he once had seemed to have vanished. He finally told Cohn that he would play the part for nothing, and Cohn gave him a screen test. Sinatra then flew back to Africa to be with Gardner, and Columbia soon sent word that he had been given the part for a $10,000 salary. Sinatra was to receive an Oscar for the role.

Deborah Kerr was also not the first choice for Karen Holmes, the promiscuous army wife. Joan Crawford was cast and would have played the part, but one day in the early stages of filming she stormed off the set, never to return. Kerr immediately declared that she wanted the role, but people scoffed at the idea. The role was completely different from the high-class women she normally played. Kerr had always wanted to play something a little less refined, and she got the part after the producer, the director, and the screenwriter convinced Harry Cohn that she could play it. She ended up having the most famous scene in the film, a love scene with Burt Lancaster on the beach as waves roll over them. Apparently, though, the scene was not fun to make. It was so cold that the two performers had to keep ice cubes under their tongues in order to keep their breath from showing on the screen.

Another bit of unlikely casting was that of Donna Reed as Alma, the "hostess" with the mostest. Reed had spent her time playing "good" characters in films like *They Were Expendable* (1945) and *It's a Wonderful Life* (1946). She desperately wanted to try something new, so she tested for the role. Director Fred Zinnemann remained unconvinced and wanted Julie Harris to play Alma, but this time Harry Cohn insisted, so Reed was tested again. She was also rejected again. Cohn, behind Zinnemann's back, had her do a third test, this time with Montgomery Clift, doing the scene where she explains that she wants to lead a respectable life. This time Zinnemann relented. He still seemed nervous with Reed and avoided close-ups of her during filming. Reed kept notes of this, and at the end of the film Harry Cohn forced Zinnemann to retake the necessary close-ups. Apparently it paid off, because Reed took away an Oscar for best supporting actress.

GIANT

1956
Director, George Stevens
Producers, George Stevens and Henry Ginsburg

At one time director George Stevens had considered Richard Burton for the James Dean part in *Giant*, but Alan Ladd was his first choice. Stevens wished many times that Ladd had accepted, because he and Dean did not get along. He swore Dean would never appear in another picture of his, and he never did, for not long after the picture was completed Dean died in an automobile accident on the way to Salinas, California.

To pay for the film rights to Edna Ferber's book, Stevens entered into a partnership with the author, and to bring *Giant* to the screen Stevens asked Warner Brothers' head, Jack Warner, for help. Warner gave him $1 million. When Stevens later went back for another $2.5 million, Warner took out of his pocket a check already endorsed for that amount, explaining, "I thought that was just about what you needed." It was a good investment. *Giant* did very well at the box office.

The film company of 250 nearly outnumbered the townspeople on location in Marfa, Texas, where Dean shared a house for three summer months with Rock Hudson and Chill Wills. To get into the character of Jett Rink (loosely based on Clem McCarthy, oil magnate and owner/builder of the famous Houston watering hole The Shamrock Hotel), Dean arrived early to the Texas location to mingle with the natives, who taught him how to twirl a lariat. He was quite proud of his accomplishment, as can be seen in a well-known photograph taken of Dean by Sanford Roth. (Roth also took the last photograph of Dean on the fatal trip to Salinas.)

Director Stevens enjoyed the epic touches of shipping in 4100 head of cattle and a Christmas tree for the movie, but Dean also had ways of making a statement. During one scene, Stevens looked through the camera to see a red convertible parked in the midst of the cattle herd. He knew without being told who the car belonged to.

There is one scene in *Giant* in which Jett Rink is invited to a party at his employer's house. Director Stevens wanted Dean to walk up to the bar and

help himself. Dean argued that since Rink always carried a flask in his back pocket, he would more likely eschew his employer's whiskey for his own flask. Stevens prevailed, but years later when he was viewing *Giant* and that scene came up on the screen, he realized that Dean had been right all along. He also realized that Dean was "too good for it. Anybody could have played that part." Dean's final words in *Giant* belong to someone else. In the final scene, the banquet scene, his words were unclear and he had to be dubbed, but by the time dubbing took place he was dead.

Critics have praised and panned *Giant*, but it won for Stevens the Oscar for best director. For James Dean, who had hoped to do more westerns, *Giant* stands as his only one.

Gigi

GIGI

1958
Director, Vincente Minnelli
Producer, Arthur Freed

For a light musical *Gigi* deals with a risqué subject—mistresses. The story, by Colette, is set at the turn of the century when many Frenchmen had mistresses and proudly displayed them in public. Yet by focusing on Gigi herself, a girl who becomes a woman in the course of the film, the story retains an atmosphere of innocence. The problem was how to get it past the censors. The initial objections were that all of the characters were unmarried and, worse still, were anti-marriage. Director Vincente Minnelli had long arguments with Geoffrey Sherlock, who was administering the produc-

tion code at this time. Minnelli argued that the film ultimately came out in favor of marriage, because the perpetually bored Gaston finally marries Gigi. Sherlock was eventually worn down, with the exception of one incident. He objected to a scene where Gaston asks Gigi to be nice to him. Gigi objects, saying, "To be nice to you means that I should have to sleep in your bed. Then when you get tired of me I would have to go to some other gentleman's bed." This time an impasse was reached, and as a compromise Minnelli suggested that they shoot the scene as is and then Sherlock could pass judgment. Sherlock was won over by Leslie Caron's innocent reading of the line.

Most of *Gigi* was shot on location in Paris. A variety of old French townhouses were redec-

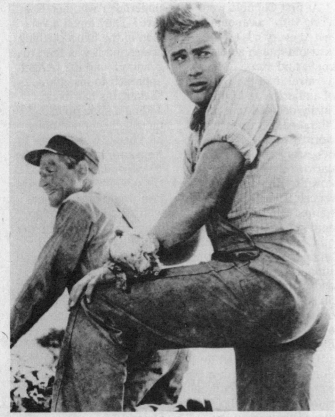

Giant

orated in the style of the period. However, nothing could substitute for Maxim's. The famous French restaurant agreed to close for filming, but only for three days and not an hour longer. Since the crew had to shoot two musical numbers as well as several dramatic scenes, the time factor presented difficulties. The scenes would have to be filmed neatly and quickly, and there would be no time for experimentation. To plan out the filming Minnelli took cameraman Joe Ruttenberg to Maxim's for lunch. Ruttenberg immediately began talking about covering up the mirrors with black drapes to avoid lighting problems. The depressing news from Minnelli was that the wall of mirrors was the trademark of Maxim's and had to be seen. Ruttenberg would have to find a way to light the set without reflecting into the mirrors. The cameraman eventually put suction cups on lights and stuck them on the ceiling and in other out of the way places.

When *Gigi* came out many people compared it to *My Fair Lady*, the musical version of George Bernard Shaw's *Pygmalion.* *My Fair Lady* had been a big success on the stage (it would not be made into a film until 1964), and there were certain similarities between the two stories: *My Fair Lady* concerns the conversion of a cockney flower-seller into a refined lady, while *Gigi* depicts the transformation of a schoolgirl into a sophisticated woman of the world. All the same, the makers of *Gigi* were not happy about all the comparisons that were made between the two.

The Godfather

THE GODFATHER

1972
Director, Francis Ford Coppola
Producer, Al Ruddy

Marlon Brando mumbling "make him an offer he can't refuse" through a mouthful of cotton wool is undoubtably one of the most memorable images in *The Godfather*. Ironically, it almost did not happen. Although Brando was the first choice of both author and co-scenarist Mario Puzo and director Francis Ford Coppola, the executives at Paramount refused even to consider him. Brando had not made a successful picture in years and was felt to be washed-up and hard to control.

At first Coppola went along with Paramount and tested every 60- to 70-year-old Italian actor he could find. None of them, however, had the right air of authority, and Coppola finally decided that only "the greatest actor in the world" would have the necessary charisma. This narrowed the choices down to Brando or Laurence Olivier. Paramount wanted Olivier, but finally agreed to consider Brando on three conditions: that he take no salary, that he submit to a screen test, and that he personally finance any budget overruns due to his own antics. Surprisingly, Brando accepted.

Coppola went out to Brando's house with a cameraman and actor Salvatore Corsitto, who played the part of the

undertaker who needs a favor. They taped a version of the film's opening scene and it was then that Brando found the perfect approach to his character, slicking his hair back, adding a shoe-polish moustache, and stuffing his cheeks with tissues to transform himself into the 70-year-old Don Corleone. On screen this transformation would be achieved with the aid of make-up artist Dick Smith, who performed similar special effects for Dustin Hoffman in *Little Big Man* (1970) and David Bowie in *The Hunger* (1983). Dick Smith was also responsible for the more elaborate make-up in Linda Blair's possession scenes in *The Exorcist* (1973) and for William Hurt's regressions in the 1980 movie *Altered States*.

GOLDFINGER

1964
Director, Guy Hamilton
Producers, Harry Saltzman and Albert R. Broccoli

Fans of the James Bond movies generally agree that *Goldfinger* is the best. Third in the series, which began in 1962 with *Dr. No, Goldfinger* introduced the first Bond car, the silver Aston Martin DB-5 (initialed for David Brown, its designer), which established the trend that led to the Lotus car-submarine, the portable helicopter "Little Nellie," and the Astrojet. The Aston Martin had several clever features, one of which was that oil could be squirted from its exhaust pipes to discourage tailgating. Originally tacks were to be discharged instead of oil, but someone suggested that little children might copy the idea, resulting in a international spate of flat tires.

Shirley Eaton played the girl whom Goldfinger murders by covering her body with gold paint, an idea originally used in 1946 in the movie *Bedlam* with Boris Karloff. A six-inch square was left unpainted on Eaton's abdomen, however, in order that she not be sacrificed for the sake of her art. Gert Frobe was the evil Goldfinger, but his thick German accent required that his voice be dubbed throughout the movie.

One day in the middle of shooting a major scene in *Goldfinger*, the publicity man brought a French woman to interview Sean Connery. She asked Connery the name of the film. He told her. Then she asked what part Connery was playing. He told her. Then she wanted to know who else was starring, and when Connery replied that the cast included a very famous German actor, Gert Frobe, the woman replied, "Well, I've never heard of her." Connery, who has never cared for publicity people, did not change his mind that day.

Connery's salary for *Dr. No* was around $45,000 and it did not increase appreciably on the next Bond movie, *From Russia With Love* (1964). By the time he got to *Goldfinger* he was ready for a raise, but the producers balked. However, when Connery injured his back during the Fort Knox scene in which Oddjob (Harold Sakata) throws him against the wall, he took a couple of days off and let it be known that he was not coming back to work until he received a raise. He got it. For *Never Say Never Again* (1983), he reportedly earned $5 million up front and a healthy percent of the gross. Not bad for playing, as Dr. No said, "a stupid policeman."

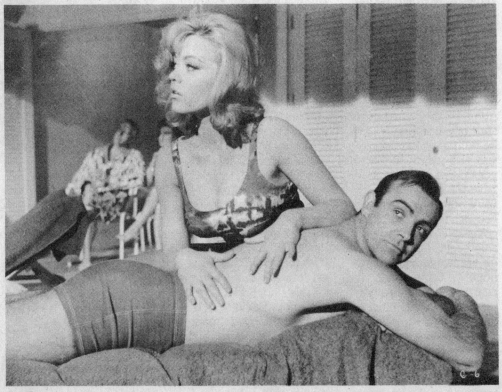

Goldfinger

GONE WITH THE WIND

1939
Director, Victor Fleming
Producer, David O. Selznick

David O. Selznick was the man behind *Gone With the Wind* and was responsible for everything from the casting down to the costumes. When Selznick read Margaret Mitchell's bestseller about the Civil War and its aftermath he was convinced that it had enormous cinematic potential and that it would make the greatest and grandest picture ever. Selznick thought big.

Clark Gable was the first choice for Rhett Butler. The public seemed to picture Gable when they read the book, although Margaret Mitchell didn't particularly want him. When asked whom she would have preferred she replied, "Groucho Marx." MGM, which had Gable's contract, was being stubborn about releasing him, and for a time Selznick toyed with the Warner Brothers' offer to have the film star both Errol Flynn and Bette Davis. MGM relented, though, when Selznick agreed to release the film through that studio.

The rest of the casting was not that simple. Selznick decided he needed a new face to play Scarlett O'Hara, and a nationwide talent search was begun. In the meantime, every actress in Hollywood from Lana Turner to Katharine Hepburn tested for the role. At one point Selznick narrowed the choice down to Norma Shearer, Jean Arthur, and Paulette God-

Gone With the Wind

who would play Scarlett O'Hara. She was Vivien Leigh, and the search for Scarlett was over.

Gone With the Wind went through an unusual number of directors. George Cukor was originally involved with the project, but was replaced when Selznick felt he was taking control of the picture away from him. This delighted Gable, who considered that Cukor was giving too much screen time to Leigh and Olivia de Havilland and not enough to him. Cukor was replaced by Victor Fleming, who was yanked off of *The Wizard of Oz* (1939), where he had replaced Richard Thorpe and would himself be replaced by King Vidor. Fleming had shot most of *Gone With the Wind* when he became ill and was temporarily replaced by Sam Wood, the director of *A Night at the Opera* (1935). Even Selznick directed one or two scenes when Wood was away.

After the film opened it was such a staggering success that Selznick considered doing a sequel. Margaret Mitchell, however, told him in no uncertain terms that she would not permit a sequel. Strangely enough, however, the very success of *Gone With the Wind* later became a curse to Selznick. He felt that his subsequent films had to top *Gone With the Wind*, but how can you top *Gone With the Wind*? His greatest fear was that when his obituary appeared it would talk about David O. Selznick, the man who made *Gone With the Wind*, and his fears were realized because that is exactly what happened when he died in 1965.

THE GRADUATE

1967
Director, Mike Nichols
Producer, Lawrence Turman

The Graduate is especially remembered for two things: the Simon and Garfunkel music—"Sounds of Silence" and "Mrs. Robinson"—and the famous line—"Ben, I want to say one word to you, just one word—plastics"— by screenwriters Buck Henry and Calder Willingham.

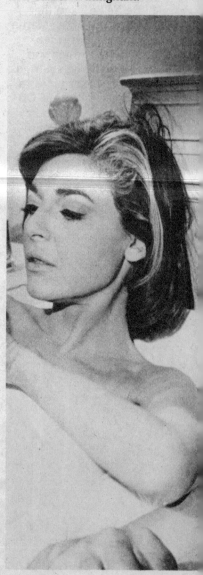

The Graduate

dard, with Goddard the favorite. However, Goddard had recently married Charlie Chaplin and there were indications that the marriage wasn't legitimate, so she lost the part.

The casting of Ashley proved even more difficult. Melvyn Douglas was considered the only halfway decent choice for the role, until he screen-tested for the part. Selznick was convinced that Leslie Howard would be right for the role, but he was equally convinced that Howard wouldn't want the part. Selznick was right on both counts. Finally Selznick dangled in front of Howard a lure that he couldn't refuse. If Howard appeared in *Gone With the Wind*, Selznick would let him produce and star in his own film. When the time

came to take Selznick up on his offer, Howard picked *Intermezzo* (1939) co-starring opposite the young Ingrid Bergman.

Gone With the Wind started filming without a Scarlett. The burning of Atlanta was the first scene shot because Tara was to be built after the debris was cleaned up, and it was considered too risky to have the fire when there were other sets nearby. Facades were used to cover over the old Hollywood sets which were set on fire, while stunt men doubling for the main characters rode through the scene. In the midst of this filming Selznick's brother Myron, one of Hollywood's leading talent agents, appeared with a woman whom he introduced as the woman

Dustin Hoffman (named for silent screen cowboy Dustin Farnum) decided at age 18 to be an actor, and he studied at the Pasadena Playhouse where he was told he would definitely make it in the movies—in ten or fifteen years. Hoffman had been bitten by the acting bug when he played Tiny Tim in seventh grade and, accepting a dare from a ninth grader, broke up the audience with the line, "God bless us everyone, goddammit." The ad-lib got him suspended.

Hoffman's Aunt Pearl once told him, "You can't be an actor. You're not good-looking enough." Hoffman felt that Aunt Pearl just might have been right about the role of Benjamin Braddock that director Mike Nichols wanted him to test for. He was not "good-looking enough" to play a romantic lead. When he made the test with Katharine Ross, he had never acted in a romantic scene before. He became very nervous and inexplicably grabbed Ross on the derriere. The test over, he mumbled apologies and left, never expecting to hear from Mike Nichols. Well-known producer Joe Levine thought Hoffman was just one of the studio messenger boys, and even the crew was unimpressed. When Hoffman dropped his subway token, a cameraman picked it up and said, "Here, kid, you're going to need this."

The Graduate earned for Mike Nichols the Oscar for best director and for Dustin Hoffman $17,000 and an Academy Award nomination. He lost out to Rod Steiger. In Los Angeles to attend the ceremonies, Hoffman—not quite the star he is today—stood around afterward with nowhere to go. Finally he called a friend who picked him up and let him spend the night.

When Hoffman went on to do *Midnight Cowboy* (1969) director Nichols was aghast, feeling that the role of Ratso Rizzo would be detrimental to Hoffman's image. But Hoffman had his eye on character acting, and by accepting roles as diverse as Ratso and Benjamin he was eventually able to play any role—even *Tootsie* (1982).

Grand Hotel

GRAND HOTEL

1932
Director, Edmund Goulding
Producer, Irving Thalberg

Grand Hotel was the movie that MGM dreaded making. It was an impressively star-studded vehicle, even for MGM which boasted it had more stars than there are in heaven. The movie featured Greta Garbo as Grusinskaya the ballerina; John Barrymore as the poor nobleman Baron von Gaigern; Joan Crawford as the secretary Flaemmchen; Wallace Beery as the unscrupulous businessman Preysing; Lionel Barrymore as Kringelein, the man with two months to live; and Lewis Stone as Dr. Otternschlag who delivers the immortal line, "Nothing ever happens at the Grand Hotel."

Everyone was convinced that there would be conflicts between the various stars as each tried to maneuver for extra screen time. The unenviable job of managing this impressive and potentially explosive lineup went to Edmund Goulding, who had already directed Garbo in *Love* (1927) and was considered well qualified to handle tempestuous performers.

The major clashes were expected to be between Garbo and Crawford. Garbo had been brought to MGM from Sweden after Louis Mayer saw *The Saga of Gosta Berling* (1924). Mayer had wanted to sign the film's director, Mauritz Stiller, but Stiller would not agree until his protégée, Garbo, was also given a contract. Stiller was unhappy in Hollywood and soon returned to Sweden, but Garbo was a huge success. She quickly became one of MGM's biggest stars, and one of the most difficult. She demanded that her films have closed sets, meaning that only the necessary technicians could watch the filming (which once meant excluding the powerful Irving Thalberg from the studio). She didn't like to rehearse, and she often showed up late and left early. During *Grand Hotel*, though, Goulding noticed a remarkable change in Garbo. She now rehearsed fanatically, especially the love scene with Barrymore where she uttered the classic line, "I vant to be alone." She watched the daily rushes and suggested changes, and was generally cooperative. The person responsible for this change in Garbo was Crawford. Crawford was a star on the rise, and Garbo was convinced that she would steal the picture from her. Goulding did his part to keep things running smoothly by making sure that Crawford and Garbo never appeared together in a scene.

Wallace Beery and John Barrymore also gave problems with their scene stealing. Beery would unnerve the other actors by ad-libbing, hoping that his co-stars would concentrate more on listening for their cues than on their own performances. Barrymore's technique for upstaging others was a fixed stare, which could crumble a lesser talent. However, since everyone in the film was a star, and since everyone knew all about everyone else's attention-getting techniques, no one actor truly stood out or was overshadowed and all were pleased with the final film.

The Grapes of Wrath

THE GRAPES OF WRATH

1940
Director, John Ford
Producer, Nunnally Johnson

By the time Henry Fonda was asked to play Tom Joad in *The Grapes of Wrath*, he had read everything written by the book's author, John Steinbeck. And he did not need prodding to work again with director John Ford in a role that seemed to have been written for him. His enthusiasm knew no bounds.

Darryl Zanuck, who bought *The Grapes of Wrath* for 20th Century-Fox, used the movie as bait to force Fonda to sign a seven-year contract with Fox—sign or say goodbye to the movie. Fonda considered himself a freelancer who owed his soul to no one, but he wanted desperately to play Tom Joad. He signed.

Although the movie was about the Oklahoma

"Okies," the location scenes were shot no farther east than Needles, California, and the Okie camps were filmed near Pomona. Gregg Toland, the fine cinematographer who in *Citizen Kane* (1941) first included ceilings in a movie, was also innovative on *The Grapes of Wrath*. During the last scene, Tom wakes his mother (Jane Darwell) to say goodbye, and lights a match. Toland rigged a small light to fit into Fonda's palm, and it provided just the amount of illumination needed to catch Ma Joad's face. The scene that followed—"I'll be there"—will never be forgotten.

Jane Darwell won an Academy Award for best supporting actress, but Fonda was passed over. Jimmy Stewart, Fonda's buddy from the time they began their careers together, won the Oscar that year for *The Philadelphia Story*. But the Academy made up for its oversight by awarding Fonda the Oscar for *On Golden Pond*—41 years later in 1981.

GUNGA DIN

1939
Director/Producer,
George Stevens

The idea of making a movie out of "Gunga Din," Rudyard Kipling's poem about an Indian water boy, had been kicked around since 1928. MGM was originally interested, but since the poem only has enough plot for a ten-minute film the task of coming up with a script was difficult and MGM finally dropped the project. The poem then went from studio to studio and along the way writers, including William Faulkner, took a stab at it. When the project landed at RKO, Ben Hecht and Charles MacArthur wrote a script which was eventually adapted into the final film. Howard Hawks was to have directed, and the film was to have starred Robert Montgomery as Ballentine and Spencer Tracy as McChesney. When Hawks left RKO, though, the direction was handed over to George Stevens, and the offer to Montgomery was withdrawn.

Cary Grant was offered the role of Ballentine, the soldier who wants to leave the Regiment in order to marry and settle down, but the part went to Douglas Fairbanks, Jr. Grant, however, chose to take the part of Cutter, the boisterous Cockney. Cutter had been seen as a secondary role, but when Grant got his hands on it he turned it into a classic comic characterization and, by doing so, paved his way to more varied roles in the future.

The film was shot in the Sierras, which caused many problems because the weather constantly shifted. Windstorms damaged the sets, dust storms prevented photography, the temperature changed abruptly from 115°F to 30°F, and snowstorms destroyed the illusion of an Indian village. As a result the film went over schedule and the crew was called back before shooting was completed. The studio, however, was so delighted by the footage that the filmmakers were sent back to the Sierras, and an all-out battle scene was added as a climax.

This added battle, between the British Regiment and the followers of the Guru (played by Eduardo Ciannelli), was the most complicated section of the film to shoot. It involved 1500 men, four elephants, and several hundred horses. To make things run smoothly, George Stevens first planned the battle out on paper, then rehearsed the cast in small groups and in slow motion. Finally, everything was put together and speeded up. As a precaution, however, first aid facilities were located just beyond camera range; fortunately, they went unused.

After the film was finished, Rudyard Kipling's widow demanded that one change be made. In the original version Kipling appeared as a character, took part in the battle, and was seen at the end composing the poem "Gunga Din." Mrs. Kipling felt that people would laugh when he appeared on the screen, and that the role generally exposed Kipling to ridicule. RKO obliged her by editing out the sequences in which the character of Kipling appeared alone, and matting him out optically in scenes with other actors.

Halloween

Gunga Din

HALLOWEEN

1978
Director, John Carpenter
Producer, Debra Hill

Made in just three weeks on a budget of $320,000, Halloween has grossed more than fifty million dollars, thus becoming the most profitable independent film ever made. It was also a tremendously influential trendsetter, spawning a spate (which is only now beginning to slack off) of mad-slasher schlockers in which promiscuous teenagers are done in by heavy-breathing psychos.

The flood of imitations has tended to obscure Halloween's virtues as a film, making it seem much worse in retrospect. For instance, there is actually very little overt violence in Halloween; director John Carpenter achieves most of his shock effects through suggestion—and so successfully does he do so that, for example, people who watched the scene in which Nancy Loomis is attacked in her car will swear that they saw her throat slashed and blood spurting out; in fact the shot is cut before the knife touches her.

Another aspect of the film that merits comment is (unlikely as it may seem in view of the subject) its sense of humor. Dedicated movie buff Carpenter slipped in a number of playful allusions to favorite films: a television set shows appropriate scenes from the 1957 *The Thing* (which Carpenter would later remake) and *Forbidden Planet* (1956); the psychiatrist in *Halloween* is named Sam Loomis, the name of the John Gavin character in *Psycho* (1960); and the sheriff is named Lee Brackett after screenwriter Leigh Brackett, who worked on *The Big Sleep* (1946) and *Rio Bravo* (1959). Carpenter used similar "in" jokes in his later films, too. In *Escape From New York* (1981) minor characters are named after fellow horror-film directors George Romero and David Cronenberg. In *The Fog* (1980) someone mentions a trip to Bodega Bay, where Hitchcock's *The Birds* (1963) was set; the coroner is named Dr. Phibes after the character played by Vincent Price in *The Abominable Dr. Phibes* (1971); and a minor character is named for Dan O'Bannon who cowrote, edited, designed, and acted in Carpenter's first film *Dark Star* (1974) and later wrote *Alien* (1979).

Although *Halloween* supposedly takes place on Halloween night in "Haddonfield, Illinois," it was actually shot in May in a suburb of Los Angeles. Bushels of dead leaves were scattered on the lawns in an effort to create an autumnal effect (although if you look carefully you will notice that the trees are still green). Even the pumpkins had to be faked; the art director sent to South America for pumpkin-shaped gourds and then had them painted orange.

High Noon

HIGH NOON

1952
Director, Fred Zinnemann
Producers, Carl Foreman and Stanley Kramer

High Noon—at 85 minutes one of the shortest contemporary movies ever made—follows minute by minute the story of the aging ex-sheriff who protects a town that does not want to protect itself. Based loosely on "The Tin Star," a short story in *Collier's* magazine, it was the last movie from Stanley Kramer's company to be filmed at United Artists. The movie debuted in the midst of the era of the Communist scare and Hollywood blacklists, and writer and co-producer Carl Foreman used *High Noon* to make a statement. Masking his ideologies in allegory, Foreman paral-

leled the isolated movie world of Hollywood with the isolated western town of Hadleyville, New Mexico. Because of trouble with the House Un-American Activities Committee Foreman would soon move to England, where he would write, uncredited, the script for *The Bridge on the River Kwai* (1957).

For Grace Kelly *High Noon* was her second movie and her first starring role. Gary Cooper was not first choice to play Sheriff Will Kane. The script was sent to Marlon Brando, Montgomery Clift, and Charlton Heston. But the movie's chief backer—a lettuce grower in the San Joaquin Valley—wanted Cooper, and it is difficult to imagine anyone else in the role. *High Noon* will always be remembered as Gary Cooper's movie. The tall man who was equally at home in

white tie and tails caught the public's fancy wearing chaps and spurs. Cooper accepted a much lower salary, $60,000 and a percentage, because the script was "a natural" for him. It rekindled fond memories of the stories his father, a Montana Supreme Court judge, used to tell him about sheriffs.

Gary Cooper received his first Academy Award in 1941 for *Sergeant York*. Coop's friend, John Wayne, picked up Cooper's second Oscar for *High Noon*. Cooper, convinced he would lose to Marlon Brando in *Viva Zapata!* was vacationing and recovering from an illness and did not attend the awards ceremony. *High Noon* was also rewarded for its music score by Dimitri Tiomkin and its Oscar-winning title song ("Do not forsake me, oh my darling").

HUD

1963
Director, Martin Ritt
Producers, Martin Ritt and Irving Ravetch

Hud was created from a novel titled *Horseman, Pass By* by Larry McMurtry (*The Last Picture Show*). The movie brought back to a western Brandon de Wilde, who ten years earlier had played Joey in *Shane*. In that movie he had fallen under the influence of Shane and now in *Hud* the influence would come from maverick Hud Bannon (Paul Newman) and his idealistic father Homer (Melvyn Douglas).

Screenwriters Irving Ravetch and Harriet Frank had earlier worked with director Martin Ritt on *The Long Hot Summer* (1958), and Joanne Woodward's line to Paul Newman in that movie—"No, thanks, I've had one cold-hearted bastard in my life, I don't need another"—is the same line Patricia Neal as Alma delivers to Newman in *Hud*. The writers included some cryptic words for Newman: "I'll remember you, honey. You're the one who got away."

Author McMurtry was unhappy with the memora-ble scene where Homer and Hud drive their diseased cattle into a ditch to be killed. He felt that director Ritt had not made clear either that the cattle being slaughtered were irreplaceable breeding cattle, or that Homer had died because his life's work had died.

Audience reaction to *Hud* was overwhelmingly favorable, and it was well received by many critics. But while Bosley Crowther of *The New York Times* praised the movie, he had problems with the title. It was so short that he worried lest a slip of a typesetter's hand change *Hud* to *Mud* or worse. He might have rested easier had Paramount stuck with the working title, *Hud Bannon Against the World*.

Two of the movie's principals—Melvyn Douglas and Patricia Neal—won Academy Awards, as did James Wong Howe for his superb black and white cinematography. Miss Neal could not attend the awards ceremony because she was home in England having a baby. A few years later she suffered a stroke, but came back to be nominated for the best actress Oscar for her work in the movie *The Subject Was Roses* (1968).

It Happened One Night

IT HAPPENED ONE NIGHT

1934
Director/Producer, Frank Capra

It Happened One Night started a movie trend that became known as screwball comedy.

When it opened at Radio City Music Hall in 1934, the movie was dismissed as just another bus picture. Considering that it was originally a short story in *Cosmopolitan* magazine entitled "Night Bus," bus picture was an accurate moniker. Director Frank Capra read the story one day at his barber's, and he suggested that Columbia buy it. They did, for $5000, but studio head Harry Cohn insisted that Capra get rid of the word bus. Cohn wasn't too happy with Capra's alternative, however, figuring it was too long to fit on the marquee.

An already successful Clark Gable played opposite star Claudette Colbert in *It Happened One Night*, and his star rose even higher as a direct result of the movie. Early in his career Gable had been passed over by studio executive Sam Goldwyn, who said Gable's ears were too big, but after *It Happened One Night*, for which he won an Academy Award, he was sought after for many roles, including that of Rhett Butler in *Gone With the Wind* (1939). Colbert was nominated for the best actress Oscar for her role in *It Happened One Night*, but since she had no expectations of winning she scheduled a train trip to New York for the night of the awards ceremony. When she heard on the radio that she had won, she paused long enough on the way to the station to give the shortest acceptance speech in the history of the Academy: "I'm happy enough to cry but can't take the time to do it. A taxi is waiting outside and the engine is running." They held the train for her and she and Oscar made it to New York as scheduled. Director Capra received his first Oscar that night. In 1936 he received his second Oscar for *Mr. Deeds Goes to Town*, and in 1938 he picked up his third for *You Can't Take It With You*.

Hud

It's a Wonderful Life

IT'S A WONDERFUL LIFE

1946
Director/Producer, Frank Capra

Actor/director John Cassavetes has said that, "Maybe there never was an America in the thirties. Maybe it was all Frank Capra." Director Frank Capra, whose greatest contribution to movies was in the 1930s, has been lauded and maligned for embodying Capraesque stylishness and the corniness of Capracorn.

Although the bulk of his movies were made in the '30s, his most famous movie, *It's a Wonderful Life*, was directed after World War II. The war had left him disillusioned with the world to the point where he thought perhaps

the critics who labeled his movies Capracorn were right, that he was a Polly-anna after all, blindly looking only at the good side in everything. But today's critics now believe that Capra's movies are a balm to the bad times, that in filling the screen with humor and good times Capra has soothed man's sadly sagging spirit and given him hope.

Jimmy Stewart was Capra's choice to play George Bailey in *It's a Wonderful Life* and he got together with him one day to explain the script. As he was explaining it the story became less and less clear until Capra gave up, yelling "Forget it. I haven't got a story." He need not have made such a fuss. Stewart was ready to sign even without a run-through. Capra also had to have Lionel Barrymore and Donna Reed from MGM—and a blonde. He viewed some tests and

found her, Gloria Grahame, whom he could have "for a cuppa coffee," according to MGM casting director Billy Grady. The rest of his actors, except newcomer Sheldon Leonard and the angel Henry Travers, were well known in Capra movies.

It's a Wonderful Life received mixed reviews from the critics, and audiences were not turning out in the hoped-for numbers. In order to hype the movie, Capra and Jimmy Stewart agreed to make a tour of Texas. On the flight from Beaumont to Dallas with ceiling zero Stewart had to assist the pilot with the landing gear. Taking sledgehammer in hand, they beat the wheels into place. Stewart had flown many missions both in the war and in the movies, but he had never been so worried about the outcome.

It's a Wonderful Life received Oscar nominations for best picture, best director, and best actor.

JAWS

1975
Director, Steven Spielberg
Producers, Richard Zanuck and David Brown

The author of the best-selling novel *Jaws*, Peter Benchley (who had a small part in the movie as a TV reporter), is the son of screenwriter Nathaniel Benchley (*The Russians Are Coming, The Russians Are Coming* in 1966) and grandson of humorist Robert Benchley. Director Steven Spielberg became interested in Benchley's book when Universal optioned it, and he was hired after a couple of prospective directors had been interviewed (one lost the job because he kept referring to the shark as a whale). Producers David Brown and Richard Zanuck are responsible for seeing the potential for a movie in the book, and they were confident that they could find a Great White that was trainable. They soon discovered that dolphins are trainable; sharks are not.

The production team did not expect to be able to find a shark the size of Jaws—25 feet—but 10- to 15-footers are quite common. Reasoning that if you can't find a big shark, use a small stunt man, they hired former jockey Carl Rizzo. The scenes in which Richard Dreyfuss as Matt Hooper goes underwater in a cage off "Amity Island" actually show jockey Rizzo in a $5/8$-size cage off the Great Barrier Reef in Australia. Shot by well-known underwater photographers Ron and Valerie Taylor, the scenes emphasize the terrifying size of the shark.

Jaws

KING KONG

1933
Directors, Ernest B. Schoedsack and Merian C. Cooper
Producer, Merian C. Cooper

King Kong was the brainchild of Merian C. Cooper. Cooper was a journalist, an explorer, and a former war pilot, and the story as he formed it in his mind combined all his interests. There would be an expedition to the prehistoric Skull Island where Kong, a giant ape ten times the size of a man, would be found and brought back to New York: there he would be shot down by airplanes. Cooper joined with his friend Ernest B. Schoedsack, with whom he had co-directed *Chang* (1927) and *The Four Feathers* (1933), and they were in business.

Cooper wasn't sure how to go about making a believable giant ape—until he met Willis O'Brien. O'Brien was working at RKO on a film called *Creation*, about a group of men who find prehistoric life inside a volcano. He had been working on miniatures for a year and had produced some impressive footage, which included a man being chased by a triceratops (a three-horned dinosaur). This so impressed Cooper that he had O'Brien taken off *Creation* (which was then abandoned) and put to work on *King Kong*. Some of *Creation*'s footage can be spotted in *King Kong* and *Son of Kong* (1933).

While the long shots of King Kong were miniatures, it was necessary to create a life-size bust of Kong's head and hand. The head was incredibly detailed and allowed for a full range of facial expressions. It took forty bearskins to provide enough fur to cover the bust. The hand was even more complex, because it had to be able to grab Fay Wray. Wray had to spend hours standing in this hand, ten feet above the ground, and this caused all kinds of problems. She had to kick, scream, and squirm around in Kong's paw, and in doing so unfortunately loosed the great ape's mechanical

Jaws was shot on Martha's Vineyard, off Cape Cod, Massachusetts—a former whaling town where all the houses were built at the best slant to view the returning sea captains—and it proved to be a perfect Amity. Filming was on Cow Bay, where the low tides and physical layout were right for sheltering the camera crew and installing the 12-ton underwater runner for the model shark. To make the model—affectionately named "Bruce," after Spielberg's attorney—Universal brought out of retirement Bob Mattey, who created Flash Gordon's rockets and the squid that fights with the *Nautilus* crew in *20,000 Leagues Under the Sea*

(1954). Three 25-foot models were made—one completely closed and two open to run on a trolley on the ocean's bottom.

The Coast Guard was of such great assistance that when the movie was completed Universal asked what it could do in return. The answer: design new uniforms for the female members of the crew. No sooner said than done. It may be the only Coast Guard contingent whose women wear Edith Head originals. *Jaws* cost $7 million to produce, made history for Universal and Spielberg, and managed to make swimmers as scared to go in the water as *Psycho* (1960) had made bathers scared to go in the shower.

King Kong

grip. Every so often she would kick so hard that the hand would open completely and Wray would be left dangling, hanging on to Kong's thumb for dear life.

One element that contributed greatly to the film's believability was the soundtrack. Murray Spivak, the sound supervisor, worked long and hard trying to find a voice for Kong. Kong's roar, for instance, was created by taking a tape of a lion's roar, running it backwards at slow speed, and rerecording it. The high spots and the loud peaks were taken and spliced together and then rerecorded several times. When spliced together this produced a roar majestic enough for the likes of Kong.

An important set for the film was the great wall that separated the natives of Skull Island from Kong. It had to be huge and majestic. Cooper wanted to avoid the expense of building such a set and explored the back lots of Hollywood in search of something suitable. He found it in the skeleton of the huge gate that Cecil B. de Mille had built in 1927 for *King of Kings*. Apart from the addition of a giant door, only minor alterations were needed and the wall was used. This wall finally met its end when it was destroyed in the burning of Atlanta sequence in *Gone With the Wind* (1939).

A last footnote to the film: in the touching final scene when Kong is shot down on top of the Empire State Building, there's one brief glimpse of the pilot and co-pilot of that fatal plane. The two men are Merian C. Cooper and Ernest B. Schoedsack.

Kramer vs. Kramer

KRAMER VS. KRAMER

1979
Director, Robert Benton
Producer, Stanley Jaffe

When producer Stanley Jaffe first sent Dustin Hoffman a copy of Avery Corman's novel *Kramer vs. Kramer* and asked him if he would be interested in starring in a film version, Hoffman turned the offer down. He still said no after reading writer/director Robert Benton's initial screenplay. Gradually though, as Benton went through rewrite after rewrite, Hoffman was coaxed into doing it—finally persuaded by the promise that he would be able to collaborate with Benton on the creation of

his character. Ironically, *Kramer vs. Kramer* also gave him the opportunity to play a character going through an untidy divorce just at the time his own marriage to dancer Anne Byrne was breaking up.

For Benton this movie presented an unusual working environment. He had gotten his start in movies as a writer—usually in collaboration with David Newman, whom he had met when they were both on the staff of *Esquire* (they originated that magazine's "Dubious Achievement" awards). He and Newman wrote *There Was a Crooked Man* (1960) and *Bonnie and Clyde* (1967) and later worked on the script for the first *Superman* (1978) film. Benton broke into directing with two well-regarded but commercially

unsuccessful features, *Bad Company* (1972) and *The Late Show* (1977), and was offered the chance to direct *Kramer vs. Kramer* after François Truffaut turned it down. Benton wasn't accustomed to having actors tamper with his dialogue, but soon found that adapting his lines to fit Hoffman's speech patterns (so that Hoffman's improvisations would not stand out) became an interesting challenge.

Originally Benton and Jaffe had wanted Kate Jackson to play Mrs. Kramer, but the actress was committed to TV's *Charlie's Angels* and couldn't accept the role. So the part went to Meryl Streep, whose performance won her an Oscar for best supporting actress. The film also marked the screen debut of JoBeth Williams in the small role of the woman with whom Hoffman has a brief affair, which causes him to confront an unexpected touch of reality when his son finds this new woman wandering around the house naked.

Hoffman quarrelled frequently with Benton during the shooting, and it began to be rumored on the set that he had only taken the part because he feared that if he let it go Al Pacino would get it. The story—although it was totally unfounded—soon developed into a running gag; the crew even gave Hoffman a coffee mug with Pacino's name on it. In an effort to get even one day, Hoffman approached a crew member and remarked, "Did you know you look just like Al Pacino?" But the joke backfired; without missing a beat the man replied, "*You*? Or the *real* Pacino?"

THE LADY EVE

1941
Director, Preston Sturges
Producer, Paul Jones

The Lady Eve

Between 1940 and 1944 Preston Sturges wrote and directed an astonishing eight features, including such undisputed comic masterpieces as *The Great McGinty* (1940), *The Lady Eve* (1941), *Sullivan's Travels* (1941), and *The Palm Beach Story* (1942). At his peak he was the third highest-paid executive in the country. He owned The Players, a popular Hollywood restaurant; an engineering firm; and a half interest in a movie studio (Howard Hughes owned the other half). Yet before the decade was up Sturges was considered a has-been. He directed only four more films and when he died in 1959 at the age of 61 he was almost broke.

Sturges' short-lived success had been a long time coming. For much of his life he was just a dilettante. His adoptive father, Solomon Sturges, was a successful Chicago stockbroker. His mother, Mary Desti (originally Dempsey), was a woman of vaguely artistic pretensions who ran perfumeries in Paris and New York and was an intimate of Isadora Duncan; in fact, it was she who gave Duncan the scarf that became entangled in the wheel of her Bugatti and strangled her.

When his parents separated, Sturges divided his time between his mother's cultural odysseys across Europe and his father's business, a combination of experiences that undoubtedly nurtured the cynicism toward both highbrow pre-

tension and middle-class propriety that was to become the hallmark of his films. It was not a way of life, however, likely to help him form a clear idea of what he wanted to do with his life. He dabbled in business and tried to make a name for himself as an inventor (devising a prototype autogyro, a new type of diesel engine, and a kiss-proof lipstick) before trying his hand at writing plays.

The success of his play *Strictly Dishonorable* took him to Hollywood, where he soon became Paramount's top scriptwriter. Then, weary of watching talentless directors wreck his scripts, he made a deal with his bosses: he'd give them his new script for a token ten dollars—but only if he could direct it himself. The script, *The Great McGinty*, made a successful film, and so did

its follow-up, *Christmas in July* (1940), which paved the way for Sturges' first major picture, *The Lady Eve*.

Sturges tailored *Eve* to leading lady Barbara Stanwyck, adjusting the timing of the whole film to suit her brash delivery. Henry Fonda, who was not generally thought of as a comic actor, proved an excellent foil for Stanwyck, and his all-American earnestness was perfect for the role of the straight-laced herpetologist who declares "Snakes are my life!" (To which Stanwyck replies, "What a life!") Sturges surrounded the stars with members of his familiar "stock company," among them William Demarest, Franklin Pangborn, and Jimmy Conlin. The supporting performers, however, did not get the kid-glove handling Sturges afforded his stars. At one

point, employing his most persuasive tactics in a fruitless endeavor to coax a different line reading out of Fonda and Stanwyck, he stalked over to Demarest, who was not even in the scene, and yelled, "And don't talk so damn fast!"

Although Sturges was successful with *Eve* and with his next two pictures, his temperament eventually got the better of him. He left Paramount after the failure of *The Great Moment* (1944) and went into business with Hughes, with whom his first film, *The Sin of Harold Diddlebock* (alternate title *Mad Wednesday*), in 1947 starred the silent film comedian Harold Lloyd and used some of the footage from Lloyd's 1925 classic, *The Freshman*. It was a ruinously expensive failure that started Sturges on a swift slide into obscurity.

LAST TANGO IN PARIS

1972
Director, Bernardo
Bertolucci
Producer, Alberto
Grimaldi

That Bernardo Berto-
lucci's *Last Tango in
Paris* would be a major
cinematic event was
assured before the film
even opened. Critic
Pauline Kael's 4000-word
rave in *The New Yorker* (in
which she compared *Last
Tango*'s New York Film
Festival debut to the premiere of Stravinsky's *Rites
of Spring*) was reprinted in
its entirety across two
pages of *The New York
Times* by the film's dis-
tributor, United Artists.
And reviewers began a
crazy scramble search for
adjectives in their efforts
to outdo each other in
proclaiming its praises.

The critical hoo-hah
was almost trivial, though,
in comparison with the
controversy over the film's
sex scenes. The film was
shown uncut in France
and the United States.
(There were many at-
tempts to ban it in the
States, but United Artists
was always able to avert
them.) Only the sodomy
scene was cut in Great
Britain. But the reaction in
Bertolucci's native Italy
was much more extreme.
The Catholic church con-
demned *Last Tango* in the
harshest possible terms
and the film was banned
for two months. Even its
eventual release was
short-lived, and it was ultimately banned perma-
nently. All prints were
seized; the negative was
burnt (luckily Bertolucci
had made duplicate nega-

Last Tango in Paris

tives); stars Marlon Brando
and Maria Schneider were
officially condemned for
appearing in it; and Ber-
tolucci was given a four-
year suspended prison
sentence and had his civil
rights revoked for five
years. What more could
anyone have done to
assure the film success?

Bertolucci had intended
the film as a reunion vehicle for Jean-Louis Trin-
tignant and Dominique
Sanda, the stars of his previous picture, *The Con-
formist* (1971). Sanda,
however, became pregnant
and had to bow out.
Catherine Deneuve was all
set to take Sanda's place
when she also became
pregnant. Bertolucci then
chose for the role an
unknown actress named
Maria Schneider, whom he
described as "a Lolita—
but more perverse." Even

with his female star
assured, Bertolucci's casting problems were not
over. Trintignant also
dropped out. Bertolucci,
hunting for a replacement,
wandered into an exhibi-
tion of paintings by British
artist Francis Bacon, and
something in their images
of despair reminded him
of Brando. (One of the
paintings appears in the
film's credit sequence.)

Brando, fresh from the
success of his comeback
performance in *The God-
father* (for which he would
win—and refuse to
accept—the 1972 Acad-
emy Award for best actor),
agreed to appear in the
film and took the part over
completely, improvising
most of his own lines.
Unfortunately, it was to be
his last great performance
before he degenerated into
grotesque self-parody.

LAURA

1944
Director/Producer, Otto
Preminger

No one was particularly
enthusiastic about making
Laura. It was seen as just
another detective story
with a gimmick—the
detective falling in love
with a portrait of the girl
whose death he is inves-
tigating. Only Otto Preminger thought that the film
had potential and could be
something great, and he
was proved right. When
20th Century-Fox bought
the script, Preminger
latched onto it and
arranged to produce the
film. He also wanted to
direct the movie but Dar-
ryl Zanuck, the head of
20th Century-Fox, forbade
it. Zanuck had given Preminger his big chance
some years earlier when
he asked him to direct
Kidnapped (1938), but
problems on the film led
to Preminger's being
replaced. Now back at
20th Century-Fox, Zanuck
announced that Preminger
would never direct a film
as long as he was there.

For a while it looked as
though no one—other
than Preminger—wanted
to direct *Laura*. Lewis
Milestone, Walter Lang,
and John Brahm were
among the many who
turned down the job.
Finally Rouben Mamoulian,
the man who directed
Oklahoma! and *Porgy
and Bess* on Broadway,
accepted and started work.
He filmed for 18 days and
was taken off by Zanuck.
Depending on whom you
believe, Mamoulian either
did a job not to Zanuck's
liking or was undermined
by producer Preminger. In
any event, Mamoulian left

and, stuck with a film without a director, Zanuck relented and allowed Preminger to take over.

Dana Andrews desperately wanted the role of Mark, the detective. He was convinced that it would make him a star. However, Zanuck had John Hodiak in mind for the part. Andrews embarked on a mini-campaign to get himself chosen and clinched the deal when he ran into Zanuck's wife, Virginia. They talked together for a long time and Andrews brought the conversation around to *Laura*. He explained that it was a different part from the ones he normally received and that he would play it differently. Apparently he convinced Virginia, because two days later Zanuck gave the word that Andrews had been cast.

Perhaps most people's most lasting memory of *Laura* is its haunting love theme, which was written by David Raksin and later given lyrics by Johnny Mercer. Preminger, however, wanted to use Duke Ellington's "Sophisticated Lady" as *Laura's* theme. Raksin tried to talk Preminger out of it, but the best he could do was get Preminger to agree to listen to Raksin's tune. However, Raksin was only given the weekend to write it. Under this intense pressure, Raksin went home and tried to compose, but nothing would come. Then, according to Raksin, he received a letter from his wife. He propped it up on the piano and read it. His wife was leaving him; his marriage was over. The moment this news sunk in he found he was playing the piano. He was playing the theme from *Laura*.

Lost Horizon

LOST HORIZON

1937
Director/Producer, Frank Capra

Lost Horizon was by far the most ambitious film that Columbia Pictures had made up to that point. Columbia was a poor little studio, nicknamed "poverty row," which made do on a staple of Grade B films and the likes of the Three Stooges. However, Frank Capra (Columbia's most successful director who was responsible for among others, *It Happened One Night* in 1934 and *Mr. Deeds Goes to Town* in 1936) read James Hilton's novel about the utopian community of Shangri-La, where war does not exist, and decided he had to make it into a movie.

The casting of the film proved relatively simple. Ronald Colman, after some initial hesitations about working at Columbia, agreed to play the lead, which was crucial because Colman assured box office success. They had trouble casting the High Lama, though. For the man who was supposedly two hundred years old, an actor by the name of A. E. Anson was chosen. Unfortunately, he died. The same fate overtook the second candidate for the role, silent star Henry B. Walthall. On the third try, Capra decided to test someone a bit younger who might stand a better chance of surviving the production. Broadway actor Sam Jaffe was finally chosen, and extensive makeup was used to make him look ancient. Everything from dry oatmeal to cigarette paper was applied to his face in order to give his skin the texture of extreme age. Eventually a mask of his face was sculpted into that of an old man.

Laura

The early scenes of the film are supposed to take place in the frozen tundra of the Himalayas, and Capra concluded that it was essential that the viewers "feel" the cold. Blocks of cornstarch were out, as far as Capra was concerned. He wanted real snow. But how to do it in southern California? Eventually Capra sought out a warehouse with a freezer system used for storing meat. He emptied it out, brought in snow-blowing machinery and constructed an entire set inside the warehouse. The effect of cold was achieved, successfully— you could see the actors' breath. This caused other problems, however. It was so cold that film in the camera kept jamming because the oil had frozen. The crew finally figured out that heaters placed on the film cannisters would keep the cameras rolling. The cold caused other problems, too; the actors were afraid of getting pneumonia through going from the freezing warehouse into the hot California sun.

Once the three-hour epic was finished, Capra held a preview and was shocked to discover that the audience was laughing at the movie. He left the theatre and went over every scene in the picture to try to determine what was wrong. At last he came back and gave orders to splice the opening credits onto the third reel of the film, thus lopping about 20 minutes off the running time. At the next preview, the film closed to thunderous applause. For whatever reason, by throwing away the opening scenes Capra had saved the picture.

The Maltese Falcon

THE MALTESE FALCON

1941
Director, John Huston
Producer, Henry Blanke

Screenwriter John Huston had never directed a movie when he was hired to direct *The Maltese Falcon,* taken from the book by popular writer Dashiell Hammett. Because Huston was as yet untried and because *The Maltese Falcon* was not "an important picture," George Raft refused the role of laconic flatfoot Sam Spade. Other actors were considered— Edward G. Robinson, Fred MacMurray, and Henry Fonda—but Humphrey Bogart got the part. For the Brigid O'Shaughnessy role, which Mary Astor won, Olivia de Havilland, Rita Hayworth, and Ingrid Bergman had been suggested. The role of the fat man, Kasper Gutman, was Sydney Greenstreet's first job in the movies. The ship's captain who delivered the Maltese falcon to Sam Spade was played by director Huston's father, Walter, who would work

with his son again in *The Treasure of the Sierra Madre* (1948).

Huston worked with the actors on a nearly closed set, and he storyboarded the entire movie so that it went along like clockwork. One scene that did not was that in which his father delivers the falcon to Spade's office. Huston had his father do it twenty times, until Huston *père* was tired out and anxious to go home. As a joke, when the poor fellow returned home he was called back to do the scene again.

The 1941-era censorship of the Hays Office, arbiter of moviedom's morality, insisted that Spade and his partner's widow not appear to be lovers and that Peter Lorre's Joe Cairo tone down his "pansy" characterization.

The movie, originally titled *The Gent From Frisco,* was filmed as a B picture in 34 days, for $381,000. It did so well at the box office that Warner Brothers considered making a sequel, *Further Adventures of the Maltese Falcon.* Fortunately that idea never took shape.

THE MAN WHO WOULD BE KING

1975
Director, John Huston
Producer, John Foreman

Director John Huston had been without a good movie for several years when he brought *The Man Who Would Be King* to the screen. Rudyard Kipling wrote a good yarn and audiences were ready for the old-fashioned epic adventure recounted by the movie. Kipling's poems and short stories have been a well-used fount of movie inspiration over the years. His poem "Gunga Din" was the basis for the 1939 film classic, and Frank Capra's first job as director was a 12-minute movie based on the Kipling poem "The Ballad of Fisher's Boarding House."

For 20 years John Huston had dreamed of bringing Rudyard Kipling's short story, "The Man Who Would Be King," to the screen. He had first wanted Clark Gable and Humphrey Bogart for the roles of Daniel Dravot and Peachey Carnehan, but when Bogie died in 1957 Huston put the project aside. The project was reactivated in the 1970s with Robert Redford and Paul Newman in mind. But when the script was sent to Newman, he wired Huston with the perfect casting solution: "For Christ's sake, John, get Connery and Caine." With a budget of $5 million, not an inconsiderable amount in 1975, it was difficult finding financing. Allied Artists, one of the movie's backers, went into bank-

The Man Who Would Be King

ruptcy and Sean Connery and Michael Caine had to sue to get paid.

For *The Man Who Would Be King* dress designer Edith Head created 40,000 costumes, more than she had ever done for any other movie. The movie was shot entirely on location in Morocco. The Khyber Pass of Kipling's story, which was written in the 1880s, is now a multi-lane highway with traffic and telephone poles, so the Atlas Mountains were used instead. Huston began scouting Marrakesh for natives to fill some of the roles. One day he saw an old man—it turned out he was over 100—leaning on a cane in the market square. He was just right for the role of Kafu Selim, the High Priest, and Huston found two other fellows to act as his assistants. None of them took direction very well, but they played their scenes with a natural instinct. After the movie was in the can and Huston was about to preview it he invited the three old men to watch it with him. Huston was anxious to get their

reactions to seeing themselves on the screen, and through the translator he asked, "What did you think of the movie?" The High Priest's eloquent answer, "We will never die," thrilled Huston. One other casting note: Caine's non-actress wife, Shakira, also appears in the movie.

The critics were divided on *The Man Who Would Be King*. Some thought it was too personal a portrayal of the two men, that it should have concentrated more on the epic. Even with the talents of Huston, Connery, Caine, Christopher Plummer as Kipling, and Saeed Jaffrey as Billy Fish, and with Maurice Jarre's music and Edith Head's costumes, it received no awards. *One Flew Over the Cuckoo's Nest* won all five major Academy Awards that year—best picture, best director, best actor, best actress, and best screenplay (adaptation)—a feat accomplished only once before by *It Happened One Night* in 1934. But *The Man Who Would Be King* has come to be regarded as a wonderful story and one of Huston's best pictures.

MARY POPPINS

1964
Director, Robert Stevenson
Producers, Bill Walsh and Walt Disney

When Julie Andrews received her Oscar for best actress for *Mary Poppins* she thanked Jack Warner for all his help. His help had taken the unlikely form of making sure that she didn't get the role of Eliza in the 1964 movie version of *My Fair Lady*. Andrews was such a hit on Broadway that everyone assumed she would be cast. Warner, however, didn't want to take a chance by using a screen newcomer in such an important film, so Audrey Hepburn was cast in her place. Hepburn, it should be noted, didn't

even do her own singing in the film—she was dubbed by Marni Nixon (Hepburn did sing her own songs in the 1957 film *Funny Face*). As a result of losing Eliza, Andrews was free when Disney offered her Mary Poppins.

Mary Poppins was Walt Disney's most ambitious live-action film to date, and it became his most successful (although *Splash*, released in 1984, will probably break the studio's record). *Mary Poppins* featured the most complex mixing of live action and animation to date (which created some confusion for the actors, as many dances occurred on a white set while the animators brainstormed and told them what to do). It also featured the best score of the Sherman brothers, Richard M. and Robert B., with "Chim

Mary Poppins

Chim Cher-ee," "Supercali-fragilisticexpialidocious," and others which became hits. (The Sherman brothers have written songs for most of the Disney films since then, but their most notable achievement may be the song "It's a Small World" which is sung by computerized puppets every three minutes at both Disney World and Disneyland.)

Virtually every role in *Mary Poppins* is played by a well-known character actor. At the beginning of the film the current Nanny resigns: she is played by Elsa Lanchester, who is best known for the title role in *Bride of Franken-stein* (1935). The bird woman, who scarcely has a speaking role, is played by Jane Darwell, who played Ma Joad in *The Grapes of Wrath* (1940). Glynis Johns, who plays Mrs. Banks, has made many movies but is perhaps best known for introducing the song "Send in the Clowns" in *A Little Night Music* on Broadway. Ed Wynn made one of his few screen appearances as the floating Uncle Albert. Wynn (father of Keenan Wynn) preferred Broadway, radio, and television to movies.

Any discussion of the *Mary Poppins* cast must include mention of Dick Van Dyke's amiable and cheerful performance as Bert, the chimney sweep. Van Dyke was currently riding high both in the movies and on TV. The year *Mary Poppins* came out he won an Emmy Award for his highly successful *Dick Van Dyke Show*, and he was to win two more Emmys in the two successive years—an impressive three-in-a-row achievement.

*M*A*S*H*

M*A*S*H

1970
Director, Robert Altman
Producer, Ingo Preminger

*M*A*S*H* was a complete fluke; few people had any confidence in the movie and it surprised everyone by becoming a major hit and eventually the basis for the incredibly successful TV series.

Ring Lardner, Jr. had read the book by Richard Hooker, which was the pseudonym of a doctor who had served during the Korean War and written a book based on his experiences. Lardner took the book and made the rounds of the studios with it, but most weren't interested. At the last studio, 20th Century-Fox, Lardner at last found someone who liked it, Ingo Preminger (brother of Otto). Preminger got 20th Century-Fox to agree to make the film. The problems did not end there, however; no one wanted to direct it. Over a dozen directors were approached and all gave the project a thumbs

down. As a desperate measure, the studio turned to a young filmmaker who only had a few movies to his credit: taking a major chance, they gave the job to the young Robert Altman.

Altman had started his film career directing industrial films for the Calvin Company in Kansas City. From there he branched into low-budget films such as *The Delinquents* (1957) and *The James Dean Story* (1957), which he co-directed. His next move was to television, where he did such series as *Alfred Hitchcock Presents* and *Bonanza*. After a ten-year period during which he made very few movies, he made *That Cold Day in the Park* in 1969. Ingo Preminger says that had he seen *That Cold Day in the Park*, he would never have offered Altman *M*A*S*H*.

For a relatively unknown film director, Altman was very clear about his ideas on movie making. But he didn't always get to carry them out. For example, he wanted to shoot *M*A*S*H* on location

in Korea, but 20th Century-Fox turned down the plan. Instead they offered him a site in Malibu. Altman reluctantly accepted this, but then decided that the golf scene at least should be shot in Japan. Again he was rebuffed and the golf scene was filmed on a public golf course across from the studio. To give the scene authenticity, a number of Japanese women were dressed up as caddies.

The battles Altman did win concerned the script. Altman virtually abandoned Lardner's script, preferring instead to have the actors improvise. At first, the actors balked at this and tried to get Altman taken off the film. When that didn't work they had no choice but to go along with Altman's methods. Another Altman trademark which caused some consternation was his overlapping dialogue, where characters speak simultaneously and the audience has to reach for the meaning of the words. Altman has said that "words are not necessarily supposed to be heard," and he demonstrated this in *M*A*S*H*. Ironically, Lardner won an Oscar for best screenplay.

*M*A*S*H* catapulted Altman to fame, and it did the same for Donald Sutherland, who played Hawkeye Pierce. Gary Burghoff, who played Radar O'Reilly, became popular when he repeated the role in the TV series. He was the only performer featured in both the movie and TV versions.

A trivia footnote: *M*A*S*H* is one of the few films to have the closing credits spoken out loud— they are announced over the P.A. system.

MEET ME IN ST. LOUIS

1944
Director, Vincente Minnelli
Producer, Arthur Freed

Meet Me in St. Louis

When Judy Garland was presented with the script of *Meet Me in St. Louis* she initially turned it down. The story called for her to play an emergent teenager and Garland felt it was time to play more adult roles. She also agreed with MGM head Louis B. Mayer, who was of the opinion that the script, based on a series of pieces Sally Benson had written for *The New Yorker*, had no plot. However, Arthur Freed, the head of musical productions, held firm. He wanted to make the film and he wanted to make it with Garland. Reluctantly, Garland gave in and made the movie, little realizing the effect it would have both on her career and on her personal life.

Garland and Vincente Minnelli, who was directing the film, did not get off to a good start because Garland didn't understand the character she was playing and insisted on "acting." Minnelli wanted her to be herself, and Garland wasn't sure how to do that. At first their working relationship was stormy—she ridiculed the script, and often when her frustrations grew too great she walked off the set. However, Minnelli gradually won her over and eventually she came to grips with the part. To call a truce, they went out on a double date together. This led to single dates together and finally, even though Gar-

land was still married, they moved in together. Their eventual marriage, which was to last for several years, produced a daughter—current superstar Liza Minnelli.

One of the most intriguing characters in the film is Tootie, the youngest child in the family, played by Margaret O'Brien. Although O'Brien was only seven years old she was already quite the actress with several films to her credit, including *Journey for Margaret* (1942). However, she had to go to great lengths to achieve her performance. Before she started a scene her mother would whisper to her, and then she would go out and act. Before they started shooting the classic Christmas sequence where Tootie runs outside and destroys her snowman, her mother came to Minnelli with the news that Minnelli would

have to do the briefing. O'Brien, it seemed, was angry with her mother. Her mother instructed Minnelli that he must tell O'Brien that someone was going to kill her little dog. Minnelli was naturally reluctant, but the film had to get done, so he went to O'Brien and told her the unfortunate news about her dog. O'Brien asked, "Is there going to be lots of blood?" Minnelli elaborated further. He found himself forced to embellish the story until O'Brien was reduced to tears. Then Minnelli ordered the cameras to start filming. When the take was finished O'Brien skipped happily off the set; Minnelli, however, took several hours to calm down.

When a film was finished it was customary to screen the rough cut print. Most of the people involved agreed that *Meet*

Me in St. Louis was too long, but a dispute arose over what to cut. Several people suggested that the Halloween sequence be eliminated because it had nothing to do with the plot, but Minnelli resisted this strenuously. It was this very scene that had made him decide to do the picture. As a compromise, the scene was deleted and the film shown to see how it looked without it. After the lights came up Minnelli nervously awaited the verdict. Arthur Freed agreed that it wasn't the same film without the Halloween sequence, and the scene was restored. Instead, they cut "Boys and Girls Like You and Me," a song that had been previously dropped from the Broadway show *Oklahoma!* All doubts about *Meet Me in St. Louis* were resolved when it opened to unanimous popular and critical acclaim.

MIDNIGHT COWBOY

1969
Director, John Schlesinger
Producer, Jerome Hellman

In 1967 in *The Graduate*, Dustin Hoffman did what most actors only dream of—he became a movie star overnight. So when he was offered the role of Ratso Rizzo, the dying, two-bit con man in *Midnight Cowboy*, his business agents tried to talk him out of it. Why throw away his new-found stardom to take a supporting role in what showed all the signs of turning into an obscure art-house movie? Audiences would think that his original success had been just a fluke. Hoffman, though, fearful of being typecast as one or another of Benjamin Braddock's alter egos for the rest of his career, insisted on taking the job.

Time, of course, proved that Hoffman made a wise choice. Although tame by today's standards, at the time, *Midnight Cowboy*'s sordid subject matter, nudity, and crude dialogue made it one of the most daring films ever to be put out by a major studio. Add to this the arty direction of expatriate English filmmaker John Schlesinger, and you couldn't find a more "happening" film. Audiences flocked to it and it became the first (and probably last) "X"-rated film to win an Oscar.

The major source of the film's success was the touching and finely detailed relationship between Ratso and Joe Buck (Jon Voight). During the making of the film Hoffman and Voight developed a certain lighthearted rivalry, effectively illustrated in the following anecdote: One day Schlesinger asked Hoffman, playing a character dying of tuberculosis, to work on his cough. Hoffman took this advice so literally and coughed so violently that he fell down vomiting in the street. "Wow!" said Voight, "How am I gonna upstage *that*?"

A Night at the Opera

A NIGHT AT THE OPERA

1935
Director, Sam Wood
Producer, Irving Thalberg

A Night at the Opera marked a drastic change for the Marx Brothers. Their previous film, *Duck Soup* (1933), although now acknowledged as a comedy classic, opened to a confused response and did little business. Paramount dumped the Marx Brothers and, at the suggestion of producer Irving Thalberg, MGM picked them up. Thalberg, the legendary "Boy Wonder," was one of the most powerful men at MGM and he knew how to save the Marx Brothers. The problem with *Duck Soup*, according to Thalberg, was that it didn't have a plot or a love interest. He thought it was a funny film, but figured that more people would go to see a funny film about real people. He won over the Marx Brothers to this point of view and was proved right when *A Night at the Opera* became their most successful film.

After welcoming them to MGM, Thalberg set up a meeting with the Marx Brothers. Thalberg, however, was notorious for making people wait to see him. Most people suffered this in silence, but not the Marx Brothers. They showed up for their appointment only to be told that Thalberg was busy. They conferred briefly, then each lit two cigars and began puffing them under the crack in Thalberg's doorframe. Minutes later he came out, thinking the building was on fire, and he was less than delighted to find the three brothers waiting. He told them in no uncertain terms that he did not want them to blow smoke under his door ever again, so for their next meeting they tried a different approach. Thalberg again could not see them at the appointed time, so the Marx Brothers

Midnight Cowboy

simply picked up all the file cabinets in the office, placed them in front of his door, and left.

Another Thalberg trait which the Marx Brothers didn't appreciate was his habit of conducting several story conferences simultaneously. He would work on one script and suggest changes to the writers, then move to the next room and return in twenty or thirty minutes. When he tried this on the Marx Brothers he was chagrined, on his return, to find the three brothers sitting on the floor, naked, roasting potatoes over the carpet. This time Thalberg gave up and ordered some butter from the cafeteria.

One idea which developed out of the conference with Thalberg was to test the comedy material before it was included in the film. The Marx Brothers' first two films, *The Cocoanuts* (1929) and *Animal Crackers* (1930), had been done on Broadway, and all of the jokes were tried and true. So for *A Night at the Opera*, the tour was born. The comedy scenes for the film were gathered together and mounted as a mini revue; depending on audience response, jokes were retained or thrown out. As a result of the tour, one line, which all the writers agreed was funny, never made it into the film: Groucho is sitting in his opera box watching the opera when suddenly a horde of policemen descend on the stage. Groucho's line was "Either there are cops in *La Traviata* or the jig is up." The tour audience didn't agree with the writers that the line was amusing, and it was thrown out of the script.

NIGHT OF THE LIVING DEAD

1968
Director, George A. Romero
Producers, Russell Streinger and Karl Hardman

With its murky black and white photography, graphic violence, and acting that runs the gamut from amateurish to nonexistent, *Night of the Living Dead*, shot on a shoestring budget in—of all places—Pittsburgh, is nonetheless one of the most effective and influential horror films of all time. Its success can be attributed almost entirely to one man: its director, co-writer, cinematographer, and editor, George A. Romero.

Romero grew up a movie-obsessed kid in the Parchester section of the Bronx. When he was 14 he was arrested for throwing a burning dummy off a tenement roof (the climax of an amateur sci-fi epic entitled *The Man From the Meteor*). He later attended the Carnegie-Mellon Institute in Pittsburgh, where

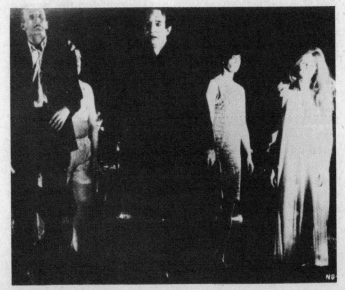

Night of the Living Dead

he studied drama and painting. Except for a brief stint in 1959 as a grip on Alfred Hitchcock's *North by Northwest*, which instilled in him a lifelong hatred of the studio system, he has lived and worked in Pittsburgh ever since. Once, when someone asked him, "Why Pittsburgh?" he replied, "I like the beer."

After leaving school Romero and a group of friends formed Latent Image, a production company which specialized in commercials and sports documentaries. For Latent Image, Romero directed commercials for U.S. Steel, Gulf Oil, Alcoa, and Heinz, and for Richard Nixon's 1968 presidential campaign. His most elaborate effort, however, was a parody of the 1966 film *Fantastic Voyage*, in which the crew of a miniaturized submarine witnesses first hand the effects of Calgon detergent.

All this, however, was just a warm-up. In 1968 Romero began shooting *Night of the Living Dead*, using $60,000 (only two-thirds the cost of the Calgon commercial) raised

from private investors, and another $54,000 in deferred credit. One of the investors was a butcher, who was able to supply Romero with all the bones and entrails he needed.

After thirty days shooting—mostly on weekends—the film was finished. But when it was first shown the response was far from favorable. The trade paper *Variety* panned it unmercifully, saying that the film ". . . casts serious aspersions on the integrity and social responsibility of its Pittsburgh-based makers, distrib Walter Reade, the film industry as a whole, and exhibs who book the pic, [and it raises] doubts about the future of the regional cinema movement, and about the moral health of filmgoers who cheerfully opt for this unrelieved orgy of sadism . . . amateurism of the first order."

Chicago movie critic Roger Ebert wrote an impassioned article in *Reader's Digest* warning audiences about the film and leveling charges of moral irresponsibility not only at the filmmakers and exhibitors, but at parents who allowed their children to see the movie. (It may be noted here that Ebert later did his bit for cinematic decency by writing the screenplay for Russ Meyer's *Beyond the Valley of the Dolls* in 1970.)

Despite the negative outpourings of the critics, *Night of the Living Dead* eventually developed a cult following. It was even shown in the Museum of Modern Art's Cineprobe series in 1969, thus paving the way for *Martin* (1978), *Dawn of the Dead* (1979), *Creepshow* (1982), and (soon) *Day of the Dead*.

North by Northwest

NORTH BY NORTHWEST

1959
Director/Producer, Alfred Hitchcock

North by Northwest was conceived as part of a trilogy, along with *Vertigo* (1958) and *Psycho* (1969). Originally titled *In a Northerly Direction* and later *Breathless*, producer/director Alfred Hitchcock changed the name to fit his ideas about movie titles: they should be easy to remember, intriguing, suggest action, give a clue without giving away the plot.

When Jimmy Stewart heard that Hitchcock had a movie on the boards he wanted to star in it, not even knowing what it was,

having done *Vertigo* for him so successfully. However Ernest Lehman had written the screenplay with Cary Grant in mind, and Hitchcock did not want to hurt Stewart's feelings by telling him that he had already decided on Grant. Hitchcock stalled until Stewart signed to do *Bell, Book, and Candle*.

MGM wanted Hitchcock to cast Cyd Charisse as the female lead but, following his credo of signing blonde women opposite dark men, Hitchcock wanted Eva Marie Saint. When he saw the dowdy wardrobe created by the costume designer for Saint, similar to what she wore in *On the Waterfront* (1954), Hitchcock took the actress on a shopping spree at Bergdorf Goodman's and chose her clothes for the movie. He

even supervised her sophisticated hairdo and makeup. After grooming her so carefully for *North by Northwest*, Hitchcock was disappointed to see Saint go into a grimy movie like *Exodus* (1960).

Cary Grant received $450,000 plus a percentage of the gross, and $5000 for every day that went past the scheduled ending date. He became a wealthy man when shooting was delayed. Hitchcock's ten percent of the movie's profits would in twenty years' time amount to over $20 million.

There are two well-remembered scenes in *North by Northwest*: the crop-dusting sequence—ostensibly depicting Indiana farmland but in reality shot near Bakersfield, California—and the Mount Rushmore climax. Hitchcock was limited by the United States Department of the Interior in how he could shoot the Mount Rushmore sequence, however. Although the presidents' faces were reconstructed in the studio, the government mandated that there be no shots of actors stepping directly on the faces. They could slide between them—which is what they did—but any action on the faces would be considered a desecration to a shrine of democracy. Certain outdoor scenes were shot on location in Rapid City, at the cafeteria, for instance, and even there the Interior Department was careful to see that Hitchcock did not take advantage of the area. For ten years Hitchcock had wanted to do a movie involving Mount Rushmore, and he got his chance in the final ten minutes of *North by Northwest*.

ON THE WATERFRONT

1954
Director, Elia Kazan
Producer, Sam Spiegel

Marlon Brando began his acting career on the Broadway stage with *I Remember Mama*. Four years later he was playing in the stage production of *A Streetcar Named Desire*. By the time he received his first Academy Award, for *On the Waterfront*, he had been nominated three times in three successive years—for the movie version of *A Streetcar Named Desire* in 1951, *Viva Zapata!* in 1952, and *Julius Caesar* in 1953.

Harry Cohn, studio head at Columbia, originally had Frank Sinatra in mind for the role of Terry Malloy in *On the Waterfront*. It was his idea to link the movie with Sinatra's success in *From Here To Eternity* (1953). When Cohn changed his mind, after already offering the part to Sinatra, the actor sued. The offer then went to Montgomery Clift, who turned it down, calling the Elia Kazan-Budd Schulberg script overblown and corny. And as usually happened when Clift turned down a part, it was next offered to Marlon Brando.

Clift and Brando were the two most sought-after actors of the 1950s. Along with James Dean, they were products of Elia Kazan's Actors' Studio in New York. Known as Method actors, which could mean anything between antiheroic and self-indulgent, the two men fit the same mold and were offered the same types of parts. What Clift

THE PHILADELPHIA STORY

1940
Director, George Cukor
Producer, Joseph L. Mankiewicz

On the Waterfront

would refuse, Brando would usually accept. Because Clift was extremely choosy, his leavings were high-class. He had also turned down the leads in *Sunset Boulevard* (1950), *East of Eden* (1955), and *Somebody Up There Likes Me* (1956). Brando held Clift in such esteem that he would often call to get his response to Brando's latest movie.

Montgomery Clift did Brando a favor by refusing *On the Waterfront*. Although Brando had already made a name for himself after only two movies, *The Men* (1950) and *A Streetcar Named Desire*, the role of Terry Malloy was probably his best and the one for which he is best remembered.

Brando, the only survivor of that gifted trio, has not starred in a critically-acclaimed movie since 1972, the year of *Last*

Tango in Paris and *The Godfather*, for which he won his second Academy Award for best actor. Rod Steiger, who played Brando's brother in *On the Waterfront*, has said of him, "Marlon was in a unique position. He could have done anything, *anything*, however difficult or uncommercial, on the screen and taken the critics, the industry, and the fans with him. But he didn't choose to. I don't know why."

Eva Marie Saint, also a graduate of the Actors' Studio, came to *On the Waterfront*, her first movie, after a successful year on Broadway in *The Trip to Bountiful*, for which she won the Drama Critics' award.

On the Waterfront was labeled a social problem movie. It appeared at a time when Hollywood was still feeling the sting of the

House Un-American Activities Committee, when certain movies had to be made outside the country. *On the Waterfront* was not one of them. According to Kazan, the final scene, in which Terry (Brando) receives the support of his fellow dockworkers after he is beaten, is a demonstration of "vital democracy."

On the Waterfront was an outstanding success, receiving eight Oscars, including best picture, best director to Kazan, best actor to Brando, and best supporting actress to Eva Marie Saint. Leonard Bernstein, whose first movie this was, received a nomination but did not win for best score. Lee J. Cobb, Rod Steiger, and Karl Malden all received nominations for best supporting actor, but lost to Edmond O'Brien in *The Barefoot Contessa*.

Katharine Hepburn was successfully starring on Broadway in Philip Barry's play, *The Philadelphia Story*, when she agreed to do the movie version at MGM. She had wisely purchased the movie rights to the play, and when the play became a major stage hit a number of movie studios tried to buy the rights from Hepburn. The actress sold the rights to MGM only when the studio agreed that she would star in the film. Although she requested Clark Gable and Spencer Tracy for her male leads, she got Jimmy Stewart and Cary Grant instead.

It was producer Joseph L. Mankiewicz's idea to tape the reactions of the play's Broadway audience before starting to film the movie. From the tapes, director George Cukor and screenwriter Donald Ogden Stewart could decide where the play lagged, and speed up the movie's pace in those areas. Three nights before the play closed, with the consent of all concerned and paying the stage actors an extra week's wages, Mankiewicz ordered his crew to wire New York's Broadhurst Theatre for sound. Although the audience was unaware of the taping, the stage actors knew it was going to happen, but they did not know which night they would be taped. One

49

result of the experiment was the addition to the movie of the library scene.

Hepburn had quit her five-year RKO contract—leaving behind bad feelings and the label "box office poison"—for Broadway, and the play had made her wealthier than Hollywood ever had. MGM was not sure what to expect from their star, but "the new Katharine Hepburn" turned out to be surprisingly cooperative. Reporting to MGM ahead of schedule and posing for publicity stills on her day off, she remarked, "If the picture's a success, I'll probably revert to type."

Hepburn, ever the farceur, further surprised the MGM brass when on the first day of shooting she brought to the studio a beautifully wrapped box containing a dead skunk, which she presented to her script man. After he had accepted the gift with mixed emotions, Hepburn dug a hole and buried the animal on Metro soil. No doubt it lies there still.

Audiences and critics alike cheered what *The New York Times* critic Bosley Crowther labeled "a blue-chip comedy." It was refreshing to have a movie with the wit and charm of *The Philadelphia Story* in a year when studios were putting their money into "outdoor epics" and "rugged individualist" films. If Hepburn was box office poison, Crowther smirked, then "a lot of people don't read labels."

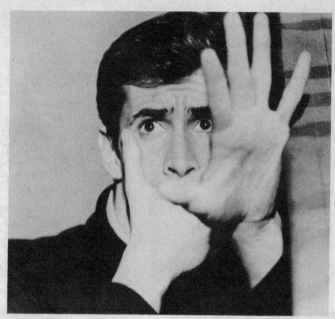

Psycho

PSYCHO

1960
Director/Producer, Alfred Hitchcock

When police searched the isolated Wisconsin farmhouse of Ed Gein, they finally found the grisly answer to a number of missing persons cases that had baffled local authorities throughout the mid- and late-fifties. They found the poorly-preserved corpse of Gein's mother, two chairs upholstered in human skin, an ashtray decorated with used chewing gum and human noses, items made from human bones, and other similarly gruesome *objets d'art*. The horrifying search revealed evidence of over a dozen murders. The exact number of the killer's victims (mostly young women) is unknown; the police were unable to make an accurate count and Gein would not talk.

The case, naturally enough, caused something of a stir at the time and, shorn of its more sensa-tional elements, formed the basis for Robert Bloch's novel *Psycho*, upon which Alfred Hitchcock in turn was to base his most notorious film (Gein's exploits would make it to the screen more explicitly in 1974 in Tobe Hooper's *The Texas Chainsaw Massacre*, in which the Gein character was presented not as a single small-town recluse but as a trio of pathological hillbilly entrepreneurs).

Before *Psycho* Hitchcock had never done a straight, no-holds-barred horror film, and the possibilities offered by the script were irresistible. Since low-budget shockers were popular at the time, he saw the film as an opportunity to beat American International and Hammer Films at their own game. With the irony typical of all Hitchcock undertakings, however, *Psycho*, shot by a television crew for a mere $800,000, was to be his most successful film.

The film's most famous moment, of course, occurs when "Mrs. Bates" brutally

The Philadelphia Story

murders Janet Leigh in the shower. Using 78 separate camera setups to produce less than a minute of completed footage, the sequence is so brilliantly cut that most viewers do not realize that at no time does the knife actually touch the victim's body. In fact, the body was that of a double; Leigh was willing to do the scene, but Hitchcock felt that leading ladies should not have to do nude scenes. "Mrs. Bates," by the way, was also played by a double—when the scene was shot Anthony Perkins was appearing in a play in New York. It may come as a surprise to many movie-goers who have this scene tagged as "typical Hitchcock" to learn that the shower sequence was not conceived by Hitchcock but by title designer Saul Bass (who also did the titles for *The Man With the Golden Arm* in 1956, *Vertigo* in 1958, and *Walk on the Wild Side* in 1962). Hitchcock, though, did add the shots of the blood swirling dcwn the drain. And Bass originally directed the scene where Martin Balsam enters the Bates house before he is murdered, but Hitchcock was dissatisfied with the result and reshot it himself.

And Ed Gein? He died in July 1984, having spent his last years living quietly in a mental institution in Wisconsin, where he had been considered a model inmate. Theoretically he had been eligible for release for some time, but he had no living relatives to speak up in favor of freeing him, so whenever the topic came up the authorities cleared their throats and changed the subject.

Raiders of the Lost Ark

RAIDERS OF THE LOST ARK

1981
Director, Steven Spielberg
Producer, George Lucas

Raiders of the Lost Ark—the result of a conspiracy of talent among director Steven Spielberg, producer George Lucas, and screenwriter Lawrence Kasdan—was Steven Spielberg's Bond movie, albeit Indiana Jones was more Humphrey Bogart than 007. After Spielberg directed *Sugarland Express* in 1974 for United Artists he asked to do a Bond, but he was told only Britons do Bonds. But Indy (played by Harrison Ford) could throw away lines—"I'm just making this up as I go"—with the best of them. It was Lucas' wish that the movie begin with a pre-title bang, just as did the Bond movies, and thus was devised the 12-minute scene in which Indy is chased by a huge boulder.

It actually was a 300-pound boulder and it chased Harrison Ford for ten different takes. Fortunately he survived, for it was only the second week of shooting.

George Lucas knew what kind of hero he wanted down to his hat, and he wanted an old-fashioned serial. It took Philip Kaufman *(The Right Stuff)* to come up with the kicker to the movie—the lost Ark of the Covenant—about which his orthodontist had told him when he was nine.

Spielberg was forever conscious of using his friend George Lucas' money to shoot *Raiders of the Lost Ark*, and he would shoot up to 35 setups and 15 scenes a day in the heat of the Tunisian location. The British crew—cinematographer Douglas Slocombe and second unit man Michael Moore among them—were unflappable. But filming in Tunisia where it was 130 degrees in the shade very soon became tiresome. There

was one long scene left to shoot—the whip vs. scimitar scene in the marketplace where Indy rescues Marion (Karen Allen). Harrison Ford suggested that rather than shoot the scene as planned, which would require at least another day in Tunisia, why not have Indy whip out a gun and kill the Turk; "Shoot the guy and save the girl." It turned out to be one of the favorite scenes in the movie, and Spielberg brought the movie in early in 73 shooting days.

Shooting was also done in London's Elstree Studios and in La Rochelle, France. There Spielberg borrowed the submarine from *Das Boot* (1981), but he was restricted to using it in waves no higher than one meter.

United Artists brought out *Raiders of the Lost Ark* and the Bond offering, *For Your Eyes Only*, in June of 1981, and *Raiders* beat Bond three to one at the box office. Spielberg had made a better Bond.

REBECCA

1940
Director, Alfred Hitchcock
Producer, David O. Selznick

Although Alfred Hitchcock began his career in his native England, his first film job—designing silent-film title cards—was for an American company, Famous Players-Lasky (later Paramount). Twenty years later he finally came to America at the invitation of David O. Selznick to do a film on the sinking of the *Titanic*.

As it happened, the *Titanic* film never came off, and instead Hitchcock was given the task of translating to the screen Daphne du Maurier's bestseller *Rebecca*. Selznick intended *Rebecca* to be his follow-up movie to the phenomenally successful *Gone With the Wind*, and although he gave Hitchcock more freedom than Selznick's directors usually enjoyed, he was very insistent that Hitchcock stick as closely as possible to the novel and avoid a lot of "personal" touches. But Hitchcock still had the last laugh; his customary method of preplanning a film down to the last shot and shooting only what was necessary meant Selznick could not make any changes in the editing room, causing him to complain bitterly about Hitchcock's "goddamn jigsaw cutting."

Selznick did give Hitchcock a free hand in casting, though, agreeing to his choice of Laurence Olivier as Max de Winter (Selznick had suggested, among others, David Niven and William Powell). Just as he had done for *Gone*

Rebecca

With the Wind, Selznick mounted a nationwide talent search to find a lead actress to play the nameless heroine. Olivier tried to get Vivien Leigh the part, but Hitchcock wanted Joan Fontaine, and he got her. (Hitchcock even considered giving a name to the "nameless" heroine; his idea was to call her Daphne de Winter—a play on the original author's name.) Besides Fontaine, the only other American in the cast was Florence Bates, a Texas lawyer who decided she wanted to get into show business. She played the rich American for whom Fontaine works as a paid companion at the start of the film.

One of the most curious aspects of *Rebecca* is that it is the only one of the 51 films Hitchcock made since *The Lodger* in 1926 in which he does not appear. Hitchcock was often very subtle about slipping in his cameo appearances. For instance, he can be seen in a newspaper advertisement in *Lifeboat* (1944) and in a college reunion photograph in *Dial M for Murder* (1954). But even though publicity stills for *Rebecca* show Hitchcock in costume lurking outside a telephone booth as George Sanders makes a call, there is no such cameo in the completed film.

Now there's a mystery.

REBEL WITHOUT A CAUSE

1955
Director, Nicholas Ray
Producer, David Weisbart

When Nicholas Ray, the director of *In a Lonely Place* (1950) and *Johnny Guitar* (1954), described the film that he wanted to make out of *Rebel Without a Cause* Warner Brothers was ecstatic. The story, about misunderstood teenagers trying to find meaning in their lives, seemed to offer a perfect way to capitalize on the youth market. Warners had some reservations, though, particularly about the casting. Ray wanted to cast two then unknowns—James Dean and Natalie Wood. The studio didn't like that idea and wanted to use Jayne Mansfield and Tab Hunter because both were being groomed for stardom. Ray was adamant, and when *East of Eden* was released in 1955 and catapulted the young Dean to superstardom, the studio dropped all resistance.

For an actor, Dean had more than the usual amount of influence on *Rebel Without a Cause*. He was directly responsible for finding both the composer and the screenwriter for the film. The composer was Leonard Rosenman, who was Dean's piano teacher. Rosenman had never thought of movie composing until one day when James Dean brought Elia Kazan to a concert given by Rosenman. Kazan was working with Dean on *East of Eden* and was so impressed with the concert that he hired Rosenman on the spot. Rosenman wrote the music for *East of Eden* and was carried over to work on *Rebel Without a Cause*.

The movie's screenwriter was Stewart Stern, who had one screenplay to his credit. One day when he went to visit his cousin, James Dean was there. Stern took an immediate liking to Dean. In the evening they went to a sneak preview of *East of Eden* and Stern said that he'd never seen so impressive a screen debut. Then Dean took a liking to Stern. Dean introduced Stern to Nicholas Ray; Ray spent a night explaining what he wanted, and then hired Stern. To research the assignment, Stern went to a Juvenile Hall and spent ten days posing as a social worker.

The two most famous scenes in the film are the scene where Dean takes out his frustration on a desk, and the scene where

the youths play "chicken" with their cars. Dean spent an entire day getting ready to film the desk scene, which was one of the first shots in the movie. The whole crew waited until he got into the mood, and Ray gave instructions that Dean was not to be disturbed, no matter how much money the delay was costing. Finally, Dean signified that the moment had come. He walked out of his dressing room and came to the set, and filming began. Dean started to pound on the desk, finally breaking it to splinters. The scene was shot in one take, and after everyone finished congratulating him it was discovered that Dean had broken two bones in his hand.

The "chicken" scene gained greater fame when James Dean died in an auto accident at the age of 24—the same year that *Rebel* was released. *Giant*, his last film, was released in 1956 after his death.

Rocky

ROCKY

1978
Director, John G. Avildsen
Producers, Gene Kirkwood, Irwin Winkler, and Robert Chartoff

Rocky is the story of a small-time boxer who, against all odds, fights his way to the top and wins boxing's greatest prize. Perhaps the most fascinating thing about the picture, though, is how the film parallels the story of *Rocky*'s creator, Sylvester Stallone.

Stallone was just another New York nobody before *Rocky* was made—one more would-be actor/writer, trying without much success to peddle scripts and find work. He finally made the big career commitment and came to Hollywood, where he got bit parts and cameos (he can be glimpsed as a subway thug in Woody Allen's 1971 *Bananas*).

Even when he got his first substantial role (in 1974 in *The Lords of Flatbush* with Henry Winkler, then also unknown) he caused little stir. Sylvester Stallone seemed doomed to obscurity.

The crucial moment occurred when Stallone

was sitting in his room watching television and happened to switch to a boxing match between Mohammed Ali and Chuck Wepner. Ali was the odds-on favorite; Wepner was a nobody, a part-time professional fighter from New Jersey who wasn't expected to last more than two rounds with the Champ. But Wepner surprised everyone by lasting the entire bout and inspired Stallone with the idea for a film about an underdog boxer.

Stallone dashed out the script in three days and got it to producers Irwin Winkler and Robert Chartoff. They offered him $75,000 for the script but Stallone, incredibly, turned it down. He refused to sell the script unless he could star in it, a remarkable piece of audacity on the part of an unknown writer. But Winkler and Chartoff wanted the script so badly that they bought it and agreed to his condition. Stallone got the part, and the picture made oodles of money and ultimately won Hollywood's own heavyweight title, the Oscar. It's the sort of rags-to-riches story that Frank Capra was so fond of, and in fact *Rocky* was Capra's favorite film of that year.

Rebel Without a Cause

ROSEMARY'S BABY

1968
Director, Roman Polanski
Producer, William Castle

While he was growing up in war-torn Poland, Roman Polanski dreamed of some day going to Hollywood, so when Paramount offered him the chance to write and direct *Rosemary's Baby* it was natural that he should jump at the opportunity. Producer/director William Castle, who gave audiences such schlock classics as *The House on Haunted Hill* (1958) and *The Tingler* (1959), had bought the rights to Ira Levin's best-seller and then sold them to Paramount for a tidy profit. (Castle originally wanted to direct *Rosemary's Baby* himself, but Paramount decided they needed a "real" director. Instead, Castle produced the film and made a sinister cameo appearance, lurking outside a telephone booth in the scene where Mia Farrow tries to call her doctor.)

At first Polanski was concerned about how he would adapt to Hollywood working methods; he was so worried about how his long, detailed script would go over that he asked a veteran Paramount secretary if it could be typed single-spaced "to make it look shorter." "The last man to ask that," she said nostalgically, "was Mr. von Sternberg!"

Despite his jitters, the script was approved, and Polanski set about casting the film. It was Paramount head honcho Robert Evans who suggested Mia Farrow for Rosemary, and Polanski liked her right away. Casting Rosemary's husband Guy was not so simple. Polanski wanted a wholesome TV-commercial type, but he had a hard time finding someone who looked the part *and* could act. Warren Beatty, his first choice, met Polanski's criteria in terms of both looks and talent, but Beatty turned him down. Polanski rejected a then-unknown horror-film actor named Jack Nicholson because he looked too sinister. He almost hired Robert Redford, but at the time Paramount was suing Redford for walking off the set of *Blue*, and when Redford and Polanski met for lunch to discuss the film their meeting was interrupted by a Paramount process server; this put something of a damper on Redford's enthusiasm for the role.

Polanski finally cast John Cassavetes as Guy, and Cassavetes' Method approach to acting became a considerable headache for the director. The problem of dealing with Cassavetes, though, paled into insignificance beside the upheavals caused by Mia Farrow's then-husband Frank Sinatra. Sinatra was set to star in *The Detective* later that year and wanted Farrow as his co-star. As Polanski's painstaking shooting methods caused *Rosemary's Baby* to lag farther and farther behind schedule, it became obvious that Farrow would not be free in time to do *The Detective*. Sinatra began putting pressure on her to leave the film but Farrow, realizing what *Rosemary's Baby* meant to her career, refused to quit. Their marriage deteriorated, and finally, without even telling her, Sinatra began divorce proceedings; he even had a flunky deliver the papers to her. This personal turmoil certainly accounts at least in part for Farrow's convincingly haggard and persecuted demeanor as the film progressed: it was precisely the way she felt.

Rosemary's Baby

SHANE

1953
Director, George Stevens
Producers, George Stevens and Ivan Moffat

Filmed on location in Jackson Hole, Wyoming, *Shane* was Alan Ladd's most memorable movie and has been labeled the best western ever made. Brandon de Wilde as Joey, observing the western landscape, would ten years later again be a western observer, as Lon in *Hud*.

Two of Ladd's children had small roles in *Shane*. Daughter Alana was given a part in which she had to lug a ten-pound sack of potatoes, but she enjoyed the experience. Alan Ladd, Jr. was paid, but did not make it to the screen. Years later, he would send other movies to the screen as head of The Ladd Company, a division of Warner Brothers.

Ladd and director George Stevens worked very well together, each respecting the other. And Ladd and fellow actor Van Heflin became very good friends and continued that way over the years. Ladd was never sure of himself, even about his performance in *Shane*. That his performance did not net him an Academy Award nomination served to strengthen his insecurity. The cast believed they had made a fine movie, but it was not until two years later, when Paramount released *Shane*, that they knew just how fine.

Shane was Alan Ladd's final movie as a contract player for Paramount. The studio had treated Ladd shabbily over the years, sticking him into any movie because they knew

Shane

SINGIN' IN THE RAIN

1952
Directors, Gene Kelly and Stanley Donen
Producer, Arthur Freed

One of the reasons that MGM produced such great musicals in the 1940s and 1950s was that songwriters were allowed to take part in the production. And it was an impressive lineup of talent that assembled to make *Singin' in the Rain*. Associate producer Roger Edens had been musical supervisor on many MGM movies; screenwriters Betty Comden and Adolph Green had collaborated on the books and lyrics for stage and screen productions; and Arthur Freed, the greatest producer of them all, was a songwriter. It can easily be understood why the MGM musical unit put all its efforts behind *Singin' in the Rain*. The movie was to be a tribute to Freed, using all of the great songs he wrote in the 1920s and 1930s. If ever there was a way to please the boss, this was it.

Comden and Green were given the task of creating a screenplay based on Freed's songs and they immediately concluded that songs like "The Wedding of the Painted Doll" and "All I Do the Whole Night Through (is Dream of You)" would only be accepted in the period in which they were written, the 1920s. Then they conceived the idea of a film about Hollywood when sound came in. To research this subject, they had to look no further than their own backyard. MGM was full of survivors

of that hectic period, each with horror stories about microphones in potted plants and extraneous soundtrack noises which drove the engineers crazy. Arthur Freed knew his share of stories, because he had written songs for the very first all-talking musical, *The Broadway Melody* (1929). In one of the scenes in that film (which won the second Academy Award for best picture) the elaborate costumes designed for the chorus were made out of glass beads. After the first day's shooting, however, it was discovered that the beads sounded like an avalanche on the soundtrack and the costumes had to be changed. All of the sound-related incidents in *Singin' in the Rain* are based on real-life problems.

The casting for *Singin' in the Rain* was completed quickly. Gene Kelly was an obvious choice for silent movie star Don Lockwood, but Arthur Freed wanted Oscar Levant to play Lockwood's friend, Cosmo Brown. Kelly felt that Levant's dour countenance would give a sour note to this bouncy musical, and with Comden's and Green's help Levant was excluded—they rewrote the character so that only a professional dancer could play it, thus ruling Levant out. Donald O'Connor was deemed the perfect choice to play Cosmo, and he got the part. O'Connor was a child vaudeville star who shifted to films in 1937. His biggest role as a child was the young Beau Geste in the 1939 film of the same name. As he grew older he signed with Universal, where he never had a chance to display his con-

he would make money for them. Even Cecil B. de Mille did not like Ladd; he did not like any short man, and made even his six-foot-tall actors wear shoe lifts. Ladd left Paramount to accept a better deal with Warner Brothers— $150,000 per picture plus ten percent of the gross at one picture a year for ten years, plus residual and loan-out rights and story approval. He made very few movies for Warners; most of his work was on loan-out. For Paramount, Ladd had made his first 23 movies, including *This Gun*

for Hire (1942), *Whispering Smith* (1948), and *The Great Gatsby* (1949), and it was at Paramount that he would make his last one, *The Carpetbaggers* (1964).

Alan Ladd was not nominated for an Academy Award for *Shane*, which, considering it is the movie for which he is best remembered and his best role, was a tremendous oversight. And although director Stevens and actors Brandon de Wilde and Jack Palance were nominated, the only category in which *Shane* won was for cinematography.

Singin' in the Rain

SOME LIKE IT HOT

1959
Director/Producer, Billy Wilder

Some Like It Hot proves that some comedies are not much fun to make. Billy Wilder's film about two musicians (Tony Curtis and Jack Lemmon) who dress up as women to escape a gangster, is now recognized as a comic masterpiece, but no one was laughing during shooting.

The problems all revolved around the leading lady, Marilyn Monroe. Monroe was now a star and seemed to feel that this gave her a free rein to do whatever she felt like doing. She rarely came to the set on time, and often never showed up at all. One time she arrived two hours late and went into her dressing room, where she remained for another hour. Finally an assistant director made a hesitant attempt to coax Monroe out of her dressing room; after all, hundreds of people were standing around waiting for her. He found her in her room reading a book. When he asked her to come out, her reply was short and simple: "Drop dead," she said.

On another occasion Monroe arrived four hours late and again barricaded herself in her dressing room. This time the crew

siderable dancing skills except in loan-outs like *Singin' in the Rain*. At his home studio, he was best known for the Francis the Talking Mule pictures.

The love interest, Kathy Selden, was played by then unknown Debbie Reynolds. Reynolds had only made five films before *Singin' in the Rain*. In *Three Little Words* (1950) she only had one line, "Boop boop a doop," and that was dubbed, but in *Two Weeks With Love* (1950) she stole the film singing "Abba Dabba Honeymoon" with Carleton Carpenter. MGM was taking a chance in giving her a leading role, but the studio's gamble paid off.

The movie, at times, took its toll on the performers. After performing the strenuous dance

"Make 'Em Laugh," which he improvised himself, O'Connor collapsed and was bedridden for three days. When he came back to the set he discovered that the film had been spoiled in the developing process, which meant the number had to be reshot. Again O'Connor had to spend three days recuperating. If that happened to O'Connor, a professional dancer, imagine the toll the movie took on Debbie Reynolds. She collapsed after working an entire day on the "Good Morning" number.

For the climactic "Broadway Rhythm" ballet, an unknown contract player was brought in to play the non-speaking role of the vamp. It was the start of a long career for Cyd Charisse.

Some Like It Hot

was ready for her. Billy Wilder closed down the production and everyone went home; by the time Monroe came out, the set was deserted.

Even when Monroe did make it to the set, she caused her share of problems. She had a tendency to blow her lines and twenty or thirty takes on a scene were not uncommon. In her scenes with Tony Curtis it would take Monroe at least twenty takes to warm up. Curtis, however, got steadily worse after each take. As a result, when Wilder edited their scenes together he was forced to give Monroe more footage than Curtis.

The scene which caused the biggest problem was a simple one where Monroe had to walk into a room belonging to Jack Lemmon and Tony Curtis and say "Where's the bourbon?" For some reason Monroe could not get this line right. She would substitute any word she felt like, and by the 59th take it seemed hopeless. The solution came when Wilder changed the action. In the film she walks into the room, opens a few drawers in a cabinet, and then utters the not particularly memorable line. Inside each drawer was a card that said "Where's the bourbon?" Even with this prompting it still took eight attempts before she got it right.

Small wonder, then, that Wilder swore never to work with her again. Commenting on the experience, Wilder said that as the only director to work with Monroe twice (*The Seven Year Itch*, made four years earlier, was a Wilder film) he should be awarded a Purple Heart.

Stagecoach

STAGECOACH

1939
Director, John Ford
Producer, Walter Wanger

Stagecoach was the first movie director John Ford ever filmed in Monument Valley, an area which became his trademark and which he claimed to have discovered. John Wayne argued that fact, for he believed that he had discovered it in 1929. And entrepreneur Harold Goulding is sure *he* is the man who introduced Ford to the Valley. Goulding claimed that Ford gave him a check for $5000 to make arrangements for filming there and that Ford eventually spent $60,000 in the Navajo territory. Goulding subsequently created a tourist paradise out of the area, and today the amenities are much more pleasurable than they were when *Stagecoach* was shot in 1939.

The April 10, 1937 issue of *Collier's* magazine produced two short stories that were turned into movies. In 1938 "Bringing Up Baby" became a screwball comedy with the same title, and a year later "Stage to Lordsburg" became *Stagecoach*. It was not John Wayne's first starring role. He had come to the movies as a prop man and stuntman, and when director Raoul Walsh saw him on the set one day he hired him for *The Big Trail* (1930), the epic movie which nearly ruined Fox studios when William Fox decided he wanted it shot in 70mm rather than the common 35mm. It was an innovative idea and one that would catch on 50 years later, but at the time no one was willing to make the expensive changes required. John Wayne went from that extravaganza to budget westerns at Republic, where he learned his craft and met stuntman Yakima Canutt. Wayne introduced Ford to Canutt, who performed in *Stagecoach* one of the most magnificent and daring stunts ever attempted when he dropped down between the team of horses pulling the stagecoach.

John Ford began in the movie business directing silent films, where he established the ritual of using music on the set to put the actors in the mood appropriate to the scene. He became known as much for his use of Irish music as for his use of Monument Valley. Ford wished to instill moviemaking with the romance and pageantry of the theatre, and to do that he maintained another ritual—this time one which sometimes riled those who did not know him very well. He would arrive late to the set each day in his chauffeur-driven limousine, alighting to accordionist Danny Borzage's rendition of "Bringing in the Sheaves" or some similarly inspiring tune.

Thomas Mitchell won the only Academy Award *Stagecoach* received, for 1939 was a year of memorable movies, including *Gone With the Wind*. Although John Ford and John Wayne went on to other collaborations, *Stagecoach* would always remain one of their favorites.

A Star Is Born

A STAR IS BORN

1954
Director, George Cukor
Producer, Sidney Luft

A Star Is Born contains Judy Garland's finest screen performance, and it's ironic that it came about only because of her excesses at MGM, the studio that discovered her. Garland, whose weight was a constant obsession, was addicted to weight-reducing pills (which contributed to her demise). After missing too many rehearsals and film days, and after driving herself to a point of physical exhaustion, Garland was dismissed by MGM at the conclusion of *Summer Stock* (1950).

Garland needed a screen vehicle to prove that she could act, and Warner Brothers offered her *A Star Is Born*. Eventually the same problems which had occurred at MGM cropped up again, and despite her brilliant performance she was never trusted with a major film again.

Garland's *A Star Is Born* was actually the third version of a tale of parallel careers—a young starlet on her way up, and her alcoholic husband on the way down. The first version was *What Price Hollywood?*, directed in 1932 by George Cukor, who was also to direct the Garland version. *What Price Hollywood?* was originally conceived as a comeback vehicle for Clara Bow. Bow was rejected, though, because she was too fat and run-down. The story was written by columnist Adela Rogers St. John, who patterned the leads on Colleen Moore and Moore's alcoholic producer/husband, John McCormick. In the second version of the story, *A Star Is Born*, which was made in 1937 and starred Janet Gaynor and Fredric March, the Norman Maine char-

acter was made into a combination of John Bowers and John Barrymore. Bowers, a star in the days of silent movies, committed suicide by renting a boat and sailing out to sea; in the screenplay this was turned into Norman Maine's walk into the ocean. Barrymore was a notorious alcoholic, and the scene where Maine is in a sanitarium drying out was based directly on an episode in Barrymore's life. Barrymore was in a sanitarium, trying to dry out so that he could play Mercutio in the 1936 film *Romeo and Juliet*. George Cukor went to see him about a part, but quickly dropped the notion of using him when he saw the pathetic condition the actor was in. Cukor later related this scene to the film's producer, David O. Selznick, who immediately added it to the script of the Gaynor version of *A Star Is Born*. Ironically, Cukor himself directed this very scene in the Garland version.

When *A Star Is Born* was completed, it ran approximately 2 hours and 40 minutes. Then, over Cukor's protests, the movie was lengthened even further by the addition of "Born in a Trunk," a 20-minute musical number directed by Richard Barstow, the film's choreographer. Now that the film ran over three hours the studio had to shorten it. Moss Hart, the screenwriter, and Cukor both offered to edit the movie themselves, but they were turned down. The studio literally hacked away at the film and it was only recently that the lost portions, which included two very good Garland songs, were restored.

STAR TREK—THE MOTION PICTURE

1979
Director, Robert Wise
Producer, Gene Roddenberry

Star Trek—The Motion Picture was a film created by its audience. For years, fans of the television show (or Trekkies, as they're known) had demanded that the series be brought back, so Gene Roddenberry, who created the series, was approached by Paramount Pictures to write a screenplay, which he did. The studio, however, decided it would be far too controversial to film. In Roddenberry's script the starship *Enterprise* comes across a creature which is causing a disturbance in space. The creature claims to be God.

Once a script was found, the original cast of the television series was reunited. The company brought together everyone from William Shatner, as Kirk, to Grace Lee Whitney, who played Yeoman Rand on the first few episodes of the show. The most important addition to the cast was Leonard Nimoy as Mr. Spock, easily the show's most popular character. At first Nimoy didn't want to make the film. He had already had enough trouble trying to disassociate himself from the character, as is clear from the title of Nimoy's book *I Am Not Spock*. However, the deal was made so sweet for him that he eventually gave in. Incidentally, the price for

STAR WARS

1977
Director, George Lucas
Producer, Gary Kurtz

Star Trek

The *Star Wars* saga was George Lucas' baby, and he directed the first one of the series, which he expects eventually to include nine movies. Lucas was exhausted by the start of the second one, *The Empire Strikes Back* (1980), and he asked Irvin Kershner to direct. Lucas laments that even though he has given up the directorial chores, "I'm the only one who knows where we've been and where we're going." His wife, Marcia Lucas, won an Academy Award as one of the editors of *Star Wars*.

Makeup artist Stuart Freeborn, looking for a model for Yoda, noticed a slug crawling in his garden and used its sliminess to depict Yoda. Yoda's face, Freeborn insists, is his own, although the eyes are thought to be Albert Einstein's.

The actors who played Chewbacca and C-3PO received little initial publicity because Lucas wanted audiences to perceive them as characters, not people. Chewbacca's alter ego, Peter Mayhew—7 feet 2 inches tall and 242 pounds, with size 16EEEE shoes—hopes the saga continues. He does not receive many movie offers.

Anthony Daniels is C-3PO. His costume for *Star Wars* weighed 28 pounds and was very constricting, but a $300,000 lightweight version was created for *The Empire Strikes Back*. Originally, producer Lucas did not want to use Daniels' voice for C-3PO. He thought the

getting Nimoy involved in the subsequent *Star Trek* pictures has grown higher and higher, and he only agreed to appear in the third film when he was promised that he could direct it.

The most distinctive feature of Mr. Spock was his pointed ears. Fred Phillips, who did the makeup for both the TV series and the movie, had saved the casts of Nimoy's ears from 15 years before. But Nimoy's ears had grown slightly in the meantime, so the old casts couldn't be used. New ones were made, and they were put to heavy use. The ears were made of a more lifelike, more fragile material and Nimoy went through three sets of ears a day. During the days of the TV show one pair of ears would last for several months. Also, the temperature on the set had to be kept under 70 degrees, otherwise Nimoy's ears would melt. Phillips dealt with this ear inflation by baking new sets of ears in a kiln every morning. One weekend he left the oven

on, leaving instructions for a watchman to turn it off after five hours. When Phillips came back he found the oven still on and the molds exploded and useless. Fortunately he had a few extra pairs of ears left over, and he worked round the clock to make new molds. Spock didn't miss a minute of shooting.

An incredible amount of detail went into the film, much of which went unnoticed by the audiences. For example, Bob Fletcher, who did the costumes, wanted to create uniforms with a slight but not obvious futuristic look. He decided that in the future people wouldn't wear shoes. Instead, a shoe-like article would be found at the end of each pants leg. To achieve this realistically, Fletcher engaged an Italian shoemaker who built each shoe by hand and sewed it into the costume.

Another example of the filmmakers' attention to detail concerned the various aliens that appeared throughout the film. In

addition to the Vulcans and the Klingons (Mark Leonard appears as a Klingon at the beginning of the film, making him the only person to play a Klingon, a Vulcan, and a Romulan, the three most popular alien species), there are such exotic creatures as Aaamazzarites, Kazarites and Zaranites. Separate latex masks were designed for these creatures, as well as special clothing. Fletcher hunted through the studio's back lot in search of exotic clothes and uncovered a bolt of material which had been purchased by Cecil B. de Mille in 1938. It was a red, black, silver, and gold brocade, with real gold and silver thread, woven with a design of leopards and falcons. Its value was estimated at $20,000. Twelve yards of this material went into the costume for the ambassador from Betelgeuse, making it one of the most expensive costumes ever made. Unfortunately, these aliens can hardly be seen in the finished film.

Star Wars

A STREETCAR NAMED DESIRE

1951
Director, Elia Kazan
Producer, Charles K. Feldman

A Streetcar Named Desire was a phenomenal Broadway success, clearly establishing Tennessee Williams as a major American playwright, and it seemed natural that Hollywood would bring it to the screen. However, the play was very frank and when the script was submitted to Joseph Breen's office, which was in charge of Hollywood censorship, there were three objections. Blanche's husband could not have been a homosexual; Blanche could not be a nymphomaniac; and most important of all, Blanche could not be raped by Stanley Kowalski.

Tennessee Williams and director Elia Kazan agreed that there was no need to mention homosexuality, and the script was rewritten so that the husband's problem was that he couldn't face the reality of life. They also agreed to cuts concerning Blanche's sexual proclivities, leaving only a hint of her promiscuous behavior. Williams, however, was adamant that the rape scene remain. He pointed out that the rape was the central metaphor in the play: the ravishment of the tender and sensitive by the brutal forces of modern society. The censors were torn; they didn't want to expose children to such a shocking scene, but they realized that Williams was an important playwright and they wouldn't look good if their objections blocked the making of the film. So they searched for a compromise, and they found one. Blanche would be raped by Stanley, but as a result Stanley would be rejected by his wife, Stella. This compromise marked the beginning of the end of movie censorship.

Elia Kazan's next battle was the casting of the film. He wanted to use the

role called for the fast-pitch style of Stan Freberg, and Daniels had to talk Lucas into letting the actor use his own voice.

As a result of *Star Wars* a special effects company, Industrial Light and Magic (ILM), was founded, and later a research and development company called Sprocket Systems was created. *Star Wars*, being the first of the series, began small. Sound man Ben Burtt created most of the movie's sound effects in George Lucas' basement, using a tape recorder. He collects artillery and explosion sounds from firing ranges and missile bases and has occasionally set off blocks of TNT for the effect. The engine noise for the *Millennium Falcon* is that of a P-51 World War II Mustang. The library of *Star Wars* sounds now includes 160 explosion noises, and Burtt is forever on the lookout for the ultimate. For all of his laborious research, however, one of the best sounds in his repertoire came from the air conditioner in his Arizona motel room.

A Streetcar Named Desire

actors who did the play on Broadway, which Kazan had also directed. There was studio opposition even after the screen tests were made, but at length Kazan got his way. The exception was Jessica Tandy, who played Blanche on Broadway but was passed over in favor of Vivien Leigh. Leigh was playing Blanche in a London production directed by her husband Laurence Olivier, and she didn't particularly want the film part. She had played Blanche for so long that she was tired of the role. In addition, she didn't want to have to move to America and be separated from Olivier. Olivier, however, was asked to play in William Wyler's *Carrie* (1952), which provided a convenient excuse for both of them to "go Hollywood."

After *A Streetcar Named Desire* was finished and previewed, word came through that the Legion of Decency—the movie rating service for the Catholic Church—was going to give the film a "C," or Condemned, rating. This would mean that Roman Catholics would be instructed not to see the film. An emergency meeting was set up with the Legion and they suggested cuts that could be made to reduce the rating to a "B"—objectionable in part for all. Without Kazan's or William's consent, four minutes were cut out of the film. The cuts included deleting the words "on the mouth" from the line "I would like to kiss you softly and sweetly..." and cutting the line that Stanley utters before he rapes Blanche: "You know, you might not be bad to interfere with."

Sunset Boulevard

SUNSET BOULEVARD

1950
Director, Billy Wilder
Producer, Charles Brackett

So thoroughly is Gloria Swanson identified with the role of Norma Desmond, the aging silent-movie queen living on her forgotten reputation, that it may come as a surprise to learn that when Billy Wilder made *Sunset Boulevard* in 1950 not only was she not a has-been, but she was not even originally considered for the part.

Wilder's first choice was Mae West, who turned him down, as did Pola Negri and Mary Pickford (who was willing to do the film, but only if she could have complete control over the production as she had had in her United Artists heyday—a concession which Wilder was naturally unwilling to make). It was only then that Wilder turned to Swanson. The actress, although perhaps not as popular as she had been, was still working steadily on stage and in films.

The casting was fortuitous—the similarities between Swanson and Desmond give the film an eerie resonance. Norma declares at the end of the film "I'm ready for my close-up, Mr. de Mille!" And it is the audience's realization of the parallels between truth and fiction that adds poignancy to the scene. Swanson really *did* work with Cecil B. de Mille (who plays himself in a brief cameo in this film). And De Mille was instrumental in transforming her from a Mack Sennett comedienne (not a bathing beauty, as is often claimed) into the personification of '20s glamour in such films as *Male and Female* (1919) and *Why Change Your Wife?* (1920).

What ultimately gives *Sunset Boulevard* its power is that so much of it is literally or figuratively true. Silent films flourished in Hollywood during a brief period from 1907 to 1927. Fortunes were made overnight—and, after the coming of sound, lost overnight. One effect of the introduction of sound was that the studios now had the leverage they needed to squeeze out actors or directors they considered too temperamental or independently minded. Many people found themselves washed up and forgotten while still in their twenties or thirties, and for years these former stars hovered on the fringe of Hollywood society, doing bit parts and trying to convince themselves they were still remembered.

Nowhere is this fact driven home more succinctly than in the scene in *Sunset Boulevard* where Norma throws a bridge party for three old friends: Anna Q. Nilsson, H. B. Warner, and Buster Keaton, all playing themselves. (It seems grimly appropriate that Keaton, now reduced to writing gags for Red Skelton and the like, should have only one line—"Pass.")

The film's bitterest irony, however, is in the casting of Max von Mayerling—formerly Norma's husband and director, now her butler and chauffeur—

who is played by the brilliant silent director Erich von Stroheim. Von Stroheim was notorious for his arrogant manner (which was cultivated while playing villainous Prussians in World War I melodramas like D. W. Griffith's *Hearts of the World* in 1918, ultimately earning him the nickname "the man you love to hate") and for his extravagant shooting methods. His films were habitually over budget and behind schedule, and his passion for accuracy occasionally led him to such lunatic extremes as insisting that the casino doorbells in the silent *Foolish Wives* (1922) work, or that the Austrian uniforms in *The Merry Widow* (1925) be correct down to the underwear. He ran afoul of Universal's Irving Thalberg while shooting *The Merry-Go-Round* (1923) and became the first director ever fired from a production. He fared no better at MGM, especially after Thalberg moved there too, and his epic adaptation of *Greed* (1925) was taken out of his hands and cut from ten hours to two. Von Stroheim's last silent was an independent production, *Queen Kelly* (1928)—produced by and starring none other than Gloria Swanson. Swanson ultimately fired him as well, completing the film herself and releasing it in Europe but not in the United States.

When Norma screens one of her films for Joe Gillis (William Holden), actual clips from *Queen Kelly* are shown, provoking her famous line "I *am* big—it's the pictures that got small!" The audience may be tempted to agree with her.

Superman

SUPERMAN

1978
Director, Richard Donner
Producers, Ilya and Alexander Salkind and Pierre Spengler

Richard Donner, who replaced Guy Hamilton of the James Bond series as director on *Superman*, was not sure it was the right movie for him until one day wardrobe sent him a Superman costume to look at. He took it home, tried it on in front of the mirror, and his apprehension dissolved. For the part of Superman, writers David and Leslie Newman had a young Burt Reynolds in mind. (Mario Puzo and Robert Benton also worked on the screen-

play.) For Lex Luthor, they were thinking of Dustin Hoffman; they got Gene Hackman, who, with Hoffman, had been voted least likely to succeed by their alma mater, Pasadena Playhouse.

Casting was a big headache. Robert Redford was first choice for Superman, but he turned it down. Paul Newman was offered either Superman or Lex Luthor. He said no to both. The producers knew that once they signed one big name, other actors would begin to take the movie seriously. They signed Marlon Brando—a big name indeed—to play Superman's father, Jor-El, for $4 million. The *Superman* crew calculated Brando's salary to be $8 per second; or, to put it

another way, if he were to buy a Rolls Royce, by the time it reached the set at Shepperton Studios it would be paid for. Gene Hackman came on board for $2 million.

But they still hadn't found Superman. Bruce Jenner was tested, even producer Ilya Salkind's wife's dentist was tested. Things were desperate. But Chris Reeve, skinny at the time, had possibilities. They signed him and he began a muscle- and weight-building regimen with the result that he did not need to pad his Superman suit. In the search for someone to play Lois Lane, Carrie Fisher, who had just completed *Star Wars* the year before, was suggested. But when Margot Kidder was brought to London from her home in Montana for a test, they had their Lois.

Many of the people who had put *Star Wars* together were employed on *Superman*, a fact which helped immensely in holding the behemoth production together. It took 350 shooting days and 1,250,000 feet of film to complete, but in an innovative move the producers filmed scenes for *Superman* and *Superman II* (1980) at the same time. The 007 stage—one of the largest in the world—was used to film Superman's icy Fortress of Solitude. To create the ice effect, $6000 of salt was scattered. The submarine from the 1977 Bond movie, *The Spy Who Loved Me*, was rigged to support several ice floes. Although some cameramen cynically predicted filming on *Superman* would continue until 1981, it was completed in 1978—almost on time and only three years after it had begun.

A TALE OF TWO CITIES

1935
Director, Jack Conway
Producer, David O.
Selznick

A *Tale of Two Cities*
opened Christmas Day,
1935, at one of New York's
largest theatres, the Capitol. Produced by David O.
Selznick, who had just
made the move from RKO
to MGM, the movie starred
Ronald Colman as the
sympathetic and self-sac-
rificing Sydney Carton,
who gave up his life to
save the husband of the
woman he loved. The
Charles Dickens book had
been brought to the
screen several times
before, but this was the
first sound version. Selznick received a lot of flak
from MGM's New York
office for the expense of
the film, for he had to go

to Europe for backdrop
photographs, but Selznick
argued that the expenses
were not outrageous and
that the movie was worth
every penny.

Selznick was known for
his penchant for travel,
and he took a boat trip
from California to New
York in order to rest. He
brought along two sec-
retaries and scriptwriter
Donald Ogden Stewart,
and by the time they
reached New York the first
draft of *A Tale of Two
Cities* was completed.
(Screenplay credit went to
W. P. Lipscomb and S. N.
Behrman.)

The movie took five
months to film, which was
quite a stretch of time in
1935 terms. When Colman
was signed to do *A Tale of
Two Cities*, he had built a
reputation as an actor in
roles less serious than that
of Sydney Carton, the man
about to be executed for
something he did not do.
But Colman sufficiently

restrained his usually
ebullient self to capture
the sincerity and humility
of Carton, and one critic
wrote that for once it was
not Colman playing Col-
man. Isabel Jewell, a newcomer and light come-
dienne, had to overcome
Selznick's reluctance in
order to play the girl who
goes to the guillotine with
Carton.

At one point con-
sideration was given to
letting Colman play both
Carton and the man he
saves, but Selznick and
Colman believed this dual-
ity would confuse the
audience, and the idea was
scrapped. Although *A Tale
of Two Cities* was nom-
inated for an Academy
Award for best picture, it
lost to *The Great Ziegfeld*.
What has forever remained
a mystery within the in-
dustry is why Ronald Col-
man was not nominated.
Sydney Carton was one of
his best and most memor-
able roles.

TAXI DRIVER

1976
Director, Martin Scorsese
Producers, Michael and
Julia Philips

One year after *Taxi
Driver* hit the screen,
along came the block-
buster movie *Close En-
counters of the Third Kind*.
Although both movies
were produced by Michael
and Julia Philips, they
were complete opposites.

Director Martin Scor-
sese came to movies from
a background filming television commercials and
editing CBS-TV news. His
first feature film was *Who's
That Knocking at My
Door?* (1968). In 1972, he
directed (for $5000) a film
called *Boxcar Bertha* for
Roger Corman, king of the
B movies.

For *Taxi Driver*,
Scorsese hired two actors
he had directed in *Alice
Doesn't Live Here Anymore*
(1975)—12-year-old Jodie
Foster for the role of 12-
year-old prostitute Iris,
and Harvey Keitel as her
pimp. Robert de Niro, who
played taxi driver Travis
Bickel, had also worked
with Scorsese before, in
Mean Streets in 1973.

Foster had previously
appeared in three movies
for Disney Productions
and was hesitant about
playing Iris; she felt it was
a part for an older girl. It
was Foster's mother, a
former Hollywood press
agent, who talked her into
taking the part. She liked
the idea of Jodie working
again with Keitel and
Scorsese.

Several precautionary
measures were agreed to
before Foster could accept
the part: Foster was interviewed by a psychiatrist to
establish her maturity and

A Tale of Two Cities

Taxi Driver

THE TEN COM-MANDMENTS

1956
Director, Cecil B. de Mille
Producers, Cecil B. de Mille and Henry Wilcoxon

For his last film Cecil B. de Mille chose to go back into his past and remake one of his greatest successes from the silent period, *The Ten Commandments*. It was only a partial remake, though, because while the remake concerned itself with the entire story of the Exodus, the 1923 silent version had only used the Ten Commandments sequence as a prologue, followed by a modern story about two brothers, one of whom mocks the Ten Commandments while the other defends them.

One of De Mille's joys in remaking *The Ten Commandments* was throwing his weight around as far as the budget was concerned. The first version of *The Ten Commandments* had many budgetary restraints. The scenes of the Israelites fleeing the Egyptians, for example, was originally filmed in California. The remake was filmed on location in Egypt. For a time the plan to shoot on location was in doubt because negotiations were conducted with President Naguib, who was promptly overthrown by Colonel Nasser. However, De Mille gained the full support of the new Egyptian government, who even volun-

The Ten Commandments

stability; the child welfare board was on the set every day and viewed the rushes in order to protect Foster from any psychological trauma; and Foster's 20-year-old sister, Connie, replaced her in certain scenes.

Taxi Driver would have received an "X" rating had Scorsese not followed the MPAA mandate to desaturate the color of the final scene, toning down the red of the spurting blood.

Young Foster, rather than being sickened by the gore, thought the sugary blood, styrofoam bones, and blood pump were "neat."

When an injured actor had to be replaced in the role of De Niro's disturbed passenger, Scorsese took his place. (Scorsese had once been offered and had turned down the role of Charles Manson in the 1976 television movie *Helter Skelter*.)

teered the Egyptian army to drive the chariots.

Remaking the film also gave De Mille the chance to learn from experience. In the first version many people were injured when some of the chariot drivers lost control of their horses during the Exodus scene. Off to the side there had been a 30-piece orchestra playing march music (it was common to play music while filming silent films to set the tempo for the actors and to get them into the right mood for the scene). One riderless horse, pulling a chariot, came charging straight toward the orchestra. They continued playing and the frightened horse crashed into the musicians, causing many injuries. De Mille swore that this type of thing would not happen again, and he was true to his word; the chase sequence went flawlessly even though it now involved 12,000 people, not to mention 1500 animals.

Only one major problem occurred during the filming of *The Ten Commandments*. One of the cameras, which was stationed at the top of a 100-foot-high gate, broke; De Mille decided to check it out himself, and as he reached the top he felt a stabbing pain in his heart. He blacked out briefly, then controlled the pain and descended the ladder. He was rushed home and seen by a doctor who said that he would not be able to direct the rest of the film. According to De Mille, he refused to accept the doctor's ultimatum and spent most of the night praying. When he woke up he knew he was going to be fine, and he completed the film.

THE THIRTY-NINE STEPS

1935
Director, Alfred Hitchcock
Producer, Michael Balcon

For a time it seemed that *The Thirty-Nine Steps* would not be made. Alfred Hitchcock had made several disappointing films and was losing some of his box office pull in England. However, he had just finished *The Man Who Knew Too Much* (1934), which he considered his best film to date and guaranteed to change his fortunes. In this mood of optimism, he started work on the screenplay for *The Thirty-Nine Steps*. But things were not to be so simple.

The head of Gaumont-British pictures was a man by the name of Michael Balcon, and Balcon was a Hitchcock supporter. However, before he could screen *The Man Who Knew Too Much* he had to go to America, leaving C. M. Woolf in charge of the studio. Woolf and

The Thirty-Nine Steps

Hitchcock had crossed paths before when Hitchcock made his first important film, *The Lodger* (1926). Woolf hated *The Lodger*, was convinced that no one would understand it, and refused to release it. Eventually he was overruled and *The Lodger* not only established Hitchcock's career, but put British cinema on the map. This time Woolf, true to form, screened *The Man Who Knew Too Much*, hated it, and said that he wasn't going to release it. Hitchcock's career seemed to be on the skids. However, once again Woolf was persuaded to open the film for a limited press run, and to his shock the movie garnered phenomenally good reviews. He had no choice but to relent and give the film a wide release, allowing Hitchcock to finish *The Thirty-Nine Steps*.

Hitchcock was a notorious practical joker, and he perpetrated a characteristic joke on the stars of *The Thirty-Nine Steps*, Madeleine Carroll and Robert Donat, soon after filming began. In the film Carroll and Donat spend

much of the time handcuffed together. As soon as they started rehearsing Hitchcock handcuffed them, then announced that he'd mislaid the key and promptly vanished. For the next five hours, until Hitchcock showed up again, Carroll and Donat had to contend with such basic problems as going to the bathroom chained together. Perhaps, though, they didn't object to the enforced proximity: it was rumored that Carroll and Donat were having an affair during the shooting.

In one scene, where Donat is befriended by a Scottish crofter's wife, played by Peggy Ashcroft, Donat and Ashcroft could not keep from giggling. Ashcroft started it, but Donat soon caught on and they ruined several takes. After the fifth take Hitchcock, never a man to be caught off guard, coolly surveyed the pair, then swiftly walked over to a lamp and smashed his fist into the bulb. The loud noise sobered everyone up and stopped the giggles. The next take went without a hitch.

After *The Thirty-Nine Steps* was finished Hitchcock made a slight change in the ending. As it now stands, the film ends in the theatre after Mr. Memory has been shot. Originally, though, the film contained a subsequent scene where Donat and Carroll ride away in a taxi. Donat tells Carroll that under Scottish law they're actually married, since all you have to do is say that you're married for the marriage to be legal. Then they register at the inn as man and wife. Hitchcock, however, felt that the scene lacked the punch of the current ending.

To Have and Have Not

TO HAVE AND HAVE NOT

1944
Director/Producer,
Howard Hawks

"You know you don't have to act with me, Steve. You don't have to say anything, and you don't have to do anything. Not a thing. Oh, maybe just whistle. You know how to whistle, don't you, Steve? You just put your lips together and blow." With this come-on began one of Hollywood's most memorable romances—both on screen and off.

It all started one day when director Howard Hawks went fishing with Ernest Hemingway. Hawks was trying to convince Hemingway to write for the movies but Hemingway was reluctant. Finally Hawks challenged him, claiming that he could make a good movie out of the worst thing Hemingway ever wrote, even "that piece of junk *To Have and Have Not*." The two of them then proceeded to throw out most of the novel and concoct a completely new story, using only the title and some of

the characters. Later William Faulkner (along with Jules Furthman) was brought in to write the screenplay, making *To Have and Have Not* the only Hollywood film to boast the participation of two Nobel Prize winners.

Meanwhile, Hawks saw a photograph of a young model named Betty Perske in a copy of *Harper's Bazaar* magazine. He asked his secretary to find out if she could act, but the secretary misunderstood and brought Perske out to Hollywood. She was so eager to go to work that Hawks did not have the heart to ship her back, so he sent her off for some voice training to see if she could do anything about the high, nasal tone that Hawks found so irritating. She came back with a husky voice that was destined to become her trademark, but at that point Hawks still had no idea what to do with her. Finally, one night at a party at Hawks' house, Hawks asked her to find someone else to give her a ride home as he wanted to do some serious drinking that night. She said that she never did too well with men, no matter how nice she tried to be.

Hawks said that her very niceness might be her problem; maybe she should try being less nice. The next day Perske reported to Hawks that his idea had worked. She had approached a man and asked him where he had bought his tie; she wanted to know so that she could warn her friends to buy *their* ties somewhere else. The man—Clark Gable by name—gave her a ride.

This started Hawks thinking—how about pairing Humphrey Bogart with a girl as tough and insolent as he? He gave the idea to Furthman to work into *To Have and Have Not*; thus Betty Perske became Lauren Bacall and was introduced to Bogart. Hawks' hunch was proven a winner as soon as the two met; it was love at first sight—Bogart did not even care that Bacall was stealing the picture right out from under him. The pair made three more films together, *The Big Sleep* in 1946, *Dark Passage* in 1947, and *Key Largo* in 1948, and in 1955 were going to make another (to be called *Melville Goodman, USA*) until Bogart's illness caused the plan to be shelved.

Incidentally, one commonly circulated rumor—that Bacall's singing voice in *To Have and Have Not* was dubbed by Andy Williams—is false. Hawks *did* have Williams record the movie's songs (he could not find a woman with a low enough voice) and had Bacall mouth the words as they were shooting. She sang along as she did this and Hawks was so taken by the sound of her voice that he let her sing the part herself.

TOP HAT

1935
Director, Mark Sandrich
Producer, Pandro S. Berman

Fred Astaire and Ginger Rogers were the most popular dancing team of the 1930s, and in *Top Hat*, their greatest film, it's easy to see why. Astaire and Rogers complemented each other perfectly. Katharine Hepburn once defined their appeal by saying that Astaire gave Rogers class while Rogers gave Astaire sex appeal.

The original teaming of Fred Astaire and Ginger Rogers was almost accidental. After a very successful Broadway career Astaire had come to Hollywood, but Hollywood didn't know what to do with him. In his first film, *Dancing Lady* (1933), he appears for approximately five minutes, performing one dance with his first screen partner, Joan Crawford. His second film, though, was *Flying Down to Rio* (1933), where Ginger Rogers and Astaire received fourth and fifth billing respectively. The irony is that Rogers wouldn't have appeared at all if Dorothy Jordan, who was scheduled to play the part, hadn't married the film's producer, Merian C. Cooper, and dropped out. So Astaire and Rogers got to dance "The Carioca" in *Flying Down to Rio* and as a result were lifted out of movie obscurity. Their performance together was so popular that they were teamed together in nine more movies.

Top Hat marked the first time Irving Berlin wrote for Fred Astaire. As well as being a great dancer, Astaire was one of the foremost vocal interpreters of his or any day, and was a favorite of the Gershwins, Jerome Kern, and Cole Porter—Astaire had introduced songs by all of them. Astaire later appeared in such Berlin films as *Follow the Fleet* (1936), *Carefree* (1938), *Holiday Inn* (1942), and *Easter Parade* (1948).

More than anything else, what one remembers about *Top Hat* are the musical numbers. When Astaire started work on a film, he and his choreographer, Hermes Pan, would work out the choreography together. Astaire didn't care about the script or any other aspect of a film that didn't involve dancing—perhaps this is why a terrible film like *Follow the Fleet* can contain such wonderful dancing.

Of the musical numbers in *Top Hat*, "Cheek to Cheek" presented the only real problem. Ginger Rogers wears a stunning dress made out of feathers, but if you look carefully you'll notice that the

feathers shed like crazy when she dances, leaving a trail behind her. Astaire wanted her to wear something else for just that reason—at times it was like dancing with a dust cloud—but Rogers was adamant and the dress stayed. Retakes of the dance scenes were often troublesome. After a take the shiny marble floors would be scuffed up, and the performers would have to wait around while the floors were reshined before they could do the number again. Some of the dances were filmed late into the night.

The choreography for "Top Hat, White Tie and Tails" was borrowed from *Smiles*, the only Astaire Broadway musical to have a short run. The dance was taken from a song called "Say, Young Man of Manhattan" where Astaire faced a line of men in top hats, white ties, and tails and shot them all down, using his cane and the sound of his taps. As can be seen in the film, the sequence was borrowed almost step for step.

Twelve Angry Men

TWELVE ANGRY MEN

1957
Director, Sidney Lumet
Producers, Henry Fonda and Reginald Rose.

Henry Fonda, who had never produced a movie before, decided to produce *Twelve Angry Men* when he first viewed it as a television play. He chose for his director Sidney Lumet, who made his directorial debut with the film. Thus, there came to the project a producer who had never produced and a director who had never directed—not the sort of team usu-

ally guaranteed to spell success. Nor was the movie filmed with flashy sets and exotic locations; it took place within the confines of one room, the jury room. As if doing a stage play, Fonda and the other eleven actors rehearsed for two weeks before shooting began. Sidney Lumet would later use this technique on all of his films.

A few days before shooting was to begin, neophyte producer Fonda was getting the jitters. He was not as sure of himself or of this production as he had been in the beginning, and when he saw the painted backdrop for an exterior shot he hit the

Top Hat

roof. He had worked with directors like Alfred Hitchcock whose backdrops had been so realistically drawn that actors would walk into them, thinking they were the real thing. Lumet had been assured by the cameraman that these backdrops would photograph perfectly, but his reassurances had no effect on Fonda, who continued to rant.

The first day's shooting was strenuous because of problems with the lighting, and the next day when the producer and director were to look at the rushes, Fonda confessed to Lumet that he couldn't stand to see himself on the screen, that he never watched the rushes and sometimes never saw his films. But as producer he knew he had to view them, so he got up his courage and sat down in the projection room to watch as the film rolled. All of a sudden Lumet felt someone squeezing his neck. Fonda leaned forward and said, "Sidney, it's magnificent." He never came to the rushes again.

Twelve Angry Men became an unforgettable movie, but it didn't do well at the box office. That is because United Artists went against Fonda's wishes to open it at small theatres around the country. The studio executives were so taken with the movie that they decided to open it Easter Week at theatres the size of New York's Capitol, which seated 4600. The opening-day audience did not fill the first four rows, and the movie closed in a week. Fonda was sure his career as a producer, maybe even as an actor, was over—until the movie began winning acclaim at film festivals around the world.

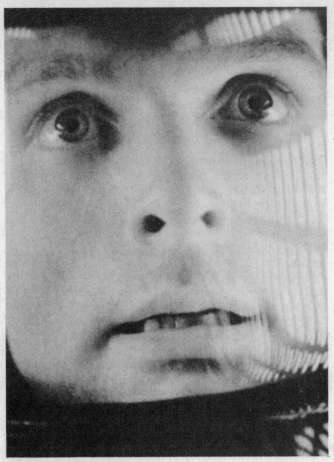

2001: A Space Odyssey

2001: A SPACE ODYSSEY

1968
Director, Stanley Kubrick
Producers, Stanley Kubrick and Victor Lyndon

2001: A Space Odyssey was based on a short story by Arthur C. Clarke called "The Sentinel," in which an alien artifact discovered on the moon supposedly notifies its creators that Earth has discovered space flight and is now worthy of their interest. The film expanded considerably on this premise, and the story became just one of many episodes.

Originally, *2001* was to have opened with a ten-minute prologue in which scientists like Freeman Dyson discussed the possibility of life on other planets. However, after filming this sequence, director Stanley Kubrick concluded that it would add little to an already long movie.

The special effects for *2001* were the most advanced that had been used in any film up to this point. Douglas Trumbull supervised the project, which involved complicated miniatures and full-sized sets. The miniatures of the spaceships were meticulous down to the finest detail. After the modeling was done, tiny parts from thousands of plastic model kits were glued onto the ships so the camera could get as close as it wanted without losing any detail.

Everything about the movie caused problems, even the simple things. In the scene where Bowman (Keir Dullea) tries to rescue Poole's lifeless body, they discovered that a dummy did not float realistically. As a result a stunt man had to lie in a contorted position in the arms of the pod spaceship for the length of the scene. To give these space scenes the proper feeling of weightlessness, they were shot at four times the regular speed of film and then projected at normal speed.

In *2001*, humans are the least interesting characters. The star of the picture is the HAL 9000 computer. HAL stands for Heuristically Programmed Algorithmic Computer; actually the letters were IBM taken one letter down. Many actors, including Martin Balsam, were auditioned for HAL's voice. The role finally went to Douglas Rain, a Canadian actor, who completed his work for *2001* in nine hours—surprisingly fast work when you consider that HAL virtually dominates the third section of the movie.

The end of the film, where Bowman turns into the Star Child, has been a source of much confusion. The original ending called for Bowman to confront the Black Monolith, change into the Star Child (which represents the next stage of human evolution), and then return to Earth and destroy the nuclear weapons which are circling the globe. Kubrick felt, however, that since four years ago he had already ended one film (*Dr. Strangelove*) with an atomic blast, that was quite enough.

WEST SIDE STORY

1961
Directors, Robert Wise and Jerome Robbins
Producer, Robert Wise

West Side Story, with songs by newcomers Stephen Sondheim and Leonard Bernstein, was a smash Broadway hit. It's a modern version of the Romeo and Juliet story, with the feuding families translated into rival gangs of teenagers, the Jets and the Sharks. Jerome Robbins had directed and choreographed the stage production, and was approached to do a film version. Robbins, however, had never directed a movie before, so Robert Wise was brought onto the project. Wise's career had started as a film editor on such movies as *The Hunchback of Notre Dame* (1939) and *Citizen Kane* (1941), and as a director he had done such diverse projects as *The Day the Earth Stood Still* (1951) and *I Want to Live* (1958). Wise and Robbins collaborated on the film and received co-directing credits—a rarity in films.

When casting began for the movie version of *West Side Story*, the cast of the Broadway musical was entirely ignored because the actors were all in their twenties. While one could get away with older actors playing teenagers on Broadway, the camera's eye could not be so easily fooled. Thus Carole Lawrence and Larry Kert were passed over in favor of Natalie Wood and Richard Beymer. Wise himself admits that Beymer was completely miscast as Tony, giving a performance that can only be described as leaden. Wise had no qualms about Natalie Wood, but she was not as confident as the director. She felt she was a terrible choice for Maria because she was not Puerto Rican and she could not sing, and she fought to be taken off the film. The studio tried to help her look Puerto Rican through not very successful makeup, and tried to solve the singing problem by having queen of the dubbers Marni Nixon sing for her.

Chita Rivera, who played Anita on Broadway, was replaced in the movie by Rita Moreno, who won an Oscar for her performance. Moreno had appeared in bit parts in many Hollywood films—including *Singin' in the Rain* (1952), where she played a vamp—but *West Side Story* was her breakthrough. Once she won her award, however, she found that she was hopelessly typecast as a Spanish or Mexican spitfire. Moreno abandoned Hollywood for Broadway, although she came back occasionally to appear in films like *Carnal Knowledge* in 1971 and *The Ritz* in 1976.

One of the most striking things about *West Side Story* is the opening, with a helicopter shot of New York followed by the scene where the gang members walk through the streets of New York and suddenly break into dance. It was Robert Wise's idea to film the scene on location in New York. Wise figured that since 80 percent of the film had to be shot in the studio in California, the opening needed to establish enough of a sense of New York that the audience would forget it was seeing reproductions most of the time. Jerome Robbins was concerned about how the actors would look dancing in direct sunlight, so he rehearsed the dances on an open stage in California and then in downtown Los Angeles before he came to New York. Interestingly enough, Wise was to use the identical concept in 1965 for the opening of his next film, *The Sound of Music*, with a long shot of the Alps which then zooms into a picture of Julie Andrews singing. Wise claims, though, that the opening for *The Sound of Music* was not his idea but that of screenwriter Ernest Lehman. Wise just couldn't think of anything better.

West Side Story

WHATEVER HAPPENED TO BABY JANE?

1962
Director/Producer, Robert Aldrich

The story goes that when director Robert Aldrich approached Bette Davis about starring with her long-time rival Joan Crawford in *Whatever Happened to Baby Jane?*, Davis demanded to know if Aldrich was having an affair with Crawford. Assured that this was not the case and therefore the director wouldn't be likely to give Crawford all the best footage, Davis agreed to do the movie.

In truth, neither Davis nor Crawford could really afford to pass up the film, because both their careers were then at a pretty low ebb. Nor, for Crawford, was it the first time she had been in career trouble. She had suffered a similar reversal in the '40s when, after starring for MGM first in flapper roles and then in a series of working-girl-makes-good movies, her popularity nose-dived to the point where she was labelled "box office poison." She moved over to Warner Brothers, where she became the studio's number two female star—after Davis. At Warners, Crawford's career was revitalized when she won an Oscar in 1945 for her role in *Mildred Pierce*. All the same, the seeds of her rivalry with Davis had taken root.

Although the gossip columnists had a field day with the "feud" between the two stars, speculating

Whatever Happened to Baby Jane?

WHO'S AFRAID OF VIRGINIA WOOLF?

1966
Director, Mike Nichols
Producer, Ernest Lehman

When faced with the prospect of doing the movie version of *Who's Afraid of Virginia Woolf?*, Edward Albee's powerful stage play, Richard Burton initially turned it down. He felt that he didn't know how to approach the character of George, a man apparently intent on torturing his wife and destroying his marriage. But there was another and more important reason for Burton's reluctance. He was to appear opposite his current wife, Elizabeth Taylor, who would play George's wife and equal in viciousness, Martha. Burton was afraid that with constant on-screen hostility between the two of them, some of the anger would spill over into their private life. Burton knew about the power of movies to make and break marriages. After all, he had met Taylor during the

for weeks as to which one of them would walk off the set first, the shooting went smoothly. Davis, who had delighted in playing unsympathetic heroines ever since *Of Human Bondage* in 1934, threw herself into the role with abandon. She even created her own make-up for the role, using dense white pancake with kohl-rimmed eyes and thick, red lips to create the impression that Baby Jane never really washed, but just trowelled on another layer of make-up each morning. She crowned the effect with a Mary Pickford-style fright wig to create the right impression of infantile ghastliness. In addition, the clips of "Baby Jane" movies too bad to release (shown during the 1938 segment) were actually from two of Davis' less memorable features made in 1933, *Ex-Lady* and *Parachute Jumper*. When Crawford, as Blanche, watches one of *her* old films on television, the excerpt is from *Sadie McKee* (1934).

Baby Jane provided a career boost for both Davis and Crawford, and in 1964 they were due to team up again under Aldrich's direction for another exercise in gothicry, *Hush . . . Hush, Sweet Charlotte*. But Crawford contracted viral pneumonia and her part went to Olivia de Havilland. Upon her recovery, Crawford was able to satisfy her new-found public's taste for the macabre with *I Saw What You Did* (1965), *Berserk* (1967), and *Trog* (1970).

Who's Afraid of Virginia Woolf?

traumatic filming of *Cleopatra* (1963), after which they both divorced their current spouses to marry each other. As a result, Burton was adamant in his refusal of the role; no amount of coaxing from director Mike Nichols could get him to change his mind. As usual, however, Burton melted like butter when Taylor tried to convince him that he should play George. She soon wore him down and he accepted the part.

During filming both Burton's major concerns about the movie were laid to rest. Instead of seeing George as Albee's lean and hungry man, he thought of him as a decaying, seedy, obese intellectual. This proved his key to the character and he was able to give a fine performance. As for the bickering of George and Martha (who incidentally are named for the nation's first first family, George and Martha Washington), it had an effect quite opposite to the one Burton had feared. The two stars found that after venting their anger in the film, they didn't have time or energy for such hostilities when they went home, and they were becoming gentler people off the set. Their marriage was still shaky, though, and they divorced a few years later.

Elizabeth Taylor won the Oscar for best actress for her portrayal of Martha; Burton was nominated as best actor, but lost out to Paul Scofield for *A Man for All Seasons*. In her acceptance speech Taylor said that it was nice to win but that "the edge was taken off because Richard didn't win, and he was the best actor of the year."

WITNESS FOR THE PROSECUTION

1957
Director, Billy Wilder
Producer, Arthur Hornblow, Jr.

Billy Wilder didn't particularly want to make *Witness for the Prosecution*, a film based on the Agatha Christie stage play. He had nothing against the project; it just didn't inspire him. He was urged to take it on by his friend Marlene Dietrich, whom he had directed in 1948 in *A Foreign Affair*, and she succeeded in persuading him to accept the assignment. Dietrich, however, had an ulterior motive; she wanted the choice role of the wife, and she got it.

Wilder then set out to rewrite the play as a movie. He added the character played by Elsa Lanchester, who continually feuds with the attorney played by Charles Laughton. Lanchester was married to Laughton in real life, although they had a strange relationship since he was a homosexual.

Wilder also added a scene where Tyrone Power first meets Marlene Dietrich. There is a barroom brawl with hundreds of extras, and when the dust has cleared the purpose of the scene is made evident—one of Dietrich's trouser legs has been ripped off. Dietrich's legs were considered the best in Hollywood, and at one point they were insured for a million dollars.

The set of the Old Bailey, where virtually all of the action takes place, proved to be fairly difficult to construct. It was built by a man named Trauner, who went to England to take photographs of the famous courthouse from which to work. On his arrival he was forbidden to take photographs and had to make do with numerous hasty drawings. The set he built was remarkable not only because it was so faithful to the original, but also because it was so cleverly designed to meet the demands of the cameramen. The walls, the floor, and the ceiling could all be removed if necessary so that the camera could shoot the characters from any angle and extend the action beyond the limits of the theater stage where it had originated.

Witness for the Prosecution was Tyrone Power's final Hollywood film. Power had started in Hollywood in the '30s and had gradually moved up from bit roles to featured parts. His days of actual stardom were interrupted by the start of World War II. After he returned from fighting in the war he made several films, but he never regained his popularity. He died in 1958 during the filming of *Solomon and Sheba*, and was replaced in that movie by Yul Brynner.

Witness for the Prosecution

THE WIZARD OF OZ

1939
Director, Victor Fleming
Producer, Mervyn LeRoy

Although *The Wizard of Oz* is now recognized as a classic and seen by millions of people yearly, on its initial release for MGM it lost money. The film, with its multitude of special effects, was expensive to make, and the audience for a children's movie was not there. In addition, the valuable foreign market for the film was diminished because of the start of World War II. Although it took over a decade for the film to go into the black, it has more than caught up on its slow start and is still a moneymaker for MGM.

The casting of the film is a story in itself. W. C. Fields was originally considered for the role of the Wizard, but Fields had a disagreement with the studio and was passed over in favor of Frank Morgan. Gale Sondergaard was the original choice for the Wicked Witch of the West, but fortunately the role went to Margaret Hamilton.

Opinion differs as to whether or not Judy Garland was the first choice for the role of Dorothy. Many movie buffs believe that MGM wanted to use their number one child star, Shirley Temple. However, Garland was being groomed for stardom and the studio was itching for a chance to use her. Interestingly enough, her screen debut was in 1936 in a short film called *Every Sunday*, where she was teamed with another

The Wizard of Oz

young unknown female singer named Deanna Durbin. MGM let the young Durbin go because they felt they couldn't sign up two teenage singers, and she was promptly snapped up by Universal.

The original Tin Woodsman was played by Buddy Ebsen, who was a song and dance man before the days of *The Beverly Hillbillies*, and Ebsen even shot some scenes for the movie. But during the course of filming Ebsen became very ill and it was soon discovered that he was allergic to the silver paint which covered his body for the role; he had to be hospitalized. Jack Haley, who at that time was playing the Scarecrow, had secretly wanted to

play the Woodsman, so he shifted parts and Broadway performer Ray Bolger was brought in to replace him as the Scarecrow.

The special effects for *The Wizard of Oz* were state-of-the-art for 1939, but some effects weren't complicated—they just required ingenuity. For example, in one scene the Wicked Witch of the West skywrites "Surrender Dorothy" over the Emerald City. This effect was achieved by filling a glass-bottomed tank with milk. Then a mixture of black dye and sheep dip was put into a stylus, with a miniature of the Witch and her broom fastened to the end. The camera was placed under the tank, shooting up, and a prop man wrote

the words from above, backwards. The mixture released from the pen gave a cloudy effect just like smoke in the sky.

After filming was completed the studio made several cuts. An entire dance number, "The Jitterbug," was deleted, as well as a reprise of "Ding Dong the Witch is Dead" sung after the second witch is killed. However, MGM also wanted to cut "Over the Rainbow"; executives felt it was entirely inappropriate. A fierce battle raged and at various previews the song was taken out and then immediately put back in. Arthur Freed, who was an assistant producer at the time, fought the longest and the hardest for the song and, of course, it stayed in; it also won an Oscar for best song.

Although the film is technically almost flawless, some mistakes can be seen. In the opening scene in Oz, Munchkins come out to visit Dorothy as she is emerging from her house. One Munchkin climbs up from under a manhole cover in the middle of the yellow brick road. However, when Dorothy walks up this same road in search of the Wizard, this manhole has disappeared. Another mistake concerns Judy Garland's hair. When she leaves Munchkinland her hair is shoulder length. When she meets the Scarecrow it's five inches longer, but when he sings "If I Only Had a Brain" her hair shrinks again, then grows after the number. And in the entrance scene to the Emerald City, when Dorothy is carried by the horse of a different color, the purple horse can be seen trying to lick off its jello coating.

QUOTES FROM
THE MOVIES

You have a good mind, Tracy. You have a pretty face, a fine disciplined body that does what you tell it. You have everything it takes to make a lovely woman—except the one essential: an understanding heart. Without it, you might just as well be made of bronze.

> —John Halliday to Katharine Hepburn in *The Philadelphia Story*
> —Also Sidney Blackmer to Grace Kelly in the 1956 musical remake, *High Society*

Isn't it enough that you've gathered every other man's heart today? You've always had mine. You cut your teeth on it.

> —Leslie Howard to Vivien Leigh in *Gone With the Wind*

A relationship, I think is—is like a shark. You know, it has to constantly move forward or it dies, and I think what we got on our hands is a dead shark.

> —Woody Allen, analyzing his failing romance with Diane Keaton in *Annie Hall*

Oh, but anyway, Toto, we're home! And this is my room—and you're all here! And I'm not going to leave here ever, ever again because I love you all! And—Oh, Auntie Em, there's no place like home.

> —Judy Garland in *The Wizard of Oz*

Mr. Maryk, you may tell the crew for me there are four ways of doing things on board my ship: the right way, the wrong way, the Navy way—and my way. If they do things my way, we'll get along.

> —Humphrey Bogart, as Captain Queeg, explains the status quo to his crew in *The Caine Mutiny*

Here's looking at you, kid.

> —Humphrey Bogart to Ingrid Bergman in *Casablanca*

Was that cannonfire—or is it my heart pounding?

> —Ingrid Bergman to Humphrey Bogart in *Casablanca*

Louis, I think this is the beginning of a beautiful friendship.

> —Humphrey Bogart to Claude Rains as they walk into the dark at the end of *Casablanca*

Nice speech, Eve. But I wouldn't worry too much about your heart. You can always put that award where your heart ought to be.

> —Bette Davis to Anne Baxter in *All About Eve*

I coulda had class! I coulda been a contender! I coulda been somebody! Instead of a bum which is what I am! Let's face it. It was you Charley!

> —Marlon Brando to Rod Steiger in *On the Waterfront*

73

THE
BOX OFFICE
CHAMPIONS

It's fascinating to learn which actors and actresses have been the biggest box office attractions over the years, and to see which films have been most successful in luring audiences into the movie theatres. Take a look at the lists that follow and you'll get some surprises. You'll also be able to monitor the loyalty audiences accorded some of their all-time idols. The top box office stars are named each year by film exhibitors throughout the United States. We list the top ten for each year from 1932. The top moneymaking films are listed according to their rental earnings as reported by Variety. We list the top three moneymakers (or four, in case of a tie) each year from 1947.

TOP BOX OFFICE STARS*

1932

Marie Dressler
Janet Gaynor
Joan Crawford
Charles Farrell
Greta Garbo
Norma Shearer
Wallace Beery
Clark Gable
Will Rogers
Joe E. Brown

1933

Marie Dressler
Will Rogers
Janet Gaynor
Eddie Cantor
Wallace Beery
Jean Harlow
Clark Gable
Mae West
Norma Shearer
Joan Crawford

1934

Will Rogers
Clark Gable
Janet Gaynor
Wallace Beery
Mae West
Joan Crawford
Bing Crosby
Shirley Temple
Marie Dressler
Norma Shearer

1935

Shirley Temple
Will Rogers
Clark Gable
Fred Astaire and
    Ginger Rogers
Joan Crawford
Claudette Colbert
Dick Powell
Wallace Beery
Joe E. Brown
James Cagney

1936

Shirley Temple
Clark Gable
Fred Astaire and
    Ginger Rogers
Robert Taylor
Joe E. Brown
Dick Powell
Joan Crawford
Claudette Colbert
Jeanette MacDonald
Gary Cooper

1937

Shirley Temple
Clark Gable
Robert Taylor
Bing Crosby
William Powell
Jane Withers
Fred Astaire and
    Ginger Rogers
Sonja Henie
Gary Cooper
Myrna Loy

1938

Shirley Temple
Clark Gable
Sonja Henie
Mickey Rooney
Spencer Tracy
Robert Taylor
Myrna Loy
Jane Withers
Alice Faye
Tyrone Power

1939

Mickey Rooney
Tyrone Power
Spencer Tracy
Clark Gable
Shirley Temple
Bette Davis
Alice Faye
Errol Flynn
James Cagney
Sonja Henie

1940

Mickey Rooney
Spencer Tracy
Clark Gable
Gene Autry
Tyrone Power
James Cagney
Bing Crosby
Wallace Beery
Bette Davis
Judy Garland

1941

Mickey Rooney
Clark Gable
Abbott and Costello
Bob Hope
Spencer Tracy
Gene Autry
Gary Cooper
Bette Davis
James Cagney
Judy Garland

1942

Abbott and Costello
Clark Gable
Gary Cooper
Mickey Rooney
Bob Hope
James Cagney
Gene Autry
Betty Grable
Greer Garson
Spencer Tracy

1943

Betty Grable
Bob Hope
Abbott and Costello
Bing Crosby
Gary Cooper
Greer Garson
Humphrey Bogart
James Cagney
Mickey Rooney
Clark Gable

Alice Faye

Mickey Rooney

Bette Davis

*Source: Quigley Publications

1944

Bing Crosby
Gary Cooper
Bob Hope
Betty Grable
Spencer Tracy
Greer Garson
Humphrey Bogart
Abbott and Costello
Cary Grant
Bette Davis

1945

Bing Crosby
Van Johnson
Greer Garson
Betty Grable
Spencer Tracy
Humphrey Bogart/
  Gary Cooper
Bob Hope
Judy Garland
Margaret O'Brien
Roy Rogers

1946

Bing Crosby
Ingrid Bergman
Van Johnson
Gary Cooper
Bob Hope
Humphrey Bogart
Greer Garson
Margaret O'Brien
Betty Grable
Roy Rogers

1947

Bing Crosby
Betty Grable
Ingrid Bergman
Gary Cooper
Humphrey Bogart
Bob Hope
Clark Gable
Gregory Peck
Claudette Colbert
Alan Ladd

1948

Bing Crosby
Betty Grable
Abbott and Costello
Gary Cooper
Bob Hope
Humphrey Bogart
Clark Gable
Cary Grant
Spencer Tracy
Ingrid Bergman

1949

Bob Hope
Bing Crosby
Abbott and Costello
John Wayne
Gary Cooper
Cary Grant
Betty Grable
Esther Williams
Humphrey Bogart
Clark Gable

1950

John Wayne
Bob Hope
Bing Crosby
Betty Grable
James Stewart
Abbott and Costello
Clifton Webb
Esther Williams
Spencer Tracy
Randolph Scott

1951

John Wayne
Dean Martin and Jerry
  Lewis
Betty Grable
Abbott and Costello
Bing Crosby
Bob Hope
Randolph Scott
Gary Cooper
Doris Day
Spencer Tracy

1952

Dean Martin and Jerry
  Lewis
Gary Cooper
John Wayne
Bing Crosby
Bob Hope
James Stewart
Doris Day
Gregory Peck
Susan Hayward
Randolph Scott

1953

Gary Cooper
Dean Martin and Jerry
  Lewis
John Wayne
Alan Ladd
Bing Crosby
Marilyn Monroe
James Stewart
Bob Hope
Susan Hayward
Randolph Scott

1954

John Wayne
Dean Martin and Jerry
  Lewis
Gary Cooper
James Stewart
Marilyn Monroe
Alan Ladd
William Holden
Bing Crosby
Jane Wyman
Marlon Brando

1955

James Stewart
Grace Kelly
John Wayne
William Holden
Gary Cooper
Marlon Brando
Dean Martin and Jerry
  Lewis
Humphrey Bogart
June Allyson
Clark Gable

Ingrid Bergman

Gregory Peck

Marilyn Monroe

1956

William Holden
John Wayne
James Stewart
Burt Lancaster
Glenn Ford
Dean Martin and Jerry
    Lewis
Gary Cooper
Marilyn Monroe
Kim Novak
Frank Sinatra

1957

Rock Hudson
John Wayne
Pat Boone
Elvis Presley
Frank Sinatra
Gary Cooper
William Holden
James Stewart
Jerry Lewis
Yul Brynner

1958

Glenn Ford
Elizabeth Taylor
Jerry Lewis
Marlon Brando
Rock Hudson
William Holden
Brigitte Bardot
Yul Brynner
James Stewart
Frank Sinatra

1959

Rock Hudson
Cary Grant
James Stewart
Doris Day
Debbie Reynolds
Glenn Ford
Frank Sinatra
John Wayne
Jerry Lewis
Susan Hayward

1960

Doris Day
Rock Hudson
Cary Grant
Elizabeth Taylor
Debbie Reynolds
Tony Curtis
Sandra Dee
Frank Sinatra
Jack Lemmon
John Wayne

1961

Elizabeth Taylor
Rock Hudson
Doris Day
John Wayne
Cary Grant
Sandra Dee
Jerry Lewis
William Holden
Tony Curtis
Elvis Presley

1962

Doris Day
Rock Hudson
Cary Grant
John Wayne
Elvis Presley
Elizabeth Taylor
Jerry Lewis
Frank Sinatra
Sandra Dee
Burt Lancaster

1963

Doris Day
John Wayne
Rock Hudson
Jack Lemmon
Cary Grant
Elizabeth Taylor
Elvis Presley
Sandra Dee
Paul Newman
Jerry Lewis

1964

Doris Day
Jack Lemmon
Rock Hudson
John Wayne
Cary Grant
Elvis Presley
Shirley MacLaine
Ann-Margret
Paul Newman
Richard Burton

1965

Sean Connery
John Wayne
Doris Day
Julie Andrews
Jack Lemmon
Elvis Presley
Cary Grant
James Stewart
Elizabeth Taylor
Richard Burton

1966

Julie Andrews
Sean Connery
Elizabeth Taylor
Jack Lemmon
Richard Burton
Cary Grant
John Wayne
Doris Day
Paul Newman
Elvis Presley

1967

Julie Andrews
Lee Marvin
Paul Newman
Dean Martin
Sean Connery
Elizabeth Taylor
Sidney Poitier
John Wayne
Richard Burton
Steve McQueen

1968

Sidney Poitier
Paul Newman
Julie Andrews
John Wayne
Clint Eastwood
Dean Martin
Steve McQueen
Jack Lemmon
Lee Marvin
Elizabeth Taylor

1969

Paul Newman
John Wayne
Steve McQueen
Dustin Hoffman
Clint Eastwood
Sidney Poitier
Lee Marvin
Jack Lemmon
Katharine Hepburn
Barbra Streisand

Barbra Streisand and Robert Redford

1970

Paul Newman
Clint Eastwood
Steve McQueen
John Wayne
Elliott Gould
Dustin Hoffman
Lee Marvin
Jack Lemmon
Barbra Streisand
Walter Matthau

1971

John Wayne
Clint Eastwood
Paul Newman
Steve McQueen
George C. Scott
Dustin Hoffman
Walter Matthau
Ali McGraw
Sean Connery
Lee Marvin

1972

Clint Eastwood
George C. Scott
Gene Hackman
John Wayne
Barbra Streisand
Marlon Brando
Paul Newman
Steve McQueen
Dustin Hoffman
Goldie Hawn

1973

Clint Eastwood
Ryan O'Neal
Steve McQueen
Burt Reynolds
Robert Redford
Barbra Streisand
Paul Newman
Charles Bronson
John Wayne
Marlon Brando

1974

Robert Redford
Clint Eastwood
Paul Newman
Barbra Streisand
Steve McQueen
Burt Reynolds
Charles Bronson
Jack Nicholson
Al Pacino
John Wayne

1975

Robert Redford
Barbra Streisand
Al Pacino
Charles Bronson
Paul Newman
Clint Eastwood
Burt Reynolds
Woody Allen
Steve McQueen
Gene Hackman

1976

Robert Redford
Jack Nicholson
Dustin Hoffman
Clint Eastwood
Mel Brooks
Burt Reynolds
Al Pacino
Tatum O'Neal
Woody Allen
Charles Bronson

1977

Sylvester Stallone
Barbra Streisand
Clint Eastwood
Burt Reynolds
Robert Redford
Woody Allen
Mel Brooks
Al Pacino
Diane Keaton
Robert de Niro

1978

Burt Reynolds
John Travolta
Richard Dreyfuss
Warren Beatty
Clint Eastwood
Woody Allen
Diane Keaton
Jane Fonda
Peter Sellers
Barbra Streisand

1979

Burt Reynolds
Clint Eastwood
Jane Fonda
Woody Allen
Barbra Streisand
Sylvester Stallone
John Travolta
Jill Clayburgh
Roger Moore
Mel Brooks

1980

Burt Reynolds
Robert Redford
Clint Eastwood
Jane Fonda
Dustin Hoffman
John Travolta
Sally Field
Sissy Spacek
Barbra Streisand
Steve McQueen

1981

Burt Reynolds
Clint Eastwood
Dudley Moore
Dolly Parton
Jane Fonda
Harrison Ford
Alan Alda
Bo Derek
Goldie Hawn
Bill Murray

1982

Burt Reynolds
Clint Eastwood
Sylvester Stallone
Dudley Moore
Richard Pryor
Dolly Parton
Jane Fonda
Richard Gere
Paul Newman
Harrison Ford

1983

Clint Eastwood
Eddie Murphy
Sylvester Stallone
Burt Reynolds
John Travolta
Dustin Hoffman
Harrison Ford
Richard Gere
Chevy Chase
Tom Cruise

Sally Field and Paul Newman

TOP MONEYMAKING MOTION PICTURES*

1947

The Best Years of Our Lives	$11,500,000
Duel in the Sun	10,750,000
The Jolson Story	8,000,000
Forever Amber	8,000,000

1948

The Road to Rio	$4,500,000
Easter Parade	4,200,000
Red River	4,150,000

1949

Jolson Sings Again	$5,500,000
Pinky	4,200,000
I Was a Male War Bride	4,100,000
The Snake Pit	4,100,000
Joan of Arc	4,100,000

1950

Samson and Delilah	$11,000,000
Battleground	4,550,400
King Solomon's Mines	4,400,000

1951

David and Bathsheba	$7,000,000
Showboat	5,200,000
An American in Paris	4,500,000
The Great Caruso	4,500,000

1952

The Greatest Show on Earth	$12,000,000
Quo Vadis	10,500,000
Ivanhoe	7,000,000

1953

The Robe	$20–30,000,000
From Here to Eternity	12,500,000
Shane	8,000,000

*Source: Variety, Inc.

Easter Parade

An American in Paris

From Here to Eternity

Shane

White Christmas

20,000 Leagues Under the Sea

Giant

Sayonara

1954

White Christmas	$12,000,000
The Caine Mutiny	8,700,000
The Glenn Miller Story	7,000,000

1955

Cinerama Holiday	$10,000,000
Mister Roberts	8,500,000
Battle Cry	8,000,000
20,000 Leagues Under the Sea	8,000,000

1956

Guys and Dolls	$9,000,000
The King and I	8,500,000
Trapeze	7,500,000

1957

The Ten Commandments	$18,500,000
Around the World in 80 Days	16,200,000
Giant	12,000,000

1958

The Bridge on the River Kwai	$18,000,000
Peyton Place	12,000,000
Sayonara	10,500,000

1959

Auntie Mame	$8,800,000
Shaggy Dog	7,800,000
Some Like It Hot	7,000,000

Auntie Mame

1960

Ben-Hur	$17,300,000
Psycho	8,500,000
Operation Petticoat	6,800,000

1961

The Guns of Navarone	$8,600,000
The Absent-Minded Professor	8,200,000
The Parent Trap	8,000,000

1962

Spartacus	$13,500,000
West Side Story	11,000,000
Lover Come Back	8,500,000
That Touch of Mink	8,500,000

1963

Cleopatra	$15,700,000
The Longest Day	12,750,000
Irma La Douce	9,250,000

1964

The Carpetbaggers	$13,000,000
It's a Mad Mad Mad Mad World	10,000,000
The Unsinkable Molly Brown	7,500,000

1965

Mary Poppins	$28,500,000
The Sound of Music	20,000,000
Goldfinger	19,700,000

1966

Thunderball	$26,000,000
Doctor Zhivago	15,000,000
Who's Afraid of Virginia Woolf?	10,300,000

1967

The Dirty Dozen	$18,200,000
You Only Live Twice	16,300,000
Casino Royale	10,200,000

1968

The Graduate	$39,000,000
Guess Who's Coming to Dinner?	25,100,000
Gone With the Wind (reissue)	23,000,000

1969

The Love Bug	$17,000,000
Funny Girl	16,500,000
Bullitt	16,400,000

1970

Airport	$37,650,796
M*A*S*H	22,000,000
Patton	21,000,000

1971

Love Story	$50,000,000
Little Big Man	15,000,000
Summer of '42	14,000,000

Mary Poppins

Thunderball

1972

The Godfather	$81,500,000
Fiddler on the Roof	25,100,000
Diamonds Are Forever	21,000,000

1973

The Poseidon Adventure	$40,000,000
Deliverance	18,000,000
The Getaway	17,500,000

1974

The Sting.	$68,450,000
The Exorcist	66,300,000
Papillon.	19,750,000

1975

Jaws.	$102,650,000
The Towering Inferno.	55,000,000
Benji	30,800,000

1976

One Flew Over the Cuckoo's Nest	$56,500,000
All the President's Men	29,000,000
The Omen.	27,851,000

1977

Star Wars	$127,000,000
Rocky.	54,000,000
Smokey and the Bandit	39,744,000

1978

Grease	$83,091,000
Close Encounters of the Third Kind	54,000,000
National Lampoon's Animal House.	32,368,000

1979

Superman	$81,000,000
Every Which Way But Loose	48,000,000
Rocky II.	43,049,274

1980

The Empire Strikes Back	$120,000,000
Kramer vs. Kramer	60,528,000
The Jerk	43,000,000

1981

Raiders of the Lost Ark	$90,434,000
Superman II	64,000,000
Stir Crazy	58,408,000

1982

E.T. The Extra-Terrestrial	$190,000,000
Rocky III	63,400,000
On Golden Pond	63,000,000

1983

Return of the Jedi	$165,500,000
Tootsie	94,571,613
Trading Places	40,600,000

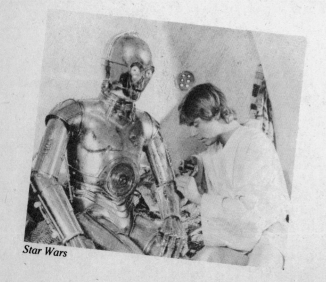

Star Wars

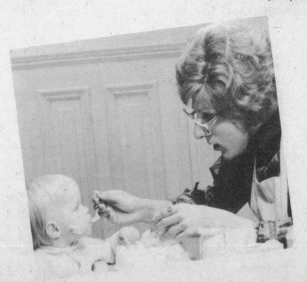

Tootsie

THE
AWARDS

Actors and actresses in the live theatre can hear the audience cheer. Their colleagues in the movies, in front of the cameras or behind them, learn how their work is received from the reviews, the box office take—and the awards. A number of bodies honor major film achievements with annual awards. We list here the awards made by four of them: the Academy, the New York Film Critics Circle, the British Academy of Film and Television Arts, and the National Society of Film Critics. The most famous award, of course, is the Academy's Oscar. Controversy arises periodically over the validity of the Academy's choices, but few who are awarded the coveted little golden statuette ever say, 'No, thank you.'

THE ACADEMY AWARDS

The Academy of Motion Picture Arts and Sciences —generally known simply as "the Academy"—was formed in 1927 for the purpose of raising the "cultural, educational, and scientific standards" of the movies offered to the American audience.

The Academy started out with 36 charter members, led by Douglas Fairbanks as their president, and one of the new organization's first undertakings was to make annual achievement awards to notable films and filmmakers. Thus the coveted Academy Awards came into being.

The Academy Awards can take the form of a statuette, a plaque, or a certificate, but it's the statuette—which came to be known as the Oscar— which fills the dreams of the award nominees. The Oscar was designed by MGM's art director, Cedric Gibbons, and although to many who receive it the award is worth its weight in gold, only the exterior is actually gold: beneath the 24K gold surface, the statuette is composed of a secret mix of metals. (During World War II, when precious metals were in short supply, the Oscar was made of ordinary plaster.)

The system by which award nominations and final selections are made has undergone many changes since the first days, when only a handful of Academy members determined who should be so honored. Subsequently various procedures were tried and rejected, and in 1957 it was decided that all nominations and final votes should be the prerogative of the Academy. Nominations are made by specific branches of the Academy—for instance, nominations for best director are made by the Academy Directors Branch. Then all Academy members are eligible to participate in the final vote.

Although periodic outbreaks occur over the validity (or lack of it) of the Academy's selections, the Oscar remains a significant prize, not only in terms of personal gratification for the winners but also in terms of box office impact—audiences go to see Oscar-winning movies. Whatever rumblings of criticism may be heard beneath the clamor of acclaim and excitement, Academy Awards night remains a glittering occasion in the old, glamorous Hollywood tradition. And very few who are offered it ever actually turn down an Academy Award.

Listed here are Academy Award winners from 1927/28* to 1983 in the fol-

	BEST PICTURE	BEST ACTOR	BEST ACTRESS	BEST SUPPORTING ACTOR	BEST SUPPORTING ACTRESS	BEST DIRECTOR
1927/28	Wings	Emil Jannings, The Way of All Flesh and The Last Command	Janet Gaynor, Seventh Heaven; Street Angel; and Sunrise			Frank Borzage, Seventh Heaven Comedy Director: Lewis Milestone, Two Arabian Knights
1928/29	The Broadway Melody	Warner Baxter, In Old Arizona	Mary Pickford, Coquette			Frank Lloyd, The Divine Lady
1929/30	All Quiet on the Western Front	George Arliss, Disraeli	Norma Shearer, The Divorcee			Lewis Milestone, All Quiet on the Western Front
1930/31	Cimarron	Lionel Barrymore, A Free Soul	Marie Dressler, Min and Bill			Norman Taurog, Skippy
1931/32	Grand Hotel	Fredric March, Dr. Jekyll and Mr. Hyde Wallace Beery, The Champ	Helen Hayes, The Sin of Madelon Claudet			Frank Borzage, Bad Girl

lowing categories: best film, best actor, best actress, best supporting actor, best supporting actress, and best director. (A separate listing of awards for best original song from a movie is given at the end of this section.) These are, of course, only the major categories in which awards are made— to cover every category is beyond the scope of this book.

*Note that from 1927 to 1933 awards were made on a seasonal basis, covering a period from August 1 of one year to July 31 of the following year. From 1934 on, awards have been made on a calendar year basis.

Clark Gable and Charles Laughton in *Mutiny on the Bounty*, best picture of 1935.

	BEST PICTURE	BEST ACTOR	BEST ACTRESS	BEST SUPPORTING ACTOR	BEST SUPPORTING ACTRESS	BEST DIRECTOR
1932/33	*Cavalcade*	Charles Laughton, *The Private Life of Henry VIII*	Katharine Hepburn, *Morning Glory*			Frank Lloyd, *Cavalcade*
1934	*It Happened One Night*	Clark Gable, *It Happened One Night*	Claudette Colbert, *It Happened One Night*			Frank Capra, *It Happened One Night*
1935	*Mutiny on the Bounty*	Victor McLaglen, *The Informer*	Bette Davis, *Dangerous*			John Ford, *The Informer*
1936	*The Great Ziegfeld*	Paul Muni, *The Story of Louis Pasteur*	Luise Rainer, *The Great Ziegfeld*	Walter Brennan, *Come and Get It*	Gale Sondergaard, *Anthony Adverse*	Frank Capra, *Mr. Deeds Goes to Town*
1937	*The Life of Emile Zola*	Spencer Tracy, *Captains Courageous*	Luise Rainer, *The Good Earth*	Joseph Schildkraut, *The Life of Emile Zola*	Alice Brady, *In Old Chicago*	Leo McCarey, *The Awful Truth*

Gary Cooper in the title role of *Sergeant York*, for which he won the 1941 best actor award.

James Cagney and Joan Leslie in *Yankee Doodle Dandy*; Cagney's performance won him the 1942 best actor Oscar.

	BEST PICTURE	BEST ACTOR	BEST ACTRESS	BEST SUPPORTING ACTOR	BEST SUPPORTING ACTRESS	BEST DIRECTOR
1938	*You Can't Take It With You*	Spencer Tracy, *Boys Town*	Bette Davis, *Jezebel*	Walter Brennan, *Kentucky*	Fay Bainter, *Jezebel*	Frank Capra, *You Can't Take It With You*
1939	*Gone With the Wind*	Robert Donat, *Goodbye, Mr. Chips*	Vivien Leigh, *Gone With the Wind*	Thomas Mitchell, *Stagecoach*	Hattie McDaniel, *Gone With the Wind*	Victor Fleming, *Gone With the Wind*
1940	*Rebecca*	James Stewart, *The Philadelphia Story*	Ginger Rogers, *Kitty Foyle*	Walter Brennan, *The Westerner*	Jane Darwell, *The Grapes of Wrath*	John Ford, *The Grapes of Wrath*
1941	*How Green Was My Valley*	Gary Cooper, *Sergeant York*	Joan Fontaine, *Suspicion*	Donald Crisp, *How Green Was My Valley*	Mary Astor, *The Great Lie*	John Ford, *How Green Was My Valley*
1942	*Mrs. Miniver*	James Cagney, *Yankee Doodle Dandy*	Greer Garson, *Mrs. Miniver*	Van Heflin, *Johnny Eager*	Teresa Wright, *Mrs. Miniver*	William Wyler, *Mrs. Miniver*

Dorothy McGuire and Gregory Peck in *Gentleman's Agreement*, best picture of 1947.

	BEST PICTURE	BEST ACTOR	BEST ACTRESS	BEST SUPPORTING ACTOR	BEST SUPPORTING ACTRESS	BEST DIRECTOR
1943	*Casablanca*	Paul Lukas, *Watch on the Rhine*	Jennifer Jones, *The Song of Bernadette*	Charles Coburn, *The More the Merrier*	Katina Paxinou, *For Whom the Bell Tolls*	Michael Curtiz, *Casablanca*
1944	*Going My Way*	Bing Crosby, *Going My Way*	Ingrid Bergman, *Gaslight*	Barry Fitzgerald, *Going My Way*	Ethel Barrymore, *None But the Lonely Heart*	Leo McCarey, *Going My Way*
1945	*The Lost Weekend*	Ray Milland, *The Lost Weekend*	Joan Crawford, *Mildred Pierce*	James Dunn, *A Tree Grows in Brooklyn*	Anne Revere, *National Velvet*	Billy Wilder, *The Lost Weekend*
1946	*The Best Years of Our Lives*	Fredric March, *The Best Years of Our Lives*	Olivia de Havilland, *To Each His Own*	Harold Russell, *The Best Years of Our Lives*	Anne Baxter, *The Razor's Edge*	William Wyler, *The Best Years of Our Lives*
1947	*Gentleman's Agreement*	Ronald Colman, *A Double Life*	Loretta Young, *The Farmer's Daughter*	Edmund Gwenn, *Miracle on 34th Street*	Celeste Holm, *Gentleman's Agreement*	Elia Kazan, *Gentleman's Agreement*

John Wayne and Maureen O'Hara in *The Quiet Man*, for which John Ford won the 1952 Oscar for best director.

	BEST PICTURE	BEST ACTOR	BEST ACTRESS	BEST SUPPORTING ACTOR	BEST SUPPORTING ACTRESS	BEST DIRECTOR
1948	*Hamlet*	Laurence Olivier, *Hamlet*	Jane Wyman, *Johnny Belinda*	Walter Huston, *The Treasure of the Sierra Madre*	Claire Trevor, *Key Largo*	John Huston, *The Treasure of the Sierra Madre*
1949	*All the King's Men*	Broderick Crawford, *All the King's Men*	Olivia de Havilland, *The Heiress*	Dean Jagger, *Twelve O'Clock High*	Mercedes McCambridge, *All the King's Men*	Joseph L. Mankiewicz, *A Letter to Three Wives*
1950	*All About Eve*	José Ferrer, *Cyrano de Bergerac*	Judy Holliday, *Born Yesterday*	George Sanders, *All About Eve*	Josephine Hull, *Harvey*	Joseph L. Mankiewicz, *All About Eve*
1951	*An American in Paris*	Humphrey Bogart, *The African Queen*	Vivien Leigh, *A Streetcar Named Desire*	Karl Malden, *A Streetcar Named Desire*	Kim Hunter, *A Streetcar Named Desire*	George Stevens, *A Place in the Sun*
1952	*The Greatest Show Ever Made*	Gary Cooper, *High Noon*	Shirley Booth, *Come Back, Little Sheba*	Anthony Quinn, *Viva Zapata!*	Gloria Grahame, *The Bad and the Beautiful*	John Ford, *The Quiet Man*

Ingrid Bergman as *Anastasia*, the role which won her the best actress Oscar in 1956.

	BEST PICTURE	BEST ACTOR	BEST ACTRESS	BEST SUPPORTING ACTOR	BEST SUPPORTING ACTRESS	BEST DIRECTOR
1953	From Here to Eternity	William Holden, Stalag 17	Audrey Hepburn, Roman Holiday	Frank Sinatra, From Here to Eternity	Donna Reed, From Here to Eternity	Fred Zinnemann, From Here to Eternity
1954	On the Waterfront	Marlon Brando, On the Waterfront	Grace Kelly, The Country Girl	Edmond O'Brien, The Barefoot Contessa	Eva Marie Saint, On the Waterfront	Elia Kazan, On the Waterfront
1955	Marty	Ernest Borgnine, Marty	Anna Magnani, The Rose Tattoo	Jack Lemmon, Mister Roberts	Jo Van Fleet, East of Eden	Delbert Mann, Marty
1956	Around the World in 80 Days	Yul Brynner, The King and I	Ingrid Bergman, Anastasia	Anthony Quinn, Lust for Life	Dorothy Malone, Written on the Wind	George Stevens, Giant
1957	The Bridge on the River Kwai	Alec Guinness, The Bridge on the River Kwai	Joanne Woodward, The Three Faces of Eve	Red Buttons, Sayonara	Miyoshi Umeki, Sayonara	David Lean, The Bridge on the River Kwai

Shirley MacLaine and Jack Lemmon in *The Apartment*, best picture of 1960; the film also won Billy Wilder an Oscar for best director.

Elizabeth Taylor in *Butterfield 8*, for which she won the 1960 best actress award.

	BEST PICTURE	BEST ACTOR	BEST ACTRESS	BEST SUPPORTING ACTOR	BEST SUPPORTING ACTRESS	BEST DIRECTOR
1958	*Gigi*	David Niven, *Separate Tables*	Susan Hayward, *I Want to Live!*	Burl Ives, *The Big Country*	Wendy Hiller, *Separate Tables*	Vincente Minnelli, *Gigi*
1959	*Ben-Hur*	Charlton Heston, *Ben-Hur*	Simone Signoret, *Room at the Top*	Hugh Griffith, *Ben-Hur*	Shelley Winters, *The Diary of Anne Frank*	William Wyler, *Ben-Hur*
1960	*The Apartment*	Burt Lancaster, *Elmer Gantry*	Elizabeth Taylor, *Butterfield 8*	Peter Ustinov, *Spartacus*	Shirley Jones, *Elmer Gantry*	Billy Wilder, *The Apartment*
1961	*West Side Story*	Maximilian Schell, *Judgment at Nuremberg*	Sophia Loren, *Two Women*	George Chakiris, *West Side Story*	Rita Moreno, *West Side Story*	Robert Wise and Jerome Robbins, *West Side Story*
1962	*Lawrence of Arabia*	Gregory Peck, *To Kill a Mockingbird*	Anne Bancroft, *The Miracle Worker*	Ed Begley, *Sweet Bird of Youth*	Patty Duke, *The Miracle Worker*	David Lean, *Lawrence of Arabia*

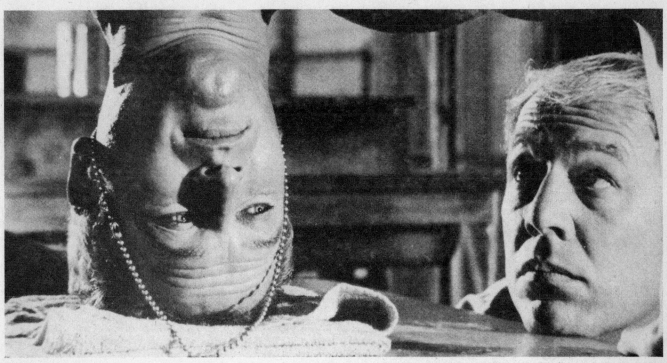

George Kennedy, best supporting actor of 1967 for *Cool Hand Luke*, with Paul Newman in a scene from the film.

	BEST PICTURE	BEST ACTOR	BEST ACTRESS	BEST SUPPORTING ACTOR	BEST SUPPORTING ACTRESS	BEST DIRECTOR
1963	Tom Jones	Sidney Poitier, *Lilies of the Field*	Patricia Neal, *Hud*	Melvyn Douglas, *Hud*	Margaret Rutherford, *The V.I.P.s*	Tony Richardson, *Tom Jones*
1964	My Fair Lady	Rex Harrison, *My Fair Lady*	Julie Andrews, *Mary Poppins*	Peter Ustinov, *Topkapi*	Lila Kedrova, *Zorba the Greek*	George Cukor, *My Fair Lady*
1965	The Sound of Music	Lee Marvin, *Cat Ballou*	Julie Christie, *Darling*	Martin Balsam, *A Thousand Clowns*	Shelley Winters, *A Patch of Blue*	Robert Wise, *The Sound of Music*
1966	A Man for All Seasons	Paul Scofield, *A Man for All Seasons*	Elizabeth Taylor, *Who's Afraid of Virginia Woolf?*	Walter Matthau, *The Fortune Cookie*	Sandy Dennis, *Who's Afraid of Virginia Woolf?*	Fred Zinnemann, *A Man for All Seasons*
1967	In the Heat of the Night	Rod Steiger, *In the Heat of the Night*	Katharine Hepburn, *Guess Who's Coming to Dinner?*	George Kennedy, *Cool Hand Luke*	Estelle Parsons, *Bonnie and Clyde*	Mike Nichols, *The Graduate*

Liza Minnelli in the 1972 musical *Cabaret*, which won her a best actress Oscar.

	BEST PICTURE	BEST ACTOR	BEST ACTRESS	BEST SUPPORTING ACTOR	BEST SUPPORTING ACTRESS	BEST DIRECTOR
1968	*Oliver!*	Cliff Robertson, *Charly*	Katharine Hepburn, *The Lion in Winter* Barbra Streisand, *Funny Girl*	Jack Albertson, *The Subject Was Roses*	Ruth Gordon, *Rosemary's Baby*	Carol Reed, *Oliver!*
1969	*Midnight Cowboy*	John Wayne, *True Grit*	Maggie Smith, *The Prime of Miss Jean Brodie*	Gig Young, *They Shoot Horses, Don't They?*	Goldie Hawn, *Cactus Flower*	John Schlesinger, *Midnight Cowboy*
1970	*Patton*	George C. Scott, *Patton* (award declined)	Glenda Jackson, *Women in Love*	John Mills, *Ryan's Daughter*	Helen Hayes, *Airport*	Franklin J. Schaffner, *Patton*
1971	*The French Connection*	Gene Hackman, *The French Connection*	Jane Fonda, *Klute*	Ben Johnson, *The Last Picture Show*	Cloris Leachman, *The Last Picture Show*	William Friedkin, *The French Connection*
1972	*The Godfather*	Marlon Brando, *The Godfather* (award declined)	Liza Minnelli, *Cabaret*	Joel Grey, *Cabaret*	Eileen Heckart, *Butterflies Are Free*	Bob Fosse, *Cabaret*

Peter Finch in *Network*; his performance won him the 1976 award for best actor.

	BEST PICTURE	BEST ACTOR	BEST ACTRESS	BEST SUPPORTING ACTOR	BEST SUPPORTING ACTRESS	BEST DIRECTOR
1973	The Sting	Jack Lemmon, *Save the Tiger*	Glenda Jackson, *A Touch of Class*	John Houseman, *The Paper Chase*	Tatum O'Neal, *Paper Moon*	George Roy Hill, *The Sting*
1974	The Godfather, Part II	Art Carney, *Harry and Tonto*	Ellen Burstyn, *Alice Doesn't Live Here Anymore*	Robert de Niro, *The Godfather, Part II*	Ingrid Bergman, *Murder on the Orient Express*	Francis Ford Coppola, *The Godfather, Part II*
1975	One Flew Over the Cuckoo's Nest	Jack Nicholson, *One Flew Over the Cuckoo's Nest*	Louise Fletcher, *One Flew Over the Cuckoo's Nest*	George Burns, *The Sunshine Boys*	Lee Grant, *Shampoo*	Milos Forman, *One Flew Over the Cuckoo's Nest*
1976	Rocky	Peter Finch, *Network*	Faye Dunaway, *Network*	Jason Robards, *All the President's Men*	Beatrice Straight, *Network*	John Avildsen, *Rocky*
1977	Annie Hall	Richard Dreyfuss, *The Goodbye Girl*	Diane Keaton, *Annie Hall*	Jason Robards, *Julia*	Vanessa Redgrave, *Julia*	Woody Allen, *Annie Hall*

Jessica Lange, best supporting actress of 1982 for *Tootsie*, with Dustin Hoffman in the movie's final scene.

	BEST PICTURE	BEST ACTOR	BEST ACTRESS	BEST SUPPORTING ACTOR	BEST SUPPORTING ACTRESS	BEST DIRECTOR
1978	*The Deer Hunter*	Jon Voight, *Coming Home*	Jane Fonda, *Coming Home*	Christopher Walken, *The Deer Hunter*	Maggie Smith, *California Suite*	Michael Cimino, *The Deer Hunter*
1979	*Kramer vs. Kramer*	Dustin Hoffman, *Kramer vs. Kramer*	Sally Field, *Norma Rae*	Melvyn Douglas, *Being There*	Meryl Streep, *Kramer vs. Kramer*	Robert Benton, *Kramer vs. Kramer*
1980	*Ordinary People*	Robert de Niro, *Raging Bull*	Sissy Spacek, *Coal Miner's Daughter*	Timothy Hutton, *Ordinary People*	Mary Steenburgen, *Melvin and Howard*	Robert Redford, *Ordinary People*
1981	*Chariots of Fire*	Henry Fonda, *On Golden Pond*	Katharine Hepburn, *On Golden Pond*	John Gielgud, *Arthur*	Maureen Stapleton, *Reds*	Warren Beatty, *Reds*
1982	*Gandhi*	Ben Kingsley, *Gandhi*	Meryl Streep, *Sophie's Choice*	Louis Gosset, Jr., *An Officer and a Gentleman*	Jessica Lange, *Tootsie*	Richard Attenborough, *Gandhi*
1983	*Terms of Endearment*	Robert Duvall, *Tender Mercies*	Shirley MacLaine, *Terms of Endearment*	Jack Nicholson, *Terms of Endearment*	Linda Hunt, *The Year of Living Dangerously*	James L. Brooks, *Terms of Endearment*

ACADEMY AWARDS FOR BEST SONG

1934 "The Continental" from *The Gay Divorcee*; Con Conrad and Herb Magidson

1935 "Lullaby of Broadway" from *Gold Diggers of 1935*; Harry Warren and Al Dubin

1936 "The Way You Look Tonight" from *Swing Time*; Jerome Kern and Dorothy Fields

1937 "Sweet Leilani" from *Waikiki Wedding*; Harry Owens

1938 "Thanks for the Memory" from *The Big Broadcast of 1938*; Ralph Rainger and Leo Robin

1939 "Over the Rainbow" from *The Wizard of Oz*; Harold Arlen and E. Y. Harburg

1940 "When You Wish Upon a Star" from *Pinocchio*; Leigh Harline and Ned Washington

1941 "The Last Time I Saw Paris" from *Lady Be Good*; Jerome Kern and Oscar Hammerstein II

1942 "White Christmas" from *Holiday Inn*; Irving Berlin

1943 "You'll Never Know" from *Hello, Frisco, Hello*; Harry Warren and Mack Gordon

1944 "Swinging on a Star" from *Going My Way*; James Van Heusen and Johnny Burke

1945 "It Might As Well Be Spring" from *State Fair*;

Richard Rodgers and Oscar Hammerstein II

1946 "On the Atchison, Topeka and Santa Fe" from *The Harvey Girls*; Harry Warren and Johnny Mercer

1947 "Zip-A-Dee-Doo-Dah" from *Song of the South*; Allie Wrubel and Ray Gilbert

1948 "Buttons and Bows" from *Paleface*; Jay Livingston and Ray Evans

1949 "Baby, It's Cold Outside" from *Neptune's Daughter*; Frank Loesser

1950 "Mona Lisa" from *Captain Carey, USA*; Ray Evans and Jay Livingston

1951 "In the Cool, Cool, Cool of the Evening" from *Here Comes the Groom*; Hoagy Carmichael and Johnny Mercer

1952 "High Noon" from *High Noon*; Dimitri Tiomkin and Ned Washington

1953 "Secret Love" from *Calamity Jane*; Sammy Fain and Paul Francis Webster

1954 "Three Coins in the Fountain" from *Three Coins in the Fountain*; Jule Styne and Sammy Cahn

1955 "Love Is a Many-Splendored Thing" from *Love Is a Many-Splendored Thing*; Sammy Fain and Paul Francis Webster

1956 "Whatever Will Be, Will Be" from *The Man Who Knew Too Much*; Jay Livingston and Ray Evans

1957 "All the Way" from *The Joker Is Wild*; James Van Heusen and Sammy Cahn

1958 "Gigi" from *Gigi*;

Frederick Loewe and Alan Jay Lerner

1959 "High Hopes" from *A Hole in the Head*; James Van Heusen and Sammy Cahn

1960 "Never on Sunday" from *Never on Sunday*; Manos Hadjidakis

1961 "Moon River" from *Breakfast at Tiffany's*; Henry Mancini and Johnny Mercer

1962 "Days of Wine and Roses" from *Days of Wine and Roses*; Henry Mancini and Johnny Mercer

1963 "Call Me Irresponsible" from *Papa's Delicate Condition*; James Van Heusen and Sammy Cahn

1964 "Chim Chim Cheree" from *Mary Poppins*; Richard M. Sherman and Robert B. Sherman

1965 "The Shadow of Your Smile" from *The Sandpiper*; Johnny Mandel and Paul Francis Webster

1966 "Born Free" from *Born Free*; John Barry and Don Black

1967 "Talk to the Animals" from *Doctor Doolittle*; Leslie Bricusse

1968 "The Windmills of Your Mind" from *The Thomas Crown Affair*; Michel Legrand and Alan and Marilyn Bergman

1969 "Raindrops Keep Fallin' on My Head" from *Butch Cassidy and the Sundance Kid*; Burt Bacharach and Hal David

1970 "For All We Know" from *Lovers and Other Strangers*; Fred Karlin, Robb Wilson, and Arthur James

1971 "Theme from Shaft" from *Shaft*; Isaac Hayes

1972 "The Morning After" from *The Poseidon Adventure*; Al Kasha and Joel Hirschhorn

1973 "The Way We Were" from *The Way We Were*; Marvin Hamlisch and Alan and Marilyn Bergman

1974 "We May Never Love Like This Again" from *The Towering Inferno*; Al Kasha and Joel Hirschhorn

1975 "I'm Easy" from *Nashville*; Keith Carradine

1976 "Evergreen" from *A Star Is Born*; Barbra Streisand and Paul Williams

1977 "You Light Up My Life" from *You Light Up My Life*; Joseph Brooks

1978 "Last Dance" from *Thank God It's Friday*; Paul Jabara

1979 "It Goes Like It Goes" from *Norma Rae*; David Shire and Norman Gimbel

1980 "Fame" from *Fame*; Michael Gore and Dean Pitchford

1981 "Arthur's Theme (Best That You Can Do)" from *Arthur*; Burt Bacharach, Carole Bayer Sager, Christopher Cross, and Peter Allen

1982 "Up Where We Belong" from *An Officer and a Gentleman*; Jack Nitzsche, Buffy Sainte-Marie, and Will Jennings

1983 "Flashdance . . . What a Feeling" from *Flashdance*; Giorgio Moroder, Keith Forsey, and Irene Cara

THE NEW YORK FILM CRITICS AWARDS

The New York Film Critics Circle, founded in 1935, professed a dual purpose: to honor major achievements in the film industry, and to maintain the status of film criticism. Early in its history, leading *New York Times* film critic Bosley Crowther became the most significant figure in the organization's decision-making processes, and he remained so until 1968 when he left the *Times*.

After Crowther's departure, the Circle expanded its membership and made some changes in both the categories in which awards are made and in its voting procedures. At present, each critic may cast one vote in each category. If this system does not produce a winner, each critic then lists his or her three top choices in order of preference, and on this basis a final decision is reached.

Greta Garbo as *Camille*, for which she won the 1937 best actress award.

	BEST PICTURE	BEST ACTOR	BEST ACTRESS	BEST FOREIGN FILM	SPECIAL AWARD	BEST DIRECTOR
1935	*The Informer*	Charles Laughton, *Mutiny on the Bounty* and *Ruggles of Red Gap*	Greta Garbo, *Anna Karenina*			John Ford, *The Informer*
1936	*Mr. Deeds Goes to Town*	Walter Huston, *Dodsworth*	Luise Rainer, *The Great Ziegfeld*	*La Kermesse Héroique* (France)		Rouben Mamoulian, *The Gay Desperado*
1937	*The Life of Emile Zola*	Paul Muni, *The Life of Emile Zola*	Greta Garbo, *Camille*	*Mayerling* (France)		Gregory La Cava, *Stage Door*
1938	*The Citadel*	James Cagney, *Angels With Dirty Faces*	Margaret Sullavan, *Three Comrades*	*Grand Illusion* (France)	*Snow White and the Seven Dwarfs*	Alfred Hitchcock, *The Lady Vanishes*
1939	*Wuthering Heights*	James Stewart, *Mr. Smith Goes to Washington*	Vivien Leigh, *Gone With the Wind*	*Harvest* (France)		John Ford, *Stagecoach*

Charles Chaplin, voted best actor for *The Great Dictator* in 1940, declined the award.

	BEST PICTURE	BEST ACTOR	BEST ACTRESS	BEST FOREIGN FILM	SPECIAL AWARD	BEST DIRECTOR
1940	*The Grapes of Wrath*	Charles Chaplin, *The Great Dictator* (award declined)	Katharine Hepburn, *The Philadelphia Story*	*The Baker's Wife* (France)	Walt Disney, *Fantasia*	John Ford, *The Grapes of Wrath* and *The Long Voyage Home*
1941	*Citizen Kane*	Gary Cooper, *Sergeant York*	Joan Fontaine, *Suspicion*			John Ford, *How Green Was My Valley*
1942	*In Which We Serve*	James Cagney, *Yankee Doodle Dandy*	Agnes Moorehead, *The Magnificent Ambersons*			John Farrow, *Wake Island*
1943	*Watch on the Rhine*	Paul Lukas, *Watch on the Rhine*	Ida Lupino, *The Hard Way*			George Stevens, *The More the Merrier*
1944	*Going My Way*	Barry Fitzgerald, *Going My Way*	Tallulah Bankhead, *Lifeboat*			Leo McCarey, *Going My Way*

Laurence Olivier as *Hamlet*, the 1948 role which won him his second best actor award for a Shakespearean performance.

Olivia de Havilland in *The Heiress*, for which she won her second consecutive best actress award in 1949.

	BEST PICTURE	BEST ACTOR	BEST ACTRESS	BEST FOREIGN FILM	SPECIAL AWARD	BEST DIRECTOR
1945	*The Lost Weekend*	Ray Milland, *The Lost Weekend*	Ingrid Bergman, *Spellbound* and *The Bells of St. Mary's*		*The True Glory* and *The Fighting Lady* (U.S. documentaries)	Billy Wilder, *The Lost Weekend*
1946	*The Best Years of Our Lives*	Laurence Olivier, *Henry V*	Celia Johnson, *Brief Encounter*	*Open City* (Italy)		William Wyler, *The Best Years of Our Lives*
1947	*Gentleman's Agreement*	William Powell, *Life With Father* and *The Senator Was Indiscreet*	Deborah Kerr, *Black Narcissus* and *The Adventuress*	*To Live in Peace* (Italy)		Elia Kazan, *Gentleman's Agreement* and *Boomerang*
1948	*The Treasure of the Sierra Madre*	Laurence Olivier, *Hamlet*	Olivia de Havilland, *The Snake Pit*	*Paisan* (Italy)		John Huston, *The Treasure of the Sierra Madre*
1949	*All the King's Men*	Broderick Crawford, *All the King's Men*	Olivia de Havilland, *The Heiress*	*The Bicycle Thief* (Italy)		Carol Reed, *The Fallen Idol*

Rear Window, in which she's seen here with James Stewart, was one of the three films that won Grace Kelly the 1954 best actress award.

	BEST PICTURE	BEST ACTOR	BEST ACTRESS	BEST FOREIGN FILM	SPECIAL AWARD	BEST DIRECTOR
1950	All About Eve	Gregory Peck, Twelve O'Clock High	Bette Davis, All About Eve	Ways of Love (Italy/France)		Joseph L. Mankiewicz, All About Eve
1951	A Streetcar Named Desire	Arthur Kennedy, Bright Victory	Vivien Leigh, A Streetcar Named Desire	Miracle in Milan (Italy)		Elia Kazan, A Streetcar Named Desire
1952	High Noon	Ralph Richardson, Breaking the Sound Barrier	Shirley Booth, Come Back, Little Sheba	Forbidden Games (France)		Fred Zinnemann, High Noon
1953	From Here to Eternity	Burt Lancaster, From Here to Eternity	Audrey Hepburn, Roman Holiday	Justice Is Done (France)		Fred Zinnemann, From Here to Eternity
1954	On the Waterfront	Marlon Brando, On the Waterfront	Grace Kelly, The Country Girl; Rear Window; and Dial M for Murder	Gate of Hell (Japan)		Elia Kazan, On the Waterfront

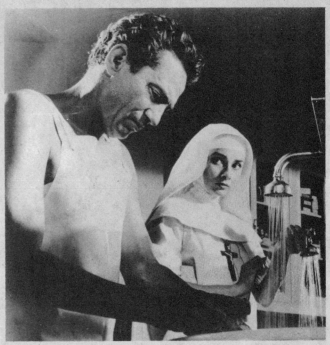

Ingrid Bergman as *Anastasia*, the performance for which she was voted best actress of 1956.

Audrey Hepburn, seen here with Peter Finch, was the 1959 choice as best actress for *The Nun's Story*.

	BEST PICTURE	BEST ACTOR	BEST ACTRESS	BEST FOREIGN FILM	SPECIAL AWARD	BEST DIRECTOR
1955	*Marty*	Ernest Borgnine, *Marty*	Anna Magnani, *The Rose Tattoo*	*Umberto D.* (Italy) *Diabolique* (France)		David Lean, *Summertime*
1956	*Around the World in 80 Days*	Kirk Douglas, *Lust for Life*	Ingrid Bergman, *Anastasia*	*La Strada* (Italy)		John Huston, *Moby Dick*
1957	*The Bridge on the River Kwai*	Alec Guinness, *The Bridge on the River Kwai*	Deborah Kerr, *Heaven Knows, Mr. Allison*	*Gervaise* (France)		David Lean, *The Bridge on the River Kwai*
1958	*The Defiant Ones*	David Niven, *Separate Tables*	Susan Hayward, *I Want to Live!*	*Mon Oncle* (France)		Stanley Kramer, *The Defiant Ones*
1959	*Ben-Hur*	James Stewart, *Anatomy of a Murder*	Audrey Hepburn, *The Nun's Story*	*The 400 Blows* (France)		Fred Zinnemann, *The Nun's Story*

Burt Lancaster as *Elmer Gantry*, the performance for which he was voted best actor of 1960.

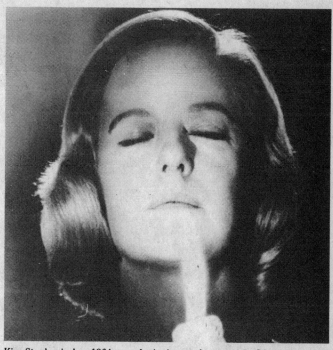

Kim Stanley in her 1964 award-winning performance in *Séance on a Wet Afternoon.*

	BEST PICTURE	BEST ACTOR	BEST ACTRESS	BEST FOREIGN FILM	SPECIAL AWARD	BEST DIRECTOR
1960	*The Apartment Sons and Lovers*	Burt Lancaster, *Elmer Gantry*	Deborah Kerr, *The Sundowners*	*Hiroshima, Mon Amour* (France/Japan)		Billy Wilder, *The Apartment* Jack Cardiff, *Sons and Lovers*
1961	*West Side Story*	Maximilian Schell, *Judgment at Nuremberg*	Sophia Loren, *Two Women*	*La Dolce Vita* (Italy)		Robert Rossen, *The Hustler*
1962	no awards given this year					
1963	*Tom Jones*	Albert Finney, *Tom Jones*	Patricia Neal, *Hud*	*8½* (Italy)		Tony Richardson, *Tom Jones*
1964	*My Fair Lady*	Rex Harrison, *My Fair Lady*	Kim Stanley, *Séance on a Wet Afternoon*	*That Man From Rio* (France)		Stanley Kubrick, *Dr. Strangelove, or How I Learned to Stop Worrying and Love the Bomb*

Joanne Woodward, best actress choice for 1968 for *Rachel, Rachel*.

	BEST PICTURE	BEST ACTOR	BEST ACTRESS	BEST FOREIGN FILM	SPECIAL AWARD	BEST DIRECTOR
1965	*Darling*	Oskar Werner, *Ship of Fools*	Julie Christie, *Darling*	*Juliet of the Spirits* (Italy)		John Schlesinger, *Darling*
1966	*A Man for All Seasons*	Paul Scofield, *A Man for All Seasons*	Elizabeth Taylor, *Who's Afraid of Virginia Woolf?* Lynn Redgrave, *Georgy Girl*	*The Shop on Main Street* (Czechoslovakia)		Fred Zinnemann, *A Man for All Seasons*
1967	*In the Heat of the Night*	Rod Steiger, *In the Heat of the Night*	Edith Evans, *The Whisperers*	*La Guerre Est Finie* (France)	Bosley Crowther	Mike Nichols, *The Graduate*
1968	*The Lion in Winter*	Alan Arkin, *The Heart Is a Lonely Hunter*	Joanne Woodward, *Rachel, Rachel*	*War and Peace* (Russia)		Paul Newman, *Rachel, Rachel*

The New York Film Critics Circle made changes in award categories between 1968 and 1969. The earlier practice of making separate awards for best American film and best foreign film was dropped; the categories were combined to give a single "best picture" award. Also, new best supporting actor and best supporting actress categories were introduced.

Jane Fonda, winner of the best actress award for *Klute* in 1971, pictured with co-star Donald Sutherland.

	BEST PICTURE	BEST ACTOR	BEST ACTRESS	BEST SUPPORTING ACTOR	BEST SUPPORTING ACTRESS	BEST DIRECTOR
1969	Z	Jon Voight, *Midnight Cowboy*	Jane Fonda, *They Shoot Horses, Don't They?*	Jack Nicholson, *Easy Rider*	Dyan Cannon, *Bob & Carol & Ted & Alice*	Costa-Gavras, *Z*
1970	*Five Easy Pieces*	George C. Scott, *Patton*	Glenda Jackson, *Women in Love*	Chief Dan George, *Little Big Man*	Karen Black, *Five Easy Pieces*	Bob Rafelson, *Five Easy Pieces*
1971	*A Clockwork Orange*	Gene Hackman, *The French Connection*	Jane Fonda, *Klute*	Ben Johnson, *The Last Picture Show*	Ellen Burstyn, *The Last Picture Show*	Stanley Kubrick, *A Clockwork Orange*
1972	*Cries and Whispers*	Laurence Olivier, *Sleuth*	Liv Ullmann, *Cries and Whispers* and *The Emigrants*	Robert Duvall, *The Godfather*	Jeannie Berlin, *The Heartbreak Kid*	Ingmar Bergman, *Cries and Whispers*
1973	*Day for Night*	Marlon Brando, *Last Tango in Paris*	Joanne Woodward, *Summer Wishes, Winter Dreams*	Robert de Niro, *Bang the Drum Slowly*	Valentina Cortese, *Day for Night*	François Truffaut, *Day for Night*

Amarcord, chosen as best film of 1974, also won a best director award for Federico Fellini.

	BEST PICTURE	BEST ACTOR	BEST ACTRESS	BEST SUPPORTING ACTOR	BEST SUPPORTING ACTRESS	BEST DIRECTOR
1974	Amarcord	Jack Nicholson, *Chinatown* and *The Last Detail*	Liv Ullmann, *Scenes from a Marriage*	Charles Boyer, *Stavisky*	Valerie Perrine, *Lenny*	Federico Fellini, *Amarcord*
1975	Nashville	Jack Nicholson, *One Flew Over the Cuckoo's Nest*	Isabelle Adjani, *The Story of Adele H.*	Alan Arkin, *Hearts of the West*	Lily Tomlin, *Nashville*	Robert Altman, *Nashville*
1976	All the President's Men	Robert de Niro, *Taxi Driver*	Liv Ullmann, *Face to Face*	Jason Robards, *All the President's Men*	Talia Shire, *Rocky*	Alan Pakula, *All the President's Men*
1977	Annie Hall	John Gielgud, *Providence*	Diane Keaton, *Annie Hall*	Maximilian Schell, *Julia*	Sissy Spacek, *Three Women*	Woody Allen, *Annie Hall*
1978	The Deer Hunter	Jon Voight, *Coming Home*	Ingrid Bergman, *Autumn Sonata*	Christopher Walken, *The Deer Hunter*	Colleen Dewhurst, *Interiors*	Terrence Malick, *Days of Heaven*

Sophie's Choice won Meryl Streep the best actress award for 1982; she's seen here with co-star Kevin Kline.

	BEST PICTURE	BEST ACTOR	BEST ACTRESS	BEST SUPPORTING ACTOR	BEST SUPPORTING ACTRESS	BEST DIRECTOR
1979	*Kramer vs. Kramer*	Dustin Hoffman, *Kramer vs. Kramer*	Sally Field, *Norma Rae*	Melvyn Douglas, *Being There*	Meryl Streep, *Kramer vs. Kramer* and *The Seduction of Joe Tynan*	Woody Allen, *Manhattan*
1980	*Ordinary People*	Robert de Niro, *Raging Bull*	Sissy Spacek, *Coal Miner's Daughter*	Joe Pesci, *Raging Bull*	Mary Steenburgen, *Melvin and Howard*	Jonathan Demme, *Melvin and Howard*
1981	*Reds*	Burt Lancaster, *Atlantic City*	Glenda Jackson, *Stevie*	John Gielgud, *Arthur*	Mona Washbourne, *Stevie*	Sidney Lumet, *Prince of the City*
1982	*Gandhi*	Ben Kingsley, *Gandhi*	Meryl Streep, *Sophie's Choice*	John Lithgow, *The World According to Garp*	Jessica Lange, *Tootsie*	Sydney Pollack, *Tootsie*
1983	*Terms of Endearment*	Robert Duvall, *Tender Mercies*	Shirley MacLaine, *Terms of Endearment*	Jack Nicholson, *Terms of Endearment*	Linda Hunt, *The Year of Living Dangerously*	Ingmar Bergman, *Fanny and Alexander*

THE BRITISH ACADEMY AWARDS

The British Film Academy was founded in 1948, with film critic and historian Roger Manvell at its helm, to promote and improve creative work among filmmakers. In 1959 the organization cast in its lot with the Guild of Television Producers and Directors, thus forming the Society for Film and Television Arts. For the next ten years, both bodies made separate awards. Since 1968, however, the awards have been presented for notable work in both the film and television areas. Further reorganization took place in 1975, and the result was the British Academy of Film and Television Arts.

In 1967 the British Academy's statuette was named Stella—a name chosen through a poll conducted by a major television periodical. Note that only the film awards—not those made for achievements in TV—are listed here.

The Italian movie *The Bicycle Thief* won the best picture award for 1949.

	BEST PICTURE	BEST BRITISH PICTURE	BEST BRITISH ACTOR	BEST BRITISH ACTRESS	BEST FOREIGN ACTOR	BEST FOREIGN ACTRESS
1947	*The Best Years of Our Lives* (U.S.A.)	*Odd Man Out*				
1948	*Hamlet* (Great Britain)	*The Fallen Idol*				
1949	*The Bicycle Thief* (Italy)	*The Third Man*				
1950	*All About Eve* (U.S.A.)	*The Blue Lamp*				
1951	*La Ronde* (France)	*The Lavender Hill Mob*				

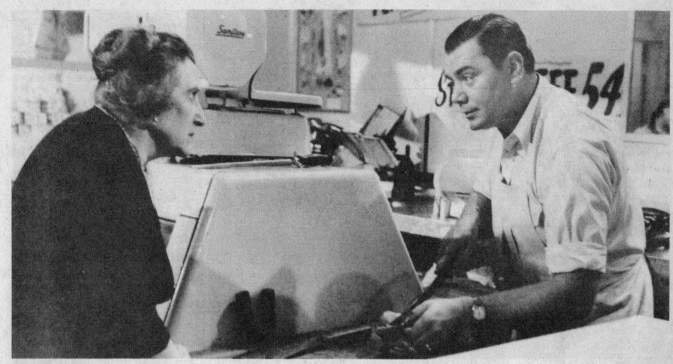

The 1955 award for best foreign actor went to Ernest Borgnine for his performance as *Marty*.

	BEST PICTURE	BEST BRITISH PICTURE	BEST BRITISH ACTOR	BEST BRITISH ACTRESS	BEST FOREIGN ACTOR	BEST FOREIGN ACTRESS
1952	*The Sound Barrier* (Great Britain; U.S. title *Breaking the Sound Barrier*)	*The Sound Barrier*	Ralph Richardson, *The Sound Barrier*	Vivien Leigh, *A Streetcar Named Desire*	Marlon Brando, *Viva Zapata!*	Simone Signoret, *Casque d'Or*
1953	*Forbidden Games* (France)	*Genevieve*	John Gielgud, *Julius Caesar*	Audrey Hepburn, *Roman Holiday*	Marlon Brando, *Julius Caesar*	Leslie Caron, *Lili*
1954	*The Wages of Fear* (France)	*Hobson's Choice*	Kenneth More, *Doctor in the House*	Yvonne Mitchell, *The Divided Heart*	Marlon Brando, *On the Waterfront*	Cornell Borchers, *The Divided Heart*
1955	*Richard III* (Great Britain)	*Richard III*	Laurence Olivier, *Richard III*	Katie Johnson, *The Ladykillers*	Ernest Borgnine, *Marty*	Betsy Blair, *Marty*
1956	*Gervaise* (France)	*Reach for the Sky*	Peter Finch, *A Town Like Alice*	Virginia McKenna, *A Town Like Alice*	François Périer, *Gervaise*	Anna Magnani, *The Rose Tattoo*

Lawrence of Arabia, the best picture of 1962, also won a best British actor award for Peter O'Toole.

Best foreign actor of 1962 was Burt Lancaster for Birdman of Alcatraz.

	BEST PICTURE	BEST BRITISH PICTURE	BEST BRITISH ACTOR	BEST BRITISH ACTRESS	BEST FOREIGN ACTOR	BEST FOREIGN ACTRESS
1957	The Bridge on the River Kwai (Great Britain)	The Bridge on the River Kwai	Alec Guinness, The Bridge on the River Kwai	Heather Sears, The Story of Esther Costello	Henry Fonda, Twelve Angry Men	Simone Signoret, The Witches of Salem
1958	Room at the Top (Great Britain)	Room at the Top	Trevor Howard, The Key	Irene Worth, Orders to Kill	Sidney Poitier, The Defiant Ones	Simone Signoret, Room at the Top
1959	Ben-Hur (U.S.A.)	Sapphire	Peter Sellers, I'm All Right, Jack	Audrey Hepburn, The Nun's Story	Jack Lemmon, Some Like It Hot	Shirley MacLaine, Ask Any Girl
1960	The Apartment (U.S.A.)	Saturday Night and Sunday Morning	Peter Finch, The Trials of Oscar Wilde	Rachel Roberts, Saturday Night and Sunday Morning	Jack Lemmon, The Apartment	Shirley MacLaine, The Apartment
1961	Ballad of a Soldier (U.S.S.R.) The Hustler (U.S.A.)	A Taste of Honey	Peter Finch, No Love for Johnny	Dora Bryan, A Taste of Honey	Paul Newman, The Hustler	Sophia Loren, Two Women
1962	Lawrence of Arabia (Great Britain)	Lawrence of Arabia	Peter O'Toole, Lawrence of Arabia	Leslie Caron, The L-Shaped Room	Burt Lancaster, Birdman of Alcatraz	Anne Bancroft, The Miracle Worker

Dr. Strangelove, starring Peter Sellers in a triple role, won the 1964 best picture award.

Audrey Hepburn as Eliza Dolittle and Stanley Holloway as her father in *My Fair Lady*, best picture of 1965.

	BEST PICTURE	BEST BRITISH PICTURE	BEST BRITISH ACTOR	BEST BRITISH ACTRESS	BEST FOREIGN ACTOR	BEST FOREIGN ACTRESS
1963	*Tom Jones* (Great Britain)	*Tom Jones*	Dirk Bogarde, *The Servant*	Rachel Roberts, *This Sporting Life*	Marcello Mastroianni, *Divorce—Italian Style*	Patricia Neal, *Hud*
1964	*Dr. Strangelove, or How I Learned to Stop Worrying and Love the Bomb* (Great Britain)	*Dr. Strangelove, or How I Learned to Stop Worrying and Love the Bomb*	Richard Attenborough, *Guns at Batasi* and *Séance on a Wet Afternoon*	Audrey Hepburn, *Charade*	Marcello Mastroianni, *Yesterday, Today and Tomorrow*	Anne Bancroft, *The Pumpkin Eater*
1965	*My Fair Lady* (U.S.A.)	*The Ipcress File*	Dirk Bogarde, *Darling*	Julie Christie, *Darling*	Lee Marvin, *The Killers* and *Cat Ballou*	Patricia Neal, *In Harm's Way*
1966	*Who's Afraid of Virginia Woolf?* (U.S.A.)	*The Spy Who Came in From the Cold*	Richard Burton, *The Spy Who Came in From the Cold* and *Who's Afraid of Virginia Woolf?*	Elizabeth Taylor, *Who's Afraid of Virginia Woolf?*	Rod Steiger, *The Pawnbroker*	Jeanne Moreau, *Viva Maria!*
1967	*A Man for All Seasons* (Great Britain)	*A Man for All Seasons*	Paul Scofield, *A Man for All Seasons*	Edith Evans, *The Whisperers*	Rod Steiger, *In the Heat of the Night*	Anouk Aimée, *A Man and a Woman*

Note that after 1967 the categories in which awards were made changed. The distinctions between British and foreign films and performers were dropped in favor of a single listing in each area—best picture, best actor, and best actress. Also, categories for best supporting actor and best supporting actress were introduced.

Guess Who's Coming to Dinner? won Katharine Hepburn and Spencer Tracy the best actress and best actor awards for 1968. Hepburn is seen here with Sidney Poitier and Katharine Houghton.

	BEST PICTURE	BEST ACTOR	BEST ACTRESS	BEST SUPPORTING ACTOR	BEST SUPPORTING ACTRESS	BEST DIRECTOR
1968	*The Graduate* (U.S.A.)	Spencer Tracy, *Guess Who's Coming to Dinner?*	Katharine Hepburn, *Guess Who's Coming to Dinner?* and *The Lion in Winter*	Ian Holm, *The Bofors Gun*	Billie Whitelaw, *The Twisted Nerve* and *Charlie Bubbles*	Mike Nichols, *The Graduate*
1969	*Midnight Cowboy* (U.S.A.)	Dustin Hoffman, *Midnight Cowboy* and *John and Mary*	Maggie Smith, *The Prime of Miss Jean Brodie*	Laurence Olivier, *Oh! What a Lovely War*	Celia Johnson, *The Prime of Miss Jean Brodie*	John Schlesinger, *Midnight Cowboy*
1970	*Butch Cassidy and the Sundance Kid* (U.S.A.)	Robert Redford, *Tell Them Willie Boy Is Here* and *Butch Cassidy and the Sundance Kid*	Katharine Ross, *Tell Them Willie Boy Is Here* and *Butch Cassidy and the Sundance Kid*	Colin Welland, *Kes*	Susannah York, *They Shoot Horses, Don't They?*	George Roy Hill, *Butch Cassidy and the Sundance Kid*
1971	*Sunday Bloody Sunday* (Great Britain)	Peter Finch, *Sunday Bloody Sunday*	Glenda Jackson, *Sunday Bloody Sunday*	Edward Fox, *The Go-Between*	Margaret Leighton, *The Go-Between*	John Schlesinger, *Sunday Bloody Sunday*
1972	*Cabaret* (U.S.A.)	Gene Hackman, *The French Connection* and *The Poseidon Adventure*	Liza Minnelli, *Cabaret*	Ben Johnson, *The Last Picture Show*	Cloris Leachman, *The Last Picture Show*	Bob Fosse, *Cabaret*

Jack Nicholson won the 1974 best actor award for performances in *Chinatown* and in *The Last Detail*, in which he's shown here with Otis Young.

	BEST PICTURE	BEST ACTOR	BEST ACTRESS	BEST SUPPORTING ACTOR	BEST SUPPORTING ACTRESS	BEST DIRECTOR
1973	Day for Night (France)	Walter Matthau, *Pete 'n' Tillie* and *Charley Varrick*	Stéphane Audran, *The Discreet Charm of the Bourgeoisie* and *Juste Avant la Nuit*	Arthur Lowe, *O Lucky Man!*	Valentina Cortese, *Day for Night*	François Truffaut, *Day for Night*
1974	Lacombe, Lucien (France)	Jack Nicholson, *Chinatown* and *The Last Detail*	Joanne Woodward, *Summer Wishes, Winter Dreams*	John Gielgud, *Murder on the Orient Express*	Ingrid Bergman, *Murder on the Orient Express*	Roman Polanski, *Chinatown*
1975	Alice Doesn't Live Here Anymore (U.S.A.)	Al Pacino, *The Godfather, Part II* and *Dog Day Afternoon*	Ellen Burstyn, *Alice Doesn't Live Here Anymore*	Fred Astaire, *The Towering Inferno*	Diane Ladd, *Alice Doesn't Live Here Anymore*	Stanley Kubrick, *Barry Lyndon*
1976	One Flew Over the Cuckoo's Nest (U.S.A.)	Jack Nicholson, *One Flew Over the Cuckoo's Nest*	Louise Fletcher, *One Flew Over the Cuckoo's Nest*	Brad Dourif, *One Flew Over the Cuckoo's Nest*	Jodie Foster, *Bugsy Malone* and *Taxi Driver*	Milos Forman, *One Flew Over the Cuckoo's Nest*
1977	Annie Hall (U.S.A.)	Peter Finch, *Network*	Diane Keaton, *Annie Hall*	Edward Fox, *A Bridge Too Far*	Jenny Agutter, *Equus*	Woody Allen, *Annie Hall*

Kagemusha won Akira Kurosawa the best director award in 1980.

Ben Kingsley as *Gandhi* was the best actor of 1982.

	BEST PICTURE	BEST ACTOR	BEST ACTRESS	BEST SUPPORTING ACTOR	BEST SUPPORTING ACTRESS	BEST DIRECTOR
1978	*Julia* (U.S.A.)	Richard Dreyfuss, *The Goodbye Girl*	Jane Fonda, *Julia*	John Hurt, *Midnight Express*	Geraldine Page, *Interiors*	Alan Parker, *Midnight Express*
1979	*Manhattan* (U.S.A.)	Jack Lemmon, *The China Syndrome*	Jane Fonda, *The China Syndrome*	Robert Duvall, *Apocalypse Now*	Rachel Roberts, *Yanks*	Francis Ford Coppola, *Apocalypse Now*
1980	*The Elephant Man* (U.S.A.)	John Hurt, *The Elephant Man*	Judy Davis, *My Brilliant Career*			Akira Kurosawa, *Kagemusha*
1981	*Chariots of Fire* (Great Britain)	Burt Lancaster, *Atlantic City*	Meryl Streep, *The French Lieutenant's Woman*	Ian Holm, *Chariots of Fire* (best supporting artist)		Louis Malle, *Atlantic City*
1982	*Gandhi* (Great Britain)	Ben Kingsley, *Gandhi*	Katharine Hepburn, *On Golden Pond*	Jack Nicholson, *Reds*	Maureen Stapleton, *Reds* Rohini Hattangady, *Gandhi*	Richard Attenborough, *Gandhi*
1983	*Educating Rita* (Great Britain)	Michael Caine, *Educating Rita*	Julie Walters, *Educating Rita*	Denholm Elliott, *Trading Places*	Jamie Lee Curtis, *Trading Places*	Bill Forsyth, *Local Hero*

THE NATIONAL SOCIETY OF FILM CRITICS AWARDS

The National Society of Film Critics is a relatively young body, founded in 1966. Its professed aims were fourfold: to recognize major achievements in film by means of annual awards; to promote films the members considered worthy of attention; to protest against practices in moviemaking or distribution that the Society felt to be against the best interests either of the industry or of the audience; and to foster friendly relations between American moviemakers and critics and those of other countries. Each member has one vote in each category; if the first ballot does not produce a winner, each critic lists his or her three top choices in order of preference and on this basis a final decision is reached.

Her role in *Women in Love* won Glenda Jackson the best actress award for 1970.

	BEST PICTURE	BEST ACTOR	BEST ACTRESS	BEST SUPPORTING ACTOR	BEST SUPPORTING ACTRESS	BEST DIRECTOR
1966	Blow-Up	Michael Caine, Alfie	Sylvie, The Shameless Old Lady			Michelangelo Antonioni (no film indicated)
1967	Persona	Rod Steiger, In the Heat of the Night	Bibi Andersson, Persona	Gene Hackman, Bonnie and Clyde	Marjorie Rhodes, The Family Way	Ingmar Bergman, Persona
1968	Shame	Per Oscarsson, Hunger	Liv Ullmann, Shame	Seymour Cassel, Faces	Billie Whitelaw, Charlie Bubbles	Ingmar Bergman, Shame and Hour of the Wolf
1969	Z	Jon Voight, Midnight Cowboy	Vanessa Redgrave, The Loves of Isadora	Jack Nicholson, Easy Rider	Sian Phillips, Goodbye, Mr. Chips	François Truffaut, Stolen Kisses
1970	M*A*S*H	George C. Scott, Patton	Glenda Jackson, Women in Love	Chief Dan George, Little Big Man	Lois Smith, Five Easy Pieces	Ingmar Bergman, The Passion of Anna
1971	Claire's Knee	Peter Finch, Sunday Bloody Sunday	Jane Fonda, Klute	Bruce Dern, Drive, He Said	Ellen Burstyn, The Last Picture Show	Bernardo Bertolucci, The Conformist

The 1972 best actress award went to Cicely Tyson for her performance in *Sounder*.

	BEST PICTURE	BEST ACTOR	BEST ACTRESS	BEST SUPPORTING ACTOR	BEST SUPPORTING ACTRESS	BEST DIRECTOR
1972	The Discreet Charm of the Bourgeoisie	Al Pacino, *The Godfather*	Cicely Tyson, *Sounder*	Joel Grey, *Cabaret* Eddie Albert, *The Heartbreak Kid*	Jeannie Berlin, *The Heartbreak Kid*	Luis Buñuel, *The Discreet Charm of the Bourgeoisie*
1973	Day for Night	Marlon Brando, *Last Tango in Paris*	Liv Ullmann, *The New Land*	Robert de Niro, *Mean Streets*	Valentina Cortese, *Day for Night*	François Truffaut, *Day for Night*
1974	Scenes from a Marriage	Jack Nicholson, *The Last Detail* and *Chinatown*	Liv Ullmann, *Scenes from a Marriage*	Holger Lowenadler, *Lacombe, Lucien*	Bibi Andersson, *Scenes from a Marriage*	Francis Ford Coppola, *The Conversation* and *The Godfather, Part II*
1975	Nashville	Jack Nicholson, *One Flew Over the Cuckoo's Nest*	Isabelle Adjani, *The Story of Adele H.*	Henry Gibson, *Nashville*	Lily Tomlin, *Nashville*	Robert Altman, *Nashville*
1976	All the President's Men	Robert de Niro, *Taxi Driver*	Sissy Spacek, *Carrie*	Jason Robards, *All the President's Men*	Jodie Foster, *Taxi Driver*	Martin Scorsese, *Taxi Driver*
1977	Annie Hall	Art Carney, *The Late Show*	Diane Keaton, *Annie Hall*	Edward Fox, *A Bridge Too Far*	Ann Wedgeworth, *Handle With Care*	Luis Buñuel, *That Obscure Object of Desire*

Debra Winger, seen here with Huckleberry Fox, was the best actress of 1983 for *Terms of Endearment*.

	BEST PICTURE	BEST ACTOR	BEST ACTRESS	BEST SUPPORTING ACTOR	BEST SUPPORTING ACTRESS	BEST DIRECTOR
1978	*Get Out Your Handkerchiefs*	Gary Busey, *The Buddy Holly Story*	Ingrid Bergman, *Autumn Sonata*	Richard Farnsworth, *Comes a Horseman* Robert Morley, *Who Is Killing the Great Chefs of Europe?*	Meryl Streep, *The Deer Hunter*	Terrence Malick, *Days of Heaven*
1979	*Breaking Away*	Dustin Hoffman, *Kramer vs. Kramer* and *Agatha*	Sally Field, *Norma Rae*	Frederic Forrest, *The Rose* and *Apocalypse Now*	Meryl Streep, *Kramer vs. Kramer; Manhattan;* and *The Seduction of Joe Tynan*	Robert Benton, *Kramer vs. Kramer* Woody Allen, *Manhattan*
1980	*Melvin and Howard*	Peter O'Toole, *The Stunt Man*	Sissy Spacek, *Coal Miner's Daughter*	Joe Pesci, *Raging Bull*	Mary Steenburgen, *Melvin and Howard*	Martin Scorsese, *Raging Bull*
1981	*Atlantic City*	Burt Lancaster, *Atlantic City*	Marilia Pera, *Pixote*	Robert Preston, *S.O.B.*	Maureen Stapleton, *Reds*	Louis Malle, *Atlantic City*
1982	*Tootsie*	Dustin Hoffman, *Tootsie*	Meryl Streep, *Sophie's Choice*	Mickey Rourke, *Diner*	Jessica Lange, *Tootsie*	Steven Spielberg, *E.T. The Extra-Terrestrial*
1983	*The Night of the Shooting Stars*	Gerard Depardieu, *Danton* and *The Return of Martin Guerre*	Debra Winger, *Terms of Endearment*	Jack Nicholson, *Terms of Endearment*	Sandra Bernhard, *The King of Comedy*	Paolo and Vittorio Taviani, *The Night of the Shooting Stars*

ACTORS
AND
ACTRESSES
WHO MAKE THE MOVIES GREAT

A decade or so ago this chapter might have been headed simply 'Biographies of the Stars.' But what is a movie 'star' today? In the past, studios used to groom a handful of performers (some tremendously talented and some just tremendously successful) to be stars. Today different criteria apply. What every actor and actress listed in this chapter has in common is that he or she is an important contributor to the film world, whose presence in a movie can be expected to add significantly to the quality of the entertainment offered to the audience. There are far more performers who meet that criterion than we can list here—we couldn't include everyone, but we've done our best.

The classic comedy team of Bud Abbott and Lou Costello share a private offscreen joke.

ABBOTT AND COSTELLO

BUD ABBOTT
Born William Alexander Abbott on October 2, 1895 in Asbury Park, NJ
Died on April 24, 1974
Married to Jennie Mae "Betty" Pratt in 1916; adopted son, William Harry "Bud"; adopted daughter, Rae Victoria

Book *The Abbott & Costello Book* by Jim Mulholland

LOU COSTELLO
Born Louis Francis Cristillo on March 6, 1906 in Paterson, NJ
Died on March 4, 1959
Married to Ann Battler in 1934; son Lou Jr. born in 1942 (drowned in pool in 1943); daughter Patricia; daughter Carole Lou; daughter Christine

Biography *Lou's on First* by Chris Costello and Raymond Strait

First Film (Abbott and Costello) *One Night in the Tropics*, 1940

Major Films include *Buck Privates*, 1941; *In the Navy*, 1941; *Keep 'em Flying*, 1941; *Rio Rita*, 1942; *The Naughty Nineties*, 1945; *Abbott and Costello Meet Frankenstein*, 1948; *Abbott and Costello Meet Dr. Jekyll and Mr. Hyde*, 1953; *Dance With Me Henry*, 1956; *The Thirty-Foot Bride of Candy Rock* (Costello only), 1959

BRIAN AHERNE

Born William Brian DeLacy Aherne on May 2, 1902 in King's Norton, Worcestershire, England
Married to actress Joan Fontaine in 1939; divorced in 1944
Married to Eleanor DeLiagre Labrot in 1946

First Film *The Eleventh Commandment*, 1924
Major Films include *Underground*, 1928; *Song of Songs*, 1933; *Sylvia Scarlett*, 1935; *Beloved Enemy*, 1936; *Merrily We Live*, 1938; *Juarez*, 1939; *Captain Fury*, 1939; *Hired Wife*, 1940; *My Sister Eileen*, 1942; *A Night to Remember*, 1943; *The Locket*, 1946; *Smart Woman*, 1948; *Titanic*, 1953; *Prince Valiant*, 1954; *The Swan*, 1956; *The Best of Everything*, 1959; *Susan Slade*, 1961; *Rosie*, 1967

Academy Award Nomination for best supporting actor: *Juarez*, 1939

Autobiography *A Proper Job*, 1969

ALAN ALDA

Born Alan Alda on January 28, 1936 in New York City, NY
Married to Arlene Weiss in 1957; daughter Eve born in 1958; daughter Elizabeth born in 1959; daughter Beatrice born in 1960

First Film *Gone Are the Days*, 1963
Major Films include *The Mephisto Waltz*, 1971; *Same Time, Next Year*, 1978; *California Suite*, 1978; *The Seduction of Joe Tynan*, 1979; *The Four Seasons*, 1981

Book *Alan Alda—A Biography* by Raymond Strait

JANE ALEXANDER

Born Jane Quigley on October 28, 1939 in Boston, MA
Married to Robert Alexander in 1962; divorced in 1969; son Jason born in 1963
Married to Edwin Sherin in 1975

First Film *The Great White Hope*, 1970
Major Films include *All the President's Men*, 1976; *Kramer vs. Kramer*, 1979; *Brubaker*, 1980; *Testament*, 1983

Academy Award Nominations for best actress: *The Great White Hope*, 1970; *Testament*, 1983
Nominations for best supporting actress: *All the President's Men*, 1976; *Kramer vs. Kramer*, 1979

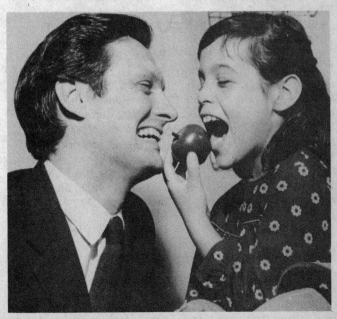

Alan Alda with daughter Eve—then eight years old—in a personal moment off the set.

Woody Allen, the gifted comedian to whom life is a state of perpetual psychological conflict, in a scene from *Stardust Memories* (1980).

WOODY ALLEN

Born Allen Stewart Konigsberg on December 1, 1935 in Brooklyn, NY
Married to Harlene Rosen in 1954; divorced in 1958
Married to actress Louise Lasser in 1966; divorced in 1970

First Film *What's New, Pussycat?*, 1965
Major Films include *What's Up, Tiger Lily?*, 1966; *Casino Royale*, 1967; *Take the Money and Run*, 1969; *Bananas*, 1971; *Play It Again, Sam*, 1972; *Everything You Always Wanted to Know About Sex (But Were Afraid to Ask)*, 1972; *Sleeper*, 1973; *Love and Death*, 1975; *The Front*, 1976; *Annie Hall*, 1977; *Manhattan*, 1979; *Stardust Memories*, 1980; *A Midsummer Night's Sex Comedy*, 1982; *Zelig*, 1983; *Broadway Danny Rose*, 1984

Academy Award for best director: *Annie Hall*, 1977
Academy Award for best original screenplay: *Annie Hall* (co-written with Marshall Brickman), 1977

Nomination for best actor: *Annie Hall*, 1977
Nomination for best director: *Interiors*, 1978
Nominations for best original screenplay: *Interiors*, 1978; *Manhattan* (co-written with Marshall Brickman), 1979

Biography *On Being Funny* by Eric Lax

JUNE ALLYSON

Born Ella Geisman on October 7, 1917 in Bronx, NY
Married to Dick Powell in 1945; widowed in 1963; stepdaughter, Ellen; adopted daughter, Pamela; son Richard Jr. born in 1950
Married to Alfred Glenn Maxwell in 1963; divorced in 1965
Remarried to Alfred Glenn Maxwell in 1966; divorced in 1970
Married to David Ashrow in 1976

First Film *Best Foot Forward*, 1953
Major Films include *Two Girls and a Sailor*, 1944; *Music for Millions*, 1945; *Good News*, 1947; *Little Women*, 1949; *Strategic Air Command*, 1955; *The Shrike*, 1955; *Interlude*, 1957

Biography *June Allyson* by Frances S. Leighton

DANA ANDREWS

Born Carver Daniel Andrews on January 1, 1909 in Collins, MS
Married to Janet Murray in 1932; widowed in 1935; son David born in 1934 (died in 1964)
Married to Mary Todd in 1939; son Stephen born in 1944; daughter Katharine born in 1948; daughter Susan born in 1949

First Film *Lucky Cisco Kid*, 1940
Major Films include *The Ox-Bow Incident*, 1943; *Laura*, 1944; *State Fair*, 1945; *Fallen Angel*, 1945; *The Best Years of Our Lives*, 1946; *My Foolish Heart*, 1949; *Where the Sidewalk Ends*, 1950; *While the City Sleeps*, 1956; *Brainstorm*, 1965; *Airport 1975*, 1974; *The Last Tycoon*, 1976; *The Pilot*, 1979

JULIE ANDREWS

Born Julia Elizabeth Wells Andrews on October 1, 1934 in Walton-on-Thames, Surrey, England
Married to designer Tony Walton in 1959; divorced in 1968; daughter Emma born in 1962
Married to director Blake Edwards in 1969

First Film *Mary Poppins*, 1964
Major Films include *The Sound of Music*, 1965; *Torn Curtain*, 1966; *Thoroughly Modern Millie*, 1967; *Darling Lili*, 1970; *The Tamarind Seed*, 1974; *10*, 1979; *Victor/Victoria*, 1982; *S.O.B.*, 1983; *The Man Who Loved Women*, 1984

Academy Award for best actress: *Mary Poppins*, 1964
Nominations for best

Julie Andrews, star of *Mary Poppins* and *The Sound of Music*—both perennial favorites with children—has also written a children's book. It's about a young girl called *Mandy*.

Ann-Margret, a glamor girl who established herself as a serious, Academy Award-nominated actress, in a pensive mood in *Looking to Get Out* (1982).

actress: *The Sound of Music*, 1965; *Victor/Victoria*, 1982

Biography *Julie Andrews—A Biography* by Raymond Strait
Children's Book by Andrews *Mandy*

ANN-MARGRET

Born Ann-Margaret Olsson on April 28, 1941 in Valsjobyn, Jamtland, Sweden
Married to actor/manager Roger Smith in 1967; stepson, Jordan; stepdaughter, Tracey; stepson, Dallas Thomas

First Film *A Pocketful of Miracles*, 1961
Major Films include *Bye Bye Birdie*, 1963; *The Cincinnati Kid*, 1965; *Carnal Knowledge*, 1971; *Tommy*, 1975; *Joseph Andrews*, 1977; *Magic*, 1978; *I Ought to Be in Pictures*, 1982

Academy Award Nomination for best actress: *Tommy*, 1975
Nomination for best supporting actress: *Carnal Knowledge*, 1971

JEAN ARTHUR

Born Gladys Georgianne Greene on October 17, 1905 in New York City, NY
Married to Julian Anker in 1928; annulled in 1928
Married to producer Frank J. Ross in 1932; divorced in 1949

First Film *Cameo Kirby*, 1923
Major Films include *The Saturday Night Kid*, 1929; *The Whole Town's Talking*, 1935; *Diamond Jim*, 1935; *Mr. Deeds Goes to Town*, 1936; *Easy Living*, 1937; *You Can't Take It With You*, 1938; *Only Angels Have Wings*, 1939; *Mr. Smith Goes to Washington*, 1939; *The Devil and Miss Jones*, 1941; *The More the Merrier*, 1943; *A Foreign Affair*, 1948; *Shane*, 1953

Academy Award Nomination for best actress: *The More the Merrier*, 1943

FRED ASTAIRE

Born Frederick Austerlitz on May 10, 1899 in Omaha, NE (brother of Adele Astaire, his first dancing partner; they were very successful on Broadway and in London until she retired in 1932 to marry Lord Charles Cavendish)
Married to Phyllis Baker Potter in 1933; widowed in 1954; stepson, Peter Potter; son Fred Jr. born in 1941; daughter Ava born in 1942
Married to Robyn Smith in 1980

First Film *Dancing Lady*, 1933
Major Films include *Flying Down to Rio*, 1933; *The Gay Divorcee*, 1934; *Top Hat*, 1935; *Swing Time*, 1936; *Shall We Dance*, 1937; *The Story of Vernon & Irene Castle*, 1939; *You'll Never Get Rich*, 1941; *Holiday Inn*, 1942; *Blue Skies*, 1946; *Easter Parade*, 1948; *The Barkleys of Broadway*, 1949; *Three Little Words*, 1950; *The Band Wagon*, 1953; *Funny Face*, 1957; *Finian's Rainbow*, 1968; *The Towering Inferno*, 1974; *Ghost Story*, 1981

Academy Award Nomination for best supporting actor: *The Towering Inferno*, 1974
Special Academy Award "for his unique artistry and his contributions to the technique of musical pictures," 1949

Autobiography *Steps in Time*, 1959
Book *Fred Astaire and Ginger Rogers* by Arlene Croce

GENE AUTRY

Born Orvon Gene Autry on September 29, 1907 in Tioga, TX
Married to Ina Mae Spivey in 1932; widowed in 1980
Married to Jacqueline Ellam in 1981

First Film *In Old Santa Fe*, 1934
Major Films include *The Singing Cowboy*, 1937; *South of the Border*, 1939; *Melody Ranch*, 1940; *Down Mexico Way*, 1941; *Cowboy Serenade*, 1942; *Robin Hood of Texas*, 1947; *Loaded Pistols*, 1949; *Mule Train*, 1950; *Texans Never Cry*, 1951; *Apache Country*, 1952; *On Top of Old Smoky*, 1953

Autobiography *Back in the Saddle Again*, 1978

Jean Arthur in clearly thought-provoking conversation with Jack Holt (father of actor Tim Holt) in the 1934 movie *The Defense Rests*.

Anne Bancroft stars as a ballerina facing the end of her stage career in *The Turning Point*; her performance in the 1977 film brought Bancroft her third Academy Award nomination for best actress.

LAUREN BACALL

Born Betty Perske on September 16, 1924 in Bronx, NY
Married to actor Humphrey Bogart in 1945; widowed in 1957; son Stephen born in 1948; daughter Leslie born in 1952
Married to actor Jason Robards, Jr. in 1961; divorced in 1969; son Sam born in 1962

First Film *To Have and Have Not*, 1944
Major Films include *The Big Sleep*, 1946; *Key Largo*, 1948; *How to Marry a Millionaire*, 1953; *Written on the Wind*, 1956; *Harper*, 1966; *Murder on the Orient Express*, 1974; *The Shootist*, 1976

Autobiography *Lauren Bacall by Myself*, 1978

LUCILLE BALL

Born Lucille Ball on August 6, 1911 in Jamestown, NY
Married to Desi Arnaz in 1940; divorced in 1960; daughter Lucie Desirée born in 1951; son Desiderio (Desi) Alberto IV born in 1953
Married to Gary Morton in 1961

First Film *Broadway Thru a Keyhole*, 1933
Major Films include *Stage Door*, 1937; *The Affairs of Annabel*, 1938; *Too Many Girls*, 1940; *The Big Street*, 1942; *Du Barry Was a Lady*, 1943; *Easy to Wed*, 1946; *Lured*, 1947; *Fancy Pants*, 1950; *The Long, Long Trailer*, 1954; *The Facts of Life*, 1960; *Yours, Mine and Ours*, 1968; *Mame*, 1974

Biography *Lucy* by Edward Epstein and Joseph Morella

ANNE BANCROFT

Born Anna Maria Luisa Italiano on September 17, 1931 in Bronx, NY
Married to Marty May in 1954; divorced in 1957
Married to actor/director Mel Brooks in 1964; stepdaughter, Stefanie; stepson, Nicholas; stepson, Edward; son Maximilian born in 1972

First Film *Don't Bother to Knock*, 1952
Major Films include *Nightfall*, 1956; *The Miracle Worker*, 1962; *The Pumpkin Eater*, 1964; *The Graduate*, 1967; *Young Winston*, 1972; *The Turning Point*, 1977; *The Elephant Man*, 1980; *To Be or Not To Be*, 1983

Academy Award for best actress: *The Miracle Worker*, 1962
Nominations for best actress: *The Pumpkin Eater*, 1964; *The Graduate*, 1967; *The Turning Point*, 1977

Biography *Seesaw: A Dual Biography of Anne Bancroft and Mel Brooks* by Will Holtzman

TALLULAH BANKHEAD

Born Tallulah Brockman Bankhead on January 31, 1902 in Huntsville, AL

(daughter of William Brockman Bankhead, Speaker of the House of Representatives)
Died on December 12, 1968
Married to actor John Emery in 1937; divorced in 1941; adopted daughter, Barbara Nicholai Emery

First Film *When Men Betray*, 1918
Major Films include *His House in Order*, 1928; *Tarnished Lady*, 1931; *Devil and the Deep*, 1932; *Stage Door Canteen*, 1943; *Lifeboat*, 1944; *A Royal Scandal*, 1945; *Main Street to Broadway*, 1953; *Die! Die! My Darling!*, 1965; *The Daydreamer* (voice only), 1966

Autobiography *Tallulah*, 1952

BRIGITTE BARDOT

Born Camille Javal Bardot on September 28, 1934 in Paris, France
Married to director Roger Vadim in 1952; divorced in 1957
Married to actor Jacques

The classic and mysterious beauty of Tallulah Bankhead is caught dramatically in this shot from *Devil and the Deep*, which she made in 1932.

Brigitte Bardot, who once claimed that she'd never been a good actress, has been the subject of books by two serious French authors, Françoise Sagan and Simone de Beauvoir.

Charrier in 1959; divorced in 1963; son Nicholas Jacques born in 1960
Married to millionaire Gunther Sachs in 1966; divorced in 1969; stepson, Rolf

First Film *Le Trou Normand*, 1952
Major Films include *And God Created Woman*, 1956; *The Truth*, 1961; *Love on a Pillow*, 1962; *Contempt*, 1963; *Viva Maria!*, 1965; *The Novices*, 1970; *Ms. Don Juan*, 1973

Books *Brigitte Bardot—A Close-up* by Françoise Sagan; *Brigitte Bardot and the Lolita Syndrome* by Simone de Beauvoir

ETHEL BARRYMORE

Born Ethel Mae Blythe Barrymore on August 15, 1879 in Philadelphia, PA (daughter of actor Herbert Blythe—stage name Maurice Barrymore—and actress Georgiana Drew; sister of actors John and Lionel Barrymore)
Died on June 18, 1959
Married to New York

socialite Russell Griswold Colt in 1905; divorced in 1923; son Samuel born in 1910; son John born in 1911; daughter Ethel (actress under name Louise Kinlock) born in 1912 (died in 1977)

First Film *The Nightingale*, 1914
Major Films include *Rasputin and the Empress*, 1932; *None But the Lonely Heart*, 1944; *The Spiral Staircase*, 1946; *The Farmer's Daughter*, 1947; *The Paradine Case*, 1947; *Pinky*, 1949; *Kind Lady*, 1951; *Deadline U.S.A.*, 1952

Academy Award for best supporting actress: *None But the Lonely Heart*, 1944
Nominations for best supporting actress: *The Spiral Staircase*, 1946; *The Paradine Case*, 1947; *Pinky*, 1949

Autobiography *Memories*, 1956

JOHN BARRYMORE

Born John Sidney Blythe Barrymore on February 15,

1882 in Philadelphia, PA (son of actor Herbert Blythe—stage name Maurice Barrymore—and actress Georgiana Drew; brother of actress Ethel and actor Lionel Barrymore)
Died on May 29, 1942
Married to Katherine Corri Harris in 1910; divorced in 1917
Married to Blanche Oelrichs Thomas (writer under pseudonym Michael Strange) in 1920; divorced in 1928; daughter Diana Blanche (actress) born in 1921 (died in 1960)
Married to actress Dolores Costello in 1928; divorced in 1935; daughter Dolores Ethel Mae born in 1932; son John Blythe Jr. (actor under name John Drew Barrymore) born in 1932
Married to Elaine Jacobs in 1936; divorced in 1940

First Film *An American Citizen*, 1913
Major Films include *Dr. Jekyll and Mr. Hyde*, 1920; *Don Juan*, 1926; *Moby Dick*, 1930; *Svengali*, 1931; *Grand Hotel*, 1932; *A Bill of Divorcement*, 1932; *Rasputin and the Empress*, 1932; *Dinner at Eight*, 1933;

Twentieth Century, 1934; *Romeo and Juliet*, 1936; *Maytime*, 1937; *The Great Man Votes*, 1939; *The Great Profile*, 1940

Autobiography *Confessions of an Actor*, 1926
Biographies *Good Night Sweet Prince*, by Gene Fowler; *Damned in Paradise* by John Kobler

LIONEL BARRYMORE

Born Lionel Blythe Barrymore on April 28, 1878 (son of actor Herbert Blythe—stage name Maurice Barrymore—and actress Georgiana Drew; brother of actress Ethel and actor John Barrymore)
Died on November 15, 1954
Married to Doris Rankin in 1904; divorced in 1923; daughter Ethel born in 1908
Married to actress Irene Frizzel (stage name Irene Fenwick) in 1923; widowed in 1936

First Film *Friends*, 1909
Major Films include *The*

John Barrymore, whose private life was as dramatic as his on-screen performances, discussed his performing career in his 1926 autobiography, *Confessions of an Actor*.

121

Lionel Barrymore, eldest of the famous sibling trio (the others, of course, are Ethel and John), in *Yellow Ticket*. His co-star in the 1931 film is Elissa Landi.

Temptress, 1926; *Sadie Thompson*, 1928; *A Free Soul*, 1931; *Grand Hotel*, 1932; *Rasputin and the Empress*, 1932; *Dinner at Eight*, 1933; *Treasure Island*, 1934; *David Copperfield*, 1935; *Ah, Wilderness*, 1935; *You Can't Take It With You*, 1938; *Young Dr. Kildare* (first of 15 Kildare films with Barrymore as Dr. Gillespie), 1938; *It's a Wonderful Life*, 1946; *Duel in the Sun*, 1947; *Key Largo*, 1948; *Down to the Sea in Ships*, 1949 (From 1938 onward Barrymore continued to act in a wheelchair to which he was confined as a result of paralysis caused by arthritis and a hip injury.)

Academy Award for best actor: *A Free Soul*, 1930/31
Nomination for best director: *Madame X*, 1928/29

Autobiography *We Barrymores*, 1951

ALAN BATES

Born Alan Arthur Bates on March 17, 1934 in Derbyshire, England
Married to Victoria Ward in 1970; twin sons born in 1970

First Film *The Entertainer*, 1959
Major Films include *Whistle Down the Wind*, 1961; *Nothing But the Best*, 1964; *Zorba the Greek*, 1965; *Georgy Girl*, 1966; *Far From the Madding Crowd*, 1967; *The Fixer*, 1968; *Women in Love*, 1970; *The Go-Between*, 1971; *Royal Flash*, 1975; *An Unmarried Woman*, 1978; *The Rose*, 1978; *Nijinsky*, 1979; *Quartet*, 1981

Academy Award Nomination for best actor: *The Fixer*, 1968

ANNE BAXTER

Born Anne Baxter on May 7, 1923 in Michigan City, IN
Married to actor John Hodiak in 1946; divorced in 1953; daughter Katrina born in 1951
Married to Australian rancher Randolph Galt in 1960; widowed in 1975; daughter Melissa born in 1963; daughter Maginel born in 1964

Married to Daniel Klee in 1977

First Film *Twenty Mule Team*, 1940
Major Films include *The Magnificent Ambersons*, 1942; *Sunday Dinner for a Soldier*, 1944; *The Razor's Edge*, 1946; *All About Eve*, 1950; *The Ten Commandments*, 1956; *Cimarron*, 1960

Academy Award for best supporting actress: *The Razor's Edge*, 1946
Nomination for best actress: *All About Eve*, 1946

Autobiography *Intermission*, 1976

THE BEATLES

GEORGE HARRISON
Born George Harrison on February 25, 1943 in Liverpool, England
Married to model Patti Boyd in 1966; divorced
Married to Olivia Arias in 1978; son Dhani born in 1978

JOHN LENNON
Born John Winston Lennon on October 9, 1940 in Liverpool, England
Died on December 8, 1980
Married to Cynthia Powell in 1962; divorced; son John Charles Julian born in 1963
Married to Yoko Ono in 1969; son Sean born in 1975

Books by Lennon *In His Own Write; A Spaniard in the Works*

PAUL MCCARTNEY
Born James Paul McCartney on June 18, 1942 in Liverpool, England
Married to Linda Eastman in 1969; stepdaughter, Heather; daughter Mary born in 1969; daughter Stella born in 1971; son James Louis born in 1977

RINGO STARR
Born Richard Starkey on July 7, 1940 in Liverpool, England
Married to Maureen Cox in 1965; divorced in 1975; son Zak born in 1965; son Jason; daughter Lee
Married to actress Barbara Bach in 1981

First Film (The Beatles) *A Hard Day's Night*, 1964
Major Films include *Help!*, 1965; *How I Won the War* (Lennon only), 1967;

Alan Bates, a British actor with a powerful screen personality, as he appeared in *The Rose*, playing the hard-driving manager of a rock superstar portrayed by Bette Midler.

Warren Beatty, brother of actress Shirley MacLaine, as he appeared in *Bonnie and Clyde* in 1967 with co-star Faye Dunaway.

Yellow Submarine (voices only), 1968; *Let It Be*, 1970; *The Magic Christian*, (Starr only), 1970; *Concert for Bangladesh* (Harrison and Starr only), 1972; *That'll Be the Day* (Starr only), 1974; *Caveman* (Starr only), 1981

Autobiographies *Beatlemania: 1963 to 1966*; *Beatlemania: 1967 to 1970*

WARREN BEATTY

Born Warren Beaty on March 30, 1937 in Richmond, VA (brother of actress Shirley MacLaine)

First Film *Splendor in the Grass*, 1961
Major Films include *The Roman Spring of Mrs. Stone*, 1961; *Lilith*, 1964; *Bonnie and Clyde*, 1967; *McCabe and Mrs. Miller*, 1971; *The Parallax View*, 1974; *Shampoo*, 1975; *Heaven Can Wait*, 1978; *Reds*, 1981

Academy Award for best director: *Reds*, 1981

Nominations for best actor: *Bonnie and Clyde*, 1967; *Heaven Can Wait*, 1978; *Reds*, 1981
Nomination for best director: *Heaven Can Wait* (with Buck Henry), 1978
Nominations for best original screenplay: *Shampoo* (with Robert Towne), 1975; *Reds* (with Trevor Griffiths), 1981
Nomination for best screenplay adaptation: *Heaven Can Wait* (with Elaine May), 1978 (*Heaven Can Wait* in 1978 and *Reds* in 1981, both of which Beatty produced, were nominated for Academy Awards for best picture.)

Biographies *Warren Beatty—His Life, Loves, and Work* by Suzanne Munchower; *Warren Beatty* by Jim Burke

WALLACE BEERY

Born Wallace Beery on April 1, 1885 in Kansas City, MO (brother of actor Noah Beery, Sr.)

Died on April 17, 1949
Married to actress Gloria Swanson in 1916; divorced in 1918
Married to actress Rita Gilman in 1924; divorced in 1939; adopted daughter, Carol Ann

First Film *Sweedie, the Swatter*, 1913
Major Films include *The Little American*, 1917; *The Unpardonable Sin*, 1919; *The Last of the Mohicans*, 1920; *Richard the Lion-Hearted*, 1923; *The Sea Hawk*, 1924; *The Lost World*, 1925; *We're in the Navy Now*, 1926; *The Big House*, 1929; *Billy the Kid*, 1930; *Min and Bill*, 1930; *The Champ*, 1931; *Grand Hotel*, 1932; *Viva Villa!*, 1934; *Treasure Island*, 1934; *China Seas*, 1935; *A Message to Garcia*, 1936; *Stand Up and Fight*, 1939; *Wyoming*, 1940; *Jackass Mail*, 1942; *Bad Bascomb*, 1946; *A Date With Judy*, 1948; *Big Jack*, 1949

Academy Award for best actor: *The Champ*, 1931/32
Nomination for best actor: *The Big House*, 1929/30

WILLIAM BENDIX

Born William Bendix on January 14, 1906 in New York City, NY
Died on December 15, 1964
Married to Teresa Stefanotti in 1928; adopted daughter, Stephanie; daughter Lorraine

First Film *Woman of the Year*, 1941
Major Films include *Wake Island*, 1942; *The Glass Key*, 1942; *Lifeboat*, 1944; *The Hairy Ape*, 1944; *A*

Bell for Adano, 1945; *The Blue Dahlia*, 1946; *The Dark Corner*, 1946; *Calcutta*, 1947; *The Babe Ruth Story*, 1948; *A Connecticut Yankee in King Arthur's Court*, 1949; *The Life of Riley*, 1949

Academy Award Nominations for best supporting actor: *Wake Island*, 1942; *Lifeboat*, 1944

CONSTANCE BENNETT

Born Constance Campbell Bennett on October 22, 1905 in New York City, NY (daughter of actor Richard Bennett; sister of actress Joan Bennett)
Died on July 26, 1965
Married to Chester Hirst Moorhead in 1922; annulled in 1924
Married to millionaire Philip Morgan Hayward Plant in 1925; divorced in 1930; adopted son, Peter
Married to Marquis Henri de la Falaise de la Coudray in 1931; divorced in 1940
Married to actor Gilbert Roland in 1941; divorced in 1945; daughter Lorinda Alonzo born in 1942; daughter Gyl Christina born in 1943
Married to U.S. Air Force General John Coulter in 1946

First Film *The Valley of Decision*, 1916
Major Films include *Reckless Youth*, 1922; *Cytherea*, 1924; *Code of the West*, 1925; *Sally, Irene and Mary*, 1925; *This Thing Called Love*, 1929; *Three Faces East*, 1930; *Born to Love*, 1931; *Bought*, 1931; *Lady With a Past*, 1932; *What Price Hollywood?*, 1932; *After Tonight*, 1933; *Moulin Rouge*, 1934; *After*

Jack Benny, who made his first film in 1929, followed a successful screen career by becoming an even more successful television personality with *The Jack Benny Show*.

Office Hours, 1935; *Ladies in Love*, 1936; *Topper*, 1937; *Merrily We Live*, 1938; *Topper Takes a Trip*, 1939; *Two-Faced Woman*, 1941; *Paris Underground*, 1945; *Centennial Summer*, 1946; *The Unsuspected*, 1947; *As Young as You Feel*, 1951; *Madame X*, 1966

Biography *Constance Bennett* by M. H. McBride

JOAN BENNETT

Born Joan Bennett on February 27, 1910 in Palisades, NJ (daughter of actor Richard Bennett; sister of actress Constance Bennett)
Married to John Martin Fox in 1926; divorced in 1928; daughter Adrienne born in 1928
Married to screenwriter Gene Markey in 1932; divorced in 1937; daughter Melinda born in 1934
Married to producer Walter Wanger in 1940; divorced in 1962; daughter Stephanie born in 1943;

daughter Shelley born in 1948
Married to David Wilde in 1978

First Film *The Valley of Decision*, 1916
Major Films include *Disraeli*, 1929; *Moby Dick*, 1930; *Little Women*, 1933; *Private Worlds*, 1935; *Big Brown Eyes*, 1936; *Trade Winds*, 1939; *Man Hunt*, 1941; *The Woman in the Window*, 1944; *Scarlet Street*, 1945; *The Macomber Affair*, 1947; *Woman on the Beach*, 1947; *The Reckless Moment*, 1949; *Father of the Bride*, 1950; *Father's Little Dividend*, 1951; *We're No Angels*, 1955; *Desire in the Dust*, 1960; *House of Dark Shadows*, 1970; *Suspiria*, 1977

Autobiography *The Bennett Playbill*, 1970

JACK BENNY

Born Benjamin Kubelsky on February 14, 1894 in Waukegan, IL
Died on December 26, 1974

Married to actress Sadye Marks (stage name Mary Livingstone) in 1928; adopted daughter, Joan Naomi

First Film *The Hollywood Revue of 1929*, 1929
Major Films include *Broadway Melody of 1936*, 1935; *Artists and Models*, 1937; *Love Thy Neighbor*, 1940; *Charley's Aunt*, 1941; *To Be or Not To Be*, 1942; *George Washington Slept Here*, 1942; *The Horn Blows at Midnight*, 1945; *It's in the Bag*, 1945; *A Guide for the Married Man*, 1967

Biography *Jack Benny: An Intimate Biography* by Irving A. Fein

INGRID BERGMAN

Born Ingrid Bergman on August 29, 1915 in Stockholm, Sweden
Died on August 29, 1982
Married to Dr. Peter Lindstrom in 1937; divorced in 1950; daughter Pia born in 1938

Married to director Roberto Rossellini in 1950; divorced in 1957; son Roberto Jr. born in 1950; twin daughters Isabella and Ingrid Isotta born in 1952
Married to Lars Schmidt in 1958; separated

First Film *The Count From the Monk's Bridge*, 1934
Major Films include *Intermezzo* (in Swedish), 1936; *Intermezzo: A Love Story* (in English), 1939; *Dr. Jekyll and Mr. Hyde*, 1941; *Casablanca*, 1943; *For Whom the Bell Tolls*, 1943; *Gaslight*, 1944; *Spellbound*, 1945; *Saratoga Trunk*, 1945; *The Bells of St. Mary's*, 1945; *Notorious*, 1946; *Joan of Arc*, 1948; *Stromboli*, 1950; *Anastasia*, 1956; *Indiscreet*, 1958; *Cactus Flower*, 1969; *Murder on the Orient Express*, 1974; *Autumn Sonata*, 1978

Academy Awards for best actress: *Gaslight*, 1944; *Anastasia*, 1956
Academy Award for best supporting actress: *Murder on the Orient Express*, 1974
Nominations for best

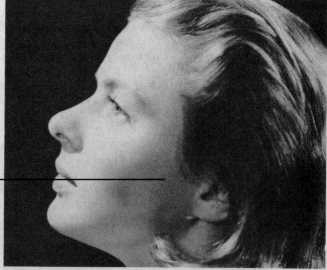

A classic profile study of Ingrid Bergman, whose impressive screen career spanned over forty years, winning her three Academy Awards and four nominations.

THE ACTORS AND ACTRESSES

Humphrey Bogart played opposite Lauren Bacall for the first time in *To Have and Have Not* in 1944; they married the following year and named their son, born in 1948, after Bogart's character in the movie.

actress: *For Whom the Bell Tolls*, 1943; *The Bells of St. Mary's*, 1945; *Joan of Arc*, 1948; *Autumn Sonata*, 1978

Autobiography *Ingrid Bergman: My Story* (with Alan Burgess), 1980
Biography *Ingrid Bergman* by John Russell Taylor

DIRK BOGARDE

Born Derek Niven van den Bogaerde on March 28, 1921 in London, England

First Film *Come On George*, 1939
Major Films include *Quartet*, 1948; *Doctor in the House*, 1954; *A Tale of Two Cities*, 1958; *Libel*, 1959; *Song Without End*, 1960; *Victim*, 1961; *The Servant*, 1963; *Darling*, 1965; *The Fixer*, 1968; *Oh! What a Lovely War*, 1969; *Death in Venice*, 1971; *Providence*, 1977; *Despair*, 1978

Autobiographies *A Postillion Struck by Light-*ning, 1977; *An Orderly Man*, 1983
Novels by Bogarde *Voices in the Garden; A Gentle Occupation*

HUMPHREY BOGART

Born Humphrey DeForest Bogart on January 23, 1899 in New York City, NY
Died on January 14, 1957
Married to actress Helen Menken in 1926; divorced in 1927
Married to actress Mary Phillips in 1928; divorced in 1937
Married to actress Mayo Methot in 1938; divorced in 1945
Married to actress Lauren Bacall in 1945; son Stephen born in 1948; daughter Leslie born in 1952

First Film *A Devil With Women*, 1930
Major Films include *The Petrified Forest*, 1936; *Marked Woman*, 1937; *Dead End*, 1937; *Angels With Dirty Faces*, 1938; *High Sierra*, 1941; *The Mal-*tese Falcon, 1941; *Casablanca*, 1943; *To Have and Have Not*, 1944; *The Big Sleep*, 1946; *The Treasure of the Sierra Madre*, 1948; *Key Largo*, 1948; *In a Lonely Place*, 1950; *The African Queen*, 1951; *Beat the Devil*, 1954; *The Caine Mutiny*, 1954; *The Barefoot Contessa*, 1954; *The Desperate Hours*, 1955; *The Harder They Fall*, 1956

Academy Award for best actor: *The African Queen*, 1951
Nominations for best actor: *Casablanca*, 1943; *The Caine Mutiny*, 1954

Biographies *Bogart & Bacall, A Love Story* by Joseph Hyams; *Screen Greats: Bogart* by M. Samuels

PAT BOONE

Born Charles Eugene Boone on June 1, 1934 in Jacksonville, FL
Married to Shirley Foley in 1953; daughter Cheryl Lynn; daughter Linda Lee; daughter Deborah Ann (singer); daughter Laura Gene

First Film *Bernardine*, 1957
Major Films include *April Love*, 1957; *Mardi Gras*, 1958; *Journey to the Center of the Earth*, 1959; *All Hands on Deck*, 1961; *State Fair*, 1962; *Goodbye Charlie*, 1964; *The Greatest Story Ever Told*, 1965; *The Perils of Pauline*, 1967; *The Cross and the Switchblade*, 1970; *Matilda* (voice only), 1978

Autobiography *The Honeymoon Is Over*, 1977

ERNEST BORGNINE

Born Ermès Effron Borgnine on January 24, 1917 in Hamden, CT
Married to Rhoda Kemins in 1949; divorced in 1958; daughter Nancy born in 1953
Married to actress Katy Jurado in 1959; divorced in 1961
Married to actress Ethel Merman in 1964; divorced in 1964
Married to Donna Granoucci Rancourt in 1965; divorced in 1972; son

Ernest Borgnine, here projecting a tough-guy image in *Bad Day at Black Rock* in 1954, the following year won a best actor Academy Award for a very different role—the gentle, lonely hero of *Marty*.

125

Christopher born in 1966; daughter Sharon born in 1967
Married to Tove Newman in 1972

First Film *China Corsair*, 1951
Major Films include *From Here to Eternity*, 1953; *Bad Day at Black Rock*, 1954; *Marty*, 1955; *The Catered Affair*, 1956; *The Badlanders*, 1958; *McHale's Navy*, 1964; *The Flight of the Phoenix*, 1965; *The Dirty Dozen*, 1967; *The Wild Bunch*, 1969; *Willard*, 1971; *The Poseidon Adventure*, 1972; *The Devil's Rain*, 1975; *Escape From New York*, 1981

Academy Award for best actor: *Marty*, 1955

CHARLES BOYER

Born Charles Boyer on August 28, 1897 in Figeac, France
Died (suicide) on August 26, 1978
Married to actress Pat Paterson in 1934; widowed on August 24, 1978; son Michael born in 1944 (died in 1965)

First Film *L'Homme du Large*, 1920
Major Films include *Private Worlds*, 1935; *Mayerling*, 1936; *Conquest*, 1937; *History Is Made at Night*, 1937; *Algiers*, 1938; *Love Affair*, 1939; *All This and Heaven Too*, 1940; *Back Street*, 1941; *Gaslight*, 1944; *Confidential Agent*, 1945; *Cluny Brown*, 1946; *The Earrings of Madame de*, 1953; *Fanny*, 1961; *Barefoot in the Park*, 1967; *Lost Horizon*, 1973; *A Matter of Time*, 1976

Academy Award Nominations for best actor: *Conquest*, 1937; *Algiers*, 1938; *Gaslight*, 1944; *Fanny*, 1961
Special Academy Award "for his progressive cultural achievement in establishing the French Research Foundation in Los Angeles as a source of reference for the Hollywood Motion Picture Industry," 1942

Biography *The Reluctant Lover* by Larry Swindell

MARLON BRANDO

Born Marlon "Bud" Brando, Jr. on April 30, 1924 in Omaha, NE
Married to actress Anna Kashfi in 1947; divorced in 1960; son Christian Devi born in 1958
Married to actress Movita Castaneda in 1960; divorced in 1961; son Miko born in 1960; daughter Rebecca born in 1961; son Tehoto born in 1961
Married to Tarita Terripain in 1962; divorced; daughter Cheyenne "Tarita" born in 1970

First Film *The Men*, 1950
Major Films include *A Streetcar Named Desire*, 1951; *Viva Zapata!*, 1952; *Julius Caesar*, 1953; *The Wild One*, 1953; *On the Waterfront*, 1954; *Sayonara*, 1957; *One-Eyed Jacks*, 1961; *Mutiny on the Bounty*, 1962; *The Chase*, 1966; *Reflections in a Golden Eye*, 1967; *The Godfather*, 1972; *Last Tango in Paris*, 1973; *Apocalypse Now*, 1979

Academy Awards for best actor: *On the Waterfront*, 1954; *The Godfather*, 1972 (refused)

Nominations for best actor: *A Streetcar Named Desire*, 1951; *Viva Zapata!*, 1952; *Julius Caesar*, 1953; *Sayonara*, 1957; *Last Tango in Paris*, 1973

Biography *Brando for Breakfast* by Anna K. Brando and E. P. Stein

JEFF BRIDGES

Born Jeff Bridges on December 4, 1949 in Los Angeles, CA (son of actor Lloyd Bridges; brother of actor Beau Bridges)

First Film *Halls of Anger*, 1970
Major Films include *The Last Picture Show*, 1971; *Bad Company*, 1972; *The Last American Hero*, 1973; *The Iceman Cometh*, 1973; *Thunderbolt and Lightfoot*, 1974; *Hearts of the West*, 1975; *Somebody Killed Her Husband*, 1978; *Winter Kills*, 1979; *Cutter's Way*, 1981; *Against All Odds*, 1984

Academy Award Nominations for best supporting actor: *The Last Picture Show*, 1971; *Thunderbolt and Lightfoot*, 1974

CHARLES BRONSON

Born Charles Buchinsky on November 3, 1921 in Ehrenfeld, PA
Married to Harriet Tendler in 1949; divorced in 1965; daughter Suzanne born in 1955; son Anthony born in 1961
Married to actress Jill Ireland in 1968; three stepsons; daughter Zuleika born in 1971

First Film *You're in the Navy Now*, 1951
Major Films include *Pat and Mike*, 1952; *Machine Gun Kelly*, 1958; *The Magnificent Seven*, 1960; *The Great Escape*, 1963; *The Dirty Dozen*, 1967; *Once Upon a Time in the West*, 1969; *The Valachi Papers*, 1972; *Death Wish*, 1975; *Hard Times*, 1975; *The White Buffalo*, 1977; *Love and Bullets*, 1979; *Death Wish II*, 1982

Book *The Films of Charles Bronson* by Jerry Vermilye

Charles Bronson has turned in fine performances in a number of films over the course of his career but is probably still best known to many western movie buffs as one of *The Magnificent Seven* (1960).

George Burns, the indestructible star of *The Sunshine Boys* (1975) for which he won the best supporting actor Oscar, is also the author of several books.

YUL BRYNNER

Born Youl Bryner on July 11, 1915 on the island of Sakhalin (east of Siberia and north of Japan)
Married to actress Virginia Gilmore in 1944; divorced in 1960; son Yul "Rocky" born in 1945
Married to Doris Kleiner in 1960; divorced; daughter Victoria born in 1962
Married to Jacqueline de Croisset in 1971; adopted daughters, Mia and Melody

First Film *Port of New York*, 1949
Major Films include *The King and I*, 1956; *Anastasia*, 1956; *The Ten Commandments*, 1956; *The Sound and the Fury*, 1959; *The Magnificent Seven*, 1960; *Return of the Seven*, 1966; *The Madwoman of Chaillot*, 1969; *Westworld*, 1973

Academy Award for best actor: *The King and I*, 1956

Book by Brynner *The Yul Brynner Cookbook* (with Susan Reed)

GEORGE BURNS

Born Nathan Birnbaum on January 20, 1896 in New York City, NY
Married to vaudeville partner Hannah Siegel; divorced
Married to actress Gracie Allen in 1926; widowed in 1964; adopted daughter, Sandra Jean; adopted son, Roland Jon

First Film *The Big Broadcast*, 1932
Major Films include *International House*, 1933; *College Holiday*, 1936; *A Damsel in Distress*, 1937; *Honolulu*, 1939; *The Sunshine Boys*, 1975; *Oh, God!*, 1977; *Sergeant Pepper's Lonely Hearts Club Band*, 1978; *Just You and Me, Kid*, 1979; *Going in Style*, 1979

Academy Award for best supporting actor: *The Sunshine Boys*, 1975

Books by Burns *I Love Her, That's Why* (with Cynthia Hobart Lindsay); *Living It Up: or They Still Love Me in Altoona; The Third Time Around; How to Live to 100 or More*

RAYMOND BURR

Born Raymond William Stacey Burr on May 21, 1917 in New Westminster, British Columbia, Canada
Married to Annette Sutherland in 1939; widowed in 1943 when she died in a plane crash; son Michael Evan born in 1940 (died in 1950)
Married to Isabella Ward in 1946; divorced
Married to Laura Andrina Morgan in 1950; widowed in 1955

First Film *San Quentin*, 1946
Major Films include *Raw Deal*, 1948; *Walk a Crooked Mile*, 1948; *Abandoned*, 1949; *Key to the City*, 1950; *Borderline*, 1950; *A Place in the Sun*, 1951; *Meet Danny Wilson*, 1952; *The Blue Gardenia*, 1953; *Rear Window*, 1954; *You're Never Too Young*, 1955; *Godzilla*, 1956; *Please Murder Me*, 1956; *Crime of Passion*, 1957; *Desire in the Dust*, 1960; *Tomorrow Never Comes*, 1978; *Out of the Blue*, 1980

ELLEN BURSTYN

Born Edna Rae Gillooly on December 7, 1932 in Detroit, MI
Married to William Alexander in 1950; divorced
Married to Paul Roberts in 1957; divorced
Married to Neil Burstyn in 1961; divorced in 1970; son Jefferson born in 1962

First Film *For Those Who Think Young*, 1964
Major Films include *The Last Picture Show*, 1971; *The Exorcist*, 1973; *Harry and Tonto*, 1974; *Alice Doesn't Live Here Anymore*, 1974; *Same Time, Next Year*, 1978; *Resurrection*, 1979

Ellen Burstyn won a best actress Oscar for *Alice Doesn't Live Here Anymore* in 1974, and followed this with best actress nominations for *The Exorcist* (1973) and *Same Time, Next Year* (1978).

127

Academy Award for best actress: *Alice Doesn't Live Here Anymore*, 1974
Nominations for best actress: *The Exorcist*, 1973; *Same Time, Next Year*, 1978
Nomination for best supporting actress: *The Last Picture Show*, 1971

RICHARD BURTON

Born Richard Walter Jenkins on November 10, 1925 in Pontrhydyfen, Wales
Died on August 5, 1984
Married to actress Sybil Williams in 1949; divorced in 1963; daughter Kate (actress); daughter Jessica
Married to actress Elizabeth Taylor in 1964; divorced in 1974
Remarried to Elizabeth Taylor in 1975; divorced in 1976
Married to model Susan Hunt in 1976; divorced in 1982
Married to Sally Hay in 1983

First Film *The Last Days of Dolwyn*, 1948
Major Films include *My Cousin Rachel*, 1952; *The Robe*, 1953; *Prince of Players*, 1954; *Alexander the Great*, 1956; *Look Back in Anger*, 1958; *Cleopatra*, 1963; *Becket*, 1964; *The Night of the Iguana*, 1964; *The Spy Who Came in From the Cold*, 1965; *Who's Afraid of Virginia Woolf?*, 1966; *Where Eagles Dare*, 1969; *Anne of the Thousand Days*, 1969; *Equus*, 1977; *The Wild Geese*, 1978; *Circle of Two*, 1980

Academy Award Nominations for best actor: *The Robe*, 1953; *Becket*, 1964; *The Spy Who Came in From the Cold*, 1965; *Who's Afraid of Virginia Woolf?*, 1966; *Anne of the Thousand Days*, 1969; *Equus*, 1977

Nomination for best supporting actor: *My Cousin Rachel*, 1952

JAMES CAAN

Born James Caan on March 26, 1939 in New York City, NY
Married to Dee Jay Mattis in 1961; divorced in 1966; daughter Tara Alisa born in 1964
Married to Sheila Ryan in 1976; separated in 1978; son Scott Andrew born in 1976

First Film *Irma La Douce*, 1963
Major Films include *Lady in a Cage*, 1964; *Red Line 7000*, 1965; *El Dorado*, 1967; *The Rain People*, 1969; *Rabbit, Run*, 1970; *The Godfather*, 1972; *Cinderella Liberty*, 1974; *The Gambler*, 1974; *Funny Lady*, 1975; *Comes a Horseman*, 1978; *Thief*, 1981

Academy Award Nomination for best supporting actor: *The Godfather*, 1972

JAMES CAGNEY

Born James Francis Cagney, Jr. on July 17, 1899 in New York City, NY
Married to Frances Willard (Billie) Vernon in 1920; adopted daughter, Cathleen; adopted son, Jimmy

First Film *Sinner's Holiday*, 1930
Major Films include *The Public Enemy*, 1931; *Foot-light Parade*, 1933; *A Midsummer Night's Dream*, 1935; *Angels With Dirty Faces*, 1938; *The Roaring Twenties*, 1939; *Yankee Doodle Dandy*, 1942; *Blood on the Sun*, 1946; *13 Rue Madeleine*, 1947; *White Heat*, 1949; *Love Me or Leave Me*, 1955; *Mister Roberts*, 1955; *Man of a Thousand Faces*, 1957; *One Two Three*, 1962; *Ragtime*, 1981

Academy Award for best actor: *Yankee Doodle Dandy*, 1942
Nominations for best actor: *Angels With Dirty Faces*, 1938; *Love Me or Leave Me*, 1955

Autobiography *Cagney by Cagney*
Biography *James Cagney, The Authorized Biography* by Douglas Warren

MICHAEL CAINE

Born Maurice Joseph Micklewhite on March 14, 1933 in London, England

Married to actress Patricia Haines in 1955; divorced; daughter Dominique born in 1956
Married to Shakira Baksh in 1973; divorced; daughter Natasha born in 1974

First Film *A Hill in Korea*, 1956
Major Films include *Zulu*, 1964; *The Ipcress File*, 1965; *Alfie*, 1966; *Funeral in Berlin*, 1966; *Sleuth*, 1972; *The Man Who Would Be King*, 1975; *The Eagle Has Landed*, 1977; *California Suite*, 1978; *Dressed to Kill*, 1980; *Victory*, 1981; *Educating Rita*, 1983

Academy Award Nominations for best actor: *Alfie*, 1966; *Sleuth*, 1972

Biography *Raising Caine* by William Hall

DYAN CANNON

Born Samille Diane (Frosty) Friesen on January 4, 1937 in Tacoma, WA

Richard Burton, twelfth of thirteen children of a Welsh coal miner, took his professional name from the man who became his mentor and his foster father—schoolmaster Philip Burton.

Dyan Cannon is seen here with Charles Grodin in a scene from *Heaven Can Wait*, the 1978 movie which won her an Oscar nomination for best supporting actress.

Married to actor Cary Grant in 1965; divorced in 1968; daughter Jennifer born in 1966

First Film *The Rise and Fall of Legs Diamond*, 1960
Major Films include *Bob & Carol & Ted & Alice*, 1969; *Such Good Friends*, 1971; *The Last of Sheila*, 1973; *Shamus*, 1973; *Heaven Can Wait*, 1978; *Revenge of the Pink Panther*, 1978; *Deathtrap*, 1982

Academy Award Nominations for best supporting actress: *Bob & Carol & Ted & Alice*, 1969; *Heaven Can Wait*, 1978 (*Number One*, which Cannon wrote, directed, and co-produced with Vince Cannon in 1976, was nominated for an Academy Award for best live-action short film.)

ART CARNEY

Born Arthur William Matthew Carney on November 4, 1918 in Mt. Vernon, NY

Married to Jean Meyers in 1940; divorced; daughter Eileen born in 1941; son Brian born in 1942; son Paul born in 1952
Married to Barbara Isaacs in 1979; divorced

First Film *Pot o' Gold*, 1941
Major Films include *The Yellow Rolls-Royce*, 1964; *Harry and Tonto*, 1974; *W.W. and the Dixie Dance Kings*, 1975; *The Late Show*, 1977; *House Calls*, 1978

Academy Award for best actor: *Harry and Tonto*, 1974

LESLIE CARON

Born Leslie Claire Margaret Caron on July 1, 1931 in Paris, France
Married to meat-packing heir George Hormel in 1951; divorced in 1954
Married to producer/director Peter Hall in 1956; divorced in 1966; son Christopher John born in 1957; daughter Jennifer born in 1958

Married to producer Michael Laughlin in 1969

First Film *An American in Paris*, 1951
Major Films include *The Story of Three Loves*, 1953; *Lili*, 1953; *The Glass Slipper*, 1955; *Daddy Long Legs*, 1955; *Gigi*, 1958; *Fanny*, 1961; *The L-Shaped Room*, 1963; *Father Goose*, 1964; *Is Paris Burning?*, 1966; *The Man Who Loved Women*, 1977; *Goldengirl*, 1979

Academy Award Nominations for best actress: *Lili*, 1953; *The L-Shaped Room*, 1963

MADELEINE CARROLL

Born Marie Madeleine Bernadette O'Carroll on February 26, 1906 in West Bromwich, Staffordshire, England
Married to Philip Astley in 1931; divorced in 1938

Married to producer Henri Lavorel in 1939; divorced in 1942
Married to actor Sterling Hayden in 1942; divorced in 1946
Married to *Life* magazine publisher Andrew Heiskell in 1950; divorced in 1965; daughter Anne-Madeleine

First Film *The Guns of Loos*, 1928
Major Films include *I Was a Spy*, 1931; *The Thirty-Nine Steps*, 1935; *Secret Agent*, 1936; *Lloyds of London*, 1936; *On the Avenue*, 1937; *The Prisoner of Zenda*, 1937; *My Son, My Son*, 1940; *North West Mounted Police*, 1940; *Virginia*, 1941; *Bahama Passage*, 1942; *My Favorite Blonde*, 1942; *An Innocent Affair*, 1948; *The Fan*, 1949

JEFF CHANDLER

Born Ira Grossel on December 15, 1918 in

Madeleine Carroll, whose major films include the 1935 version of *The Thirty-Nine Steps*, is seen here in *Bahama Passage* (1942).

Cyd Charisse, believed at the height of her career to have the most beautiful legs in Hollywood, is seen here with Gene Kelly in *It's Always Fair Weather* in 1955.

Brooklyn, NY
Died on June 17, 1961
Married to Marjorie Hoshelle in 1946; divorced in 1954; son Jamie born in 1947; son Dana born in 1948

First Film *Johnny O'Clock*, 1949
Major Films include *Broken Arrow*, 1950; *The Iron Man*, 1951; *Female on the Beach*, 1955; *Away All Boats*, 1956; *Thunder in the Sun*, 1959; *Return to Peyton Place*, 1961; *Merrill's Marauders*, 1962

Academy Award Nomination for best supporting actor: *Broken Arrow*, 1950

CHARLIE CHAPLIN

Born Charles Spencer Chaplin, Jr. on April 16, 1889 in Walworth, London, England
Died on December 25, 1977
Married to actress Mildred Harris in 1918; divorced in 1920; son born in 1919 (died when three days old)
Married to actress Lita Grey in 1924; divorced in 1927; son Charles Spencer born in 1925 (died in 1968): son Sydney Earle born in 1926
Married to actress Paulette Goddard in 1936; divorced in 1942
Married to Oona O'Neill (daughter of playwright Eugene O'Neill) in 1943; daughter Geraldine (actress) born in 1944; son Michael born in 1945; daughter Josephine born in 1946; daughter Victoria born in 1947; daughter Jane born in 1948; daughter Annette born in 1949; son Eugene born in 1950; son Christopher born in 1951

First Film *Making a Living* (short), 1914
Major Films include (shorts) *Tillie's Punctured Romance*, 1914; *The Tramp*, 1915; *The Rink*, 1916; *Easy Street*, 1917; *The Immigrant*, 1917; *Shoulder Arms*, 1918; (features) *The Kid*, 1921; *The Gold Rush*, 1925; *The Circus*, 1927; *City Lights*, 1931; *Modern Times*, 1936; *The Great Dictator*, 1940; *Monsieur Verdoux*, 1947; *Limelight*, 1952; *A King in New York*, 1957; *A Countess From Hong Kong*, 1967

Academy Award Nominations for best actor: *The Circus*, 1927/28; *The Great Dictator*, 1940
Nomination for best comedy direction: *The Circus*, 1927/28
Special Academy Awards "for versatility and genius in writing, acting, directing, and producing *The Circus*," 1927/28; "for the incalculable effect he has had in making motion pictures the art form of this century," 1971

Knighted in 1975

Autobiography *My Autobiography*, 1964
Biography *Charles Chaplin* by Theodore Huff
Book *The Films of Charlie Chaplin* by Gerald D. McDonald

CYD CHARISSE

Born Tula Ellice Finklea on March 8, 1922 in Amarillo, TX
Married to ballet teacher Nico Charisse in 1939; divorced in 1947; son Nicky born in 1940
Married to singer Tony Martin in 1948; son Tony Jr. born in 1950

First Film *Mission to Moscow*, 1943
Major Films include *The Harvey Girls*, 1946; *Words and Music*, 1948; *Singin' in the Rain*, 1952; *The Band Wagon*, 1953; *Brigadoon*, 1954; *It's Always Fair Weather*, 1955; *Meet Me in Las Vegas*, 1956; *Silk Stockings*, 1957

Autobiography *The Two of Us* by Charisse and Tony Martin, as told to Dick Kleiner, 1976

MAURICE CHEVALIER

Born Maurice Auguste Chevalier on September 12, 1888 in Menilmontante, France
Died on January 1, 1972
Married to actress Yvonne Vallée in 1926; annulled in 1935

Maurice Chevalier, always the image of the debonair Frenchman, took on a new persona in the Walt Disney adaptation of Jules Verne's *In Search of the Castaways*. He's seen here with co-star Hayley Mills.

First Film *Trop Crédule* (short), 1908
Major Films include *Innocents of Paris*, 1929; *The Love Parade*, 1930; *The Big Pond*, 1930; *One Hour With You*, 1932; *Love Me Tonight*, 1932; *A Bedtime Story*, 1933; *The Merry Widow*, 1934; *Folies Bergère*, 1935; *The Beloved Vagabond*, 1937; *Le Silence Est d'Or*, 1947; *Gigi*, 1958; *A Breath of Scandal*, 1960; *Fanny*, 1961; *In Search of the Castaways*, 1962

Academy Award Nominations for best actor: *The Love Parade*, 1929/30; *The Big Pond*, 1929/30
Special Academy Award "for his contributions to the world of entertainment for more than half a century," 1958

Autobiographies *The Man in the Straw Hat*, 1949; *With Love*, 1960; *I Remember It Well*, 1972

JULIE CHRISTIE

Born Julie Christie on April 14, 1940 in Chukur, Assam, India

First Film *Crooks Anonymous*, 1962
Major Films include *Darling*, 1965; *Doctor Zhivago*, 1965; *Far From the Madding Crowd*, 1967; *Petulia*, 1968; *The Go-Between*, 1971; *McCabe and Mrs. Miller*, 1971; *Don't Look Now*, 1973; *Shampoo*, 1975; *Heaven Can Wait*, 1978; *Heat and Dust*, 1983

Academy Award for best actress: *Darling*, 1965
Nomination for best actress: *McCabe and Mrs. Miller*, 1971

MONTGOMERY CLIFT

Born Edward Montgomery Clift on October 17, 1920 in Omaha, NE
Died on July 24, 1966

First Film *Red River*, 1948
Major Films include *The Search*, 1948; *The Heiress*, 1949; *A Place in the Sun*, 1951; *I Confess*, 1952; *From Here to Eternity*, 1953; *Suddenly Last Summer*, 1959; *The Misfits*, 1961; *Judgment at Nuremberg*, 1961; *Freud*, 1962; *The Defector*, 1966

Academy Award Nominations for best actor: *The Search*, 1948; *A Place in the Sun*, 1951; *From Here to Eternity*, 1953
Nomination for best supporting actor: *Judgment at Nuremberg*, 1961

Biographies *Monty* by Robert Laguardia; *Montgomery Clift* by Pat Bosworth
Book *The Films of Montgomery Clift* by Judith M. Kass

JAMES COBURN

Born James Coburn on August 31, 1928 in Laurel, NE
Married to Beverly Kelly in 1958; daughter Lisa; son James

First film *Ride Lonesome*, 1959
Major Films include *The Magnificent Seven*, 1960; *The Great Escape*, 1963; *Charade*, 1963; *The Americanization of Emily*, 1964; *Our Man Flint*, 1966; *In Like Flint*, 1967; *Midway*, 1976; *Cross of Iron*, 1977; *Goldengirl*, 1979; *The Baltimore Bullet*, 1979; *Firepower*, 1980

CLAUDETTE COLBERT

Born Lily Claudette Chauchoin on September 13, 1905 in Paris, France
Married to actor/director Norman Foster in 1928; divorced in 1935
Married to Joel Pressman in 1935; widowed in 1968

First Film *For the Love of Mike*, 1928
Major Films include *The Smiling Lieutenant*, 1931; *The Sign of the Cross*, 1932; *It Happened One Night*, 1934; *Cleopatra*, 1934; *The Gilded Lily*, 1935; *Private Worlds*, 1935; *She Married Her Boss*, 1935; *Tovarich*, 1937; *Midnight*, 1939; *Boom Town*, 1940; *The Palm Beach Story*, 1942; *Since You Went Away*, 1944; *Tomorrow Is Forever*, 1946; *The Egg and I*, 1947; *Three Came Home*, 1950; *Texas Lady*, 1955; *Parrish*, 1961

Academy Award for best actress: *It Happened One Night*, 1934
Nominations for best actress: *Private Worlds*, 1935; *Since You Went Away*, 1944

Biography *Claudette Colbert* by William K. Everson

JOAN COLLINS

Born Joan Collins on May 23, 1933 in London, England (sister of novelist Jackie Collins)
Married to Maxwell Reed in 1942; divorced in 1957
Married to actor Anthony Newley in 1953; divorced; daughter Tara born in 1963; son Anthony Jr. born in 1965
Married to producer Ron Kass in 1972; divorced; daughter Katharine born in 1972

First Film *I Believe in You*, 1952

Julie Christie, seen here in *Heat and Dust* (1983), won a best actress Academy Award for her performance in *Darling* (1965) and a best actress nomination for *McCabe and Mrs. Miller* (1971).

Major Films include *Decameron Nights*, 1952; *The Good Die Young*, 1954; *Land of the Pharaohs*, 1955; *The Girl in the Red Velvet Swing*, 1955; *The Opposite Sex*, 1956; *The Wayward Bus*, 1957; *Island in the Sun*, 1957; *The Bravados*, 1958; *Rally 'Round the Flag, Boys*, 1958; *Seven Thieves*, 1960; *Road to Hong Kong*, 1962; *Warning Shot*, 1967; *Tales from the Crypt*, 1972; *The Stud*, 1978; *The Big Sleep*, 1978; *Sunburn*, 1979; *The Bitch*, 1979

Autobiography *Past Imperfect*, 1984

RONALD COLMAN

Born Ronald Charles Colman on February 9, 1891 in Richmond, Surrey, England
Died on April 20, 1958
Married to Victoria Maud (stage name Thelma Ray) in 1919; divorced in 1934
Married to actress Benita Hume in 1938; daughter Juliet born in 1939

First Film *Sheba*, 1918
Major Films include *The White Sister*, 1923; *The Dark Angel*, 1925; *Beau Geste*, 1926; *Bulldog Drummond*, 1929; *Condemned*, 1929; *Raffles*, 1930; *Arrowsmith*, 1931; *A Tale of Two Cities*, 1935; *Lost Horizon*, 1937; *The Prisoner of Zenda*, 1937; *The Talk of the Town*, 1942; *Random Harvest*, 1942; *A Double Life*, 1947; *Champagne for Caesar*, 1949

Academy Award for best actor: *A Double Life*, 1947
Nominations for best actor: *Bulldog Drummond*, 1929/30; *Condemned*, 1929/30; *Random Harvest*, 1942

Biography *A Very Private Person* by Juliet Colman

SEAN CONNERY

Born Thomas Connery on August 25, 1930 in Edinburgh, Scotland
Married to actress Diane Cilento in 1962; divorced in 1974; son Jason born in 1963; daughter Giovanna born in 1964
Married to Micheline Roquebrune in 1974; divorced in 1975
Remarried to Micheline Roquebrune in 1975

First Film *No Road Back*, 1956
Major Films include *Dr. No*, 1962; *From Russia With Love*, 1963; *Marnie*, 1964; *Goldfinger*, 1964; *Thunderball*, 1965; *You Only Live Twice*, 1967; *The Molly Maguires*, 1970; *Diamonds Are Forever*, 1971; *Murder on the Orient Express*, 1974; *The Man Who Would Be King*, 1975; *Robin and Marian*, 1976; *The Great Train Robbery*, 1979; *Time Bandits*, 1981; *Wrong Is Right*, 1982; *Never Say Never Again*, 1983

Biography *Sean Connery: A Biography* by Kenneth Passingham
Book *The Films of Sean Connery* by Emma Andrews

JACKIE COOGAN

Born John Leslie Coogan on October 26, 1914 in Los Angeles, CA
Died on March 2, 1984
Married to actress Betty Grable in 1936; divorced in 1939

Married to Flower Parry in 1941; divorced in 1943; son John Anthony born in 1942
Married to Ann McCormack in 1946; divorced in 1951; daughter Joann Dolliver born in 1948
Married to Dorothea Lamphere in 1952; daughter Leslie Diane born in 1954; son Christopher Fenton born in 1967

First Film *Skinner's Baby*, 1917
Major Films include *A Day's Pleasure*, 1919; *The Kid*, 1921; *Peck's Bad Boy*, 1921; *A Boy of Flanders*, 1924; *Buttons*, 1927; *Tom Sawyer*, 1930; *Huckleberry Finn*, 1931; *Home on the Range*, 1935; *Million Dollar Legs*, 1939; *The Proud Ones*, 1956; *The Joker Is Wild*, 1957; *Lonelyhearts*, 1958; *John Goldfarb Please Come Home*, 1964; *A Fine Madness*, 1966; *Marlowe*, 1969; *The Manchu Eagle Murder Caper Mystery*, 1975; *Human Experiments*, 1979

GARY COOPER

Born Frank James Cooper on May 7, 1901 in Helena, MT
Died on May 13, 1961
Married to socialite Veronica Balfe in 1933; daughter Maria Veronica born in 1937

First Film *The Winning of Barbara Worth*, 1926
Major Films include *The Shopworn Angel*, 1929; *The Virginian*, 1929; *Morocco*, 1930; *City Streets*, 1931; *A Farewell to Arms*, 1932; *One Sunday Afternoon*, 1933; *The Lives of a Bengal Lancer*, 1935; *Mr. Deeds Goes to Town*, 1936; *The Plainsman*, 1937; *Bluebeard's Eighth Wife*, 1938; *Beau Geste*, 1939; *The Westerner*, 1940; *Sergeant York*, 1941; *The Pride of the Yankees*, 1942; *For Whom the Bell Tolls*, 1943; *Saratoga Trunk*, 1945; *The Fountainhead*, 1949; *You're in the Navy Now*, 1951; *High Noon*,

Sean Connery, who—somewhat unwillingly—became known throughout the moviegoing world as Ian Fleming's super-suave James Bond, is seen here with Brooke Adams in *Cuba* (1979).

For those who tend to forget that Gary Cooper ever appeared outside of a western—a portrait of the star as a handsome, romantic leading man in modern dress.

1952; *Vera Cruz*, 1954; *Friendly Persuasion*, 1956; *They Came to Cordura*, 1959; *The Naked Edge*, 1961

Academy Awards for best actor: *Sergeant York*, 1941; *High Noon*, 1952
Nominations for best actor: *Mr. Deeds Goes to Town*, 1936; *The Pride of the Yankees*, 1942; *For Whom the Bell Tolls*, 1943
Special Academy Award "for his many memorable screen performances and for the international recognition he, as an individual, has gained for the film industry," 1960

Biographies *The Cooper Story* by George Carpozi, Jr.; *The Last Hero* by Larry Swindell

JOSEPH COTTEN

Born Joseph Cotten on May 13, 1905 in Petersburg, VA
Married to Lenore Kip in 1931; widowed in 1960; stepdaughter, Judith Kip

1952; *Vera Cruz*, 1954; **Married** to actress Patricia Medina in 1960

First Film *Citizen Kane*, 1941
Major Films include *The Magnificent Ambersons*, 1942; *Journey Into Fear*, 1942; *Shadow of a Doubt*, 1943; *Gaslight*, 1944; *Duel in the Sun*, 1946; *The Farmer's Daughter*, 1947; *Portrait of Jennie*, 1948; *Under Capricorn*, 1949; *The Third Man*, 1949; *September Affair*, 1950; *Niagara*, 1953; *Hush . . . Hush, Sweet Charlotte*, 1965; *The Money Trap*, 1966; *Petulia*, 1968; *Soylent Green*, 1973; *Airport '77*, 1977

JEANNE CRAIN

Born Jeanne Crain on May 25, 1925 in Barstow, CA
Married to Paul Brinkman in 1945; son Paul Frederick born in 1947; son Michael Anthony born in 1948; son Christopher born in 1950; daughter Jeanine born in 1952; daughter Lisabette born in 1957; daughter Maria born in 1960; son Timothy born in 1965

First Film *The Gang's All Here*, 1943
Major Films include *Home in Indiana*, 1944; *State Fair*, 1945; *Leave Her to Heaven*, 1945; *Margie*, 1946; *You Were Meant for Me*, 1948; *Apartment for Peggy*, 1948; *A Letter to Three Wives*, 1949; *Pinky*, 1949; *Cheaper by the Dozen*, 1950; *The Model and the Marriage Broker*, 1952; *O. Henry's Full House*, 1952; *Gentlemen Marry Brunettes*, 1955; *The Joker Is Wild*, 1957; *Madison Avenue*, 1962; *Hot Rods to Hell*, 1967; *Skyjacked*, 1972; *The Night God Screamed*, 1975

Academy Award Nomination for best actress: *Pinky*, 1949

BRODERICK CRAWFORD

Born William Broderick Pendergast on December 9, 1911 in Philadelphia, PA (son of actress Helen Broderick and actor Lester Crawford—a stage name; Crawford combined the names of both parents in his own stage name)
Married to singer Kay Griffith in 1940; divorced in 1961; adopted son, Kim; son Christopher born in 1948; son Kelly born in 1951
Married to actress Joan Tabor in 1962; divorced in 1967; stepdaughter, Lauren Gold
Married to Mary Alice Mitchell in 1973

First Film *Woman Chases Man*, 1937
Major Films include *Eternally Yours*, 1939; *Seven Sinners*, 1940; *Larceny, Inc.*, 1942; *All the King's Men*, 1949; *Born Yesterday*, 1950; *Human Desire*, 1954; *Not as a Stranger*, 1955; *A House Is Not a Home*, 1964; *The Oscar*, 1966; *Ransom Money*, 1971; *Embassy*, 1972; *Terror in the Wax Museum*, 1973; *The Private Files of J. Edgar Hoover*, 1978; *A Little Romance*, 1979

Academy Award for best actor: *All the King's Men*, 1949

JOAN CRAWFORD

Born Lucille Fay Le Sueur on March 23, 1904 in San Antonio, TX
Died on May 10, 1977
Married to actor Douglas Fairbanks, Jr. in 1929; divorced in 1933
Married to actor Franchot Tone in 1935; divorced in 1939
Married to actor Phillip Terry in 1942; divorced in 1946; adopted son, Christopher; adopted daughter, Christina; adopted daughter, Catharine; adopted daughter, Cynthia
Married to Alfred N. Steele (chairman of the Pepsi-Cola Company) in 1955; widowed in 1959

First Film *Lady of the Night*, 1925
Major Films include *Sally, Irene and Mary*, 1925; *Our Dancing Daughters*, 1928; *Our Modern Maidens*, 1929; *Laughing Sinners*, 1931; *Grand Hotel*, 1932; *Dancing Lady*, 1933; *Forsaking All Others*, 1934; *The Women*, 1939; *A Woman's Face*, 1941; *Mildred Pierce*, 1945; *Humoresque*, 1946; *Possessed*, 1947; *Sudden Fear*, 1952; *Johnny Guitar*, 1954; *Autumn Leaves*, 1956; *Whatever Happened to Baby Jane?*, 1972

A striking study of a striking performer: Joan Crawford, who won a best actress Academy Award for *Mildred Pierce* in 1945 and best actress nominations for *Possessed* (1947) and *Sudden Fear* (1952).

Academy Award for best actress: *Mildred Pierce*, 1945

Nominations for best actress: *Possessed*, 1947; *Sudden Fear*, 1952

Autobiographies *A Portrait of Joan*, 1962; *My Way of Life*, 1971

Biographies *Crawford— The Last Years* by Cal Johnes; *Mommie Dearest* by Christina Crawford

BING CROSBY

Born Harry Lillis Crosby on May 2, 1901 in Tacoma, WA

Died on Oct. 14, 1977

Married to singer Dixie Lee in 1930; widowed in 1952; son Gary born in 1933; twin sons Philip and Dennis born in 1934; son Lindsay born in 1937

Married to actress Kathryn Grant in 1957; daughter Mary Frances born in 1959; son Harry Lillis born in 1960; son Nathaniel Pat born in 1961

First Film *King of Jazz*, 1930

Major Films include *The Big Broadcast*, 1932; *Anything Goes*, 1936; *Pennies From Heaven*, 1936; *Road to Singapore*, 1940; *Holiday Inn*, 1942; *Going My Way*, 1944; *Here Come the Waves*, 1944; *The Bells of St. Mary's*, 1945; *Blue Skies*, 1946; *Road to Rio*, 1947; *A Connecticut Yankee in King Arthur's Court*, 1949; *The Country Girl*, 1954; *White Christmas*, 1954; *High Society*, 1956; *Road to Hong Kong*, 1962; *Stagecoach*, 1966

Academy Award for best actor: *Going My Way*, 1944

Nominations for best actor: *The Bells of St. Mary's*, 1945; *The Country Girl*, 1954

Autobiography *Call Me Lucky*, 1953

Biographies *Going My Way* by Gary Crosby and Ross Firestone; *Bing and Other Things* by Kathryn Crosby; *My Life With Bing* by Kathryn Crosby

ROBERT CUMMINGS

Born Clarence Robert Orville Cummings on June 9, 1908 in Joplin, MO

Married to Edna Emma Myers; divorced

Married to Vivienne Audrey Janis in 1933; divorced in 1943

Married to Mary Elliott in 1945; divorced in 1969; daughter Laurel born in 1946; daughter Sharon Patricia born in 1948; daughter Mary Lelinda born in 1951; daughter Michelle Helene born in 1955; son Robert Richard born in 1955; son Anthony born in 1957; son Charles Clarence born in 1959

Married to Regina Young in 1971

First Film *The Virginia Judge*, 1935

Major Films include *Three Smart Girls Grow Up*, 1937; *The Devil and Miss Jones*, 1941; *It Started With Eve*, 1941; *King's Row*, 1941; *Saboteur*, 1942; *The Lost Moment*, 1947; *Dial M for Murder*, 1954; *The Carpetbaggers*, 1964; *Stagecoach*, 1966

TONY CURTIS

Born Bernard Schwartz on June 1, 1925 in New York City, NY

Married to actress Janet Leigh in 1951; divorced in 1962; daughter Kelly born in 1956; daughter Jamie Lee (actress) born in 1958

Married to actress Christine Kauffmann in 1963; divorced in 1967; daughter Alexandra born in 1964; daughter Allegra born in 1966

Married to Leslie Allen in 1968; divorced; son Nicholas born in 1970; son Benjamin born in 1973

First Film *Criss Cross*, 1949

Major Films include *The Prince Who Was a Thief*, 1951; *Houdini*, 1953;

Tony Curtis with Gina Lollobrigida in one of his early leading roles— in *Trapeze* (1956).

Linda Darnell, star of such movies as *Blood and Sand* (1941) and *Forever Amber* (1947), strikes a seductive pose for the cameraman.

Trapeze, 1956; *The Sweet Smell of Success*, 1957; *The Defiant Ones*, 1958; *Some Like It Hot*, 1959; *Sex and the Single Girl*, 1964; *The Great Race*, 1965; *The Boston Strangler*, 1968; *The Last Tycoon*, 1976; *Little Miss Marker*, 1979; *The Mirror Crack'd*, 1980

Academy Award Nomination for best actor: *The Defiant Ones*, 1958

Novel by Curtis *Kid Andrew Cody and Julie Sparrow*

DAN DAILEY

Born Dan Dailey, Jr. on December 14, 1917 in New York City, NY
Died on October 16, 1978
Married to Esther Rodier; divorced in 1941
Married to Elizabeth Hofert in 1942; divorced in 1951; son Dan born in 1947
Married to Gwen Carter in 1954; divorced
Married to Nora Warner in 1968

First Film *The Mortal Storm*, 1940
Major Films include *Mother Wore Tights*, 1947; *Give My Regards to Broadway*, 1948; *When My Baby Smiles at Me*, 1948; *The Pride of St. Louis*, 1952; *There's No Business Like Show Business*, 1954; *It's Always Fair Weather*, 1955; *The Best Things in Life Are Free*, 1956; *The Wings of Eagles*, 1957; *Pepe*, 1960; *Hemingway's Adventures of a Young Man*, 1962

Academy Award Nomination for best actor: *When My Baby Smiles at Me*, 1948

LINDA DARNELL

Born Monetta Eloyse Darnell on October 16, 1921 in Dallas, TX
Died on April 11, 1965
Married to cameraman J. Perevell Marley in 1943; divorced in 1951; adopted daughter, Charlotte "Lola" Mildred

Married to Philip Liebman in 1954; divorced in 1955
Married to Merle Robertson in 1957; divorced in 1963

First Film *Hotel for Women*, 1939
Major Films include *The Mark of Zorro*, 1940; *Blood and Sand*, 1941; *It Happened Tomorrow*, 1944; *Summer Storm*, 1945; *Hangover Square*, 1945; *My Darling Clementine*, 1946; *Forever Amber*, 1947; *A Letter to Three Wives*, 1949; *Second Chance*, 1953; *Black Spurs*, 1965

BETTE DAVIS

Born Ruth Elizabeth Davis on April 5, 1908 in Lowell, MA
Married to Harmon O. Nelson, Jr. in 1932; divorced in 1938
Married to Arthur Farnsworth in 1940; widowed in 1943
Married to William Grant Sherry in 1945; divorced in 1949; daughter Barbara born in 1946

Married to actor Gary Merrill in 1950; divorced in 1960; adopted son, Michael; adopted daughter, Margot

First Film *Bad Sister*, 1931
Major Films include *Of Human Bondage*, 1934; *Bordertown*, 1935; *Dangerous*, 1935; *The Petrified Forest*, 1936; *Marked Woman*, 1937; *Jezebel*, 1938; *Dark Victory*, 1939; *The Old Maid*, 1939; *The Letter*, 1940; *The Little Foxes*, 1941; *Now, Voyager*, 1942; *Old Acquaintance*, 1943; *Mr. Skeffington*, 1944; *The Corn Is Green*, 1945; *A Stolen Life*, 1946; *All About Eve*, 1950; *The Star*, 1952; *The Virgin Queen*, 1955; *A Pocketful of Miracles*, 1961; *Whatever Happened to Baby Jane?*, 1962; *Hush . . . Hush, Sweet Charlotte*, 1965; *Death on the Nile*, 1978

Academy Awards for best actress: *Dangerous*, 1935; *Jezebel*, 1938
Nominations for best actress: *Dark Victory*, 1939; *The Letter*, 1940; *The Little Foxes*, 1941; *Now, Voyager*,

Bette Davis, with two best actress Academy Awards and eight nominations to her credit, in 1977 became the first woman to receive the American Film Institute's Life Achievement Award.

135

Yvonne de Carlo fascinates Rock Hudson in *Scarlet Angel*, a 1952 Civil War period piece which gave De Carlo a chance to exhibit her particular brand of sultry sophistication.

1942; *Mr. Skeffington*, 1944; *All About Eve*, 1950; *The Star*, 1952; *Whatever Happened to Baby Jane?*, 1962

Autobiography *The Lonely Life*, 1962
Book *Bette Davis—Mother Goddam* by Whitney Stine with Bette Davis

DORIS DAY

Born Doris von Kappelhoff on April 3, 1924 in Cincinnati, OH
Married to Al Jordan in 1941; divorced in 1943; son Terry (later changed his last name to Melcher) born in 1942
Married to George Weidler in 1946; divorced in 1949
Married to agent Martin Melcher in 1951; widowed in 1968
Married to Barry Comden in 1976; divorced

First Film *Romance on the High Seas*, 1948
Major Films include *Young Man With a Horn*, 1950; *Tea for Two*, 1950; *Lullaby of Broadway*, 1951; *Calamity Jane*, 1953; *Young at Heart*, 1954; *Love Me or Leave Me*, 1955; *The*

Man Who Knew Too Much, 1956; *The Pajama Game*, 1957; *Pillow Talk*, 1959; *Please Don't Eat the Daisies*, 1960; *That Touch of Mink*, 1962; *Move Over Darling*, 1963

Academy Award Nomination for best actress: *Pillow Talk*, 1959

Book *Doris Day—Her Own Story* by A. E. Hotchner

JAMES DEAN

Born James Byron Dean on February 8, 1931 in Marion, IN
Died on September 30, 1955 (auto accident)

First Film *Fixed Bayonets*, 1951
Major Films include *East of Eden*, 1955; *Rebel Without a Cause*, 1955; *Giant*, 1956

Academy Award Nominations for best actor: *East of Eden*, 1955; *Giant*, 1956

Biographies *James Dean: A Portrait* by Roy Schatt; *James Dean: The Mutant King* by David Dalton

YVONNE DE CARLO

Born Peggy Yvonne Middleton on September 1, 1922 in Vancouver, British Columbia, Canada
Married to stuntman Robert Morgan in 1955; widowed; son Bruce born in 1956; son Michael born in 1957

First Film *Harvard Here I Come*, 1942
Major Films include *This Gun for Hire*, 1942; *The Deerslayer*, 1943; *Salome—Where She Danced*, 1945; *The Song of Scheherazade*, 1947; *Criss Cross*, 1949; *Hotel Sahara*, 1951; *The Captain's Paradise*, 1953; *The Ten Commandments*, 1956; *Band of Angels*, 1957; *McLintock!*, 1963

OLIVIA DE HAVILLAND

Born Olivia de Havilland on July 1, 1916 in Tokyo, Japan (sister of actress Joan Fontaine)

Married to novelist Marcus Goodrich in 1946; divorced in 1952; son Benjamin born in 1949
Married to Pierre Paul Calante (editor of *Paris Match*) in 1955; divorced; daughter Giselle born in 1956

First Film *A Midsummer Night's Dream*, 1935
Major Films include *Captain Blood*, 1935; *The Charge of the Light Brigade*, 1936; *The Adventures of Robin Hood*, 1938; *Gone With the Wind*, 1939; *Hold Back the Dawn*, 1941; *They Died With Their Boots On*, 1941; *Dark Mirror*, 1946; *To Each His Own*, 1946; *The Snake Pit*, 1948; *The Heiress*, 1949; *My Cousin Rachel*, 1952; *The Proud Rebel*, 1958; *Hush . . . Hush, Sweet Charlotte*, 1964; *The Swarm*, 1978

Academy Awards for best actress: *To Each His Own*, 1946; *The Heiress*, 1949
Nominations for best actress: *Hold Back the Dawn*, 1941; *The Snake Pit*, 1948
Nomination for best supporting actress: *Gone With the Wind*, 1939

James Dean's exciting movie career was cut short when he was killed in an auto accident before his last film, *Giant*, was released.

Olivia de Havilland was instrumental in winning a landmark legal decision that limited the length of a player's contract with a studio to seven years, including suspensions.

Book by De Havilland *Every Frenchman Has One*, 1963
Biography *Olivia de Havilland* by Judith Kass
Book *The Films of Olivia de Havilland* by Tony Thomas

CATHERINE DENEUVE

Born Catherine Dorléac on October 22, 1943 in Paris, France (sister of actress Françoise Dorléac)
Son Christian Deneuve by director Roger Vadim born in 1963
Married to photographer David Bailey in 1965; divorced in 1970
Daughter Chiara-Charlotte Deneuve by actor Marcello Mastroianni born in 1972

First Film *Les Collégiennes*, 1956
Major Films include *Les Portes Claquent*, 1960; *The Umbrellas of Cherbourg*, 1964; *Repulsion*, 1965; *Belle de Jour*, 1967; *Benjamin*, 1968; *Mississippi*

Mermaid, 1969; *Tristana*, 1970; *Le Grande Bourgeoise*, 1974; *Hustle*, 1975; *The Last Metro*, 1980; *The Hunger*, 1983

ROBERT DE NIRO

Born Robert de Niro, Jr. on August 17, 1943 in New York City, NY
Married to actress Diahnne Abbott in 1976; divorced; stepdaughter, Drina; son Raphael Eugene

First Film *The Wedding Party*, 1967 (released in 1969)
Major Films include *Bloody Mama*, 1970; *Bang the Drum Slowly*, 1973; *The Godfather, Part II*, 1974; *Taxi Driver*, 1976; *1900*, 1976; *The Last Tycoon*, 1976; *New York, New York*, 1977; *The Deer Hunter*, 1978; *Raging Bull*, 1980; *The King of Comedy*, 1983; *Once Upon a Time in America*, 1984

Academy Award for best actor: *Raging Bull*, 1980

Academy Award for best supporting actor: *The Godfather, Part II*, 1974
Nomination for best actor: *The Deer Hunter*, 1978

SANDY DENNIS

Born Sandra Dale Dennis on April 27, 1937 in Hastings, NE
Married to musician Gerry Mulligan in 1965; separated in 1976

First Film *Splendor in the Grass*, 1961
Major Films include *Who's Afraid of Virginia Woolf?*, 1966; *Up the Down Staircase*, 1967; *The Out-of-Towners*, 1970; *The Four Seasons*, 1981; *Come Back to the Five and Dime, Jimmy Dean, Jimmy Dean*, 1982

Academy Award for best supporting actress: *Who's Afraid of Virginia Woolf?*, 1966

MARLENE DIETRICH

Born Maria Magdalene Dietrich von Losch on December 27, 1901 in Berlin, Germany
Married to Rudolph Sieber in 1924; widowed in 1975; daughter Maria (stage name Maria Riva) born in 1925

First Film *Der Kleine Napoleon*, 1923
Major Films include *The Blue Angel*, 1930; *Morocco*, 1930; *Shanghai Express*, 1932; *The Song of Songs*, 1933; *The Scarlet Express*, 1934; *The Devil Is a Woman*, 1935; *Desire*, 1936; *The Garden of Allah*, 1936;

Destry Rides Again, 1939; *A Foreign Affair*, 1948; *Stage Fright*, 1950; *Rancho Notorious*, 1952; *Around the World in 80 Days*, 1956; *Witness for the Prosecution*, 1958; *Judgment at Nuremberg*, 1961; *Just a Gigolo*, 1978

Academy Award Nomination for best actress: *Morocco*, 1930/31

Book by Dietrich *Marlene Dietrich's ABC*
Biography *The Life of Marlene Dietrich* by Charles Higham

ROBERT DONAT

Born Robert Donat on March 18, 1905 in Manchester, England
Died on June 9, 1958
Married to Ella Annesley Voysey in 1929; divorced in 1946
Married to actress Renée Asherson in 1953; separated in 1956

First Film *Men of Tomorrow*, 1932
Major Films include *The Private Life of Henry VIII*, 1933; *The Count of Monte Cristo*, 1934; *The Thirty-Nine Steps*, 1935; *The Ghost Goes West*, 1936; *The Citadel*, 1938; *Goodbye, Mr. Chips*, 1939; *The Young Mr. Pitt*, 1942; *Perfect Strangers*, 1945; *The Winslow Boy*, 1948; *The Magic Box*, 1951; *The Inn of the Sixth Happiness*, 1958

Academy Award for best actor: *Goodbye, Mr. Chips*, 1939
Nomination for best actor: *The Citadel*, 1938

Biography *Robert Donat* by J. C. Trewin

Kirk Douglas, winner of three best actor Academy Award nominations (*Champion*, 1949; *The Bad and the Beautiful*, 1952; *Lust for Life*, 1956), saw his son Michael follow him into the film business.

KIRK DOUGLAS

Born Issur Danielovitch Demsky on December 9, 1916 in Amsterdam, NY
Married to Diana Dill in 1943; divorced in 1950; son Michael (actor/producer) born in 1945; son Joel born in 1947
Married to Anne Buydens in 1954; son Vincent born in 1955; son Eric born in 1958; son Peter born in 1960

First Film *The Strange Love of Martha Ivers*, 1946
Major Films include *Out of the Past*, 1947; *A Letter to Three Wives*, 1949; *Champion*, 1949; *Young Man With a Horn*, 1950; *The Glass Menagerie*, 1950; *Ace in the Hole* (retitled *The Big Carnival*), 1951; *Detective Story*, 1951; *The Bad and the Beautiful*, 1952; *20,000 Leagues Under the Sea*, 1954; *Lust for Life*, 1956; *Gunfight at the O.K. Corral*, 1957; *Paths of Glory*, 1957; *Spartacus*, 1960; *Lonely Are the Brave*, 1962; *Seven Days in May*, 1964; *Once Is Not Enough*, 1975; *The Fury*, 1978; *Saturn 3*, 1980

Academy Award Nominations for best actor: *Champion*, 1949; *The Bad and the Beautiful*, 1952; *Lust for Life*, 1956

MELVYN DOUGLAS

Born Melvyn Edouard Hesselberg on April 5, 1901 in Macon, GA
Died on August 4, 1981
First marriage and divorce; son Gregory born in 1920; son Melvyn Jr. born in 1921
Married to actress and Congresswoman Helen Gahagan in 1931; widowed in 1980; son Pierre "Peter" born in 1933; daughter Mary Helen born in 1935

First Film *Tonight or Never*, 1931
Major Films include *As You Desire Me*, 1932; *She Married Her Boss*, 1935; *Annie Oakley*, 1935; *Theodora Goes Wild*, 1936; *Angel*, 1937; *Ninotchka*, 1939; *A Woman's Face*, 1941; *Two-Faced Woman*, 1942; *Sea of Grass*, 1947; *Hud*, 1963; *I Never Sang for My Father*, 1970; *The Candidate*, 1972; *The Seduction of Joe Tynan*, 1979; *Being There*, 1979

Academy Awards for best supporting actor: *Hud*, 1963; *Being There*, 1979
Nomination for best actor: *I Never Sang for My Father*, 1970

MICHAEL DOUGLAS

Born Michael Douglas on September 25, 1945 in New Brunswick, NJ (son of actor Kirk Douglas)
Married to Diandra Murrell Luker in 1977

First Film *Hail, Hero*, 1969
Major Films include *Coma*, 1978; *The China Syndrome*, 1979; *It's My Turn*, 1980; *Romancing the Stone*, 1984

(*One Flew Over the Cuckoo's Nest*, which Douglas co-produced, won the Academy Award for best picture in 1975.)

RICHARD DREYFUSS

Born Richard Dreyfuss on October 29, 1945 in Brooklyn, NY
Married in 1983

First Film *Valley of the Dolls*, 1967
Major Films include *Dillinger*, 1973; *American Graffiti*, 1973; *The Apprenticeship of Duddy Kravitz*, 1974; *Jaws*, 1975; *Close Encounters of the Third Kind*, 1977; *The Goodbye Girl*, 1977; *The Competition*, 1980; *Whose Life Is It Anyway?*, 1981

Academy Award for best actor: *The Goodbye Girl*, 1977

FAYE DUNAWAY

Born Dorothy Faye Dunaway on January 14, 1941 in Bascom, FL
Married to rock singer Peter Wolf in 1974; separated

First Film *Hurry Sundown*, 1967
Major Films include *Bon-*

Actor/producer Michael Douglas, son of actor Kirk Douglas, co-produced *One Flew Over the Cuckoo's Nest* (1975) which won five Oscars. He also produced and starred in *The China Syndrome* (1979).

Irene Dunne, as she appeared in *A Guy Named Joe* with Spencer Tracy in 1943.

nie and Clyde, 1967; *The Thomas Crown Affair*, 1969; *The Three Musketeers*, 1973; *Chinatown*, 1974; *The Towering Inferno*, 1974; *Three Days of the Condor*, 1975; *Network*, 1976; *The Eyes of Laura Mars*, 1978; *Mommie Dearest*, 1981

Academy Award for best actress: *Network*, 1976
Nominations for best actress: *Bonnie and Clyde*, 1967; *Chinatown*, 1974

IRENE DUNNE

Born Irene Marie Dunn on December 20, 1904 in Louisville, KY
Married to Francis Griffin in 1928; widowed in 1965; adopted daughter, Mary Frances

First Film *Leathernecking*, 1930
Major Films include *Cimarron*, 1931; *Back Street*, 1932; *Magnificent Obsession*, 1935; *Show Boat*, 1936; *Theodora Goes Wild*, 1936; *The Awful Truth*, 1937; *Love Affair*,

1939; *My Favorite Wife*, 1940; *Penny Serenade*, 1941; *A Guy Named Joe*, 1943; *Anna and the King of Siam*, 1946; *Life With Father*, 1947; *I Remember Mama*, 1948

Academy Award Nominations for best actress: *Cimarron*, 1930/31; *Theodora Goes Wild*, 1936; *The Awful Truth*, 1937; *Love Affair*, 1939; *I Remember Mama*, 1948

ROBERT DUVALL

Born Robert Duvall on January 5, 1931 in San Diego, CA (son of Rear Admiral William Howard Duvall)
Married to Barbara Duvall; divorced in 1975
Married to Gail MacLachlan Youngs in 1982

First Film *To Kill a Mockingbird*, 1963
Major Films include *Bullitt*, 1968; *The Detective*, 1968; *True Grit*, 1969; *The Rain People*, 1969;

M*A*S*H, 1970; *The Godfather*, 1972; *The Godfather, Part II*, 1973; *The Seven Percent Solution*, 1976; *Network*, 1976; *The Betsy*, 1978; *Apocalypse Now*, 1979; *The Great Santini*, 1980; *True Confessions*, 1981; *Tender Mercies*, 1983

Academy Award for best actor: *Tender Mercies*, 1983
Nomination for best actor: *The Great Santini*, 1980
Nominations for best supporting actor: *The Godfather*, 1972; *Apocalypse Now*, 1979

CLINT EASTWOOD

Born Clinton Eastwood, Jr. on May 31, 1930 in San Francisco, CA
Married to Maggie Johnson in 1953; divorced in 1984; son Kyle Clinton born in 1968 (co-starred with his father in *Honkytonk Man* in 1982); daughter Alison born in 1972

(co-starred with her father in *Tightrope* in 1984)

First Film *Revenge of the Creature*, 1955
Major Films include *A Fistful of Dollars*, 1964; *For a Few Dollars More*, 1965; *The Good, the Bad and the Ugly*, 1966; *Coogan's Bluff*, 1968; *Paint Your Wagon*, 1969; *Kelly's Heroes*, 1970; *Play Misty for Me*, 1971; *Dirty Harry*, 1971; *Magnum Force*, 1973; *The Outlaw Josey Wales*, 1976; *The Gauntlet*, 1977; *Every Which Way But Loose*, 1978; *Escape From Alcatraz*, 1979; *Any Which Way You Can*, 1980; *Firefox*, 1982; *Honkytonk Man*, 1982; *Sudden Impact*, 1983; *Tightrope*, 1984

Biography *Clint Eastwood—Movin' On* by Peter Douglas

DOUGLAS FAIRBANKS, JR.

Born Douglas Elton Ulman, Jr. on December 9, 1909 in New York City, NY

Robert Duvall won the 1983 best actor Oscar for his portrayal of an alcoholic country music performer who finds a new way of living through the young widow he meets in *Tender Mercies*.

Alice Faye was the first of a series of blonde box office stars in 20th Century-Fox musicals. Among her successors were Betty Grable and Marilyn Monroe.

(son of actor Douglas Fairbanks, Sr.)
Married to actress Joan Crawford in 1929; divorced in 1933
Married to Mary Lee Hartford Epling in 1939; daughter Melissa born in 1940; daughter Daphne born in 1942; daughter Victoria born in 1947

First Film *Stephen Steps Out*, 1923
Major Films include *Stella Dallas*, 1925, *The Power of the Press*, 1927; *A Woman of Affairs*, 1928; *Our Modern Maidens*, 1929; *The Dawn Patrol*, 1930; *Little Caesar*, 1930; *Morning Glory*, 1933; *The Prisoner of Zenda*, 1937; *The Young in Heart*, 1938; *Gunga Din*, 1939; *The Corsican Brothers*, 1941; *Sinbad the Sailor*, 1947; *The Exile*, 1948

Knighted in 1949

Biography *Knight Errant* by Brian Connell

MIA FARROW

Born Maria de Lourdes Villiers Farrow on February 9, 1946 in Los Angeles, CA (daughter of actress Maureen O'Sullivan and writer/director John Farrow)
Married to singer/actor Frank Sinatra in 1966; divorced in 1968
Married to conductor André Previn in 1970; divorced in 1979; twin sons Matthew Phineas and Sascha Villiers born in 1970; son Kym Lark born in 1974; also adopted a number of children

First Film *Guns at Batasi*, 1964
Major Films include *Rosemary's Baby*, 1968; *Secret Ceremony*, 1968; *The Great Gatsby*, 1974; *The Wedding*, 1978; *Death on the Nile*, 1978; *Hurricane*, 1979; *A Midsummer Night's Sex Comedy*, 1982; *Zelig*, 1983; *Broadway Danny Rose*, 1984

ALICE FAYE

Born Ann Jeanne (Alice) Leppert on May 5, 1912 in New York City, NY
Married to singer Tony Martin in 1937; divorced in 1940

Married to bandleader Phil Harris in 1941; stepson, Phil Jr.; daughter Alice born in 1942; daughter Phyllis born in 1944

First Film *George White's Scandals*, 1934
Major Films include *Wake Up and Live*, 1937; *You Can't Have Everything*, 1937; *In Old Chicago*, 1938; *Alexander's Ragtime Band*, 1938; *Rose of Washington Square*, 1939; *Hollywood Cavalcade*, 1939; *Tin Pan Alley*, 1940; *Weekend in Havana*, 1941; *Fallen Angel*, 1945; *State Fair*, 1962; *The Magic of Lassie*, 1978

Book *The Films of Alice Faye* by W. Franklyn Moshier

JOSÉ FERRER

Born José Vincente Ferrer de Otero y Cintron on January 8, 1912 in Santurce, Puerto Rico
Married to actress Uta Hagen in 1938; divorced in 1948; daughter Leticia

Thyra
Married to Phyllis Hill in 1948; divorced in 1953
Married to singer Rosemary Clooney in 1953; divorced in 1967; son Miguel born in 1954; son Raphael born in 1955; daughter Maria born in 1956; son Gabriel born in 1957; daughter Monsita born in 1958
Married to Stella Daphne Magree

First Film *Joan of Arc*, 1948
Major Films include *Cyrano de Bergerac*, 1950; *Moulin Rouge*, 1952; *The Caine Mutiny*, 1954; *The Shrike*, 1955; *Lawrence of Arabia*, 1962; *The Greatest Story Ever Told*, 1965; *Ship of Fools*, 1965; *Voyage of the Damned*, 1976; *A Midsummer Night's Sex Comedy*, 1982

Academy Award for best actor: *Cyrano de Bergerac*, 1950
Nomination for best actor: *Moulin Rouge*, 1952
Nomination for best supporting actor: *Joan of Arc*, 1948

José Ferrer in one of his best-known roles, as the French painter Toulouse-Lautrec in the 1952 film *Moulin Rouge*.

Sally Field, best actress Oscar winner for Norma Rae (1979), is seen here in the 1981 film *Absence of Malice* in which she plays an overzealous newspaper reporter.

SALLY FIELD

Born Sally Field on November 6, 1946 in Pasadena, CA
Married to Steve Craig in 1968; divorced; son Peter born in 1969; son Eli born in 1972

First Film *The Way West*, 1967
Major Films include *Stay Hungry*, 1976; *Smokey and the Bandit*, 1977; *Heroes*, 1977; *Hooper*, 1978; *Norma Rae*, 1979; *Absence of Malice*, 1981

Academy Award for best actress: *Norma Rae*, 1979

W. C. FIELDS

Born William Claude Dukenfield on February 10, 1879 in Philadelphia, PA
Died on December 25, 1946
Married to Harriet V. Hughes in 1900; divorced; son William Claude Jr.

First Film *Pool Sharks* (short), 1915
Major Films include *Sally of the Sawdust*, 1925; *It's the Old Army Game*, 1926; *Million Dollar Legs*, 1932; *Tillie and Gus*, 1933; *Six of a Kind*, 1934; *The Old-Fashioned Way*, 1934; *It's a Gift*, 1934; *David Copperfield*, 1935; *The Man on the Flying Trapeze*, 1935; *You Can't Cheat an Honest Man*, 1939; *My Little Chickadee*, 1939; *The Bank Dick*, 1940; *Never Give a Sucker an Even Break*, 1941

Autobiography *Fields for President*, 1940
Biography *W. C. Fields by Himself* edited by Ronald J. Fields (the actor's grandson)

ALBERT FINNEY

Born Albert Finney, Jr. on May 9, 1936 in Salford, Lancashire, England
Married to actress Jane Wenham in 1957; divorced in 1961; son Simon born in 1958
Married to actress Anouk Aimée in 1970; divorced in 1978

First Film *The Entertainer*, 1960
Major Films include *Saturday Night and Sunday Morning*, 1960; *Tom Jones*, 1963; *Two for the Road*, 1967; *Charlie Bubbles*, 1968; *Scrooge*, 1970; *Murder on the Orient Express*, 1974; *The Duellists*, 1977; *Shoot the Moon*, 1982; *Annie*, 1982; *The Dresser*, 1983; *Under the Volcano*, 1984

Academy Award Nominations for best actor: *Tom Jones*, 1963; *Murder on the Orient Express*, 1974; *The Dresser*, 1983

CARRIE FISHER

Born Carrie Fisher on October 21, 1956 in Los Angeles, CA (daughter of actress Debbie Reynolds and singer Eddie Fisher)
Married to singer/songwriter Paul Simon in 1983

First Film *Shampoo*, 1975
Major Films include *Star Wars*, 1977; *Wise Blood*, 1979; *The Empire Strikes Back*, 1980; *The Blues Brothers*, 1981; *Return of the Jedi*, 1983

BARRY FITZGERALD

Born William Joseph Shields on March 10, 1888 in Dublin, Ireland (brother of actor Arthur Shields, who died in 1970)
Died on January 4, 1961

First Film *Juno and the Paycock*, 1930
Major Films include *The Plough and the Stars*, 1937; *Bringing Up Baby*, 1938; *The Dawn Patrol*, 1938; *The Long Voyage Home*, 1940; *The Sea Wolf*, 1941; *How Green Was My Valley*, 1941; *Going My Way*, 1944; *None But the Lonely Heart*, 1944; *And Then There Were None*, 1945; *Welcome Stranger*, 1947; *The Naked City*, 1948; *Union Station*, 1950; *The Quiet Man*, 1952

Academy Award for best supporting actor: *Going My Way*, 1944
Nomination for best actor: *Going My Way*, 1944

Carrie Fisher, daughter of actress Debbie Reynolds and singer Eddie Fisher, in her first movie—*Shampoo* in 1975. She later became famous as Princess Leia in the *Star Wars* series.

Errol Flynn, who was to become one of the most romantic leading men of movie history, in a pensive mood in an early portrait.

ERROL FLYNN

Born Errol Leslie Flynn on June 20, 1909 in Hobart, Tasmania, Australia
Died on October 14, 1959
Married to actress Lili Damita in 1936; divorced in 1942; son Sean Leslie (photojournalist and actor) born in 1941 (disappeared in 1970 in Cambodia while covering the Vietnam War, presumed captured or dead)
Married to Nora Eddington in 1943; divorced in 1949; daughter Deirdre born in 1945; daughter Rory born in 1947
Married to actress Patrice Wymore in 1950; daughter Arletta born in 1953

First Film *In the Wake of the Bounty*, 1933
Major Films include *Captain Blood*, 1935; *The Charge of the Light Brigade*, 1936; *The Adventures of Robin Hood*, 1938; *The Dawn Patrol*, 1938; *The Sea Hawk*, 1940; *They Died With Their Boots On*, 1941; *Gentleman Jim*, 1942; *Objective Burma!*, 1945; *That Forsyte Woman*, 1949; *Kim*, 1950; *The Sun Also Rises*, 1957; *Too Much, Too Soon*, 1958

Autobiographies *Beam Ends*, 1937; *My Wicked, Wicked Ways*, 1959
Novel by Flynn *Showdown*, 1946

HENRY FONDA

Born Henry Jaynes Fonda on May 16, 1905 in Grand Island, NE
Died on August 12, 1982
Married to actress Margaret Sullavan in 1931; divorced in 1933
Married to Frances Seymour Brokaw in 1936; widowed in 1950; stepdaughter, Frances De Villers Brokaw; daughter Jane (actress) born in 1937; son Peter (actor) born in 1939
Married to Susan Blanchard in 1950; divorced in 1956; adopted daughter, Amy
Married to Alfreda Franchetti in 1957; divorced in 1962
Married to Shirlee Mae Adams in 1965

First Film *The Farmer Takes a Wife*, 1935
Major Films include *The Trail of the Lonesome Pine*, 1936; *You Only Live Once*, 1937; *Jezebel*, 1938; *Young Mr. Lincoln*, 1939; *The Grapes of Wrath*, 1940; *The Lady Eve*, 1941; *The Male Animal*, 1942; *The Ox-Bow Incident*, 1943; *My Darling Clementine*, 1946; *Fort Apache*, 1948; *Mister Roberts*, 1955; *War and Peace*, 1956; *The Wrong Man*, 1956; *Twelve Angry Men*, 1957; *Advise and Consent*, 1962; *How the West Was Won*, 1962; *Fail-Safe*, 1964; *Madigan*, 1969; *Yours, Mine and Ours*, 1969; *The Boston Strangler*, 1969; *Sometimes a Great Notion*, 1971; *Midway*, 1976; *On Golden Pond*, 1981

Academy Award for best actor: *On Golden Pond*, 1981
Nomination for best actor: *The Grapes of Wrath*, 1940

Special Academy Award to "the consummate actor, in recognition of his brilliant accomplishments and enduring contribution to the art of motion pictures," 1980

Books *The Fondas—The Films and Careers of Henry, Jane and Peter* by John Springer; *The Films of Henry Fonda* by Tony Thomas

JANE FONDA

Born Jayne Seymour Fonda on December 21, 1937 in New York City, NY (daughter of actor Henry Fonda; sister of actor Peter Fonda)
Married to director Roger Vadim in 1965; divorced in 1973; daughter Vanessa born in 1968
Married to political activist Thomas Hayden in 1973; son Troy born in 1973

First Film *Tall Story*, 1960
Major Films include *Cat Ballou*, 1965; *Barefoot in the Park*, 1967; *Barbarella*, 1968; *They Shoot Horses,*

Henry Fonda's performance in *The Grapes of Wrath* (1940), in which he is seen here, won him a best actor Oscar nomination. It wasn't until over forty years later, however, that he won an Oscar.

Jane Fonda, daughter of actor Henry Fonda, in *The China Syndrome* (1979), for which she won a best actress Academy Award nomination. She had already won two best actress Oscars and two nominations.

Don't They?, 1969; *Klute*, 1971; *Steelyard Blues*, 1973; *Fun With Dick and Jane*, 1977; *Julia*, 1977; *Coming Home*, 1978; *The Electric Horseman*, 1979; *The China Syndrome*, 1979; *9 to 5*, 1980; *On Golden Pond*, 1981

Academy Awards for best actress: *Klute*, 1971; *Coming Home*, 1978
Nominations for best actress: *They Shoot Horses, Don't They?*, 1969; *Julia*, 1977; *The China Syndrome*, 1979

Biography *The Fabulous Fondas* by James Brough
Book *The Fondas—The Films and Careers of Henry, Jane and Peter* by John Springer
Books by Fonda *Jane Fonda's Workout Book*; *Jane Fonda's Year of Fitness, Health, and Nutrition*

PETER FONDA

Born Peter Henry Fonda on February 23, 1939 in New York City, NY (son of actor Henry Fonda; brother of actress Jane Fonda)
Married to Susan Brewer in 1961; divorced in 1974; daughter Bridget; son Justin

First Film *Tammy and the Doctor*, 1963
Major Films include *Lilith*, 1964; *Easy Rider*, 1969; *The Hired Hand*, 1971; *Dirty Mary, Crazy Larry*, 1974; *Futureworld*, 1976; *Wanda Nevada*, 1979; *The Cannonball Run*, 1982

Biography *The Fabulous Fondas* by James Brough
Book *The Fondas—The Films and Careers of Henry, Jane and Peter* by John Springer

JOAN FONTAINE

Born Joan de Beauvoir de Havilland on October 22, 1917 in Tokyo, Japan (sister of actress Olivia de Havilland)

Married to actor Brian Aherne in 1939; divorced in 1944
Married to producer William Dozier in 1946; divorced in 1951; daughter Deborah Leslie born in 1947
Married to Collier Young in 1952; divorced in 1961
Married to journalist Alfred Wright, Jr. in 1964; divorced

First Film *No More Ladies*, 1935
Major Films include *A Damsel in Distress*, 1937; *The Women*, 1939; *Rebecca*, 1940; *Suspicion*, 1941; *The Constant Nymph*, 1943; *Jane Eyre*, 1944; *The Affairs of Susan*, 1945; *Letter from an Unknown Woman*, 1948; *September Affair*, 1951; *Something to Live For*, 1952; *Until They Sail*, 1957; *Tender Is the Night*, 1962

Academy Award for best actress: *Suspicion*, 1941
Nominations for best actress: *Rebecca*, 1940; *The Constant Nymph*, 1943

Autobiography *No Bed of Roses*, 1978

GLENN FORD

Born Gwyllyn Samuel Newton Ford on May 1, 1916 in Quebec, Canada
Married to dancer Eleanor Powell in 1943; divorced in 1959; son Peter born in 1945
Married to Kathryn Hayes in 1966; divorced in 1968
Married to actress Cynthia Hayward in 1977

First Film *Heaven With a Barbed Wire Fence*, 1939
Major Films include *So Ends Our Night*, 1941; *Destroyer*, 1943; *Gilda*, 1946; *A Stolen Life*, 1946; *Lust for Gold*, 1949; *The Big Heat*, 1953; *The Blackboard Jungle*, 1955; *The Teahouse of the August Moon*, 1956; *The Gazebo*, 1959; *A Pocketful of Miracles*, 1961; *The Courtship of Eddie's Father*, 1963; *Fate Is the Hunter*, 1964; *Smith*, 1969; *Midway*, 1976

Autobiography *Glenn Ford, R.F.D. Beverly Hills*, 1970

CLARK GABLE

Born William Clark (Billy) Gable on February 1, 1901 in Cadiz, OH
Died on November 16, 1960
Married to drama coach Josephine Dillon in 1924; divorced in 1930
Married to Texas socialite Rhea Lucas Langham in 1931; divorced in 1939
Married to actress Carole Lombard in 1939; widowed in 1942 when the plane on which Lombard was returning from a War Bond drive crashed
Married to Lady Sylvia Hawkes Ashley in 1949; divorced in 1952
Married to Kay Williams Spreckels in 1955; son John Clark born in 1960

First Film *The Painted Desert*, 1931
Major Films include *A Free Soul*, 1931; *Susan Lennox: Her Fall and Rise*, 1931; *Red Dust*, 1932; *Dancing Lady*, 1933; *It Happened One Night*, 1934; *Call of the Wild*, 1935; *Mutiny on the Bounty*, 1935; *San Francisco*, 1936; *Test Pilot*, 1937; *Gone With the Wind*, 1939; *Boom Town*, 1940; *Somewhere I'll Find You*, 1942; *Adventure*, 1945; *The Hucksters*, 1947; *Key to the City*, 1950; *Mogambo*, 1953; *The Tall*

143

Clark Gable, acknowledged "King of Hollywood" at the height of his career, in a portrait that proves he never lost the charm that helped him to that title.

Men, 1955; *Run Silent, Run Deep*, 1958; *It Started in Naples*, 1960; *The Misfits*, 1961

Academy Award for best actor: *It Happened One Night*, 1934
Nominations for best actor: *Mutiny on the Bounty*, 1935; *Gone With the Wind*, 1939

Biography *The King* by Charles Samuels

GRETA GARBO

Born Greta Louisa Gustafsson on September 18, 1905 in Stockholm, Sweden

First Film *Peter the Tramp*, 1922
Major Films include *The Saga of Gösta Berling*, 1924; *The Joyless Street*, 1925; *The Torrent*, 1926; *The Temptress*, 1926; *Flesh and the Devil*, 1927; *Love*, 1927; *The Divine Woman*, 1928; *A Woman of Affairs*, 1928; *The Kiss*, 1929; *Anna Christie*, 1930; *Romance*, 1930; *Susan Lennox: Her Fall and Rise*, 1931; *Mata Hari*, 1931; *Grand Hotel*, 1932; *Queen Christina*, 1933; *Anna Karenina*, 1935; *Camille*, 1937; *Ninotchka*, 1939

Academy Award Nominations for best actress: *Anna Christie*, 1929/30; *Romance*, 1929/30; *Camille*, 1937; *Ninotchka*, 1939
Special Academy Award "for her unforgettable screen performances," 1954

Biography *Garbo* by John Bainbridge

AVA GARDNER

Born Ava Lavinia Gardner on December 24, 1922 in Smithfield, NC
Married to actor Mickey Rooney in 1942; divorced in 1943
Married to bandleader Artie Shaw in 1945; divorced in 1947
Married to singer/actor Frank Sinatra in 1951; divorced in 1954

First Film *We Were Dancing*, 1942
Major Films include *The Killers*, 1946; *The Hucksters*, 1947; *Show Boat*, 1951; *Pandora and the Flying Dutchman*, 1951; *The Snows of Kilimanjaro*, 1952; *Mogambo*, 1953; *The Barefoot Contessa*, 1954; *The Sun Also Rises*, 1957; *The Night of the Iguana*, 1964; *Mayerling*, 1968; *Earthquake*, 1974; *The Cassandra Crossing*, 1977

Academy Award Nomination for best actress: *Mogambo*, 1953

Biographies *Ava* by Charles Higham; *Ava Gardner* by John Daniell

JOHN GARFIELD

Born Julius Garfinkle on March 4, 1913 in New York City, NY
Died on May 21, 1952
Married to Roberta Mann in 1933; son John Jr. born in 1943; daughter Julie born in 1946

First Film *Footlight Parade*, 1933
Major Films include *Four Daughters*, 1938; *They Made Me a Criminal*, 1939; *The Sea Wolf*, 1941; *Tortilla Flat*, 1942; *The Pride of the Marines*, 1945; *The Postman Always Rings Twice*, 1946; *Humoresque*, 1946; *Body and Soul*, 1947; *Gentleman's Agreement*, 1947; *The Breaking Point*, 1950; *He Ran All the Way*, 1952

Academy Award Nomination for best actor: *Body and Soul*, 1947
Nomination for best supporting actor: *Four Daughters*, 1938

Biography *Body and Soul* by Larry Swindell
Book *John Garfield: His Life and Films* by James N. Beaver

JUDY GARLAND

Born Frances Ethel Gumm on June 10, 1922 in Grand Rapids, MN

A classic study of a classic beauty—Greta Garbo, winner of three best actress Oscar nominations and, in 1954, a special Academy Award "for her unforgettable screen performances."

James Garner, a performer equally at home in westerns or romantic comedies, here stars in the 1969 movie *Support Your Local Sheriff.*

Died on June 23, 1969
Married to musician David Rose in 1941; divorced in 1944
Married to director Vincente Minnelli in 1945; divorced in 1951; daughter Liza (actress/singer) born in 1946
Married to promoter Sid Luft in 1952; divorced in 1965; daughter Lorna (singer) born in 1952; son Joseph born in 1955
Married to actor Mark Herron in 1966; divorced in 1967
Married to club manager Mickey Deans in 1969

First Film *Pigskin Parade,* 1939
Major Films include *Broadway Melody of 1938,* 1937; *Love Finds Andy Hardy,* 1938; *The Wizard of Oz,* 1939; *Strike Up the Band,* 1940; *Ziegfeld Girl,* 1941; *For Me and My Gal,* 1942; *Meet Me in St. Louis,* 1944; *The Harvey Girls,* 1946; *Easter Parade,* 1948; *Summer Stock,* 1950; *A Star Is Born,* 1954; *Judgment at Nuremberg,* 1961; *I Could Go on Singing,* 1963

Special Academy Award (miniature) "for her outstanding performance as a screen juvenile during the past year," 1939
Academy Award Nomination for best actress: *A Star Is Born,* 1954
Nomination for best supporting actress: *Judgment at Nuremberg,* 1961

Biographies *I Remember It Well* by Vincente Minnelli; *Judy: A Remembrance* by David Melton

JAMES GARNER

Born James Scott Baumgarner on April 7, 1928 in Norman, OK
Married to Lois Clarke in 1956; stepdaughter, Kimberly; daughter Greta born in 1958

First Film *The Girl He Left Behind,* 1956
Major Films include *Sayonara,* 1957; *The Children's Hour,* 1962; *The Thrill of It All,* 1963; *The Americanization of Emily,* 1964; *How Sweet It Is,* 1968; *Support Your Local Sheriff,* 1969; *Health,* 1979; *The Fan,* 1982; *Victor/Victoria,* 1982; *Tank,* 1984

GREER GARSON

Born Greer Garson on September 29, 1908 in County Down, N. Ireland
Married to Edwin A. Snelson in 1932; divorced in 1937
Married to actor Richard Ney in 1943; divorced in 1947
Married to E. E. Fogelson in 1949

First Film *Goodbye, Mr. Chips,* 1939
Major Films include *Pride and Prejudice,* 1940; *Blossoms in the Dust,* 1941; *Mrs. Miniver,* 1942; *Random Harvest,* 1942; *Madame Curie,* 1943; *Mrs. Parkington,* 1944; *The Valley of Decision,* 1945; *Adventure,* 1946; *That Forsyte Woman,* 1949; *Strange Lady in Town,* 1955; *Sunrise at Campobello,* 1960; *The Singing Nun,* 1966

Academy Award for best actress: *Mrs. Miniver,* 1942
Nominations for best actress: *Goodbye, Mr. Chips,* 1939; *Blossoms in the Dust,* 1941; *Madame Curie,* 1943; *Mrs. Parkington,* 1944; *The Valley of Decision,* 1945; *Sunrise at Campobello,* 1960

JANET GAYNOR

Born Laura Gainor on November 6, 1906 in Philadelphia, PA
Died on September 14, 1984
Married to Lydell Peck in 1929; divorced in 1934
Married to Gilbert Adrian (MGM's top dress designer) in 1939; widowed in 1959; son Robin born in 1940

Married to stage producer Paul Gregory in 1964

First Film *The Johnstown Flood,* 1926
Major Films include *Seventh Heaven,* 1927; *Sunrise,* 1927; *Street Angel,* 1928; *Sunny Side Up,* 1929; *Daddy Long Legs,* 1931; *State Fair,* 1933; *Carolina,* 1934; *The Farmer Takes a Wife,* 1935; *A Star Is Born,* 1937; *The Young in Heart,* 1938

First ever Academy Award for best actress, given for three films, *Sunrise; Seventh Heaven;* and *Street Angel,* 1927/28

JOHN GIELGUD

Born Arthur John Gielgud on April 14, 1904 in London, England

First Film *Who Is the Man?,* 1924
Major Films include *Secret Agent,* 1936; *Julius Caesar,* 1953; *Richard III,* 1955; *The Barretts of Wimpole Street,* 1957; *Saint Joan,* 1957; *Becket,* 1964; *Falstaff,* 1966; *The Charge of the Light Brigade,* 1968; *Julius Caesar,* 1970; *Murder on the Orient Express,* 1974; *Providence,* 1977; *Murder by Decree,* 1979; *The Elephant Man,* 1980; *Arthur,* 1981; *Chariots of Fire,* 1981; *Gandhi,* 1982

Academy Award for best supporting actor: *Arthur,* 1981
Nomination for best supporting actor: *Becket,* 1964

Knighted in 1953

Autobiographies *Early Stages,* 1939; *Stage Directions,* 1963; *Distinguished Company,* 1972

PAULETTE GODDARD

Born Pauline Marion Goddard Levy on June 3, 1911 in Great Neck, Long Island, NY
Married to Edgar James in 1925; divorced in 1931
Married to actor/director Charlie Chaplin in 1936; divorced in 1942
Married to actor Burgess Meredith in 1943; divorced in 1948
Married to author Erich Maria Remarque in 1958; widowed in 1970

First Film *City Streets*, 1929
Major Films include *Modern Times*, 1936; *The Young in Heart*, 1938; *The Women*, 1939; *The Great Dictator*, 1940; *Nothing But the Truth*, 1941; *So Proudly We Hail*, 1943; *Kitty*, 1946; *Diary of a Chambermaid*, 1946; *Hazard*, 1948; *Vice Squad*, 1953; *Time of Indifference*, 1964

Academy Award Nomination for best supporting actress: *So Proudly We Hail*, 1943

ELLIOTT GOULD

Born Eliott Goldstein on August 29, 1938 in Brooklyn, NY
Married to actress/singer Barbra Streisand in 1963; divorced in 1971; son Jason born in 1966
Married to Jennifer Bogard in 1973; daughter Molly born in 1971; son Sam born in 1973

First Film *Quick, Let's Get Married*, 1964 (released in 1971)

Major Films include *The Night They Raided Minsky's*, 1968; *Bob & Carol & Ted & Alice*, 1969; *M*A*S*H*, 1970; *Getting Straight*, 1970; *The Touch*, 1971; *The Long Goodbye*, 1973; *A Bridge Too Far*, 1976; *Capricorn One*, 1978; *The Lady Vanishes*, 1979; *The Devil and Max Devlin*, 1981

Academy Award Nomination for best supporting actor: *Bob & Carol & Ted & Alice*, 1969

BETTY GRABLE

Born Elizabeth Ruth Grable on December 18, 1916 in St. Louis, MO
Died on July 2, 1973
Married to actor Jackie Coogan in 1937; divorced in 1940
Married to bandleader Harry James in 1943; divorced in 1965; daughter Victoria; daughter Jessica

First Film *Happy Days*, 1930
Major Films include *Kiki*, 1931; *The Sweetheart of Sigma Chi*, 1933; *The Gay Divorcee*, 1934; *Pigskin Parade*, 1936; *College Swing*, 1938; *Tin Pan Alley*, 1940; *A Yank in the RAF*, 1941; *Pin Up Girl*, 1944; *The Dolly Sisters*, 1946; *Mother Wore Tights*, 1947; *Wabash Avenue*, 1950; *How to Marry a Millionaire*, 1953; *How to Be Very Very Popular*, 1955

Biography *Betty Grable— The Reluctant Movie Queen* by Doug Warren

CARY GRANT

Born Archibald Alexander Leach on January 18, 1904

in Bristol, England
Married to actress Virginia Cherrill in 1933; divorced in 1935
Married to Woolworth heiress Barbara Hutton in 1942; divorced in 1945
Married to actress Betsy Drake in 1949; divorced in 1959
Married to actress Dyan Cannon in 1965; divorced in 1968; daughter Jennifer born in 1966
Married to Barbara Harris in 1981

First Film *This Is the Night*, 1932
Major Films include *Blonde Venus*, 1932; *She Done Him Wrong*, 1933; *Sylvia Scarlett*, 1936; *Topper*, 1937; *The Awful Truth*, 1937; *Bringing Up Baby*, 1938; *Gunga Din*, 1939; *Only Angels Have Wings*, 1939; *His Girl Friday*, 1940; *The Philadelphia Story*, 1940; *Penny Serenade*, 1941; *Suspicion*, 1941; *None But the Lonely Heart*, 1944; *Arsenic and Old Lace*, 1944; *Notorious*, 1946; *I Was a Male War Bride*, 1949; *Room for One More*, 1952; *To Catch a Thief*, 1955; *An Affair to Remember*, 1957; *Indiscreet*, 1958; *North by Northwest*, 1959; *That Touch of Mink*, 1962;

Charade, 1963; *Walk Don't Run*, 1966

Special Academy Award "for his unique mastery of the art of screen acting, with the respect and affection of his colleagues," 1969
Academy Award Nominations for best actor: *Penny Serenade*, 1941; *None But the Lonely Heart*, 1944

Book *The Films of Cary Grant* by Donald Deschner
Biographies *Haunted Idol* by Geoffrey Wansell; *Cary Grant* by Richard Schickel

KATHRYN GRAYSON

Born Zelma Kathryn Hedrick on February 9, 1922 in Winston-Salem, NC
Married to actor John Shelton in 1940; divorced in 1946
Married to singer Johnny Johnston in 1947; divorced in 1951; daughter Patricia Kathryn born in 1948

First Film *Andy Hardy's Private Secretary*, 1941
Major Films include *Thousands Cheer*, 1943;

Paulette Goddard, one of the screen's legendary heroines, proves in a scene from *Kitty* (1946) that true heroines have a natural bent for self-defense.

Alec Guinness in a scene from *The Bridge on the River Kwai* (1957); his performance won him an Academy Award for best actor.

Anchors Aweigh, 1945; *Till the Clouds Roll By*, 1946; *It Happened in Brooklyn*, 1947; *That Midnight Kiss*, 1949; *Show Boat*, 1951; *Kiss Me Kate*, 1952; *The Vagabond King*, 1956

ALEC GUINNESS

Born Alec Guinness on April 2, 1914 in London, England
Married to Nerula Salaman in 1938; son Matthew born in 1938

First Film *Great Expectations*, 1946
Major Films include *Oliver Twist*, 1948; *Kind Hearts and Coronets*, 1949; *Last Holiday*, 1950; *The Lavender Hill Mob*, 1952; *The Ladykillers*, 1955; *The Bridge on the River Kwai*, 1957; *Tunes of Glory*, 1960; *Lawrence of Arabia*, 1962; *Doctor Zhivago*, 1965; *Scrooge*, 1970; *Star Wars*, 1977; *The Empire Strikes Back*, 1980

Academy Award for best actor: *The Bridge on the River Kwai*, 1957
Nomination for best actor: *The Lavender Hill Mob*, 1952
Nomination for best supporting actor: *Star Wars*, 1977
Special Academy Award "for advancing the art of screen acting through a host of memorable and distinguished performances," 1979

Knighted in 1959

Biography *Guinness* by Kenneth Tynan

GENE HACKMAN

Born Eugene Alden Hackman on January 30, 1931 in San Bernardino, CA
Married to Kay Maltese in 1956; daughter Elizabeth; daughter Leslie; son Christopher

First Film *Mad Dog Coll*, 1961
Major Films include *Lilith*, 1964; *Bonnie and Clyde*, 1967; *The Gypsy Moths*, 1969; *I Never Sang for My Father*, 1970; *The French Connection*, 1971; *The Poseidon Adventure*, 1972; *The Conversation*, 1974; *A Bridge Too Far*, 1976; *Superman*, 1978; *Reds*, 1982, *Uncommon Valor*, 1983

Academy Award for best actor: *The French Connection*, 1971
Nominations for best supporting actor: *Bonnie and Clyde*, 1967; *I Never Sang for My Father*, 1970

JEAN HARLOW

Born Harlean Carpenter on March 3, 1911 in Kansas City, MO
Died on June 7, 1937
Eloped with Charles F. McGrew in 1927; annulled in 1930
Married to director Paul Bern in 1932; widowed in 1932
Married to director of photography Harold Rosson in 1933; divorced in 1934
Eloped with actor William Powell in 1936 but did not marry

First Film *Moran of the Marines*, 1928
Major Films include *Hell's Angels*, 1931; *Platinum Blonde*, 1931; *Red Dust*, 1932; *Bombshell*, 1933; *Dinner at Eight*, 1934; *Libeled Lady*, 1936

Biography *Harlow* by Irving Shulman

RICHARD HARRIS

Born Richard St. John Harris on October 1, 1933 in Limerick, Ireland
Married to Joan Elizabeth Reese-Williams in 1957; divorced in 1969; son Damian born in 1958; son Jared born in 1961; son Jamie born in 1964
Married to actress Ann Turkel in 1974; separated

First Film *Alive and Kicking*, 1958
Major Films include *The Wreck of the Mary Deare*, 1959; *Mutiny on the Bounty*, 1961; *The Guns of Navarone*, 1961; *This Sporting Life*, 1963; *Red*

Jean Harlow, born Harlean Carpenter, adopted her mother's maiden name as her stage name.

Goldie Hawn embarks on matrimony with Albert Brooks in *Private Benjamin* (1980); the role won her a best actress Oscar nomination to add to her 1969 best supporting actress award for *Cactus Flower.*

Desert, 1964; *Camelot,* 1967; *A Man Called Horse,* 1970; *A Man in the Wilderness,* 1971; *Robin and Marian,* 1976; *The Return of a Man Called Horse,* 1976; *The Wild Geese,* 1978; *Game for Vultures,* 1979

Academy Award Nomination for best actor: *This Sporting Life,* 1963

Book *Love, Honor and Dismay* by Joan Elizabeth Reese-Williams
Book (Poetry) by Harris *I in the Membership of My Days*

REX HARRISON

Born Reginald Carey Harrison on March 5, 1908 in Huyton, Lancashire, England
Married to Marjorie Thomas in 1934; divorced in 1942; son Noel born in 1935
Married to actress Lilli Palmer in 1943; divorced in 1957; son Carey born in 1944
Married to actress Kay

Kendall in 1957; widowed in 1959
Married to actress Rachel Roberts in 1962; divorced in 1971
Married to Joan Elizabeth Harris (ex-wife of actor Richard Harris) in 1971; divorced
Married to Mercia Tinker in 1978

First Film *The Great Game,* 1930
Major Films include *Storm in a Teacup,* 1937; *The Citadel,* 1939; *Night Train to Munich,* 1940; *Major Barbara,* 1941; *Blithe Spirit,* 1945; *Anna and the King of Siam,* 1946; *The Ghost and Mrs. Muir,* 1947; *The Reluctant Debutante,* 1958; *Cleopatra,* 1963; *My Fair Lady,* 1964; *Dr. Doolittle,* 1967; *The Prince and the Pauper,* 1977

Academy Award for best actor: *My Fair Lady,* 1964
Nomination for best actor: *Cleopatra,* 1963

Autobiography *Rex: An Autobiography,* 1975
Book *Love, Honor and Dismay* by Joan Elizabeth Reese-Williams

GOLDIE HAWN

Born Goldie Jean Hawn on November 21, 1945 in Washington, D.C.
Married to screenwriter/director Gus Trikonis in 1969; divorced in 1974
Married to singer Bill Hudson in 1976; divorced in 1979; son Oliver born in 1976; daughter Kate born in 1979

First Film *The One and Only Genuine Original Family Band,* 1968
Major Films include *Cactus Flower,* 1969; *Butterflies are Free,* 1972; *Shampoo,* 1975; *Foul Play,* 1978; *Private Benjamin,* 1980; *Best Friends,* 1982; *Swing Shift,* 1984

Academy Award for best supporting actress: *Cactus Flower,* 1969
Nomination for best actress: *Private Benjamin,* 1980

STERLING HAYDEN

Born John Hamilton on March 26, 1916 in Montclair, NJ
Married to actress Madeleine Carroll in 1942; divorced in 1946
Married to Betty Ann De-Noon in 1947; divorced in 1954; son Christian born in 1948; daughter Dana born in 1950; daughter Gretchen born in 1952
Married to Catherine McConnell in 1960; son Matthew born in 1961

First Film *Virginia,* 1941
Major Films include *The Asphalt Jungle,* 1950; *The Star,* 1953; *Johnny Guitar,* 1954; *Suddenly,* 1954; *The Killing,* 1956; *Dr. Strangelove, or How I*

Learned to Stop Worrying and Love the Bomb, 1964; *The Godfather,* 1972; *The Long Goodbye,* 1973; *1900,* 1976; *9 to 5,* 1980

Autobiography *The Wanderer,* 1963

HELEN HAYES

Born Helen Hayes Brown on October 10, 1900 in Washington, D.C.
Married to writer Charles MacArthur in 1928; widowed in 1956; daughter Mary born in 1930 (died in 1949); adopted son, James (actor)

First Film *The Weavers of Life,* 1917
Major Films include *The Sin of Madelon Claudet,* 1931; *Arrowsmith,* 1931; *A Farewell to Arms,* 1932; *The White Sister,* 1933; *Anastasia,* 1956; *Airport,* 1970; *Herbie Rides Again,* 1974; *Candleshoe,* 1978

Academy Award for best actress: *The Sin of Madelon Claudet,* 1931
Academy Award for best supporting actress: *Airport,* 1970

Autobiographies *A Gift of Joy,* 1965; *On Reflection,* 1969; *Twice Over Lightly* (with Anita Loos), 1971

SUSAN HAYWARD

Born Edythe Marrener on June 30, 1918 in Brooklyn, NY
Died on March 14, 1975
Married to Jess Barker in 1944; divorced in 1954; twin sons Timothy and Gregory born in 1945
Married to attorney Floyd

Susan Hayward, one of whose biographies is titled *Portrait of a Survivor*, won an Oscar for best actress for *I Want to Live!* (1958), after receiving four best actress nominations between 1947 and 1956.

Eaton Chalkley in 1957; widowed in 1966

First Film *Hollywood Hotel*, 1937
Major Films include *Beau Geste*, 1939; *Adam Had Four Sons*, 1941; *The Hairy Ape*, 1944; *Smash-Up: The Story of a Woman*, 1947; *My Foolish Heart*, 1950; *I Can Get It for You Wholesale*, 1951; *With a Song in My Heart*, 1952; *The Snows of Kilimanjaro*, 1952; *Garden of Evil*, 1954; *I'll Cry Tomorrow*, 1956; *I Want to Live!*, 1958; *Back Street*, 1961; *Valley of the Dolls*, 1967

Academy Award for best actress: *I Want to Live!*, 1958
Nominations for best actress: *Smash-Up: The Story of a Woman*, 1947; *My Foolish Heart*, 1950; *With a Song in My Heart*, 1952; *I'll Cry Tomorrow*, 1956

Biographies *The Divine Bitch* by Doug McClelland; *Portrait of a Survivor—Susan Hayward* by Beverly Linet
Book *The Films of Susan Hayward* by Eduardo Moreno

RITA HAYWORTH

Born Margarita Carmen Cansino on October 17, 1918 in New York City, NY (daughter of dancer Eduardo Cansino)
Married to Edward Judson in 1937; divorced in 1943
Married to actor Orson Welles in 1943; divorced in 1947; daughter Rebecca born in 1944
Married to Prince Aly Khan in 1949; divorced in 1951; daughter Yasmin born in 1950
Married to singer Dick Haymes in 1953; divorced in 1955
Married to producer James Hill in 1958; divorced in 1961

First Film *Under the Pampas Moon*, 1935
Major Films include *Only Angels Have Wings*, 1939; *Strawberry Blonde*, 1941; *Blood and Sand*, 1941; *You'll Never Get Rich*, 1941; *You Were Never Lovelier*, 1942; *Cover Girl*, 1944; *Gilda*, 1946; *The Lady From Shanghai*, 1948; *Salome*, 1953; *Pal Joey*, 1957; *Separate Tables*, 1958; *The Circus World*, 1964

Biography *Rita* by John Kobal
Book *The Films of Rita Hayworth: The Legend & Career of a Love Goddess* by Gene Ringgold

AUDREY HEPBURN

Born Audrey Hepburn-Ruston on May 4, 1929 in Brussels, Belgium
Married to actor Mel Ferrer in 1954; divorced in 1968; son Sean born in 1960
Married to psychiatrist Andrea Dotti in 1969; divorced; son Luca born in 1970

First Film *One Wild Oat*, 1951
Major Films include *Roman Holiday*, 1953; *Sabrina*, 1954; *War and Peace*, 1956; *Funny Face*, 1957; *The Nun's Story*, 1959; *Breakfast at Tiffany's*, 1961; *The Children's Hour*, 1962; *Charade*, 1963; *My Fair Lady*, 1964; *Two for the Road*, 1967; *Wait Until Dark*, 1967; *Robin and Marian*, 1976; *Bloodline*, 1979

Academy Award for best actress: *Roman Holiday*, 1953
Nominations for best actress: *Sabrina*, 1954; *The Nun's Story*, 1959; *Breakfast at Tiffany's*, 1961; *Wait Until Dark*, 1967

Biography *Audrey Hepburn* by Caroline Latham

KATHARINE HEPBURN

Born Katharine Houghton Hepburn on November 8, 1907 in Hartford, CT
Married to Ludlow Ogden Smith in 1928; divorced in 1934

First Film *A Bill of Divorcement*, 1932
Major Films include *Morning Glory*, 1933; *Little Women*, 1933; *Alice Adams*, 1935; *Sylvia Scarlett*, 1936; *Stage Door*, 1937; *Bringing*

Audrey Hepburn, pictured with co-star Sean Connery, proves that even legendary characters don't stay young for ever in *Robin and Marian* (1976), an update on the Robin Hood adventure tale.

Charlton Heston, seen here with Sophia Loren in *El Cid* (1961), has served as president of the Screen Actors' Guild and as chairman of the American Film Institute.

Up Baby, 1938; *Holiday*, 1938; *The Philadelphia Story*, 1940; *Woman of the Year*, 1942; *The Sea of Grass*, 1947; *Adam's Rib*, 1949; *The African Queen*, 1951; *Summertime*, 1955; *The Rainmaker*, 1956; *Suddenly Last Summer*, 1959; *Long Day's Journey into Night*, 1962; *Guess Who's Coming to Dinner?*, 1967; *The Lion in Winter*, 1968; *Rooster Cogburn*, 1975; *On Golden Pond*, 1981

Academy Awards for best actress: *Morning Glory*, 1932/33; *Guess Who's Coming to Dinner?*, 1967; *The Lion in Winter*, 1968; *On Golden Pond*, 1981
Nominations for best actress: *Alice Adams*, 1935; *The Philadelphia Story*, 1940; *Woman of the Year*, 1942; *The African Queen*, 1951; *Summertime*, 1955; *The Rainmaker*, 1956; *Suddenly Last Summer*, 1959; *Long Day's Journey into Night*, 1962

Biography *Kate: The Life of Katharine Hepburn* by Charles Higham
Book *The Films of Katharine Hepburn* by Homer Dickens

CHARLTON HESTON

Born Charlton Carter on October 4, 1924 in Evanston, IL
Married to Lydia Clarke in 1944; son Fraser born in 1955; adopted daughter, Holly Ann

First Film *Dark City*, 1950
Major Films include *The Greatest Show on Earth*, 1952; *Ruby Gentry*, 1952; *The President's Lady*, 1953; *The Ten Commandments*, 1956; *Touch of Evil*, 1958; *The Big Country*, 1958; *Ben-Hur*, 1959; *El Cid*, 1961; *The Agony and the Ecstasy*, 1965; *Will Penny*, 1968; *Planet of the Apes*, 1968; *Antony and Cleopatra*, 1972; *Earthquake*, 1974; *Airport 1975*, 1974; *Midway*, 1976; *Two-Minute Warning*, 1976; *Gray Lady Down*, 1978

Academy Award for best actor: *Ben-Hur*, 1959
Jean Hersholt Humanitarian Award, 1977

Autobiography *The Actor's Life*, 1978

Biography *Charlton Heston* by Michael Druxman

DUSTIN HOFFMAN

Born Dustin Hoffman on August 8, 1937 in Los Angeles, CA
Married to dancer Anne Byrne in 1969; divorced in 1979; daughter Jennifer Celia born in 1970
Married to Lisa Gottsegan in 1980; daughter Karina

First Film *The Tiger Makes Out*, 1967
Major Films include *The Graduate*, 1967; *Midnight Cowboy*, 1969; *Little Big Man*, 1971; *Papillon*, 1973; *Lenny*, 1974; *All the President's Men*, 1976; *Marathon Man*, 1976; *Straight Time*, 1978; *Kramer vs. Kramer*, 1979; *Tootsie*, 1982

Academy Award for best actor: *Kramer vs. Kramer*, 1979
Nominations for best actor: *The Graduate*, 1967; *Midnight Cowboy*, 1969; *Lenny*, 1974; *Tootsie*, 1982

Biography *Dustin Hoffman: Hollywood's Antihero* by Len Lenburg
Book *The Films of Dustin Hoffman* by Jeff Brodes

WILLIAM HOLDEN

Born William Franklin Beedle, Jr. on April 17, 1918 in O'Fallon, IL
Died on November 16, 1981
Married to actress Brenda Marshall in 1941; divorced in 1970; stepdaughter, Virginia; son Peter born in 1943; son Scott born in 1946

First Film *Prison Farm*, 1938
Major Films include *Golden Boy*, 1939; *Our Town*, 1940; *The Man from Colorado*, 1948; *The Dark Past*, 1949; *Sunset Boulevard*, 1950; *Born Yesterday*, 1950; *The Turning Point*, 1952; *The Moon Is Blue*, 1953; *Stalag 17*, 1953; *Sabrina*, 1954; *Love Is a Many-*

William Holden in *The Bridge on the River Kwai* (1957). J. D. Salinger, author of *Catcher in the Rye*, named his protagonist, Holden Caulfield, after William Holden and Joan Caulfield, who co-starred in two films.

Leslie Howard, born in London and the model of the perfect Englishman, was English only by accident; his parents were Hungarian immigrants. Here Howard appears in *Romeo and Juliet.*

Splendored Thing, 1955; *Picnic*, 1956; *The Bridge on the River Kwai*, 1957; *The Counterfeit Traitor*, 1962; *The Wild Bunch*, 1969; *The Towering Inferno*, 1974; *Network*, 1976; *S.O.B.*, 1981

Academy Award for best actor: *Stalag 17*, 1953
Nominations for best actor: *Sunset Boulevard*, 1950; *Network*, 1976

Biography *Golden Boy: The Untold Story of William Holden* by Bob Thomas
Book *The Films of William Holden* by Lawrence Quirk

JUDY HOLLIDAY

Born Judith Tuvim on June 21, 1922 in New York City, NY
Died on June 7, 1965
Married to David Oppenheim in 1948; divorced in 1958; son Jonathan born in 1949

First Film *Greenwich Village*, 1944

Major Films include *Winged Victory*, 1944; *Adam's Rib*, 1949; *Born Yesterday*, 1950; *The Marrying Kind*, 1952; *It Should Happen to You*, 1954; *The Solid Gold Cadillac*, 1956; *Bells Are Ringing*, 1960

Academy Award for best actress: *Born Yesterday*, 1950

Biographies *Judy Holliday* by Gary Carey; *Judy Holliday: Only Child* by Will Holtzman

BOB HOPE

Born Leslie Townes Hope on May 29, 1903 in Eltham, London, England
Married to Dolores Reade in 1933; adopted daughter, Linda; adopted daughter, Honora; adopted son, Anthony; adopted son, William

First Film *The Big Broadcast of 1938*, 1938
Major Films include *Never Say Die*, 1939; *The Cat and the Canary*, 1939; *Road to Singapore*, 1940; *Road to Zanzibar*, 1941; *My Favorite Blonde*, 1942; *Road to Morocco*, 1942; *The Princess and the Pirate*, 1944; *Monsieur Beaucaire*, 1946; *Road to Rio*, 1947; *The Paleface*, 1948; *Fancy Pants*, 1950; *The Lemon Drop Kid*, 1951; *Road to Bali*, 1953; *The Facts of Life*, 1960; *The Road to Hong Kong*, 1962; *Critic's Choice*, 1963; *How to Commit Marriage*, 1969; *Cancel My Reservation*, 1972

Special Academy Awards for his many services to the motion picture industry and to the Academy, 1940, 1944, 1952, 1965
Jean Hersholt Humanitarian Award, 1959

Autobiography *The Road to Hollywood*, 1977
Books by Hope *I Never Left Home; They Got Me Covered; So This Is Peace; Have Tux Will Travel; I Owe Russia $1200*

LESLIE HOWARD

Born Leslie Howard Stainer on April 3, 1893 in London, England
Died on June 2, 1943 returning from a wartime mission, when his plane was shot down by Nazis who believed Winston Churchill was also aboard
Married to Ruth Evelyn Martin in 1916; son Ronald (actor) born in 1918; daughter Leslie Ruth born in 1924

First Film *The Happy Warrior*, 1917
Major Films include *Outward Bound*, 1930; *Five and Ten*, 1931; *Service for Ladies*, 1932; *The Animal Kingdom*, 1932; *Berkeley Square*, 1933; *Of Human Bondage*, 1934; *The Scarlet Pimpernel*, 1935; *The Petrified Forest*, 1936; *Romeo and Juliet*, 1936; *Pygmalion*, 1938; *Gone With the Wind*, 1939; *Intermezzo: A Love Story*, 1939; *49th Parallel*, 1941; *The First of the Few*, 1942

Academy Award Nominations for best actor: *Berkeley Square*, 1932/33; *Pygmalion*, 1938

Biography *A Quite Remarkable Father* by Leslie Ruth Howard

ROCK HUDSON

Born Roy Scherer, Jr. on November 17, 1925 in Winnetka, IL
Married to Phyllis Gates in 1955; divorced in 1958

First Film *Fighter Squadron*, 1948
Major Films include *Bend of the River*, 1952; *Horizons West*, 1952; *Magnificent Obsession*, 1954; *All That Heaven Allows*, 1956; *Giant*, 1956; *A Farewell to Arms*, 1957; *Pillow Talk*, 1959; *Lover Come Back*, 1962; *Man's Favorite Sport?*, 1964; *Seconds*, 1966; *Tobruk*, 1967; *Ice Station Zebra*, 1968; *Darling Lili*, 1970; *Pretty Maids All in a Row*, 1971; *The Mirror Crack'd*, 1980

Academy Award Nomination for best actor: *Giant*, 1956

WALTER HUSTON

Born Walter Houghston on April 6, 1884 in To-

British actress Glenda Jackson has won best actress Oscars for *Women in Love* (1969) and *A Touch of Class* (1973), and nominations for *Sunday Bloody Sunday* (1971), and *Hedda* (1975).

ronto, Canada
Died on April 7, 1950
Married to newspaperwoman Rhea Gore in 1905; divorced in 1913; son John (director/screenwriter) born in 1906
Married to vaudeville partner Bayonne Whipple in 1914; divorced
Married to actress Nan Sunderland in 1931

First Film *Gentlemen of the Press*, 1929
Major Films include *The Virginian*, 1929; *Abraham Lincoln*, 1930; *The Ruling Voice*, 1931; *Law and Order*, 1932; *American Madness*, 1932; *Rain*, 1932; *Dodsworth*, 1936; *The Light That Failed*, 1940; *All That Money Can Buy*, 1941; *The Maltese Falcon*, 1941; *Yankee Doodle Dandy*, 1942; *The Outlaw*, 1943; *And Then There Were None*, 1945; *The Treasure of the Sierra Madre*, 1947; *The Furies*, 1950

Academy Award for best supporting actor: *The Treasure of the Sierra Madre*, 1947
Nominations for best actor: *Dodsworth*, 1936; *All That Money Can Buy*, 1941

Nomination for best supporting actor: *Yankee Doodle Dandy*, 1942

BETTY HUTTON

Born Elizabeth June Thornbug on February 26, 1921 in Battle Creek, MI
Married to Ted Briskin in 1945; divorced in 1951; daughter Lindsay born in 1946; daughter Candice born in 1948
Married to dance director Charles O'Curran in 1952; divorced in 1954
Married to Alan Livingston in 1955; divorced in 1958
Married to musician Pete Candoli in 1961; divorced in 1968; daughter Carolyn born in 1962

First Film *The Fleet's In*, 1942
Major Films include *The Miracle of Morgan's Creek*, 1944; *Incendiary Blonde*, 1945; *Dream Girl*, 1948; *Annie Get Your Gun*, 1950; *The Greatest Show on Earth*, 1952; *Spring Reunion*, 1957

BURL IVES

Born Burle Icle Ivanhoe on June 14, 1909, in Hunt, IL
Married to Helen Ehrlich in 1945; divorced
Married to Dorothy Koster in 1971; son Alexander born in 1972

First Film *Smoky*, 1946
Major Films include *East of Eden*, 1955; *Desire Under the Elms*, 1958; *The Big Country*, 1958; *Cat on a Hot Tin Roof*, 1958; *Our Man in Havana*, 1959; *Ensign Pulver*, 1964; *Just You and Me, Kid*, 1978

Academy Award for best supporting actor: *The Big Country*, 1958

Autobiography *The Wayfaring Stranger's Notebook*

GLENDA JACKSON

Born Glenda Jackson on May 9, 1936 in Birkenhead, Cheshire, England
Married to Roy Hodges in 1958; divorced in 1976; son Daniel born in 1969

First Film *The Persecution and Assassination of Jean-Paul Marat as Performed by the Inmates of the Asylum of Charenton Under the Direction of the Marquis de Sade*, 1967
Major Films include *Women in Love*, 1969; *Sunday Bloody Sunday*, 1971; *Mary, Queen of Scots*, 1971; *A Touch of Class*, 1973; *Hedda*, 1975; *House Calls*, 1978; *Stevie*, 1978

Academy Awards for best actress: *Women in Love*, 1969; *A Touch of Class*, 1973

Nominations for best actress: *Sunday Bloody Sunday*, 1971; *Hedda*, 1975

VAN JOHNSON

Born Charles Van Johnson on August 25, 1916 in Newport, RI
Married to Eve Abbott Wynn (ex-wife of his friend Keenan Wynn) in 1947; divorced in 1968; daughter Schuyler born in 1948

First Film *Too Many Girls*, 1942
Major Films include *A Guy Named Joe*, 1943; *The White Cliffs of Dover*, 1944; *Two Girls and a Sailor*, 1944; *Weekend at the Waldorf*, 1945; *State of the Union*, 1948; *In the Good Old Summertime*, 1949; *Battleground*, 1949; *The Caine Mutiny*, 1954; *Brigadoon*, 1954; *Wives and Lovers*, 1963; *Divorce American Style*, 1967; *Yours, Mine and Ours*, 1968

JAMES EARL JONES

Born James Earl Jones on January 17, 1931 in Arkabutla, MS (son of boxer-turned-actor Robert Earl Jones)
Married to Julianne Marie in 1967; divorced
Married to Cecilia Hart in 1982; daughter born in 1983

First Film *Dr. Strangelove, or How I Learned to Stop Worrying and Love the Bomb*, 1964
Major Films include *The Comedians*, 1967; *The Great White Hope*, 1970; *The Man*, 1972; *Claudine*, 1974; *The Bingo Long*

The young Jennifer Jones in the film which made her famous and won her a best actress Academy Award: *The Song of Bernadette* in 1943. She later won four nominations—three for best actress.

Traveling All-Stars and Motor Kings, 1976; *Conan the Barbarian*, 1982

Academy Award Nomination for best actor: *The Great White Hope*, 1970

JENNIFER JONES

Born Phyllis Isley on March 2, 1919 in Tulsa, OK
Married to actor Robert Walker in 1939; divorced in 1945; son Robert Jr. (actor) born in 1940; son Michael born in 1941
Married to producer David O. Selznick in 1949; widowed in 1965; daughter Mary Jennifer born in 1954 (died in 1976)
Married to millionaire Norton Simon in 1971

First Film *New Frontier*, 1939 (as Phyllis Isley)
Major Films include *The Song of Bernadette*, 1943; *Since You Went Away*, 1944; *Love Letters*, 1945; *Cluny Brown*, 1946; *Duel in the Sun*, 1946; *Madame Bovary*, 1949; *Carrie*, 1952;

Ruby Gentry, 1953; *Beat the Devil*, 1954; *Love Is a Many-Splendored Thing*, 1955; *The Barretts of Wimpole Street*, 1957; *Tender Is the Night*, 1962; *The Towering Inferno*, 1974

Academy Award for best actress, *The Song of Bernadette*, 1943
Nominations for best actress: *Love Letters*, 1945; *Duel in the Sun*, 1946; *Love Is a Many-Splendored Thing*, 1955
Nomination for best supporting actress: *Since You Went Away*, 1944

Book *The Films of Jennifer Jones* by Franklyn Moshier

SHIRLEY JONES

Born Shirley Mae Jones on March 31, 1934 in Smithton, PA
Married to actor/singer Jack Cassidy in 1956; divorced in 1975; stepson, David (actor/singer); son Shaun (actor/singer) born in 1959; son Patrick born

in 1962; son Ryan John born in 1966
Married to actor/agent Marty Ingels in 1977

First Film *Oklahoma!*, 1955
Major Films include *Carousel*, 1956; *Elmer Gantry*, 1960; *The Music Man*, 1962; *The Courtship of Eddie's Father*, 1963; *The Cheyenne Social Club*, 1970

Academy Award for best supporting actress: *Elmer Gantry*, 1960

LOUIS JOURDAN

Born Louis Gendre on June 19, 1919 in Marseilles, France
Married to Berthe Frédérique in 1946; son Louis Henry born in 1951

First Film *Le Corsaire*, 1939
Major Films include *The Paradine Case*, 1948; *Letter From an Unknown Woman*, 1948; *Madame Bovary*, 1949; *Three Coins in the Fountain*, 1954; *Julie*, 1956; *Gigi*, 1958; *The Best of Everything*, 1959; *The V.I.P.s*, 1963; *The Count of Monte Cristo*, 1976; *Octopussy*, 1983

BORIS KARLOFF

Born William Henry Pratt on November 23, 1887 in Dulwich, England
Died on February 2, 1969
Married to Olive de Wilton in 1913; divorced
Married to Helen Soule in 1923; divorced in 1928
Married to Dorothy Stine in 1928; divorced in 1946; daughter Sara Jane born in 1929
Married to Evelyn Helmore in 1946

First Film *The Dumb Girl of Portici*, 1916
Major Films include *Parisian Nights*, 1925; *The Unholy Night*, 1929; *The Criminal Code*, 1931; *Frankenstein*, 1931; *Scarface*, 1932; *The Old Dark House*, 1932; *The Mask of Fu Manchu*, 1932; *The*

Shirley Jones, seen here in *The Cheyenne Social Club* in 1970, has seen two members of her family—stepson David Cassidy and son Shaun Cassidy—follow her into show business.

153

Danny Kaye, here shown in the title role of *Hans Christian Andersen,* (1952), numbers among his offscreen activities participation in UNICEF and charity appearances as an orchestral guest conductor.

Mummy, 1932; *The Lost Patrol,* 1934; *The Black Cat,* 1934; *The Bride of Frankenstein,* 1935; *The Walking Dead,* 1936; *Mr. Wong—Detective,* 1938; *The Climax,* 1944; *The Body Snatcher,* 1945; *The Secret Life of Walter Mitty,* 1947; *The Comedy of Terrors,* 1963; *The Venetian Affair,* 1967; *Targets,* 1968

Biography *Dear Boris* by Cynthia Lindsay
Book *The Films of Boris Karloff* by Richard Bojarski

DANNY KAYE

Born David Daniel Kaminski on January 18, 1913 in Brooklyn, NY
Married to songwriter Sylvia Fine in 1940; daughter Dena born in 1946

First Film *Up in Arms,* 1944
Major Films include *Wonder Man,* 1945; *The Secret Life of Walter Mitty,* 1947; *A Song Is Born,* 1948; *On the Riviera,* 1951; *Hans*

Christian Andersen, 1952; *White Christmas,* 1954; *The Five Pennies,* 1959; *The Madwoman of Chaillot,* 1969

Special Academy Award "for his unique talents, his service to the Academy, the motion picture industry, and the American people," 1954
Jean Hersholt Humanitarian Award, 1981

Biography *Danny Kaye* by Kurt D. Singer

DIANE KEATON

Born Diane Hall on January 5, 1946 in Los Angeles, CA

First Film *Lovers and Other Strangers,* 1970
Major Films include *The Godfather,* 1972; *Play It Again, Sam,* 1972; *Sleeper,* 1973; *Annie Hall,* 1977; *Looking for Mr. Goodbar,* 1977; *Interiors,* 1978;

Manhattan, 1979; *Reds,* 1981; *Shoot the Moon,* 1982

Academy Award for best actress: *Annie Hall,* 1977
Nomination for best actress: *Reds,* 1981

Book by Keaton *Reservation,* 1980 (photographs)

HOWARD KEEL

Born Harold Clifford Leek on April 13, 1917 in Gillespie, IL
Married to Rosemary Cooper in 1943; divorced in 1948
Married to Helen Anderson in 1949; divorced in 1970; daughter Kaija Liane born in 1950; son Gunnar born in 1955; daughter Kristine born in 1957
Married to Judy Magamoll in 1970; daughter Leslie Grace born in 1974

First Film *The Small Voice,* 1948
Major Films include *Annie Get Your Gun,* 1950; *Show Boat,* 1951; *Calamity Jane,* 1953; *Kiss Me Kate,* 1953; *Seven Brides for*

Seven Brothers, 1954; *Kismet,* 1955; *The War Wagon,* 1967

GENE KELLY

Born Eugene Curran Kelly on August 23, 1912 in Pittsburgh, PA
Married to actress Betsy Blair in 1940; divorced in 1957; daughter Kerry born in 1942
Married to Jeanne Coyne in 1960; widowed in 1973; son Timothy born in 1962; daughter Bridget born in 1963

First Film *For Me and My Gal,* 1942
Major Films include *Cover Girl,* 1944; *Anchors Aweigh,* 1945; *Ziegfeld Follies,* 1946; *The Three Musketeers,* 1948; *Words and Music,* 1948; *Take Me Out to the Ball Game,* 1949; *On the Town,* 1949; *Summer Stock,* 1950; *An American in Paris,* 1951; *Singin' in the Rain,* 1952; *Brigadoon,* 1954; *Invitation to the Dance,* 1956; *Inherit the Wind,* 1960; *40 Carats,* 1973; *That's Entertainment*

Diane Keaton, perhaps best-known as Woody Allen's favorite leading lady, is here seen in *Shoot the Moon,* a 1982 study of a failing marriage in which she played opposite Albert Finney.

In *High Society*, the 1956 musical remake of the 1940 film *The Philadelphia Story*, Grace Kelly plays Tracy, the role played in the original by Katharine Hepburn.

(narration), 1974; *That's Entertainment, Part II* (narration), 1976; *Xanadu*, 1980

Academy Award Nomination for best actor: *Anchors Aweigh*, 1945
Special Academy Award "in appreciation of his versatility as an actor, singer, director and dancer, and especially for his brilliant achievements in the art of choreography on film," 1951

Biography *Gene Kelly* by Clive Hirschhorn

GRACE KELLY

Born Grace Patricia Kelly on November 12, 1928 in Philadelphia, PA
Died on September 14, 1982
Married to Prince Rainier III of Monaco in 1956; daughter Caroline born in 1957; son Albert born in 1958; daughter Stephanie born in 1965

First Film *Fourteen Hours*, 1951

Major Films include *High Noon*, 1952; *Mogambo*, 1953; *Rear Window*, 1954; *The Country Girl*, 1954; *To Catch a Thief*, 1955; *High Society*, 1956

Academy Award for best actress: *The Country Girl*, 1954
Nomination for best actress: *Mogambo*, 1953

Biographies *Princess Grace* by Gwen Robyns; *Grace of Monaco* by Steven Englund

GEORGE KENNEDY

Born George Kennedy on February 18, 1926 in New York City, NY
Married to Norma Jean Wurman in 1959; daughter Karianne born in 1962; son Christopher George born in 1965

First Film *The Little Shepherd of Kingdom Come*, 1961
Major Films include *Lonely Are the Brave*, 1962; *Charade*, 1963; *Mirage*, 1965; *The Sons of Katie Elder*, 1965; *The Flight of the Phoenix*, 1966; *The Dirty Dozen*, 1967; *Cool Hand Luke*, 1967; *The Boston Strangler*, 1968; *Airport*, 1970; *Lost Horizon*, 1973; *Thunderbolt and Lightfoot*, 1974; *Earthquake*, 1974; *The Eiger Sanction*, 1975; *Death on the Nile*, 1978; *Airport '79 Concorde*, 1979

Academy Award for best supporting actor: *Cool Hand Luke*, 1967

DEBORAH KERR

Born Deborah J. Kerr-Trimmer on September 30, 1921 in Helensburgh, Scotland
Married to Anthony Bartley in 1945; divorced in 1959; daughter Melanie Jane born in 1947; daughter Frances born in 1951
Married to writer Peter Viertel in 1960; divorced in 1968

First Film *Major Barbara*, 1941
Major Films include *The Life and Death of Colonel Blimp*, 1943; *Black Narcissus*, 1947; *Edward My Son*, 1949; *Quo Vadis*, 1951; *From Here to Eternity*, 1953; *The King and I*, 1956; *Heaven Knows, Mr. Allison*, 1957; *An Affair to Remember*, 1957; *Separate Tables*, 1958; *The Sundowners*, 1960; *The Innocents*, 1961; *The Night of the Iguana*, 1964; *Casino Royale*, 1967

Academy Award Nominations for best actress: *Edward My Son*, 1949; *From Here to Eternity*, 1953; *The King and I*, 1956; *Heaven Knows, Mr. Allison*, 1957; *Separate Tables*, 1958; *The Sundowners*, 1960

Biography *Deborah Kerr* by Eric Braun

Deborah Kerr with Robert Mitchum and Peter Ustinov in a scene from *The Sundowners*; the 1960 film won Kerr her sixth Academy Award nomination for best supporting actress.

ALAN LADD

Born Alan Walbridge Ladd on September 3, 1913 in Hot Springs, AR
Died on January 30, 1964
Married to Marjorie June Harrold in 1930; divorced in 1942; son Alan Jr. (producer) born in 1937
Married to actress/agent Sue Carol in 1942; daughter Alana born in 1943; son David (actor) born in 1947

First Film *Once in a Lifetime*, 1932
Major Films include *Citizen Kane*, 1941; *This Gun for Hire*, 1942; *The Glass Key*, 1942; *Salty O'Rourke*, 1945; *The Blue Dahlia*, 1946; *Calcutta*, 1947; *Saigon*, 1948; *The Great Gatsby*, 1949; *Shane*, 1953; *The Big Land*, 1957; *The Proud Rebel*, 1958

Biography *Ladd* by Beverly Linet

VERONICA LAKE

Born Constance Frances Marie Ockelman on November 14, 1919 in Brooklyn, NY
Died on July 7, 1973
Married to art director John Detlie in 1940; divorced in 1943; daughter Elaine born in 1942; son William Anthony born in 1943
Married to director André de Toth in 1944; divorced in 1952; daughter Diane born in 1948
Married to music publisher Joseph Allan McCarthy in 1955; divorced in 1959
Married to Ron House in 1962; divorced
Married to Robert Carlton-Munroe in 1972; di-

vorce pending when she died

First Film *Sorority House*, 1939 (as Constance Keane)
Major Films include *Sullivan's Travels*, 1941; *This Gun for Hire*, 1942; *The Glass Key*, 1942; *I Married a Witch*, 1942; *The Blue Dahlia*, 1946; *Saigon*, 1948; *Slattery's Hurricane*, 1949

Autobiography *Veronica—The Autobiography of Veronica Lake* (with Donald Bain), 1971
Biography *Peekaboo: The Story of Veronica Lake* by Jeff Lemburg

HEDY LAMARR

Born Hedwig Eva Maria Kiesler on November 9, 1913 in Vienna, Austria
Married to millionaire Fritz Mandl in 1933; divorced in 1937
Married to screenwriter Gene Markey in 1939; divorced in 1940
Married to actor John Loder in 1943; divorced in 1948; daughter Denise born in 1945; son Anthony born in 1947
Married to Ernest Stauffer in 1951; divorced in 1952
Married to W. Howard Lee in 1953; divorced in 1959
Married to Lewis Boles in 1963; divorced in 1965

First Film *Die Blumenfrau von Lindenau*, 1931
Major Films include *Ecstasy*, 1933; *Algiers*, 1938; *Boom Town*, 1940; *H. M. Pulham, Esq.*, 1941; *Tortilla Flat*, 1942; *Experiment Perilous*, 1944; *Samson and Delilah*, 1949; *The Female Animal*, 1958

Autobiography *Ecstasy and Me*, 1966
Book *The Films of Hedy Lamarr* by Christopher Young

DOROTHY LAMOUR

Born Mary Leta Dorothy Kaumeyer on December 10, 1914 in New Orleans, LA
Married to band leader Herbie Kaye in 1935; divorced in 1939
Married to William Ross Howard in 1943; widowed; son John Ridgely born in 1946; son Richard born in 1949

First Film *The Jungle Princess*, 1936
Major Films include *Swing High Swing Low*, 1937; *The Hurricane*, 1937; *Spawn of the North*, 1938; *Road to Singapore*, 1940; *Road to Zanzibar*, 1941; *The Fleet's In*, 1942; *Road to Morocco*, 1942; *Dixie*, 1943; *My Favorite Brunette*, 1947; *Road to Rio*, 1947; *The Greatest Show on Earth*, 1952; *Donovan's Reef*, 1963

Autobiography *My Side of the Road* (with Dick McInnes), 1980

BURT LANCASTER

Born Burton Stephen Lancaster on November 2, 1913 in New York City, NY
Married to June Ernst in 1935; divorced in 1936
Married to Norma Anderson in 1946; divorced in 1969; son William born in 1947; son James born in 1949; daughter Susan born in 1951; daughter Joanna born in 1954; daughter Sighle born in 1956

First Film *The Killers*, 1946
Major Films include *All*

Burt Lancaster has been making movies for nearly forty years. He's seen here as the head of a Texas oil company who wants to turn a Scottish village into a refinery in *Local Hero* (1982).

Jessica Lange as actress Frances Farmer in the 1982 movie *Frances*. The film won her a best actress nomination in the same year that she won the best supporting actress Oscar for *Tootsie*.

My Sons, 1948; *The Flame and the Arrow*, 1950; *The Crimson Pirate*, 1952; *Come Back, Little Sheba*, 1952; *From Here to Eternity*, 1953; *Vera Cruz*, 1954; *The Rose Tattoo*, 1955; *Gunfight at the O.K. Corral*, 1957; *Separate Tables*, 1958; *Elmer Gantry*, 1960; *Birdman of Alcatraz*, 1962; *Airport*, 1970; *Ulzana's Raid*, 1972; *Atlantic City*, 1981; *Local Hero*, 1982

Academy Award for best actor: *Elmer Gantry*, 1960
Nominations for best actor: *From Here to Eternity*, 1953; *Birdman of Alcatraz*, 1962; *Atlantic City*, 1981

Biography *Burt Lancaster* by Tony Thomas

JESSICA LANGE

Born Jessica Lange on April 20, 1949 in Cloquet, MN
Married to photographer Paco Grande; separated
Daughter Alexandra by dancer Mikhail Baryshnikov born in 1981

First Film *King Kong*, 1976
Major Films include *All That Jazz*, 1979; *How to Beat the High Cost of Living*, 1980; *The Postman Always Rings Twice*, 1981; *Frances*, 1982; *Tootsie*, 1982

Academy Award for best supporting actress: *Tootsie*, 1982
Nomination for best actress: *Frances*, 1982

ANGELA LANSBURY

Born Angela Brigid Lansbury on October 16, 1925 in London, England
Married to actor Richard Cromwell in 1945; divorced in 1946
Married to Peter Shaw in 1949; son Anthony born in 1952; daughter Dierdre born in 1953

First Film *Gaslight*, 1944
Major Films include *National Velvet*, 1944; *The Picture of Dorian Gray*, 1945; *State of the Union*, 1948; *The Court Jester*, 1956; *The Long Hot Summer*, 1958; *The Dark at the Top of the Stairs*, 1960; *The Manchurian Candidate*, 1962; *Dear Heart*, 1964; *Bedknobs and Broomsticks*, 1971; *Death on the Nile*, 1978; *The Lady Vanishes*, 1979; *The Pirates of Penzance*, 1983

Academy Award Nominations for best supporting actress: *Gaslight*, 1944; *The Picture of Dorian Gray*, 1945; *The Manchurian Candidate*, 1962

CHARLES LAUGHTON

Born Charles Laughton on July 1, 1899 in Scarborough, England
Died on December 15, 1962
Married to actress Elsa Lanchester in 1929

First Film *Bluebottles* (short), 1928
Major Films include *Piccadilly*, 1929; *The Sign of the Cross*, 1932; *Island of Lost Souls*, 1932; *The Private Life of Henry VIII*, 1933; *The Barretts of Wimpole Street*, 1934; *Ruggles of Red Gap*, 1935; *Les Misérables*, 1935; *Mutiny on the Bounty*, 1935; *The Hunchback of Notre Dame*, 1939; *The Suspect*, 1945; *The Big Clock*, 1948; *Hobson's Choice*, 1954; *Witness for the Prosecution*, 1957; *Advise and Consent*, 1962

Academy Award for best actor: *The Life of Henry VIII*, 1932/33
Nominations for best actor: *Mutiny on the Bounty*, 1935; *Witness for the Prosecution*, 1957

Autobiography *Tell Me a Story*, 1957
Biography *Charles Laughton and I* by Elsa Lanchester, 1938
Book *Elsa Lanchester: Herself* by Elsa Lanchester

LAUREL AND HARDY

STAN LAUREL
Born Arthur Stanley Jefferson on June 16, 1890 in Ulverston, Lancashire, England
Died on February 24, 1965

Angela Lansbury is Agatha Christie's spinster super-sleuth Miss Marple in *The Mirror Crack'd* (1980). Lansbury's career has brought her three best supporting actress Oscar nominations.

Stan Laurel and Oliver Hardy mourn the sad fate of a bent cigar. In 1960, after Hardy's death, Laurel won a special Academy Award "for his creative pioneering in the field of cinema comedy."

Married to Raemond Walbern; divorced
Married to Lois Nelson; divorced in 1933; daughter Lois born in 1931
Married to Virginia Ruth Rogers in 1935; divorced in 1937
Remarried to Virginia Ruth Rogers in 1938; divorced in 1939
Married to dancer Vera Illiana in 1940; divorced in 1966
Married to singer Ida Kitaeva in 1946; divorced

Special Academy Award "for his creative pioneering in the field of cinema comedy," 1960

Biographies *The Comedy World of Stan Laurel* by John McCabe; *Stan—The Life of Stan Laurel* by Fred Lawrence

OLIVER HARDY

Born Oliver Norvell Hardy on January 18, 1892 in Harlem, GA
Died on August 8, 1957
Married to Myrtle Reeves

in 1921; divorced in 1937
Married to Lucille Jones in 1940

First Film (Hardy) *Outwitting Dad* (short), 1914
First Film (Laurel) *Nuts in May* (short), 1917
Major Films include (shorts) *Lucky Dog* (not as team), 1917; *Slipping Wives* (not as team), 1926; *Putting Pants on Philip* (first as team), 1927; *Two Tars*, 1928; *Liberty*, 1929; *Another Fine Mess*, 1930; *Laughing Gravy*, 1931; *The Music Box* (Academy Award for best comedy short subject, 1931/32), 1932; (features) *Pardon Us*, 1931; *Sons of the Desert*, 1933; *Babes in Toyland*, 1934; *Bonnie Scotland*, 1935; *Blockheads*, 1938; *A Chump at Oxford*, 1940; *The Bullfighters*, 1945; *Riding High* (Hardy only), 1950

Books *The Films of Laurel and Hardy* by William K. Everson; *Mr. Laurel and Mr. Hardy* by John McCabe

PETER LAWFORD

Born Peter Aylen Lawford on September 7, 1923 in London, England
Married to Patricia Kennedy (sister of President John F. Kennedy) in 1954; divorced in 1966; son Christopher born in 1955; daughter Sydney born in 1957; daughter Victoria Frances born in 1959; daughter Robin born in 1961
Married to Mary Rowan (daughter of comedian Dan Rowan) in 1971; divorced in 1973
Married to Deborah Gould in 1976

First Film *Poor Old Bill*, 1931
Major Films include *Mrs. Miniver*, 1942; *The White Cliffs of Dover*, 1944; *Cluny Brown*, 1946; *It Happened in Brooklyn*, 1947; *Good News*, 1947; *Easter Parade*, 1948; *Little Women*, 1949; *Royal Wedding*, 1951; *It Should Happen to You*, 1954; *Exodus*, 1960; *Advise and Consent*, 1962; *Salt and Pepper*, 1968; *That's Entertainment* (narration), 1974

CLORIS LEACHMAN

Born Cloris Leachman on April 30, 1926 in Des Moines, IA
Married to producer/director George Englund in 1953; son Adam born in 1953; son Bryan born in 1954; son George Jr. born in 1956; son Morgan born in 1962; daughter Dinah born in 1966

First Film *Kiss Me Deadly*, 1955
Major Films include *Butch Cassidy and the Sundance Kid*, 1969; *Lovers and Other Strangers*, 1970; *The Last Picture Show*, 1971; *Dillinger*, 1973; *Young Frankenstein*, 1974; *Daisy Miller*, 1974; *High Anxiety*, 1977

Academy Award for best supporting actress: *The Last Picture Show*, 1971

JANET LEIGH

Born Jeanette Helen Morrison on July 26, 1927 in Merced, CA
Married to John K. Carlyle

Cloris Leachman had experienced a moment of fame of a different kind before she went into movies: she had been a runner-up in the 1946 Miss America pageant.

Vivien Leigh, winner of best actress Oscars for *Gone With the Wind* (1939) and *A Streetcar Named Desire* (1951), is seen here with Robert Taylor in the 1940 film *Waterloo Bridge*.

in 1942; annulled in 1942
Married to Stanley Reames in 1946; divorced in 1948
Married to actor Tony Curtis in 1951; divorced in 1962; daughter Kelly born in 1956; daughter Jamie Lee (actress) born in 1958
Married to Robert Brant in 1962

First Film *The Romance of Rosy Ridge*, 1947
Major Films include *Little Women*, 1949; *Holiday Affair*, 1949; *Scaramouche*, 1952; *Prince Valiant*, 1954; *My Sister Eileen*, 1955; *Jet Pilot*, 1957; *Touch of Evil*, 1958; *The Perfect Furlough*, 1959; *Psycho*, 1960; *The Manchurian Candidate*, 1962; *Bye Bye Birdie*, 1963; *An American Dream*, 1966; *One Is a Lonely Number*, 1972; *The Fog*, 1979

Academy Award Nomination for best supporting actress: *Psycho*, 1960

VIVIEN LEIGH

Born Vivian Mary Hartley on November 5, 1913 in Darjeeling, India
Died on July 8, 1967
Married to Herbert Leigh Holman in 1932; divorced in 1937; daughter Suzanne born in 1933
Married to actor Laurence Olivier in 1940; divorced in 1960

First Film *Things Are Looking Up*, 1934
Major Films include *Gentleman's Agreement*, 1935; *A Yank at Oxford*, 1938; *Gone With the Wind*, 1939; *Waterloo Bridge*, 1940; *That Hamilton Woman*, 1941; *Caesar and Cleopatra*, 1945; *Anna Karenina*, 1948; *A Streetcar Named Desire*, 1951; *The Deep Blue Sea*, 1955; *The Roman Spring of Mrs. Stone*, 1961; *Ship of Fools*, 1965

Academy Awards for best actress: *Gone With the Wind*, 1939; *A Streetcar Named Desire*, 1951

Biographies *Vivien Leigh* by Anne Edwards; *The Oliviers* by Felix Barker

JACK LEMMON

Born John Uhler Lemmon III on February 8, 1925 in Boston, MA
Married to Cynthia Stone in 1950; divorced in 1956; son Christopher born in 1954
Married to actress Felicia Farr in 1962; daughter Courtney born in 1966

First Film *It Should Happen to You*, 1954
Major Films include *Mister Roberts*, 1955; *Some Like It Hot*, 1959; *The Apartment*, 1960; *Days of Wine and Roses*, 1962; *Good Neighbor Sam*, 1964; *How to Murder Your Wife*, 1965; *The Odd Couple*, 1968; *Save the Tiger*, 1973; *The China Syndrome*, 1979; *Tribute*, 1980; *Missing*, 1982

Academy Award for best actor: *Save the Tiger*, 1973
Academy Award for best supporting actor: *Mister Roberts*, 1955
Nominations for best actor: *Some Like It Hot*, 1959; *The Apartment*, 1960; *Days of Wine and Roses*, 1962; *The China Syndrome*, 1979; *Tribute*, 1980

Book *The Films of Jack Lemmon* by Joe Baltake

JERRY LEWIS

Born Josef Levitch on March 16, 1926 in Newark, NJ
Married to singer Patti Palmer in 1944; divorced in 1983; son Gary born in 1945; son Ronald born in 1949; son Scott born in 1956; son Christopher born in 1957; son Anthony born in 1959; son Joseph born in 1964
Married to Sandy P. Lewis in 1983

First Film *My Friend Irma*, 1949
Major Films include *Sailor Beware*, 1952; *The*

Jack Lemmon's performance in *The China Syndrome* won him one of his five best actor Oscar nominations. Lemmon won the best actor award in 1973 for *Save the Tiger*.

159

Gina Lollobrigida, pictured here in *Come September* (1961), made her last movie in 1975 and switched careers to become a photographer—working behind instead of in front of a camera.

Caddy, 1953; *Artists and Models*, 1955; *Hollywood or Bust*, 1956; *The Delicate Delinquent*, 1957; *The Bellboy*, 1960; *The Nutty Professor*, 1963; *Which Way to the Front?*, 1970; *King of Comedy*, 1983

Autobiography *Jerry Lewis in Person* (with Herb Gluck), 1982
Book by Lewis *The Complete Film-maker*, 1971

GINA LOLLOBRIGIDA

Born Gina Lollobrigida on July 4, 1928 in Subiaco, Italy
Married to Milko Skofic in 1949; divorced in 1968; son Milko Jr. born in 1957
Married to George Kaufman in 1969

First Film *Elisir d'Amore*, 1946
Major Films include *Fan-*

fan the Tulip, 1952; *Bread, Love and Dreams*, 1954; *Beat the Devil*, 1954; *Trapeze*, 1956; *Come September*, 1961; *Hotel Paradiso*, 1966; *Buona Sera Mrs. Campbell*, 1968; *Bad Man's River*, 1971

CAROLE LOMBARD

Born Jane Alice Peters on October 6, 1908 in Fort Wayne, IN
Died on January 16, 1942 when the plane on which she was returning from a War Bond drive crashed
Married to actor William Powell in 1931; divorced in 1933
Married to actor Clark Gable in 1939

First Film *A Perfect Crime*, 1921
Major Films include *Fast and Loose*, 1930; *Man of the World*, 1931; *No Man of*

Her Own, 1932; *Twentieth Century*, 1934; *Hands Across the Table*, 1935; *My Man Godfrey*, 1936; *True Confession*, 1937; *Nothing Sacred*, 1937; *Made for Each Other*, 1939; *They Knew What They Wanted*, 1940; *To Be or Not To Be*, 1942

Biography *Gable & Lombard* by Warren G. Harris

SOPHIA LOREN

Born Sofia Villani Scicolone on September 20, 1934 in Naples, Italy
Married to producer Carlo Ponti in 1957; annulled in 1962
Remarried to Carlo Ponti in 1966; son Carlo Jr. born in 1968; son Edouardo born in 1973

First Film *Cuori sul Mare*, 1950
Major Films include *Aida*, 1953; *Gold of Naples*, 1954; *Boy on a Dolphin*, 1957; *Houseboat*, 1958; *The*

Black Orchid, 1959; *It Started in Naples*, 1960; *Two Women*, 1961; *Yesterday, Today and Tomorrow*, 1963; *Marriage Italian Style*, 1964; *Arabesque*, 1966; *Man of La Mancha*, 1972; *The Verdict*, 1975; *A Special Day*, 1977; *Revenge*, 1979

Academy Award for best actress: *Two Women*, 1961
Nomination for best actress: *Marriage Italian Style*, 1964

Autobiography *Sophia—Living and Loving: Her Own Story*, 1979
Book *The Films of Sophia Loren* by Tony Crawley

PETER LORRE

Born Laszlo Löwenstein on June 26, 1904 in Rosenberg, Hungary
Died on March 24, 1964
Married to Cecilie Lvovsky in 1933; divorced in 1945
Married to actress Karen Verne in 1945; divorced
Married to Anna Brenning

When Carole Lombard died in a plane crash in 1942, President Roosevelt cabled "...she gave unselfishly of time and talent to serve her government in peace and war. She loved her country...."

Myrna Loy, seen here with Pat O'Brien in *Consolation Marriage* (1931), took a leave of absence from movies during World War II to work for the Red Cross. She was also a U.S. representative to UNESCO.

1975, 1974; *Just Tell Me What You Want*, 1979

Book *The Films of Myrna Loy* by Lawrence J. Quirk

Biography *Lugosi: The Man Behind the Cape* by Robert Cremer

Book *The Films of Bela Lugosi* by Richard Bojarski

BELA LUGOSI

Born Béla Lugosi Blasko on October 20, 1882 in Lugos, Hungary
Died on August 16, 1956
Married to Beatrice Weeks in 1924; divorced
Married to Lillian Arch in 1933; divorced in 1953; son Bela Jr. born in 1934
Married to Hope Lininger in 1955

First Film *A Leopard*, 1917
Major Films include *Dracula*, 1931; *Murders in the Rue Morgue*, 1932; *The Black Cat*, 1934; *Mark of the Vampire*, 1935; *The Raven*, 1935; *Son of Frankenstein*, 1939; *Ninotchka*, 1939; *The Wolf Man*, 1941; *The Body Snatcher*, 1945; *Genius at Work*, 1946; *Abbott and Costello Meet Frankenstein*, 1948; *The Black Sleep*, 1956

IDA LUPINO

Born Ida Lupino on February 4, 1918 in London, England (daughter of actor Stanley Lupino; sister of actress Rita Lupino)
Married to actor Louis Hayward in 1938; divorced in 1945
Married to Columbia executive Collier Young in 1948; divorced in 1950
Married to actor Howard Duff in 1952; divorced; daughter Bridget Marelia

First Film *Her First Affair*, 1933
Major Films include *The Light That Failed*, 1940; *High Sierra*, 1941; *The Sea Wolf*, 1941; *Ladies in Retirement*, 1941; *The Hard Way*, 1943; *In Our Time*, 1944; *Devotion*, 1946; *On Dangerous Ground*, 1952; *The Big Knife*, 1955; *While the City Sleeps*, 1956; *Junior Bonner*, 1972

Ida Lupino came from a family whose theatrical roots dated back to the seventeenth century. Here she stars with Louis Hayward, her husband from 1938 to 1945, in *Ladies in Retirement* (1941).

in 1952; daughter Kathryn born in 1953

First Film *Pioneer in Inoplastadt*, 1928
Major Films include *M*, 1931; *The Man Who Knew Too Much*, 1934; *Mad Love*, 1935; *Crime and Punishment*, 1935; *Secret Agent*, 1936; *Think Fast Mr. Moto*, 1937; *Mr. Moto Takes A Vacation*, 1939; *Strange Cargo*, 1940; *The Maltese Falcon*, 1941; *Casablanca*, 1942; *The Constant Nymph*, 1943; *The Mask of Dimitrios*, 1944; *Confidential Agent*, 1945; *The Verdict*, 1946; *My Favorite Brunette*, 1947; *20,000 Leagues Under the Sea*, 1954; *Silk Stockings*, 1957; *The Big Circus*, 1959; *Voyage to the Bottom of the Sea*, 1961; *The Patsy*, 1964

Book *The Films of Peter Lorre* by Stephen D. Youngkin

MYRNA LOY

Born Myrna Williams on August 2, 1905 in Raidersburg, MT
Married to producer Arthur Hornblow, Jr. in 1936; divorced in 1942
Married to car-rental heir John Hertz, Jr. in 1942; divorced in 1945
Married to screenwriter Gene Markey in 1946; divorced in 1950
Married to Deputy Assistant Secretary of State Howland Sergeant in 1952; divorced in 1960

First Film *Pretty Ladies*, 1925
Major Films include *Don Juan*, 1926; *The Desert Song*, 1929; *Arrowsmith*, 1931; *The Mask of Fu Manchu*, 1932; *The Animal Kingdom*, 1932; *The Thin Man*, 1934; *Broadway Bill*, 1934; *Libeled Lady*, 1936; *After the Thin Man*, 1936; *Double Wedding*, 1938; *Test Pilot*, 1939; *Love Crazy*, 1941; *The Best Years of Our Lives*, 1946; *Mr. Blandings Builds His Dream House*, 1948; *Cheaper by the Dozen*, 1950; *Belles on Their Toes*, 1952; *Lonelyhearts*, 1958; *Midnight Lace*, 1960; *The April Fools*, 1969; *Airport*

Dorothy McGuire with Robert Young in her first movie, *Claudia*, which was made in 1943. Four years later she won a best actress Academy Award nomination for *Gentleman's Agreement* (1947).

JEANETTE MACDONALD

Born Jeanette Ann MacDonald on June 18, 1901 in Philadelphia, PA (sister of actress Blossom MacDonald—known as Blossom Rock and Marie Blake—and dancer Elsie MacDonald)
Died on January 14, 1965
Married to actor Gene Raymond in 1937

First Film *The Love Parade*, 1929
Major Films include *Monte Carlo*, 1930; *Love Me Tonight*, 1932; *The Merry Widow*, 1934; *Naughty Marietta*, 1935; *Rose Marie*, 1936; *San Francisco*, 1936; *Sweethearts*, 1938; *New Moon*, 1940; *I Married an Angel*, 1942; *Follow the Boys*, 1944; *Three Daring Daughters*, 1948; *The Sun Comes Up*, 1949

Book *The Films of Jeanette MacDonald and Nelson Eddy* by Phillip Castanza

DOROTHY MCGUIRE

Born Dorothy Hackett McGuire on June 14, 1918 in Omaha, NE
Married to photographer John Swope in 1943; daughter Mary "Topo" (actress) born in 1944; son Mark born in 1945

First Film *Claudia*, 1943
Major Films include *A Tree Grows in Brooklyn*, 1945; *The Spiral Staircase*, 1946; *Gentleman's Agreement*, 1947; *Three Coins in the Fountain*, 1954; *Friendly Persuasion*, 1956; *A Summer Place*, 1959; *This Earth Is Mine*, 1959; *The Dark at the Top of the Stairs*, 1960; *Swiss Family Robinson*, 1960; *Summer Magic*, 1963; *Flight of the Doves*, 1971; *Jonathan Livingston Seagull* (voice only), 1973

Academy Award Nomination for best actress: *Gentleman's Agreement*, 1947

VICTOR MCLAGLEN

Born Victor McLaglen on December 10, 1886 in Tunbridge Wells, Kent, England (son of a clergyman who later became Bishop of Claremont, South Africa; brother of actors Cyril, Leopold, Clifford, Arthur, and Kenneth McLaglen)
Died on November 7, 1959
Married to Enid Lamont in 1919; widowed in 1942; daughter Sheila born in 1920; son Andrew (director) born in 1921
Married to his secretary Suzanne M. Brueggemann in 1943; divorced in 1948
Married to Margaret Pumphrey in 1948

First Film *The Call of the Road*, 1920
Major Films include *The Glorious Adventure*, 1922; *The Beloved Brute*, 1924; *The Unholy Three*, 1925; *What Price Glory?*, 1926; *A Girl in Every Port*, 1928; *The Black Watch*, 1929; *The Cock-Eyed World*, 1929; *Dishonored*, 1931; *The Lost Patrol*, 1934; *The Informer*, 1935; *Klondike Annie*, 1936; *Under Two Flags*, 1936; *Wee Willie Winkie*, 1937; *Gunga Din*, 1939; *China Girl*, 1943; *The Foxes of Harrow*, 1947; *Fort Apache*, 1948; *She Wore a Yellow Ribbon*, 1949; *Rio Grande*, 1950; *The Quiet Man*, 1952; *Many Rivers to Cross*, 1955; *Sea Fury*, 1958

Academy Award for best actor: *The Informer*, 1935
Nomination for best supporting actor: *The Quiet Man*, 1952

Autobiography *Express to Hollywood*, 1934

SHIRLEY MACLAINE

Born Shirley MacLean Beaty on April 24, 1934 in Richmond, VA (sister of actor Warren Beatty)

Fred MacMurray began his career as a saxophonist but, starting as an extra in films to supplement his income, found himself a movie star instead. He's seen here in *Pushover* (1954), in which he played a detective.

Married to Steve Parker in 1954; divorced in 1984; daughter Stephanie Sachiko (actress) born in 1955

First Film *The Trouble with Harry*, 1955
Major Films include *Around the World in 80 Days*, 1956; *The Matchmaker*, 1958; *Some Came Running*, 1958; *Ask Any Girl*, 1959; *The Apartment*, 1960; *The Children's Hour*, 1961; *Irma La Douce*, 1963; *Gambit*, 1966; *Sweet Charity*, 1969; *Desperate Characters*, 1972; *The Turning Point*, 1977; *Being There*, 1979; *Terms of Endearment*, 1983

Academy Award for best actress: *Terms of Endearment*, 1983
Nominations for best actress: *Some Came Running*, 1958; *The Apartment*, 1960; *Irma La Douce*, 1963; *The Turning Point*, 1977 (*The Other Half of the Sky: A China Memoir*, which MacLaine wrote, produced, and co-directed with Claudia Weill, was nominated for the 1975 Academy Award for best documentary feature.)

Autobiographies *Don't Fall Off the Mountain*, 1970; *You Can Get There From Here*, 1975; *Out on a Limb*, 1983

FRED MACMURRAY

Born Frederick Martin MacMurray on August 30, 1908 in Kankakee, IL
Married to dancer Lillian Lamont in 1936; widowed in 1953; adopted daughter, Susan; adopted son, Robert
Married to actress June

Haver in 1954; adopted twin daughters, Laurie and Katherine

First Film *Girls Gone Wild*, 1926
Major Films include *Friends of Mr. Sweeney*, 1934; *The Gilded Lily*, 1935; *Alice Adams*, 1935; *The Trail of the Lonesome Pine*, 1936; *True Confession*, 1937; *Honeymoon in Bali*, 1939; *No Time for Love*, 1943; *Double Indemnity*, 1944; *The Egg and I*, 1947; *The Caine Mutiny*, 1954; *A Woman's World*, 1955; *The Shaggy Dog*, 1959; *The Apartment*, 1960; *The Absent-Minded Professor*, 1961; *The Happiest Millionaire*, 1967; *The Swarm*, 1978

STEVE MCQUEEN

Born Terrence Stephen McQueen on March 24, 1930 in Slater, MO
Died on November 7, 1980
Married to dancer Neile Adams in 1956; divorced in 1972; daughter Terry born in 1959; son Chadwick born in 1960
Married to actress Ali MacGraw in 1973; divorced
Married to Barbara Minty

First Film *Somebody Up There Likes Me*, 1956
Major Films include *The Great St. Louis Bank Robbery*, 1959; *The Magnificent Seven*, 1960; *The War Lover*, 1962; *The Great Escape*, 1963; *Love With the Proper Stranger*, 1963; *Baby, the Rain Must Fall*, 1965; *The Cincinnati Kid*, 1965; *The Sand Pebbles*, 1966; *Bullitt*, 1969; *Junior Bonner*, 1972; *Papillon*, 1973; *The Towering Inferno*, 1974; *The Hunter*, 1980

Academy Award Nomination for best actor: *The Sand Pebbles*, 1966

Biography *McQueen* by William F. Nolan

ANNA MAGNANI

Born Anna Magnani on March 7, 1907 in Alexandria, Egypt
Died on September 26, 1973
Married to director Goffredo Alessandrini in 1935; separated in 1940; annulled in 1950
Son by actor Massimo Serato born in 1942

First Film *Scampolo*, 1927
Major Films include *Doctor Beware*, 1941; *Open City*, 1945; *Angelina*, 1947; *Bellissima*, 1951; *The Golden Coach*, 1953; *The Rose Tattoo*, 1955; *Wild Is the Wind*, 1957; *The Fugitive Kind*, 1960; *The Secret of Santa Vittoria*, 1969

Academy Award for best actress: *The Rose Tattoo*, 1955

Nomination for best actress: *Wild Is the Wind*, 1957

DOROTHY MALONE

Born Dorothy Eloise Maloney on January 30, 1925 in Chicago, IL
Married to actor Jacques Bergerac in 1959; divorced in 1964; daughter Mimi born in 1960; daughter Diane born in 1961
Married to Robert Tomarkin in 1969; annulled in 1969
Married to Charles H. Bell in 1971

First Film *The Falcon and the Co-Eds*, 1943
Major Films include *The Big Sleep*, 1946; *One Sunday Afternoon*, 1948; *Convicted*, 1950; *Young at Heart*, 1954; *Battle Cry*, 1955; *Written on the Wind*, 1956; *Man of a Thousand Faces*, 1957; *Too Much, Too Soon*, 1958; *Fate Is the Hunter*, 1964; *The Man Who Would Not Die*, 1975; *Winter Kills*, 1979

Steve McQueen starred with Lee Remick in the 1965 movie *Baby, the Rain Must Fall*. The actor, who won an Oscar nomination for best actor for *The Sand Pebbles* in 1966, died in 1980.

Academy Award for best supporting actress: *Written on the Wind*, 1956

FREDRIC MARCH

Born Ernest Frederick McIntyre Bickel on August 31, 1897 in Racine, WI
Died on April 14, 1975
Married to Ellis Baker in 1924; divorced in 1927
Married to actress Florence Eldridge in 1927; adopted daughter, Penelope; adopted son, Anthony

First Film *Paying the Piper*, 1921
Major Films include *Paris Bound*, 1929; *The Royal Family of Broadway*, 1930; *Dr. Jekyll and Mr. Hyde*, 1931; *Strangers in Love*, 1932; *The Eagle and the Hawk*, 1933; *Design for Living*, 1933; *Death Takes a Holiday*, 1934; *The Barretts of Wimpole Street*, 1934; *Les Misérables*, 1935; *Anna Karenina*, 1935; *Anthony Adverse*, 1936; *A Star Is Born*, 1937; *Nothing Sacred*, 1937; *I Married a Witch*, 1942; *The Best Years of Our Lives*, 1946; *Death of a Salesman*, 1951; *The Desperate Hours*, 1955; *The Man in the Gray Flannel Suit*, 1956; *Inherit the Wind*, 1960; *Hombre*, 1967

Academy Awards for best actor: *Dr. Jekyll and Mr. Hyde*, 1931/32; *The Best Years of Our Lives*, 1946
Nominations for best actor: *The Royal Family of Broadway*, 1930/31; *A Star Is Born*, 1937; *Death of a Salesman*, 1951

Book *The Films of Fredric March*, by Lawrence J. Quirk

DEAN MARTIN

Born Dino Paul Crocetti on June 17, 1917 in Steubenville, OH
Married to Betty McDonald in 1940; divorced in 1949; daughter Gail born in 1941; daughter Deana born in 1942; son Craig born in 1943; daughter Claudia born in 1946
Married to model Jeanne Bieggers in 1949; divorced in 1969; son Dean "Dino" born in 1951; son Ricci born in 1953; daughter Gina born in 1956
Married to Kathy Hawn in 1973; divorced in 1976

First Film *My Friend Irma*, 1949
Major Films include *The Stooge*, 1952; *The Caddy*, 1953; *Pardners*, 1956; *Some Came Running*, 1959; *Rio Bravo*, 1959; *Toys in the Attic*, 1963; *The Silencers*, 1966; *Airport*, 1970; *Showdown*, 1973; *Mr. Ricco*, 1975

Biography *Everybody Loves Somebody Sometime* by Arthur Marx

LEE MARVIN

Born Lee Marvin on February 19, 1924 in New York City, NY
Married to Betty Edeling in 1951; divorced in 1967; son Christopher born in 1952; daughter Courtenay born in 1954; daughter Cynthia born in 1956; daughter Claudia born in 1958
Married to Pamela Freeley in 1970; divorced

First Film *You're in the Navy Now*, 1951
Major Films include *Eight Iron Men*, 1952; *The Wild One*, 1954; *The Caine Mutiny*, 1954; *Attack!*, 1956; *The Man Who Shot Liberty Valance*, 1962; *The Killers*, 1964; *Ship of Fools*, 1965; *Cat Ballou*, 1965; *The Dirty Dozen*, 1967; *Paint Your Wagon*, 1969; *The Iceman Cometh*, 1973; *The Great Scout and Cathouse Thursday*, 1976; *The Big Red One*, 1979

Academy Award for best actor: *Cat Ballou*, 1965

THE MARX BROTHERS

CHICO MARX
Born Leonard Marx on March 22, 1887 in New York City, NY
Died on October 11, 1961
Married to Betty Karp in 1910; divorced; daughter Maxine born in 1911
Married to Mary Divithas in 1958

GROUCHO MARX
Born Julius Henry Marx on October 2, 1890 in New York City, NY
Died on August 19, 1977
Married to Ruth Johnson in 1920; divorced in 1942; son Arthur (writer) born in 1925; daughter Miriam born in 1932
Married to Katherine Marvis in 1945; divorced in 1951; daughter Melinda born in 1945
Married to Eden Hartford in 1954; divorced in 1970

Special Academy Award "in recognition of his brilliant creativity and for the unequalled achievements of the Marx Brothers in the art of motion picture comedy," 1973

Autobiographies *Groucho and Me*, 1959; *Memoirs of a Mangy Lover*, 1964; *The Groucho Letters*, 1967

HARPO MARX
Born Adolph "Arthur" Marx on November 23, 1888 in New York City, NY
Died on September 28, 1964
Married to Susan Fleming in 1936; adopted children, William; Alexander; twins Minnie and James

Lee Marvin squares up to Gene Hackman in *Prime Cut* (1972). Marvin won a best actor Academy Award for his performance as a drunken has-been gunslinger in the 1965 movie *Cat Ballou*.

James Mason in *The Desert Fox* (1951). Three years later Mason was nominated for the best actor Oscar for his performance in *A Star Is Born* (1954). He was also nominated twice for best supporting actor.

Autobiography *Harpo Speaks!*, 1961

ZEPPO MARX
Born Herbert Marx on February 25, 1901 in New York City, NY
Died on November 30, 1979
Married to Marian Benda in 1927; divorced in 1954; son Timothy born in 1928
Married to Barbara Blakely in 1959; divorced

First Film (Harpo) *Too Many Kisses*, 1925
First Film (The Marx Brothers) *The Cocoanuts*, 1929
Major Films include *Animal Crackers*, 1930; *Horse Feathers*, 1932; *Duck Soup* (Zeppo's last appearance), 1933; *A Night at the Opera*, 1935; *Room Service*, 1938; *The Big Store*, 1941; *The Story of Mankind* (not as team), 1957; *Skidoo* (Groucho only), 1968

Note: Gummo (Milton) Marx appeared with his brothers in vaudeville but left the act before it reached Broadway or Hollywood.

JAMES MASON

Born James Neville Mason on May 15, 1909 in Huddersfield, England
Died on July 27, 1984
Married to actress Pamela Ostrer Kellino in 1940; divorced in 1964; daughter Portland born in 1948; son Alexander Morgan born in 1949
Married to Clarissa Kaye in 1971

First Film *Late Extra*, 1935
Major Films include *The Mill on the Floss*, 1937; *I Met a Murderer*, 1939; *The Man in Grey*, 1943; *The Seventh Veil*, 1945; *Odd Man Out*, 1947; *The Reckless Moment*, 1949; *The Desert Fox*, 1951; *The Prisoner of Zenda*, 1952; *Julius Caesar*, 1953; *A Star Is Born*, 1954; *20,000 Leagues Under the Sea*, 1954; *North by Northwest*, 1959; *Journey to the Center of the Earth*, 1959; *Lolita*, 1962; *Lord Jim*, 1965; *Georgy Girl*, 1966; *Mandingo*, 1975; *Heaven Can Wait*, 1978; *Murder by Decree*, 1979; *The Verdict*, 1982

Academy Award Nomination for best actor: *A Star Is Born*, 1954
Nominations for best supporting actor: *Georgy Girl*, 1966; *The Verdict*, 1982

Autobiography *Cats in Our Lives* (with Pamela Kellino Mason)
Book *The Films of James Mason* by Clive Hirschhorn

WALTER MATTHAU

Born Walter Matuschanskavasky on October 1, 1920 in New York City, NY
Married to Grace Geraldine Johnson in 1948; divorced in 1958; son David born in 1949; daughter Jennifer born in 1950
Married to Carol Grace Marcus Saroyan in 1959; son Charles born in 1960

First Film *The Kentuckian*, 1955
Major Films include *Bigger Than Life*, 1956; *King Creole*, 1958; *Lonely Are the Brave*, 1962; *Charade*, 1963; *The Fortune Cookie*, 1966; *The Odd Couple*, 1968; *Hello, Dolly!*, 1969; *Cactus Flower*, 1969; *Kotch*, 1971; *Pete 'n' Tillie*, 1972; *The Taking of Pelham One Two Three*, 1974; *The Front Page*, 1974; *The Sunshine Boys*, 1975; *The Bad News Bears*, 1976; *House Calls*, 1978; *First Monday in October*, 1981; *I Ought to Be in Pictures*, 1982

Academy Award for best supporting actor: *The Fortune Cookie*, 1966
Nominations for best actor: *Kotch*, 1971; *The Sunshine Boys*, 1975

BURGESS MEREDITH

Born Burgess George Meredith on November 16, 1908 in Cleveland, OH
Married to Helen Derby in 1932; divorced in 1935
Married to Margaret Perry in 1936; divorced in 1938
Married to actress Paulette Goddard in 1943; divorced in 1948
Married to Kaja Sundsten in 1949; son Jonathan born

Burgess Meredith, who has been making movies since 1936, is shown here in his role as an aging and bitter Monsignor in the 1981 release *True Confessions*.

in 1950; daughter Tala Beth born in 1952

First Film *Winterset*, 1936
Major Films include *Idiot's Delight*, 1939; *Castle on the Hudson*, 1940; *Of Mice and Men*, 1940; *That Uncertain Feeling*, 1941; *Tom, Dick and Harry*, 1941; *The Story of G.I. Joe*, 1945; *The Diary of a Chambermaid*, 1946; *Mine Own Executioner*, 1947; *The Man on the Eiffel Tower*, 1949; *Advise and Consent*, 1962; *The Cardinal*, 1963; *In Harm's Way*, 1965; *Madame X*, 1966; *Hurry Sundown*, 1967; *Mackenna's Gold*, 1969; *The Reivers* (narration only), 1969; *There Was a Crooked Man*, 1970; *The Day of the Locust*, 1975; *Rocky*, 1976; *Foul Play*, 1978; *Rocky II*, 1979; *True Confessions*, 1981; *Rocky III*, 1982

Academy Award Nominations for best supporting actor: *The Day of the Locust*, 1975; *Rocky*, 1976

ETHEL MERMAN

Born Ethel Agnes Zimmermann on January 16, 1909 in Astoria, NY
Died on February 15, 1984
Married to agent William B. Smith in 1940; divorced in 1941
Married to Robert D. Levitt in 1941; divorced in 1952; daughter Ethel born in 1942; son Robert Jr. born in 1943
Married to Robert F. Six in 1953; divorced in 1960
Married to actor Ernest Borgnine in 1964; divorced in 1964

First Film *Follow the Leader*, 1930

Major Films include *Kid Millions*, 1934; *The Big Broadcast of 1936*, 1935; *Anything Goes*, 1936; *Alexander's Ragtime Band*, 1938; *Call Me Madam*, 1953; *There's No Business Like Show Business*, 1954; *It's a Mad Mad Mad Mad World*, 1963; *The Art of Love*, 1965; *Rudolph and Frosty's Christmas in July* (voice only), 1979

Autobiographies *Who Could Ask for Anything More?*, 1955; *Merman—An Autobiography* (with George Eells), 1978

RAY MILLAND

Born Reginald Truscott-Jones on January 3, 1905 in Neath, Glamorgan, Wales
Married to Muriel Webster in 1931; son Daniel David born in 1940; daughter Victoria Francesca born in 1941

First Film *The Plaything*, 1929
Major Films include *Payment Deferred*, 1932; *The Gilded Lily*, 1935; *Next Time We Love*, 1936; *Easy Living*, 1937; *Everything Happens at Night*, 1939; *The Major and the Minor*, 1942; *Ministry of Fear*, 1944; *The Lost Weekend*, 1945; *Kitty*, 1946; *The Big Clock*, 1948; *Night into Morning*, 1951; *The Thief*, 1952; *Dial M for Murder*, 1954; *Love Story*, 1970; *The Last Tycoon*, 1976; *Oliver's Story*, 1978

Academy Award for best actor: *The Lost Weekend*, 1945

Autobiography *Wide-Eyed in Babylon*, 1974

ANN MILLER

Born Lucille Ann Collier on April 12, 1923 in Chireno, TX
Married to millionaire Reese L. Milner in 1946; divorced in 1947
Married to Texas oilman William Moss in 1958; divorced in 1961
Married to Texas oilman Arthur Cameron in 1961; annulled in 1962

First Film *Anne of Green Gables*, 1934
Major Films include *Stage Door*, 1937; *You Can't Take It With You*, 1938; *Too Many Girls*, 1940; *Carolina Blues*, 1944; *Easter Parade*, 1948; *On the Town*, 1949; *Kiss Me Kate*, 1953; *Deep in My Heart*, 1954; *Hit the Deck*, 1955; *The Great American Pastime*, 1956

Autobiography *Miller's High Life*, 1972

LIZA MINNELLI

Born Liza May Minnelli on March 12, 1946 in Los Angeles, CA (daughter of actress Judy Garland and director Vincente Minnelli)
Married to entertainer Peter Allen in 1967; divorced in 1972
Married to producer Jack Haley, Jr. in 1974; divorced in 1978
Married to Mark Gero in 1979

First Film *In the Good Old Summertime*, 1947
Major Films include *Charlie Bubbles*, 1967; *The Sterile Cuckoo*, 1969; *Tell Me That You Love Me, Junie Moon*, 1970; *Cabaret*, 1972; *New York, New York*, 1977; *Arthur*, 1981

Academy Award for best actress: *Cabaret*, 1972
Nomination for best actress: *The Sterile Cuckoo*, 1969

Biography *Liza!* by James R. Parrish, 1975

ROBERT MITCHUM

Born Robert Charles Duran Mitchum on August 6, 1917 in Bridgeport, CT

Liza Minnelli imparts some of her highly-colored views on life to Marisa Berenson in *Cabaret*, the 1972 musical film version of Christopher Isherwood's *I Am a Camera*. The role won Minnelli an Oscar.

Marilyn Monroe as her admirers love to remember her—the most dazzling of the movie world's dizzy blondes.

Married to Dorothy Spencer in 1940; daughter Petrine; son Jim (actor); son Chris (actor)

First Film *Hoppy Serves a Writ*, 1943
Major Films include *The Story of G.I. Joe*, 1945; *Till the End of Time*, 1946; *Crossfire*, 1947; *Out of the Past*, 1947; *Rachel and the Stranger*, 1948; *Blood on the Moon*, 1948; *His Kind of Woman*, 1951; *River of No Return*, 1954; *Not as a Stranger*, 1955; *The Night of the Hunter*, 1955; *Heaven Knows, Mr. Allison*, 1957; *Thunder Road*, 1958; *The Sundowners*, 1960; *El Dorado*, 1967; *Ryan's Daughter*, 1970; *The Friends of Eddie Coyle*, 1973; *Farewell, My Lovely*, 1975; *Midway*, 1976; *That Championship Season*, 1982

Academy Award Nomination for best supporting actor: *The Story of G.I. Joe*, 1945

Biography *Robert Mitchum* by George Eells
Book *Robert Mitchum on the Screen* by Alvin H. Marill

MARILYN MONROE

Born Norma Jean Baker on June 1, 1926 in Los Angeles, CA
Died on August 5, 1962
Married to Jim Dougherty in 1944; divorced in 1946
Married to baseball player Joe DiMaggio in 1954; divorced in 1955
Married to playwright Arthur Miller in 1956; divorced in 1961

First Film *Scudda Hoo! Scudda Hay!*, 1948
Major Films include *The Asphalt Jungle*, 1950; *All About Eve*, 1950; *Niagara*, 1953; *Gentlemen Prefer Blondes*, 1953; *How to Marry a Millionaire*, 1953; *The Seven Year Itch*, 1955; *Bus Stop*, 1956; *The Prince and the Showgirl*, 1957; *Some Like It Hot*, 1959; *The Misfits*, 1961

Biography *Norma Jean* by Fred Lawrence Guiles
Books *Screen Greats: Monroe* by M. Samuels; *Monroe—Her Life in Pictures* by James Spada

ROBERT MONTGOMERY

Born Henry Montgomery, Jr. on May 21, 1904 in Beacon, NY
Died on September 27, 1981
Married to Elizabeth Bryan Allen in 1928; divorced in 1950; son Robert Jr. born in 1930; daughter Elizabeth (actress) born in 1933
Married to Elizabeth Grant Harkness in 1950

First Film *The Single Standard*, 1929
Major Films include *Their Own Desire*, 1929; *The Big House*, 1930; *Inspiration*, 1931; *Private Lives*, 1931; *Letty Lynton*, 1932; *Riptide*, 1934; *Piccadilly Jim*, 1936; *Night Must Fall*, 1937; *The Earl of Chicago*, 1940; *Here Comes Mr. Jordan*, 1941; *They Were Expendable*, 1945; *Lady in the Lake*, 1946; *June Bride*, 1948; *Once More My Darling*, 1949; *Your Witness*, 1950

Academy Award Nominations for best actor: *Night Must Fall*, 1937; *Here Comes Mr. Jordan*, 1941

MARY TYLER MOORE

Born Mary Tyler Moore on December 29, 1937 in Brooklyn, NY
Married to Richard Meeker in 1960; divorced; son Richard Jr. born in 1961 (died in 1980)
Married to television executive Grant Tinker in 1963; divorced in 1981
Married to doctor S. Robert Levine in 1984

First Film *X-15*, 1961
Major Films include *Thoroughly Modern Millie*, 1967; *Don't Just Stand There!*, 1968; *What's So Bad About Feeling Good?*, 1968; *Change of Habit*, 1969; *Ordinary People*, 1980; *Six Weeks*, 1982

Academy Award Nomination for best actress: *Ordinary People*, 1980

ROGER MOORE

Born Roger Moore on October 14, 1928 in London,

British actor Roger Moore as super-hero James Bond, the role he took over from (and later gave back to) another British actor, Sean Connery. Here, Moore plays 007 in *Octopussy* (1983).

Paul Muni faces significant odds in one of his early movies, *Scarface* (1932). Muni won a best actor Academy Award for *The Story of Louis Pasteur* in 1936, and has been nominated four times.

England
Married to Doorn Van Steyn; divorced in 1953
Married to singer Dorothy Squires in 1953; divorced in 1969
Married to Luisa Mattioli in 1969; daughter Deborah; son Geoffrey; son Christian

First Film *Caesar and Cleopatra*, 1945
Major Films include *Interrupted Melody*, 1955; *Diane*, 1956; *The Sins of Rachel Cade*, 1961; *Live and Let Die*, 1973; *The Man With the Golden Gun*, 1974; *The Spy Who Loved Me*, 1977; *Moonraker*, 1979; *For Your Eyes Only*, 1981; *Octopussy*, 1983

PAUL MUNI

Born Muni Weisenfreund on September 22, 1895 in Lemberg, Austria (later Lwow, Poland; now Lvov, USSR)
Died on August 28, 1967
Married to Bella Finkle in 1921

First Film *The Valiant*, 1929
Major Films include *Scar-*

face, 1932; *I Am a Fugitive from a Chain Gang*, 1932; *Bordertown*, 1935; *The Story of Louis Pasteur*, 1936; *The Good Earth*, 1937; *The Life of Emile Zola*, 1937; *Juarez*, 1939; *Hudson's Bay*, 1941; *The Commandos Strike at Dawn*, 1943; *A Song to Remember*, 1945; *The Last Angry Man*, 1959

Academy Award for best actor: *The Story of Louis Pasteur*, 1936
Nominations for best actor: *The Valiant*, 1928/29; *I Am a Fugitive From a Chain Gang*, 1931/32; *The Life of Emile Zola*, 1937; *The Last Angry Man*, 1959

Biography *Actor—The Life and Times of Paul Muni* by Jerome Lawrence

PATRICIA NEAL

Born Patricia Louise Neal on January 20, 1926 in Packard, KY
Married to writer Roald Dahl in 1953; divorced in 1983; daughter Olivia (died in 1962); daughter Tessa Sophia; son Theodore

Matthew Roald born in 1960; daughter Ophelia Magdalene born in 1964; daughter Lucille Neal born in 1965

First Film *John Loves Mary*, 1949
Major Films include *The Fountainhead*, 1949; *The Breaking Point*, 1950; *The Day the Earth Stood Still*, 1951; *Diplomatic Courier*, 1952; *A Face in the Crowd*, 1957; *Breakfast at Tiffany's*, 1961; *Hud*, 1963; *In Harm's Way*, 1965; *The Subject Was Roses*, 1968; *Happy Mother's Day, Love George*, 1973; *The Passage*, 1979; *Ghost Story*, 1981

Academy Award for best actress: *Hud*, 1963
Nomination for best actress: *The Subject Was Roses*, 1968

Biography *Pat and Roald* by Barry Farrell

PAUL NEWMAN

Born Paul L. Newman on January 26, 1925 in Cleveland, OH
Married to actress Jacqueline Witte in 1947; di-

vorced in 1956; son Allan Scott born in 1950 (acted under name of William Scott; died in 1978); daughter Susan born in 1951; daughter Stephanie born in 1952
Married to actress Joanne Woodward in 1958; daughter Elinor Terese born in 1959; daughter Melissa Stewart born in 1960; daughter Clea Olivia born in 1961

First Film *Silver Chalice*, 1955
Major Films include *Somebody Up There Likes Me*, 1956; *The Long Hot Summer*, 1958; *Cat on a Hot Tin Roof*, 1958; *From the Terrace*, 1960; *The Hustler*, 1961; *Hud*, 1963; *Harper*, 1966; *Cool Hand Luke*, 1967; *Butch Cassidy and the Sundance Kid*, 1969; *The Sting*, 1972; *The Towering Inferno*, 1974; *Slap Shot*, 1977; *Absence of Malice*, 1981; *The Verdict*, 1982

Academy Award Nominations for best actor: *Cat on a Hot Tin Roof*, 1958; *The Hustler*, 1961; *Hud*, 1963; *Cool Hand Luke*, 1967; *Absence of Malice*, 1981; *The Verdict*, 1982

Paul Newman totes a gun again in *Hombre* (1967). Over the course of his career Newman has racked up six Academy Award nominations for best actor, the last being for *The Verdict* in 1982.

Jack Nicholson, who specializes in sinister or unpredictable characters, runs true to form in the 1981 remake of *The Postman Always Rings Twice*, in which he starred opposite Jessica Lange.

JACK NICHOLSON

Born Jack Nicholson on April 22, 1937 in Neptune, NJ
Married to Sandra Knight in 1961; divorced in 1966; daughter Jennifer born in 1963

First Film *The Cry Baby Killer*, 1958
Major Films include *The Raven*, 1963; *Easy Rider*, 1969; *On a Clear Day You Can See Forever*, 1970; *Five Easy Pieces*, 1970; *Carnal Knowledge*, 1971; *The Last Detail*, 1973; *Chinatown*, 1974; *The Passenger*, 1975; *Tommy*, 1975; *One Flew Over the Cuckoo's Nest*, 1975; *Goin' South*, 1978; *The Shining*, 1980; *The Postman Always Rings Twice*, 1981; *Reds*, 1981; *Terms of Endearment*, 1983

Academy Award for best actor: *One Flew Over the Cuckoo's Nest*, 1975
Academy Award for best supporting actor: *Terms of Endearment*, 1983

Nominations for best actor: *Five Easy Pieces*, 1970; *The Last Detail*, 1973; *Chinatown*, 1974
Nominations for best supporting actor: *Easy Rider*, 1969; *Reds*, 1981

DAVID NIVEN

Born James David Graham Niven on March 1, 1909 in Kirriemuir, Angus, Scotland
Died on July 29, 1983
Married to Primula Rollo in 1940; widowed in 1946; son James born in 1942; son David Jr. born in 1945
Married to Hjordis Tersmeden in 1948; adopted daughter, Kristina; adopted daughter, Fiona

First Film *Mutiny on the Bounty*, 1935
Major Films include *The Charge of the Light Brigade*, 1936; *Dinner at the Ritz*, 1937; *The Dawn Patrol*, 1938; *Wuthering Heights*, 1938; *Bachelor Mother*, 1939; *The First of the Few*, 1942; *Stairway to Heaven*, 1946; *The Elusive Pimpernel*, 1950; *The Moon Is Blue*, 1953; *Around the World in 80 Days*, 1956; *Separate Tables*, 1958; *Please Don't Eat the Daisies*, 1960; *The Guns of Navarone*, 1961; *The Pink Panther*, 1964; *Casino Royale*, 1967; *Murder by Death*, 1976; *Death on the Nile*, 1978; *Curse of the Pink Panther*, 1983

Academy Award for best actor: *Separate Tables*, 1958

Autobiographies *The Moon's a Balloon*, 1971; *Bring on the Empty Horses*, 1975

KIM NOVAK

Born Marilyn Pauline Novak on February 13, 1933 in Chicago, IL
Married to actor Richard Johnson in 1965; divorced in 1966
Married to veterinarian Robert Mallory in 1976

First Film *The French Line*, 1954
Major Films include *The Man With the Golden Arm*, 1955; *Picnic*, 1955; *The Eddie Duchin Story*, 1956; *Jeanne Eagels*, 1957; *Pal Joey*, 1957; *Vertigo*, 1958; *Bell, Book and Candle*, 1958; *Middle of the Night*, 1959; *The Notorious Landlady*, 1962; *Of Human Bondage*, 1964; *The Amorous Adventures of Moll Flanders*, 1965; *Just a Gigolo*, 1979; *The Mirror Crack'd*, 1980

MERLE OBERON

Born Estelle Merle O'Brien Thompson on February 19, 1911 in Tasmania, Australia
Died on November 23, 1979
Married to producer Alexander Korda in 1939; divorced in 1945
Married to cinematographer Lucien Ballard in 1945; divorced in 1949
Married to Bruno Pagliai in 1957; divorced in 1973; adopted son, Bruno Jr.; adopted daughter, Francesca
Married to actor Robert Wolders in 1973

First Film *Alf's Button*, 1930

David Niven, winner of the 1958 best actor Oscar for his performance in *Separate Tables*, plays here opposite Shirley MacLaine in *Around the World in 80 Days* (1956).

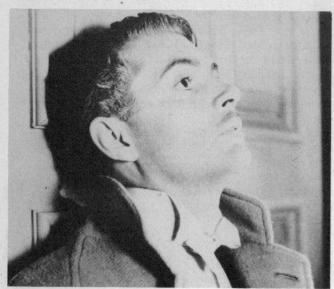

Laurence Olivier, one of the greatest classical actors of stage and screen, strikes a classic attitude in *Rebecca* (1940).

Major Films include *The Private Life of Henry VIII*, 1933; *The Scarlet Pimpernel*, 1935; *The Dark Angel*, 1935; *These Three*, 1936; *Beloved Enemy*, 1936; *Wuthering Heights*, 1939; *Till We Meet Again*, 1940; *That Uncertain Feeling*, 1941; *The Lodger*, 1944; *A Song to Remember*, 1945; *Berlin Express*, 1948; *Desirée*, 1954; *Deep in My Heart*, 1954; *The Price of Fear*, 1956; *The Oscar*, 1966; *Hotel*, 1967; *Interval*, 1973

Academy Award Nomination for best actress: *The Dark Angel*, 1935

MAUREEN O'HARA

Born Maureen FitzSimmons on August 17, 1920 in Millwall (near Dublin), Ireland
Married to director George Hanley Brown in 1938; annulled in 1941
Married to director Will Price in 1941; divorced in 1953; daughter Bronwyn born in 1944

Married to Charles F. Blair, Jr. in 1968 (first pilot to fly solo over the Arctic Ocean and the North Pole); widowed in 1978

First Film *Kicking the Moon Around*, 1938
Major Films include *The Hunchback of Notre Dame*, 1939; *How Green Was My Valley*, 1941; *The Black Swan*, 1942; *This Land Is Mine*, 1943; *Miracle on 34th Street*, 1947; *Sitting Pretty*, 1948; *Rio Grande*, 1950; *The Quiet Man*, 1952; *The Long Gray Line*, 1955; *Our Man in Havana*, 1959; *The Parent Trap*, 1961; *Mr. Hobbs Takes a Vacation*, 1962; *Spencer's Mountain*, 1963; *Big Jake*, 1971

LAURENCE OLIVIER

Born Laurence Kerr Olivier on May 22, 1907 in Dorking, Surrey, England
Married to actress Jill Esmond in 1930; divorced in 1940; son Tarquin born in 1936
Married to actress Vivien Leigh in 1940; divorced in 1960
Married to actress Joan Plowright in 1961; son Richard born in 1961; daughter Tamsin born in 1963; daughter Julie-Kate born in 1966

First Film *The Temporary Widow*, 1930
Major Films include *Westward Passage*, 1932; *As You Like It*, 1936; *Fire Over England*, 1937; *Wuthering Heights*, 1939; *Rebecca*, 1940; *Pride and Prejudice*, 1940; *That Hamilton Woman*, 1941; *Henry V*, 1944; *Hamlet*, 1948; *Carrie*, 1952; *Richard III*, 1956; *The Prince and the Showgirl*, 1957; *The Entertainer*, 1960; *Spartacus*, 1960; *Othello*, 1965; *The Shoes of the Fisherman*, 1968; *Nicholas and Alexandra*, 1971; *Sleuth*, 1972; *Marathon Man*, 1976; *The Boys From Brazil*, 1978; *A Little Romance*, 1979; *Clash of the Titans*, 1981; *The Jigsaw Man*, 1984

Academy Award for best actor: *Hamlet*, 1948
Academy Award for best supporting actor: *Marathon Man*, 1976
Nominations for best actor: *Wuthering Heights*, 1939; *Rebecca*, 1940; *Henry V*, 1946; *Richard III*, 1956; *The Entertainer*, 1960; *Othello*, 1965; *Sleuth*, 1972; *The Boys From Brazil*, 1978
Nomination for best director: *Hamlet*, 1948
Special Academy Awards "for his outstanding achievement as actor, producer and director in bringing *Henry V* to the screen," 1946; "for the full body of his work, for the unique achievements of his entire career and his lifetime of contribution to the art of film," 1978

Knighted in 1947; elevated to the peerage in 1970

Autobiography *Confessions of an Actor*, 1982

PETER O'TOOLE

Born Peter Seamus O'Toole on August 2, 1933 in Connemara, Ireland
Married to actress Sian Phillips in 1959; divorced in 1979; daughter Catherine born in 1960; daugh-

Peter O'Toole is seen here as King Henry II in *Becket* (1964). Both O'Toole and Richard Burton, who played Becket, won best actor Academy Award nominations for their roles.

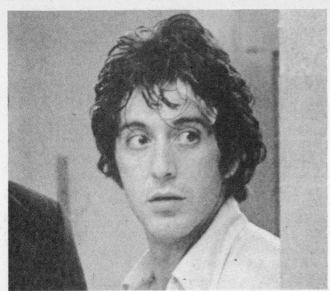

Al Pacino in *Dog Day Afternoon* (1975), for which he won a best actor Oscar nomination. He was also nominated for *Serpico* (1973); *The Godfather, Part II* (1974); and . . . *And Justice for All* (1979).

ter Patricia born in 1963
Son Lorcan Patrick by Karen Brown born in 1983

First Film *The Savage Innocents*, 1960
Major Films include *Kidnapped*, 1960; *Lawrence of Arabia*, 1962; *Becket*, 1964; *Lord Jim*, 1965; *How to Steal a Million*, 1966; *The Lion in Winter*, 1968; *Goodbye, Mr. Chips*, 1969; *The Ruling Class*, 1972; *Caligula*, 1977; *The Stuntman*, 1980; *My Favorite Year*, 1982

Academy Award Nominations for best actor: *Lawrence of Arabia*, 1962; *Becket*, 1964; *The Lion in Winter*, 1968; *Goodbye, Mr. Chips*, 1969; *The Ruling Class*, 1972; *The Stuntman*, 1980; *My Favorite Year*, 1982

AL PACINO

Born Alberto Pacino on April 25, 1940 in New York City, NY
Reported married to Joanne-Alex Skylar in 1976; marriage reported a hoax

in 1976

First Film *Me Natalie*, 1969
Major Films include *The Panic in Needle Park*, 1971; *The Godfather*, 1972; *Serpico*, 1973; *The Godfather, Part II*, 1974; *Scarecrow*, 1974; *Dog Day Afternoon*, 1975; *Bobby Deerfield*, 1977; . . . *And Justice for All*, 1979; *Cruising*, 1980; *Author! Author!*, 1982; *Scarface*, 1983

Academy Award Nominations for best actor: *Serpico*, 1973; *The Godfather, Part II*, 1974; *Dog Day Afternoon*, 1975; . . . *And Justice for All*, 1979
Nomination for best supporting actor: *The Godfather*, 1972

JACK PALANCE

Born Walter Jack Palahnuik on February 18, 1919 in Lattimer, PA
Married to Virginia Baker in 1949; divorced in 1966; daughter Holly born in 1950; daughter Brook Gabrielle born in 1951; son

Cody John born in 1955

First Film *Panic in the Streets*, 1950
Major Films include *Sudden Fear*, 1952; *Shane*, 1953; *Arrowhead*, 1953; *Sign of the Pagan*, 1954; *The Big Knife*, 1955; *I Died a Thousand Times*, 1955; *Attack!*, 1956; *The Lonely Man*, 1957; *Ten Seconds to Hell*, 1959; *Contempt*, 1963; *The Professionals*, 1966; *The Desperados*, 1969; *The Horseman*, 1971; *Chato's Land*, 1972; *Oklahoma Crude*, 1973; *The Shape of Things to Come*, 1979

Academy Award Nominations for best supporting actor: *Sudden Fear*, 1952; *Shane*, 1953

GREGORY PECK

Born Eldred Gregory Peck on April 5, 1916 in La Jolla, CA
Married to Greta Rice Konen in 1942; divorced in 1955; son Stephen born in 1944; son Jonathan born in 1946 (died in 1954); son Carey born in 1949

Married to Veronique Passani in 1955; son Anthony born in 1956; daughter Cecilia born in 1958

First Film *Days of Glory*, 1944
Major Films include *The Keys of the Kingdom*, 1945; *Spellbound*, 1945; *The Yearling*, 1946; *The Macomber Affair*, 1947; *Gentleman's Agreement*, 1947; *Twelve O'Clock High*, 1949; *The Gunfighter*, 1950; *The Snows of Kilimanjaro*, 1952; *Roman Holiday*, 1953; *The Man in the Gray Flannel Suit*, 1956; *The Big Country*, 1958; *The Guns of Navarone*, 1961; *To Kill a Mockingbird*, 1962; *MacArthur*, 1977; *The Boys From Brazil*, 1978

Academy Award for best actor: *To Kill a Mockingbird*, 1962
Nominations for best actor: *The Keys of the Kingdom*, 1945; *The Yearling*, 1946; *Gentleman's Agreement*, 1947; *Twelve O'Clock High*, 1949
Jean Hersholt Humanitarian Award, 1967

Autobiography *An Actor's Life*, 1978

Gregory Peck as novelist F. Scott Fitzgerald and Deborah Kerr as Hollywood columnist Sheilah Graham in *Beloved Infidel* (1959). The film is based on Graham's efforts to curb Fitzgerald's alcoholism.

In *Psycho II* (1983), Anthony Perkins as Norman Bates returns to the infamous Bates Motel after a sojourn in a mental institution. This sequel to the classic 1960 chiller has ample shock value itself.

ANTHONY PERKINS

Born Anthony Perkins on April 4, 1932 in New York City, NY (son of actor Osgood Perkins)
Married to photographer Berinthia Berenson (sister of actress Marisa Berenson) in 1973; son Osgood Robert born in 1974; son Elvis Brooke born in 1976

First Film *The Actress*, 1953
Major Films include *Friendly Persuasion*, 1956; *Fear Strikes Out*, 1957; *The Matchmaker*, 1958; *Psycho*, 1960; *The Trial*, 1962; *Pretty Poison*, 1968; *Catch-22*, 1970; *Play It As It Lays*, 1972; *Murder on the Orient Express*, 1974; *Mahogany*, 1975; *The Black Hole*, 1979; *Psycho II*, 1983

Academy Award Nomination for best supporting actor: *Friendly Persuasion*, 1956

WALTER PIDGEON

Born Walter David Pidgeon on September 23, 1897 in East St. John, New Brunswick, Canada
Died on September 25, 1984
Married to artist Edna Pickles in 1922; widowed in 1923; daughter Edna Verne born in 1923
Married to Ruth Walker in 1930

First Film *Mannequin*, 1926
Major Films include *Bride of the Regiment*, 1930; *Too Hot to Handle*, 1938; *Man Hunt*, 1941; *How Green Was My Valley*, 1941; *Mrs. Miniver*, 1942; *Madame Curie*, 1943; *Mrs. Parkington*, 1944; *The Secret Heart*, 1946; *Command Decision*, 1948; *That Forsyte Woman*, 1949; *Forbidden Planet*, 1956; *Advise and Consent*, 1962; *Funny Girl*, 1968; *Skyjacked*, 1972; *Harry in Your Pocket*, 1973

Academy Award Nominations for best actor: *Mrs. Miniver*, 1942; *Madame Curie*, 1943

CHRISTOPHER PLUMMER

Born Arthur Christopher Orme Plummer on December 13, 1929 in Toronto, Ontario, Canada
Married to actress Tammy Grimes in 1956; divorced in 1960; daughter Amanda (actress) born in 1957
Married to journalist Patricia Lewis in 1962; divorced in 1968
Married to actress Elaine Taylor in 1970

First Film *Stage Struck*, 1958
Major Films include *The Fall of the Roman Empire*, 1964; *The Sound of Music*, 1965; *Oedipus the King*, 1968; *The Royal Hunt of the Sun*, 1969; *The Man Who Would Be King*, 1975; *The Return of the Pink Panther*, 1975; *Murder by Decree*, 1978; *International Velvet*, 1978; *Eyewitness*, 1981; *The Amateur*, 1982; *Dreamscape*, 1984

SIDNEY POITIER

Born Sidney Poitier on February 20, 1924 in Miami, FL
Married to dancer Juanita Hardy in 1950; divorced; daughter Beverly born in 1951; daughter Pamela born in 1952; daughter Sherry born in 1953
Married to actress Joanna Shimkus in 1976

First Film *No Way Out*, 1950
Major Films include *The Blackboard Jungle*, 1955; *Edge of the City*, 1957; *The Defiant Ones*, 1958; *Porgy and Bess*, 1959; *A Raisin in the Sun*, 1961; *Lilies of the Field*, 1963; *To Sir With Love*, 1967; *In the Heat of the Night*, 1967; *Guess Who's Coming to Dinner?*, 1967; *For Love of Ivy*, 1968; *Buck and the Preacher*, 1972; *Uptown Saturday Night*, 1974; *The Wilby*

Sidney Poitier, winner of the best actor Oscar for *Lilies of the Field* in 1963, is seen here in *To Sir With Love*, which was released in 1967 and had him cast as a teacher who wins over his unruly students.

Dick Powell, whose movie career began in 1932, is seen here in the 1948 film *Rogues' Regiment*. He later successfully turned to television and directed several films.

Conspiracy, 1975; *A Piece of the Action*, 1977

Academy Award for best actor: *Lilies of the Field*, 1963
Nomination for best actor: *The Defiant Ones*, 1958

DICK POWELL

Born Richard E. Powell on November 14, 1904 in Mountain View, AR
Died on January 2, 1963
Married to Mildred Maund in 1925; divorced in 1933
Married to actress Joan Blondell in 1936; divorced in 1944; stepson, Norman Scott Barnes; daughter Ellen born in 1938
Married to actress June Allyson in 1945; adopted daughter, Pamela; son Richard Keith Jr. born in 1950

First Film *Blessed Event*, 1932
Major Films include *42nd Street*, 1933; *Footlight Parade*, 1933; *Gold Diggers of 1935*, 1935; *Colleen*, 1936; *Going Places*, 1938;

Christmas in July, 1940; *It Happened Tomorrow*, 1944; *Murder My Sweet*, 1945; *The Bad and the Beautiful*, 1952; *Susan Slept Here*, 1954

WILLIAM POWELL

Born William Horatio Powell on July 29, 1892 in Pittsburgh, PA
Died on March 5, 1984
Married to actress Eileen Wilson in 1915; divorced in 1931; son William David born in 1925 (died in 1968)
Married to actress Carole Lombard in 1931; divorced in 1933
Married to actress Diana Lewis in 1940

First Film *Sherlock Holmes*, 1922
Major Films include *Romola*, 1924; *The Great Gatsby*, 1926; *The Last Command*, 1928; *Interference*, 1928; *The Canary Murder Case*, 1929; *For the Defense*, 1930; *One Way Passage*, 1932; *The Thin*

Man, 1934; *Reckless*, 1935; *The Great Ziegfeld*, 1936; *My Man Godfrey*, 1936; *Libeled Lady*, 1936; *Love Crazy*, 1941; *Life With Father*, 1947; *The Senator Was Indiscreet*, 1947; *Mister Roberts*, 1955

Academy Award Nominations for best actor: *The Thin Man*, 1934; *My Man Godfrey*, 1936; *Life With Father*, 1947

TYRONE POWER

Born Tyrone Edmund Power, Jr. on May 5, 1913 in Cincinnati, OH (son of actor Tyrone Power, Sr.; great-grandson of actor Tyrone Power)
Died on November 15, 1958 while filming *Solomon and Sheba*
Married to actress Suzanne Carpentier (stage name Annabella) in 1939; divorced in 1948; stepdaughter, Anne
Married to actress Linda Christian in 1949; divorced in 1955; daughter Romina (actress) born in 1949; daughter Taryn (actress) born in 1953

Married to actress Deborah Minardos in 1958; son Tyrone born in 1959

First Film *Tom Brown of Culver*, 1932
Major Films include *Lloyds of London*, 1936; *Alexander's Ragtime Band*, 1938; *Jesse James*, 1939; *The Mark of Zorro*, 1940; *Blood and Sand*, 1941; *The Black Swan*, 1942; *The Razor's Edge*, 1946; *Nightmare Alley*, 1947; *Diplomatic Courier*, 1952; *The Eddie Duchin Story*, 1956; *The Sun Also Rises*, 1957; *Witness for the Prosecution*, 1958

ELVIS PRESLEY

Born Elvis Aron Presley on January 8, 1935 in Tupelo, MS (the survivor of identical twins)
Died on August 16, 1977
Married to Priscilla Beaulieu in 1967; divorced in 1973; daughter Lisa Marie born in 1968

First Film *Love Me Tender*, 1956
Major Films include *Jailhouse Rock*, 1957; *King*

Elvis Presley flashes the smile that had teenage girls swooning in the aisles during *Jailhouse Rock* (1957), *King Creole* (1958), and all those other great Elvis-gets-the-girl movies.

Vincent Price in a mood suitably somber for the star of such bone-chillers as *The Pit and the Pendulum* (1961) and *The Raven* (1963). His career, however, was not restricted to horror movies.

Creole, 1958; *G.I. Blues*, 1960; *Blue Hawaii*, 1961; *Kid Galahad*, 1962; *Viva Las Vegas*, 1964; *Girl Happy*, 1965; *Easy Come, Easy Go*, 1967; *The Trouble With Girls*, 1969; *Change of Habit*, 1969

Biography *Elvis* by Jerry Hopkins

ROBERT PRESTON

Born Robert Preston Meservey on June 8, 1918 at Newton Highlands, MA
Married to actress Kay Feltus (stage name Catherine Craig) in 1940

First Film *King of Alcatraz*, 1938
Major Films include *Beau Geste*, 1939; *Typhoon*, 1940; *This Gun for Hire*, 1942; *Wake Island*, 1942; *The Macomber Affair*, 1947; *The Big City*, 1948; *Tulsa*, 1949; *The Dark at the Top of the Stairs*, 1960; *The Music Man*, 1962; *All the Way Home*, 1963; *Mame*, 1974; *Semi-Tough*,

1977; *S.O.B.*, 1981; *Victor/Victoria*, 1982; *The Last Starfighter*, 1984

Academy Award Nomination for best supporting actor: *Victor/Victoria*, 1982

VINCENT PRICE

Born Vincent Price on May 27, 1911 in St. Louis, MO
Married to actress Edith Barrett in 1938; divorced in 1948; son Vincent (journalist) born in 1939
Married to Mary Grant in 1949; divorced in 1972; daughter Mary Victoria born in 1962
Married to actress Coral Browne in 1974

First Film *Service de Luxe*, 1938
Major Films include *The House of the Seven Gables*, 1940; *The Song of Bernadette*, 1943; *Laura*, 1944; *Leave Her to Heaven*, 1945; *Dragonwyck*, 1946; *Champagne for Caesar*, 1950; *The Baron of Arizona*,

1950; *House of Wax*, 1953; *The Ten Commandments*, 1956; *House on Haunted Hill*, 1959; *The House of Usher*, 1960; *The Pit and the Pendulum*, 1961; *Tower of London*, 1962; *The Raven*, 1963; *The Masque of the Red Death*, 1964; *The Tomb of Ligeia*, 1964; *The Conqueror Worm*, 1968; *The Abominable Dr. Phibes*, 1971; *Theatre of Blood*, 1973; *The Monster Club*, 1980

Autobiography *I Like What I Know*, 1959

RICHARD PRYOR

Born Richard Pryor on December 1, 1940 in Peoria, IL
Son Richard Jr. born in 1962
Married in 1967; divorced; daughter Elizabeth Anne born in 1967; daughter Rain born in 1970
Married to Deborah McGuire in 1977; divorced; daughter Renee
Married to Jennifer Lee in 1982; divorced in 1982

First Film *The Busy Body*, 1968
Major Films include *Lady Sings the Blues*, 1972; *Some Call It Loving*, 1973; *Uptown Saturday Night*, 1974; *Silver Streak*, 1976; *The Wiz*, 1978; *California Suite*, 1978; *Richard Pryor Live in Concert*, 1979; *Stir Crazy*, 1980; *Bustin' Loose*, 1981; *Richard Pryor Live on the Sunset Strip*, 1982; *Some Kind of Hero*, 1982; *Superman III*, 1983

Academy Award Nomination for best supporting actor: *Lady Sings the Blues*, 1972

ANTHONY QUINN

Born Anthony Rudolph Oaxaco Quinn on April 21, 1915 in Chihuahua, Mexico
Married to actress Katherine de Mille (adopted daughter of director Cecil B. de Mille) in 1937; divorced in 1965; son Christopher born in 1938 (died in 1941); daughter Christina born in 1941; daughter Kathleen born in

Richard Pryor's wild comic talent is showcased, as here, in his one-man performances. He's also turned in great teamwork in movies from *Lady Sings the Blues* (1972) to *Superman III* (1983).

George Raft worked as a prizefighter and a dancer before he became a movie star and established himself as a sleek, tough gangster. He once estimated that he'd met a violent death in over 80 (75%) of his films.

1942; son Duncan born in 1945; daughter Valentina born in 1952
Son Francesco by Jolanda Addolari born in 1963
Daughter Daniele by Jolanda Addolari born in 1964
Married to Jolanda Addolari in 1965; son Lorenzo born in 1966

First Film *Parole*, 1936
Major Films include *Union Pacific*, 1939; *The Ghost Breakers*, 1940; *Blood and Sand*, 1941; *The Ox-Bow Incident*, 1943; *Back to Bataan*, 1945; *Tycoon*, 1947; *Viva Zapata!*, 1952; *La Strada*, 1954; *Lust for Life*, 1956; *Wild Is the Wind*, 1957; *The Guns of Navarone*, 1961; *Lawrence of Arabia*, 1962; *Zorba the Greek*, 1964; *The Secret of Santa Vittoria*, 1969; *The Greek Tycoon*, 1978

Academy Awards for best supporting actor: *Viva Zapata!*, 1952; *Lust for Life*, 1956
Nominations for best actor: *Wild Is the Wind*, 1957; *Zorba the Greek*, 1964

Autobiography *The Original Sin*, 1972

GEORGE RAFT

Born George Raft on September 27, 1895 in New York City, NY
Died on November 24, 1980
Married to Grace Mulrooney in 1916

First Film *Queen of the Night Clubs*, 1929
Major Films include *Scarface*, 1932; *Night After Night*, 1932; *Bolero*, 1934; *Souls at Sea*, 1937; *You and Me*, 1938; *Each Dawn I Die*, 1939; *They Drive by Night*, 1940; *Manpower*, 1941; *Johnny Angel*, 1945; *Johnny Allegro*, 1949; *Black Widow*, 1954; *A Bullet for Joey*, 1955; *Some Like It Hot*, 1959; *Casino Royale*, 1967; *Hammersmith Is Out*, 1972

Biography *The George Raft File* by James Robert Parrish and Steven Whitney

CLAUDE RAINS

Born William Claude Rains on November 10, 1889 in London, England
Died on May 30, 1967

Married to actress Isabel Jeans in 1913; divorced
Married to Marie Hemingway in 1920; divorced in 1920
Married to actress Beatrix Thomson in 1924; divorced in 1935
Married to Frances Propper in 1935; divorced in 1959; daughter Jennifer born in 1936
Married to Agi Jambor in 1959; divorced in 1960
Married to Rosemary Clark in 1960

First Film *The Invisible Man*, 1933
Major Films include *Crime Without Passion*, 1934; *The Man Who Reclaimed His Head*, 1935; *The Prince and the Pauper*, 1937; *The Adventures of Robin Hood*, 1938; *Four Daughters*, 1938; *Mr. Smith Goes to Washington*, 1939; *The Sea Hawk*, 1940; *Here Comes Mr. Jordan*, 1941; *Now, Voyager*, 1942; *Casablanca*, 1943; *The Phantom of the Opera*, 1943; *Mr. Skeffington*, 1944; *Caesar and Cleopatra*, 1945; *Notorious*, 1946; *This Earth Is Mine*, 1959; *Lawrence of Arabia*, 1962; *The Greatest Story Ever Told*, 1965

Academy Award Nominations for best supporting actor: *Mr. Smith Goes to Washington*, 1939; *Casablanca*, 1943; *Mr. Skeffington*, 1944; *Notorious*, 1946

TONY RANDALL

Born Leonard Rosenberg on February 26, 1920 in Tulsa, OK
Married to Florence Mitchell in 1942

First Film *Oh Men! Oh Women!*, 1957
Major Films include *Will Success Spoil Rock Hunter?*, 1957; *The Mating Game*, 1959; *Pillow Talk*, 1959; *Lover Come Back*, 1961; *Boys' Night Out*, 1962; *The Seven Faces of Dr. Lao*, 1964; *The Alphabet Murders*, 1966; *Hello Down There*, 1969; *Everything You Always Wanted to Know About Sex (But Were Afraid to Ask)*, 1972; *Scavenger Hunt*, 1979

Claude Rains, whose extensive film career won him four best supporting actor nominations: for *Mr. Smith Goes to Washington* (1939); *Casablanca* (1943); *Mr. Skeffington* (1944); and *Notorious* (1946).

ROBERT REDFORD

Born Charles Robert Redford, Jr. on August 18, 1937 in Santa Maria, CA
Married to Lola van Wangemen in 1958; son Scott born in 1959 (died as baby); daughter Shauna born in 1961; son Jamie born in 1963; daughter Amy born in 1972

First Film *War Hunt*, 1962
Major Films include *Barefoot in the Park*, 1967; *Butch Cassidy and the Sundance Kid*, 1969; *The Candidate*, 1972; *The Way We Were*, 1973; *The Sting*, 1973; *The Great Gatsby*, 1974; *All the President's Men*, 1976; *The Electric Horseman*, 1979; *The Natural*, 1984

Academy Award for best director: *Ordinary People*, 1980
Academy Award Nomination for best actor: *The Sting*, 1973

Biography *The Superstar Nobody Knows* by David Hanna

MICHAEL REDGRAVE

Born Michael Scudamore Redgrave on March 20, 1908 in Bristol, England
Married to actress Rachel Kempson in 1935; daughter Vanessa (actress) born in 1937; son Colin (actor) born in 1939; daughter Lynn (actress) born in 1943

First Film *The Lady Vanishes*, 1938
Major Films include *The Stars Look Down*, 1939;

Kipps, 1941; *Thunder Rock*, 1942; *The Way to the Stars*, 1945; *Dead of Night*, 1945; *The Captive Heart*, 1946; *Mourning Becomes Electra*, 1947; *The Browning Version*, 1951; *The Importance of Being Earnest*, 1952; *The Sea Shall Not Have Them*, 1954; *The Quiet American*, 1958; *Shake Hands With the Devil*, 1959; *The Loneliness of the Long Distance Runner*, 1962; *Oh! What a Lovely War*, 1969; *Nicholas and Alexandra*, 1971

Academy Award Nomination for best actor: *Mourning Becomes Electra*, 1947

Knighted in 1959

Autobiographies *The Actor's Ways and Means*, 1955; *Mask or Face*, 1958
Novel by Redgrave *The Mountebank's Tale*, 1959

VANESSA REDGRAVE

Born Vanessa Redgrave on January 30, 1937 in London, England (daughter of actor Michael Redgrave and actress Rachel Kempson; sister of actor Colin and actress Lynn Redgrave)
Married to director Tony Richardson in 1962; divorced in 1967; daughter Natasha born in 1963; daughter Joely Kim born in 1965
Son Carlo Nero by actor Franco Nero born in 1969

First Film *Behind the Mask*, 1958
Major Films include *Morgan!*, 1966; *Blow-Up*, 1966; *Camelot*, 1967; *Isadora*, 1968; *The Trojan Women*, 1971; *Mary, Queen of Scots*, 1971; *Murder on the Orient Express*,

1974; *The Seven Percent Solution*, 1976; *Julia*, 1977; *Yanks*, 1979

Academy Award for best supporting actress: *Julia*, 1977
Nominations for best actress: *Morgan!*, 1966; *Isadora*, 1968; *Mary, Queen of Scots*, 1971

DONNA REED

Born Donna Belle Mullenger on January 27, 1921 in Denison, IA
Married to makeup expert William Tuttle in 1943; divorced in 1945
Married to agent/producer Tony Owen in 1945; divorced in 1971; daughter Penny born in 1947; daughter Mary Ann born in 1948; son Tony Jr. born in 1949; son Timothy born in 1950
Married to Colonel Grover Asmus in 1974

First Film *The Getaway*, 1941 (as Donna Adams)
Major Films include *The Courtship of Andy Hardy*, 1942; *See Here, Private*

Hargrove, 1944; *The Picture of Dorian Gray*, 1945; *They Were Expendable*, 1945; *It's a Wonderful Life*, 1946; *Green Dolphin Street*, 1947; *Chicago Deadline*, 1949; *Scandal Sheet*, 1952; *From Here to Eternity*, 1953; *The Far Horizons*, 1955; *The Benny Goodman Story*, 1956; *The Whole Truth*, 1958

Academy Award for best supporting actress: *From Here to Eternity*, 1953

OLIVER REED

Born Oliver Reed on February 13, 1938 in Wimbledon, England (nephew of film director Carol Reed)
Married to Kathleen Byrne in 1960; divorced in 1970; son Mark born in 1962; daughter Sarah born in 1970

First Film *The Angry Silence*, 1960
Major Films include *The Curse of the Werewolf*, 1962; *The Trap*, 1966; *Oliver!*, 1968; *Women in Love*, 1969; *The Devils*,

Vanessa Redgrave, the maverick elder daughter of a theatrical family (her father, mother, sister, and brother are all actors) is seen here in Michelangelo Antonioni's *Blow-Up* (1966).

1971; *The Three Mus-keteers*, 1974; *The Four Musketeers*, 1975; *Tommy*, 1975; *The Prince and the Pauper*, 1977; *The Big Sleep*, 1978; *Condorman*, 1981; *The Sting II*, 1983

BURT REYNOLDS

Born Burt Reynolds on February 11, 1936 in Way-cross, GA
Married to actress Judy Carne in 1963; divorced in 1965

First Film *Angel Baby*, 1961
Major Films include *Sam Whiskey*, 1969; *Deliver-ance*, 1972; *Shamus*, 1973; *The Longest Yard*, 1973; *Gator*, 1976; *Smokey and the Bandit*, 1977; *Semi-Tough*, 1977; *Hooper*, 1978; *Starting Over*, 1979; *The Cannonball Run*, 1981; *Best Friends*, 1982; *The Best Lit-tle Whorehouse in Texas*, 1982; *Cannonball Run II*, 1984

DEBBIE REYNOLDS

Born Mary Frances Rey-nolds on April 1, 1932 in El Paso, TX
Married to singer Eddie Fisher in 1955; divorced in 1959; daughter Carrie (actress) born in 1956; son Todd born in 1958
Married to Harry Karl in 1960; divorced in 1975
Married to Richard Ham-lett in 1984

First Film *June Bride*, 1948
Major Films include *Singin' in the Rain*, 1952; *The Tender Trap*, 1955;

The Catered Affair, 1956; *Tammy and the Bachelor*, 1957; *The Rat Race*, 1960; *The Unsinkable Molly Brown*, 1964; *The Singing Nun*, 1966; *Divorce Ameri-can Style*, 1967; *How Sweet It Is*, 1968; *What's the Mat-ter with Helen?*, 1971; *That's Entertainment* (nar-ration), 1974

Academy Award Nomina-tion for best actress: *The Unsinkable Molly Brown*, 1964

Autobiography *If I Knew Then*, 1962

JASON ROBARDS

Born Jason Nelson Robards, Jr. on July 26, 1922 in Chicago, IL (son of actor Jason Robards, Sr.)
Married to Eleanor Pit-man in 1946; divorced in 1958; daughter Sara Louise born in 1947; son Jason born in 1948; son David born in 1949
Married to Rachel Taylor in 1959; divorced in 1961
Married to actress Lauren Bacall in 1961; divorced in 1969; son Sam born in 1962
Married to Lois O'Connor in 1970; daughter Shannon born in 1972; son Jake born in 1974

First Film: *The Journey*, 1959
Major Films include *Long Day's Journey Into Night*, 1962; *Tender Is the Night*, 1962; *Act One*, 1963; *A Thousand Clowns*, 1965; *Any Wednesday*, 1966; *Isadora*, 1968; *Julius Caesar*, 1970; *Pat Garrett and Billy the Kid*, 1973; *All the President's Men*, 1976; *Julia*, 1977; *Comes a Horseman*, 1978; *Melvin*

and Howard, 1979; *Max Dugan Returns*, 1983

Academy Awards for best supporting actor: *All the President's Men*, 1976; *Julia*, 1977

CLIFF ROBERTSON

Born Clifford Parker Robertson, III on Septem-ber 9, 1925 in La Jolla, CA
Married to Cynthia Stone in 1957; divorced; daughter Stephanie born in 1959
Married to actress Dina Merrill in 1966; daughter Heather born in 1968

First Film *Picnic*, 1955
Major Films include *Autumn Leaves*, 1956; *The Naked and the Dead*, 1958; *Gidget*, 1959; *The Interns*, 1962; *The Best Man*, 1964; *The Honey Pot*, 1967; *Charly*, 1968; *J. W. Coop*, 1972; *Three Days of the Condor*, 1975; *Obsession*, 1976; *The Pilot*, 1979; *Class*, 1983

Academy Award for best actor: *Charly*, 1968

EDWARD G. ROBINSON

Born Emmanuel Gold-enberg on December 12, 1893 in Bucharest, Romania
Died on January 26, 1973
Married to artist Gladys Lloyd in 1927; divorced in 1956; son Emmanuel Jr. (actor under name Edward G. Robinson, Jr.) born in 1934 (died in 1974)
Married to Jane Adler in 1958

First Film *The Bright Shawl*, 1923
Major Films include *Little Caesar*, 1931; *The Little Giant*, 1933; *The Whole Town's Talking*, 1935; *Bar-bary Coast*, 1935; *Kid Galahad*, 1937; *Confessions of a Nazi Spy*, 1939; *Dr. Ehrlich's Magic Bullet*, 1940; *The Sea Wolf*, 1941; *Larceny Inc.*, 1942; *Double Indemnity*, 1944; *The Woman in the Window*, 1944; *Our Vines Have Ten-der Grapes*, 1945; *Scarlet Street*, 1945; *The Stranger*, 1946; *Key Largo*, 1948; *Illegal*, 1955; *The Ten Commandments*, 1956; *The*

In *Julia* (1977), Jason Robards played writer Dashiell Hammett oppo-site Jane Fonda as Lillian Hellman. His performance won him his sec-ond best supporting actor Academy Award.

177

Ginger Rogers, more frequently pictured on the dance floor with long-time partner Fred Astaire, here assumes a more sedentary role in *Kitty Foyle* (1940).

Prize, 1963; *The Cincinnati Kid*, 1965; *Mackenna's Gold*, 1969; *Soylent Green*, 1973

Special Academy Award for achieving "greatness as a player, a patron of the arts, and a dedicated citizen . . . in sum, a Renaissance man. From his friends in the industry he loves," 1972

Autobiography *All My Yesterdays*, 1973
Biography *My Father—My Son* by Edward G. Robinson, Jr.

GINGER ROGERS

Born Virginia Katherine McMath on July 16, 1911 in Independence, MO
Married to vaudeville partner Jack Culpepper in 1929; divorced in 1931
Married to actor Lew Ayres in 1934; divorced in 1941
Married to Jack Briggs in 1942; divorced in 1949
Married to actor Jacques Bergerac in 1953; divorced in 1957

Married to actor/director/producer William Marshall in 1961; divorced in 1972

First Film *Young Man of Manhattan*, 1930
Major Films include *42nd Street*, 1933; *Flying Down to Rio*, 1933; *The Gay Divorcee*, 1934; *Top Hat*, 1935; *Swing Time*, 1936; *Stage Door*, 1937; *Carefree*, 1938; *Bachelor Mother*, 1939; *Kitty Foyle*, 1940; *Tom, Dick and Harry*, 1941; *The Major and the Minor*, 1942; *Lady in the Dark*, 1944; *The Barkleys of Broadway*, 1949; *We're Not Married*, 1952; *Forever Female*, 1953; *Tight Spot*, 1955; *Harlow*, 1965

Academy Award for best actress: *Kitty Foyle*, 1940

Biography *Ginger Rogers* by Patrick McGilligan

GILBERT ROLAND

Born Luis Antonio Damaso de Alonso on December 11, 1905 in Juarez, Mexico
Married to actress

Constance Bennett in 1941; divorced in 1946; daughter Gyl Christina born in 1942; daughter Lorinda Alonso born in 1943
Married to Guillermina Cantu in 1954

First Film *The Plastic Age*, 1925
Major Films include *Camille*, 1927; *New York Nights*, 1929; *Men of the North*, 1930; *The Woman in Room 13*, 1932; *She Done Him Wrong*, 1933; *Mystery Woman*, 1935; *The Last Train From Madrid*, 1937; *Juarez*, 1939; *The Sea Hawk*, 1940; *Captain Kidd*, 1945; *King of the Bandits*, 1947; *We Were Strangers*, 1949; *The Furies*, 1950; *The Bullfighter and the Lady*, 1951; *The Bad and the Beautiful*, 1952; *Three Violent People*, 1957; *Cheyenne Autumn*, 1964; *Islands in the Stream*, 1977

MICKEY ROONEY

Born Joe Yule, Jr. on September 23, 1920 in Brooklyn, NY
Married to actress Ava Gardner in 1942; divorced in 1943

Married to Betty Jane Rase in 1944; divorced in 1949; son Mickey Jr. born in 1944; son Timothy born in 1947
Married to actress Martha Vickers in 1949; divorced in 1951; son Theodore born in 1949
Married to Elaine Mahnken in 1952; divorced in 1959
Married to Barbara Ann Thomasen in 1959; divorced; daughter Kelly Ann born in 1959; daughter Kerry born in 1960; son Kyle born in 1961; daughter Kimmy Sue born in 1962
Married to Margaret Lang in 1966; divorced in 1967
Married to Carolyn Hockett in 1969; divorced in 1974
Married to singer Janice Darlene Chamberlain in 1978

First Film *Not to Be Trusted*, 1926
Major Films include *Orchids and Ermine*, 1927; *My Pal the King*, 1932; *A Midsummer Night's Dream*, 1935; *Ah Wilderness!*, 1935; *Little Lord Fauntleroy*, 1936; *A Family Affair*, 1937; *Captains Courageous*, 1937; *Love Finds Andy Hardy*, 1938; *Boys Town*, 1938; *The Adven-*

Gilbert Roland, seen here with Jane Russell in *Underwater!* (1955), was born Luis Antonio Damaso de Alonso, the son of a Mexican bullfighter, and once made a movie called *The Bullfighter and the Lady*.

Gena Rowlands plays a tough girl who attempts to beat the mob at their own game in *Gloria* (1980), which won her a second best actress Oscar nomination. The first was for *A Woman Under the Influence*.

tures of *Huckleberry Finn*, 1939; *Babes in Arms*, 1939; *Young Tom Edison*, 1940; *Babes on Broadway*, 1941; *The Human Comedy*, 1943; *National Velvet*, 1944; *Off Limits*, 1953; *The Bold and the Brave*, 1956; *Baby Face Nelson*, 1957; *Requiem for a Heavyweight*, 1962; *It's a Mad Mad Mad Mad World*, 1963; *The Black Stallion*, 1979

Special Academy Awards for "significant contribution in bringing to the screen the spirit and personification of youth, and as juvenile players setting a high standard of ability and achievement," (shared with Deanna Durbin) 1938; "in recognition of sixty years of versatility in a variety of memorable film performances," 1982
Academy Award Nominations for best actor: *Babes in Arms*, 1939; *The Human Comedy*, 1943
Nomination for best supporting actor: *The Bold and the Brave*, 1956

GENA ROWLANDS

Born Virginia Cathryn Rowlands on June 19, 1934 in Cambria, WI
Married to actor/director John Cassavetes in 1954; daughter Alexandra born in 1965; son Nicholas born in 1967; daughter Zoe born in 1970

First Film *High Cost of Loving*, 1958
Major Films include *Lonely Are the Brave*, 1962; *The Spiral Road*, 1962; *A Child Is Waiting*, 1963; *Tony Rome*, 1967; *Faces*, 1968; *Minnie and Moskowitz*, 1971; *A Woman Under the Influence*, 1974; *Two-Minute Warning*, 1976; *Opening Night*, 1978; *The Brink's Job*, 1978; *Gloria*, 1980; *Tempest*, 1982

Academy Award Nominations for best actress: *A Woman Under the Influence*, 1974; *Gloria*, 1980

JANE RUSSELL

Born Ernestine Jane Geraldine Russell on June 21, 1921 in Bemidji, MN
Married to football player Bob Waterfield in 1943; divorced in 1967; adopted son, Thomas; adopted daughter, Tracy; adopted son Robert Jr.
Married to Roger Barrett in 1968; widowed in 1968
Married to John Peoples in 1974

First Film *The Outlaw*, 1943 (not officially released until 1950)
Major Films include *The Paleface*, 1948; *His Kind of Woman*, 1951; *Macao*, 1952; *Son of Paleface*, 1952; *Gentlemen Prefer Blondes*, 1953; *The French Line*, 1954; *The Tall Men*, 1955; *The Revolt of Mamie Stover*, 1956; *The Fuzzy Pink Nightgown*, 1957; *Waco*, 1966; *Darker Than Amber*, 1970

ROSALIND RUSSELL

Born Rosalind Russell on June 4, 1908 in Waterbury, CT (daughter of lawyer James Russell and Clara McKnight, editor of *Vogue* magazine)
Died on November 28, 1976
Married to producer Frederick Brisson in 1941; son Lance born in 1943

First Film *Evelyn Prentice*, 1934
Major Films include *China Seas*, 1935; *Rendezvous*, 1935; *Craig's Wife*, 1936; *Night Must Fall*, 1937; *The Citadel*, 1938; *The Women*, 1939; *His Girl Friday*, 1940; *The Feminine Touch*, 1941; *My Sister Eileen*, 1942; *Sister Kenny*, 1946; *Mourning Becomes Electra*, 1947; *The Velvet Touch*, 1948; *Picnic*, 1956; *Auntie Mame*, 1958; *Gypsy*, 1962; *The Trouble With Angels*, 1966; *Mrs. Pollifax—Spy*, 1971

Academy Award Nomination for best actress: *My Sister Eileen*, 1942; *Sister Kenny*, 1946; *Mourning Becomes Electra*, 1947; *Auntie Mame*, 1958
Jean Hersholt Humanitarian Award, 1972

Autobiography *Life Is a Banquet*, 1977

Jane Russell, who co-starred with Marilyn Monroe in *Gentlemen Prefer Blondes* in 1953, is seen here in less sophisticated form in the 1952 western *Montana Belle*.

179

ROBERT RYAN

Born Robert Bushnell Ryan on November 11, 1909 in Chicago, IL
Died on July 11, 1973
Married to actress Jessica Cadwalder in 1939; widowed in 1972; son Timothy born in 1946; son Cheney born in 1948; daughter Lisa born in 1951

First Film *Queen of the Mob*, 1940
Major Films include *The Woman on the Beach*, 1947; *Crossfire*, 1947; *Act of Violence*, 1949; *The Set-Up*, 1949; *Born to Be Bad*, 1950; *On Dangerous Ground*, 1952; *Clash by Night*, 1952; *The Tall Men*, 1955; *God's Little Acre*, 1958; *Billy Budd*, 1962; *The Professionals*, 1966; *The Wild Bunch*, 1969; *The Iceman Cometh*, 1973

Academy Award Nomination for best supporting actor: *Crossfire*, 1947

EVA MARIE SAINT

Born Eva Marie Saint on July 4, 1924 in Newark, NJ
Married to director Jeffrey Hayden in 1951; son Darrell born in 1955; daughter Laurette born in 1958

First Film *On the Waterfront*, 1954
Major Films include *That Certain Feeling*, 1956; *A Hatful of Rain*, 1957; *North by Northwest*, 1959; *Exodus*, 1960; *All Fall Down*, 1962; *The Sandpiper*, 1965; *The Russians Are Coming, the Russians Are Coming*, 1966; *The Stalking Moon*, 1969; *Loving*, 1970; *Cancel My Reservation*, 1972

Academy Award for best supporting actress: *On the Waterfront*, 1954

GEORGE SANDERS

Born George Sanders on July 3, 1906 in St. Petersburg, Russia (brother of actor Tom Conway)
Died (suicide) on April 25, 1972
Married to actress Elsie M. Poole (stage name Susan Larsen) in 1940; divorced in 1947
Married to actress Zsa Zsa Gabor in 1949; divorced in 1954
Married to actress Benita Hume in 1959; widowed in 1967
Married to Magda Gabor in 1970; divorced in 1970

First Film *Find the Lady*, 1936
Major Films include *Lloyds of London*, 1937; *The Saint Strikes Back*, 1939; *Confessions of a Nazi Spy*, 1939; *Rebecca*, 1940; *The House of the Seven Gables*, 1940; *The Gay Falcon*, 1941; *Man Hunt*, 1941; *The Moon and Sixpence*, 1942; *The Picture of Dorian Gray*, 1945; *The Ghost and Mrs. Muir*, 1947; *Lured*, 1947; *Samson and Delilah*, 1949; *All About Eve*, 1950; *Ivanhoe*, 1952; *Call Me Madam*, 1953; *That Certain Feeling*, 1956; *Village of the Damned*, 1960; *A Shot in the Dark*, 1964; *The Jungle Book* (voice only), 1967; *The Kremlin Letter*, 1970

Academy Award for best supporting actor: *All About Eve*, 1950

Autobiography *Memoirs of a Professional Cad*, 1960

ROY SCHEIDER

Born Roy Scheider on November 10, 1935 in Orange, NJ
Married to film editor Cynthia Eddenfield Bebout in 1964; daughter Maximilia born in 1964

First Film *Curse of the Living Corpse*, 1964
Major Films include *Klute*, 1971; *The French Connection*, 1971; *Jaws*, 1975; *Marathon Man*, 1976; *Sorcerer*, 1977; *All That Jazz*, 1979; *Still of the Night*, 1982; *Blue Thunder*, 1983

Academy Award Nomination for best actor: *All That Jazz*, 1979
Nomination for best supporting actor: *The French Connection*, 1971

MAXIMILIAN SCHELL

Born Maximilian Schell on December 8, 1930 in Vienna, Austria (brother of actress Maria Schell)

First Film *Kinder Mütter und ein General*, 1955
Major Films include *The Young Lions*, 1958; *Judgment at Nuremberg*, 1961; *Five Finger Exercise*, 1962; *Topkapi*, 1964; *The Deadly Affair*, 1967; *The Castle*, 1968; *Krakatoa East of Java*, 1969; *The Odessa File*, 1974; *The Man in the Glass Booth*, 1975; *Cross of Iron*, 1977; *Julia*, 1977; *The Black Hole*, 1979

Academy Award for best actor: *Judgment at Nuremberg*, 1961
Nomination for best actor: *The Man in the Glass Booth*, 1975
Nomination for best supporting actor: *Julia*, 1977

GEORGE C. SCOTT

Born George Campbell Scott on October 18, 1927 in Wise, VA
Married to actress Carolyn Hughes; divorced
Married to singer Patricia Reed; divorced
Married to actress Colleen Dewhurst in 1960; divorced in 1965; son Alexander born in 1961; son

Roy Scheider won a best actor Academy Award nomination for his lead role in *All That Jazz* (1979), director Bob Fosse's autobiographical backstage musical drama.

George C. Scott, pictured here in *The Changeling* (1980), was awarded a best actor Oscar for his 1970 performance as *Patton* but refused to accept the honor.

Campbell born in 1962
Remarried to Colleen Dewhurst in 1967; divorced in 1972
Married to actress Trish Van Devere in 1972

First Film *The Hanging Tree*, 1959
Major Films include *Anatomy of a Murder*, 1959; *The Hustler*, 1961; *Dr. Strangelove, or How I Learned to Stop Worrying and Love the Bomb*, 1964; *The Bible*, 1966; *Petulia*, 1968; *Patton*, 1970; *Jane Eyre*, 1971; *The Hospital*, 1971; *The New Centurions*, 1972; *The Prince and the Pauper*, 1977; *Movie Movie*, 1978; *Hardcore*, 1979; *Taps*, 1982

Academy Award for best actor: *Patton*, 1970 (refused)
Nomination for best actor: *The Hospital*, 1971
Nominations for best supporting actor: *Anatomy of a Murder*, 1959; *The Hustler*, 1961

RANDOLPH SCOTT

Born George Randolph Crane Scott on January 23, 1903 in Orange County, VA
Married to Marion Dupont Somerville in 1926; divorced in 1938
Married to Patricia Stillman in 1944; son Christopher; daughter Sandra

First Film *The Far Call*, 1929
Major Films include *Hot Saturday*, 1932; *Roberta*, 1935; *She*, 1935; *The Last of the Mohicans*, 1936; *Rebecca of Sunnybrook Farm*, 1938; *Western Union*, 1941; *Abilene Town*, 1946; *Return of the Badmen*, 1948; *Man in the Saddle*, 1951; *The Bounty Hunter*, 1954; *A Lawless Street*, 1955; *The Tall T*, 1957; *Ride Lonesome*, 1959; *Comanche Station*, 1960; *Ride the High Country*, 1962

GEORGE SEGAL

Born George Segal on February 13, 1934 in Great Neck, NY
Married to Marion Sobol in 1956; divorced; daughter Elizabeth born in 1957; daughter Patricia born in 1958
Married in 1983

First Film *The Young Doctors*, 1961
Major Films include *Invitation to a Gunfighter*, 1964; *Ship of Fools*, 1965; *Who's Afraid of Virginia Woolf?*, 1966; *The St. Valentine's Day Massacre*, 1967; *The Owl and the Pussycat*, 1970; *A Touch of Class*, 1973; *Blume in Love*, 1973; *Fun With Dick and Jane*, 1977; *Who Is Killing the Great Chefs of Europe?*, 1978; *Lost and Found*, 1979; *Carbon Copy*, 1981

Academy Award Nomination for best supporting actor: *Who's Afraid of Virginia Woolf?*, 1966

PETER SELLERS

Born Richard Henry Sellers on September 8, 1925 in Southsea, England
Died on July 24, 1980
Married to actress Anne Howe in 1951; divorced in 1964; daughter Sarah Jane born in 1952; son Michael Peter Anthony born in 1953
Married to actress Britt Ekland in 1964; divorced in 1969; daughter Victoria born in 1965
Married to Miranda Quarry in 1970; divorced in 1974
Married to actress Lynne Frederick in 1977

First Film *Penny Points to Paradise*, 1951
Major Films include *The Ladykillers*, 1955; *The Naked Truth*, 1957; *The Mouse That Roared*, 1959; *I'm All Right Jack*, 1959; *Only Two Can Play*, 1962; *Lolita*, 1962; *The Pink Panther*, 1963; *Dr. Strangelove, or How I Learned to Stop Worrying and Love the Bomb*, 1964; *What's New Pussycat?*, 1965; *I Love You Alice B. Toklas*, 1968; *The Magic Christian*, 1969; *The Return of the Pink Panther*, 1975; *Murder by Death*, 1976; *Revenge of the Pink Panther*, 1978; *The Prisoner of Zenda*, 1979; *Being There*, 1979

Academy Award Nominations for best actor: *Dr. Strangelove, or How I Learned to Stop Worrying and Love the Bomb*, 1964; *Being There*, 1979

Peter Sellers, seen here in *Lolita* (1962), was nominated for best actor Oscars for his triple role in *Dr. Strangelove, or How I Learned to Stop Worrying and Love the Bomb* (1964), and *Being There* (1979).

Robert Shaw, who co-starred with a Great White shark in *Jaws* (1975), received a best supporting actor Oscar nomination for a very different role—as King Henry VIII in *A Man for All Seasons* (1966).

ROBERT SHAW

Born Robert Shaw on August 9, 1927 in Liverpool, England
Died on August 28, 1978
Married to Jennifer Bourke in 1952; divorced
Married to actress Mary Ure in 1964; widowed in 1975
Married to Virginia Dewitt Jansen in 1975
Father of ten children, natural and adopted

First Film *The Dam Busters*, 1954
Major Films include *Sea Fury*, 1959; *From Russia With Love*, 1963; *The Luck of Ginger Coffey*, 1964; *Battle of the Bulge*, 1965; *A Man for All Seasons*, 1966; *The Royal Hunt of the Sun*, 1969; *The Sting*, 1973; *Jaws*, 1975; *Swashbuckler*, 1976; *Black Sunday*, 1977; *Force 10 from Navarone*, 1978

Academy Award Nomination for best supporting actor: *A Man for All Seasons*, 1966

NORMA SHEARER

Born Edith Norma Shearer on August 10, 1904 in Montreal, Quebec, Canada
Died on June 12, 1983
Married to producer Irving Thalberg in 1927; widowed in 1937; son Irving Jr. born in 1930; daughter Katharine born in 1935
Married to Martin Arrouge in 1942

First Film *The Flapper*, 1920
Major Films include *The Man Who Paid*, 1922; *He Who Gets Slapped*, 1924; *The Trial of Mary Dugan*, 1929; *Their Own Desire*, 1929; *The Divorcee*, 1930; *A Free Soul*, 1930; *Private Lives*, 1930; *Strange Interlude*, 1932; *Smilin' Through*, 1932; *The Barretts of Wimpole Street*, 1934; *Romeo and Juliet*, 1936; *Marie Antoinette*, 1938; *The Women*, 1939; *Escape*, 1940; *Her Cardboard Lover*, 1942

Academy Award for best actress: *The Divorcee*, 1929/30
Nominations for best actress: *Their Own Desire*, 1929/30; *A Free Soul*, 1930/31; *The Barretts of Wimpole Street*, 1934; *Romeo and Juliet*, 1936; *Marie Antoinette*, 1938

ANN SHERIDAN

Born Clara Lou Sheridan on February 21, 1915 in Denton, TX
Died on January 21, 1967
Married to actor Edward Norris in 1936; divorced in 1939
Married to actor George Brent in 1942; divorced in 1943
Married to James Owens in 1956; divorced
Married to actor Scott McKay in 1966

First Film *Search for Beauty*, 1934 (as Clara Lou Sheridan)
Major Films include *Behold My Wife*, 1935; *The Great O'Malley*, 1937; *Angels With Dirty Faces*, 1938; *They Made Me a Criminal*, 1939; *Torrid Zone*, 1940; *They Drive by Night*, 1940; *The Man Who Came to Dinner*, 1942; *King's Row*, 1942; *George Washington Slept Here*, 1942; *Shine On Harvest Moon*, 1944; *The Unfaithful*, 1947; *I Was a Male War Bride*, 1949; *Woman on the Run*, 1950; *Take Me to Town*, 1953; *Come Next Spring*, 1956; *The Opposite Sex*, 1956

JEAN SIMMONS

Born Jean Merilyn Simmons on January 31, 1929 in London, England
Married to actor Stewart Granger in 1950; divorced in 1960; daughter Tracy born in 1956
Married to director Richard Brooks in 1960; daughter Kate born in 1961

First Film *Give Us the Moon*, 1944
Major Films include *Great Expectations*, 1946; *Black Narcissus*, 1947; *Hamlet*,

Jean Simmons is pictured here with Stewart Granger, to whom she was married from 1950 to 1960. Simmons won a best actress Oscar nomination for *The Happy Ending* (1969).

A very young Frank Sinatra displays the charm that—along with that famous voice—made him an idol who has stayed at the top of his profession for over forty years.

RED SKELTON

Born Richard Bernard Skelton on July 18, 1913 in Vincennes, IN (son of circus clown Joseph Skelton)
Married to writer Edna Stillwell in 1932; divorced in 1943
Married to model Georgia Maureen David in 1945; divorced in 1971; daughter Valentina born in 1947; son Richard born in 1948 (died in 1958)
Married to Lothian Ioland in 1973

First Film *Having Wonderful Time*, 1938
Major Films include *Whistling in the Dark*, 1941; *Lady Be Good*, 1941; *Ship Ahoy*, 1942; *Panama Hattie*, 1942; *DuBarry Was a Lady*, 1943; *Thousands Cheer*, 1943; *Bathing Beauty*, 1944; *The Show-Off*, 1946; *Merton of the Movies*, 1947; *The Fuller Brush Man*, 1948; *Neptune's Daughter*, 1949; *Three Little Words*, 1950; *Lovely to Look At*, 1952; *The Clown*, 1953; *Public Pigeon Number One*, 1957; *Those Magnificent Men in Their Flying Machines*, 1965

MAGGIE SMITH

Born Margaret Smith on December 28, 1934 in Ilford, Essex, England
Married to actor Robert Stephens in 1967; divorced in 1974; son Christopher born in 1967; son Toby born in 1969
Married to screenwriter Beverley Cross in 1974

First Film *Nowhere to Go*, 1958
Major Films include *Go to Blazes*, 1962; *The V.I.P.s*, 1963; *Othello*, 1965; *Hot Millions*, 1968; *The Prime of Miss Jean Brodie*, 1969; *Travels With My Aunt*, 1972; *Love and Pain and the Whole Damn Thing*, 1973; *Murder by Death*, 1976; *Death on the Nile*, 1978; *California Suite*, 1978; *Clash of the Titans*, 1980; *Evil Under the Sun*, 1982

Academy Award for best actress: *The Prime of Miss Jean Brodie*, 1969
Academy Award for best supporting actress: *California Suite*, 1978

1948; *The Blue Lagoon*, 1949; *Angel Face*, 1952; *The Actress*, 1953; *The Robe*, 1953; *Guys and Dolls*, 1955; *The Big Country*, 1958; *Home Before Dark*, 1958; *Elmer Gantry*, 1960; *Spartacus*, 1960; *All the Way Home*, 1963; *Divorce American Style*, 1967; *The Happy Ending*, 1969; *Mr. Sycamore*, 1975

Academy Award Nomination for best actress: *The Happy Ending*, 1969
Nomination for best supporting actress: *Hamlet*, 1948

FRANK SINATRA

Born Francis Albert Sinatra on December 12, 1915 in Hoboken, NJ
Married to Nancy Barbato in 1939; divorced in 1951; daughter Nancy (singer) born in 1940; son Frank Jr. born in 1944; daughter Christine born in 1948
Married to actress Ava Gardner in 1951; divorced in 1957

Married to actress Mia Farrow in 1966; divorced in 1968
Married to Barbara Blakely Marx in 1976

First Film *Las Vegas Nights*, 1941
Major Films include *Anchors Aweigh*, 1945; *The House I Live In* (Oscar-winning short), 1945; *It Happened in Brooklyn*, 1947; *Take Me Out to the Ball Game*, 1949; *On the Town*, 1949; *From Here to Eternity*, 1953; *Young at Heart*, 1955; *The Man With the Golden Arm*, 1955; *High Society*, 1956; *Pal Joey*, 1957; *Some Came Running*, 1959; *The Manchurian Candidate*, 1962; *None But the Brave*, 1965; *The Detective*, 1968; *Dirty Dingus Magee* 1970; *That's Entertainment* (narration), 1974; *The First Deadly Sin*, 1980

Academy Award for best supporting actor: *From Here to Eternity*, 1953
Nomination for best actor: *The Man With the Golden Arm*, 1955
Jean Hersholt Humanitarian Award, 1970

Maggie Smith, who won a best actress Academy Award for *The Prime of Miss Jean Brodie* in 1969, is seen here with Michael Palin in a more recent movie, *The Missionary* (1982).

Nomination for best actress: *Travels With My Aunt*, 1972
Nomination for best supporting actress: *Othello*, 1965

SISSY SPACEK

Born Mary Elizabeth Spacek on December 25, 1950 in Quitman, TX (cousin of actor Rip Torn)
Married to director Jack Fisk in 1974; daughter Schuyler Elizabeth born in 1982

First Film *Prime Cut*, 1972
Major Films include *Badlands*, 1973; *Carrie*, 1976; *Three Women*, 1977; *Coal Miner's Daughter*, 1979; *Raggedy Man*, 1981; *Missing*, 1982

Academy Award for best actress: *Coal Miner's Daughter*, 1979
Nominations for best actress: *Carrie*, 1976; *Missing*, 1982

SYLVESTER STALLONE

Born Michael Sylvester Stallone on July 6, 1946 in New York City, NY
Married to Sasha Czack; son Sage Moon Blood born in 1976; son Seth

First Film *Bananas*, 1971 (uncredited)
Major Films include *The Lords of Flatbush*, 1974; *Rocky*, 1976; *Paradise Alley*, 1978; *Rocky II*, 1979; *Victory*, 1981; *Rocky III*, 1982; *First Blood*, 1982

Academy Award Nomination for best actor: *Rocky*, 1976

Nomination for best original screenplay: *Rocky*, 1976

BARBARA STANWYCK

Born Ruby Stevens on July 16, 1907 in Brooklyn, NY
Married to actor Frank Fay in 1928; divorced in 1935; stepson, Anthony; adopted son, Dion
Married to actor Robert Taylor in 1939; divorced in 1952

First Film *Broadway Nights*, 1927
Major Films include *Ten Cents a Dance*, 1931; *The Miracle Woman*, 1931; *Forbidden*, 1932; *Baby Face*, 1933; *Gambling Lady*, 1934; *Annie Oakley*, 1935; *Stella Dallas*, 1937; *Union Pacific*, 1939; *Golden Boy*, 1939; *Remember the Night*, 1940; *The Lady Eve*, 1941; *Meet John Doe*, 1941; *Ball of Fire*, 1941; *Lady of Burlesque*, 1942; *Double Indemnity*, 1944; *The Strange Love of Martha Ivers*, 1946; *Sorry, Wrong Number*, 1948; *The Furies*, 1950; *Clash by Night*, 1952; *Executive Suite*, 1954; *There's Always Tomorrow*, 1956; *Walk on the Wild Side*, 1962; *The Night Walker*, 1965

Academy Award Nominations for best actress: *Stella Dallas*, 1937; *Ball of Fire*, 1941; *Double Indemnity*, 1944; *Sorry, Wrong Number*, 1948
Special Academy Award "for superlative creativity and unique contribution to the art of screen acting," 1981

ROD STEIGER

Born Rodney Stephen Steiger on April 14, 1925 in Westhampton, NY
Married to Sally Gracie in 1952; divorced in 1954
Married to actress Claire Bloom in 1959; divorced in 1969; daughter Anna Justine born in 1960
Married to Sherry Nelson in 1973; divorced in 1979

First Film *Teresa*, 1951
Major Films include *On the Waterfront*, 1954; *Oklahoma!*, 1955; *Jubal*, 1956; *The Harder They Fall*, 1956; *Across the Bridge*, 1958; *Al Capone*, 1959; *The Longest Day*, 1962; *The Pawnbroker*, 1965; *The Loved One*, 1965; *Doctor Zhivago*, 1965; *In the Heat of the Night*, 1967; *The Amityville Horror*, 1979; *The Chosen*, 1982

Academy Award for best actor: *In the Heat of the Night*, 1967
Nomination for best actor: *The Pawnbroker*, 1965
Nomination for best supporting actor: *On the Waterfront*, 1954

JAMES STEWART

Born James Maitland Stewart on May 20, 1908 in Indiana, PA
Married to Gloria Hatrick McLean in 1949; twin daughters Kelly and Judy born in 1951; adopted son, Michael; adopted son, Ronald (died)

First Film *The Murder Man*, 1935
Major Films include *Born to Dance*, 1936; *The Shopworn Angel*, 1938; *You Can't Take It With You*, 1938; *Made for Each Other*, 1939; *It's a Wonderful World*, 1939; *Mr. Smith Goes to Washington*, 1939; *Destry Rides Again*, 1939; *The Shop Around the Corner*, 1940; *The Philadelphia Story*, 1940; *It's a Wonderful Life*, 1946; *Harvey*, 1950; *The Greatest Show on Earth*, 1952; *Rear Window*, 1954; *Strategic Air Command*, 1955; *The Man Who Knew Too Much*, 1956; *Vertigo*, 1958; *Anatomy of a Murder*, 1959; *The Man Who Shot Liberty Valance*, 1962;

Rod Steiger, one of the screen's most compelling dramatic figures, in the 1956 release *The Harder They Fall*. Steiger won the 1967 best actor Oscar for *In the Heat of the Night*.

Since she made her first movie, *Julia* in 1977, Meryl Streep has won two Oscars and three nominations. For *Silkwood* (in which she's seen here) she won a 1983 best actress nomination.

Shenandoah, 1965; *The Shootist*, 1976; *The Big Sleep*, 1978

Academy Award for best actor: *The Philadelphia Story*, 1940
Nominations for best actor: *Mr. Smith Goes to Washington*, 1939; *It's a Wonderful Life*, 1946; *Harvey*, 1950; *Anatomy of a Murder*, 1959

Book *The Films of James Stewart* by Kenneth D. Jones

MERYL STREEP

Born Mary Louise Streep on June 27, 1949 in Summet, NJ
Married to sculptor Donald Gummer in 1978; son Henry born in 1978; daughter born in 1983

First Film *Julia*, 1977
Major Films include *The Deer Hunter*, 1978; *Manhattan*, 1979; *The Seduction of Joe Tynan*, 1979; *Kramer vs. Kramer*, 1979; *The French Lieutenant's Woman*, 1981; *Sophie's Choice*, 1982; *Still of the Night*, 1982; *Silkwood*, 1983

Academy Award for best actress: *Sophie's Choice*, 1982
Academy Award for best supporting actress: *Kramer vs. Kramer*, 1979
Nominations for best actress: *The French Lieutenant's Woman*, 1981; *Silkwood*, 1983
Nomination for best supporting actress: *The Deer Hunter*, 1978

BARBRA STREISAND

Born Barbara Joan Streisand on April 24, 1942 in Brooklyn, NY
Married to actor Elliott Gould in 1963; divorced in 1971; son Jason born in 1966

First Film *Funny Girl*, 1968
Major Films include *Hello, Dolly!*, 1969; *On a Clear Day You Can See Forever*, 1970; *The Owl and the Pussycat*, 1970; *What's Up, Doc?*, 1972; *Up the Sandbox*, 1972; *The Way We Were*, 1973; *For Pete's Sake*, 1974; *Funny Lady*, 1975; *A Star Is Born*, 1976; *The Main Event*, 1979; *Yentl*, 1983

Academy Award for best actress: *Funny Girl*, 1968
Nomination for best actress: *The Way We Were*, 1973
Academy Award for best song: "Evergreen" from *A Star Is Born* (music by Streisand, lyrics by Paul Williams), 1976

ERICH VON STROHEIM

Born Erich Oswald Stroheim on September 22, 1886 in Vienna, Austria
Died on May 12, 1957
Married to Marguerite Knox; widowed
Married to May Jones in 1915; divorced; son Erich Jr. born in 1916
Married to Valerie Marguerite Germonprez in 1930; divorced; son Josef Erich born in 1931
Married to Sheila Darcy in 1943

First Film *Captain McLean*, 1914
Major Films include *His Picture in the Papers*, 1916; *For France*, 1917; *Hearts of the World*, 1918; *The Hun Within*, 1918; *Blind Husbands*, 1919; *Foolish Wives*, 1921; *The Wedding March*, 1928; *The Great Gabbo*, 1929; *Three Faces East*, 1930; *The Lost Squadron*, 1932; *As You Desire Me*, 1932; *Grand Illusion*, 1937; *L'Alibi*, 1937; *Boy's School*, 1938; *Personal Column*, 1939; *Paris—New York*, 1940; *So Ends Our Night*, 1941; *Five Graves to Cairo*, 1943; *Storm Over Lisbon*, 1944; *La Danse de Mort*, 1947; *Sunset Boulevard*, 1950; *Napoléon*, 1955

Academy Award Nomination for best supporting actor: *Sunset Boulevard*, 1950

DONALD SUTHERLAND

Born Donald Sutherland on July 17, 1934 in St. John, New Brunswick, Canada
Married to Lois May Hardwick in 1959; divorced
Married to actress Shirley Douglas in 1966; divorced in 1971; daughter Rachel born in 1966; son Kiefer born in 1966
Children by Francine Racette; son Roeg born in 1974; son Rossis born in 1978; son born in 1982

First Film *Castle of the Living Dead*, 1964
Major Films include *The Dirty Dozen*, 1967; *M*A*S*H*, 1970; *Kelly's Heroes*, 1970; *Klute*, 1971; *Don't Look Now*, 1973; *The Day of the Locust*, 1975; *1900*, 1976; *Fellini's Casanova*, 1976; *Invasion of the Body Snatchers*, 1978; *The Great Train Robbery*, 1978; *Murder by Decree*, 1979; *Ordinary People*, 1980; *Eye of the Needle*, 1981; *Threshold*, 1983

ELIZABETH TAYLOR

Born Elizabeth Taylor on February 27, 1932 in London, England

Elizabeth Taylor's newsworthy private life sometimes overshadows her acting achievements; in fact, she's won two best actress Academy Awards and three nominations in the same category.

Married to Conrad Nicholson Hilton, Jr. in 1950; divorced in 1951

Married to actor Michael Wilding in 1952; divorced in 1957; son Michael Howard Jr. born in 1953; son Christopher Edward born in 1955

Married to producer Michael Todd in 1957; widowed in 1958; daughter Elizabeth Frances born in 1957

Married to singer Eddie Fisher in 1959; divorced in 1964; adopted daughter, Maria-Petra

Married to actor Richard Burton in 1964; divorced in 1974

Remarried to Richard Burton in 1975; divorced in 1976

Married to Senator John William Warner, Jr., in 1976; divorced

First Film *There's One Born Every Minute*, 1942
Major Films include *Lassie Come Home*, 1943; *National Velvet*, 1944; *Life With Father*, 1947; *A Date With Judy*, 1948; *Little Women*, 1949; *Father of the Bride*, 1950; *A Place in the Sun*, 1951; *Ivanhoe*, 1952; *The Last Time I Saw Paris*, 1954; *Giant*, 1956; *Raintree County*, 1957; *Cat on a Hot Tin Roof*, 1958; *Suddenly Last Summer*, 1959; *Butterfield 8*, 1960; *Cleopatra*, 1963; *The V.I.P.s*, 1964; *Who's Afraid of Virginia Woolf?*, 1966; *The Taming of the Shrew*, 1967; *Reflections in a Golden Eye*, 1967; *Ash Wednesday*, 1973; *The Blue Bird*, 1976; *A Little Night Music*, 1977

Academy Awards for best actress: *Butterfield 8*, 1960; *Who's Afraid of Virginia Woolf?*, 1966
Nominations for best actress: *Raintree County*, 1957; *Cat on a Hot Tin Roof*, 1958; *Suddenly Last Summer*, 1959

Biography *Richard and Elizabeth* by Lester David and Jahn Robbins

SHIRLEY TEMPLE

Born Shirley Jane Temple on April 23, 1928 in Santa Monica, CA

Married to actor John Agar in 1945; divorced in 1949; daughter Linda Susan born in 1947
Married to Charles A. Black in 1950; son Charles Alden Jr., born in 1952; daughter Lori Alden born in 1954

First Film *The Red-Haired Alibi*, 1932
Major Films include *Stand Up and Cheer*, 1934; *Little Miss Marker*, 1934; *Bright Eyes*, 1934; *The Little Colonel*, 1935; *Curly Top*, 1935; *The Littlest Rebel*, 1935; *Captain January*, 1936; *Poor Little Rich Girl*, 1936; *Stowaway*, 1936; *Wee Willie Winkie*, 1937; *Heidi*, 1937; *Rebecca of Sunnybrook Farm*, 1938; *The Little Princess*, 1939; *Since You Went Away*, 1944; *Kiss and Tell*, 1946; *The Bachelor and the Bobby Soxer*, 1947; *Fort Apache*, 1948; *The Story of Seabiscuit*, 1949

Special Academy Award "in grateful recognition of her outstanding contribution to screen entertainment during the year 1934," 1934

Autobiography *My Young Life*, 1945

GENE TIERNEY

Born Gene Eliza Tierney on November 20, 1920 in Brooklyn, NY
Married to fashion designer Oleg Cassini in 1941; divorced in 1952; daughter Daria born in 1943; daughter Christina born in 1944
Married to W. Howard Lee in 1960; widowed

First Film *The Return of Frank James*, 1940
Major Films include *Belle Starr*, 1941; *The Shanghai Gesture*, 1942; *Heaven Can Wait*, 1943; *Laura*, 1944; *Leave Her to Heaven*, 1945; *The Razor's Edge*, 1946; *The Ghost and Mrs. Muir*, 1947; *Whirlpool*, 1950; *Never Let Me Go*, 1953; *The Left Hand of God*, 1955, *Advise and Consent*, 1962; *The Pleasure Seekers*, 1964

Academy Award Nomination for best actress: *Leave Her to Heaven*, 1945

Autobiography *Self Portrait*, 1979

FRANCHOT TONE

Born Stanislaus Pascal Franchot Tone on February 27, 1905 in Niagara Falls, NY
Died on September 18, 1968
Married to actress Joan Crawford in 1935; divorced in 1939
Married to actress Jean Wallace in 1941; divorced in 1948; son Thomas Jefferson born in 1942; son Pascal born in 1943
Married to actress Barbara Payton in 1951; divorced in 1952
Married to actress Dolores Dorn-Heft in 1956; divorced in 1959

First Film *The Wiser Sex*, 1932
Major Films include *Dancing Lady*, 1933; *Moulin Rouge*, 1934; *Gentlemen Are Born*, 1934; *The Lives of a Bengal Lancer*, 1935; *Mutiny on the Bounty*, 1935; *Love on the Run*, 1936; *Quality Street*, 1937; *They Gave Him a Gun*, 1937; *Three Comrades*, 1938; *This*

John Travolta, who won a best actor Academy Award nomination for the musical *Saturday Night Fever* (1977), is seen here in a straight acting role in *Blow Out* (1981).

JOHN TRAVOLTA

Born John Travolta on February 18, 1954 in Englewood, NJ

First Film *The Devil's Rain*, 1975
Major Films include *Carrie*, 1976; *Saturday Night Fever*, 1977; *Grease*, 1978; *Moment by Moment*, 1978; *Urban Cowboy*, 1980; *Blow Out*, 1981; *Staying Alive*, 1983

Academy Award Nomination for best actor: *Saturday Night Fever*, 1977

LANA TURNER

Born Julia Jean Mildred Frances Turner on February 8, 1920 in Wallace, ID
Married to bandleader Artie Shaw in 1940; divorced in 1942
Married to actor Stephen Crane in 1943; divorced in 1944; daughter Cheryl born in 1944
Married to millionaire Henry J. (Bob) Topping in 1948; divorced in 1952
Married to actor Lex Barker in 1953; divorced in 1957
Married to Fred May in 1960; divorced in 1962
Married to Robert Eaton in 1965; divorced in 1969
Married to Ronald Dante in 1969; divorced in 1972

First Film *A Star Is Born*, 1937
Major Films include *They Won't Forget*, 1937; *Calling Dr. Kildare*, 1939; *Dr. Jekyll and Mr. Hyde*, 1941; *Honky Tonk*, 1941; *Johnny Eager*, 1942; *The Postman Always Rings Twice*, 1946; *Cass Timberlane*, 1947; *The Three Musketeers*, 1948; *The Bad and the Beautiful*, 1952; *Peyton Place*, 1957; *Imitation of Life*, 1959; *Madame X*, 1966; *Bittersweet Love*, 1976

Academy Award Nomination for best actress: *Peyton Place*, 1957

Woman Is Mine, 1941; *Five Graves to Cairo*, 1943; *Phantom Lady*, 1944; *Every Girl Should Be Married*, 1948; *The Man on the Eiffel Tower*, 1950; *Advise and Consent*, 1962; *Nobody Runs Forever*, 1968

Academy Award Nomination for best actor: *Mutiny on the Bounty*, 1935

SPENCER TRACY

Born Spencer Bonaventure Tracy on April 5, 1900 in Milwaukee, WI
Died on June 10, 1967
Married to actress Louise Treadwell in 1923; son John born in 1924; daughter Louise born in 1932

First Film *Up the River*, 1930
Major Films include *Quick Millions*, 1931; *20,000 Years in Sing Sing*, 1933; *The Power and the Glory*, 1933; *A Man's Castle*, 1933; *The Show-Off*, 1934; *Fury*, 1936; *San Francisco*, 1936; *Captains Courageous*, 1937; *Boys Town*, 1938; *Stanley and Livingstone*, 1939; *Boom Town*, 1940; *Dr. Jekyll and Mr. Hyde*, 1941; *Woman of the Year*, 1942; *A Guy Named Joe*, 1943; *Adam's Rib*, 1949; *Father of the Bride*, 1950; *The Actress*, 1953; *Bad Day at Black Rock*, 1955; *The Old Man and the Sea*, 1958; *The Last Hurrah*, 1958; *Inherit the Wind*, 1960; *Judgment at Nuremberg*, 1961; *Guess Who's Coming to Dinner?*, 1967

Academy Awards for best actor: *Captains Courageous*, 1937; *Boys Town*, 1938
Nominations for best actor: *San Francisco*, 1936; *Father of the Bride*, 1950; *Bad Day at Black Rock*, 1955; *The Old Man and the Sea*, 1958; *Inherit the Wind*, 1960; *Judgment at Nuremberg*, 1961; *Guess Who's Coming to Dinner?*, 1967

Biography *Spencer Tracy* by Larry Swindell

A blonde bombshell study of Lana Turner, who proved she had talent as well as beauty by winning an Academy Award nomination for best actress for her performance in *Peyton Place* in 1957.

Peter Ustinov, a man of many talents, in *Billy Budd* (1962). Ustinov won best supporting actor Oscars for *Spartacus* (1960) and *Topkapi* (1964), and was nominated for *Quo Vadis* (1951).

PETER USTINOV

Born Peter Alexander Ustinov on April 15, 1921 in London, England
Married to actress Isolde Denham in 1940; divorced; daughter Tamara born in 1941
Married to actress Suzanne Cloutier in 1954; divorced in 1971; son Igor born in 1956; daughter Pavia born in 1959
Married to press agent Hélène du Lau d'Alleman in 1972

First Film *Hullo Fame*, 1940
Major Films include *The Way Ahead*, 1944; *Private Angelo*, 1949; *Hotel Sahara*, 1951; *Quo Vadis*, 1951; *Beau Brummel*, 1954; *We're No Angels*, 1955; *Spartacus*, 1960; *The Sundowners*, 1960; *Romanoff and Juliet*, 1961; *Billy Budd*, 1962; *Topkapi*, 1964; *Hot Millions*, 1968; *One of Our Dinosaurs Is Missing*, 1975; *Death on the Nile*, 1978; *Evil Under the Sun*, 1981

Academy Awards for best supporting actor: *Spartacus*, 1960; *Topkapi*, 1964
Nomination for best supporting actor: *Quo Vadis*, 1951
Nomination for best original screenplay: *Hot Millions* (with Ira Wallach), 1968

Autobiography *Dear Me*, 1977

JON VOIGHT

Born Jon Voight on December 29, 1938 in Yonkers, NY
Married to Lauri Peters in 1962; divorced
Married to Marcelline Bertrand in 1971; son James born in 1972; daughter Angelina

First Film *Hour of the Gun*, 1967
Major Films include *Midnight Cowboy*, 1969; *The Revolutionary*, 1970; *Deliverance*, 1972; *Conrack*, 1974; *The Odessa File*, 1974; *Coming Home*, 1978; *The Champ*, 1979; *Lookin'*

to Get Out, 1982; *Table for Five*, 1983

Academy Award for best actor: *Coming Home*, 1978
Nomination for best actor: *Midnight Cowboy*, 1969

ROBERT WAGNER

Born Robert Wagner, Jr. on February 10, 1930 in Detroit, MI
Married to actress Natalie Wood in 1957; divorced in 1962
Married to actress Marion Marshall in 1963; divorced in 1971; daughter Katherine born in 1964
Remarried to Natalie Wood in 1972; widowed in 1981; stepdaughter, Natasha Gregson; daughter Courtney Brooke born in 1974

First Film *The Happy Years*, 1950
Major Films include *Titanic*, 1953; *Prince Valiant*, 1954; *The True Story of Jesse James*, 1957; *The Pink Panther*, 1964; *Harper*, 1966; *Banning*, 1967; *Winning*, 1969; *The Towering Inferno*, 1974; *Midway*, 1976; *Airport '79 Concorde*, 1979

JOHN WAYNE

Born Marion Michael Morrison on May 26, 1907 in Winterset, IA
Died on June 11, 1979
Married to Josephine Saenz in 1932; divorced in 1944; son Michael A. Morrison (producer under name of Michael Wayne) born in 1934; son Patrick Morrison (actor under name of Patrick Wayne) born in 1939; daughter Antonia Morrison born in 1940; daughter Melinda Morrison born in 1941
Married to actress Esperanza Bauer in 1946; divorced in 1954
Married to Pilar Palette in 1954; daughter Aissa Morrison born in 1955; son Ethan Morrison born in

John Wayne was not one of the movie world's overnight stars; he had spent ten years making B westerns for various studios before scoring his first big success in *Stagecoach* in 1939.

1962; daughter Marisa Morrison born in 1966

First Film *The Drop Kick*, 1927
Major Films include *The Big Trail*, 1930; *Baby Face*, 1933; *The Oregon Trail*, 1936; *Stagecoach*, 1939; *The Long Voyage Home*, 1940; *Seven Sinners*, 1940; *The Spoilers*, 1942; *They Were Expendable*, 1945; *Fort Apache*, 1948; *Red River*, 1948; *She Wore a Yellow Ribbon*, 1949; *Sands of Iwo Jima*, 1949; *Rio Grande*, 1950; *The Quiet Man*, 1952; *The Searchers*, 1956; *Rio Bravo*, 1959; *The Man Who Shot Liberty Valance*, 1962; *The Sons of Katie Elder*, 1965; *The Green Berets*, 1969; *True Grit*, 1969; *The Cowboys*, 1972; *The Shootist*, 1976

Academy Award for best actor: *True Grit*, 1969
Nomination for best actor: *Sands of Iwo Jima*, 1949

Biography *Duke* by Mike Tomkin
Book *The Complete Films of John Wayne* by Mark Ricci

CLIFTON WEBB

Born Webb Parmalee Hollenbeck on November 9, 1891 in Indianapolis, IN
Died on October 13, 1966

First Film *Polly With a Past*, 1920
Major Films include *New Toys*, 1925; *Laura*, 1944; *The Razor's Edge*, 1946; *Sitting Pretty*, 1948; *Mr. Belvedere Goes to College*, 1949; *Cheaper by the Dozen*, 1950; *Dreamboat*, 1952; *Titanic*, 1953; *Three Coins in the Fountain*,

1954; *Woman's World*, 1954; *The Man Who Never Was*, 1956; *Boy on a Dolphin*, 1957; *The Remarkable Mr. Pennypacker*, 1959; *Satan Never Sleeps*, 1962

Academy Award Nomination for best actor: *Sitting Pretty*, 1948
Nominations for best supporting actor: *Laura*, 1944; *The Razor's Edge*, 1946

JOHNNY WEISSMULLER

Born Peter John Weissmuller on June 2, 1904 in Windber, PA
Died on January 20, 1984
Married to Camilla Louier; divorced
Married to singer Bobbe Arnst in 1930; divorced in 1932
Married to actress Lupe Velez in 1933; divorced in 1938
Married to Beryl Scott in 1939; divorced in 1943; daughter Wendy born in 1939; son John Jr. born in 1940; daughter Heidi born in 1942
Married to Allene Gates in 1948; divorced in 1962
Married to Maria Brock Mandell in 1963

First Film *Glorifying the American Girl*, 1929
Major Films include *Tarzan the Ape Man*, 1932; *Tarzan and His Mate*, 1934; *Tarzan Escapes*, 1936; *Tarzan Finds a Son*, 1939; *Tarzan's Secret Treasure*, 1941; *Tarzan's New York Adventure*, 1942; *Tarzan Triumphs*, 1943; *Tarzan's Desert Mystery*, 1943; *Tarzan and the Amazons*, 1945; *Tarzan and the Leopard Woman*, 1946; *Tarzan and the Huntress*, 1947; *Tarzan and*

the Mermaids, 1948; *Jungle Jim*, 1948; *The Lost Tribe*, 1949; *Captive Girl*, 1950; *Fury of the Congo*, 1951; *Savage Mutiny*, 1953; *Devil Goddess*, 1955

Autobiography *Water, World and Weissmuller*, 1967

ORSON WELLES

Born George Orson Welles on May 6, 1915 in Kenosha, WI
Married to actress Virginia Nicholson in 1934; divorced in 1940; son Christopher born in 1938
Married to actress Rita Hayworth in 1943; divorced in 1947; daughter Rebecca born in 1944
Married to Paola Mari in 1955; daughter Beatrice born in 1956

First Film *Citizen Kane*, 1941
Major Films include *Jane Eyre*, 1944; *The Stranger*, 1946; *The Lady From*

Shanghai, 1948; *Macbeth*, 1948; *The Third Man*, 1949; *The Black Rose*, 1950; *Othello*, 1952 (released in U.S. in 1955); *Mr. Arkadin*, 1955 (released in U.S. in 1962); *Moby Dick*, 1956; *Touch of Evil*, 1958; *Compulsion*, 1959; *The Trial*, 1962; *A Man for All Seasons*, 1966; *Falstaff*, 1966; *Oedipus the King*, 1968; *Catch-22*, 1970; *F for Fake*, 1975; *Voyage of the Damned*, 1976; *The Muppet Movie*, 1979

Academy Award for best original screenplay: *Citizen Kane* (with Herman J. Mankiewicz), 1941
Nomination for best actor: *Citizen Kane*, 1941
Nomination for best director: *Citizen Kane*, 1941
Special Academy Award "for superlative artistry and versatility in the creation of motion pictures," 1970

Biography *Orson Welles* by Joseph McBride
Books *Orson Welles* by Peter Bogdanovich; *The Magic World of Orson Welles* by James Navemore

Actor/director Orson Welles' first and most famous film, *Citizen Kane*, won him nominations for both best actor and best director. Welles also co-wrote the Award-winning screenplay.

MAE WEST

Born Mae West on August 17, 1892 in Brooklyn, NY
Died on November 23, 1980
Married to Frank Wallace in 1911; divorced in 1943

First Film *Night After Night*, 1932
Major Films include *She Done Him Wrong*, 1933; *I'm No Angel*, 1933; *Belle of the Nineties*, 1934; *Goin' to Town*, 1935; *Klondike Annie*, 1936; *Go West Young Man*, 1936; *Every Day's a Holiday*, 1938; *My Little Chickadee*, 1940; *The Heat's On*, 1943; *Myra Breckinridge*, 1970; *Sextette*, 1978

Autobiographies *Goodness Had Nothing to Do With It*, 1959; *Life, Sex and ESP*, 1975

RICHARD WIDMARK

Born Richard Widmark on December 26, 1914 in Sunrise, MN
Married to actress/screenwriter Jean Hazelwood in 1942; daughter Anne (married to baseball player Sandy Koufax)

First Film *Kiss of Death*, 1947
Major Films include *The Street With No Name*, 1948; *Down to the Sea in Ships*, 1949; *Panic in the Streets*, 1950; *No Way Out*, 1950; *Don't Bother to Knock*, 1952; *Broken Lance*, 1954; *The Cobweb*, 1955; *Time Limit*, 1957; *Tunnel of Love*, 1958; *The Alamo*, 1960; *The Secret Ways*, 1961; *How the West Was Won*, 1963; *Cheyenne Autumn*, 1964; *The Bedford

Incident, 1965; *Madigan*, 1968; *When the Legends Die*, 1972; *Murder on the Orient Express*, 1974; *Coma*, 1978; *Against All Odds*, 1984

Academy Award Nomination for best supporting actor: *Kiss of Death*, 1947

BILLY DEE WILLIAMS

Born Billy Dee Williams on April 6, 1937 in New York City, NY
Married to Audrey Sellers; divorced; son Corey
Married to Marlene Clark; divorced
Married to Teruko Nakagami in 1972; daughter Hanaku born in 1973

First Film *The Last Angry Man*, 1959
Major Films include *The Out-of-Towners*, 1970; *Lady Sings the Blues*, 1972; *Hit!*, 1973; *The Take*, 1974; *Mahogany*, 1975; *The Bingo Long Traveling All-Stars and Motor Kings*, 1976; *Scott Joplin*, 1977; *The Empire Strikes Back*, 1980; *Nighthawks*, 1981; *Return of the Jedi*, 1983

ESTHER WILLIAMS

Born Esther Jane Williams on August 8, 1923 in Los Angeles, CA
Married to Leonard Kovner in 1941; divorced in 1944
Married to radio announcer Ben Gage in 1945; divorced in 1957; son Benjamin born in 1949; son Kimball born in 1950; daughter Susan born in 1953

Married to actor Fernando Lamas in 1963; widowed in 1982; stepdaughter Alejandre; stepson Lorenzo Fernando (actor)

First Film *Andy Hardy's Double Life*, 1942
Major Films include *Bathing Beauty*, 1944; *Thrill of a Romance*, 1945; *The Hoodlum Saint*, 1946; *Fiesta*, 1947; *On an Island With You*, 1948; *Take Me Out to the Ball Game*, 1949; *Neptune's Daughter*, 1949; *Duchess of Idaho*, 1950; *Pagan Love Song*, 1950; *Texas Carnival*, 1951; *Million Dollar Mermaid*, 1952; *Dangerous When Wet*, 1953; *Jupiter's Darling*, 1955; *The Unguarded Moment*, 1956; *Raw Wind in Eden*, 1958; *The Big Show*, 1961

SHELLEY WINTERS

Born Shirley Schrift on August 18, 1922 in St. Louis, MO

Married to Mack Meyer in 1942; divorced in 1948
Married to actor Vittorio Gassman in 1952; divorced in 1954; daughter Vittoria born in 1953
Married to actor Anthony Franciosa in 1957; divorced in 1960

First Film *What a Woman!*, 1943
Major Films include *A Double Life*, 1948; *The Great Gatsby*, 1949; *A Place in the Sun*, 1951; *Phone Call From a Stranger*, 1952; *Executive Suite*, 1954; *I Am a Camera*, 1955; *The Night of the Hunter*, 1955; *I Died a Thousand Times*, 1955; *The Diary of Anne Frank*, 1959; *Lolita*, 1962; *A Patch of Blue*, 1965; *Alfie*, 1966; *Wild in the Streets*, 1968; *Bloody Mama*, 1970; *The Poseidon Adventure*, 1972; *Next Stop, Greenwich Village*, 1976; *Pete's Dragon*, 1977; *King of the Gypsies*, 1979; *S.O.B.*, 1981

Academy Awards for best supporting actress: *The Diary of Anne Frank*, 1959; *A Patch of Blue*, 1965

The Royal Air Force honored the glamorous Mae West in an original manner: they named an inflatable lifesaving device the "Mae West" after her. West became an entertainer young—she was only five.

Nomination for best actress: *A Place in the Sun*, 1951
Nomination for best supporting actress: *The Poseidon Adventure*, 1972

Autobiography *Shelley, Also Known as Shirley*, 1980

NATALIE WOOD

Born Natasha Gurdin on July 20, 1938 in San Francisco, CA
Died in a drowning accident on November 29, 1981
Married to actor Robert Wagner in 1957; divorced in 1962
Married to Richard Gregson in 1969; divorced; daughter Natasha born in 1970
Remarried to Robert Wagner in 1972; daughter Courtney Brooke born in 1974

First Film *Happy Land*, 1943 (as Natasha Gurdin)
Major Films include *Tomorrow Is Forever*, 1946; *Miracle on 34th Street*, 1947; *No Sad Songs for Me*, 1950; *The Star*, 1953; *Rebel Without a Cause*, 1955; *Marjorie Morningstar*, 1958; *Splendor in the Grass*, 1961; *West Side Story*, 1961; *Gypsy*, 1962; *Love With the Proper Stranger*, 1963; *The Great Race*, 1965; *Bob & Carol & Ted & Alice*, 1969; *Peeper*, 1976; *Meteor*, 1979; *Brainstorm*, 1983

Academy Award Nominations for best actress: *Splendor in the Grass*, 1961; *Love With the Proper Stranger*, 1963
Nomination for best supporting actress: *Rebel Without a Cause*, 1955

JOANNE WOODWARD

Born Joanne Gignilliat Woodward on February 27, 1930 in Thomasville, GA
Married to actor Paul Newman in 1958; daughter Elinor Terese born in 1959; daughter Melissa Stewart born in 1960; daughter Clea Olivia born in 1961

First Film *Count Three and Pray*, 1955
Major Films include *A Kiss Before Dying*, 1956; *The Three Faces of Eve*, 1957; *No Down Payment*, 1957; *The Long Hot Summer*, 1958; *The Sound and the Fury*, 1959; *From the Terrace*, 1960; *The Stripper*, 1963; *A Big Hand for the Little Lady*, 1966; *Rachel, Rachel*, 1968; *WUSA*, 1970; *The Effect of Gamma Rays on Man-in-the-Moon Marigolds*, 1972; *Summer Wishes, Winter Dreams*, 1973; *The Drowning Pool*, 1975; *The End*, 1978

Academy Award for best actress: *The Three Faces of Eve*, 1957
Nominations for best actress: *Rachel, Rachel*, 1968; *Summer Wishes, Winter Dreams*, 1973

JANE WYMAN

Born Sarah Jane Fulks on January 4, 1914 in St. Joseph, MO
Married to Myron Futterman in 1937; divorced in 1938
Married to actor Ronald Reagan (later President of the United States) in 1940; divorced in 1948; adopted son, Michael; daughter Maureen born in 1942
Married to bandleader

Fred Karger in 1952; divorced in 1954
Remarried to Fred Karger in 1961; divorced

First Film *Gold Diggers of 1937*, 1936
Major Films include *Brother Rat*, 1938; *Larceny Inc.*, 1942; *Princess O'Rourke*, 1943; *The Lost Weekend*, 1945; *The Yearling*, 1946; *Magic Town*, 1947; *Johnny Belinda*, 1948; *Stage Fright*, 1950; *The Glass Menagerie*, 1950; *The Blue Veil*, 1951; *Just for You*, 1952; *So Big*, 1953; *Magnificent Obsession*, 1954; *All That Heaven Allows*, 1956; *Pollyanna*, 1960; *Bon Voyage!*, 1962; *How to Commit Marriage*, 1969

Academy Award for best actress: *Johnny Belinda*, 1948
Nominations for best actress: *The Yearling*, 1946; *The Blue Veil*, 1951; *Magnificent Obsession*, 1954

LORETTA YOUNG

Born Gretchen Michaela Young on January 6, 1913 in Salt Lake City, UT (sister of actress Elizabeth Jane Young—stage name Sally Blane)
Married to actor Grant Withers in 1930; annulled in 1931
Adopted daughters Jane and Judy in 1937
Married to producer/writer Thomas H. A. Lewis in 1940; divorced in 1969; son Christopher born in 1944; son Peter born in 1945

First Film *Naughty But Nice*, 1927
Major Films include *Laugh Clown Laugh*, 1928; *The Squall*, 1929; *Loose Ankles*, 1930; *Taxi*, 1932; *A Man's Castle*, 1933; *The House of Rothschild*, 1934; *Call of the Wild*, 1935; *Ladies in Love*, 1936; *Love Is News*, 1937; *A Night to*

Natalie Wood, who died in a drowning accident in 1981 at the age of 43, was twice nominated for the best actress Oscar—for *Splendor in the Grass* (1961), and *Love With the Proper Stranger* (1963).

Loretta Young, seen here snuggling up to Tyrone Power, won a best actress Academy Award for *The Farmer's Daughter* (1947). She was also nominated for *Come to the Stable* (1949).

Remember, 1942; *The Stranger*, 1946; *The Farmer's Daughter*, 1947; *Rachel and the Stranger*, 1948; *Come to the Stable*, 1949; *Cause for Alarm*, 1951; *It Happens Every Thursday*, 1953

Academy Award for best actress: *The Farmer's Daughter*, 1947
Nomination for best actress: *Come to the Stable*, 1949

Autobiography *The Things I Had to Learn*, 1961

ROBERT YOUNG

Born Robert George Young on February 22, 1907 in Chicago, IL
Married to Elizabeth Louise Henderson in 1933; daughter Carol Ann born in 1933; daughter Barbara Queen born in 1937; daughter Elizabeth Louise born in 1943; daughter Kathleen born in 1945

First Film *The Black Camel*, 1931
Major Films include *The Sin of Madelon Claudet*, 1931; *Unashamed*, 1932; *Tugboat Annie*, 1933; *Spitfire*, 1934; *The House of Rothschild*, 1934; *Secret Agent*, 1936; *Navy Blue and Gold*, 1937; *Three Comrades*, 1938; *Northwest Passage*, 1940; *H. M. Pulham, Esq.*, 1941; *Journey for Margaret*, 1942; *Claudia*, 1943; *The Enchanted Cottage*, 1945; *Crossfire*, 1947; *That Forsyte Woman*, 1951; *Secret of the Incas*, 1954

QUOTES FROM
ACTORS (AND SOME OTHERS) ON ACTING

French director Jean Renoir has said, "I like to start with actors. I consider that my profession as a director is not exactly like supervision. No. We are, simply, midwives." And, on another occasion, Renoir said of the actor's task, "An actor must have the feeling that he wrote the part. It's not true; he didn't write it—but he must believe it. He must reject what doesn't seem to come from him."

The following quotes tell how some performers and others in the movie business feel about their calling.

What is acting but lying, and what is good acting but convincing lying?

—Laurence Olivier

People always say that you cannot change the Bible and you cannot change Shakespeare. But me? I always change things. I am like that.

—Klaus Kinski

You've got to be neurotic, insane, or totally obsessed to make it in this business.

—Albert S. Ruddy, producer

I do a part because I feel something for it . . . not because it builds my image.

—Robert Redford

Great men are marvelous to play. You feel a great inadequacy, sort of suspended inside this vast figure, straining desperately to fill it.

—Charlton Heston

I went into this business for the money and the art grew out of it.

—Charles Chaplin

I wasn't driven to acting by an inner compulsion. I was running away from the sporting goods business.

—Paul Newman

It's really like the Army. You're uncomfortable. You're never fed at the hour. You have to take orders.

—Norman Mailer on acting in *Ragtime*

Some parts you fall into like an old glove. Elmer really wasn't acting—that was me!

—Burt Lancaster on preparing for the title role in *Elmer Gantry*

The end of the original play of Mr. Maugham's is the line: "I still love the man I killed." We couldn't end it there because it was a big censorship era and if you murdered anybody you had to die yourself. Of course, it was ridiculous, because to live on with your own guilt is a far worse hell than having somebody happily put you out of your misery.

—Bette Davis on the making of *The Letter*

Doing this picture gripes the hell out of me. . . . It's too commercial, it's in bad taste. Everyone is crazy, mixed-up sick— except for the part Eddie [Fisher, her husband at that time] plays.

—Elizabeth Taylor on her feelings about making *Butterfield 8*, for which she won an Academy Award as best actress

It's all so political. Keep the director happy. Keep the unit happy. Because in the end it's you up there on the screen.

—Peter O'Toole

Doing a moving picture is like telling a very personal experience to someone in your own living room. You don't have to project so much but it's just as powerful: the atom bomb is pretty small, too.

—Shirley Booth on her feelings about making the film version of *Come Back, Little Sheba*

My favorite line I've ever had to say . . . came out of Cabin in the Cotton: *"Ah'd love to kiss ya, but ah jest washed mah hair."*

—Bette Davis

It takes more than greasepaint and footlights to make an actress. It takes heartbreak as well.

—Constance Collier in *Stage Door*

I didn't have the heart to tell him [writer/ director Jason Miller] until the last day that I've never seen a whole basketball game. Christ, who'd ever want to see a whole basketball game?"

—Robert Mitchum talking about *That Championship Season*

I choose my roles carefully so that when my career is finished, I will have covered all our recent history of oppression.

—Vanessa Redgrave

The character I played was symbolic of what people would like to be. He was not a black character or a white character: he was all characters, you see. He was the man that all people can look upon and wish they were like. He was a strong man. He was a just man. He was a well-loved man. He was a happy full-of-life man. He spread love and glad tidings wherever he moved. Everyone would like to be like that. And these ingredients of his character made his color invisible.

—Sidney Poitier on the character he played in *Edge of the City*

All right, you warm, bloody bastards, what's good for one is good for all! I'm not shooting till I see every one of you down to your jockey shorts.

—Carole Lombard, required to wear light silk garments in freezing midwinter weather, to the film crew and director of *From Hell to Heaven.*

I think the best training for an actor at a certain age is not to study acting. The best training for an actor is to study the humanities, to study literature, to study history, to travel, to get a sense of who he is and what his relationship is to his environment and his relationship to his time. That's the passion he should develop. Then you learn the craft and, God willing, you have the craft and you have an understanding of yourself and the times in which you live. Then you can be an actor.

—Gilbert Cates, director

QUOTES FROM
ACTORS ON THEMSELVES

Things aren't always what they seem to be, and nor are people. The audience's image of an actor or actress may differ significantly from that performer's image of himself or herself. Here's what some performers, and others involved in the world of the movies, have to say about themselves.

I've had a fascinating life. I don't think I'm the least bit peculiar, but people tell me that I am.

—Katharine Hepburn

I was an ugly kid with a big mouth, an obnoxious show-off. Nobody liked me. I was bossy, prim, and determined. I looked middle-aged, and the other kids thought I was one of the teachers!

—Meryl Streep

I'm pretty introspective. I'm not what I'd call a hedonist: just ignore what you read—I do.

—Warren Beatty

I gave my best performance, perhaps, during the war—pretending to be an officer and a gentleman.

—Alec Guinness

Do you know what I like doing as much as anything in the whole wide world? Signing autographs. Writing my own name. Burt Reynolds. Over and over. Burt Reynolds. It's soothing. I feel like a mystic. It gives me power.

—Burt Reynolds

My face looks like two miles of country road. Every night I've stayed up late, every woman I've ever chased, every drink I've taken—shows. But, hell, man, I don't work in spite of my face, I work because of it—and I know that to be true.

—Warren Oates

It's because I'm one of the only non-neurotic women in Hollywood.

—Bette Davis on why she was so good at portraying neurotic women

I never thought to be an actor. I was in London in the Mr. Universe contest, and looking for something else to do. I had an offer to try for the Manchester United football team, but I was 22, a bit old for that. Then someone told me they were looking for people to fill the chorus of South Pacific. *So I found out where to go to audition, I got a job, and that was that.*

—Sean Connery

I've at last learned to relax. The emotional crises are finished so one can concentrate more on one's work which is all, finally, I care about.

—John Gielgud

As a dancer, I can't compete with Ginger Rogers or Eleanor Powell. As a singer, I'm no Doris Day. As an actress, I don't take myself seriously. I have some looks, without being in the big beauty league.

—Betty Grable

I've done everything I've wanted to do . . . . I've played Hamlet *in London; I've had every woman I ever wanted; I have a son to carry on my name . . . . I'm bored and I'm tired.*

—John Barrymore

You can't get spoiled if you do your own ironing.

—Meryl Streep

My idea of cooking is doing the dishes.

—Teri Garr

I think my performance [in Deliverance*] has probably ruined the movie. How's* The Godfather? *Worst acting I've ever done. I just hope the picture will slip out and not be seen by too many people. It's my only chance.*

—Jon Voight and Al Pacino discussing their performances in, respectively, *Deliverance* and *The Godfather*

All my life I have been impassioned, driven by my instincts. I can never be satisfied because my desire continues.

—Klaus Kinski

I kissed more soldiers than any woman in the world.

—Marilyn Monroe

No matter how tough things got, I could still walk into a restaurant anywhere in the world and get a good table.

—Buster Keaton

I started out as a lousy actress and have remained one.

—Brigitte Bardot

I'm a wonderful housekeeper. Every time I get a divorce, I keep the house.

—Zsa Zsa Gabor

For a man who has been dead fifteen years I am in remarkable health.

—John Barrymore

I have often thought that my tombstone might well read: "Here lies Paul Newman, who died a failure because his eyes suddenly turned brown."

—Paul Newman

If I feel someone is exploiting me, I think about it and consider whether I'm willing to go along with it. If it bothers me, I throw it out. If it's reasonable, I go with it.

—Jacqueline Bisset

I knew I was a homely kid. They don't call you Goofus and Dumbo for nothing.

—Donald Sutherland

There is one thing I'm tired of, and that's folks coming up and shouting out, "Hello, Dolly!" I wish they'd say "Dolly, hi, how are you?"

—Dolly Parton

As an actor, I don't get a chance to stretch at all.

—Burt Reynolds

QUOTES FROM
ACTORS (AND SOME OTHERS) ON OTHERS

Performers' opinions of themselves can be most illuminating. So can their views on other members of the moviemaking profession. Here actors talk about others in their field.

His talent is so abundant and fertile that I think it sometimes does him a disservice. Things come so easily to him and he can think of so many fruitful solutions to directing problems that he perhaps doesn't find which is the best because they are all so much better than what anyone else would think up. . . . He's an extremely complicated, utterly charming, unpredictable, and in some respects I'm afraid I'd have to say unreliable man. But I learned more from him about acting and about filmmaking than any other director.

—Charlton Heston on working with Orson Welles

She was an absolute magician in her medium and had every right to get rid of me.

—Laurence Olivier on Greta Garbo after she called him to Hollywood to co-star with her in *Queen Christina* and then fired him

Richard Burton is so discriminating that he won't go to see a play with anybody in it but himself.

—Elizabeth Taylor

If I come back in another life, I want to be Warren Beatty's fingertips.

—Woody Allen

[Woody Allen] is a genius, a fabulous film-maker. Years ago, I was running a company called Embassy Pictures, and the executive vice-president came into my office and said, "There's a crazy-looking guy out here with sneakers on who's been bothering me for three days. He wants to see you." I didn't even answer him. That was Woody Allen. If he hadn't worn sneakers, he'd be working for me today.

—Joseph E. Levine, producer

Marlene Dietrich is a professional—*a professional actress, a professional dress designer, a professional cameraman.*

—Alfred Hitchcock, director

That's what's so scary about him—nothing seems to faze him. He arrives on time and knows his lines. He sits and waits like an empty vessel and when they need him he fills up, does his thing and sits down... I'm 44 years old and still he can reduce me to feeling abject helplessness.

—Jane Fonda on father Henry Fonda

[I told him] what a great figure he is. While Larry sat in total silence, I went on and on comparing him to other artistic geniuses of our time like Picasso and Stravinsky. When I finally finished, Larry looked at me and said, "Well, don't stop. I'm rather enjoying this."

—Lilli Palmer reporting a conversation with long-time friend Laurence Olivier

Paul Newman, a lad who resembles Marlon Brando, delivers his lines with the emotional fervor of a Putnam Division conductor announcing local stops.

—The New Yorker magazine

He was able to do a very emotional scene with tears in his eyes and pinch my fanny at the same time.

—Shelley Winters on Fredric March

Ava [Gardner] is a lady of strong passions, something which has mixed merit, one of her passions being rage.

—Mickey Rooney

You can really call Irene Dunne the first lady of Hollywood, because she's the first real *lady Hollywood has ever seen.*

—Leo McCarey, director

I will always remember two compliments he paid me. He said I had perfect timing in comedy and that I was the sweetest-smelling actress he ever worked with.

—Irene Dunne on Cary Grant

She took the rough with the smooth with apparent serenity. I never noticed that she was quietly sharpening her claws.

—Director Roger Vadim on Catherine Deneuve

Bogart's a helluva nice guy till 11:30 P.M. After that he thinks he's Bogart.

—Dave Chasen, restauranteur

He wore baldness like an expensive hat, as if it were out of the question for him to have hair like other men.

—Gloria Swanson on director Cecil B. de Mille

I declared pontifically that that young man did not have what it takes for a successful career in films.

—Director Cecil B. de Mille on Clark Gable

I came out here with one suit and everybody thought I was a bum; when Brando came out with one sweat shirt, the town drooled over him.

—Humphrey Bogart on Marlon Brando

Interviewing Warren Beatty is like asking a hemophiliac for a pint of blood.

—Rex Reed, critic

Working with her is like being hit over the head with a Valentine's card.

—Christopher Plummer on Julie Andrews

Faye Dunaway says she is being haunted by mother's ghost. After her performance in Mommie Dearest, *I can understand why.*

—Christina Crawford, adopted daughter of Joan Crawford

Keeping in touch with Nastassja Kinski is like trying to find a pearl in fettuccine: impossible.

—Jodie Foster

She's seven going on twenty-nine.

—Director Steven Spielberg on Drew Barrymore in E.T. The Extra-Terrestrial

Debbie remains the girl-next-door, whereas I live somewhere down the street.

—Carrie Fisher on her mother, Debbie Reynolds

I've known Jane [Fonda] since she was a French housewife.

—Gore Vidal, author

Her horoscope suggests that Olivia would have fared better as an only child.

—Joan Fontaine on her sister, Olivia de Havilland

In real life, [Diane] Keaton believes in God. But she also thinks the radio works because there are tiny people inside it.

—Woody Allen

He is the nearest we are ever likely to get to a human Mickey [Mouse], near enough for many critics to have noted the resemblance.

—Writer Graham Greene on Fred Astaire

Fred Astaire can give an audience pleasure just by walking across the floor.

—Gene Kelly

Warren [Beatty] has an interesting psychology. He has always fallen in love with girls who have just won or been nominated for an Academy Award.

—Leslie Caron

CHARACTER ACTORS
THE FACE IS FAMILIAR...

How many times have you watched a movie and missed part of the action while you tried to remember just who a certain performer was and where you'd seen that face before? The performers known as 'character actors' frequently put the viewer in that dilemma. They are the actresses and actors who have spent their careers as second or third leads, as the star's best friend or the comic foil—always the bridesmaid, never the bride. The one hundred character actors profiled here are just a handful of those who spent their careers just out of the spotlight, in the shadow of the stars. They never became stars themselves, but they could make a mediocre film look good and a good film look great.

Iris Adrian

IRIS ADRIAN

Few actresses have been equipped with such a barbed and biting tongue as Iris Adrian, and few actresses could match her portrayals of cheap blondes—though some tried, among them Veda Ann Borg and Marian Martin. Adrian started her show business career as a chorus girl, moved up to the Ziegfeld Follies, and from there made it to the movies. Starting with *Paramount on Parade* in 1930 she has made over a hundred films, usually playing chorus girls, gangsters' molls, waitresses, etc. She still works when she's offered a part that interests her. Among her movie credits are *Gold Diggers of 1937* (1936), *Roxie Hart* (1942), and, more recently, *The Odd Couple* (1968). TV viewers remember her for her many guest appearances on *The Jack Benny Show*.

The actress was born Iris Adrian Hofstadter in Los Angeles on May 29, 1912. She never finished grade school—she was educated, as they say, in the school of life. She had already been through a couple of unsuccessful marriages before she married her present husband, former professional football player "Fido" Murphy,

over 25 years ago. None of her marriages produced any children.

Eddie Albert

EDDIE ALBERT

Eddie Albert is an American actor who made the transition from radio and stage work to films with his appearance in *Brother Rat* in 1938. He had played the cadet on the stage and repeated the role in the movie. Albert has appeared in over a hundred movies, usually in character roles and most often cast as the "good old buddy" to the star. He received Academy Award nominations as best supporting actor for his performances in *Roman Holiday* (1953) and in *The Heartbreak Kid* (1972). His other major films include *Oklahoma!* (1955), *I'll Cry Tomorrow* (1955), *The Teahouse of the August Moon* (1956), and *The Roots of Heaven* (1958). Albert's screen career has been long and busy, and he is thought of as a right guy in the industry. Although Albert's movie career gained him respect, it took a television series, *Green Acres*, to make him famous.

Albert was born Eddie Albert Heimberger on April 22, 1908 in Rock Island,

Illinois, the son of Frank and Julia Heimberger. In 1945 he married Maria Margarita Bolado, an actress who changed her name to Margo and was rewarded with brief fame in the movie *Lost Horizon* (1937). The couple have a son, Edward, who followed his father into movies (among his credits are *Butterflies Are Free*, in which he appeared opposite Goldie Hawn in 1972, and *Forty Carats*, opposite Liv Ullmann in 1973), and an adopted daughter, Marisa.

Sara Allgood

SARA ALLGOOD

If ever a name suited its owner, Allgood certainly suited Sara. She was a lovely actress, perfectly equipped for the kindly mother roles in which she was so often cast. Before Allgood ever came to Hollywood she had established a solid reputation as one of Ireland's greatest actresses, playing for many years with the Abbey Theatre in Dublin. She made her first screen appearance in 1918 in *Just Peggy*, then was not seen on the screen for over a decade. Her first important film opportunity occurred when she recreated her stage role in the film ver-

sion of *Juno and the Paycock* in 1930. A long list of movie roles followed, including the one that she will always be remembered for: the Welsh mother in *How Green Was My Valley* (1941). Her warm, loving portrayal of Mrs. Morgan won her an Academy Award nomination for best supporting actress. Other films in which Allgood appeared include *Jane Eyre* (1944) and *The Spiral Staircase* (1945).

Allgood was born in Dublin, Ireland on October 31, 1893 to middle-class parents. She never married. She died of a heart attack on September 13, 1950.

Leon Ames

LEON AMES

Leon Ames is an accomplished American actor who has made a career out of presenting on the screen a succession of exasperated but loving fathers, doctors, and assorted professional men. Ames made his first movie, *The Murders in the Rue Morgue*, in 1932. Although he has made over a hundred films he has been quoted, strangely enough, as being of the opinion that not much of his work was really very good. His most famous roles were as Judy Garland's father in

Meet Me in St. Louis (1944), and as the district attorney in *The Postman Always Rings Twice* (1946). Toward the end of his career, Ames turned his attention to television and did well with *Life With Father, Father of the Bride*, and *Mr. Ed*. He has not worked for the past few years, but his best friend continues to be someone in the business—actor Lloyd Nolan.

Ames was born to Russian immigrant parents, Charles and Cora Waycoff, in Portland, Indiana on January 20, 1903 (sources differ as to the year). He changed his name from Leon Waycoff to Leon Ames in 1935. Three years later he married starlet Christine Gossett. They have a daughter, Shelly, and a son, Leon Jr.

Eve Arden

EVE ARDEN

Eve Arden, the lanky American comedienne who was to make her name in movies as the satirical, wisecracking friend of a long line of heroines, started her own career as a performer on the stage at the age of 16. Billed under her real name, Eunice Quedens, she had bit parts in the films *Song of Love* (1929) and *Dancing Lady* (1933). As Eve Arden, she made her first

appearance on the New York stage in *The Ziegfeld Follies of 1934* (she also appeared in the 1936 *Follies*). Arden then returned to her home state of California to embark on a lengthy film career. She's probably appeared as best friend to more movie heroines than any other actress in film history, and many a 1940s near-flop was rescued from disaster by Arden's quick tongue and sparkling wit. She won recognition for her work in *Cover Girl* (1944), *The Doughgirls* (1944), and *Mildred Pierce* (1945). The latter won her an Academy Award nomination for best supporting actress. Other big movies in which she appeared include *Anatomy of a Murder* (1959) and *The Dark at the Top of the Stairs* (1960). More recently she was seen as the unshockable high school principal in *Grease* (1978). Like a number of other much admired character performers, it took a television series, *Our Miss Brooks*, to get Arden top billing. The popular '50s series won her an Emmy award. Arden has not yet ended her long career. She is still acting and also appears in TV commercials.

Arden was born Eunice Quedens on April 30, 1912 in Mill Valley, California, the daughter of Charles and Lucille Quedens. Her first marriage, to Edward G. Bergen in 1939, produced a daughter, Elizabeth; the couple also adopted a daughter, Constance. They divorced in 1948, and three years later Arden married actor Brooks West. They had a son, Douglas Brooks West, and adopted another boy, Duncan Paris West. Brooks West died in 1984.

Edward Arnold

EDWARD ARNOLD

A stout but commanding American actor, Edward Arnold was one of the movie industry's most dignified and skillful performers. His favorite roles were those of public officials who operated just on the edge of corruption. He also played a succession of businessmen and fathers. Arnold made his stage debut at 17 in *A Midsummer Night's Dream*. He also had the distinction of appearing on the stage with Ethel Barrymore. In 1915 Arnold joined the Essanay Studios as a cowboy and made 50 silent two-reelers. He went back to the stage in 1919 and moved to Hollywood in 1932, playing lead roles in such films as *Sadie McKee* (1934) and *Diamond Jim* (1935). He never became a star, but by the '40s was solidly established as a superb character actor. One of his biggest successes was his portrayal of a corrupt politician in *Mr. Smith Goes to Washington* (1939). Among his other most notable films were *Sutter's Gold* (1936) and *You Can't Take It With You* (1938). Throughout his screen career, Arnold was a public-spirited Hollywood citizen and at one

time was president of the Screen Actors' Guild. In the 1940s he had even considered running for Senator of California, but finally came to the decision that an actor could never win public office. Time, of course, has proved him wrong in this assumption.

Arnold was born Guenther Edward Arnold Schneider, of German parents, on February 18, 1890 in New York City. He was married three times and had two daughters and a son, Edward Arnold, Jr. He died of a cerebral hemorrhage on April 26, 1956.

Mischa Auer

MISCHA AUER

Mischa Auer, a gangling Russian comedian with colossal eyes and a sorrowful face, was brought to the United States by his maternal grandfather in 1920, after the Russian Revolution. He started his career on the stage, then in 1928 he went to Hollywood where he played minor roles until his joyful performance (and his impersonation of a gorilla) in *My Man Godfrey* (1936) made him a celebrity and won him an Oscar nomination for best supporting actor. He became one of Hollywood's most in-demand character actors, usually called upon to accentuate his broken English as a series of titled but somewhat incompetent foreigners in films like *You Can't Take It With You* (1938) and *Destry Rides Again* (1939). Auer made about 60 films in America and then another 40 or so in Europe, where he spent his last years.

Auer was born Mischa Ounskowski on November 17, 1905 in St. Petersburg, Russia. He changed his name to that of his grandfather—Leopold Auer, a violinist and teacher—when he embarked upon his stage career. He married four times; had one son, Anthony; and later adopted a daughter, Zoe. Auer died of a heart attack on March 5, 1967 in Rome, Italy.

Jim Backus

JIM BACKUS

Jim Backus always wanted to be an actor. A graduate of the American Academy of Dramatic Arts, he had a great deal of experience in stock, vaudeville, radio, and stage even before he made his first film appearance in *The Pied Piper* in 1942. In the course of his movie career he was in constant demand as a second lead in scores of movies, among them *Rebel Without a Cause* (1955), in which he

played James Dean's father. He originated the offscreen voice of Mr. Magoo in the cartoons of the '50s. Two of them, *When Magoo Flew* (1954) and *Mister Magoo's Puddle Jumper* (1956), won Academy Awards for best cartoon short subject. After his film career slowed down, Backus turned to television, starring in such hit shows as *I Married Joan* and *Gilligan's Island*.

Backus was born February 25, 1913 in Cleveland, Ohio to Russell and Daisy Backus. He married Henriette (Henny) Kaye in 1943, and the couple still work together on TV and writing projects.

Fay Bainter

FAY BAINTER

Fay Bainter did not make her first motion picture until the age of 41, but she had not been wasting her time before that: a long career in the theatre took her from child actress (at age 5) to ingenue to leading lady. In the course of her second career she put together a lengthy list of movie credits, frequently playing sympathetic matrons. She achieved national attention and won an Academy Award as best supporting actress for her role in *Jezebel* (1938), which starred Bette Davis and

Henry Fonda. That same year Bainter was also nominated as best actress in a leading role for her performance in the film *White Banners*. Ironically enough, she lost to Bette Davis—in *Jezebel*. (Davis has always expressed the highest admiration for Bainter's work in films.) Among the screen credits Bainter acquired over her long career are *Our Town* (1940), *State Fair* (1945), *The Secret Life of Walter Mitty* (1947), and *The Children's Hour* (1961), for which she won an Academy Award nomination for best supporting actress.

Fay Bainter was born on December 7, 1891 in Los Angeles, California, the daughter of Charles and Mary Bainter. In 1922 she married Reginald Venable, and their son, also named Reginald, was born in 1926. Venable died in 1964, and Fay Bainter died on April 16, 1968 after a long illness.

Bob Balaban

BOB BALABAN

Bob Balaban is a very contemporary character actor of a type seldom encountered any more since the demise of the studio system. His family owned the Balaban & Katz chain of theatres and his uncle, Barney Balaban, was president of Para-

mount Pictures from 1936 to 1964. Bob Balaban started acting in high school, then progressed logically enough through university, stock, and off-Broadway until at last he arrived on the Broadway stage. Balaban's first film was *Midnight Cowboy* in 1969, in which he played the nervous student who makes homosexual overtures to Jon Voight. Among his other film credits are *Close Encounters of the Third Kind* (1977) and *Absence of Malice* (1981).

He was born Robert Elmer Balaban in Chicago, Illinois on August 16, 1945. His father, Elmer Balaban, was part owner of the movie theatre chain and now heads a cable and pay TV company. His mother, Eleanor Pottasch, is an actress. Bob Balaban married Lynn Crossman in 1965, and their daughter Maviah was born in 1977.

Binnie Barnes

BINNIE BARNES

British actress Binnie Barnes had worked as a milkmaid, nurse, ropespinner, ballroom dancer, and chorus girl before she found her way into films. She made her screen debut in 1929, appearing in numerous comedy two-reelers; she had her first prominent feature role in 1931 in *A Night in Montmartre*. Two years later she drew attention to her abilities with her performance as Catherine Howard in *The Private Life of Henry VIII*, playing opposite the celebrated Charles Laughton. This role was to bring her to the attention of American audiences and win her a Hollywood contract. Her subsequent film roles, however, were mainly second leads in movies like *Three Smart Girls* (1937), *The Three Musketeers* (1939), *I Married an Angel* (1942), and *Daytime Wife* (1939). She became known as an English version of Eve Arden, who played the same sort of wisecracking lady in her movies. Unfortunately, most of Barnes' movies were undistinguished.

Binnie Barnes was born Gitelle Enoyce Barnes (or, as some sources state, Gertrude Maude Barnes) in London, England on March 25, 1905. Her first marriage, to art dealer Samuel Joseph in 1932, ended in divorce after four years. In 1940 Barnes married Mike Frankovich, UCLA football hero, sportscaster, and now famous movie producer. Theirs has been a long and successful marriage. They have three children, Michael, Peter, and Michelle.

VINCE BARNETT

Few people other than dedicated film buffs recognize Vince Barnett's name, but he is one of the many performers who have made character acting so well respected a part of the movie business. As a

Vince Barnett

Florence Bates

Charles Bickford

young man he became an airplane pilot, and he worked for some years flying mail planes. In his late 20s he decided to try a stage career, and he did do some stage work. For the most part, however, his career was based in Hollywood, where he logged a considerable list of film credits, frequently playing minor gangsters or put-upon little men. His first year of movie making—1930—gave him a role in a very important picture, *All Quiet on the Western Front*. His other film titles include *Scarface* (1932), *A Star Is Born* (1937) and *The Human Jungle* (1954). In his later years he was seen frequently on television. Barnett had a reputation in the entertainment field as a practical joker.

Barnett was born in Pittsburgh, Pennsylvania on July 4, 1902, the son of stage actor Luke Barnett. His first marriage lasted until his wife's death. Three months later he remarried. Barnett died on August 10, 1977.

FLORENCE BATES

Florence Bates had a singularly varied working life. She was a piano-playing musical prodigy as a child, and at the age of 18 graduated with a teaching degree from the University of Texas. By the time she was 26 she had become the first woman lawyer in the state of Texas. And she didn't stop there. In turn she went into the antique business, joined an oil company, and opened her own bakery. Along the way—inevitably, perhaps, for such an adventurous woman—she tried acting, and discovered that she was a born actress. It was director Alfred Hitchcock who gave her her first important film role as a rich, overbearing dowager in *Rebecca* in 1940, at which time Bates was already past 50. She continued to make movies until a year before her death in 1954. Some of her credits: *Kismet* (1944), *Saratoga Trunk* (1945), and *I Remember Mama* (1948).

Bates was born Florence Rabe in San Antonio, Texas on April 15, 1888. Her father owned an antique store. An early marriage ended in divorce, and in 1929 Bates married the real love of her life, Will Jacoby, with whom she had a daughter. Bates died on January 31, 1954, shortly after the death of her husband.

CHARLES BICKFORD

Charles Bickford started his acting career on the stage but when sound came to Hollywood, Bickford followed. A goodlooking actor with a powerful voice, he had no trouble finding film assignments and during his first years in Hollywood was able to secure some leading roles (most notably as Greta Garbo's lover in her first talkie, *Anna Christie* in 1930). Soon, however, he established a reputation as a character actor with a talent for effortlessly projecting rugged and thoughtful sincerity. His forcefulness and talent enabled him to dominate many of the films in which he appeared. At one point in his career he had a major feud with Louis B. Mayer, head of MGM. Bickford didn't want to do some of the roles Mayer selected for him, and the disagreement harmed Bickford's career considerably. Mayer had him blacklisted at all the studios and Bickford was out of work for a considerable time. All the same, in the course of his Hollywood career he was to appear in over a hundred movies, winning

Academy Award nominations as best supporting actor for three of them: *The Song of Bernadette* (1943), *The Farmer's Daughter* (1947), and *Johnny Belinda* (1948). In 1966 he became known to television viewers for the series *The Virginian*.

He was born on January 1, 1899 in Cambridge, Massachusetts, one of seven children of Lovetus and Mary Bickford. Charles Bickford married Beatrice Loring in 1919, and the marriage produced two children, Doris, born in 1920, and Rex, born in 1921. Bickford died on November 9, 1967.

Beulah Bondi

BEULAH BONDI

Beulah Bondi is one of the most respected character actresses in movie history. She started acting very young—she was about seven—and by the time she was ten was already winning honors. She worked steadily as an actress but it was not until 1925, when she was well into her thirties, that she made her Broadway debut in *One of the Family*. In 1929 she made her film debut, recreating her stage role in the film version of Elmer Rice's play *Street Scene*. Thereafter she di-

vided her professional attentions between stage and screen for many years. Because she never signed a long-term contract with any studio, she could be selective about her roles. Her characters ranged from kind and understanding to mean and nosy. Of course, like most older actresses in Hollywood, she played her share of mothers, among them James Stewart's in *Mr. Smith Goes to Washington* (1939) and *It's a Wonderful Life* (1946), Fred MacMurray's in *Remember the Night* (1940), and William Holden's in *Our Town* (1940). Her only lead role in a major film was in *Make Way for Tomorrow* (1937), which had no "stars" but was beautifully acted by its cast of character actors, including Victor Moore, Thomas Mitchell, Fay Bainter, Porter Hall, Louise Beavers, and Gene Lockhart. Bondi received best supporting actress Oscar nominations for her performances in *The Gorgeous Hussy* (1936) and *Of Human Hearts* (1938). She just missed getting the plum roles of Aunt Polly in *The Adventures of Tom Sawyer*, and Ma Joad in *The Grapes of Wrath*. (The role of Ma Joad went to Jane Darwell and won her an Oscar for best supporting actress.)

The actress was born Beulah Bondy on May 3, 1892 in Chicago, Illinois. She never married. She died on January 12, 1981.

EDGAR BUCHANAN

Edgar Buchanan made an unusual career switch

Edgar Buchanan

from dentistry—he was head of the oral surgery department at Eugene Hospital, Oregon from 1929 to 1937—to acting. The switch was not, however, unpredictable, for Buchanan had always been interested in acting, in school and later in small theatres. He had an unusual voice, rough and husky, and he was not the glamorous type—in fact, he was perfect material for a character actor. He had little reason to regret giving up his career as a dentist; he was offered so many scripts that he was soon able to pick and choose his roles. He made close to a hundred films, mostly westerns, playing an assortment of characters that included a collection of rugged old-timers. Among his films were *Arizona* (1940) and *Texas* (1941). Late in his career he entered television and found great success in the series *Petticoat Junction*. He was still going strong as an actor up to his death.

William Edgar Buchanan was born on March 21, 1903 in Humansville, Missouri, the son of a dentist. He had a long and happy marriage. He died on April 4, 1979.

Billie Burke

BILLIE BURKE

American-born Billie Burke moved to London at age eight and made her London stage debut in 1902. She fulfilled her early promise by growing up to be a most beautiful woman. Her marriage in 1914 to the flamboyant stage impresario Florenz Ziegfeld introduced her to an extraordinary life—the sort that makes movie history. (Myrna Loy portrayed her in the 1936 musical film *The Great Ziegfeld*, with William Powell in the title role.) Burke entered films in 1916, when influential producer Thomas H. Ince, one of the most important and creative men in Hollywood, offered her $300,000—then, of course, a small fortune—to star in the movie *Peggy*, a love story about a Scots maid. She starred in several more films (on the condition they be made in New York) and returned to the stage in 1921. But when Ziegfeld lost his fortune in the 1929 stockmarket crash, Burke went back to Hollywood. There she made her mark in movies with a series of portraits of fluttery matrons. She played in nearly a hundred films, winning an Academy Award nomination for her part in *Merrily We Live* (1938). And who can ever forget her 1939 performance as Glinda, the good witch in *The Wizard of Oz*? She retired in 1960.

Billie Burke was born Mary William Ethelbert Appleton Burke on August 7, 1885 in Washington, D.C. Her parents were William Burke (a clown with the Barnum & Bailey Circus) and Blanche Burke. Billie Burke's father was known professionally as Billy, and she took his stage name as her own. Her daughter, Patricia Ziegfeld, was born in 1916. Burke remained beautifully vain until she died on May 14, 1970 at the age of 84.

Spring Byington

SPRING BYINGTON

An American stage actress who turned to Hollywood in the thirties, Spring Byington played in scores of movies with great success. Performing seemed to come easily to her, and she once said of herself that she prevailed because "Lady Macbeth and I aren't friends." Her career on the stage began when she was very young, so she had had plenty of acting experience when, at age 40, she made a very impressive feature-film debut as Marmee in *Little Women* (1933). She went on to play pleasant maternal figures, sometimes a bit scatterbrained but almost always winning out by the end of the movie thanks to their down-to-earth, homespun philosophy. In 1938 she won an Academy Award nomination for best supporting actress for her role in *You Can't Take It With You*. In the fifties she was a big hit in the television series *December Bride*.

Spring Byington was born on October 17, 1893 in Colorado Springs, Colorado. Her parents were Edwin Lee Byington, a teacher, and Helen Cleghorn, a doctor. She married Roy Carey Chandler and the couple had two daughters, Phyllis and Lois, before the marriage ended in divorce. Byington died on September 7, 1971, at the age of 77.

Louis Calhern

LOUIS CALHERN

If ever one wanted to find a distinguished, handsome, and talented actor, one only had to look for Louis Calhern. He began his film career as a leading man in the silents of the 1920s and went on to become one of the most respected and in-demand character actors in the business. He certainly became one of the busiest: in fact in one year, 1950, he could be seen in seven new films. His greatest personal success was in the 1950 film *The Magnificent Yankee*, which won him an Academy Award nomination for best actor. Other films in which he appeared include *Annie Get Your Gun* (1950); *The Asphalt Jungle* (1950); *Julius Caesar* (1953), in which he played the title role; *Executive Suite* (1954); *The Blackboard Jungle* (1955); and *High Society* (1956).

Louis Calhern was born Carl Henry Vogt on February 19, 1895 in New York City, the son of Eugene Adolph Vogt and Hubertina Friese. He was not the only family member to feel the lure of the movie world: his sister Emmy also tried acting, though without much success. Calhern believed in marriage, and he liked actresses—he married (and divorced) four of them: Ilka Chase, Julia Hoyt, Natalie Schaefer, and Marianne Stewart. He died of a heart attack in Tokyo on May 12, 1956 during the filming of *The Teahouse of the August Moon*.

JOSEPH CALLEIA

Joseph Calleia was an actor with the uncanny quality of always seeming to be aware of what everybody else on the screen was thinking. Many of the movie roles assigned him were threatening char-

Joseph Calleia

acters of one kind or another—whichever side of the law they happened to be on. It's something of a surprise that Calleia became an actor at all. He had trained intensively for an operatic career and had toured in concerts, musicals, and even vaudeville. Calleia settled in Hollywood in the '30s and made his debut in *His Woman* in 1931. He did many important pictures such as *My Little Chickadee* (1940), *Jungle Book* (1942), *For Whom the Bell Tolls* (1943), *Gilda* (1946), and *Touch of Evil* (1958).

He was born Joseph Spurin-Calleia on August 4, 1897, in Malta. His father was an architect. Calleia's only marriage, in 1930, lasted almost 40 years. He and his wife never had any children. After his wife's death Calleia returned in 1970 to his native Malta, where he remained until his death on October 31, 1975.

JOHN CARRADINE

John Carradine, a towering, craggy, extraordinary-looking man, has

John Carradine

made an unbelievable number of movies—over 175 of them stretching over five decades. He has made all kinds of films. Many of them were worthless, but his credit list does include such fine movies as *Captains Courageous* (1937), *Stagecoach* (1939), and *The Grapes of Wrath* (1940). He counted among his personal friends such major stars as Tyrone Power, Henry Fonda, and John Wayne. After a run of strong character roles in the '30s and '40s, Carradine became locked into a series of inferior parts of the horror movie variety. In between film work he toured with a one-man performance of readings from Shakespeare. Today three of his sons—David, Keith, and Robert—have gained a good following on their own in films.

He was born Richmond Reed Carradine on February 5, 1906 in New York City, the son of William Reed Carradine, a well-known journalist, and Genevieve Carradine, a noted surgeon. Between 1930 and 1935 he acted under the name of John Peter Richmond. He married four times: Ardanelle Cosner, whom he married in 1935 and divorced in 1944, was the mother of his sons David and Bruce. Carradine's four other sons, John, Christopher,

Keith, and Robert, were born during Carradine's next marriage, to Sonia Sorel; the marriage lasted from 1945 to 1955. His next marriage, to Doris Rich, lasted from 1956 to 1971, and in 1975 he married his fourth wife, Emily Cisneros.

Jack Carson

JACK CARSON

Jack Carson was a beefy, brassy movie performer who showed up in a vast number of movies, mostly during the 1940s. He was a reliable but not very versatile actor, usually playing the smart guy who in reality was a lot less smart than he gave himself credit for. Carson had come to films from vaudeville and was impressive in his characterizations of opportunistic, larcenous, or just plain nasty characters. For all that, many people remember him best for the series of pleasant films that he did with Dennis Morgan, among them *The Hard Way* (1942) and *Two Guys From Milwaukee* (1946). He was also teamed with Jane Wyman in several movies—Warner Brothers thought they'd make a winning team, but the chemistry wasn't right. Carson was rumored to have had a serious romance with Doris Day dur-

ing the filming of *Romance on the High Seas*—her first film—in 1948. Other major films in which he can be seen are *The Strawberry Blonde* (1941), *The Male Animal* (1942), *Mildred Pierce* (1945), *A Star Is Born* (1954), and *Cat on a Hot Tin Roof* (1958).

Carson was born John Elmer Carson on October 27, 1910 in Carmen, Manitoba, Canada. He was married four times: to Betty Lynn; Kay St. Germaine (by whom he had two children, John and Germaine); actress Lola Albright; and Sandra Tucker. He died on the same day as film star Dick Powell, January 2, 1963.

Lon Chaney, Jr.

LON CHANEY, JR.

His father's distinguished reputation was the toughest obstacle Lon Chaney, Jr. had to contend with. That, and not having conventionally handsome looks, plagued him throughout his career. Although he made some 150 films his roles—with few exceptions—required him to follow in his father's footsteps, unfortunately in progressively inferior films. One major moment of redemption in his career was when he impressed critics with his

performance as Lennie in the movie of John Steinbeck's *Of Mice and Men* in 1939. But for the most part he was saddled with a succession of poor horror movies.

Lon Chaney, Jr. was born Creighton Chaney on February 10, 1906 in Oklahoma City, Oklahoma, the son of the famous "man of a thousand faces" and his wife, singer Cleva Creighton. Chaney Jr. married model Patsy Beck in 1937 and the marriage produced two sons, Lon Chaney III and Ronald. Chaney Jr. died of throat cancer on July 12, 1973.

Lee J. Cobb

LEE J. COBB

Lee J. Cobb made scores of movies and admitted that he didn't care for any of them. He insisted that it was the need to make money that drove him into movies and that he would have preferred to spend his time on the stage. But the heavily-built Cobb was an outstanding actor who distinguished himself on the American stage, in films, and on television. Cobb had that special talent that could make a bad movie worthwhile just because he was in it. He was known for various pieces of "business" that he introduced into his roles—

his distinctive leer; his mocking, cynical snarl; his sudden, terrifying outbursts. No one who saw his performances in movies such as *On the Waterfront* (1954) or *The Brothers Karamazov* (1958) can accept Cobb's own disenchantment with his contribution to movies. He was nominated for best supporting actor for both films. His other credits include *Golden Boy* (1939), *Twelve Angry Men* (1957), and *Coogan's Bluff* (1968).

Cobb was born Leo Jacoby on December 8, 1911 in New York City. In 1940 he married heiress Helen Beverly, but the marriage ended in divorce after 12 years. In 1957 Cobb married Mary Hirsch, by whom he had two sons, Anthony and Gerald. Cobb died on February 11, 1976.

Charles Coburn

CHARLES COBURN

Charles Coburn was an eminent American actor who had made a name for himself on the Broadway stage long before he made his first movie in 1933. In fact, since he did not come to movies till the age of 56, he never achieved major popularity except as a character actor. But he did manage the

miraculous feat of upstaging some of the more important stars of the day. His performances were characterized by a crusty benevolence, and his soft heart usually lay revealed by the end of the movie. He's most likely to be remembered for his Academy Award winning performance (for best supporting actor) in *The More the Merrier* in 1943. Earlier he had received a best supporting actor nomination for *The Devil and Miss Jones* (1941), and was to be nominated again for *The Green Years* (1946).

He was born Charles Douville Coburn on January 19, 1877 in Savannah, Georgia, the son of Moses and Emma Coburn. He married actress Ivah Wills in 1906, and together they created the Coburn Shakespeare Players. It was not until after Ivah's death in 1937 that Coburn settled in Hollywood. He married his second wife, Winifred Natzka, in 1959. Coburn died on August 30, 1961.

Hans Conreid

HANS CONRIED

Hans Conried could be found in art museums as often as on movie sets. He had a deep affection for the Old Masters and was sufficiently knowledgeable

to be regarded as an expert in the field. He began his performing career in radio, which gave him the opportunity to perfect his use of dialects and to develop a rich and versatile speaking voice. He made his first movie, *Dramatic School*, in 1938, and continued to act in movies for 40 years, during which time he also did a great deal of work in television and some work on the stage. He specialized in eccentric comedy roles. His most famous film, and the one most people will remember him for, was *The Five Thousand Fingers of Doctor T* (1953).

Conried was born on April 15, 1917 in Baltimore, Maryland. He and his wife, Margaret, had four children, Libby, Hans III, Alexander, and Edith. He died on January 5, 1982, having always maintained that his contribution to acting was diminutive and that it is a rare individual who ever contributes to life anything of real significance.

Gladys Cooper

GLADYS COOPER

Gladys Cooper, the distinguished and talented British actress, started life in less auspicious surroundings than most of us

are accustomed to seeing her in. She came from a less than fashionable suburb southeast of London, but grew up to be a maker of fashions herself. As she matured she was hailed as one of the great beauties of the 20th century and became a World War I pinup. She made some silent films in Britain in the early days of films and even one talkie, *The Iron Duke* in 1935. But she returned to the stage, which was her first love. It wasn't until 1940, when she was 52, that she went to Hollywood to make *Rebecca*. For all practical purposes, the movie launched her on a new and sparkling career as a film character actress. Among her screen credits are *Now, Voyager* (1942), *The Song of Bernadette* (1943), and *My Fair Lady* (1964); all three brought her Oscar nominations for best supporting actress.

She was born Gladys Constance Cooper on December 18, 1888 in Lewisham, England. Her parents were Charles Frederick Cooper, a prominent publisher, and Mabel Cooper. Gladys Cooper was first married to Herbert J. Buckmaster, and the couple had two children, Joan and John, before divorcing in 1922. Her second marriage, to Sir Neville Pearson in 1928, produced a daughter, Sally, but ended in divorce in 1936. Her third husband, Philip Merivale, with whom she had a son, John, died in 1946. Her daughter Joan is married to actor Robert Morley. Gladys Cooper published her autobiography, *Without Veils*, in 1953 and was made a Dame Commander of the Order of the British Empire in 1967. She died on November 17, 1971.

Jerome Cowan

Laird Cregar

July 28, 1916 in Philadelphia, Pennsylvania, the son of a wealthy importer. He never married. Cregar died on December 9, 1944.

Donald Crisp

(1955), and *Pollyanna* (1960).

Donald Crisp was born on July 27, 1880 in Aberfeldy, Scotland. He married writer Jane Murfin in 1932. The couple had no children. Crisp died on May 25, 1974 at the age of 93.

Hume Cronyn

JEROME COWAN

Productive and reliable are ideal terms to describe Jerome Cowan, who was seen everywhere in the forties, playing roles of every kind from the detective murdered by Mary Astor in *The Maltese Falcon* (1941) to Dagwood's boss in a number of *Blondie* films. He has said that he credited his movie versatility to his early years in vaudeville, stock, and radio and on Broadway. He had an easy manner that endeared him to audiences, but was not conventionally good-looking enough to become the lead in an era when leading men had to be handsome. In most of his films Cowan found himself outsmarted by the leading man or leading lady. Other films in which he appeared include *Shall We Dance* (1937), *Mr. Skeffington* (1944) and *Miracle on 34th Street* (1947). He also did some television work.

Jerome Palmer Cowan was born in New York City on October 6, 1897. He married Helen Dodge, and the couple had two daughters, Suzanne and Diane. Cowan suffered a long illness before his death on January 24, 1972.

LAIRD CREGAR

In view of the fact that his career covered a mere five years and that he has been dead now for forty years, it is amazing that Laird Cregar's name is still familiar to filmgoers. One wonders, naturally, what course his career would have taken had he lived. He was an enormous man, 6 feet 3 inches tall and weighing close to 300 pounds. He broke into films in 1940 as a villain and played the bad guy to the end. Despite his youth (he was only 24 when he made his first film, *Granny Get Your Gun*, in 1940), his voice was well suited to older roles and they were what he usually got. He appeared in—among others—*Charley's Aunt* in 1941, *The Lodger* in 1944, and *Hangover Square* also in 1944. Laird wanted desperately to be a leading man, and dieted strenuously to reduce his bulk. In a dangerously short time he lost 85 pounds, but the murderous diet he had undertaken put impossible stress on his heart. He suffered two massive heart attacks and died at the age of 28.

The actor was born Samuel Laird Cregar on

DONALD CRISP

Donald Crisp's career in the movie industry was a busy one. He first worked in films in 1906, and by 1915 he was engaged as D. W. Griffith's assistant on the landmark movie *Birth of a Nation* (in which he also appeared). Even before he came to Hollywood he had been a stage actor and singer, and once arrived on the film scene he directed and/or appeared in many silents, with stars such as Douglas Fairbanks, Lillian Gish, and Buster Keaton. He more or less gravitated to full-time acting when sound arrived, and went on to appear in more than 200 films, playing all kinds of characters. His first film was probably some silent shot in the early 1900s. His best known is certainly *How Green Was My Valley* (1941), for which he received an Oscar for best supporting actor. Other major titles in which he appeared include *Mutiny on the Bounty* (1935), *Lassie Come Home* (1943), *The Man From Laramie*

HUME CRONYN

Hume Cronyn, an unassuming-looking man and rather short at five feet six inches, became a distinguished character actor, director, and writer. In 1930, while he was still in school, he made his stage debut with the Montreal Repertory Theatre, but he did not make his screen debut until 1943 when he was cast in Alfred Hitchcock's *Shadow of a Doubt*. The following year his performance in *The Seventh Cross* won him an Academy Award nomination for best supporting actor. He went on to make a great number of films, alternating moviemaking with stage and, later, television work. In 1942 he married his second wife, English-born actress Jessica Tandy, and the couple have appeared together many times on stage, screen, and television.

Hume Blake Cronyn, Jr. was born on July 19, 1911 in London, Ontario, Canada, the youngest of five children. With his second wife, Jessica Tandy, he has two children, Christopher and Tandy. Because of a recurring eye ailment, Cronyn underwent surgery for the removal of his left eye in 1970.

Henry Daniell

HENRY DANIELL

Henry Daniell was not only a dazzling character actor, but also a highly intelligent individual. Like many fine character actors, he came from England and had had a great deal of experience on the stage both in London and on Broadway. He was known as "the Adolphe Menjou of Menace" and was in constant demand by directors; there were few performers available who could portray wicked characters with such grace. In many of his films he was much more interesting than the stars. Daniell's first film was *Jealousy* in 1929, and the movie for which he is best known is probably *Camille*, made in 1936. He made over 60 films, including *The Philadelphia Story* (1940), *The Body Snatchers* (1945), *The*

Woman in Green (1945), *The Man in the Grey Flannel Suit* (1956), and *My Fair Lady*—his last film—which came out in 1964 after his death.

He was born Charles Henry Daniell on March 5, 1894 in London, England. He married Ann Knox, an English writer. He died of a heart attack in his home on October 31, 1963.

Andy Devine

ANDY DEVINE

Andy Devine's massive size and unique raspy voice made him a very memorable character actor. Before he entered the movie business he attended Santa Clara University where he became famous as a football player. Late in 1925, however, Devine hit Hollywood in single-minded pursuit of movie work, making his first appearance in *The Collegians* in 1927. With the introduction of sound, Devine assumed that his movie career was all washed-up. In fact, though, his distinctive voice proved one of his most valuable assets and worked to his advantage. His undoubted talent, comic looks, and rough, high-pitched voice brought him thousands of new fans, and his career covered well over a hundred films, including many

westerns in which he played variations on the theme of a cowboy sidekick. Among his credits: *A Star Is Born* (1937), *Stagecoach* (1939), *The Red Badge of Courage* (1951), and *The Adventures of Huckleberry Finn* (1960). Devine also entered television very successfully as Jingles on *The Adventures of Wild Bill Hickok* series.

Andy Devine was born Jeremiah Schwartz on October 7, 1905 in Flagstaff, Arizona. His father owned a hotel. His grandfather, James Ward, was an Admiral in the U.S. Navy. In 1933 Devine married Dorothy Irene House and the couple had two sons, Denny and Tod. Devine died on February 18, 1977.

Brian Donlevy

BRIAN DONLEVY

Brian Donlevy was a hard man to get to know—a loner and always reluctant to talk about his acting career. He had had many jobs before he thought about acting. He tried military life for a while, joining General John Pershing's expedition to Mexico against Pancho Villa. He became a pilot with the famous Lafayette Escadrille during World

War I, after which he found himself in New York City with a job modeling shirts. He pushed himself in at the Pathé studios and made his film debut in 1924. He was handsome enough to become a star, even if he was also a little stocky and not too tall. In fact, he did have lead roles in a number of films, including *The Great McGinty* in 1940. But he seemed to get into a rut playing villains, especially after winning a best supporting actor nomination for his performance as the evil Sergeant Markoff—a truly contemptible villain—in *Beau Geste* (1939). Donlevy made close to a hundred films, among them *Destry Rides Again* (1939), *The Glass Key* (1942), and *An American Romance* (1944). He also appeared in the TV series *Dangerous Assignment*.

The actor was born Waldo Bruce Donlevy on February 9, 1901 in Portadown, Ireland, the son of a salesman. Donlevy was married three times. His first marriage ended in divorce. In 1936 he married singer Marjorie Lane, by whom he had a daughter, Judith. The marriage ended in 1947. In 1966 Donlevy married Lillian Arch, former wife of Bela Lugosi. Donlevy died of cancer on April 5, 1972.

DOUGLASS DUMBRILLE

Douglass Dumbrille was one of the most famous heavies that Hollywood has ever produced. Even moviegoers who never knew his name certainly recognized his face in the more than 200 films in

Douglass Dumbrille

Charles Durning

Dan Duryea

Frank Faylen

which he appeared—from the silent *What 80,000,000 Women Want* in 1916 to *Shock Treatment*, his last movie, in 1964. All told, his career spanned almost 50 years of moviemaking. Dumbrille had worked extensively on the stage before turning to films during the '30s. He normally played some kind of unscrupulous swindler, from an affluent but shifty businessman to a dishonest politician. His suave manner also made him an appropriate foil to many notable comedians. Among his more memorable films are *Mr. Deeds Goes to Town* (1936), *The Three Musketeers* (1939), and *The Ten Commandments* (1956). He appeared in the TV series *China Smith* from 1952 to 1955 and *The New Phil Silvers Show* in 1963/64.

Douglas Dumbrille was born on October 13, 1889, in Hamilton, Ontario, Canada. His first marriage, to Jessie Lawson, lasted 47 years until her death in 1958. In 1960 he married Patricia Mowbray, who was 42 years his junior and the daughter of Dumbrille's best friend, actor Alan Mowbray. Dumbrille retired in 1966, and died on April 2, 1974 in Los Angeles, California.

CHARLES DURNING

Charles Durning may be the most in-demand character actor working today. His career seems to parallel those of yesterday's charactor actors Ed Begley and Lloyd Nolan. Durning spent many years in show business before, as he puts it, he was "able to make it." He has that quality essential to good character actors: versatility. He can dance, sing, act both comedy and drama, and look good doing any of them. He started acting very young in every kind of theatrical situation and has certainly had a thorough grounding—vaudeville, burlesque, stock, singing, dancing, and straight theatre. He performed in dozens of plays before he started to do films. Included among his many film credits are *The Front Page* (1974), *Dog Day Afternoon* (1975), *Tootsie* (1982), *The Best Little Whorehouse in Texas* (1982), and *To Be or Not To Be* (1983)—the last two won him Academy Award nominations for best supporting actor. Durning also does a lot of work in television.

Charles Durning was born in Highland Falls, New York on February 28, 1933. He studied at New York University. He and his wife, Mary Ann, whom he married, divorced, and subsequently remarried, have no children.

DAN DURYEA

Dan Duryea graduated from Cornell University before embarking on an acting career that took him first to the New York stage, where he won extraordinary reviews for his performance as the weak son, Leo, in Lillian Hellman's *The Little Foxes*. When the play was made into a motion picture in 1941 he recreated his role, again to rave reviews. In his next two films, *Ball of Fire* (1941) and *Pride of the Yankees* (1942), Duryea again played nasty characters, and thereafter he was pretty much typecast as a villain for the rest of his career. Duryea was satisfied with this casting; he felt he did his best work as a heavy. In reality he was totally different from the roles he played—offscreen he was an educated, refined family man, known for his generosity and highly regarded by friends from all walks of life. He worked in films and television right up to the year of his death. Two of his best performances were in *The*

Woman in the Window (1944) and *Scarlet Street* (1945), both directed by Fritz Lang.

Dan Duryea was born on January 23, 1907 in White Plains, New York, the son of Richard Hewlett Duryea and Mabel Hoffman. In 1931 he married Helen Bryan, by whom he had two sons, Peter and Richard. Helen Bryan died in 1967, a year before Duryea's own death on June 7, 1968.

FRANK FAYLEN

Frank Faylen was a hard-working, well-known character actor who was much in demand for a number of years, acting steadily from 1936 into the late '60s. He was the son of a vaudeville team known as "Ruf and Cusik." He worked with his parents before forming his own act with Carol Hughes, who later became his wife. When he turned to film he signed with Warner Brothers and went to work for them in 1936 with the film *Bullets or Ballots*. He later worked extensively for Paramount. His best-remembered role was that of the loathsome male nurse in *The Lost Weekend* (1945). Despite his lengthy film career, however, he is probably most familiar to audiences through his television work, particularly as the father in the series *The Many Loves of Dobie Gillis*.

Faylen was born Frank Cusik on December 8, 1907 or 1909, in St. Louis, Missouri. In 1928 he married his vaudeville partner Carol Hughes, who went on to win fame as the female lead in the 1940 serial *Flash Gordon Conquers the Universe*. The couple have two daughters, Kay and Carol.

Stepin Fetchit

STEPIN FETCHIT

Here we have a piece of history: Stepin Fetchit was the first black actor to receive featured billing on the American screen. He always maintained that he took his name from a racehorse on whom he'd placed a lucky bet. He started his show business career in carnivals with a song-and-dance act. In 1927 he made his first movie, *In Old Kentucky*, in which he registered strongly as a personality and found his career on the upswing. In the early 1930s he was often teamed with Will Rogers. Also among his best-remembered films are *The Ghost Talks* (1929) and *Swing*

High (1930). Today many people find objectionable the type of slow-witted, lazy character Fetchit did so well. Nobody could roll his eyes and shake his body to express fear more effectively than Fetchit. Now, of course, such stereotypical characterizations are considered offensive. Even though Fetchit was reputed to have made millions, he declared bankruptcy in 1947.

Fetchit was born Lincoln Theodore Monroe Andrew Perry on May 30, 1902 in Key West, Florida. He was adopted when he was 11 years old. He married but never had children. In the late 1960s he converted to the Black Muslim faith. He sued CBS for $3 million in 1970 for defamation of character, claiming they had used film clips out of context to describe him as a "white man's Negro." The suit was unsuccessful. He temporarily revived his career in the early 1970s, appearing in a few films and as a stand-up comedian. However, he suffered a stroke in 1976 and has lived since then at the Motion Picture Country House in Woodland Hills, California.

REGINALD GARDINER

British actor Reginald Gardiner came from a well-heeled family who believed in a good education. He graduated with honors from London's Royal Academy of Dramatic Art. With his good looks he had no problem finding stage work. He embarked on his movie career in *The Lovelorn Lady* in 1932.

Reginald Gardiner

Dozens of film roles followed, exploiting his talent for comedy and his suave, well-bred, and elegant manner. His film credits include *Born to Dance* (1936), *The Great Dictator* (1940), and *The Man Who Came to Dinner* (1941). He was also successful on television, co-starring with Phyllis Diller in the series *The Pruitts of Southampton* in 1966/67.

Reginald Gardiner was born on February 27, 1903 in Wimbledon, Surrey, England. His first wife was actress Wyn Richards. He later married Nadia Petrova, whom he divorced after more than 25 years of marriage. In the '60s Gardiner had an accident that ruined the rest of his career. He fell down the stairs in his Hollywood home and injured his head so severely that both his speech and his equilibrium were greatly affected. He died on July 7, 1980.

WILL GEER

Will Geer was an actor who worked in more acting media than most performers cover in the course of their careers. He worked in national repertory companies, on Broadway, in films, and on radio and television. Despite his

Will Geer

varied career most fans will probably remember him best as Grandpa Walton in the TV series *The Waltons*. He made his movie debut in *The Misleading Lady* in 1932, and made occasional movies in the '30s and '40s. His film career began in earnest in 1948, but shortly afterwards he was blacklisted for refusing to cooperate with the House Un-American Activities Committee. After that he wasn't seen in films again until 1962 when director Otto Preminger cast him in *Advise and Consent*. Geer was a proven and very versatile character actor; he could do anything on screen, but his specialty was an ability to convey a sense of foreboding. One of the major accomplishments of his career lay essentially outside the acting field. He built his own theatre right out in a forest canyon. There one could sit under the bright stars and watch some of the finest plays ever written.

Will Geer was born on March 9, 1902 in Frankfort, Indiana, the son of a postal worker and a teacher. He was married three times and had seven children, three of whom followed him into the acting profession. He died on April 23, 1978.

Gladys George

GLADYS GEORGE

Gladys George was born into a theatrical family and gained a great deal of experience in vaudeville and stock and on Broadway before going into movies. All the odds were in favor of her becoming a major movie star, but it didn't happen. She was just as attractive as Claire Trevor, whose career pattern it seemed George might follow, but while Trevor seemed to be able to sidestep the "tough blonde with the heart of gold" syndrome, George could not. She remained essentially a character actress throughout her career, although it's certain that she could have contributed many fine screen performances given the opportunity of larger parts in better films. She made her Broadway debut in 1918 and appeared in several silent films until she suffered severe facial burns after a domestic accident in 1920. After her recovery, she returned to the stage until 1934 when MGM signed her. She also worked for Warner Brothers, returning to the stage whenever she felt need of a challenge. She was nominated for a best

actress Oscar for her performance in *Valiant Is the Word for Carrie* (1936). Her other credits include *The Roaring Twenties* (1939), *The Way of All Flesh* (1940), and *The Lullaby of Broadway* (1951).

Gladys George was born Gladys Anna Clare on September 13, 1904 in Patten, Maine, the only child of Shakespearean actor Sir Arthur Evans Clare and Alice Clare. She was married and divorced four times, each time marrying an actor. Her husbands were Arthur Erway, Leonard Penn, Edward Fowler, and Kenneth Bradley. She died on December 8, 1954.

Billy Gilbert

BILLY GILBERT

A truly funny performer, Billy Gilbert learned his trade in vaudeville where he eventually became a headliner drawing a respectable income. It was in vaudeville that he introduced his suspense-filled sneezing routine, which became his trademark and which he later used frequently in his films. Gilbert was a large man, weighing close to 300 pounds. He appeared in a great number of movies, generally as comic relief, and he acted as stooge for

such great comedy teams as Laurel and Hardy and the Marx Brothers. But he's probably best known not for his on-screen presence but for his voice, which was used for Sneezy in Walt Disney's *Snow White and the Seven Dwarfs* (1937). Also numbered among his credits are the 1940 *The Great Dictator* (in which he played Herring, a character based on Field Marshall Hermann Göring) and *His Girl Friday* in the same year. Twenties movie heroine Zasu Pitts and comedian Charlie Chase were two of his best friends.

Gilbert was born on September 12, 1894 in Louisville, Kentucky, the son of Metropolitan Opera singers. In 1937 he married actress Ella MacKenzie. The marriage lasted over 30 years until Gilbert's death on September 9, 1971.

Connie Gilchrist

CONNIE GILCHRIST

To find a true character actor, you need look no further than Connie Gilchrist; she added so much to the movies she took part in that you might wonder how the movie could have been made without her. Like so many fine character performers,

her ability to outshine the stars of the movie amounted to a noncombative form of scene stealing. As comedian (and former boxer) Rags Ragland once put it, "I want one of those Connie Gilchrist parts where everybody works their asses off all week and she comes in on Saturday for one scene and steals the picture." Gilchrist's acting career began on the stage, and she didn't reach Hollywood until 1940, when she herself was pushing 40. Although she made most of her films for MGM, Gilchrist eventually worked at every major film studio in Hollywood. She was usually found portraying a mother or a spirited domestic. Her film credits include *Cry Havoc* in 1943 and *A Letter to Three Wives* in 1949. She also made countless guest and supporting appearances on television.

She was born Rose Gilchrist on February 2, 1901 in Brooklyn, New York, with acting in her blood. Her mother, Martha Daniels, was an actress. Gilchrist married Edwin O'Hanlon, a film director, in 1922, and they have one daughter, Dorothy.

SYDNEY GREENSTREET

Sydney Greenstreet went to Ceylon at the age of 18 to make his fortune as a tea planter, but a drought forced him back to England. There he tried several jobs, including managing a brewery, before enrolling in acting school. In 1902 he made his London stage debut playing a villain in a Sher-

Sydney Greenstreet

lock Holmes story. He was capable of playing a variety of roles and appeared in many productions in America. He spent most of the thirties with the Lunts at New York's Theatre Guild. As a successful stage actor, Greenstreet had no intention of ever experimenting with films. He didn't want to take any chances on failing in the movies. He held to this conviction for many years before he was finally persuaded by John Huston to make his screen debut as the mysterious Kasper Guttman in *The Maltese Falcon* in 1941. His first film was all it took to prove Greenstreet's fear of movie failure to be totally off-base. Audiences were delighted by his massive size, his stunning laugh, and his mock-pompous speech ("By Gad, you are a character, sir"). He was an instant hit, and he won an Academy Award nomination for best supporting actor to prove it. He worked steadily in movies for the next nine years (frequently appearing with Peter Lorre), contributing to the success of many enjoyable films and livening up many mediocre ones. Among the major movies to which he lent his presence were *Casablanca* (1943) and *The Hucksters* (1947).

He was born Sydney Hughes Greenstreet on December 27, 1879 in the English coastal town of Sandwich. His parents were John and Ann Greenstreet. In 1918 he married Dorothy Salesman, and the couple had one son, John. Greenstreet died on January 19, 1954.

Charlotte Greenwood

CHARLOTTE GREENWOOD

Charlotte Greenwood—setting aside her considerable talent as a comedienne—was fascinating just to look at. She was very tall, with a sort of elongated look, and she was an eccentric dancer who clearly enjoyed delighting audiences with her impossibly high kicks. Her stage career began in 1905 when she was barely a teenager, and she entered films in 1915 in *Jane*. Her film roles usually presented her as the friend of the star, providing the story's comic relief, and many films wouldn't have made it without her first-rate ability to inject some necessary humor. She was always fun to watch and full of humor, but she did it all with an expression of smiling good manners. Her movie credits include *Flying High* in 1931, *Moon*

Over Miami in 1941, and *Oklahoma!* in 1955. In the '30s and '40s she divided her time between stage and screen work.

Charlotte Greenwood was born on June 25, 1893 in Philadelphia, Pennsylvania, the daughter of Frank Greenwood and Bella Jacquette Higgens. In 1924 Greenwood married Martin Broones; there were no children of the marriage. She died on January 18, 1978 after a long illness.

Sara Haden

SARA HADEN

Sara Haden's roles tended to fall into one of two categories: either she played the sort of docile, drab, downtrodden woman that you had to be sorry for; or she was such a mean, merciless character that you were happy to see her get what was coming to her. She became a stage actress at an early age and had considerable acting experience. Her screen career, however, was restricted to small character parts; she never seemed to land the good roles that went to some of her contemporaries. The only reason she's remembered is for her portrayal—over a decade—of the spinster Aunt Milly in the *Andy Hardy* series. Even here she was rele-

gated to the background, coming forward once in a while to dispense a bit of advice. All the same, Haden was a fine actress and could, given the chance, have been a class A character actress. Her other film credits include *A Family Affair* (1937), *She-Wolf of London* (1946), and *A Lion Is in the Streets* (1953).

She was born on November 17, 1897, in Galveston, Texas, to Doctor John Haden and his wife, actress Charlotte Walker. In 1921 she married Richard Abbott, whose stage name was Simon Vandenberg. They had no children, and the marriage ended in divorce. Haden died on September 15, 1981.

Alan Hale

ALAN HALE

From 1911 until sound arrived, Alan Hale was the hero of a succession of silent movies, starting with his debut in *The Cowboy and the Lady*. He was also a film director and took a stab at a career as an opera singer. He really came into his own, however, in the 1930s and '40s, often playing a lovable Irish rogue. In the course of his entire movie career his appearances can be numbered in the hundreds. A husky, cheerful figure, he had roles in many Errol Flynn films, and will probably be best remembered as Little John in *The Adventures of Robin Hood* (1938). It was the second time he had played Little John on the screen—he had done the same role in the silent 1922 Douglas Fairbanks version. He played the role a third time in *Rogues of Sherwood Forest*, released after his death in 1950. Toward the end of his career he achieved some success as an inventor.

Alan Hale was born Rufus Alan McKahan on February 10, 1892 in Washington, D.C. His first marriage, to actress Gretchen Hartman in 1914, produced three children, Alan Hale, Jr., who became an actor like his father, and daughters Jeanne and Karen. Hale's second wife was Betty Reed Doer, whom he married in 1943. He died on January 22, 1950.

Margaret Hamilton

MARGARET HAMILTON

Forty-five years after *The Wizard of Oz* enchanted its first generation of young audiences, people still bring their children up to Margaret Hamilton and introduce her by saying, "Here's the Wicked Witch of the

West." That's an indication of the impact of the movie and Hamilton's role in it. Hamilton, however, did not set out to be an actress. She wanted to be a teacher and did, in fact, become a kindergarten teacher. When she started acting it was in small theatres, from which she moved up to Broadway. In 1933 she signed with RKO and started doing films, her first being *Another Language* in 1933. For a while she alternated between stage and screen appearances, then in only two years—1937 and 1938—she appeared in 14 films. In 1939 came *Oz*, and it's interesting to note that Hamilton was not the first choice for the role which was to make her famous. Gale Sondergaard was the number one candidate to play the witch, but later the studio, MGM, decided that she was too glamorous and gave the role to Hamilton. Hamilton's other movie credits include *Babes in Arms* (1939), and *State of the Union* in 1948. She is still working and can be seen on television.

Margaret Hamilton was born on December 9, 1902 in Cleveland, Ohio, the daughter of Walter J. Hamilton, an attorney, and Jennie Adams Hamilton. In 1931 she married architect Paul Meserve. The couple had one son, Hamilton, born a year before they divorced in 1937.

CEDRIC HARDWICKE

Like so many of the character actors born in England, Cedric Hardwicke came to the United States

Cedric Hardwicke

with many years of stage experience behind him. He had made his first movie in England at the age of 20; it was a two-reeler called *Riches and Rogues* in which he played six parts because he needed the money—ten guineas. It was 13 years before he did another film, *Nelson*. Once he arrived in Hollywood in 1935, however, it took no time for him to become one of the leading character actors in the business. His first Hollywood film was *Becky Sharp* (the first feature-length film to use the full, three-color process known as Technicolor) in 1935. His favorite role, and the one for which many fans remember him, is Mr. Brink (Death) in *On Borrowed Time* (1939). The long list of films to which he lent his distinguished presence also includes *Stanley and Livingstone* (1939), *Tom Brown's School Days* (1940), *The Winslow Boy* (1948; released in the U.S. in 1950), and *Richard III* (1956). His only leading role in a Hollywood film was in *The Moon Is Down* (1943).

He was born Cedric Webster Hardwicke on February 19, 1893 in Stourbridge, Worcestershire, England, the son of physician Edwin Hardwicke and Jessie Master-

son. In 1928 he married Helena Pickard, an actress by whom he had a son (Edward Hardwicke, now with Britain's National Theatre) before the union ended in divorce in 1948. His second mariage, to Mary Scott in 1950, also ended in divorce, in 1961. Hardwicke received his knighthood for services to the arts in the New Year's Honors List of 1934. His autobiography, *A Victorian in Orbit*, was published in 1960. Toward the end of his life Hardwicke fell on hard times. He died virtually penniless on August 6, 1964; his funeral was paid for by the Actors' Relief Fund.

Fay Holden

FAY HOLDEN

There were contemporary actresses—Mildred Dunnock and Fay Bainter among them—who could play the lovely devoted mother as well as Fay Holden, but none could do it any better. Holden began her career as a child actress on the stage, progressing as she grew up to "woman of the world" characters. She was persuaded to come to Hollywood by her brother-in-law, comedian Andy Clyde, and did her first film in 1936. She worked mostly for MGM, where she was used to good advantage in old-fashioned American mother roles. She is best remembered as the mother in the highly successful series of *Andy Hardy* films. Holden made around 50 films in just over 20 years, and appeared to be enjoying herself all the way. Then in 1958, after close to 10 years away from the screen, she made her last movie, *Andy Hardy Comes Home*.

Fay Holden was born Dorothy Fay Hammerton in Birmingham, England on September 26, 1895. In 1914 she married actor/producer/manager David Clyde, who died in 1945. They had no children. Holden died on June 23, 1973.

Frieda Inescort

FRIEDA INESCORT

Frieda Inescort was a lovely-looking woman who brought high-quality performances to every film she graced. Before she embarked on an acting career she was the private lady-in-waiting to Lady Astor in London. Once she became an actress she worked steadily on the British stage before making her Broadway debut in 1922. She stayed on Broadway until 1935, when she went to Hollywood to make *The Dark Angel*. She was often

cast as a wealthy, aristocratic lady, and appeared in many major films, including *The Letter* (1940), *Pride and Prejudice* (1940), *You'll Never Get Rich* (1941), and *A Place in the Sun* (1951).

Frieda Inescort was born Frieda Wightman on June 29, 1901, in Edinburgh, Scotland. Her father was a journalist and her mother a well-known Scottish actress (Elaine Inescort). Inescort married critic/poet Ben Ray Redman in 1926, and the marriage lasted for 35 years until Redman's death in 1961. Inescort herself suffered for many years from multiple sclerosis, from which she died in 1976.

Allen Jenkins

ALLEN JENKINS

Allen Jenkins' film roles generally fell into the half-witted criminal category. He also showed up frequently as mugs, policemen, cab drivers, and bartenders. In view of the fact that he wound up making some 200 films, it's interesting to note that initially Jenkins had little inclination for an acting career. However, he was given a scholarship to the American Academy of Dramatic Arts and, with his

friend James Cagney, developed a keen interest in the craft of acting. He did a great deal of stage work before making his feature-film debut in *The Girl Habit* in 1931. His other credits include *I Am a Fugitive From a Chain Gang* (1932) and *Brother Orchid* (1940). Jenkins became very close friends with other Irish players such as Frank McHugh, Pat O'Brien, and Spencer Tracy.

Allen Jenkins was born Al McGonegal on April 19, 1900, in New York City. His parents were well-known musical comedy performers. Jenkins' only marriage ended in divorce. Bad investments left him insolvent, and he lived his last years in relative obscurity. He died on July 20, 1974.

Rita Johnson

RITA JOHNSON

Rita Johnson played "other woman" roles too well for her own good, because the result was consistent type-casting. (The characters she played were early versions of Alexis, the role played by Joan Collins in the current TV series *Dynasty*.) Johnson came to movies by way of the stage, where she pulled off an early career coup by being cho-

sen to play opposite George Murphy in the 1937 movie *London by Night*. In the movie world she was greeted as a blonde Gail Patrick—a Hollywood leading lady of the time. Johnson's other early movies include *Here Comes Mr. Jordan* in 1941. In 1948 she had an accident that required head surgery, and thereafter her film appearances were insignificant. After making her last movie, *All Mine to Give*, in 1957 she was not heard of again until eight years later, when she died of a brain hemorrhage at the age of 53.

Rita Johnson was born Rita McSean on August 13, 1912 in Worcester, Massachusetts. She married stockbroker L. Stanley Kahn in 1940, but the marriage ended in divorce in 1943. A subsequent marriage to Captain Edwin Hutzler also ended in divorce. Johnson died on October 31, 1965.

Allyn Joslyn

ALLYN JOSLYN

Allyn Joslyn was a very well-liked character actor who specialized in comedy. His career started on the stage when he was still in his teens, and he did a huge amount of radio work, logging upwards of

3000 shows. His film debut, he used to point out, "was also Lana Turner's," in the now forgotten *They Won't Forget* in 1937. In the '40s Joslyn became well-known and had thousands of admirers. In films he usually played some kind of arrogant, blustering snob, sometimes as a boss to the lead performer, a suitor, or a friend to one of the stars. His film credits include *Cafe Society* (1939) and *The Horn Blows at Midnight* (1945). As the years went on and he received less film work, he did some television. His reliable, genuine personality brought him many friends.

Joslyn was born on July 21, 1901 in Milford, Pennsylvania, the son of a mining engineer and a nurse. In 1936 he married actress Dorothy Vocket, with whom he had a daughter, Linda May. His wife died in 1978, and Joslyn died on January 21, 1981.

Patsy Kelly

PATSY KELLY

If you saw Patsy Kelly's name in the credits, you knew the film was likely to be a frolic. She was renowned for her wonderful sense of humor and her deadpan comic delivery. After extensive stage experience as a dancer and comedienne in Broadway

musicals, Kelly was brought to Hollywood in 1933 by producer/director Hal Roach (most famous for his work with Harold Lloyd, Charlie Chase, Laurel and Hardy, and the *Our Gang* comedies) to replace Zasu Pitts in a series of popular two-reel comedies co-starring Thelma Todd. Her feature films include *The Cowboy and the Lady* (1938) and *Broadway Limited* (1941). She retired in the early 1940s but returned to the screen in the '60s. Her later credits include *Please Don't Eat the Daisies* (1960) and *Freaky Friday* (1977). In 1971 Kelly returned to the stage in a very successful revival of the musical *No, No, Nanette*. She co-starred with her childhood friend, dancer Ruby Keeler, and won a Tony Award. Toward the end of her life she became ill and stopped working. She moved in with Keeler, who took care of her until she died.

Patsy Kelly was born in Brooklyn, New York on January 21, 1910. She never married. She died on September 24, 1981.

Arthur Kennedy

ARTHUR KENNEDY

There have been many Kennedys in the movies—

Burt, Douglas, Edgar, Tom, George. None, though, has been as greatly talented as Arthur Kennedy. Today he would probably be a star rather than a top-class character player. He began his career on the stage at the age of 20, and his early days as a struggling young actor saw the beginning of his close friendship with fellow character actor David Wayne. Kennedy made his film debut in *City for Conquest* in 1940, and made over a hundred movies, taking a break from time to time to return to the Broadway stage. He was nominated for a best actor Oscar for *Bright Victory* (1951). His other major film credits include *Champion* (1949), *Trial* (1955), *Peyton Place* (1957), and *Some Came Running* (1958)—all of which won him best supporting actor nominations. Today, by choice, Kennedy works less and less, although he still makes the occasional film in Europe and does some television work. He expresses little enthusiasm about his past work in films.

Kennedy was born John Arthur Kennedy in Worcester, Massachusetts on February 17, 1914, the only child of Dr. and Mrs. John Timothy Kennedy. He married Mary Cheffey in 1938, and the couple have two children, Terence and Laurie.

Victor Killian

next 20 years. He made his film debut in 1929 in *Gentlemen of the Press* along with another screen newcomer, Kay Francis. Kilian made many movies during the 1930s and '40s, among them *The Adventures of Tom Sawyer* (1938) and *Gentleman's Agreement* (1947). He lost an eye during a film brawl in the 1942 movie *Reap the Wild Wind*. In the early '50s he ran afoul of the House Un-American Activities Committee and thereafter couldn't get film work for many years. His career took an upward turn again when he began playing Mary's grandfather in the hit TV series *Mary Hartman, Mary Hartman* in 1976.

Kilian was born in Jersey City, New Jersey, on March 6, 1891. He was murdered by home invaders in his Hollywood apartment on March 11, 1979. He was 88.

VICTOR KILIAN

Victor Kilian was a towering actor with a natural aptitude for playing villains. He started acting on the stage in 1909 and continued to do so for the

LEONID KINSKEY

Leonid Kinskey was one of a kind, frequently referred to as "that crazy Russian." He usually played some kind of foreign role, most often in

Leonid Kinskey

Elsa Lanchester

Jack LaRue

Oscar Levant

a comic vein. He started acting as a young man in Russia, mostly doing mime. Soon after coming to the United States he made his film debut in *The Great Deception* in 1926. He never signed a contract with any studio, but in the 30 years following *The Great Deception* he managed to appear in hundreds of films. He's most readily identified with his role as Sascha, the bartender in *Casablanca* in 1942. During the past 20 years he has made his livelihood as a writer, producer, and director of industrial trade shows.

Kinskey was born in St. Petersburg, Russia, on April 18, 1903. His first marriage ended with his wife's death. His second wife was Iphigenie Castigloni, a Viennese actress, and he was again left a widower on her death in 1963. Neither marriage produced any children. Kinskey now lives in California, making only infrequent appearances on television.

ELSA LANCHESTER

Elsa Lanchester was never a particularly beautiful woman, but she could breathe creative life into any character she portrayed. In her early years she studied dancing with Isadora Duncan, who was to become her good friend. Lanchester then transferred her talents as an actress to the legitimate stage where she met her future husband, the celebrated Charles Laughton. Her film debut was in *One of the Best* in 1927, and she followed this with a wide range of character roles, generally giving her best performances in eccentric or comic parts. Her major films include *The Private Life of Henry VIII* (1933), *Come to the Stable* (1949), and *Witness for the Prosecution* (1958). The latter two won her Academy Award nominations for best supporting actress. After Laughton died of cancer she did not work for more than a year. In later years she has toured in her one-woman show and has appeared frequently on television. In a recent autobiography titled *Elsa Lanchester: Herself*, Lanchester revealed that her husband had been a homosexual.

Elsa Lanchester was born Elizabeth Sullivan on October 28, 1902 in London, England, the daughter of James Sullivan, an accountant, and his wife Edith. She married Laughton in 1929, and the marriage lasted until his death.

JACK LARUE

Jack LaRue developed a reputation on the questionable grounds of being just about the best in the business at portraying a sadistic killer. His dark good looks, husky voice, and penchant for sinister and brutal roles assured him a special niche in movie history. His first movie was *The Mouthpiece* in 1932, and subsequently he enriched dozens of movies with his presence. Among his notable titles were *The Story of Temple Drake* (1933) and *My Favorite Brunette* (1947). After his movie career lost momentum in the '50s he opened a successful Italian restaurant in Hollywood where many movie celebrities came to dine. He owned the restaurant for almost a decade before he finally retired.

Jack LaRue was born Gaspare Biondolillo in New York City on May 3, 1902. He ended up living with his sister in an apartment in Hollywood, and nothing was heard from him for years until he died in 1983.

OSCAR LEVANT

Oscar Levant was the guy who played the amiable but grouchy neurotic who always managed to make his neuroses appear painfully funny. He was also a very accomplished concert pianist, and was well-known as a leading interpreter of the music of George Gershwin, with whom he was close friends. Levant made his film debut in 1929 in *The Dance of Life*. He wrote scores and songs for a number of movies, then gained fame for his wit on the radio show *Information Please*. This led to film appearances. His first major role, written specially for him, was as a comic foil for Bing Crosby and Mary Martin in *Rhythm on the River* (1940). In 1945 he played himself (claiming to be miscast) in *Rhapsody in Blue*, a biography of George Gershwin. Other major movies in which Levant appeared include *Humoresque* (1946), *An American in Paris* (1951), and *The Band Wagon* (1953). He wrote three autobiographical books—*A Smattering of Ignorance*, *The Unimportance of Being Oscar*, and *The Memoirs of an Amnesiac*.

Many people considered Levant to be a hypochondriac; however, he did indeed suffer from poor mental and physical health, spending many of his last years in and out of hospitals.

Oscar Levant was born on December 27, 1906 in Pittsburgh, Pennsylvania, one of four sons of Max Levant, a jeweler, and Anne Radin. In 1932 he married dancer Barbara Smith, but the marriage lasted only a year. In 1939 he married June Gilmartin, an actress. The couple had three daughters, Marcia, Lorna, and Amanda. Levant died of a heart attack on August 14, 1972.

Gene Lockhart

GENE AND JUNE LOCKHART

This talented duo were father and daughter. Gene was born in London, Ontario, Canada (as was another famous character actor, Hume Cronyn) and was a vaudevillian, stage actor, and writer before embarking on a screen career in 1922. He made well over a hundred films, and was equally at ease in warm-hearted roles or as cowardly and corrupt characters. He was often compared to fellow actors

Cecil Kellaway and Charles Coburn. Among his best-known movies are *Algiers*, for which he won an Academy Award nomination as best supporting actor in 1938, and *Going My Way* (1944). Gene Lockhart also wrote the popular song "The World Is Waiting for the Sunrise."

June Lockhart made her film debut in 1938 when she was only 12, appearing with her parents in *A Christmas Carol*. She made her real fame elsewhere, however, as the mother in the long-running television series *Lassie*. She also played the mother in the TV series *Lost in Space*.

Gene was born Eugene Lockhart on July 18, 1891, the son of John and Ellen Lockhart. In 1924 he married actress Kathleen Arthur, and their daughter June was born in New York City on June 15, 1925. Gene Lockhart died on March 31, 1957. His wife died in 1978 at the age of 97. June Lockhart's daughter, Ann, is now carrying the family tradition into the third generation— she's also an actress.

Frank McHugh

FRANK MCHUGH

Frank McHugh, the son of prominent theatre peo-

ple, became one of the most easily recognizable character actors in the movie business. McHugh made his debut on the stage at the age of ten, and remained faithful to the live theatre for many years before settling in Hollywood. In 1930 he signed with Warner Brothers and stayed with them for over a decade. His first year in Hollywood he made *The Dawn Patrol*, and he followed it with many major films, including *Footlight Parade* (1933), *Dodge City* (1939), *Going My Way* (1944), and *The Last Hurrah* (1958). He frequently played wise-cracking character roles and was famous for his funny high-pitched laugh. McHugh was well liked in the business and numbered among his friends such notables as Spencer Tracy and James Cagney.

The actor was born Francis Curray McHugh on May 23, 1899 in Homestead, Pennsylvania, the son of actor Edward A. McHugh and his wife. In 1928 Frank McHugh married actress Dorothy Spencer, and the marriage lasted over 40 years, producing two sons and a daughter. One son was killed in an auto crash. McHugh died on September 11, 1981.

ALINE MACMAHON

Aline MacMahon's stage and screen career has spanned over 60 years. She was such a fine character actress that she set the standard for many of her contemporaries. She graduated from Barnard College in 1921, and the same year appeared on

Aline MacMahon

Broadway in *The Mirage*. She did not make her first film until ten years later, when she played Edward G. Robinson's perfect secretary in the 1931 movie *Five Star Final*. She received rave reviews and signed a contract with Warner Brothers. Although not lacking in film offers, she returned to the stage several times throughout her career. Her intelligent face and large eyes had a serious expression, so she was a natural for sad or somber roles. But she was equally adept at trading wisecracks in lighter comic parts. Among the films in which she appeared were *Gold Diggers of 1933* (1933); *Dragon Seed* (1944), which won her an Academy Award nomination in the best supporting actress category; *The Search* (1948); and *All the Way Home* (1963), recreating her stage role of Aunt Hannah.

The actress was born Aline Laveen MacMahon on May 3, 1899 in McKeesport, Pennsylvania. She was the only child of telegraph-operator-turned-journalist William MacMahon and his wife, Jennie. In 1928 she married Clarence S. Stein, an architect whom she had known for almost ten years and with whom she enjoys that Hollywood rarity—a very successful marriage. The couple has one son.

Butterfly McQueen

BUTTERFLY MCQUEEN

Although everybody knows her name and her first movie, few people can recall another movie that she ever made. Butterfly McQueen's movie debut, of course, was as the engaging but not-too-bright maid, Prissy, in *Gone With the Wind* (1939). Her portrayal brought her instant fame, and her famous line, "Miss Scarlett, ah doan' know nuthin' 'bout birthin' babies," became part of movie history. But her glory faded fast. Although she made a number of other movies, none of them did much to further her career. McQueen had had some acting and dancing experience before *Gone With the Wind*, and she continued to do sporadic theatre and movie work along with a number of other meager jobs, including factory worker, waitress, and dishwasher. She did, however, have a personal moment of success when, at the age of 64, she received her bachelor's degree in political science from New York's City College.

Butterfly McQueen was born Thelma McQueen in Tampa, Florida on January 8, 1911, the daughter of a stevedore and a maid. She never married.

Marjorie Main

MARJORIE MAIN

To see this familiar sourpuss playing a series of coarse, crusty women, you would find it hard to believe that she was actually the refined, teetotal daughter of a conservative clergyman. Marjorie Main made her movie debut in *A House Divided* in 1932, and went on to appear in well over a hundred films, among them *Dead End* (1937), *The Women* (1939), and *Meet Me in St. Louis* (1944). She was nominated for an Academy Award as best supporting actress for her performance as Ma Kettle in *The Egg and I* (1947). However, she really became widely known when she further developed the Ma Kettle character in the series of *Ma and Pa Kettle* movies opposite Percy Kilbride. At first Main had doubts about the role of Ma Kettle, but she came to enjoy and to believe in the role. She retired in 1957 and lived unpretentiously until her death.

Marjorie Main was born Mary Tomlinson on February 24, 1890 in Acton, Indiana, to Samuel and Mary Tomlinson. In 1921 she married Dr. Stanley Lefevre Krebs, a psychologist and lecturer. Their daughter, Annabelle, was born in 1922. Main died on April 10, 1975.

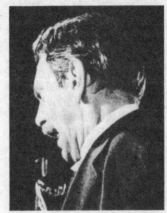
Raymond Massey

RAYMOND MASSEY

Oxford-educated and stage-trained, Raymond Massey had a lot of solid experience behind him before he came to films in 1931. His long line of screen appearances—over a hundred—included many contemptible types and a number of fanatics. He didn't always play the villain, however, and his 1940 performance as Abraham Lincoln in *Abe Lincoln in Illinois* was rewarded with an Academy Award nomination for best actor. Among his other movies are *The Scarlet Pimpernel* (1935), *The Prisoner of Zenda* (1937), *Arsenic and Old Lace* (1944), and *East of Eden* (1955).

Raymond Hart Massey was born on August 30, 1896 in Toronto, Ontario, Canada, to Chester D. Massey and Anna Vincent. His brother, Vincent Massey, became Governor General of Canada. Massey married three times. His first wife was Margery Hilda Freemantle. They married in 1921; had a son, Geoffrey, in 1922; and were divorced in 1929. His second marriage—in 1929 to actress Adrianne Allen—produced two children to carry on the family acting tradition. Their son Daniel is an actor with about 20 films to his credit, a best supporting actor Oscar nomination for *Star!* (1963), as well as stage and TV credits in Britain; their daughter Anna is well-known as a British character actress. Massey and Adrianne Allen divorced in 1939, and he married Dorothy Ludington the same year. Massey died on December 19, 1983.

Donald Meek

DONALD MEEK

Donald Meek was a character actor who could do more with one short scene than most actors could achieve with a featured part. He was seen in dozens of movies, frequently playing a timorous, nervous, or effeminate comedy role. He was ideally built for such parts, being small, bald (as a result of contracting tropical fever at the age of 18), and bespectacled. He began his career at the age of 8, as an acrobat and high-wire walker. After his arrival in the United States an accident suffered during an acrobatic performance forced him to limit his career to acting. Some of the films for which he is best remembered are *The Whole Town's Talking* (1935), *You Can't Take It With You* (1938), *Stagecoach* (1939), and *State Fair* (1945).

He was born on July 14, 1880 in Glasgow, Scotland. He never married, and he was always a very private person. He died on November 18, 1946.

Adolphe Menjou

ADOLPHE MENJOU

Adolphe Menjou was the model of a debonair and well-educated actor— he went to Cornell University. Known at a glance by his waxed black mustache and an impeccable wardrobe, he consistently appeared on the nation's list of Ten Best-Dressed Men. Menjou had had a great deal of stage experience before arriving in Hollywood, and made a name as a leading man in the silent movies of the 1920s. Later he became a much

sought after character actor in sound movies, and it was as a character actor that he gave his best performances and achieved public recognition. He's probably best known for *The Front Page*, which was made in 1931 and which brought him an Academy Award nomination for best actor, but he continued to work steadily for the next 30 years. His productive career encompassed well over a hundred movies, including a number of sophisticated drawing room comedies. Some of his credits: *A Woman of Paris* (1923), *Morning Glory* (1933), *A Star Is Born* (1937), *Roxie Hart* (1942), *State of the Union* (1948), and *Paths of Glory* (1957).

Adolphe Jean Menjou was born on February 18, 1890 in Pittsburgh, Pennsylvania, to hotel manager Albert Menjou and his wife Nora. (James Joyce, the writer, was a cousin on his mother's side.) Menjou married three times; his first two wives were Katharine Tinsley and actress Kathryn Carver. He married actress Verree Teasdale in 1934, and they co-starred in *The Milky Way* in 1936. Menjou died on October 29, 1963.

UNA MERKEL

Una Merkel's movie career started during the silent era when she was a stand-in for star Lillian Gish. She had parts in a few films but spent most of the 1920s on Broadway. With the coming of sound, she returned to Hollywood to play Ann Rutledge in D. W. Griffith's *Abraham Lincoln* (1930). However, she soon settled into

Una Merkel

comic supporting roles, typically playing a wisecracking friend of the leading lady. In this she joined a number of fine character actresses who were also doing similar second-string roles with consistent skill and success. (Eve Arden and Thelma Ritter are among those whose careers were founded on such parts.) Merkel herself will always be remembered as the woman who had the saloon fight with Marlene Dietrich in *Destry Rides Again* in 1939. Others among her many film titles are *42nd Street* (1933), *Born to Dance* (1936), *The Bank Dick* (1940), and *Summer and Smoke* (1961), for which she was nominated for a best supporting actress Oscar. Merkel returned to Broadway in the '40s and continued to intersperse stage roles among her film appearances. She once said of her career, "I was glad to do anything when the part was good. I didn't care what I was supposed to be."

Una Merkel was born in Covington, Kentucky on December 10, 1903, the daughter of traveling salesman Arnold Merkel and his wife, Phares. In 1932 she married aviator/designer Ronald L. Burla, but the marriage ended in divorce in 1945.

Agnes Moorehead

AGNES MOOREHEAD

Few character actresses could handle the role of an unlikable or neurotic woman more skillfully than Agnes Moorehead. She had had good training and a fair amount of stage experience by the time Orson Welles brought her to Hollywood for her first film assignment, playing the mother in *Citizen Kane* (1941). What had been planned as a one-picture deal developed into an interesting and varied career spanning 30 years, in the course of which Moorehead collected four Academy Award nominations— for *The Magnificent Ambersons* (1942), *Mrs. Parkington* (1944), *Johnny Belinda* (1948), and *Hush . . . Hush, Sweet Charlotte* (1964). For many years she had taught acting courses, and in the 1950s she returned to the stage herself, touring the country intermittently from 1951 to 1954 with Charles Laughton, Charles Boyer, and Cedric Hardwicke in Shaw's *Don Juan in Hell*. She later toured in her one-woman show, called *The Fabulous Redhead*, which consisted of readings from favorite books and plays. Moreover, Moorehead had a very fine career in radio and later made countless guest appearances on television. From 1964 to 1972, she appeared regularly as the mother Endora in the hit TV series *Bewitched*.

She was born Agnes Robertson Moorehead on December 6, 1906 in Clinton, Massachusetts, the daughter of the Reverend John Moorehead and Mary McCauley. She was married twice, from 1930 to 1952 to John Griffith Lee, with whom she adopted a son, Sean, and from 1953 to 1958 to Robert Gist. Moorehead died of lung cancer on April 20, 1974.

Frank Morgan

FRANK MORGAN

Frank Morgan started out as a stage performer, but rapidly found his way into films. He became known for his totally convincing portrayals of amiable but befuddled characters, the most notable of whom was the wacky wizard in *The Wizard of Oz* in 1939. Even before this, however, he'd received one Academy Award nomination for best actor for his work in *Affairs of Cellini* in 1934, and was to be nominated for best supporting actor for *Tortilla Flat* in 1942. Although he acted

character parts for most of his career, he did have a number of leading roles. Morgan had already begun work on *Annie Get Your Gun* when he died in his sleep in 1949.

Frank Morgan was born Francis Phillip Wuppermann on June 1, 1890 in New York City. His father was George Wuppermann, a prosperous manufacturer. His brother was the actor Ralph Morgan (they appeared together in the 1925 film *The Man Who Found Himself*). Frank Morgan married Alma Muller in 1914, and their son George was born in 1916. Morgan died on September 18, 1949.

Alan Napier

ALAN NAPIER

Distinguished, talented, and suave are all appropriate terms to apply to Alan Napier—another member of an extraordinarily strong army of character actors who came out of England. Like most of his actor countrymen, he had had extensive experience on the British stage. His movie debut was a minor film made in England in 1930 and titled *Caste*. He came to Hollywood in 1939, appearing that year in *We Are Not Alone*. Other credits include *The Hairy Ape* (1944), *Young Bess* (1953), and *Marnie* (1964).

In the early 1950s he had a problem with the "red scare" but continued to make movies throughout the decade. All told, however, his film career is impressive—even though he probably achieved greater recognition as Batman's butler Alfred in the *Batman* TV series from 1965 to 1967 than for any of his film roles (which, incidentally, included a number of other butlers). He has the distinction of being, at six feet five inches, one of the tallest actors in the business.

He was born Alan William Napier-Clavering on January 7, 1903 in Birmingham, England. His father was an impecunious artist, and his mother a wealthy patron of the arts. In 1930 Napier married Nancy Pettybridge, but the marriage ended in 1944 and Napier married Aileen Hawksley later the same year.

Cathleen Nesbitt

CATHLEEN NESBITT

Cathleen Nesbitt was another of the great English character actresses who crossed the ocean to grace American movie screens. Like her good friend Gladys Cooper, she was lovely, clever, and talented. She was also a very

prolific performer, appearing in hundreds of stage plays. She did her first film, *The Faithful Heart*, in 1922. In the course of the next 50 or so years she made only about 36 movies, including *An Affair to Remember* in 1957. In 1958 she appeared in the film that she personally liked most and for which most fans remember her best—*Separate Tables*. This was the only film in which she and her friend Gladys Cooper appeared together. Television viewers know Nesbitt for her work in the live dramatic-anthology series *Studio One* and as Agatha Morley, the Congressman's mother, in *The Farmer's Daughter*.

Cathleen Nesbitt was born on November 24, 1888 in Cheshire, England. In 1922 she married Cecil Ramage, a lawyer and later an actor. They had two children, Mark, who went into advertising, and Jennifer, who became a psychiatrist. Nesbitt died on August 2, 1982.

Barbara Nichols

BARBARA NICHOLS

Barbara Nichols may be the most consistently typecast performer in Hollywood. But who could be a better choice for a role as a warm-hearted floozie? She had been a showgirl and model before she made her first movie, *Miracle in the Rain* in 1956, and she went on to appear in a number of movies including *The Loved One* in 1965 and—both in 1957—*The Sweet Smell of Success* and *The Pajama Game*. She brought a touch of humor and pathos to the roles she played. She was never able to get leading roles and insisted that she was quite content to be a character actress. She also enjoyed television roles, of which she did many. Nichols never married. She once commented, "Too many men I meet confuse me with the types I've played."

Barbara Nichols was born Barbara Marie Nickerauer on December 30, 1929 in New York City, the daughter of George Nickerauer and his wife. She died on October 5, 1976 at the age of 47.

Virginia O'Brien

VIRGINIA O'BRIEN

Virginia O'Brien was not overloaded with talent but as a performer she had a certain fascination about her. She was very pretty, with a flair for comedy, and her personal contribu-

tion to movies was a deadpan singing style: she would remain completely motionless while she sang. O'Brien's whole career was spent at MGM and included fewer than 20 films. She started with *Hullabaloo* in 1940, co-starred with comedian Red Skelton in several films, and appeared in her last film, *Francis in the Navy*, in 1955. Why she didn't go further will never be known, but it's possible that she felt comfortable with her singing gimmick and was afraid to change. After some years, naturally enough, the novelty wore rather thin, and O'Brien retired from the screen.

Virginia O'Brien was born on April 18, 1921 in Los Angeles, California. Her father was a captain of detectives, and the family already had a foot in the world of movies—her mother's brother was screen director Lloyd Bacon. O'Brien married Kirk Alyn in 1942, and they had a daughter, Teresa. The marriage ended in divorce in 1955.

Mabel Paige

MABEL PAIGE

Mabel Paige's name is seldom remembered today, nor is her sweet-old-lady face. But in her heyday she was a delight

to watch in humorous, outspoken roles. In fact, she was to the penniless what Lucile Watson was to the aristocratic—Watson played sharp-tongued rich women; Paige played sharp-tongued poor women. Paige had a great deal of stage experience, starting at the age of four when she performed with her actor parents. She made a dozen or so comedy shorts in 1915 and 1916, but the demands of parenthood kept her away from the screen until the 1940s. At that time she did one of the funniest characterizations ever seen on film, the part of the boozy Annie, both touching and hilarious, in *Lucky Jordan* in 1942.

Mabel Paige was born in New York City in 1880, the daughter of Frank Roberts and Dora Paige, both actors. She married actor Charles Ritchie, with whom she had several children. She was widowed in 1931 and died on February 8, 1954.

Gail Patrick

GAIL PATRICK

Gail Patrick was a sophisticated and very feminine actress admirably suited to the sleek, sometimes snobbish, roles she played. She was a towering beauty and was generally

considered to have all the makings of a top-flight star. Somehow, however, she became the victim of her own singular style and was typecast in "Gail Patrick" parts for the rest of her performing career. Among her film credits were *Death Takes a Holiday* (1934), *My Man Godfrey* (1936), *My Favorite Wife* (1940), and *Love Crazy* (1941). Patrick, a self-confident and well-educated woman (she was once dean of women students at her alma mater, Howard College), did not content herself with an acting career that had not brought her the major success so many people expected. In the 1950s she turned to TV producing and was hugely successful, most notably as the executive producer of the *Perry Mason* series. Patrick and her third husband, Thomas Cornwall Jackson—who was Erle Stanley Gardner's literary agent—together initiated the highly successful series.

Gail Patrick was born Margaret LaVelle Fitzpatrick on June 20, 1911 in Birmingham, Alabama. In 1936 she married Robert Cobb, whom she divorced in 1940. Subsequent marriages to Navy Lieutenant Arnold White in 1944 and to Jackson—the father of her two children, Jennifer and Tom—in 1947 also failed. In 1974 she married Robert Velde. Patrick died on July 6, 1980 after a three-year fight against leukemia.

ZASU PITTS

Zasu Pitts' bizarre name (derived from combining *Eliza* and *Susan*, the names of her father's sis-

Zasu Pitts

ters) was appropriate to one of the funniest comediennes who ever appeared in films. She started her Hollywood career in silents, playing in both comedies and dramas. In her comic roles all she had to do was appear on screen to get the audience laughing. In her tragic roles she was brilliant, particularly in two films directed by Erich von Stroheim, *Greed* (1924) and *The Wedding March* (1928). With the coming of movie sound she restricted her film appearances exclusively to comedies. From 1932 to 1934 she made a very successful series of comedies with Thelma Todd as her partner. All told, Pitts made over a hundred movies, including *The Guardsman* (1931), *Mrs. Wiggs of the Cabbage Patch* (1934), and *Life With Father* (1947). Her last film was *It's a Mad Mad Mad Mad World* in 1963. She was suffering from cancer at the time the movie was made, but wouldn't pass up the chance of appearing in a picture with such a great cast of comedians.

Zasu Pitts was born on January 3, 1898 in Parsons, Kansas. Her father died when she was a baby. She married Thomas Gallery in 1921 and the couple had a daughter, Ann, and adopted a son, Marvin, be-

fore the marriage ended in divorce in 1932. The following year she married Edward Woodall. Pitts died on June 7, 1963.

John Qualen

JOHN QUALEN

John Qualen became one of Hollywood's most valuable character actors despite an inauspicious start. As a young man he began his career acting in tent shows and such against the wishes of his strongly religious parents. Persevering, Qualen made his Broadway debut in 1929, as the Swedish janitor in Elmer Rice's play *Street Scene*. He made his film debut two years later, recreating his role in the film version of the Pulitzer Prize-winning play. Also in 1931, he appeared in John Ford's *Arrowsmith*, beginning his membership in that director's stock company of players. Among his other films for Ford: *The Grapes of Wrath* (1940), *The Long Voyage Home* (1940), *The Searchers* (1956), and *The Man Who Shot Liberty Valance* (1962). Qualen worked steadily in Hollywood and almost invariably appeared as a meek or unfortunate character. He appeared in

over a hundred movies, including *His Girl Friday* (1940) and *Casablanca* (1942).

The son of a Norwegian minister, Qualen was born John Oleson in Vancouver, British Columbia, Canada on December 8, 1889. His marriage has lasted over 50 years and has produced three daughters and ten grandchildren. Qualen lost his best friend when fellow character actor Pat O'Brien died in 1983.

Frances Rafferty

FRANCES RAFFERTY

Frances Rafferty was a pretty actress who might have been expected to go on to better things, but in fact didn't really make it even in character work. She might have done a lot better today, when movie actresses are allowed a wider range of expression than they were 40 years ago. Her distinctive lip curl and caustic voice were effective, but they weren't enough to make her a popular success. Rafferty made her film debut in 1942, and had reached her peak by 1944 when she played the part of Walter Huston's daughter-in-law in the movie *Dragon Seed*—she had a

memorable scene in which she was brutally raped and murdered. When her career in films faltered she turned to television, where she lucked out by landing the part of Spring Byington's daughter in the long-running series *December Bride*.

Frances Rafferty was born on June 26, 1922 in Sioux City, Iowa, the daughter of personnel expert Maxwell Rafferty and his wife. Frances' brother, Maxwell Rafferty, Jr., became a famous politician and educator. In 1948 she married television writer Tom Baker; the couple had one daughter, Bridget.

Marjorie Rambeau

MARJORIE RAMBEAU

Marjorie Rambeau started acting at age ten and was still beguiling audiences fifty years later. Her stage career brought her recognition for her elegant looks and refined manner, though in her later film career she often played salty, promiscuous characters. Rambeau started acting in films as early as 1916 in *The Dazzling Miss Davison* but didn't settle in Hollywood until 1930. In 1931 she appeared in ten films and her character career was underway. Major films in which she appeared include *The Primrose Path* (1940), for which she won an Academy Award nomination for best supporting actress, and *Tugboat Annie Sails Again* (1940), in which she played the lead. She was working steadily when she was involved in a near-fatal auto accident in 1945. However, after three years and numerous operations, she was able to return to moviemaking, winning a second best supporting actress nomination for *Torch Song* (1953). She continued working in films until 1957.

Rambeau was born on July 15, 1889 in San Francisco, California to a French father, Marcel Rambeau, and his wife Lillian. Rambeau's first two marriages were to actor/writer Willard Mack, and Hugh Dillman. Both marriages ended in divorce. However, Rambeau's third marriage, to Francis A. Gudger in 1931, lasted until he died in 1967. Rambeau died on July 7, 1970, a week before her 81st birthday.

MARTHA RAYE

Martha Raye was one of those theatre children for whom the term "born in a trunk" was coined. She embarked on her show business career, with the help of her vaudevillian parents, at the age of three, and went on to become a working-class-style comedienne with a high-class singing voice. By 1936 when she made her first film, *Rhythm on the Range*, she had done just about everything in show

Martha Raye

business, including singing with a band. During World War II she worked hard for the war effort, entertaining American servicemen wherever they were fighting. She performed similarly during the Korean War and the Vietnam War, and for her morale-raising efforts was awarded the 1968 Jean Hersholt Humanitarian Award by the Academy of Motion Picture Arts and Sciences. She made a number of movies, including *Monsieur Verdoux* (1947) and *Jumbo* (1962), and gained popularity on both radio and TV. At one point she had her own TV series, *The Martha Raye Show*. Raye now does mainly night club and stage shows.

Martha Raye was born Margaret Theresa Yvonne Reed on August 27, 1908 in Butte, Montana. She was married and divorced six times. Her husbands were makeup artist Bud Westmore (whom she married in 1937), composer David Rose (1938), Neal Lang (1941), Nick Condos (whom she married in 1944 and with whom she had a child, Melodye), Thomas Bogley (1954) and Robert O'Shea (1958).

Thelma Ritter

THELMA RITTER

Thelma Ritter was a very good character actress who brought a fine edge to all her performances. She was testy in a satirical way—a latter day Mabel Paige. Ritter started her acting career in stock, and after marrying and having children she did some work in radio. It was through her friend and ex-neighbor, director George Seaton, that she landed a bit part in her first film, *Miracle on 34th Street* (1947). She was such a hit that movie offers began pouring in. She went on to make a number of good movies and her work in six of them brought her best supporting actress Academy Award nominations: *All About Eve* (1950), *The Mating Season* (1951), *With a Song in My Heart* (1952), *Pickup on South Street* (1953), *Pillow Talk* (1959), and *Birdman of Alcatraz* (1962).

The actress was born Thelma Adele Ritter on February 14, 1905 in Brooklyn, New York, the daughter of Charles and

Lucy Ritter. She married Joseph Moran in 1927, and the couple had two children, Joseph, born in 1937, and Monica, born in 1940. On January 27, 1969, Ritter had a heart attack from which she died nine days later, on February 5.

Cesar Romero

CESAR ROMERO

Cesar Romero began his performing career as a dancer in ballrooms, in nightclubs, and on the stage. His Latin good looks made him a natural for the screen, but may also have hampered his career: he never seemed to be able to progress beyond a series of suave character roles. He appeared in nearly a hundred films, including *The Thin Man* (1934), *The Devil Is a Woman* (1935), *Viva Cisco Kid* (1940) and others in that series, *Springtime in the Rockies* (1942), *Julia Misbehaves* (1948), and *Donovan's Reef* (1963). In later years Romero turned to television, receiving more attention for his role as The Joker on the *Batman* TV series than for any movie role he ever did. He now travels the country performing in small theatres. During his film days Romero made many good friends, among them Tyrone Power (at whose funeral Romero spoke the eulogy) and the very perplexing Joan Crawford. Romero never married but was frequently seen in the company of famous, beautiful women.

He was born Cesar Julius Butch Romero on February 15, 1907 in New York City, the son of Cesar and Maria Romero. His grandfather was José Julian Marti, a well-known poet and revolutionary.

"Slapsie" Maxie Rosenbloom

"SLAPSIE" MAXIE ROSENBLOOM

Maxie Rosenbloom can attribute his "fame" to many causes—but his acting ability isn't one of them. His colorful name and his prizefighter background helped—he was the light-heavyweight boxing champion of the world from 1932 to 1934—as did his "dese, dem, and dose" speech pattern. He made his screen debut in 1933 in *Mr. Broadway*, and made about 30 films in the course of his 30-year career. In most of his movies he was cast as a punch-drunk fighter or a

good-natured dumbbell. His last years were not fortunate; he had serious health problems and he lost all of the money he had made in the movies.

He was born Maxwell Rosenbloom on October 1, 1903 in New York City. His mother, a former dancer, had always wanted him to follow her profession, but her wish was not to be fulfilled. In 1939 Rosenbloom married Muriel Falder, a child psychologist. Six years later the marriage ended in an untidy and much-publicized divorce. Rosenbloom died on March 6, 1976 after a lengthy illness.

Selena Royle

SELENA ROYLE

Selena Royle wanted to be an actress right from the start. She had always been a beautiful girl, and even as she grew older her beauty was striking. She entered movies in 1932 with *The Misleading Lady* and began to specialize in mother roles—which were plentiful at MGM where she worked. During the forties, the most productive period of her career, she gave small but memorable and touching performances in many films,

among them *The Harvey Girls* in 1946 and *A Date With Judy* in 1948. Her career declined sharply in the fifties when exquisite but discerning mother roles went out of vogue. She retired from the screen in the middle fifties and moved to Guadalajara, Mexico. There, to keep busy, she started writing and authored *A Gringa's Guide to Mexican Cooking*.

Selena Royle was born on November 6, 1904 in New York City. She married actor George Renavent, and was widowed in 1983. She died in 1983.

S. Z. "Cuddles" Sakall

S. Z. "CUDDLES" SAKALL

Comedian S. Z. Sakall, nicknamed "Cuddles," was one of the screen's most recognizable and beloved character actors. He was one of the funniest men in show business and his talent was in constant demand. He started writing music-hall sketches when he was 16, and originally became popular as a performer in German films of the early '30s. He worked for many years on both

stage and screen in Germany, Hungary, and Austria before the rise of Nazism forced him to migrate to the United States. His stock-in-trade was his broken English, his peerless comic timing, his excitable nature, his fat wobbly cheeks, and the expression of total bewilderment that he could assume at will. He appeared in a great many of Hollywood's color musicals. Some of the most notable films in his 40-year career were *Ball of Fire* (1942), *Casablanca* (1943), *The Dolly Sisters* (1945), and *In the Good Old Summertime* (1949).

S. Z. "Cuddles" Sakall was born Eugene Gero Szakall on February 2, 1884 in Budapest, Hungary, the child of a poverty-stricken family. He married once. He died in Los Angeles on February 12, 1955.

C. Aubrey Smith

C. AUBREY SMITH

C. Aubrey Smith always looked as though he'd been born to play distinguished character parts. No doubt his background helped—he was educated at Cambridge University and had played cricket for

England's national team. He made his stage debut in 1893 and in 1915 he made his first film, a silent movie called *Builder of Bridges*. He made several more silents but really came into his own with the talkies, becoming one of the most regularly seen British character actors of the 1930s and '40s. He made a resplendent and authoritative figure, tall and imposing. C. Aubrey Smith believed in the philosophy "that immense vitality is prerequisite to professional longevity," and proved it by embarking on a 30-year film career when he was past 50. He made more than a hundred movies, among them *Morning Glory* (1933), *Little Lord Fauntleroy* (1936), *The Prisoner of Zenda* (1937), and *The Four Feathers* (1939). He was the leader of Hollywood's "British colony" and a staunch supporter of all things English. He refused to read the local papers, preferring to wait the week it took in those days without regular transatlantic air mail service to read his news from the *London Times*. Still a cricket fan, he was the captain of the Hollywood Cricket Club. His home, which sported on its roof three cricket stumps and a cricket bat and ball as a weather vane, was known as The Round Corner, after his nickname from his cricketing days, 'Round-the-Corner Smith.

Charles Aubrey Smith was born on July 21, 1863 in London, England, the son of a doctor, Charles John Smith, and his wife Sarah Ann. Smith was married in 1896 to Isabel Mary Scott Wood; they had one daughter, Honor Beryl. The actor was knighted for his

services to the theatre in 1944. He died on December 20, 1948.

Gale Sondergaard

GALE SONDERGAARD

Gale Sondergaard is one of those actresses whom people talk of as an "actress's actress," a very talented performer whose characterizations lock themselves into the memory. She had a strong voice with flawless diction, and a wonderfully expressive face. When other character actresses complained "I wish I could get a part like Gale Sondergaard gets," what they really meant was "I wish I could act like Gale Sondergaard." She was also bright, graduating from university at a time when such an accomplishment was still relatively unusual for a woman. Sondergaard then became a stage actress, doing some fine stage work before moving on to a most successful film debut—her first-screen appearance in *Anthony Adverse* in 1936 won her the Academy Award for best supporting actress, the first award that had been given in that category. Sondergaard's other major film credits

include *The Cat and The Canary* (1939), *The Letter* (1940), and *Road to Rio* (1947). Later, in the fifties, she became a victim of the anti-communist witchhunt and was blacklisted. She has done little movie work since then.

Gale Sondergaard was born Edith Holm Sondergaard on February 15, 1899, in Litchfield, Minnesota, the daughter of university professor Hans T. Sondergaard and pianist and suffragette Kristine Holm. In 1922 Sondergaard married Neil O'Malley, whom she divorced in 1930. The same year she married Herbert J. Biberman, with whom she adopted two children. Biberman died in 1971.

Lewis Stone

LEWIS STONE

Lewis Stone was a distinguished stage actor who became a matinee idol on Broadway and later a star in silent films. He played leading roles in the silent versions of *The Prisoner of Zenda* (1922)—a dual role—and *Scaramouche* (1923). (In the '50s he played supporting roles in the remakes of both films.) He co-starred with Greta Garbo in seven films—silents and talkies—and

made a successful transition to sound. But when movies began to talk, Stone was 50 years old and he began to carve out a career as the film world's favorite father figure. He will go down in film history as old Judge Hardy, Andy's father in the *Andy Hardy* film series of the '40s. Stone also holds the record for working for MGM longer than any other actor, from 1924 until he died. Apart from the *Andy Hardy* movies, his credits include *The Patriot* (1928), for which he won an Academy Award nomination for best actor; *Grand Hotel* (1932); *David Copperfield* (1935); and *State of the Union* (1948).

Louis Stone was born on November 15, 1879 in Worcester, Massachusetts, the son of Bertrand and Lucille Stone. The family was already active in the arts—young Stone's aunts, Bess, Agnes, and Mary, cofounded the Boston Opera Company. In 1909 Stone married actress Margaret Langham. After her death he married actress Florence Oakley, but the nine-year marriage ended in divorce in 1929. His last marriage, in 1930, was to Hazel Wolf, by whom he had two daughters, Virginia and Barbara. Stone died of a heart attack on September 12, 1953.

GRADY SUTTON

Grady Sutton has been a character actor for so long that the job description might have been invented for him. He's a comedian and looks like one—pudgy, with a mobile face that adapts readily to

Grady Sutton

Henry Travers

the variations on the vacuous, fussbudgety yokel theme that he has done so often. Sutton got into films almost by accident: a friend introduced him to his brother, a director who invited Sutton to appear in a picture that he was making. Sutton liked the movie world, he stayed, and he's still there. Since his first film, in 1925, he has been much sought after, appearing in some W. C. Fields films that are now considered classics, including *You Can't Cheat an Honest Man* (1939) and *The Bank Dick* (1940). He has made well over a hundred movies—to say nothing of his many TV appearances—and is still working. His best-remembered films include *Alice Adams* (1935) and *White Christmas* (1954).

Grady Sutton was born on April 5, 1908 in Chattanooga, Tennessee. He has been a confirmed bachelor all his life.

HENRY TRAVERS

It was impossible to dislike Henry Travers. Also it's more or less impossible to remember him ever being young. Like so many of Hollywood's valuable character actors, Travers developed his acting talents on the English stage. He did not come to the United States until 1917 when he was already 43, and then he spent over ten years working on the stage. When Travers finally came to Hollywood in 1933, he was going on 60. That year he appeared in four films and thereafter continued to work steadily in a variety of movies, supporting many of Hollywood's top stars, including Bette Davis in *Dark Victory* (1939), Humphrey Bogart in *High Sierra* (1941), Gary Cooper and Barbara Stanwyck in *Ball of Fire* (1942), and Bing Crosby and Ingrid Bergman in *The Bells of St. Mary's* (1945). He became Hollywood's favorite benign elderly man. Most fans recall him best as Clarence, angel second-class, who in order to earn his wings must show James Stewart that *It's a Wonderful Life* (1946). Another landmark film for Travers was *Mrs. Miniver* (1942), which won him an Academy Award nomination for best supporting actor.

He was born Travers John Heagerty on March 5, 1874 in Berwick-on-Tweed, Northumberland, England, the son of physician Daniel Heagerty and his wife Ellen Travers. In 1926

Henry Travers married stage actress Amy Rhodes Forrest. She died in 1954, and five years later Travers married Ann G. Murphy. He died on October 18, 1965.

Norma Varden

NORMA VARDEN

Norma Varden is an actress known by name to only the most ardent film buff. But everyone knows her face. This British character actress came to Hollywood in the '40s and racked up about four movies a year for over 30 years. She was at her best playing a rich lighthearted aristocrat. Some of her film roles: the Englishwoman who, with her husband, is warned "This place is full of vultures. Vultures! Everywhere!" in *Casablanca* (1942); Mrs. Cunningham, the party guest almost strangled by Robert Walker in *Strangers on a Train* (1951); and Lady Beekman, owner of the diamond tiara Marilyn Monroe covets in *Gentlemen Prefer Blondes* (1953). Toward the end of her film career she started to make more and more television appearances. Varden had always dreamed of becoming a concert pianist, and now spends her free time

playing piano. She misses her best friend, the ever-popular actress Zasu Pitts, who died in 1963. Norma Varden made some good friends during her career, people like William Beaudine, the prominent producer and director who worked in films and, later, TV from 1909 until his death in 1970, and Allan Connor, her agent.

Norma Varden was born in London in 1898 to financially secure parents. She never married.

James Whitmore

JAMES WHITMORE

Here we have a very talented performer. He had acting experience both while he was at Yale University and later on the professional stage. He was offered his first film role early in his career, in *The Undercover Man* (1949). For his second film, *Battleground* (1949), he was nominated for an Academy Award for best supporting actor. He quickly proved himself to be a fine actor and very employable, but his height (5'6") and his lack of conventional good looks meant he was never able to capture major stardom. Today, when fewer stereotypes exist to restrict a performer's image, Whitmore might be a major name, but in those days he was forced to accept character parts. The stage has proven to be Whitmore's solace, and lately he has been touring with his very highly praised one-man show *Give 'em Hell Harry*, in which he portrays President Harry S. Truman. He won an Academy Award nomination for best actor for the 1975 film version.

James Allen Whitmore, Jr. was born on October 1, 1921 in White Plains, New York, to civic official James A. Whitmore and Florence Belle Crane. In 1947 Whitmore married Nancy Mygatt, and the couple had three sons before divorcing in 1967. In 1971 Whitmore married Audra Lindley, an actress, but he later divorced her and remarried his first wife.

Dame May Whitty

DAME MAY WHITTY

Dame May Whitty was the female equivalent of Sir C. Aubrey Smith—well-educated and the very essence of a dignified British aristocrat. May Whitty first

appeared on stage at the age of 16 and had had many years of acting experience on the English stage and in occasional silent films when she was offered a co-starring role (as an old lady in a wheelchair) in a new play, titled *Night Must Fall*, by Emlyn Williams. The play opened in England to enthusiastic reviews, and when the production transferred to America Whitty went with it. Again the play was a great success, and in 1937 Whitty finally repeated her part in the movie version, earning more accolades and a best supporting actress Oscar nomination. The actress then settled in Hollywood, creating a gallery of sweet but indomitable old ladies and winning a second Academy Award nomination for best supporting actress for *Mrs. Miniver* in 1942. Her best-remembered part, however, may be Miss Froy (the title role) in the British film *The Lady Vanishes* (1939), directed by Alfred Hitchcock.

May Whitty was born on June 19, 1865 in Liverpool, England, the daughter of journalist Alfred Whitty and Mary L. Ashton. Her grandfather was Michael Whitty, who published the *Liverpool Post*. In 1892 she married actor Ben Webster, and they had a daughter, Margaret, who became a successful actress/producer and was also noted for her direction of many Shakespeare plays. May Whitty was created a Dame Commander of the British Empire in 1918 in recognition of her philanthropic services during World War I. Unlike many performers so honored, she chose to incorporate the title of Dame into her

professional name. Ben Webster died in 1947, and his wife died a year later on May 29, 1948.

Estelle Winwood

ESTELLE WINWOOD

English-born actress Estelle Winwood had a career that must break theatrical records. Until her recent death at the age of 101, she was the oldest well-known actress still working. Her memorable performing career spanned over 80 years. She made her first movie in 1933 and was still making films in the early 1980s. On her 100th birthday she was touring as Rex Harrison's mother in *My Fair Lady*. Winwood's specialty was dignified but eccentric ladies, and she was always proud to call herself eccentric off the screen, too. Her movie credits include *The Swan* (1956) and *The Producers* (1968), where she has an unforgettably funny scene in which Zero Mostel tries to seduce her on a sofa. Winwood was a very good friend of the late actress Tallulah Bankhead.

She was born Estelle Goodwin on January 24, 1883 in Lancashire, England, to George Good-

win and Rosalie Ellis. She was married four times, in 1901 to Arthur Chesney, in 1919 to Francis Bradley, in 1930 to Guthrie McClintic, and in 1945 to Robert Barton Henderson. There were no children of any of the marriages. Her brother-in-law, Edmund Gwenn, was also a successful character actor. (He won the 1947 Oscar for best supporting actor for his best remembered role, Kris Kringle, alias Santa Claus, in *Miracle on 34th Street*. He received a second nomination for the 1950 film *Mister 880*.) Winwood died of a heart attack on June 20, 1984.

Monty Woolley

MONTY WOOLLEY

Monty Woolley will always be best remembered for those polished, crusty gentlemen whom he played so well. His real-life world was not very far removed from that inhabited by his movie characters. He was born into a well-to-do family who owned, among others, the fashionable Grand Union Hotel in Saratoga Springs. He went to school at both Harvard and Yale, and later became a professor at Yale, numbering among his students Thornton Wilder and Steven Vincent Benét. At Yale he also met Cole Porter, who was to become a lifelong friend. Woolley left teaching to appear on Broadway in the musical *On Your Toes* in 1936. His first film was *Live, Love and Learn* in 1937. He was nominated for a best actor Academy Award for *The Pied Piper* (1942) and for a best supporting actor Oscar for *Since You Went Away* (1944). But the film that is most frequently associated with his name is *The Man Who Came to Dinner* (1942), in which he played the role of Sheridan Whiteside (a character based on critic Alexander Woollcott), which he had earlier played very successfully on Broadway. Once in the movie capital he soon became a well-recognized figure with his white beard and flaring mustache. Among his other movie credits are *Night and Day* (1946), *Miss Tatlock's Millions* (1948), and *Kismet* (1955).

Monty Woolley was born Edgar Montillion Woolley on August 17, 1888 in New York City in one of the hotels his father owned. He never married. He died on May 6, 1963 in Albany, New York.

KEENAN WYNN

Keenan Wynn has been a character actor throughout his career, and as such he is considered one of the best—even though he tends not to share the general acknowledgment of his ability; it took him a long time to believe that audiences accepted him as

Keenan Wynn

an actor in his own right rather than as Ed Wynn's son. Keenan Wynn's first major film was *For Me and My Gal* in 1942. Altogether he has appeared in a hundred or so movies, playing all kinds of parts except for the leads. Among his other screen credits are *Royal Wedding* (1951), *Kiss Me Kate* (1953), *Dr. Strangelove, or How I Learned to Stop Worrying and Love the Bomb* (1964), and *Just Tell Me What You Want* (1980).

Keenan Wynn was born Francis Xavier Aloysius Keenan Wynn on July 27, 1916 in New York City, the son of actor Ed Wynn and actress Hilda Keenan. His maternal grandfather was silent screen actor Frank Keenan. He married three times and has four children (his daughter Tracy became a screenwriter). Wynn was a very good friend of actor Van Johnson, until his wife divorced him and married Johnson. In recent years Wynn has suffered from a condition known as tinnitus (or ringing in the ears) that could have hurt his career; his excellent concentration, however, has enabled him to continue working and he has done some excellent TV work.

Frieda Inescort, Maureen O'Sullivan, Greer Garson, and Karen Morley in *Pride and Prejudice* (1940).

Spencer Tracy, Hedy Lamarr, Frank Morgan, Claudette Colbert, and Clark Gable in *Boom Town* (1940).

Gladys Cooper, Ginger Rogers, and Dennis Morgan in *Kitty Foyle* (1940).

FAVORITE CHARACTER PERFORMERS

The hundred character actors and actresses profiled in the preceding pages represent only a handful of the great character performers who have provided the backbone of the movies since the early silents, supporting, enhancing, putting into focus—and, sometimes, shining brighter than the stars of their films. Now, here's a selection of her favorite character performers by one of their number, Kathleen Freeman, along with her comments on her choices.

Kathleen Freeman herself is a noted character actress who has appeared in over 300 movies, among them *Singin' in the Rain* (1952), *Bonzo Goes to College* (1952), *The Fly* (1958), *The Rounders* (1965), *North to Alaska* (1960), and almost every movie Jerry Lewis ever made.

Kathleen Freeman

TEN BEST CHARACTER ACTRESSES

Sara Allgood
(1883–1950)—An accented actress, originally from Ireland. She played everyone's mother, but she was so versatile that she could also play a great nasty rat.

Mary Boland
(1880–1965)—I'll never forget her work as Mrs. Bennett in *Pride and Prejudice*. She was totally willing to make a jackass of herself.

Beulah Bondi
(1892–1981)—I admire her absolute willingness to represent anything freely. She could play an entire spectrum of characters.

Constance Collier
(1878–1955)—She was John Barrymore's leading lady at one time. She had deep opinions about the roles she portrayed. A very talented woman.

Marie Dressler
(1869–1934)—She was an absolutely great actress. She didn't care, she just did it, even if it meant making a fool of herself.

Hattie McDaniel
(1895–1952)—The stairwell scene in *Gone With the Wind* still tears me up. She was just a superb actress who never got the credit she deserved.

Agnes Moorehead
(1906–1974)—She could do it all. She had enormous range.

Edna May Oliver
(1883–1942)—She was Aunt Betsy in *David Copperfield*. She had amazing vocal range. She could play stern, disapproving socialites better than anyone else.

Jessie Ralph
(1864–1944)—She looked like a bad road map, but she could have such a warm voice. She played the best warmhearted lady you could hope to see.

Margaret Rutherford
(1892–1972)—This British comedy actress had a special talent: she always exposed the madness in any character.

TEN BEST CHARACTER ACTORS

George Arliss
(1868–1946)—A remarkable actor; the man could play anything.

Walter Brennan
(1894–1974)—A great actor. He had a total freedom in performance.

John Carradine
(1906–)—He was always interesting. His character progressed as it moved through the film. He's never the same fellow on page sixty of the script as he was on page one.

Charles Durning
(1933–)—I think he's fabulous. He has an enormous range.

Dustin Hoffman
(1937–)—To me, Hoffman has always been a character actor and always will be. I so much admire the risks he takes. And of course, he's an incredibly gifted actor.

Sam Jaffe
(1897–1984)—From his first acting days he had an absolutely incisive view of his characters. And he had a wild sense of humor.

Dean Jagger
(1903–)—An awfully strong actor. He always got to the core of his roles.

Charles Laughton
(1899–1962)—Just a brilliant man, with a willingness to expose all the parts of a human being.

Thomas Mitchell
(1892–1962)—He played Scarlett's father in *Gone With the Wind*. He was so versatile; he could do it all.

Frank Morgan
(1890–1949)—He just fascinated me. He was great in the title role of *The Wizard of Oz*. He was perfectly willing to expose his sensitivity.

FIFTY
DIRECTORS
THE WAY THEY MAKE THEIR MOVIES

Who owns a movie? The producer who organized or financed the deal? The star? The technicians? Or the director who orchestrated all the elements on the set? Ultimately, a movie belongs to its audience. It's the viewer who makes use, psychologically and emotionally, of what a movie offers: enjoyment, escape, information, an examination of values. And it is, to a great degree, the director who is responsible for how well (or how poorly) a movie satisfies its audience. Here we profile fifty directors, past and present, who represent a wide variety of styles and techniques, and give you a glimpse of what makes each one tick.

Woody Allen

WOODY ALLEN

Born 1935

Filmography:
What's Up, Tiger Lily?, 1966
Take the Money and Run, 1969
Bananas, 1971
Everything You Always Wanted to Know About Sex (But Were Afraid to Ask), 1972
Sleeper, 1973
Love and Death, 1975
Annie Hall, 1977
Interiors, 1978
Manhattan, 1979
Stardust Memories, 1980
A Midsummer Night's Sex Comedy, 1982
Zelig, 1983
Broadway Danny Rose, 1984

While success stalks him doggedly, Woody Allen flees from the glare of the public spotlight. Born Allen Stewart Konigsberg in Brooklyn, New York, Allen started his career in comedy at age 15, writing jokes for a publicity firm. At 17 he was a staff writer at NBC. After dropping out of two New York universities he continued to write comedy for other people—including Sid Caesar, Art Carney, Pat Boone, and Garry

Moore—and by the early '60s it was clear that Allen was a comedy writer of exceptional ability. However little he relished the prospect of becoming public property, there was no hope that Allen would escape the success his talent demanded—and the inevitable publicity that would follow.

With some reluctance, Allen created his own stand-up persona and began appearing in Greenwich Village clubs. Twenty years later, a world-renowned comedian, he still prefers to stay at home in Manhattan rather than to court the adulation of international audiences.

Shyness, feelings of inferiority, and social ineptitude are characteristic of Allen's roles, and are seen in such losers as Fielding Mellish (in *Sleeper*), Virgil Starkwell (in *Take the Money and Run*), or Alvy Singer (in *Annie Hall*). Throughout Allen's filmmaking, his central character tends to display the psychological anguish experienced by the intelligent and sensitive buffoon whose ego performs pratfalls more often than his backside. Ironically, Allen can't resist a parting shot, usually letting the underdog win the girl of his dreams in the final reel.

After experimentally re-editing and redubbing a Japanese spy movie in *What's Up, Tiger Lily?* (1966), Allen doubled as director and performer in *Take the Money and Run* (1969), a fake documentary about an inept bank robber. *Bananas* (1971), although still rough around the edges technically, achieved the blend of verbal and visual humor for which Allen has since become noted.

Made over the following three years, Allen's next three films, *Sleeper, Everything You Always Wanted to Know About Sex*, and *Love and Death*, (plus *Play It Again, Sam*, Allen's play directed as a film by Herbert Ross) all rely heavily upon reference and adaptation. Allen synthesized every aspect of 20th-century popular culture, from Chaplin to Bergman, but it was not until *Annie Hall* that the theme finally meshed perfectly with Allen's sophisticated technique. *Annie Hall* is a brilliantly sentimental comedy about a TV comedy writer who falls in love with a woman who virtually outgrows him. It is one case when he doesn't win the girl in the end.

Seeking to be taken seriously in his comedy, Allen followed the many-Oscared success of *Annie Hall* with a series of well-crafted personal and intellectual films, beginning with his only fully dramatic movie, the somber *Interiors*.

Using black and white film and documentary pastiche, and paying homage to Ingmar Bergman and Federico Fellini, Woody Allen's movies of the 1980s have long lost their initial naiveté. As he has grown older his comic attacks on his own weaknesses have mellowed, so that he now explores the character of the eternal underdog with true sympathy and understanding. In *A Midsummer Night's Sex Comedy*, love is treated as an ultimate mystical truth. In *Broadway Danny Rose*, Allen has come to respect the failures he knows in himself to the point where he is willing to show his char-

acter arranging a humble Thanksgiving dinner for a group of flop entertainers, a scene even Chaplin would have envied for its pathos.

As some of the early innocence has faded from his work, Woody Allen has expanded his vision of the failures of society. As he recognizes and forgives his own weaknesses through laughter, his characters are redeemed and perhaps, given time, will accept themselves to the point where they no longer need to resort to the psychiatrist's couch. But the growing-up process that has added depth to Allen's perceptions has, perhaps, also taken something away—the later movies lack some of the zany, unstructured comic feeling that makes some of his early work so attractive.

Robert Aldrich

ROBERT ALDRICH

Born 1918
Died 1983

Filmography:
The Big Leaguer, 1953
World for Ransom, 1954
Apache, 1954
Vera Cruz, 1954
Kiss Me Deadly, 1955
The Big Knife, 1955
Autumn Leaves, 1956

Attack!, 1956
The Angry Hills, 1959
Ten Seconds to Hell, 1959
The Last Sunset, 1961
Whatever Happened to Baby Jane?, 1962
Sodom and Gomorrah, 1963
Four for Texas, 1963
Hush . . . Hush, Sweet Charlotte, 1965
Flight of the Phoenix, 1966
The Dirty Dozen, 1967
The Legend of Lylah Clare, 1968
The Killing of Sister George, 1968
Too Late the Hero, 1970
The Grissom Gang, 1971
Ulzana's Raid, 1972
Emperor of the North, 1973
The Longest Yard, 1974
Hustle, 1975
Twilight's Last Gleaming, 1977
The Choirboys, 1977
The Frisco Kid, 1979
. . . All the Marbles, 1981

Throughout his career, Robert Aldrich was of two minds about his own movies. He built up a cult of dichotomy, arranging the elements of his films to reflect the most extreme of opposites: victory within defeat, failure within success, heroism within cowardice, the interrelationship between masochism and sadism or between corruption and righteousness. Even the types of movies he made veered in two wildly different directions, from the trashy melodramatic hysteria of *Whatever Happened to Baby Jane?* to the kinetic, masculine build-up of action in *The Dirty Dozen*.

At age 23 Aldrich moved from his native Rhode Island to Los Angeles, where he methodically worked his way through the Hollywood system—from clerk to assistant to production

assistant to director—first in television and then in movies. It is in a similarly methodical manner that energy and suspense grow and build in an Aldrich movie. He rarely explores suspense for its own sake (in the manner that Alfred Hitchcock so clearly enjoyed) but rather allows it to develop like a cancer in the context of his chosen subject matter, which is frequently outrageous, daring, and violent.

Aldrich couldn't merely reshape a tale, he had to explore the most bizarre characters and situations that he could find—a Jewish cowboy in *The Frisco Kid*, the torture of a former child movie star in *Whatever Happened to Baby Jane?*, football heroics by prisoners in *The Longest Yard*, and persecuted hobos on the railroad in *Emperor of the North*.

Aldrich pursued sex to extremes, frequently segregating the sexes in his films, and then justified or romanticized his unsavory discoveries. He recognized pathos in the aging lesbian soap opera star of *The Killing of Sister George*, and he found brutish comedy in the sexual off-hours antics of Los Angeles cops in *The Choirboys*. And all along he never ceased to sympathize with even the most unlovable and the loneliest of his characters.

Aldrich's movie images leave indelible imprints on the viewer's memory. It's not easy to eradicate the sound of Burt Young's horrible cackle in *The Choirboys*, or images like the constant sweating of all the cast in *The Grissom Gang*, the touchdown finale of *The Longest Yard*, or the seaside conclusion of *Baby Jane*. Most of to-

day's popular mad slasher bloodletting and pie-in-the-face teen comedy pales in comparison to the special perversity that Aldrich allowed to exercise itself in his films, even when they were rejected by Hollywood and the public alike.

It is perfectly in character for a director who chose to divide his subject matter into equal and opposite parts that Aldrich's serious attempt at social end-of-the-world relevance, in *Twilight's Last Gleaming*, literally split the screen into two, revealing the conflicts of conscience that stirred restlessly beneath his intense and intensely personal methods of filmmaking.

Robert Altman

ROBERT ALTMAN

Born 1925

Filmography:
The Delinquents, 1956
The James Dean Story, 1957
Nightmare in Chicago, 1964
Countdown, 1968
That Cold Day in the Park, 1969
M*A*S*H, 1970
Brewster McCloud, 1970
McCabe and Mrs. Miller, 1971
Images, 1972

The Long Goodbye, 1973
Thieves Like Us, 1974
California Split, 1974
Nashville, 1975
Buffalo Bill and the Indians, 1976
Three Women, 1977
A Wedding, 1978
Quintet, 1978
A Perfect Couple, 1979
Health, 1980
Popeye, 1981
Come Back to the 5 and Dime, Jimmy Dean, Jimmy Dean, 1982
Streamers, 1983

Robert Altman has said his movies are attempts to provide a different experience to every person in the audience. Perhaps that's why they are impossible to label, even though the Altman styles are distinctive and his themes frequently anything but obscure.

Altman more or less crawled his way to Hollywood from his Kansas City beginnings. He was raised and educated a Roman Catholic, he flew in 46 bombing missions during World War II, and his father was a successful insurance salesman and compulsive gambler; all three of these elements were to influence Altman's films. After the war, he returned to Missouri to make industrial documentaries, which eventually led to a seven-year stint on television. Altman directed *Combat!*, *Bonanza*, and other popular shows, and he was one of the highest-paid TV directors in the business when he quit television work. He had always wanted to make movies, and he still did.

Altman then made a number of feature films, but it wasn't until 1970 that *M*A*S*H* gave him his first smash hit movie. After

M*A*S*H he became a prolific filmmaker of the '70s, riding a critical roller coaster with unusual movies that reflected a weird sort of insanity boiling beneath the surface of life in America.

Sometimes this was expressed as a benevolent madness. M*A*S*H presents an irreverently funny side of war and suicide. In Brewster McCloud the title character is obsessed with flying inside the Astrodome. Detective Philip Marlowe in The Long Goodbye has more concern for his cat than his clients. Altman's characters gamble wildly, rob banks dumbly, or sing country and western songs out of tune, yet they do so in ways that seem simultaneously natural and unexpected, usually provoking laughter from the audience—although sometimes the reaction is an uncomprehending stare.

Altman layers his interests and his art. His films deflate genre, puncturing the western in McCabe and Mrs. Miller, the detective film in The Long Goodbye, and the war movie in M*A*S*H. His casting has always defied Hollywood; he relies upon a repertory "family" that includes unlikely movie stars such as Shelley Duvall and Bert Remsen. His casting represents only one aspect of his disrespect for the conventions of moviemaking: Altman's use of overlapping dialogue (spoken by actors who seemed to be allowed to improvise spontaneously) infuriated studio moguls. As early as Countdown (1968), Altman allowed his characters to talk all at once.

His fondness for taking new ideas to extremes led to arty abstractions in the illusions of Images, the snow-buried scenes of McCabe and Mrs. Miller and Quintet, or Millie Lammoreaux's pseudo-sophistication (represented by her dress dangling out the car door) in Three Women. With American history as a frequent target, Altman's aim can reach both the sublime and the ridiculous. Nashville, Buffalo Bill and the Indians, A Wedding, and Health each attempt—with undeniable spirit and varying degrees of success—to parody a segment of American reality.

Curiously, it may be that in Popeye Altman has stumbled upon his perfect metaphor for democracy: a comic-strip landscape of corruption and curiosity, peopled by strange characters, with Robin Williams—mumbling and overlapping improvised dialogue—as the quintessential Altman actor.

Since 1980, Altman has concentrated primarily on stage projects. The exception is Streamers, in which he tackles head-on the insanity of war, this time with more bitterness than he expressed in M*A*S*H. In refusing to stop taking risks, Altman mocks both human folly and conventional moviemaking, showing the audience in as many ways as possible the kinds of wrong-headed confidence that has made America goofy as well as great.

RICHARD ATTEN- BOROUGH

Born 1923

Richard Attenborough

Filmography:
Oh What a Lovely War!, 1969
Young Winston, 1972
A Bridge Too Far, 1977
Magic, 1978
Gandhi, 1982

As a young British actor Richard Attenborough took on many war roles, and the English audience was attracted to him despite the fact that he was typecast as a coward for many years following his premiere appearance in Noel Coward's In Which We Serve (1942). During the Second World War he served in the Royal Air Force film unit, and from there moved step by step into other aspects of filmmaking, first as a producer and then as a director. In 1976 he was knighted for his contributions to England.

As a film producer, Attenborough helped deliver Robert Aldrich's Flight of the Phoenix (1966), Robert Wise's The Sand Pebbles (1966), and Richard Fleischer's Dr. Doolittle (1967), all of which attempt to present easy, pat solutions to life's vicissitudes. But it was in the movies he directed that Attenborough's real interests were revealed: all but one of the films for which he has been responsible have dealt with the folly of war.

Oh What a Lovely War! turns war into a very British variety show, and the title clearly indicates the irony with which the film approaches the subjects of war and glory. A Bridge Too Far, a huge, expensive production, extended Attenborough's examination of blunder and madness in war. Gandhi, which represented a further step in Attenborough's expansion of his production budgets, brought together a theoretical synthesis of the pacifist themes that Attenborough explores. Gandhi has proven the most successful of Attenborough's projects, accepted by both audiences and by the voting members of the Academy—the film picked up five 1982 Academy Awards: for best picture; best actor (Ben Kingsley); best director (Attenborough); best screenplay written directly for the screen (John Briley); and best cinematography (Billy Williams and Ronnie Taylor).

Ingmar Bergman

INGMAR BERGMAN

Born 1918

Filmography:
Crisis, 1945
It Rains on Our Love, 1946
Ship to India, 1947

Port of Call, 1948
Night Is My Future, 1948
The Devil's Wanton, 1949
Three Strange Loves, 1949
This Can't Happen Here, 1950
To Joy, 1950
Summer Interlude, 1951
Secrets of Women, 1952
Summer With Monika, 1953
Sawdust and Tinsel/The Naked Night, 1953
A Lesson in Love, 1954
Journey into Autumn, 1955
Smiles of a Summer Night, 1955
The Seventh Seal, 1957
Wild Strawberries, 1957
Brink of Life, 1958
The Magician, 1958
The Virgin Spring, 1960
The Devil's Eye, 1960
Through a Glass Darkly, 1961
Winter Light, 1963
The Silence, 1963
All These Women, 1964
Persona, 1966
Hour of the Wolf, 1968
Shame, 1968
The Ritual, 1969
The Passion of Anna, 1969
The Faro Documentary, 1970
The Touch, 1971
Cries and Whispers, 1972
Scenes from a Marriage, 1973
The Magic Flute, 1974
Face to Face, 1976
The Serpent's Egg, 1978
Autumn Sonata, 1978
From the Lives of the Marionettes, 1980
Fanny and Alexander, 1983
After the Rehearsal, 1984

Ingmar Bergman stands alone as the true genius of psychological cinema. All other attempts to create on screen the processes of emotional relationships—with all the accompanying religious and moral implications—are judged against his films, harshly, and rightly so. Few filmmakers now or ever have elected to make such movies, choosing the workings of the conflicted mind as their basic subject matter.

Raised in a strict Lutheran family, Bergman lived many of the nightmares he later depicted in his self-proclaimed swan song, *Fanny and Alexander*, including being locked away in dark closets as punishment for misbehavior. Bergman's personal life has consistently surfaced in his artistic expressions; even his longstanding professional relationship with Liv Ullmann has been entangled with a personal relationship that has produced a daughter.

Other actors and actresses, even technicians, have found international acclaim through their collaboration with Bergman, including actor Max von Sydow and cinematographer Sven Nykvist.

Bergman's perennial themes may seem somber and philosophical on paper, but his visual cinematic expertise is unsurpassed for the clarity with which it peels away the layers of illusion, letting the audience understand the characters in a surprisingly intimate way. Bergman's beginnings as a scriptwriter are evident in the clear entry he allows into the minds of his characters. And he's never ceased to be a writer—he has written all his films.

Bergman's early films, naturally enough, explored the problems of youth. It was with *The Seventh Seal* and *Wild Strawberries* in 1957 that he achieved international acclaim. Both films deal with typically heavy Bergman concerns—symbolism, religious discovery, and the meaning of life and death—and both have remained major landmarks in the history of film.

Bergman continued to examine deep and eternal conflicts in this vein with a trilogy questioning the existence and meaning of God. These movies were *Through a Glass Darkly*, *Winter Light*, and *The Silence*, and they met with a less favorable response than some of Bergman's earlier work.

Several years later, with *Persona*, Bergman began to explore filmmaking itself, adding the shocking and intrusive effects of broken film and bizarre images to illuminate the story of an actress who recognizes how the realities of her onstage and offstage lives have become blurred.

Despite his fame, Bergman faced a crisis in 1976, when he was arrested in Sweden for tax evasion. The charges were dropped, but not before Bergman had fled the country and suffered a nervous breakdown. Now he claims to have concluded his filmmaking career, going out in a blaze of glory with his greatest success, *Fanny and Alexander*, which was awarded more Oscars than any foreign film before it. (Since then, however, he has made another film, *After the Rehearsal*.) After 40 years of filmmaking, Bergman could, if he wished, rest on his laurels, knowing that his films will be explored and examined for years to come, without ever exhausting the fascination of the questions and possibilities they examine. Bergman's commentary on the truths and conflicts of human existence are destined to reverberate down the years of the future of film.

Peter Bogdanovich

PETER BOGDANOVICH

Born 1939

Filmography:
Targets, 1968
The Last Picture Show, 1971
Directed by John Ford (documentary), 1971
What's Up, Doc?, 1972
Paper Moon, 1973
Daisy Miller, 1974
At Long Last Love, 1975
Nickelodeon, 1976
Saint Jack, 1979
They All Laughed, 1981

Peter Bogdanovich never studied film formally or made a big deal about being a film critic (which he was), but he's been unable to escape the stigma of being a writer turned movie director. When three of his pet movie projects flopped in a row in the mid-'70s, some people let it be known that they thought he would do better if he returned to the typewriter. In fact, Bogdanovich is much more movie fan than anything else. His intellectual interest in film has probably burdened him more than it has fattened his bankbook, but it has allowed him to display in his films a love of everything cinematic.

Born in New York to Yugoslavian immigrant

parents, Bogdanovich entered show business by studying acting and theatre. By 1959 he had directed successfully off-Broadway, but when his Broadway directorial debut, *Once in a Lifetime*, closed after one night, he turned his attention to films. In the early '60s he wrote several monographs on film directors for the Museum of Modern Art, and he later published books on Fritz Lang, John Ford, Allan Dwan, and Orson Welles.

Veteran exploitation producer Roger Corman gave Bogdanovich a stab at filmmaking, first on such B classics as *The Wild Angels* and *Voyage to the Planet of Prehistoric Women*. Then in 1968, with *Targets*, Bogdanovich directed solo, using Boris Karloff as an aging horror star pitted against a mad sniper. His second solo picture, *The Last Picture Show*, broke through, both critically and at the box office. Filmed in reverential black and white, it used movies as a metaphor for a crumbling Texas town.

His subsequent movies all reflected an intense interest in film history: screwball comedy, small-town Americana, and the big-budget musical. But Bogdanovich's rarified vision withered at the box office. (His reputation was not helped by his audiences' disenchantment with the perceived snobbery of both the director and his girlfriend Cybill Shepherd.) His earlier success had tempted him to indulge in personal overexposure, and his prospective audiences did not react positively. Bogdanovich returned to Roger Corman for financing for

Saint Jack, a smaller and more contemporary picture than the expensive period pieces he had made previously.

Burt Reynolds' films for Bogdanovich, *At Long Last Love* and *Nickelodeon*, brought such bad notices that in *Hooper* (1978) Reynolds parodied the director as an arrogant intellectual. Bogdanovich got more sympathetic treatment in Bob Fosse's 1983 movie *Star 80*, where he was portrayed (accurately) as the man who befriended actress and Playboy Playmate Dorothy Stratten before she was brutally murdered by a jealous former boyfriend. In 1981 Bogdanovich had made *They All Laughed*, with Stratten. The film is a roundabout romantic comedy set in New York, and again reflected Bogdanovich's predilection for stylistics and the wit of an earlier era of filmmaking; here he was trying to emulate the witty, clever banter of the '40s, Lubitsch-style. In fact, whatever he does, Bogdanovich buries himself in the mythology of the movies, often with the result that the finished product reflects the idiosyncrasies of the filmmaker rather than the essence of the film.

MEL BROOKS

Born 1926

Filmography:
The Producers, 1968
The Twelve Chairs, 1970
Blazing Saddles, 1974
Young Frankenstein, 1974
Silent Movie, 1976
High Anxiety, 1977
The History of the World, Part One, 1981

Mel Brooks

Mel Brooks left Brooklyn, New York and entered the Army in time for World War II. He deactivated land mines and fought in the Battle of the Bulge, returning to seek his success in show business, first as a drummer, then as a writer for nightclub and radio. Throughout the '50s he wrote for television (in particular for the Sid Caesar series *Your Show of Shows*), and for Broadway shows and comedians. By 1960 he had earned some fame with the creation of the 2000-Year-Old Man comedy routine and later co-created the successful *Get Smart* TV series with Buck Henry. Even some of his television commercials, such as the Bic Banana, are classics.

As Brooks turned to the movies, his work increasingly reflected the influence of television comedy and his penchant for parodying other genres. The earliest movies, *The Producers* and *The Twelve Chairs*, show some hysterically funny comments of true originality. But after striking pay dirt with the western send-up, *Blazing Saddles*, Brooks returned again and again to mine old movie genres and draw on other people's inventiveness.

It's interesting to observe the effect that

this has had on Brooks' movies. While *Young Frankenstein* exploits old horror movies with feeling and appreciation, *Silent Movie* and *High Anxiety* largely fail to click. By the time he made *History of the World, Part One*, Brooks had reduced his output almost entirely to degradation, derivation, and degeneration. His attempts to recycle old Hitler jokes, once fresh and audacious in *The Producers*, became tedious, and his parodies and references came across as vulgar and tasteless—a far cry from the subtle comedy of, for instance, Woody Allen.

Mel Brooks wants to be taken seriously, as is clear from the social themes—genocide, racism, class culture—that surface in his films, but he rarely takes the risk of resisting his impulse to go for the low and easy laugh. For *To Be or Not To Be*, a generally sincere remake of Ernst Lubitsch's 1942 comedy about the Resistance in Poland, Brooks relinquished the directorship to Alan Johnson. He did, however, appear in the movie, teaming up for the first time with his wife, Anne Bancroft. Her influence apparently sedated his manic flatulence, and the movie received more positive critical reaction than Brooks' other recent film projects.

TOD BROWNING

Born 1882
Died 1962

Filmography:
Jim Bludso, 1917

Tod Browning

A Love Sublime, 1917
Hands Up, 1917
Peggy the Will-o'-the-Wisp, 1917
The Jury of Fate, 1917
The Deciding Kiss, 1918
The Eyes of Mystery, 1918
The Legion of Death, 1918
Revenge, 1918
Which Woman, 1918
Brazen Beauty, 1918
Set Free, 1918
The Exquisite Thief, 1919
A Petal in the Current, 1919
The Unpainted Woman, 1919
The Wicked Darling, 1919
Bonnie, Bonnie Lassie, 1920
The Virgin of Stamboul, 1920
No Woman Knows, 1921
Outside the Law, 1921
Man Under Cover, 1922
Under Two Flags, 1922
The Wise Kid, 1922
The Day of Faith, 1923
Drifting, 1923
The White Tiger, 1923
The Dangerous Flirt, 1924
Silk Stocking Sal, 1924
Dollar Down, 1925
The Mystic, 1925
The Unholy Three, 1925
The Blackbird, 1926
The Road to Mandalay, 1926
London After Midnight, 1927
The Show, 1927
The Unknown, 1927
The Big City, 1928
West of Zanzibar, 1928
Where East Is East, 1929
The Thirteenth Chair, 1929

Outside the Law, 1930
Dracula, 1931
Iron Man, 1931
Freaks, 1932
Fast Workers, 1933
Mark of the Vampire, 1935
The Devil Doll, 1936
Miracles for Sale, 1939

Despite the many films, both silent and sound, attributed to Tod Browning, his name today is almost invariably associated with *Freaks*, a movie banned long past his death. *Freaks* was rediscovered nearly 40 years after it was made, and it was the one film that most closely paralleled Browning's own outlook on life.

A child runaway and a circus performer around the world, Browning's travels led him pretty much inevitably to movie work. He began a collaboration with Lon Chaney that continued for many years. He wrote the chilling stories of movies such as *London After Midnight* and *Where East Is East*, and Chaney found gruesome faces to match. When Chaney died, Browning turned to Bela Lugosi to play in his vampire film *Dracula*.

The real drama of *Freaks* lies to a great extent in the fact that Browning used real people in the movie. The mutants and deformed characters who people the cast were recruited from freak shows, not created by Hollywood makeup men. Also, the film is painfully compassionate; it's a melodramatic plea for the victims of deformity.

After 1939, Browning lived in isolation in Los Angeles for over 20 years. It is remarkable, sad, and ironic that so few of his best silent films with Chaney are available now.

Frank Capra

FRANK CAPRA

Born 1897

Partial Filmography:
The Strong Man, 1926
For the Love of Mike, 1927
Long Pants, 1927
The Matinee Idol, 1928
The Power of the Press, 1928
Say It With Sables, 1928
So This Is Love, 1928
Submarine, 1928
That Certain Thing, 1928
The Way of the Strong, 1928
The Donovan Affair, 1929
Flight, 1929
The Younger Generation, 1929
Ladies of Leisure, 1930
Rain or Shine, 1930
Dirigible, 1931
The Miracle Woman, 1931
Platinum Blonde, 1931
American Madness, 1932
Forbidden, 1932
The Bitter Tea of General Yen, 1933
Lady for a Day, 1933
Broadway Bill, 1934
It Happened One Night, 1934
Mr. Deeds Goes to Town, 1936
Lost Horizon, 1937
You Can't Take It With You, 1938
Mr. Smith Goes to Washington, 1939
Meet John Doe, 1941
Co-directed World War II Documentaries, among them *Prelude to War*,

1941; *The Nazis Strike*, 1942; *Divide and Conquer*, 1943; *The Negro Soldier*, 1944
Arsenic and Old Lace, 1944
It's a Wonderful Life, 1946
State of the Union, 1948
Riding High, 1950
Here Comes the Groom, 1951
A Hole in the Head, 1959
Pocketful of Miracles, 1961

The *auteur* theory is easy to substantiate when discussing the films of Frank Capra. Although he made movies in various moods and genres—war documentaries, Oriental fantasies, romantic comedies—everyone knows what a Capra movie is about and what it stands for: a fair shake for the little guy.

Capra wrote his autobiography, *The Name Above the Title*, after it had become apparent that he was, in fact, the first director whose name actually meant more than the film title itself. It was Hollywood's first acknowledgment of *auteurism*.

Raising himself up by the bootstraps, Capra qualifies as a hero of his own favorite story. Brought to America as one of seven Sicilian children, Capra helped support his family throughout his childhood. He virtually begged his way into the film industry as a means of finding a job in 1922.

Today, Capra's films seem quaint or courageous, depending upon the political spirit of the moment. Often, too, they seem to deserve the coined phrase of "Capracorn" for the sometimes ridiculous lengths to which they carry their sentimentality.

Capra was creating little film essays on small town

political upheaval as early as *American Madness*, but it wasn't until *It Happened One Night* became the surprise hit of 1934 that America realized what an entertaining reflection of itself could be found in Capra's softhearted valentines.

But Capra's softheartedness did, on occasion, lapse into softheadedness. (He almost boasted as much in later years, naming one of his films *A Hole in the Head*.) But there was no mistaking the consistent political attitude Capra wove into every film he made. No matter the title—*Mr. Deeds Goes to Town* or *Mr. Smith Goes to Washington*, *Lost Horizon* or *You Can't Take It With You*—the underlying notion was that simple American virtues should and would triumph in the end.

Even today, *It's a Wonderful Life* (Capra's personal favorite of all his films) is a landmark movie representing the kind of personal transformation Capra would expect of his Everyman, and this conviction that man can be given a second chance to make good in terms of moral values is rerun every Christmas. The idea is also copied endlessly on TV soaps. The wonderful thing about Capra is his devoted belief in a bottomless fount of forgiveness available to man in the righteous battle against huge and mindless power.

JOHN CARPENTER

Born 1948

Filmography:
Dark Star, 1974

John Carpenter

Assault on Precinct 13, 1976
Halloween, 1978
The Fog, 1980
Escape From New York, 1981
The Thing, 1982
Christine, 1983

John Carpenter, following career patterns established in film school (University of Southern California), quickly predefined and established himself within a certain commercial category. At just past 30, he's become wedged into the mold of a cult horror filmmaker, a master in an overcrowded genre. Essentially an independent, Carpenter started out making student films and became accustomed to doing everything himself: directing, writing, composing music.

His first two low-budget features demonstrated an interest in whimsy, brutality, irony, and a rough kinetic style. But when *Halloween* clicked at the box office—making over $25 million on a budget of $250,000—Carpenter became increasingly dependent on stylistics alone to conjure up a faceless and anonymous fear machine.

Carpenter's horror is something unseen, hiding just off-screen and ready to pounce: the masked killer of *Halloween*, the regenerative formlessness of *The Thing*, the mob of killers somewhere outside *Precinct 13*, the creeping and stalking silence of *The Fog*, even what's under the hood of *Christine*. While David Cronenberg finds terror within, Carpenter sees it as something outside ourselves. The real evil is some supernatural, malevolent, transformational Other, something for which we can never feel personally responsible: in a Carpenter movie the evil to be met on a dark street is an outside force, not a direct manifestation of an evil side of the human psyche.

A creator of paranoias for an indifferent generation, Carpenter could use more introspection to bring out other talents he showed early on; for instance, the audience involvement with real people rather than inhuman creatures that was evident in *Assault on Precinct 13*. Recently, though, Carpenter has tended to involve audiences with a sledgehammer. With *Christine*, however, some of the humor he first used in *Dark Star* has returned. And his music—in particular the piano tinkle in *Halloween*—is effective. Carpenter may have sold out, but there's hope for him yet.

CHARLES CHAPLIN

Born 1889
Died 1977

Filmography (features):
The Kid, 1921
A Woman of Paris, 1923
The Gold Rush, 1925
The Circus, 1928
City Lights, 1931

Charles Chaplin

Modern Times, 1936
The Great Dictator, 1940
Monsieur Verdoux, 1947
Limelight, 1952
A King in New York, 1957
A Countess From Hong Kong, 1967

A significant number of people think of Charlie Chaplin only as the pixilated little man who appeared in short silent comedies before "real" movies began. The truth, of course, is that Chaplin's slapstick is only one part (albeit an integral one) of his work. A complete filmmaker, Chaplin created a lasting collection of feature-length films with good stories, social relevance, sentimentality, and seriousness. Personally, he was deeply invested in his movies; in most instances, he not only starred in his eleven features but also wrote, directed, and produced them and composed their music.

Chaplin's early childhood established the roots for the generous humanism of his famous little tramp. The son of British entertainers, he and his half-brother were forced to dance and sing for money on the city streets before being placed in an orphanage for destitute children. At the age of eight Chaplin performed on the London stage, and at 17 joined a comedy troupe that twice toured the United States, where in 1912 he was discovered by Mack Sennett.

He acted, clowned, chose his insignia cane and mustache, became adept at pie fights, acted in 35 shorts, and began directing. By the time he was 27, his renown was bringing him the record-breaking salary of $10,000 a week for making one short a month. His most famous titles in this period were *The Rink*, *Easy Street*, *One A.M.*, *The Pawnshop*, and *The Immigrant*.

In 1921, with *The Kid*, Chaplin embarked upon feature filmmaking, establishing a core of sentiment that would be the mainstay of his work. Continuing success led him to ignore the coming of sound technology as far as possible; *Modern Times*, made nearly a decade after sound had become routine, virtually did without dialogue, relying on Chaplin's visual style plus sound effects and music (including "Smile," which Chaplin penned).

Married four times, always to teenaged girls (once to co-star Paulette Goddard, whom he married when she was 19), Chaplin became as infamous as he was beloved, facing the moralists and the anti-communists who in 1952, during the McCarthy era, succeeded in having him virtually kicked out of his adopted homeland. Returning to the United States twenty years later, he was acclaimed and honored by the country that had first made him rich and then rejected him. A few years later, in 1975, he was knighted Sir Charles Chaplin in his original homeland, England.

Chaplin's famous little tramp character appears in only half of his features, having been abandoned at the time of *Monsieur Verdoux*, which came out in 1947. Chaplin himself played no major role in the dramatic *A Woman of Paris* or in his last film, *A Countess From Hong Kong*. But even if the little tramp does not appear in person, underneath every one of Chaplin's feature films lies a concern for the underdog, accompanied by undisguised social polemic, satire, and a certain bitterness. Most certainly, Chaplin's childhood can account for some of these feelings, and that he can still make us laugh through the tears (even if we sometimes feel that he's twisting the handkerchief for us) is testimony to his genius. We still watch, in awe, the prospector eating shoe leather in *The Gold Rush*, Hitler's global ballet in *The Great Dictator*, the berserk factory worker in *Modern Times*, *Monsieur Verdoux* counting his money, and the clown watching his love leave him behind in the final shot of *The Circus*. Chaplin's films often fade into the uncertain sunset, and we smile, even when our hearts are breaking.

FRANCIS FORD COPPOLA

Born 1939

Filmography (features):
Tonight for Sure, 1961
Battle Beyond the Sun, 1963
Dementia 13, 1963
You're a Big Boy Now, 1967

Francis Ford Coppola

Finian's Rainbow, 1968
The Rain People, 1969
The Godfather, 1972
The Conversation, 1974
The Godfather, Part II, 1974
Apocalypse Now, 1979
One From the Heart, 1982
The Outsiders, 1982
Rumble Fish, 1983

The Francis Ford Coppola rollercoaster ride might be named *ART*, in italics and all capital letters. Coppola has made decisions in his life and lived with the consequences. His film school beginnings (at the University of California at Los Angeles) led to some quickie exploitation films, including two soft-core porn films and two produced by Roger Corman —a dubbed and re-edited Russian science fiction movie and an ax murder shocker. Coppola also cashed in on '60s pop art to create his Master's thesis project, the surprising *You're a Big Boy Now*, a contemporary coming-of-age comedy whose style won out over the movie's low budget.

As a result of this success in a minor key, in 1968 Coppola was given a big-budget, wide-screen musical to direct. It was *Finian's Rainbow*, and it flopped, as did *The Rain People*, a strange sexual drama of a woman involved with a mentally retarded man, which came out the following year.

Continually reversing directions, Coppola sought relief from the rainstorm and struck gold with *The Godfather*, which he backed up immediately with a smaller picture, *The Conversation*, a definitive paranoid parable and a technically superior piece. Up to this point, Coppola had made only movies that defied the audience's expectations, reversing both his successes and his failures with different plans of box office attack. After the huge critical and commercial success of *The Godfather* he chose to direct a sequel, something traditionally handed to hacks. When *The Godfather, Part II* also succeeded with the critics and the public, sequels suddenly became respectable (and prolific).

With only himself to outdo, Coppola now chose an impossibly huge project about the Vietnam War. The story was based on Joseph Conrad's novella *Heart of Darkness*. The turmoil and expense of the production led many to conclude that Coppola was another De Mille, more interested in promotion and spectacle than in the little movies he sometimes managed artfully to spin out.

After years on the teetering brink (the film was three years in the making and the original script had been around long before shooting began) *Apocalypse Now* emerged more or less successfully. Coppola's next project, *One From the Heart*, a high-tech musical filmed on the soundstage in Coppola's own studio, was the film that plunged the stake into the heart of his financial high-rolling. In response, Coppola brought his high-style dazzle to smaller projects, adapting two teenage novels by S. E. Hinton. It's anybody's guess how his next project will turn out (it's *The Cotton Club*, a period piece set in a Harlem night club). But the Coppola name—particularly on films he produces and promotes, like Abel Gance's *Napoleon* (1927, re-released in 1980) or *Koyaanisqatsi* (1983)—has achieved the distinction of boldness: people sit up and take notice.

Given all the upheaval that has been evident throughout Coppola's flamboyant career, it is not surprising that most of his characters are people facing decisions and dealing with self-doubt. Every faltering hero in a Coppola film faces his particular coming-of-age, from the Corleone sons to the soldiers in the jungles. They all ask themselves: what am I doing here?

David Cronenberg

DAVID CRONENBERG

Born 1943

Filmography:
They Came From Within, 1975
Rabid, 1977
The Brood, 1979

Scanners, 1980
Videodrome, 1983
The Dead Zone, 1983

There are horror movies, and there are David Cronenberg horror movies. The Toronto filmmaker studied biochemistry in college, a fact which should not surprise anyone who has ventured to watch his early movies. The horrors of Cronenberg's movies come from within the body itself, terror being a chemical side effect of staying alive.

Cronenberg began by making short experimental films. His first feature, *They Came From Within*, deals with a six-inch worm-like parasite that enters bodies through the sex organs and subsequently causes intense erotic desire in the bodies it inhabits. These phallic monsters invade a chic Canadian condo, precipitating a new sexual revolution as eroticism among the condo dwellers assumes epidemic proportions.

For a follow-up, the studious-looking Cronenberg cast porn actress Marilyn Chambers in *Rabid*, in which she enters a plastic surgery clinic and comes out with a side effect: an erect tissue under her arm that stabs and sucks blood from her victims. Most horrible of all, in *The Brood* Samantha Eggar plays a woman at a "psychoplasmics" clinic whose thoughts manifest themselves in the form of tiny monster babies without belly buttons. These creatures act out their "mother's" emotions, killing when she's angry. Thoughts also kill in *Scanners*, the first Cronenberg movie to open in major U.S. theatres. Yet another

chemical side effect has produced powerful telekinetic powers in the people called "scanners," whose brains can explode other people or integrate human thought with computers. In *Videodrome*, Cronenberg creates a bizarre inversion of *Rabid*, giving actor James Woods an opening in his stomach into which cassettes can be inserted for the ultimate video experience.

Cronenberg's originality is as undeniable as his special effects are astonishing. Any synopsis of his films reduces them to absurdity—which may be appropriate—but watching these sometimes laborious psychological concepts come alive gives new meaning to the idea of movie horror. Every terror is internalized and made personal; no one merely confronts Evil: it inhabits the helpless.

With *The Dead Zone*, Cronenberg faced the challenge of his first major-budget movie and his first adaptation. Again, the terrible powers come from within. Although a much more adept piece of filmmaking (one of the best adaptations of a Stephen King shocker that has been made), *The Dead Zone* probably marks the end of the truly terrifying Cronenberg insanity. Hollywood has absorbed his warped talent, swallowed it whole, and mutated it into a tame and zombie-like version of its original self.

GEORGE CUKOR

Born 1899
Died 1983

George Cukor

Filmography:
Grumpy, 1930
The Royal Family of Broadway, 1930
Virtuous Sin, 1930
Girls About Town, 1931
Tarnished Lady, 1931
A Bill of Divorcement, 1932
One Hour With You, 1932
Rockabye, 1932
What Price Hollywood?, 1932
Dinner at Eight, 1933
Little Women, 1933
Our Betters, 1933
David Copperfield, 1935
Sylvia Scarlett, 1935
Romeo and Juliet, 1936
Camille, 1937
Holiday, 1938
Zaza, 1938
The Women, 1939
The Philadelphia Story, 1940
Susan and God, 1940
Two-Faced Woman, 1941
A Woman's Face, 1941
Her Cardboard Lover, 1942
Keeper of the Flame, 1943
Gaslight, 1944
Winged Victory, 1944
A Double Life, 1947
Adam's Rib, 1949
Edward My Son, 1949
Born Yesterday, 1950
A Life of Her Own, 1950
The Marrying Kind, 1952
The Model and the Marriage Broker, 1952
Pat and Mike, 1952
The Actress, 1953
It Should Happen to You, 1954
A Star Is Born, 1954
Bhowani Junction, 1956
Les Girls, 1957
Wild Is the Wind, 1957

Heller in Pink Tights, 1960
Let's Make Love, 1960
Song Without End, 1960
The Chapman Report, 1962
My Fair Lady, 1964
Justine, 1969
Travels With My Aunt, 1973
The Blue Bird, 1976
Rich and Famous, 1981

A Broadway stage director at the age of 27, George Cukor quickly moved westward from his native New York when sound came to the movies. He took with him his theatrical sensibilities along with a talent for drawing sublime acting from the performers he directed, particularly women.

Cukor stayed loyal to his own artistic principles, making sophisticated and tasteful films when the rest of Tinseltown was indulging in unalloyed vulgarity. And he continued to elicit wonderful performances from his female stars. Just some of the women whose careers were enhanced by working with Cukor are Tallulah Bankhead, Greta Garbo, Judy Holliday, Joan Crawford, Marilyn Monroe, Sophia Loren, Judy Garland, Elizabeth Taylor, and Audrey Hepburn. And, of course, Katharine Hepburn, who is a special case and obviously delighted to have acted in no fewer than ten Cukor projects.

Cukor's long-term relationship with Hollywood was uncharacteristically civilized (by Hollywood standards) but it was not without its bumps. Ernst Lubitsch got him fired from Paramount during the filming of *One Hour With You* in 1932, and he was one of several directors who managed to get in only a few days work on *Gone With the Wind*

(1939). His 1954 version of *A Star Is Born* is the most highly regarded of his movies, and his stock as a director has soared with the recent rediscovery of lost footage from the Judy Garland cult favorite.

At the age of 65, Cukor won the best director Academy Award for *My Fair Lady*, an adaptation package deal he directed without having much personal investment in the undertaking. Although he had been nominated four times before—for *Little Women*, *The Philadelphia Story*, *A Double Life*, and *Born Yesterday*—*My Fair Lady* was his first win. He certainly deserved the Academy's recognition of his work. Cukor continued to work into his 80s. In the final analysis, what comes through in Cukor's films is the director's eminent and polite good taste rather than any overriding message or style.

Michael Curtiz

MICHAEL CURTIZ

Born 1888
Died 1962

Partial Filmography:
Noah's Ark, 1929
The Matrimonial Bed, 1930
Cabin in the Cotton, 1932
Doctor X, 1932
20,000 Years in Sing Sing, 1933

Mystery of the Wax Museum, 1933
The Keyhole, 1933
Mandalay, 1934
Black Fury, 1935
Captain Blood, 1935
Front Page Woman, 1935
Little Big Shot, 1935
The Charge of the Light Brigade, 1936
The Walking Dead, 1936
Kid Galahad, 1937
The Adventures of Robin Hood (co-directed with William Keighley), 1938
Angels With Dirty Faces, 1938
Four Daughters, 1938
Daughters Courageous, 1939
Dodge City, 1939
Four Wives, 1939
The Private Lives of Elizabeth and Essex, 1939
The Sea Hawk, 1940
Virginia City, 1940
Dive Bomber, 1941
The Sea Wolf, 1941
Casablanca, 1942
Yankee Doodle Dandy, 1942
Mission to Moscow, 1943
This Is the Army, 1943
Passage to Marseilles, 1944
Mildred Pierce, 1945
Night and Day, 1946
Life With Father, 1947
The Unsuspected, 1947
Romance on the High Seas, 1948
Flamingo Road, 1949
The Breaking Point, 1950
Force of Arms, 1951
Jim Thorpe, All-American, 1951
The Will Rogers Story, 1952
The Jazz Singer, 1953
The Boy From Oklahoma, 1954
The Egyptian, 1954
White Christmas, 1954
We're No Angels, 1955
The Best Things in Life Are Free, 1956
The Scarlet Hour, 1956
The Vagabond King, 1956
The Helen Morgan Story, 1957
King Creole, 1958

The Proud Rebel, 1958
The Hangman, 1959
The Man in the Net, 1959
The Adventures of Huckleberry Finn, 1960
A Breath of Scandal, 1960
Francis of Assisi, 1961
The Comancheros, 1961

One of the most active of Hollywood directors, Michael Curtiz functioned so fast and so efficiently that virtually none of his own personality comes through in his most famous pictures. As a result of this nonself-serving dedication, the Curtiz movie is the genuine Hollywood product: a commercial movie with no pretensions. Curtiz was far more the craftsman than the artist, efficiently taking on Warner Brothers' projects and producing the required end result—movies that people wanted to see. Look back over his long career, and you'll recognize a succession of pictures that stand on their own proven reputation, adorned with star names that command attention: *20,000 Years in Sing Sing* (Spencer Tracy, Bette Davis), *The Adventures of Robin Hood* (Errol Flynn), *Yankee Doodle Dandy* (James Cagney), *Mildred Pierce* (Joan Crawford), *White Christmas* (Bing Crosby), and, of course, *Casablanca* (Humphrey Bogart).

Curtiz, the product of a Hungarian and German background, became the most loyal of Los Angeles studio subjects. When the power of the studios waned, Curtiz—their consummate slave—was himself without direction. Curtiz viewed filmmaking as a collaborative function, with each participant—including the director—just another cog in a functioning wheel, a faceless worker in an industry founded upon starry illusion.

Cecil B. de Mille

CECIL B. DE MILLE

**Born 1881
Died 1959**

Partial Filmography:
The Squaw Man (co-directed with Oscar Apfel), 1913
The Cheat, 1915
Temptation, 1916
The Devil Stone, 1917
The Woman God Forgot, 1917
The Squaw Man, 1918
Male and Female, 1919
Why Change Your Wife?, 1920
The Affairs of Anatol, 1921
Adam's Rib, 1923
The Ten Commandments, 1923
The Golden Bed, 1925
The Volga Boatman, 1926
The King of Kings, 1927
Dynamite, 1929
Madame Satan, 1930
The Squaw Man, 1931
The Sign of the Cross, 1932
This Day and Age, 1933
Cleopatra, 1934
Four Frightened People, 1934
The Crusades, 1935
The Plainsman, 1936
The Buccaneer, 1938
Union Pacific, 1939

North West Mounted Police, 1940
Reap the Wild Wind, 1942
The Story of Dr. Wassell, 1944
Unconquered, 1947
Samson and Delilah, 1949
The Greatest Show on Earth, 1952
The Ten Commandments, 1956

Whether or not such a reputation is deserved, the name of De Mille is synonymous with cinema spectacle. As one of the founders of Hollywood, De Mille helped establish longer and more substantial film fare than had previously been made available to audiences. His first feature, *The Squaw Man*, had a running time nearly triple that of other films of the day, and was such a success that De Mille remade the film twice. His intuitive awareness of what the public wanted has never been equalled, except perhaps currently by George Lucas.

Big budgets, however, don't by any stretch of the imagination tell the whole De Mille story. His story-telling powers were involved—and capable of involving the audience—and his popularity as an entertainer lay in his shrewd editing talents and his ability to make movies that were gorgeous to look at. Even today *The Ten Commandments*, his final film, can attract a large television audience, even though the film's special effects are nearly 30 years old, and modern computer-age moviegoers have become spoiled rotten by spectacular and stunning special effects.

Religious epics were De Mille's specialty. His father had been a minister (who

wrote theatrical plays on the side), and even in the silent era De Mille made versions of *The Ten Commandments* and *The King of Kings*. His ideals frequently came across as pious and simplistic, carrying over the same sort of emotions that characterized the American wilderness and frontier films he made; his Biblical epics were flagwaving without the flags.

The De Mille heritage is carried on today in the extravaganzas of Steven Spielberg, Francis Ford Coppola, and George Lucas, all of whom bring to their films traits more often found in a producer (Dino de Laurentiis, for example) than in a director.

For all this, however, De Mille was very much a director. Without sensing any hypocrisy, he thrived on a formula that exploited many of the vices it condemned—like lust, sexual excess, and greed. With his fingers firmly on the pulse of the American filmgoing public, De Mille made huge profits from films which depicted most of the Ten Commandments being broken.

A trivia note: the director's full name is Cecil Blount de Mille.

BRIAN DE PALMA

Born 1941

Filmography:
The Wedding Party, 1966 (released in 1969)
Greetings!, 1968
Murder à la Mod, 1968
Dionysus in 69, 1970
Hi, Mom!, 1970
Get to Know Your Rabbit, 1972

Brian de Palma

Sisters, 1973
The Phantom of the Paradise, 1974
Obsession, 1976
Carrie, 1976
The Fury, 1978
Home Movies, 1979
Dressed to Kill, 1980
Blow Out, 1981
Scarface, 1984

All the movies of Brian de Palma cry out for exclamation points behind their titles. A couple of the earlier ones—brash bubbles from the pop exuberance of the '60s—actually wore them like flags. De Palma's flourishing stylistics have cluttered everything he's done since those first comic student films, although his subject matter has switched from social sarcasm to Hitchcock scrapbook. De Palma is a filmmaker in love with his own camera.

De Palma's father was an orthopedic surgeon, which could account for his clinical view of anatomy. His mother, he has noted in interviews, bequeathed to him a number of psychological hang-ups. Feminists have frequently identified misogyny in De Palma's films, although some female critics have lavished them with praise. Whatever the political substance of his movies, De Palma clearly spent the decade between 1973 and 1983 making movies that pleasingly shocked audiences with bloody extravagance, and dazzled reviewers.

Most of these films combined Hitchcockian elements—shower scenes, mixed-up or double identities, staircases, innocents entangled in intrigue, musical soundtracks by Bernard Herrmann (who did the soundtracks for, among others, *Vertigo* in 1958, *North by Northwest* in 1959, and *Psycho* in 1960)—with highly refined camerawork. Occasionally, as in *Carrie* and *Obsession*, the camera took control, spinning in dizzying circles or sweeping from vertiginous heights. Even De Palma's first shocker, *Sisters*, made use of the split screen and nested fake documentary films and television programs within the movie itself.

For a while, the excesses of De Palma's technical tomfoolery gave him a winning combination, and it worked best in *Carrie* and *The Fury*. Now and then his old comic protester days came through at the edges, and when De Palma made the "autobiographical" *Home Movies* with his students at alma mater Sarah Lawrence, it was clear that a smart aleck sophomore still existed underneath the bloodthirsty stylist.

Sadly, when he tried to break away from type with *Scarface*, De Palma was stripped of his onion layers of style and it became clear that his excesses were attempts to obscure emptiness. Perhaps even yet De Palma will grow up and give us a film worthy of his superb ability to manipulate highly-charged moving images—one that truly deserves his desired exclamation point.

Clint Eastwood

CLINT EASTWOOD

Born 1930

Filmography:
Play Misty for Me, 1971
High Plains Drifter, 1972
Breezy, 1973
The Eiger Sanction, 1975
The Outlaw Josey Wales, 1976
The Gauntlet, 1977
Bronco Billy, 1980
Firefox, 1982
Honkytonk Man, 1982
Sudden Impact, 1983

No other star/director understands his own self-image the way Clint Eastwood does. And few risk the challenges he has taken by repeatedly playing against type.

A child of the Depression, Eastwood moved around California, studied in ten different schools, played basketball, acted, and moved from one job to another, becoming in turn a farm hand, a fireman, a lumberjack, and a swimming instructor for the Army. When a Universal film crew did some shooting at the Army base, a director asked Eastwood to contact him after his service. This was Eastwood's passport to television, where for several years he played Rowdy Yates on *Rawhide*. From

there, he became known as "the man with no name" in Italian westerns, in the process developing his characteristic laconic squint and honing the image that has propelled him to international stardom. Along the way he has gradually developed into his own best director.

In the films in which he has directed himself Eastwood has played a drunken cop (*The Gauntlet*), a broken-down country singer (*Honkytonk Man*), a circus dreamer (*Bronco Billy*), and a radio disc jockey persecuted by a fan (*Play Misty for Me*). Under other directors he has tried to sing (*Paint Your Wagon* in 1969) and twice let himself be upstaged by an orangutan (*Every Which Way But Loose* in 1978 and *Any Which Way You Can* in 1980). Robert Redford, for instance, would never allow anyone to tinker so dangerously with his image. But any time audiences have rejected the Eastwood variation, he bounces back.

Eastwood learned much about action direction from Don Siegel, his favorite director, and although he has allowed slight experimentation with his image from time to time, he still has a keen awareness of how audiences expect him to behave. The perennial Eastwood theme has been revenge and retribution, getting even both to prove something to himself and to make a statement about authority and its misuse. As Dirty Harry he is so sure that evil exists everywhere he both wills and wants it to come his way—he attracts evil like a magnet. "Make my day" is the summation of his rumble invitation.

Politically, Eastwood's attitudes are broad and barefaced, with sexual, racial, and social prejudices clearly set out in *The Eiger Sanction*, *Firefox*, and *Sudden Impact*. The impulse to point the finger at minorities or get even for real or supposed injustices may be immature, but it is undeniably human. Eastwood seems calmly aware of the vicarious release the *Dirty Harry* movies afford audiences sitting and seething in the theatre. The thread of self-aware comedy pulsing through Eastwood's movies helps soften their blow, and his use of actress Sondra Locke (does anyone else *ever* hire Sondra Locke?) reinforces the unreality of the cathartic experiences he brings to the screen. Eastwood, the actor, is a genuine successor to John Wayne; Eastwood, the director, holds the reins on where and how far that image is allowed to go.

Blake Edwards

BLAKE EDWARDS

Born 1922

Filmography:
Bring Your Smile Along, 1955
He Laughed Last, 1956
Mister Cory, 1957

This Happy Feeling, 1958
Operation Petticoat, 1959
The Perfect Furlough, 1959
High Time, 1960
Breakfast at Tiffany's, 1961
Experiment in Terror, 1962
Days of Wine and Roses, 1963
The Pink Panther, 1964
A Shot in the Dark, 1964
The Great Race, 1965
What Did You Do in the War Daddy?, 1966
Gunn, 1967
The Party, 1968
Darling Lili, 1970
Wild Rovers, 1971
The Carey Treatment, 1972
The Tamarind Seed, 1974
The Return of the Pink Panther, 1975
The Pink Panther Strikes Again, 1976
Revenge of the Pink Panther, 1978
10, 1979
S.O.B., 1980
Trail of the Pink Panther, 1982
Victor/Victoria, 1982
Curse of the Pink Panther, 1983
The Man Who Loved Women, 1983

When the world falls apart around Blake Edwards, his response is to laugh at it. He works on the "fools rush in" theory, espousing mad romance where the character falls helplessly in love before the pie can hit in the face—even though it's clear that the pie is already, as it were, on the launching pad.

Edwards turned to the movies from radio, where he had been a scriptwriter, and from television, where series he had helped develop included *Peter Gunn*. His early films—several with Tony Curtis—gained critical popularity, as he developed a bright film-making style centered on his own cleverly written scripts.

Starting in the 1960s, Edwards began to expand his vision in a highly practical manner—by broadening his budget. Facing obstacles in the studios, several of his films were not released to his specifications (in particular *Darling Lili* and *The Carey Treatment*). He got his revenge with his *S.O.B.*, a sarcastic commentary on the Hollywood system which includes a parodic reference to *Darling Lili*.

In Edwards' films, change emerges out of anarchy. This is evident even in his work with his wife, Julie Andrews, whose best director he is. He has allowed her to move beyond her goody-goody image, although the ways in which this has been achieved have not always been to her best advantage.

If Edwards has allowed the action in his films to get more and more extreme, he has kept a tight rein on visual style. The *Pink Panther* slapstick is the outgrowth of Edwards' anarchy, with Peter Sellers' bumbling Inspector Clouseau a classic study of a life and a career in a state of perpetual disintegration. The success of the *Pink Panther* movies has as much (or more) to do with the composition of each comic setup as it does with the written wit of the gags. But Edwards skidded too far with that joke as well, trying to continue the *Pink Panther* line without the irreplaceable comic genius of Sellers as Clouseau.

It was in 1965, in *The Great Race*, that Edwards attempted to create the ultimate in slapstick—a world entirely without reason. But even the immense pie fight climax was nota-

ble more for color-coordination than for chaos. Now, compared to the slobbery food fights of today's teen comedies, it looks like a model of structured order.

There is still an old-fashioned romantic core to whatever Edwards does. It was evident in 1974 in *The Tamarind Seed*, and it's still there in the recent movies—in *10*, *Victor/Victoria*, *The Man Who Loved Women*. The typical Edwards character spins in a fluttering frenzy, a soul shredded equally by the demands of love and work. And the world the character inhabits confronts, with as much dignity as it can muster, its own disorder.

Rainer Werner Fassbinder

RAINER WERNER FASSBINDER

Born 1946
Died 1983

Filmography:
Katzelmacher, 1969
Love Is Colder Than Death, 1969
The American Soldier, 1970
Die Niklashauser Fahrt, 1970
Gods of the Plague, 1970
Why Does Herr R. Run Amok?, 1970

Beware of the Holy Whore, 1971
Recruits in Ingolstadt, 1971
Rio das Mortes, 1971
Whity, 1971
The Bitter Tears of Petra von Kant, 1972
The Merchant of Four Seasons, 1972
Jail Bait, 1973
Ali: Fear Eats the Soul, 1974
Effi Briest, 1974
Martha, 1974
Fox and His Friends, 1975
Mother Kusters Goes to Heaven, 1975
Chinese Roulette, 1976
Fear of Fear, 1976
Satan's Brew, 1976
Germany in August (section), 1977
The Stationmaster's Wife, 1977
Despair, 1978
In a Year of Thirteen Moons, 1978
Berlin Alexanderplatz, 1979
The Marriage of Maria Braun, 1979
The Third Generation, 1979
Lili Marleen, 1981
Lola, 1981
Veronica Voss, 1982
Querelle, 1983

German films of the 1970s flowered in neo-decadence with the prolific output of Rainer Werner Fassbinder. Compressing the labor into a decade and a half and working with a maniacal intensity, Fassbinder wrote and directed over thirty films. Fassbinder's characters inevitably come to starkly pessimistic ends, sometimes in ways never before expressed in quite the same way on the screen.

Fassbinder's earliest films were experimental offshoots of his avant-garde theatrical roots. He quickly found his stride in the launching of a new form of melodrama—based in part on the style of director Douglas Sirk (whose credits include *All That Heaven Allows* in 1955 and *Written on the Wind* in 1956). In most of Fassbinder's films made between 1972 and 1977, the characters faced the most tragic of circumstances, and rarely recovered. When Fassbinder made *Despair* in 1978, the title alone summed up his chosen theme. It was his first big-budgeted movie, written by Tom Stoppard from a Vladimir Nabokov novel and starring Dirk Bogarde.

Fassbinder's style of filmmaking left the viewer uncertain whether to laugh or to cry. With extreme acting styles, expressionistic design, and outrageous story lines, the mixed moods of a Fassbinder film made it impossible to draw clear lines of distinction between the tragic and comic aspects of a given situation: Mother Kuster's dilemmas, for instance, or Veronica Voss' loneliness. The confusion could be riveting and involving, and it could leave the viewer feeling wretched inside. Perhaps the finest example of this inextricable meshing of opposing emotions comes from *In a Year of Thirteen Moons*, a film dedicated to one of Fassbinder's two lovers (both of whom committed suicide after he left them). *Thirteen Moons* is the tale of a reluctant transsexual, a man who changes his sex on impulse and finds it impossible to live with the outcome. This intense tragedy is interrupted by a bizarre slapstick scene from a Jerry Lewis movie (the 1955 *You're Never Too Young*), and the contrast gives new meaning to the word "despair." The hero, of course, kills himself.

Homosexuality figured frequently in Fassbinder's films. He may have been the first director to present homosexual main characters (in *Fox and His Friends*) without their homosexuality being the predominant issue of the story. Instead, class relationships or romance were the themes he explored.

In 1979, Fassbinder pulled out all the stops for *Berlin Alexanderplatz*, a 15½-hour adaptation of the Alfred Dolbin novel. Fassbinder had always felt an affinity for the Dolbin hero, Franz Bieberkopf, a confused and dumbly violent man living in Germany in the 1920s. (Fassbinder had even used Bieberkopf's name as his own pseudonym on several occasions.)

Following this masterpiece, he completed between 1979 and 1982 a popular trilogy of films emphasizing the futility existing in the lives of many people in post-war Germany as symbolized through its women (*The Marriage of Maria Braun*, *Lola*, and *Veronica Voss*). His final film was an ambitious, stylized, international (in cast and locations), and melodramatic version of *Querelle*.

Fassbinder died alone in his apartment. His death was attributed to drug-related causes.

JOHN FORD

Born 1895
Died 1973

Partial Filmography:
The Iron Horse, 1924

John Ford

Kentucky Pride, 1925
Four Sons, 1928
Strong Boy, 1929
Born Reckless, 1930
Men Without Women, 1930
Up the River, 1930
Arrowsmith, 1931
Air Mail, 1932
Flesh, 1932
Doctor Bull, 1933
Judge Priest, 1934
The Lost Patrol, 1934
The Informer, 1935
Steamboat 'Round the Bend, 1935
The Whole Town's Talking, 1935
Mary of Scotland, 1936
The Plough and the Stars, 1936
The Prisoner of Shark Island, 1936
The Hurricane, 1937
Wee Willie Winkie, 1937
Four Men and a Prayer, 1938
Submarine Patrol, 1938
Drums Along the Mohawk, 1939
Stagecoach, 1939
Young Mr. Lincoln, 1939
The Grapes of Wrath, 1940
The Long Voyage Home, 1940
How Green Was My Valley, 1941
Tobacco Road, 1941
They Were Expendable, 1945
My Darling Clementine, 1946
The Fugitive, 1947
Fort Apache, 1948
Three Godfathers, 1948
She Wore a Yellow Ribbon, 1949

Rio Grande, 1950
Wagonmaster, 1950
When Willie Comes Marching Home, 1950
The Quiet Man, 1952
What Price Glory?, 1952
Mogambo, 1953
The Sun Shines Bright, 1953
The Long Gray Line, 1955
Mister Roberts, 1955
The Searchers, 1956
The Rising of the Moon, 1957
The Wings of Eagles, 1957
The Last Hurrah, 1958
Gideon of Scotland Yard, 1959
The Horse Soldiers, 1959
Sergeant Rutledge, 1960
Two Rode Together, 1961
The Man Who Shot Liberty Valance, 1962
Donovan's Reef, 1963
How the West Was Won (Civil War episode), 1963
Cheyenne Autumn, 1964
Young Cassidy (credited to Jack Cardiff), 1965
Seven Women, 1966

John Ford, the most venerable Hollywood master, fell for his own mythology by quipping, humbly, "I make westerns."

The truth, of course, was that the American pioneer legends played a major part in all the nostalgic, masculine movies helmed by Ford, but that's not the whole story of what constitutes the John Ford film. Although he might never have admitted it—keeping his mouth shut in typical John Wayne fashion—most of Ford's movies were ultra-American confections, soft with emotion at their center.

The youngest child of Irish immigrants in Maine—his father kept a saloon—Ford followed his actor brother Francis to Hollywood and got bit parts in the movies, (among them that of a hooded KKK rider in D. W. Griffith's *Birth of a Nation*). Ford started directing films at 22.

Ford's critical reputation has risen in recent years. The sheer number of his films, plus his consistent vision of the West, makes any analysis of his "message" easy to accept—although there is still something unfashionable and uncomfortable about the weight he gives to the cult of masculinity, his penchant for simple reactionary sermons, and the glib racism frequently apparent in his movies. In the apologetic *Cheyenne Autumn*, the last western that Ford made, the director made atonement to some extent for the occasions on which he had portrayed American Indians in an unsympathetic light.

Above all other considerations, Ford was a stylist of film, and his sketchbook contained many variations on the theme of filmmaking. The dustbowl drama of *The Grapes of Wrath*; the showy stylizations of *The Informer*; the editing structure evident in *Stagecoach*; the dramatic special effects in *The Hurricane*; and Shirley Temple's most expensive travel adventure, *Wee Willie Winkie*: all these have John Ford to thank for narratives that work for the audience and one-dimensional characters who speak their minds and are clearly understood.

John Wayne, who is forever associated with Ford's films, was the physical embodiment of the Ford ideal; the rectangular jutting rocks of Utah's Monument Valley stand as Ford's most visible filmic signature. Ford's most sub-

tle film, *The Searchers*, weaves all the elements with which this director worked best, as typified by the perfect framing of the action within the frontier cabin door as Dorothy Jordan looks longingly at the man she will never be able to have. By the time of *The Searchers*, Ford's direction of such scenes had become a matter of instinct rather than calculation. His legacy to the cinema has endured because, as he said, he simply made westerns, populating the plains with strong-willed characters playing out their human tales against the vastness of the Valley.

Bob Fosse

BOB FOSSE

Born 1927

Filmography:
Sweet Charity, 1969
Cabaret, 1972
Lenny, 1974
All That Jazz, 1979
Star 80, 1983

The son of vaudevillians, Bob Fosse became a dancer in his teens and rapidly became a noted choreographer. The cinematic potential of his choreography did not go unnoticed and was ac-

corded early homage by the French New Wave filmmakers—particularly Jean-Luc Godard.

When Fosse himself turned to directing films, he choreographed images with equal success and originality, albeit in dark and moody ways. *Sweet Charity* (based on Federico Fellini's 1957 film *Nights of Cabiria*) may be the lightest of his films, but its subject is far from sunny: it studies the seamy lives of prostitutes. And his subsequent movies have presented increasingly grim views of degradation and decadence.

Lenny, the story of the controversial comedian Lenny Bruce, is not a musical as such. But Lenny Bruce had been described as a jazz musician of words and Fosse's direction made full use of this image, employing jarring black-and-white photography to add power to the torrent of abuse that the character vented on his audience. Fosse's bleak vision of the human condition reached its culmination in *Star 80*, a meditation on the lowest and least savory levels of show business and, like *Lenny*, based on fact.

Fosse's most personal film, *All That Jazz*, opines autobiographically about all kinds of theatrical excess. With references to his marriage to dancer Gwen Verdon and to his own coronary bypass operation, it is certainly the most graphically morbid musical ever made.

Fosse's organization of movement in the movies has been an exercise in reshaping despair, clothing the tarnished human creatures who people his films with a kind of physical grace.

William Friedkin

WILLIAM FRIEDKIN

Born 1939

Filmography:
Good Times, 1967
The Birthday Party, 1968
The Night They Raided Minsky's, 1968
The Boys in the Band, 1970
The French Connection, 1971
The Exorcist, 1973
Sorcerer, 1977
The Brink's Job, 1979
Cruising, 1980
Deal of the Century, 1983

A basketball star in high school, William Friedkin rose from mailroom boy at a Chicago TV station to director of more than 2000 TV shows, commercials, and documentaries. One of the latter was instrumental in releasing a wrongly convicted boy, Paul Krump, from prison.

When Friedkin turned to filmmaking, he skidded through some odd vehicles before discovering his particular bent as a moviemaker with an acute perception of Evil with a capital E.

Friedkin perceives evil on a grand scale—omnipresent and addictive, in manners and in madness. *The Boys in the Band* and *The Birthday Party*—

both adapted from stage plays—revel in dark secrets, both revealed and unrevealed. Although *The French Connection* won praise mainly as an action movie, much of its fascination is rooted in the character of a suavely cold heroin smuggler. Even *The Brink's Job*, one of Friedkin's failed comedies, deals with the most ambitious form of wrongdoing—in this case, bank robbery—that Friedkin could get his hands on.

In his huge hit, *The Exorcist*, Friedkin takes on an awesome subject: that of a little girl suffering the ultimate burden of satanic possession. But Friedkin erred seriously in relying on commercial theatrics so heavily that a true inner glimpse of malevolence within the common person is obscured. In hindsight—and given the many copycat films which followed—his handling of the theme was laughable and much of the strength of the original novel was lost.

During the filming of *Cruising*, Friedkin faced so much opposition from the gay community that the subsequent cuts necessary meant the final film was virtually incomprehensible. With *Cruising* and *The Boys in the Band*, the director became forever associated with the idea of homosexual stereotypes in film, despite his claims to have sought to present his emotionally loaded subject matter objectively.

In retrospect, sheer power is the driving force behind all Friedkin's obsessions, perhaps stemming from that early pardon he achieved for Paul Krump. His movies deal with knowing the secret lives of others, with

the most killing drug kick and the biggest heroin deal, with the transportation of massive explosives, with huge heists against the biggest bank, with sexual sadomasochistic power, and finally, with the devil himself.

Deal of the Century, Friedkin's attempt to lambaste the international weapons race, showed how much further his quest to display brute power (even in a comic light) had weakened his ability as a director.

In the 1970s, Friedkin was married briefly to actress Jeanne Moreau.

Sam Fuller

SAM FULLER

Born 1911

Filmography:
I Shot Jesse James, 1949
The Baron of Arizona, 1950
The Steel Helmet, 1950
Fixed Bayonets, 1951
Park Row, 1952
Pickup on South Street, 1953
Hell and High Water, 1954
House of Bamboo, 1955
China Gate, 1957
Forty Guns, 1957
Run of the Arrow, 1957
The Crimson Kimono, 1959
Verboten!, 1959
Underworld, U.S.A., 1961
Merrill's Marauders, 1962
Shock Corridor, 1963

The Naked Kiss, 1965
Shark!, 1969
Dead Pigeon on Beethoven Street, 1972
The Big Red One, 1979
White Dog, 1982

Getting the story is everything to Sam Fuller. People and production details are secondary to Fuller's action-packed scripts and his style of storytelling in headlines.

Fuller started working for newspapers at age 12, became a crime reporter for the *San Diego Sun* at 17, and by 24 was cranking out pulp novels based on his experiences. He wrote screenplays before World War II, fought overseas and was awarded the Purple Heart and Silver Star, and returned to Hollywood to direct his first film in 1949.

Fuller's films are indeed his own. He writes, produces, and directs, and shows no mercy towards his characters or his audience. He deals in brutality, paranoia, insanity, vulgarity. But despite the subject matter there is no ignoring the visual poetry, much of it achieved by complex camera movements, that characterizes a Fuller film. His movies have been described, by British critic David Thompson, as "scenarios made from communities of rats, the camera itself a king rat, scarred and hurt, but still swooping in and out of every scuffle."

And Fuller's filmmaking packs a terrific punch. Who, once having experienced such scenes, could ever forget the breakdown of Zack in *The Steel Helmet* ("If you die I'll kill you!"), the bald prostitute attacking her pimp in *The Naked Kiss*, or the screaming journalist trapped in

a madhouse in *Shock Corridor*?

Fuller looks his part, cigar-smoking, wizened, gruff. His fiercely independent films—when he can still manage to get one produced—are always controversial. Network television dropped the idea of showing his recent *White Dog* because of its bold treatment of racial topics.

Fuller sees a corrupt world, strips it bare, pries it apart, films this whole open-heart operation, and hawks it as an educational experience for the bottom half of a drive-in double bill. The movie medium owes him more than it knows or dares admit. To the movie community he's one of those relatives that you're ashamed to be associated with, even as you acknowledge his ability—he's the vulgarian who keeps showing up at the sophisticated party and embarrassing the guests.

D. W. Griffith

D. W. GRIFFITH

Born 1875
Died 1948

Partial Filmography:
Several hundred silent films made between 1908–1914, including:

The Lonely Villa; Her First Biscuits; In Old Kentucky; Leather Stockings; The Red Man's View; A Corner in Wheat; The Lonedale Operator; Enoch Arden; The Goddess of Sagebrush Gulch; Man's Lust for Gold; The Musketeers of Pig Alley; The Battle of Elderbush Gulch; Judith of Bethulia; The Battle of the Sexes; Home Sweet Home; The Avenging Conscience
The Birth of a Nation, 1915
Intolerance, 1916
The Great Love, 1918
Hearts of the World, 1918
Broken Blossoms, 1919
The Fall of Babylon, 1919
The Girl Who Stayed at Home, 1919
The Greatest Thing in Life, 1919
The Mother and the Law, 1919
A Romance of Happy Valley, 1919
True Heart Susie, 1919
Way Down East, 1920
Dream Street, 1921
One Exciting Night, 1922
Orphans of the Storm, 1922
The White Rose, 1923
America, 1924
Isn't Life Wonderful?, 1924
Sally of the Sawdust, 1925
Sorrows of Satan, 1926
The Battle of the Sexes, 1928
Drums of Love, 1928
Lady of the Pavements, 1929
Sound films:
Abraham Lincoln, 1930
The Struggle, 1931

Sad and majestic turns of events punctuate both the personal and the professional life of D. W. Griffith (the D. W. stands for David Wark). Even today, audiences know him mostly for two films: *The Birth of a Nation* (which suffers from racial ignorance) and *Intolerance*

(which is shown in truncated pieces, if at all).

Yet Griffith, who directed perhaps 500 films in his lifetime, is the incontestable father of American and world cinema technique. The son of a Kentucky physician, legislator, and renowned Civil War fighter for the South, young David Wark nonetheless experienced times of poverty during the reconstruction. In his attempts to find his career as an actor he was often hopelessly destitute, even into his thirties. Having failed in the theatre and as a writer—his chosen careers—Griffith entered the movies reluctantly. Hollywood, though, did give him a chance to act and to write, and at the age of 33 he directed his first film for Biograph, *The Adventures of Dolly*.

After that point he was virtually unstoppable. He liberated the screen from theatrical restrictions, discovering new ways to make movies work as he directed film after film. He demolished conventions of camera style, storytelling, editing, acting methods, movement, and time. He also watched in close-up the growth of the star system, and many star names were associated with his films, among them Lillian Gish, Mary Pickford, Mabel Normand, and Harry Carey.

One of Griffith's major contributions to movies was the development of rehearsals so that the actors were not, as previously, performing virtually cold. He also increased the use of close-ups. As a result, his productions became popular with the public for their rapid pace and quality production. *Enoch Arden*, in 1911,

clocked in at double the expected attention span of audiences, and *The Birth of a Nation* ran just under three hours and was an outstanding success—even at the then outrageous admission price of $2 a ticket.

Intolerance followed, but this time Griffith had gone too far with complexity and cost. Today, his folly is still beautifully idealistic, eminently watchable (especially in reconstructed tinted versions), and immense.

With the introduction of sound, Griffith's popular stock declined. Although his two sound films, *Abraham Lincoln* and *The Struggle*, stand up favorably to other films of the day, he is more remembered for his silent moments. And most of those are rarely shown.

He died in the Hollywood Knickerbocker Hotel at the age of 73, two failed marriages behind him, his genius past its prime, alone, bitter, and virtually ignored by the industry whose artistic vision he had helped to develop.

HOWARD HAWKS

Born 1896
Died 1977

Filmography:
Fig Leaves, 1926
The Road to Glory, 1926
The Cradle Snatchers, 1927
Paid to Love, 1927
The Air Circus, 1928
Fazil, 1928
A Girl in Every Port, 1928
Trent's Last Case, 1929
The Dawn Patrol, 1930
The Criminal Code, 1931
The Crowd Roars, 1932
Scarface, 1932

Howard Hawks

Tiger Shark, 1932
Today We Live, 1933
Twentieth Century, 1934
Barbary Coast, 1935
Ceiling Zero, 1936
Come and Get It, 1936 (co-directed with William Wyler)
The Road to Glory, 1936
Bringing Up Baby, 1938
Only Angels Have Wings, 1939
His Girl Friday, 1940
Ball of Fire, 1941
Sergeant York, 1941
Air Force, 1943
To Have and Have Not, 1944
The Big Sleep, 1946
Red River, 1948
A Song Is Born, 1948
I Was a Male War Bride, 1949
The Big Sky, 1952
Monkey Business, 1952
O'Henry's Full House ("The Ransom of Red Chief" episode), 1952
Gentlemen Prefer Blondes, 1953
The Land of the Pharaohs, 1955
Rio Bravo, 1959
Hatari!, 1962
Man's Favorite Sport?, 1964
Red Line 7000, 1965
El Dorado, 1967
Rio Lobo, 1970

Howard Hawks' male cosmology was late discovered, but the fact of the matter was that he was more comfortable with male-oriented story lines. Men at work was a favorite theme of his and he approached such themes, not as an anti-feminist, but in a gallantly and optimistically masculine frame of mind. Even the heroes of his battle-of-the-sexes comedies were quintessentially American: hardworking, middle-class, brave, ordinary.

As a student, Hawks studied mechanical engineering. He raced planes and worked in an aircraft factory before deciding that he really preferred making movies. So he returned to Hollywood, where he had once spent summer vacations on a movie lot.

Hawks always insisted that films should be made with professionalism and should offer sheer entertainment, but he refused to make a fuss about his filmmaking style. He took the most direct route toward his subject, having very little to do with complicated camera angles or other directorial intervention in the work of the cameramen.

George Roy Hill

GEORGE ROY HILL

Born 1922

Filmography:
Period of Adjustment, 1962
Toys in the Attic, 1963
The World of Henry Orient, 1964
Hawaii, 1966
Thoroughly Modern Millie, 1967
Butch Cassidy and the Sundance Kid, 1969
Slaughterhouse Five, 1972
The Sting, 1973
The Great Waldo Pepper, 1975
Slap Shot, 1977
A Little Romance, 1979
The World According to Garp, 1982

George Roy Hill came to moviemaking late in life, but once set on course he became as accomplished a director as he had been successful in the other career fields which had preceded this one. Hill, in fact, had been successful in nearly everything else he set out to do. He had studied music at Yale and literature at Dublin's Trinity College, and had been a professional Shakespearean actor with Cyril Cusack's company in Dublin. He had served as a pilot in World War II and in the Korean War; he had written and directed for TV and on Broadway. And at the age of 40, he finally got around to making his first feature film.

Some critics have seen Hill as a Renaissance man, accomplished in many fields, and that broad base of talent can sometimes work against him, making his films appear glossy-surfaced, superficial, and less substantial than they really are. Woven through his style, one finds a thread of attractive pansexuality: Hill's characters are not macho, feminine, or seductive as much as they are simply sensual, sometimes maintaining physical relationships on the most innocent levels.

Beneath the most entertaining stories, each of Hill's movies contains some expression of childlike sexuality: the underage bride in *Toys in the Attic*; the flighty romances of children in *The World of Henry Orient* and *A Little Romance*; the strength of buddy-buddy relationships in *Butch Cassidy and the Sundance Kid*, *Slap Shot*, and *The Sting*; and the many forms of sexuality explored in *The World According to Garp* (including transsexualism and the nude-bouncing-baby opening credits). Hill directs these scenes with an assured flair, almost as though no sexual tensions were there at all.

If innocent sexuality is at the root of the relationships among Hill's characters, he hopes nevertheless to give other meanings to his films. The last shot of *Butch Cassidy and the Sundance Kid* is a frozen image of the duo, substantiating the image of their intimate friendship and the historical significance of their romantic adventures together. The final moments of *Garp* flying toward death are an ironically liberating image of freedom—floating away from the burden of life. Even *Slap Shot*, which contains profanity never before heard on the screen (written, incidentally, by a woman, Nancy Dowd), carries a message about teamwork and individuality within its vulgarity and its slapstick action.

Slaughterhouse Five, which more than most of his work reflects Hill's own wartime experiences, is perhaps his least typical film, particularly in its presentation of the bubbling (and topless) sexuality of Valerie Perrine. In George Roy Hill's popular entertainments, such sexy sequences are more frequently hinted at than depicted openly.

Hill was nominated for a best director Oscar for *Butch Cassidy and the Sundance Kid*, which was also nominated as best film. *The Sting*, in 1973, won the Oscar for best film and also gave Hill the award for best director.

Walter Hill

WALTER HILL

Born 1942

Filmography:
Hard Times, 1975
The Driver, 1978
The Warriors, 1979
The Long Riders, 1980
Southern Comfort, 1981
48 Hours, 1982
Streets of Fire, 1984

Walter Hill is an intellectual director who dabbles in genre, trying to disguise the basic narrative structure in his entertainments. His early ambition was to be a comic-book illustrator—which may have influenced his later moviemaking style. Educated at Michigan State, he worked in construction and oil drilling before starting to write screenplays in the early 1970s. He wrote *The*

Getaway (1972), *The Mackintosh Man* (1973), *The Drowning Pool* (1975, co-writer), and other actioners before he was allowed to direct.

Each of Hill's movies has been a disguised variation of a familiar genre. The subject matter of his movies clearly deals with a specific subject: boxing, the West, teen gangs, a private eye, policemen, soldiers. But one must look, for instance, between the vertical lines of swamp trees which fill the frames of *Southern Comfort* to recognize that the national guardsmen lost in Louisiana are really acting out Hill's metaphor for jungle warfare. On the surface, *The Long Riders* looks like a western, but in fact it deals more with family ties than with bank jobs. To emphasize this point, Hill cast actual brothers (the Carradines, the Keachs, the Quaids, and the Guests) in the roles of outlaw brothers.

Reviewers find a mixture of references—from the classics to pop art—in Hill's work. In *The Warriors* some critics found in the story a parallel to Greek mythology. Others noted that it was a comic book characterization of street gangs. *Streets of Fire* gives a Helen of Troy update to a story of monosyllabic rock and roll rumblers.

Considering that he's a screenwriter, Hill generally gives his characters little to say. Visual flair takes precedence in most cases, one exception being the wisecracks of Eddie Murphy in *48 Hours*, Hill's most commercial venture to date. Hill creates strong conflicts—brother against brother, black against white, the educated versus

the streetwise—and adds high-speed visual energy to make the fireworks fly. The chemistry worked so well in *The Warriors* that some exhibitors refused to show the film, particularly when the film was reported to be precipitating outbreaks of violence among urban audiences.

Hill wants to make pictures with both literary value and visual cinematic pizzazz. These ambitions show up most clearly in *The Driver*, which reduced its characters to simple namelessness (The Driver, The Cop, The Girl), and at the same time spun highly-charged action racing into every scene. The film was labelled pretentious, and Hill has since toned down his tendencies to mix the old with the new. But he still holds on to visual showiness, working hard to make the image paramount to the word. He wants to be a cinematic classicist, following John Ford and Howard Hawks in structuring pure entertainments with hearts of intelligence and feet of flame.

Alfred Hitchcock

ALFRED HITCHCOCK

Born 1899
Died 1980

Filmography:
Number Thirteen, 1922
The Pleasure Garden, 1925
The Lodger, 1926
The Mountain Eagle, 1926
Downhill, 1927
The Ring, 1927
Easy Virtue, 1928
Champagne, 1928
The Farmer's Wife, 1928
The Manxman, 1929
Blackmail, 1929
Elstree Calling, 1930
Juno and the Paycock, 1930
Murder, 1930
The Skin Game, 1932
Number Seventeen, 1932
Rich and Strange, 1932
Waltzes from Vienna, 1933
The Man Who Knew Too Much, 1934
The Thirty-Nine Steps, 1935
Sabotage, 1936
Secret Agent, 1936
Young and Innocent, 1937
The Lady Vanishes, 1938
Jamaica Inn, 1939
Foreign Correspondent, 1940
Rebecca, 1940
Mr. and Mrs. Smith, 1941
Suspicion, 1941
Saboteur, 1942
Shadow of a Doubt, 1943
Adventure Malagaches, 1944
Lifeboat, 1944
Spellbound, 1945
Notorious, 1946
The Paradine Case, 1947
Rope, 1948
Under Capricorn, 1949
Stage Fright, 1950
Strangers on a Train, 1951
I Confess, 1953
Dial M for Murder, 1954
Rear Window, 1954
To Catch a Thief, 1955
The Man Who Knew Too Much, 1956
The Trouble With Harry, 1955
The Wrong Man, 1957
Vertigo, 1958
North by Northwest, 1959
Psycho, 1960
The Birds, 1963
Marnie, 1964
Torn Curtain, 1966
Topaz, 1969

Frenzy, 1972
Family Plot, 1976

The recent revival of Hitchcock's "lost" films demonstrates vividly that he has never ceased to be a potent force in the history of film.

The undisputed Master could appear on television and turn a simple "Good evening" into a threat, and that's typical of the upheaval he could generate in the most simple of affairs. The willful perversity of Hitchcock's films is what makes them so effective. The most ordinary details become the source of nameless dread: a staircase, a dinner, a flight of birds, a shower, a glass of milk. And it's ordinary people who become trapped in the intrigue.

Toward the end of his career, Hitchcock's work may have been hampered by an over-dependence upon outdated styles of filmmaking, including undisguisedly artificial sets and back projection. This was all the more disappointing when one looked back on the risks he used to take, daringly experimenting with 3-D (*Dial M for Murder*) and single-take films (*Rope*). Perhaps over-generously enthusiastic critics did him a disservice in elevating his status to such heights that he could do no wrong. Before his talent was "discovered"—and then analyzed endlessly by academics—mature works such as *Vertigo* and *Rear Window* integrated perfectly all the elements of terror, obsession, suspense, observation, and psychology that Hitchcock doted upon so lovingly.

Recent biographies also have pricked holes in the Hitchcock mystique, examining his personal difficulties and exploring his unfulfilled desires. But the fact remains that no director has ever been so copied, emulated, envied . . . and watched.

As they say, all of Freud is merely a footnote to Hitchcock.

John Huston

JOHN HUSTON

Born 1906

Filmography:
The Maltese Falcon, 1941
Across the Pacific, 1942
In This Our Life, 1942
The Battle of San Pietro, 1945
Let There Be Light, 1945
Key Largo, 1948
The Treasure of the Sierra Madre, 1948
We Were Strangers, 1949
The Asphalt Jungle, 1950
The Red Badge of Courage, 1951
The African Queen, 1952
Moulin Rouge, 1953
Beat the Devil, 1954
Moby Dick, 1956
Heaven Knows, Mr. Allison, 1957
The Barbarian and the Geisha, 1958
The Roots of Heaven, 1958
The Unforgiven, 1960
The Misfits, 1961
Freud, 1962
The List of Adrian Messenger, 1963
The Night of the Iguana, 1964

The Bible, 1966
Casino Royale, 1967
Reflections in a Golden Eye, 1967
Sinful Davy, 1969
A Walk With Love and Death, 1969
The Kremlin Letter, 1970
Fat City, 1972
The Life and Times of Judge Roy Bean, 1972
The Mackintosh Man, 1973
The Man Who Would be King, 1975
Wise Blood, 1979
Phobia, 1980
Annie, 1982
Under the Volcano, 1984

More than any other attribute, rough, stubborn persistence has taken John Huston to the top. Although in a great many of his movies he seems more comfortable South of anywhere where risk and courage are daily partners, he has also daringly taken on, for intellectual or egocentric reasons, films that seemed to defy the filmmaker, among them *Moby Dick, Freud, The Bible, Annie*.

Certainly, no director has faced more critical ups and downs. Son of a famous actor father, Walter, John Huston entered the movie industry as a writer, but it wasn't until he was able to direct *The Maltese Falcon* that he made his big splash in the Hollywood pond.

From that point Huston has meandered through various phases of theatrical and literary adaptation, experimentation with color, and periods where his talents as an actor seemed to overshadow his directorial skills, but all the time he has remained relatively true to the spirit of rugged individualism.

Huston likes to brag that he acts to get the money to finance little projects that he enjoys, and it's hard to draw the line between the truth and his self-promoting mythology. He's as willing to invest his time in an independent feature that interests him—for example, Flannery O'Connor's *Wise Blood*—as he is to take on a big-budget studio film in a style completely outside his experience—such as *Annie*. Since most of his films center on rough men under pressure, *Annie* was indeed an odd vehicle for Huston; perhaps he identified with Daddy Warbucks, or found the pressure amusing. His most recent film, *Under the Volcano*, finds him back in stride with another South of the Border saga of sin and redemption.

Who is Huston? A brave, cynical, comic, robust filmmaker? Or just an armchair adventurer? Opinions seem to change with the seasons. And he appears to delight in the myths that swirl around him, encouraging stories that would have him resemble the corrupt politician he portrayed in Polanski's *Chinatown*.

To fall back on his own favorite metaphor: like whores and buildings, if you survive long enough you get respectable.

ELIA KAZAN

Born 1909

Filmography:
A Tree Grows in Brooklyn, 1945
Boomerang, 1947
Gentleman's Agreement, 1947
The Sea of Grass, 1947
Pinky, 1949
Panic in the Streets, 1950

Elia Kazan

A Streetcar Named Desire, 1951
Viva Zapata! 1952
Man on a Tightrope, 1953
On the Waterfront, 1954
East of Eden, 1955
Baby Doll, 1956
A Face in the Crowd, 1957
Wild River, 1960
Splendor in the Grass, 1961
America, America, 1963
The Arrangement, 1969
The Visitors, 1972
The Last Tycoon, 1976

Elia Kazan became a man without a medium. Bored with the theatre and resentful of Hollywood's commercialism, Kazan never seemed able to come to peaceful terms with the power of acting and how to present it. The son of Greek immigrants, he worked in the drama department at Yale, and by the 1940s had become one of Broadway's finest stage directors with *The Skin of Our Teeth* and *Death of a Salesman* featured on his impressive list of credits. In the '30s and '40s he began acting in political and agricultural documentaries before actually trying his hand at film directing.

Without being static or stagebound, Kazan's movies reflect his own theatrical roots. His first film, *A Tree Grows in Brooklyn* (1945), won critical acclaim and picked up two Academy Awards (James Dunn for best supporting actor, and Peggy Garner for outstanding child actress) plus a nomination for the screenplay. Two years later, *Gentleman's Agreement* gathered a whole fistful of honors: Academy Awards for best film, best director (Kazan), best supporting actress (Celeste Holm); and nominations for best actor (Gregory Peck), best actress (Dorothy McGuire) and best screenplay (Moss Hart). While racial, social and religious prejudices were the themes Kazan forthrightly explored, by the 1950s his social messages carried more commercial tags.

Having directed Marlon Brando on Broadway, Kazan brought the actor into the movies with *A Streetcar Named Desire*. The long list of other actors he trained, directed, or otherwise influenced includes Lee J. Cobb, Rod Steiger, Karl Malden, Eva Marie Saint, Natalie Wood, Carroll Baker, Vivien Leigh, and James Dean (whom he also discovered). As a demonstration of the kind of performance Kazan is capable of eliciting from an actor, one need only watch the strength and egotism that Andy Griffith put into his role (his first) as the small-time yokel turned TV personality in the still-effective *A Face in the Crowd* (1957).

Largely inactive in films today, Kazan did make a directorial comeback with another literary group project, *The Last Tycoon* (with a script written by Harold Pinter and based on the F. Scott Fitzgerald novel, and Robert de Niro in the lead role). However, he has made only three commercially released features in the past 20 years.

Stanley Kubrick

STANLEY KUBRICK

Born 1928

Filmography:
Fear and Desire, 1953
Killer's Kiss, 1955
The Killing, 1956
Paths of Glory, 1957
Spartacus, 1960
Lolita, 1962
Dr. Strangelove, or How I Learned to Stop Worrying and Love the Bomb, 1964
2001: A Space Odyssey, 1968
A Clockwork Orange, 1971
Barry Lyndon, 1975
The Shining, 1979

Despite the apparent differences in storyline in every one of Stanley Kubrick's projects, the same elements surface again and again: the challenges of adaptation, meticulous film technique, love of technology, closely-honed musical soundtrack, an awkwardness with women and actors, and—above all—a powerful distrust and dislike of the human race.

Kubrick became a staff photographer for *Look* magazine while still a teenager, but he turned to filmmaking as soon as he was able to finance and make a movie on his own. When his earliest effort

met with lukewarm commercial reaction, Kubrick moved to England where he believed he would have more control over his filmmaking projects. He has remained there, working painstakingly on film projects that the fanaticism of their maker imbues with a fascination that spills over into the audience.

Kubrick has become famous for the rigors of his filmmaking and the impossible demands he makes on his co-workers. For example, for the famous scene in *The Shining* where Shelley Duvall discovers a huge manuscript filled with repetitions of the line "All work and no play makes Jack a dull boy," Kubrick apparently insisted that someone actually type the phrase over and over to fill hundreds of pages. He will retake a scene as often as necessary until it satisfies him. His interest in film technology has been the momentum behind several breakthroughs, including the space effects and front-projection technique employed in *2001: A Space Odyssey*; the futuristic sets of *A Clockwork Orange*; the low-light lenses and zooms in *Barry Lyndon*, and the floor-level tracing shots in *The Shining*.

Using wide-angle close-ups in both *Dr. Strangelove* and *A Clockwork Orange* helped create comic-strip characters to people deadly serious stories, which tell of the end of civilization as we know it. Kubrick's negative attitudes toward social institutions have helped create such non-human protagonists (or human protagonists lacking in humanity) as a computer in *2001*, a wooden opportunist in *Barry Lyndon*, and a

vicious sadist in *A Clockwork Orange*. And in every case he has managed to endow these characters with some kind of audience appeal.

Through it all, with every genre Kubrick explores, the most bitter cynicism is at work. Only an elegantly expressed contempt could be responsible for the outrage done to Shelley Winters in *Lolita* or to Shelley Duvall's family instincts in *The Shining*.

And Kubrick brings the audience directly into the line of fire. We ride through the *2001* Stargate without an answer to the mysteries of the universe; we are forced to endure Alex's brutalization in *A Clockwork Orange*, and *The Shining* has the longest fuse of any horror film, with an unrelieved tension that carries through to the bitter end—perhaps the ultimate revenge of the director.

Akira Kurosawa

AKIRA KUROSAWA

Born 1910

Filmography:
Judo Saga, 1943
The Most Beautiful, 1944
Judo Saga II, 1945

The Men Who Tread on the Tiger's Tail, 1945
No Regrets for Our Youth, 1946
Those Who Make Tomorrow, 1946
One Wonderful Sunday, 1947
Drunken Angel, 1948
The Quiet Duel, 1949
Stray Dog, 1949
Rashomon, 1950
Scandal, 1950
The Idiot, 1951
Ikiru (To Live), 1952
Seven Samurai, 1954
I Live in Fear, 1955
The Lower Depths, 1957
Throne of Blood, 1957
The Hidden Fortress, 1958
The Bad Sleep Well, 1960
Yojimbo, 1961
Sanjuro, 1962
High and Low, 1963
Red Beard, 1965
Dodes 'Ka-Den, 1970
Dersu Uzala, 1975
Kagemusha, 1980
Ran, 1984

Kurosawa is perhaps the Japanese director best known to the West. Certainly, he was the first to make himself felt here. Although films had been made in Japan for decades, it was not until *Rashomon*, first released in 1950, surfaced at the Venice Film Festival in 1951 that the international spotlight focused on an awareness of the depth and beauty of Japanese cinema. Since then directors such as Kenji Mizoguchi, Nagisa Oshima, Yasujiro Ozu, and actors such as Toshiro Mifune have been "discovered" by the West, and each one of them acknowledged as a highly original genius.

Kurosawa, however, maintained a reputation as the most western (in the sense of action-packed) of Japanese directors. Although he has made several literary adaptations, even these have been born of material known to the West: *Throne of Blood* was based on Shakespeare's *Macbeth*, and *The Lower Depths* on the play by Gorky. *I Live in Fear*, a movie about a man's paranoid terror of the end of the world, may be seen as the world's first anti-nuke movie. Kurosawa's influence was such that several American films have been obvious remakes of (or clearly highly influenced by) Kurosawa films: observe the parallels between *The Magnificent Seven* and *The Seven Samurai*, *The Outrage* and *Rashomon*, *A Fistful of Dollars* and *Yojimbo*, and *One From the Heart* and *One Wonderful Sunday*.

Through the production efforts of Francis Ford Coppola (the *One From the Heart* connection), Kurosawa returned to active filmmaking, following a financial dry spell in the early '70s and a subsequent suicide attempt. Since then, he has explored the use of color stylistically and expressively, adding a brilliant new depth to his work. The widescreen compositions in *Dersu Uzala* helped the tale of an aging hunter win an Academy Award for best foreign film in 1975, and in the later *Kagemusha* colors flew across the screen in lavish battle and imaginative dream sequences. His most recent movie, *Ran*, is an adaptation of Shakespeare's *King Lear*. Whatever his source, however, the heart of Kurosawa is in his characters, who face life's deepest challenges and conflicts philosophically and open-eyed, no matter how rampant or energetic Kurosawa's style becomes.

John Landis

JOHN LANDIS

Born 1951

Filmography:
Schlock, 1976
Kentucky Fried Movie, 1977
National Lampoon's Animal House, 1978
The Blues Brothers, 1980
An American Werewolf in London, 1981
Thriller (video short), 1983
Trading Places, 1983
Twilight Zone—The Movie (introduction and the bigot episode), 1983

More, faster, bigger was the starting slogan for young John Landis, who rose to fame essentially through mere chutzpah. He first gofered on films in Spain and Yugoslavia, willing to do anything, including falling from horses. Given a chance (who could say "no" to his manic energy?), he found a way into directing by cranking out quick satire, first by parodying the "B" movies he'd been working on (in the truth-in-advertising *Schlock*) and next in the surprise hit *Kentucky Fried Movie*, a collection of wild sophomoric sketches.

One of those sketches— a kung fu parody—

showed enough sense of structure and filmmaking technique to land Landis the wildly lucrative *National Lampoon's Animal House*, a landmark in crude slapstick which continues to be mimicked ad infinitum today. Via *Animal House*, food fights became a standard in modern filmmaking syntax.

Still attempting to pull out the stops, Landis let *The Blues Brothers* go over budget, eliminating any sense of logical narrative for the sake of energy, car crashes, and music. The rock and roll sequences, with James Brown and Aretha Franklin, demonstrate that John Landis did foresee the future combination of rock and reel. His success with Michael Jackson's *Thriller* was no fluke; Landis knows precisely when to use a close-up or a crane shot for maximum thrill impact.

With *An American Werewolf in London* and *Trading Places*, Landis made a first sincere effort to add subtext to the subject matter without sacrificing his yearning for the outrageous. He depicted the most gruesome possibilities of rotting flesh, but at the same time bestowed humor and pathos on his doomed hero—something no adult director had succeeded in doing since *Frankenstein* (1931). And while *Twilight Zone—The Movie* has many prankish Landis touches in its opening and parenthetical segments, the helicopter tragedy that occurred during filming—causing the deaths of three actors— bears testament to his past history of striving for new filmmaking extremes.

For Landis, the merry-go-round of movies is a lifetime ticket.

Fritz Lang

FRITZ LANG

Born 1890
Died 1976

Partial Filmography:
Dr. Mabuse, 1922
Die Niebelungen, 1924
Metropolis, 1927
Spies, 1928
By Rocket to the Moon,
   1929
M, 1931
*The Testament of Dr.
   Mabuse*, 1932
Fury, 1936
You Only Live Once, 1937
You and Me, 1938
*The Return of Frank
   James*, 1940
Western Union, 1941
Man Hunt, 1941
Hangmen Also Die!, 1943
Ministry of Fear, 1944
*The Woman in the Win-
   dow*, 1944
Scarlet Street, 1945
Cloak and Dagger, 1946
*American Guerilla in the
   Philippines*, 1950
House by the River, 1950
Clash by Night, 1952
Rancho Notorious, 1952
The Big Heat, 1953
The Blue Gardenia, 1953
Human Desire, 1954
Moonfleet, 1955
*Beyond a Reasonable
   Doubt*, 1956
While the City Sleeps, 1956
*Journey to the Lost City
   and the Tiger of Bengal*,
   1960
*The Thousand Eyes of Dr.
   Mabuse*, 1961

Fritz Lang brought modern paranoia to the screen. Even his oldest, most dated movies project a recognizable element of today—whatever that may say about the dangers of contemporary civilization.

Lang is one of the few directors whose early German silent films have as great a popular following as do the later sound films he made in America. Lang's sensitivity to the seething streets of pre-war Berlin helps maintain audience sympathy for Peter Lorre as the compulsive child-murderer in *M*—something few directors could do today. (*M* was banned by the Nazis in 1933.) And *Metropolis*, despite story flaws and special effects with strings showing, still has significance as a vision of modern urban claustrophobia. In fact, in 1984 *Metropolis* was successfully re-released in a restored, color-tinted version with a score by Giorgio Moroder.

Lang's films tend to explode into violence in frightening ways, particularly in his American films *Fury*, *You Only Live Once*, and *The Big Heat*. The heroes of these films have injustice heaped upon them, and then they are led on to more extreme conclusions than Hitchcock would ever dare show. Glenn Ford's happy family is virtually exploded into pieces in *The Big Heat*; Henry Fonda's family is divided and destroyed (first its innocence, then its very life) in *You Only Live Once*. Lang understood persecution and knew exactly how to present it most vividly on the screen.

Despite the harshness of Lang's world view, a romantic element surfaces in almost every film. He allowed a love story to take up a good chunk of *Metropolis*; he could not bear to let husband and wife die alone in *You Only Live Once*. In fact, this romantic streak made it hard for Lang to conclude many of his films in a satisfactory manner. In many cases, several different endings were shot, but none of them satisfactorily reconciled the two moods of persecution and romance. Even *M* has two endings in distribution.

Lang is perhaps still best associated with the gritty, urban *film noir* sensibility his American films displayed (*The Woman in the Window*, *Scarlet Street*, *Human Desire*), although late in his career he attempted a fantasy two-part thriller, *Journey to the Lost City and the Tiger of Bengal*. This film was hacked up by the studios and only recently restored (in light of the success of the similarly nostalgic 1981 film, *Raiders of the Lost Ark*). Again, Lang had been ahead of his time, and had been persecuted for it.

As for a single creation, no one (or nothing) better exemplified the Lang chill of suspicion than the unsinkable *Dr. Mabuse*, an embodiment of evil and seduction. The series was sold with the slogan, "Mabuse lives," and it rings more true today than ever. Particularly on the late, late show . . . .

RICHARD LESTER

Born 1932

Filmography:
It's a Trad Dad!, 1962

Richard Lester

The Mouse on the Moon,
   1963
A Hard Day's Night, 1964
Help!, 1965
The Knack, 1965
*A Funny Thing Happened
   on the Way to the
   Forum*, 1966
How I Won the War, 1967
Petulia, 1968
The Bed Sitting Room,
   1969
Juggernaut, 1974
The Three Musketeers,
   1974
The Four Musketeers, 1975
Royal Flash, 1975
The Ritz, 1976
Robin and Marian, 1976
*Butch and Sundance: The
   Early Days*, 1979
Cuba, 1979
Superman II, 1980
Superman III, 1983
Finders Keepers, 1984

Born in Philadelphia, Richard Lester studied clinical psychology, composed music, and sang at the University of Pennsylvania, all before becoming a television director for CBS at the age of 20. His youth, his varied talents, and his restlessness drove him to wander through continental Europe, and he left America only to settle down some time later in England where, again, he found himself directing live television shows and commercials.

When, starting with comic shorts, Lester burst upon the filmmaking scene, the style he brought with him from the video medium did not go unnoticed. His multiple camera angles, jazzy editing, and hyperkinetic technical virtuosity made a timely mark on the cinema of the mid-'60s, particularly in the Beatles films, *A Hard Day's Night* and *Help!*, and in *The Knack*, a stage play that Lester transformed into a zany movie piece.

The tightly-wound Richard Lester movie toy ran down as the '70s progressed. Lester became more cautious following the critical yo-yoing he received for some extremely personal projects. *How I Won the War* and *The Bed Sitting Room* have an experimental character even today; while the funny, sad *Petulia* perhaps single-handedly captures the disillusionment of the Vietnam era better than any movie before or since. As late as 1984—decidedly back-handing the conservative and pro-military trend of moviemaking—he again tackled the Vietnam issue in a farce, *Finders Keepers*, about feeble-minded deserters and $5 million stashed in the coffin of a war hero. The bitter anti-war idea persisted, but was buried in a more temperate style that was both comic and moving.

Lester's costume adventures have modern, revisionist overtones. *Cuba* makes wry comedy of the Batista overthrow, *The Three Musketeers* is pure slapstick (with Raquel Welch showing herself to be a fine comedienne); *The Four Musketeers* is bittersweet; and the prequel *Butch and Sundance: The Early Days* remains more lyrical than active.

In Lester's twist on the Robin Hood legend, *Robin and Marian*, the pair have reached middle-age, and the arrow that flies off into infinity at the end of the film must ultimately have landed in Lester's own heart; Lester's patented filmmaking technique has become blurred by commercialism and public disinterest.

Ernst Lubitsch

ERNST LUBITSCH

Born 1892
Died 1947

American Filmography:
Rosita, 1923
The Marriage Circle, 1924
Forbidden Paradise, 1924
Kiss Me Again, 1925
Lady Windermere's Fan, 1925
Three Women, 1924
So This Is Paris, 1926
The Student Prince, 1927
The Patriot, 1928
Eternal Love, 1929
The Love Parade, 1929
Monte Carlo, 1930
Paramount on Parade, 1930
The Smiling Lieutenant, 1931
If I Had a Million, 1932
The Man I Killed, 1932
One Hour With You, 1932
Trouble in Paradise, 1932
Design for Living, 1933
The Merry Widow, 1934
Angel, 1937
Bluebeard's Eighth Wife, 1938

Ninotchka, 1939
The Shop Around the Corner, 1940
That Uncertain Feeling, 1941
To Be or Not To Be, 1942
Heaven Can Wait, 1943
Cluny Brown, 1946
That Lady in Ermine, 1948 (co-directed with Otto Preminger)

The Lubitsch Touch! Golden household words in the 1930s that referred to a kind of comedy filmmakers today have no chance of recreating, try though they may.

Ernst Lubitsch profited from making movies at a time when the censorship office held tight rein over film subject matter. His sophisticated, subtle comedies relied upon wit and maturity to make their point, and would surely have done so regardless of the censorship laws.

A German vaudevillian and comedian, Lubitsch reached international success with his silent film comedies. Mary Pickford insisted he come to America to direct her in a picture, but his American success came with a different project, *The Marriage Circle* in 1924. His themes became very American in content—dealing with the two giants of sex and money—although they remained Continental in flair.

Lubitsch found new ways to direct both Garbo (in *Ninotchka*) and Lombard (in *To Be or Not To Be*). His ability to find meaning in a raised eyebrow or a subtle glance may have ebbed, but as late as 1946 *Cluny Brown*, with Jennifer Jones and Charles Boyer, revelled in the kind of comic dialogue screenwriters no longer bother to produce.

Another comic film-maker, Preston Sturges (1898–1959), became a last-gasp sophisticated successor to Lubitsch, almost too intelligent for Hollywood's tastes. With *The Great McGinty* (1940), *Christmas in July* (1940), *The Lady Eve* (1941), *Sullivan's Travels* (1941), *The Palm Beach Story* (1942), *The Miracle of Morgan's Creek* (1944), *Hail the Conquering Hero* (1944), and others, Sturges concocted clever contrivances of wit, cramming ideas about wealth, marriage, multiple illegitimacies, and mass hysteria into brash, wise-acre movies that James Agee called as exhilarating as "taking a nun on a roller coaster."

For these two, a nudge was as good as a kick. With the floodgates opened, today's movie-makers can only feign innocence, copy, and fail.

George Lucas

GEORGE LUCAS

Born 1944

Filmography:
THX-1138, 1971
American Graffiti, 1974
Star Wars, 1977

Young George Lucas is a modern-day Homer (although, of course, far more widely accessible), casting epic spells upon an international audience of millions. The *Star Wars* saga ensures his own eternal presence in celestial celluloid. Turning 40 in 1984, Lucas can well afford to proceed in any direction he pleases, but it seems clear that his interests lie more in the development of myths—surrounding himself and others light-years away—than in the actual directing of the tales.

For such a powerful presence, Lucas has directed only three features, fewer than any of his contemporaries. The clinical, ultra-white science-fiction atmosphere of his first feature, *THX-1138*, was developed during studies at the University of Southern California film school, where Lucas soon realized that this overpowering interest in technology would have more meaning if disguised in appealing human characteristics. As a result, *Star Wars* and the sequels pay homage to humanity's assumed goodness, through a religious power named, unembarrassingly, "The Force." The irony, though, is that ultimately laser guns, the power of hyperspace, the regenerating limbs and lives of polished chrome robots, and massive special effects preserve the Rebel troups and all they stand for against the techno-heavy Empire. Jedi Knights preach purity and wear old-fashioned bathrobes, but Han Solo pulls the ultimate triggers of time.

Like a beautiful go-between, *American Graffiti* paints a spin-back, waxed-glow reflection upon many of the same themes *Star Wars* later explored: humanism, romantic ad-

venture, and nostalgia for lost eras we need never have personally known. (*Star Wars*, too, takes place "long, long ago" rather than in the future.) Constant radio waves provide an environment for 1962 Modesto, California, rather than outer space. The spiritual guru is Wolfman Jack instead of Ben Kenobi. Through the combined power of automobiles, rock and roll, and white-socked uniforms, the teens in *American Graffiti* travel in ritual quest to adulthood, typified by a Woman in White, driving her sleek Thunderbird craft.

A filmmaker exclusively of the '70s, Lucas generated magic for a bland age, bridging a gap between the political energy of the '60s and the commercial realities of the '80s. It is no surprise that he contents himself with refining pet products. If he never again risks new ground, the massive wealth generated by his personal movie industry has in itself created a mythology of modern life, a place where heroic experience in the arms of technology provides flint for sparks in eyes around the world.

Now that Lucas' focus seems so intently set on production rather than direction, it will be interesting to observe whether or not he ever returns to the directorial field—especially since he has been quoted as saying, "I hate directing." Since *Star Wars* in 1977, Lucas has acted as executive producer and co-scenarist on three major commercial successes: *The Empire Strikes Back* (1980), *Raiders of the Lost Ark* (1981), and *Return of the Jedi* (1983).

Sidney Lumet

SIDNEY LUMET

Born 1924

Filmography:
Twelve Angry Men, 1957
Stage Struck, 1958
That Kind of Woman, 1959
The Fugitive Kind, 1960
Long Day's Journey into Night, 1962
A View From the Bridge, 1962
Fail-Safe, 1964
The Pawnbroker, 1965
The Hill, 1965
The Group, 1966
The Deadly Affair, 1967
Bye Bye Braverman, 1968
The Seagull, 1968
The Appointment, 1969
Blood Kin, 1969
King: A Film Record, 1970
The Anderson Tapes, 1971
Child's Play, 1972
The Offence, 1973
Serpico, 1973
Lovin' Molly, 1974
Murder on the Orient Express, 1974
Dog Day Afternoon, 1975
Network, 1976
Equus, 1977
The Wiz, 1978
Just Tell Me What You Want, 1980
Prince of the City, 1981
Deathtrap, 1982
The Verdict, 1982
Daniel, 1983

Who is to blame for injustice in the world? This is the loaded question most frequently posed in Sidney Lumet's films.

Lumet was a child actor who followed the uphill route through summer stock, television, and theatrical directing before arriving at the movies, where he has—with few breaks—directed a film a year since 1957. *Twelve Angry Men*, a courtroom drama commissioned by Henry Fonda on the basis of Lumet's TV work, was well received, and Lumet has been carefully selective in finding tasteful projects throughout his career.

Lumet is a celebrated New Yorker, more so than any one else making films today (with the exception of Woody Allen). Most of his films have been based in New York rather than in Hollywood. His roots in the theatre have led him to take on certain projects he might better have left alone: *Equus*, *The Wiz*, *Deathtrap*. But he takes the necessary risks with film style and subject matter, using whatever means are needed to get the message across. In *The Verdict*, we watch Paul Newman stare at a developing Polaroid for what seems like minutes, as the character's awareness of his responsibility and need for involvement slowly sinks in. *Prince of the City* ran an hour longer than most cop films because Lumet wanted to explain more than one side of the story. *Network* gave a slogan to the vidiot nation ("I'm as mad as hell, and I'm not going to take it any more"), but Lumet is more interested in making us aware of the injustices that exist all around us than in actually depicting change.

For perhaps that reason, Lumet has repeatedly, throughout his career, selected subjects that show up the functions of and flaws in the judicial system. Like a good judge, he is curious in both his comedy and his drama about why people behave as they do. In *The Pawnbroker*, *Serpico*, *Dog Day Afternoon*, *Daniel*, and many other of his movies, Lumet asks himself and his audiences, where can there be justice?

Paul Mazursky

PAUL MAZURSKY

Born 1930

Filmography:
Bob & Carol & Ted & Alice, 1969
Alex in Wonderland, 1970
Blume in Love, 1973
Harry and Tonto, 1974
Next Stop Greenwich Village, 1976
An Unmarried Woman, 1978
Willie and Phil, 1980
The Tempest, 1982
Moscow on the Hudson, 1984

Paul Mazursky's name has become a buzz word over the course of three

different decades, during which he has taken it upon himself to explore contemporary relationships.

Mazursky was first known as an actor and a comic, appearing in important roles in *The Blackboard Jungle* (1955) and (more recently) in *A Star Is Born*. He also makes unusual cameo appearances in his own movies, as the homosexual cruiser in *Harry and Tonto*, for example. His collaborative screenplay for Peter Sellers in *I Love You Alice B. Toklas* started him on the road to filmmaking.

While cutting to the bone of modern relationships is his standard theme, Mazursky will sometimes sink into autobiography, affectation, and sentimentality. *Bob & Carol & Ted & Alice*, the 1969 encounter group movie, holds up remarkably well today, except for the hallucinatory worldlove ending. In 1984, *Moscow on the Hudson* shows how an immigrant learns to appreciate American friendships, but the film is peppered with moments of embarrassing flagwaving.

Mazursky tells tales about the ways all sorts of people get along, the old, the young, the divorced and barely married, native New Yorkers and aliens, even threesomes. He explores them all. References to Shakespeare, Truffaut, and Fellini notwithstanding, Mazursky's philosophy is most clearly voiced when he confronts the issues of what it means to be involved in relationships in the 20th century. Even in his less successful efforts, one feels that the confrontation has been a genuine attempt to get to grips with reality.

Vincente Minnelli

VINCENTE MINNELLI

Born 1910

Filmography:
Cabin in the Sky, 1943
I Dood It, 1943
Meet Me in St. Louis, 1944
The Clock, 1945
Yolanda and the Thief, 1945
Undercurrent, 1946
Ziegfeld Follies, 1946
The Pirate, 1948
Madame Bovary, 1949
Father of the Bride, 1950
An American in Paris, 1951
Father's Little Dividend, 1951
The Bad and the Beautiful, 1953
The Band Wagon, 1953
The Story of Three Loves ("Mademoiselle" episode), 1953
Brigadoon, 1954
The Long, Long Trailer, 1954
The Cobweb, 1955
Kismet, 1955
Lust for Life, 1956
Tea and Sympathy, 1956
Designing Woman, 1957
The Seventh Sin, 1957 (co-directed with Ronald Neame, uncredited)
Gigi, 1958

The Reluctant Debutante, 1958
Some Came Running, 1959
Bells Are Ringing, 1960
Home From the Hill, 1960
The Four Horsemen of the Apocalypse, 1962
Two Weeks in Another Town, 1962
The Courtship of Eddie's Father, 1963
Goodbye Charlie, 1964
The Sandpiper, 1965
On a Clear Day You Can See Forever, 1970
A Matter of Time, 1976

Vincente Minnelli has said, "A story must be told in the most stylistic way to allow the introduction of a little magic. The search for an appropriate style is as important for a musical comedy as for a dramatic film." Few directors have described more accurately their own methods of approaching filmmaking.

Artist, painter, photographer, and designer of costumes and sets, Minnelli became art director of New York's Radio City Music Hall in 1933. His lavish work as director on stage shows such as the *Ziegfeld Follies* and *Very Warm for May* was respected for his use of splashy color and visual design. Arthur Freed, the great producer of MGM movie musicals, lured Minnelli to Hollywood in 1940. As a moviemaking apprentice, Minnelli staged musical numbers for the Busby Berkeley films, *Strike Up the Band* (1940) and *Babes on Broadway* (1942), both with Judy Garland. Minnelli and Garland married in 1945.

Minnelli, in becoming a film director himself, created some of the most lavish and notable products of Hollywood's musical heyday in the 1940s and 1950s. His penchant for "style" became appropriate to musicals of many moods, from the nostalgic *Meet Me in St. Louis* to the ultramodern *An American in Paris*.

Virtually all of Minnelli's musicals are recognizable by name, and virtually all are memorable. Nevertheless, of all the films he directed the non-musicals outnumber the musicals. *Madame Bovary* drew on the French literary masterpiece, lavishly costumed to add visual interest.

Minnelli's inside exposés of Hollywood in *The Bad and the Beautiful* and the sequel (of sorts) *Two Weeks in Another Town* relied for effect on the flowering of exaggerated emotions rather than on elaborately drawn sets. And *Lust for Life* was the perfect vehicle for a Minnelli drama, allowing the director to tell the story of Vincent van Gogh, a colorist painter who used a different kind of canvas. Adaptation, drama or biography, dream-like touches in Minnelli's films allow style to triumph over substance.

When age and public taste threatened his productivity, Minnelli made *A Matter of Time* with Ingrid Bergman and his own daughter, Liza. But the film was so severely re-edited by the studio that it is impossible to tell what remains of the Minnelli talent for decorating his story.

Minnelli took the lead in making color sing in the movies, particularly during the '50s when the three-process Technicolor became the new standard. His images haven't faded, and Minnelli's movies seem even brighter as time goes by.

Sam Peckinpah

SAM PECKINPAH

Born 1925

Filmography:
The Deadly Companions, 1961
Ride the High Country, 1962
Major Dundee, 1965
The Wild Bunch, 1969
The Ballad of Cable Hogue, 1970
Straw Dogs, 1971
The Getaway, 1972
Junior Bonner, 1972
Pat Garrett and Billy the Kid, 1973
Bring Me the Head of Alfredo Garcia, 1974
The Killer Elite, 1975
Cross of Iron, 1977
Convoy, 1978
The Osterman Weekend, 1983

"God is a sadist," says a character in Peckinpah's *Cross of Iron*, "and He probably doesn't even know it." The quote has typical Peckinpah punch: hard-hitting, thought-provoking, brash, self-important.

Sam Peckinpah is known as the father of the blood ballet, graphic slow motion sequences of flying limbs and broken bodies. Some viewers find beauty in these scenes, because they disguise the horror of the acts with the ex-

pressiveness of sheer color and motion on the screen. Peckinpah is a film artist in spite of his chosen subject matter.

In *The Wild Bunch* Peckinpah's directorial credit appears after William Holden speaks the line, "If they move, kill them." It isn't simply that Peckinpah wants to threaten his audience; perhaps he feels threatened himself and wants to share the feeling. The paranoia of the weakling played by Dustin Hoffman in *Straw Dogs* and the characters played by James Caan in *The Killer Elite*, Rutger Hauer in *The Osterman Weekend*, and Warren Oates in *Bring Me the Head of Alfredo Garcia* are testament to justifiable fear. Each of these characters is threatened or betrayed by friends, family, or once-trusted business associates. Peckinpah's own paranoias may stem from the fact that his films have constantly been tampered with by studio heads.

After serving with the Marines in China, Peckinpah became a drama student at the University of Southern California, where he received his Master's degree. After acting and directing on the stage, he left the theatre to work in television as stagehand, screenplay writer, and director (particularly of TV westerns). When he started making feature films, the influence of his own family background became apparent. He is a descendant of two pioneer settler families, and his violent films have reflected a preoccupation with the ambivalent morality that characterized the legendary West.

Peckinpah's films are filled with graphic vio-

lence. He'll think nothing of showing a decapitated head bouncing in the back seat of a car. As his characters lose their innocence, Peckinpah introduces images of children playing or birds singing before letting the bomb explode or the bloody fireworks begin. This motif is seen in *The Wild Bunch*, in *The Killer Elite*, and in *Cross of Iron*. But by the end of a Peckinpah movie, nothing is left untainted or unscarred.

Over the years, Peckinpah's stylized vision and pessimistic reality has degenerated, because of studio pressures and his own disenchantment with the system. And increasingly, a cartoon-like style has entered his now sporadic filmmaking. The truckstop brawls in *Convoy* spatter ketchup rather than blood, and the confrontations in *The Osterman Weekend* make do with farfetched weaponry, video gimmicks, and unlikely family situations. Although his touch has weakened, the Peckinpah personality still surfaces, displaying—as *The Osterman Weekend* does so schematically—the mistrust of former friends now engaged in violent conflict.

ROMAN POLANSKI

Born 1933

Partial Filmography:
Knife in the Water, 1962
Repulsion, 1965
Cul-de-Sac, 1966
The Fearless Vampire Killers, or Pardon Me But Your Teeth Are in My Neck, 1967

Roman Polanski

Rosemary's Baby, 1968
Macbeth, 1971
What?, 1973
Chinatown, 1974
*Diary of Forbidden
    Dreams*, 1976
The Tenant, 1976
Tess, 1979

We have again and again excused the perversity of Roman Polanski on the grounds of the brilliance of his genius and the outrage of his life history. However, his recent autobiography, *Roman*, may have both obscured and exaggerated his pain, rather than shedding light on the strange facts behind Polanski's obsessions.

Polanski's mother died in a Nazi concentration camp. His childhood was filled with horrors of abandonment and terror. His wife, actress Sharon Tate, pregnant with his child, was gruesomely murdered by the Manson family. Is it any wonder that he has created some of the most powerful concepts of evil ever seen on the screen?

When we look at Polanski's films—divorced, if that is possible, from his life—we see humiliation. No matter how dreadful a life becomes, someone is around to mock it. The hero of *Knife in the Water* is given a final choice: to accept that he has killed a man, or to believe that his wife was unfaithful. *Repul-*

sion lives up to its name by turning the lovely Catherine Deneuve into a lonely butcher. In *Rosemary's Baby*, Polanski's first major hit, not only is the wife betrayed by her own husband, but in the film's final twist she actually accepts her awful fate. In *Chinatown* Faye Dunaway is forced to admit that her father had also been the father of her child.

Nothing is beyond limits for Polanski. Having seen too much, he wants the world to share the dark vision. The ideas contained in his films lodge in the mind more frighteningly and more disturbingly than the graphic gore of a dozen mad-slasher bloodbaths. And the fact that he directed a bloody version of *Macbeth* following the death of his own family is incomprehensibly callous in itself.

The emptiness, cynicism, and black humor that pervade all Polanski movies have hampered his attempts to make film comedy—*Cul-de-Sac, The Fearless Vampire Killers*, and *What?* Even *Tess*, his epic adaptation of Thomas Hardy's novel, is a tragic story of innocence betrayed—and the fact that it unleashed upon the movie world the dubious talents of Nastassja Kinski may be Polanski's last laugh at filmmaking.

Although he was driven from America following his conviction for sexual involvement with a 13-year-old girl, Polanski still hopes to return to the United States. He continues to work in Europe on both stage and film projects. One wonders, however, if he will ever make the movie that will exorcise the demons that bedevil his own life.

Martin Ritt

MARTIN RITT

Born 1920

Filmography:
Edge of the City, 1957
No Down Payment, 1957
The Long Hot Summer,
    1958
The Black Orchid, 1959
The Sound and the Fury,
    1959
Five Branded Women, 1960
Paris Blues, 1961
*Hemingway's Adventures
    of a Young Man*, 1962
Hud, 1963
The Outrage, 1964
*The Spy Who Came in
    From the Cold*, 1965
Hombre, 1967
The Brotherhood, 1968
The Great White Hope,
    1970
The Molly Maguires, 1970
Pete 'n' Tillie, 1972
Sounder, 1972
Conrack, 1974
The Front, 1976
Casey's Shadow, 1978
Norma Rae, 1979
Back Roads, 1981
Cross Creek, 1983

Martin Ritt was a Broadway actor at the age of 17, playing in *Golden Boy*. During World War II he was given leave from the USAAF Special Forces to appear in the stage and movie versions of *Winged Victory*. His early theatre experience led to directing assignments on Broadway and for television. He also

taught acting at the Actors' Studio, where one of his best pupils was Paul Newman, who later starred in several of Ritt's movies.

Ritt's movies have a reputation for dealing with intellectual subjects, but truthfully speaking, the subject matter most frequently flaunted reflects liberal stereotypes. He has certainly taken on some difficult ideas and converted them to the screen—his sources include literature, theatre, politics, racial tensions, and regional lifestyles—but many of his movies offer teary-eyed, pat solutions instead of truly satisfying conclusions. Ritt adapted for the screen Faulkner (*The Long Hot Summer, The Sound and the Fury*), Hemingway, and Kurosawa (*The Outrage* is a remake of *Rashomon*). He has also fashioned popular entertainments by using unpopular topics as pegs for comedies or romances—cancer in *Pete 'n' Tillie*, blacklisting in *The Front*, and labor unions in *Norma Rae*. Nor is he above stacking the deck (and jerking the tears) by adding children (*Conrack*) and/or animals (*Casey's Shadow*) to his scripts.

Known for fastidious craftsmanship, Ritt takes on "heavy" films and makes them commercially palatable. He also has a talent for maintaining a strong sense of period and place whenever he makes a film with an unusual location. Most recently, Ritt has again shown interest in making movies about the American South, as he had done earlier with the Faulkner films.

But what makes Ritt movies a cut above average is the naturalistic performances he elicits from actors, regardless of their emotional and political leanings. Sally Field as the feisty labor leader *Norma Rae*, Woody Allen as a prolific but fake writer in *The Front*, or Carol Burnett railing against God's unfairness in *Pete 'n' Tillie* all demonstrate Ritt's power to recognize performance jewels in the rough.

Paul Schrader

PAUL SCHRADER

Born 1946

Filmography:
Blue Collar, 1978
American Gigolo, 1979
Hardcore, 1979
Cat People, 1982

Paul Schrader has secrets. The public may not understand what he's trying to say in his films, but Schrader doesn't care because his films are designed to work on two levels, the popular level as well as the intellectual one. Crowds may flock to see Richard Gere strut and flex his muscles in *American Gigolo*, while Schrader rejoices privately in his hidden references to French religious ideas or Japanese camera angles. The very last scene of the film, in fact, is a word-for-

word recreation from Robert Bresson's 1959 film *Pickpocket*, a movie about salvation through grace.

The son of strict Calvinists, Schrader was forbidden as a child to see movies. At divinity school he became obsessed with the medium of film and eventually wrote his dissertation on the religious elements in the films of three directors: Yasujiro Ozu, Robert Bresson, and Carl Dreyer. Schrader's screenplays are filled with references to two formative influences: the repressions and guilts associated with his religious upbringing; and the three directors and their ideas of grace and fate.

On the surface Schrader's films may seem exceedingly amoral or immoral. As a screenwriter he has dealt with hopelessness and loss (*Rolling Thunder*, 1977), the emptiness of calculated revenge (*Old Boyfriends*, 1979), and responses to a corrupt world (*Taxi Driver*, 1976). His other screenwriting credits include *Obsession* (1976), *The Yakuza* (1975), and *Raging Bull* (1980).

As a screenwriter/director, Schrader has made films that expose his roots. *Blue Collar* is one of the few modern films to both honor and question the work ethic; *Hardcore* bears evidence of the sexual inhibitions of his Midwest upbringing; *American Gigolo* depicts sexual amorality redeemed by the pure love of another; and *Cat People* is nothing if not a meditation on the abject fear of sexual liberation.

With whatever graphic depictions Schrader shocks his audience (a snuff film in *Hardcore*, a

limb torn from its socket in *Cat People*), every story he writes is grounded in moral frustration, a plea for hope against all hope.

Martin Scorsese

MARTIN SCORSESE

Born 1942

Filmography:
Who's That Knocking on My Door?, 1968
Boxcar Bertha, 1972
Mean Streets, 1973
Alice Doesn't Live Here Anymore, 1974
Taxi Driver, 1976
New York, New York, 1977
The Last Waltz, 1978
Raging Bull, 1980
King of Comedy, 1983

Raised in Manhattan's Little Italy, Martin Scorsese grew up sickly in a tough neighborhood— he belonged to a neighborhood gang. He was educated by Catholic priests, and at one point considered the priesthood for himself. (Instead, however, he entered New York University and obtained two degrees in film studies.) The movies he makes today reflect the energetic, nervous, fast-talking, film-conscious, urban elements that he grew up with.

Scorsese's characters, no matter how prominent or appealing they may be,

have irritating traits that grate on the viewer. And each film he releases brings controversy with it. Perhaps the greatest controversy occurred in retrospect, when John Hinckley, Jr. reenacted elements of *Taxi Driver* and shot President Ronald Reagan. Like *Taxi Driver*, *King of Comedy* deals with the conflicts between painfully average men and their dreams of greatness. And in both films, the tables turn unexpectedly to portray the American public as a fickle mob easily manipulated by the power of the media. The killer becomes a hero, the abductor a talk show host.

Scorsese remains faithful to his film school precepts. His feature films have been commercial, but he returns to documentary shorts and features (*The Last Waltz*) from time to time. His first acclaimed hit, *Mean Streets*, replaced a story line with character, motion and color, which harmed it at the box office (despite the fact that the movie introduced both Robert de Niro and Harvey Keitel to the screen). In a campaign against Hollywood's use of deteriorating color film stock, Scorsese decided to film and release *Raging Bull* mostly in black and white.

Scorsese's films deal with urgency in motion, with characters—even those who are basically inarticulate—who speak (as Scorsese does) quickly and frantically. In *New York, New York*, most of Robert de Niro's lines were repeated at least twice, insistently, as if to make sure he was getting his idea across. "I want to be with you. I want to be with you. Do you want to be with me? Do you want to be with me?" The movie was even commercially released twice, first in 1977, and again in 1981 with the addition of "Happy Endings," Liza Minnelli's big musical number.

The truth is that it's hard to digest a Scorsese movie in just one viewing. Each film has such originality and verve that it takes time to appreciate Scorsese's special skills.

Currently Scorsese is preparing the screen version of Nikos Kazantzakis's *The Last Temptation of Christ*. It's an interesting exercise to speculate how Scorsese will turn Jesus and his disciples into irksome, inarticulate bundles of nerves.

Steven Spielberg

STEVEN SPIELBERG

Born 1947

Filmography:
Duel (originally made for TV), 1971
The Sugarland Express, 1973
Jaws, 1975
Close Encounters of the Third Kind, 1977
1941, 1979
Raiders of the Lost Ark, 1981
E.T. The Extra-Terrestrial, 1982

Twilight Zone—The Movie ("Kick the Can" episode), 1983
Indiana Jones and the Temple of Doom, 1984

Steven Spielberg, now a household name, began directing his own films almost before he could walk. All through his teens, his home movies won awards. Universal hired him to make TV films following his California State College studies, and his first endeavor, *Duel*, has proven to be a seminal and long-lived study of man against machine.

The theme of ordinary humans confronting a power of supernatural strength has persisted throughout his films. Spielberg's negative forces or villains all display awesome, seemingly unconquerable power: the driverless truck in *Duel*, the massive police force of *The Sugarland Express*, the great white shark in *Jaws*, the media and government blockade and cover-up in *Close Encounters*, and countless obstacles in both *Indiana Jones* movies. *1941*, Spielberg's attempt to make expensive slapstick of World War II, brought in all the wow-inducing effects, but the film failed to click for lack of a central human focus.

Spielberg's family protagonists, on the other hand, are folks who watch television in suburban homes, who have no pretensions, and who dream of home and hearth—even when they fail to live up to even these simple aspirations. His protectiveness of family in *The Sugarland Express* is obsessive; the police chief's family in *Jaws* gives emotional power to the threatening terror; and Spielberg's

most recent films present recombined family units, such as the unmarried makeshift trios in *Close Encounters* and *Indiana Jones and the Temple of Doom*.

Spielberg's identification with the so-called average American has recently approached arrogance, especially in the Indiana Jones character, who has become a symbol of self-important ("*Dr. Jones, to you*"), crude, and racist pandering to the ticket-buying audiences.

Spielberg's movies continue to express innocence with state-of-the-art filmmaking powers. He has a way with children, who act naturally as they are led to the edge of danger. Spielberg, ultimately, makes movies that seek to rediscover the child in all of us, and in himself. To a child, every power appears larger than life. Spielberg wants us all to gasp at his larger-than-life movies, but he recognized the limitations of this regression when, in his *Twilight Zone* segment, he portrayed old folks who were given a second chance at youth. They rejected it.

To Spielberg, obviously, pulling the power strings is as much or more fun than sitting in the audience. Perhaps that power has gotten out of hand with the gratuitous violence-for-the-sake-of-violence evidenced in *Indiana Jones and the Temple of Doom*.

As his power has grown, Spielberg has increased his visibility as a name-above-the-title producer, giving his influence but not his directorial talents to films such as *Poltergeist* (1982) and *Gremlins* (1984).

François Truffaut

FRANÇOIS TRUFFAUT

Born 1932

Filmography:
The Four Hundred Blows, 1959
Shoot the Piano Player, 1960
Jules and Jim, 1961
The Soft Skin, 1964
Fahrenheit 451, 1966
Stolen Kisses, 1968
Mississippi Mermaid, 1969
Bed and Board, 1970
The Wild Child, 1970
Two English Girls, 1971
Day for Night, 1973
The Story of Adele H., 1975
Small Change, 1976
The Man Who Loved Women, 1977
The Green Room, 1978
Love on the Run, 1979
The Last Metro, 1980
The Woman Next Door, 1981
Confidentially Yours, 1984

Love and romance and their many manifestations are the themes played out in the films of François Truffaut.

After a difficult and unhappy childhood, Truffaut's sheer fascination with movies eased his way into the movie business. He became an outspoken critic of films, and helped revitalize the French film industry as one of the New Wave of critic/directors taking up the challenge to make the kind of movies he believed in. He has made movies ever since and, in the process, has risen to international fame.

A series of his movies have been openly autobiographical, starring Jean-Pierre Leaud as his childhood surrogate (*The Four Hundred Blows*) and his alter ego through young adulthood (*Stolen Kisses, Bed and Board*). Inevitably, these tales deal with romance, although Truffaut's fondness for children—especially those who, like himself, lacked special attention—has been responsible for some sensitive, touching portraits such as *The Wild Child* and *Small Change*.

Occasionally, Truffaut still dabbles in writing or criticism, contributing to a collection of essays by his late mentor André Bazin or commenting on his extensive interviews with Alfred Hitchcock—one of the directors whom the French New Wave helped to achieve critical prominence.

Having been responsible for the best "love triangle" movies ever made (*Jules and Jim, Two English Girls*, and the more recent *The Woman Next Door*), Truffaut continues to pursue the mysteries of hopeless romance. The most extreme example of this was in *The Story of Adele H.*, in which the daughter of Victor Hugo followed her impossible love to the ends and depths of the earth. But Truffaut adds nobility to the pursuit, and his themes are bittersweet. What is true romance, after all, but an attempt to possess some fleeting emotion—even if only for a movie's two hours.

Lina Wertmuller

LINA WERTMULLER

Born 1928

Filmography:
The Lizards, 1963
Let's Talk About Men, 1965
Rita the Mosquito (musical numbers only), 1966
Don't Sting the Mosquito (musical numbers only), 1967
The Seduction of Mimi, 1972
Love and Anarchy, 1973
All Screwed Up, 1974
Swept Away . . . By an Unusual Destiny in the Blue Sea of August, 1974
Seven Beauties, 1976
The End of the World in Our Usual Bed in a Night Full of Rain, 1978
Shimmy Lagano Tarantelle e Vino, 1978
Revenge, 1979

Born Arcangela Felice Assunta Wertmuller von Elgg in Rome, Lina Wertmuller became a stage actress and director. In her early years in the theatre she met actor Giancarlo Giannini, and their later film collaboration brought international recognition to both.

After an assistantship with Fellini on *8½*, Wertmuller began to direct some of the successful screenplays that she had been writing. When two of her films, *Swept Away* and *Seven Beauties*, were successful in the mid-'70s, several of her earlier films were "rediscovered." The films she has made since then, however, have not been well received, and she returned for a time to directing in the theatre. She is married to Enrico Job, a set designer and her frequent collaborator.

The importance of Lina Wertmuller to film history is, in part, that she made her mark at a time when very few working film directors were women. Wertmuller, striking and imposing in her angular trademark eyeglasses, became the film world's "token" woman director—an acknowledgment that women could indeed write and direct commercial films. Her stories deal prominently with class systems and power plays within class structures, and, naturally enough, her work gets a lot of attention—some positive, some not—from women. Some feminists were infuriated by the fact that in *Swept Away* a male servant (played by Giannini) dominates and abuses the aristocratic woman who is shipwrecked on the island with him, yet she subsequently falls in love with him. Wertmuller explained it as a role reversal: that the male social underdog actually symbolized the women of the world. Some bought that explanation and others didn't; but despite the contradictory responses to the male/female situation the film was a great success with both male and female audiences.

Wertmuller's other films display a strong division between the sexes, and sexual humiliation (particularly in work situations) becomes her primary metaphor for society. She carried the parallel to its pinnacle in *Seven Beauties*, where a handsome Nazi concentration camp prisoner (again played by Giannini) submits to his cruel female guardian as a means of sheer survival.

Since the mid-'70s many young and independent women directors have entered the medium, among them Joan Micklin Silver, Anna Thomas, Martha Coolidge (*Valley Girl*, 1983), Joan Darling (*First Love*, 1977), and a number of documentary filmmakers.

And setting aside the sex issue, Wertmuller's films, freed of the burden of being singled out as "women's" films, stand up trenchantly as the work of a bold, intelligent, politically conscious director.

Billy Wilder

BILLY WILDER

Born 1906

American Filmography:
The Major and the Minor, 1942

Billy Wilder was born in Vienna, and he worked as a newspaper reporter while trying to succeed as a screenwriter. He was able to collaborate on and co-direct several German films before fleeing Hitler in 1933. (His family died in concentration camps.)

In Hollywood, Wilder lived with actor Peter Lorre until he learned enough English to again begin writing screenplays. His successful scripts of the '30s and '40s were frequently co-written with Charles Brackett. Later, he wrote and directed with I.A.L. Diamond.

There are two aspects of Wilder's work that are unmistakable. One is an emphasis on writing, which is evident in the several films he made about the profession, including *The Lost Weekend*, *Ace in the Hole*, and *The Front Page*. This preoccupation with the written word is also evident in the fact that many of his films use narrators—the most uncanny example being in *Sunset Boulevard*, when William Holden tells his story from beyond the grave.

The second Wilder trait is his persistent comic cynicism. On occasion his heartlessness is callous beyond belief. His reporter in *Ace in the Hole*, for instance, is so determined to get a good news story that he allows a man to die trapped underground. The alcoholic of *The Lost Weekend* is redeemed only by Hollywood's demand for a happy ending: it seemed Wilder would have preferred to fade out laughing on a man in the final stages of delirium tremens. *Sunset Boulevard* mockingly disassembles the disposable glory of stardom. The *Fortune Cookie* lambastes lawsuits and lawyers; *One, Two, Three* snipes at Cold War tensions; and *Kiss Me, Stupid* (perhaps Wilder's most precocious film and the one featuring the most contemptible character) makes mincemeat of matrimony. *Buddy Buddy*, using two of his favorite actors, Jack Lemmon and Walter Matthau, dealt with a hit man whose job is interrupted by a persistent would-be suicide.

Wilder's films have generally been very successful, despite (or because of) his utter sarcasm. Although he hasn't lost any of his bite, his recent films have seemed dated before they even opened.

The more things change, according to Wilder's filmmaking perspective, the lousier they get.

QUOTES FROM
DIRECTORS (AND SOME OTHERS) ON DIRECTING

Everyone has a theory—or, in most cases, a whole bunch of theories—about what they do for a living. Directors and others involved in the making of movies are certainly no exceptions. Here's what some of them have to say about their craft.

Cinema is the director's medium beyond all others. If you're directing, you have the opportunity to put your signature on the bottom of the frame. You have the opportunity to say, "That is what I believe."

—Richard Attenborough

What is a picture? . . . a picture is a state of mind. Often a picture, when it is good, is the result of some inner belief which is so strong that you show what you want in spite of a stupid story. . . . A picture is a whole; you cannot say this is the beginning, this is the end, and this is the middle.

—Jean Renoir

I've been waiting for Hollywood to leave me alone and stop forcing me to make these thirty-million-dollar movies, so I can get around to making something I really want to make.

—Steven Spielberg

You know when I knew I had some talent? I'll tell you the day I knew, because I remember it. It was right smack dab in the middle of shooting Apocalypse Now. *I was in the middle of the Philippines and one day I knew I had talent.*

—Francis Ford Coppola

A director should create a climate in which people can make fools of themselves with freedom.

—George Cukor

Film lovers are sick people. One goes into a movie house to seek a sense of security. One looks for something that is better organized than the world in which we live, and if one goes back to see the same film over and over, it's to be in a world where you can predict everything that is going to happen. I don't know if once one becomes a director one is cured.

—François Truffaut

It's absolutely impossible to improvise. Making a movie is a mathematical operation. It is like sending a missile to the moon. Art is a scientific operation.

—Federico Fellini

The difference between me and [Ernst] Lubitsch is that he shows you the king on his throne and then he shows the king in his bedroom. I show the king in his bedroom first. In that way, when you see him on the throne, you've no illusions about him.

—Erich von Stroheim

The reason I did Annie *was that Ray Stark called me on the telephone and asked me . . . I thought about it for all of eight seconds before saying yes. Meditative processes were not involved.*

—John Huston

Sometimes you have to lie. One often has to distort a thing to catch its true spirit.

—Robert J. Flaherty, documentary filmmaker

The director who is searching for an abstract emotion doesn't need forms, doesn't need the faces of actors. He can talk directly from his chest to the heart of a spectator. Myself, I am more in favor of the other method, which we could compare to figurative art in painting.

—Jean Renoir

I think of the medium as a people-to-people medium—not cameramen to people, not directors to people, not writers to people, but people to people.

—Frank Capra

I'm interested in directing films that no one else is going to make.

—John Sayles

You can't teach film. I don't give a goddamn who says it, you can't teach film.

—Nicholas Ray

Even if you see a film which you think is terrible and you say, "Oh that man can't direct," there's one thing he did. He finished the film!

—Tom Conti, actor

Disney, of course, has the best casting. If he doesn't like an actor, he just tears him up.

—Alfred Hitchcock on Walt Disney

If intuition is our mental instrument, the camera is our physical instrument. I think the camera is erotic. It is the most exciting little machine that exists.

—Ingmar Bergman on his relationship with the camera

In my films Marlene is not herself. Remember that. Marlene is not Marlene: I am Marlene.

—Josef von Sternberg on Marlene Dietrich

The only thing I have against Bergman, one of my gods, is that he's obtrusive. He's always telling you it's a Bergman film, a Bergman shot.

—Mel Brooks on Ingmar Bergman

You know why I favor sophisticated blondes in my films? We're after the drawing-room type, the real ladies, who become whores once they're in the bedroom.

—Alfred Hitchcock

I think Francis Coppola's The Godfather, Part II *is certainly among the five best American pictures ever made. On my list of the unforgettable ones it's way up there with Renoir's* Grand Illusion, *Wyler's* The Best Years of Our Lives, *Lean's* The Bridge on the River Kwai, *Huston's* The Maltese Falcon, *Ford's* The Informer, *and some of the old German pictures, the Murnau pictures.*

—Billy Wilder

One of the generals said that the worst tactical mistake a general can make is to underestimate his enemy. The worst mistake you can make is to underestimate your audience. You have to look up to them; you have to take for granted that they are just as smart as you are, maybe even smarter. If you carry that out, believe me, you always come out right.

—Rouben Mamoulian

I have a theory: it is not to bore the audience.

—William Wyler

I made mistakes in drama. I thought drama was when the actors cried. But drama is when the audience cries.

—Frank Capra

I learned a long while back that an audience would rather be confused than bored.

—Paul Schrader

My films have coincided with something that's in the nature of people, the admiration for the individual who has a code and abides by it, who sticks to his own moral code rigorously. I think people like that. They may not know it, but I think that's what they respond to.

—John Huston

What did Hitchcock teach me? To be a puppet and not be creative.

—Sylvia Sidney

SIGNIFICANT TENS

Ten is a nice, tidy number. Here's a selection of 'significant tens' from the movie world, an offbeat miscellany of informational tidbits to add to your mental store of movie trivia. Can you name, for instance, ten of the most famous teams in film history and all the movies they made together? Can you list ten Frankenstein or Mummy movies? Do you know which ten films were the biggest bombs at the box office? Can you name ten films you felt should have been hits but weren't? Perhaps they're in our critics' 'most unappreciated movies' list. This chapter is just for fun—but you'll probably find it prompts you to start your own lists of 'significant tens.'

TEN TOP MOVIE TEAMS

There's a certain kind of chemistry that makes movie magic happen every time certain actors appear together on the screen. Ten of the most inspired pairings in movie history are shown here, along with the number of movies they made together. How many movies can you name for each team? The answers to this "Name Their Movies" quiz are on p. 352.

Mickey Rooney and Judy Garland (9)

Spencer Tracy and Katharine Hepburn (9)

Charles Farrell and Janet Gaynor (12)

Fred Astaire and Ginger Rogers (10)

Humphrey Bogart and Lauren Bacall (4)

Bob Hope and Bing Crosby (7)

Nelson Eddy and Jeanette MacDonald (8)

Laurence Olivier and Vivien Leigh (3)

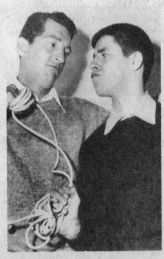

Dean Martin and Jerry Lewis (16)

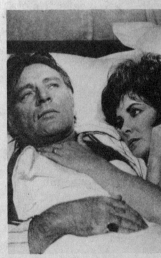

Richard Burton and Elizabeth Taylor (10)

Frank Sinatra and Faye Dunaway teamed up in *The First Deadly Sin*, but the chemistry wasn't right.

TEN MOVIE TEAMS THAT DIDN'T MAKE IT

Some inspired casting combinations make movie history—Bogart and Bacall, Astaire and Rogers. And some don't. About the best you can say for some movie partnerships is that they probably seemed a good idea at the time. Here are ten examples of teams that didn't make the ten best—ten movie couples for whom the chemistry didn't work.

James Stewart and Paulette Goddard in *Pot o' Gold* (1941)—This film has to do with a radio giveaway show that finds work for idle musicians. Stewart rarely admits to having been involved in this one—which is not even seen on the late, late, late show.

Greer Garson and Clark Gable in *Adventure* (1945)—A tough sailor marries a librarian, but doesn't realize that he really loves her until their first child is born. MGM promoted this movie with the promise that, "Gable's back and Garson's got him!" The two would have been better off if they'd never met.

Groucho Marx and Carmen Miranda in *Copacabana* (1947)— Groucho has his mustache and Carmen has her hats ...but it doesn't add up to a movie. If nothing else, *Copacabana* provides evidence that opposites don't always attract.

Humphrey Bogart and June Allyson in *Battle Circus* (1953)—Bogie plays a doctor, Allyson plays a nurse. They save lives and fall in love. It's too bad they couldn't save this movie.

Katharine Hepburn and Bob Hope in *The Iron Petticoat* (1956)—An American convinces a Russian to live for the stars and stripes. Hepburn

might have been better off in Russia.

Lana Turner and Barry Sullivan in *Another Time, Another Place* (1958)— During World War II an American newspaperwoman has an affair with a British war correspondent. He is killed in action, and she falls to pieces. Both stars should wish they had been in another place when this film was made.

Tab Hunter and Sophia Loren in *That Kind of Woman* (1959)—One critic summed this one up nicely: "The romantic reunion of Hunter and Loren resembles nothing so much as a sea scout given a luxury liner for Christmas."

Jack Lemmon and Geneviève Bujold in *Alex and the Gypsy* (1976)—Lemmon tries to civilize gypsy Bujold. They fight and scream a lot. Lemmon and Walter Matthau made a much less odd couple.

Rock Hudson and Diane Ladd in *Embryo* (1976)— Hudson, a mad scientist, injects a human fetus with a growth hormone. The monster thus created by this latter-day Frankenstein turns out to be a beautiful woman who can play chess. Of course, the scientist and his beautiful monster fall in love. But she never beats him at chess.

Frank Sinatra and Faye Dunaway in *The First Deadly Sin* (1980)—A detective (Sinatra) entertains his dying wife (Dunaway) by reading children's books to her. She finds the experience soporific. So does the audience.

TEN BOX OFFICE BOMBS

Not every movie makes money. In fact, far more lose money. The following, though not necessarily all inferior movies, are the ten biggest all-time box office losers. They're listed in descending order of how many millions each movie wound up in the red.

Heaven's Gate (1980)— between 34½ and 54 million in the red depending on whose figures you're using. This picture fared so badly, and its budget was so disorganized, that no one even seems to know (or at least to be willing to admit publicly) exactly how many millions it lost. *Heaven's Gate* was basically no more than a typical Hollywood western, and its stars included talented performers like Kris Kristofferson, Christopher Walken, John Hurt, Isabelle Huppert, and Jeff Bridges. So how could it fail so dramatically? For one thing, the shooting of the film was a fiasco. After the first six days of production director/writer Michael Cimino was already five days behind schedule. The picture was finally brought in more than 20 million dollars over budget. And it bombed completely at the box office. Despite his earlier success with *The Deer Hunter* in 1978, since *Heaven's Gate* Cimino has not directed another major picture.

Raise the Titanic! (1980)—29.2 million in the red. *Raise the Titanic!* was produced over budget,

Among the movies that bombed disastrously at the box office was the Elizabeth Taylor/Richard Burton epic *Cleopatra*.

partly because most of the budget was spent on special effects. Despite all the spectacle, the film was a total flop at the box office. Jerry Jameson directed this story about efforts to raise the famous ship. Jason Robards, Richard Jordan, and Anne Archer were the stars.

Waterloo (1970)—23.6 million in the red. As the name implies, this movie took as its subject the historical events leading up to and including the famous 1815 battle. Christopher Plummer portrayed Wellington and Rod Steiger was Napoleon. An impressive cast also included Jack Hawkins and Orson Welles. Sergei Bondarchuk directed and went way over budget. An expensive cast (in terms of both quality and quantity) combined with meager box office revenue to contribute to an astronomical financial disaster. All concerned, in fact, met their Waterloo with this one.

Honky Tonk Freeway (1981)—23.5 million in the red. Bet you never even heard of this movie. It was a complete bust at the few theatres that had the courage to show it. Director John Schlesinger (*Midnight Cowboy*) can't really be faulted for failing to make sense out of this nonsensical story about citizen efforts to secure a highway off-ramp at their small Florida community. Beau Bridges and William Devane starred.

Darling Lili (1970)—18.7 million in the red. Blake Edwards, who did the *Pink Panther* films and *Victor/Victoria*, spent years trying to live down *Darling Lili*. He wrote and directed this yarn about a World War I American pilot who falls for a German lady spy. The film isn't bad, but it did disappointing business at the box office. The big problem, reportedly, was that Edwards went millions of dollars over budget. Julie Andrews and Rock Hudson starred. One

bright spot in this movie's bleak history: Henry Mancini earned an Academy Award nomination for the song "Whistling Away the Dark."

The Fall of the Roman Empire (1964)—18.1 million in the red. This was an epic in the truest sense of the word. Everything about this film was monumental, including the budget. The huge (and expensive) cast included Alec Guinness, Christopher Plummer, Stephen Boyd, James Mason, Sophia Loren, and Omar Sharif. Dmitri Tiomkin earned an Academy Award nomination for the musical score. But American audiences, unfortunately, found this epic plain dull, and the empire fell to pieces at the box office.

Cleopatra (1963)—18 million in the red. Yes, this is the Burton/Taylor romancer. It did adequate business at the box office, but could come nowhere near recouping its huge budget—it cost 44 million dollars to make. Depending on who you talk to, either *Cleopatra* or *Heaven's Gate* holds the dubious record for the amount by which it exceeded its original budget. Joseph Mankiewicz was the director who finally completed the project, though he was only one of many involved in the course of filming. Elizabeth Taylor, of course, was Cleopatra, and Richard Burton played Marc Antony. Rex Harrison received an Academy Award nomination for his portrayal of Julius Caesar. *Cleopatra* also received a nomination for the best motion picture, and it won the Oscar for best cinema-

tography. But it certainly didn't win any awards money-wise.

Hurricane (1979)—17.5 million in the red. Dino de Laurentiis likes to spend money, and he spent 22 million making this motion picture on location on the South Pacific island of Bora Bora. The special effects are impressive, but audiences were not impressed by this tedious two-hour film. Jason Robards, Mia Farrow, Max von Sydow, and Trevor Howard starred. Jan Troell directed. As far as the box office was concerned, this *Hurricane* was, indeed, a disaster.

Sorcerer (1977)—16.1 million in the red. *Sorcerer* was a 22 million dollar remake of the 1955 French film, *Wages of Fear*, a story of four volunteers who drive nitroglycerine through the jungles of South America. William Friedkin (*The French Connection, The Exorcist*) directed and Roy Scheider starred. It's not a bad film, but it never caught on at the box office. The misleading title undoubtedly contributed to the movie's descent into obscurity.

Meteor (1979)—15.8 million in the red. This disaster epic cost 20 million to make, with super-scale special effects (earthquakes, tidal waves, and the like) and a superstar cast (Henry Fonda, Sean Connery, Natalie Wood). The story is heartwarming: American and Russian forces cooperate in order to intercept a meteor. But Ronald Neame directed a movie that simply cost more to make than it could ever hope to recoup at the box office.

TEN BIG SLEEPERS

A "sleeper" is a movie that does poor box office business—or flops altogether—when first released, but makes a comeback, sometimes years later. On re-release some sleepers make big money and may become "cult" attractions. Here are ten motion pictures that flopped when they were first released, but soared in popularity on re-release. These movies are among the ten most watched cult fims of all time. All can still be seen regularly on college campuses and in revival houses across the country. They're listed in alphabetical order.

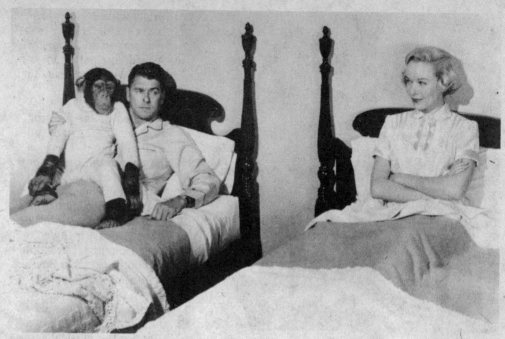

In *Bedtime for Bonzo* the character played by Ronald Reagan attempts, with the help of a chimpanzee called Bonzo, to prove that it's nurture rather than nature that determines personality. The film has done better at the box office with each release—especially since the star became President. Reagan is pictured here with Diana Lynn and their protégé.

Andy Warhol's Bad
(1977)—Film buffs enjoy watching Warhol mock Woody Allen, Federico Fellini, and others. For Warhol fans, it's one of his best. The story doesn't make much sense, and there's some violence. But it's funny. Jed Johnson directed under Warhol's watchful eye. Carroll Baker, Perry King, and Susan Tyrrell head the cast.

Bedtime for Bonzo
(1951)—This film fared much better than most cult movies first time out, but has done better still with each subsequent release. And now that the film stars the President of the United States, it's doing better than ever. It's a nature vs. nurture tale. The Ronald Reagan character attempts to prove that it's not your genetic background that counts, it's how you're reared that determines your personal-

ity. He and assistant Diana Lynn set out to prove their theory by raising a chimpanzee called Bonzo. After this movie, director Freddie de Cordova went right back into television (*The George Burns and Gracie Allen Show, The Tonight Show*). But the movie even spawned a sequel: *Bonzo Goes to College* (1952).

Emmanuelle (1974)—this French flick was promoted as the sexiest piece of art ever to be seen on a movie screen. But even a decade ago this movie was barely more risqué than the Sears catalog. About five years ago there was a renewal of interest in *Emmanuelle*. By today's standards it's pure camp. Just Jaeckin directed. Sylvia Kristel is Emmanuelle.

Freaks (1932)—Tod Browning directed and produced this story with a cast drawn from real carnival freak shows. Among

the characters—all genuine—are a bearded lady, a boy with half a torso, a turtle girl, and a living skeleton. In its day the film was considered to be in dubious taste and, in fact, MGM disowned it. As a result of early attempts to appease the censors and the management at MGM, there are at least three different versions of *Freaks* in circulation today.

Harold and Maude
(1972)—A 20-year-old boy (Bud Cort), who spends most of his time driving his mother (Vivian Pickles) crazy by faking suicide attempts, finally meets and falls in love with a member of the opposite sex (Ruth Gordon). The object of his affections happens to be 79 years old. Hal Ashby directed. Since its initial release *Harold and Maude* has grossed more than any other cult film.

King of Hearts (1967)—This French film, often shown on the same bill with *Harold and Maude*, is about a Scottish soldier who finds a war-torn city occupied by escaped lunatics. The crazy citizens want to make him their king. Philippe de Broca directed Alan Bates, Geneviève Bujold, and Jean-Claude Brialy.

The Producers (1968)—This early Mel Brooks film didn't become a box office attraction until Brooks became a star a few years after its release. The story: Broadway producer Max Bialystock (Zero Mostel) seduces an elderly widow in order to get funds to finance his play. But to make money he needs to close the show even before it opens so that he doesn't have to pay royalties. Much to Bailystock's chagrin the play, *Springtime for Hitler*, turns out to be a smash. Gene Wilder and Dick Shawn co-star.

Brooks directed and wrote the script and some of the music, but he didn't appear on the screen.

The Rocky Horror Picture Show (1975)—This movie was so bad that it wasn't even released anywhere outside of Great Britain. But somehow, some way, it caught on with American audiences, and now it's seen by more midnight show audiences than any other motion picture. Despite the fact that the film was a critical flop, audiences are still flocking to midnight shows all over the United States and Great Britain to see it. Eventually the movie generated *Rocky Horror Picture Show* fan clubs, parties, and even dolls. The only right way to see this movie is to dress up as one of the characters. It's still a craze. Jim Sharman directs; the cast includes Tim Curry, Susan Sarandon, and Barry Bostwick.

Tarzan and His Mate (1934)—Audiences at this oldie spend most of their time mimicking Tarzan's call. The costumes for the lion and gorilla are especially hokey in this Tarzan flick, but that's all part of the fun. Johnny Weissmuller is Tarzan; Maureen O'Sullivan is Jane. Cedric Gibbons directed.

Where's Poppa? (1970)—Carl Reiner directs this cult item about Jewish mama Ruth Gordon who is constantly interfering with the love life of her son (George Segal). One way to get Mom out of his hair is to do away with her but, as Segal finds out, that is easier said than done. Ron Leibman and Vincent Gardenia also star.

Blue Collar, one of critic Gene Siskel's "most unappreciated" movies, stars Harvey Keitel, Richard Pryor, and Yaphet Kotto as workers in a car factory.

TEN MOST UN-APPRECIATED MOVIES

However highly film critics recommend a movie, the movie may not do well at the box office. Every film critic has his or her own "most unappreciated" movie list. Here's such a list compiled by two well-known critics: Roger Ebert is the film critic for the *Chicago Sun Times*; Gene Siskel is the film critic for the *Chicago Tribune*; together they host the syndicated television series *At the Movies*. Here is the list of what they believe to be the ten most unappreciated movies of the last ten years or so. Ebert chose the first five; Siskel selected the rest. In both cases the movies are listed in reverse chronological order.

Gates of Heaven (1980)—This unusual movie is a commentary about pet cemeteries and includes a series of interviews with the operators of a number of pet cemeteries. It's directed by Errol Morris.

Saint Jack (1979)—Ben Gazzara portrays a pimp with a heart of gold, Jack Flowers, who is trying to run the best brothel in town. Denholm Elliott and James Villiers also appear. The director is Peter Bogdanovich.

Days of Heaven (1978)—In 1916 three poverty-stricken young people leave Chicago for the wheat fields of Texas. Written and directed by Terrence Malick, the film stars Richard Gere, Brooke Adams, Linda Manz, Sam Shepard, and Robert Wilke. Nestor Alemendros won an Academy Award for best cinematography.

Providence (1977)—In this British film from French director Alain Resnais, a famous 78-year-old writer who's dying constructs a last novel about the members of his family. Dirk Bogarde, John Gielgud, Ellen Burstyn, and Elaine Stritch star.

Heart of Glass (1976)—A German movie in which medieval European townspeople try to find the secret of how to produce the ruby glass on which the economy of the village depends. Joseph Bierbichler and Stephan Guttler star. Werner Herzog directs.

Moonlighting (1982)—In this British movie, set in England, Jeremy Irons is an English-speaking Polish foreman who tries to prevent three compatriot workers from finding out about the political overthrow in their home country. Jerzy Skolimowski directs.

Straight Time (1978)—Based on a novel by ex-convict Edward Bunker, *Straight Time* is about an ex-con (Dustin Hoffman), who just can't seem to go straight. Harry Dean Stanton and Gary Busey also appear. The director is Ulu Grosbard.

Blue Collar (1978)—Three car factory workers try to improve their lot in life. The movie stars Richard Pryor, Harvey Keitel, Yaphet Kotto, and Ed Begley, Jr. under the direction of Paul Schrader.

Lacombe, Lucien (1974)—This French movie, directed by Louis Malle, won the 1974 British Academy Award for best film. The plot has to do with a 17-year-old peasant boy who joins the French Gestapo workers and becomes a collaborator during World War II. Pierre Blaise, Aurore Clement, and Holger Lowenadler star.

Badlands (1973)—A teen-age girl and a young garbage collector wander across the country leaving a trail of murders. Martin Sheen, Sissy Spacek, and Warren Oates star. The film is directed by Terrence Malick, who also directed *Days of Heaven*—one of critic Ebert's "most unappreciated" choices.

Diana Ross in *Mahogany*. Songwriter Joel Hirschhorn believes the movie's theme song deserved an Oscar.

TEN SONGS THAT SHOULD HAVE WON OSCARS

Academy Award winning songwriter Joel Hirschhorn* lists ten songs that should have won Academy Awards, but didn't, and explains why he believes they deserved to be winners. They're listed in reverse chronological order according to when the movie was released.

"Out Here on My Own" from *Fame* (1980), performed by Irene Cara: Composer Michael Gore competed with himself in the best song category and won for the song "Fame." I think "Out Here on My Own" has more beauty and staying power.

"Nobody Does It Better" from *The Spy Who Loved Me* (1977), performed by Carly Simon: One of Marvin Hamlisch's best and most imaginative musical melodies.

"Do You Know Where You're Going To?" the theme from *Mahogany* (1975), performed by Diana Ross: This was a number one record, and the best part of that film. It should have won.

"The Look of Love" from *Casino Royale* (1967), performed by Dionne Warwick: A haunting Burt Bacharach and Hal David ballad. I don't know how this song lost to "Talk to the Animals" from *Dr. Doolittle*.

"An Affair to Remember" from *An Affair to Remember* (1957), performed by Vic Damone: This romantic tune heightened the chemistry between Cary Grant and Deborah Kerr, and, of course, became a hit song on its own.

"Friendly Persuasion (Thee I Love)" from *Friendly Persuasion* (1956), performed by Pat Boone: This song was the single factor that started this movie on the way to being a box office success. It deserved an award.

"The Man That Got Away" from *A Star Is Born* (1954), performed by Judy Garland: The greatest torch ballad in history, as far as I'm concerned. And one of Garland's most electrifying performances.

"My Foolish Heart" from *My Foolish Heart* (1949): A bittersweet and beautiful love song. To me, it's as fondly remembered as the classic "Laura."

"It's Magic" from *Romance on the High Seas* (1948), performed by Doris Day: This song made Doris Day a superstar overnight, and lifted what was a rather ordinary musical to worldwide popularity.

"The Trolley Song" from *Meet Me in St. Louis* (1944), performed by Judy Garland: A great song, a joyous masterpiece. It should have won.

*Joel Hirschhorn and Al Kasha have won two Academy Awards for best song, the first for "The Morning After," which was featured in *The Poseidon Adventure* (1972), and the second for "We May Never Love This Way Again," from *The Towering Inferno* (1974). Both songs were sung by Maureen McGovern. The songwriters also received two 1978 Oscar nominations, for best score for *Pete's Dragon*, and for the best song, "Candle on the Water" from the same movie. It was sung by Helen Reddy. In addition, Hirschhorn and Kasha have been nominated four times for Golden Globe awards and twice for Tony awards. They've written for such varied performers as Sammy Davis, Jr., Marie Osmond, Bobby Darin, the Lettermen, Tommy Roe, and Jackie Wilson.

TEN FAVORITE CARTOONS

Chuck Jones is an Academy Award winning animator who has directed and/or created, among others, Bugs Bunny, Porky Pig, Daffy Duck, Pepe LePew, and The Roadrunner. His animated TV specials include *Rikki-Tikki-Tavi* and *How The Grinch Stole Christmas*. Here, from the cartoons he has directed, Jones compiles a list of his ten favorites—the ones that he has learned most from, with his comments on why each one has a place on his "Ten Best" list:

One Froggy Evening—It was a difficult cartoon to do, and I'm most proud of the fact that the difficulty and effort doesn't show in the product.

What's Opera, Doc?—We took 14 hours and cut it down to six minutes. We played the music straight—we had a sixty-piece orchestra.

Feed The Kitty—A pugnacious dog is overcome with love for a kitten. It's just one of my favorites.

A Bear for Punishment—This was an Archie Bunker story before its time, and we had a great cast, Bea Benaderet, Billy Bletcher, and Stan Freberg.

Duck Amuck—Daffy has a long fight with the person drawing the cartoon. I had always wanted to do a story like that. It was a challenge, but it sure was fun.

Duck Dodgers in the 24½th Century—Natu-

rally, this was a Buck Rogers satire. We did a lot of experimenting. We did this in 1953, before there was a Cape Canaveral—we didn't even know what rockets were. You know, our cartoon looks just like Cape Canaveral. I'm often kidded that I'm the one who really designed Cape Canaveral.

For Scent-Imental Reasons—This won an Academy Award in 1949. The star was Pepe LePew, and this is one of my favorites because I admire Pepe so much. Really, I want to be just like he was in this cartoon.

Whoa, Be Gone—I had to include a Roadrunner picture in this list. The Roadrunner has no dialogue, so it crosses all international borders. This is my favorite Roadrunner.

The Dot and the Line—It's quite an unusual picture, and it won an Academy Award in 1965. This is the plot: A line falls in love with a dot, and a dot falls in love with a squiggle. I got this idea from a book by Norton Juster.

The Scarlet Pumpernickel— Daffy tries to sell a script to Jack Warner. We had all the characters in this one, and we really had the opportunity to play with Daffy's character. It was a lot of fun.

TEN OF THE YOUNGEST STARS

Some movie performers really started young. Here's a rundown on some of the youngsters who made it into movies between ages one and ten.

1

Dickie Moore in *The Beloved Rogue* (1927)
Baby LeRoy in *A Bedtime Story* (1933)

2

Jackie Coogan in *Skinner's Baby* (1917)
Gigi Perreau in *Madam Curie* (1943)

3

Jackie Cooper in several silent comedies and *Our Gang* episodes (1923)
Shirley Temple in a variety of short subjects (1931)
Scotty Beckett in the *Our Gang* comedies (1933)

4

Virginia Weidler in *Surrender* (1931)
Margaret O'Brien in *Babes on Broadway* (1941)

5

Natalie Wood in *Happy Land* (1943)

6

Mickey Rooney in the short *Not To Be Trusted* (1926)
Jane Withers in *Handle With Care* (1932)
Robert "Bobby" Blake in *Our Gang* comedies (1939)
Bobby Driscoll in *Lost Angel* (1943)
Jackie "Butch" Jenkins in *The Human Comedy* (1943)
Mark Lester in *Allez France!* (1964)

7

Peggy Ann Garner in *Little Miss Thoroughbred* (1938)
Darryl Hickman in *If I Were King* (1938)
Johnny Sheffield in *Tarzan Finds a Son* (1939)

8

Carl "Alfalfa" Switzer in the *Our Gang* comedies (1934)
Tommy Rettig in *Panic in the Streets* (1950)

9

Roddy McDowall in *Murder in the Family* (1938)
Dean Stockwell in *The Valley of Decision* (1945)
Tatum O'Neal in *Paper Moon* (1973)

10

Elizabeth Taylor in *There's One Born Every Minute* (1942)
Brandon de Wilde in *The Member of the Wedding* (1952)

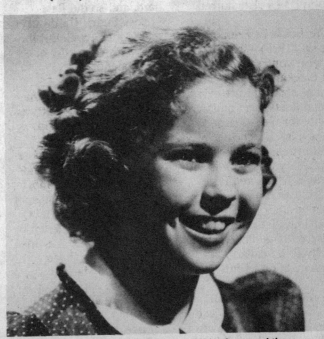

Shirley Temple began making movies at the tender age of three.

273

FRANKEN-STEIN'S MONSTER × 10

Mary Shelley's early 19th-century novel about a scientist who creates a man/monster has been translated in screen terms many times, with results varying in quality and audience appeal. From the numerous movies about Frankenstein's monster, here are ten of the best known. They're listed chronologically.

Abbott and Costello get more than they bargain for in *Abbott and Costello Meet Frankenstein.*

Frankenstein (1931)—This is the original American version, based on two sources: the German film *The Golem* (1922) and Mary Shelley's 19th-century novel. It's difficult to believe today that this movie had problems getting past the censors. James Whale directed this masterpiece, and Boris Karloff embarked upon a career playing Frankenstein's monster. Mae Clarke, Colin Clive, and John Boles also starred.

The Bride of Frankenstein (1935)—In this one, Baron von Frankenstein is blackmailed by Dr. Praetorious into reviving his monster and building a mate for him. In a dual role, Elsa Lanchester plays both the monster's bride and Mary Shelley. Director James Whale and Boris Karloff as the monster resumed their tasks for this movie. Colin Clive co-starred. The film was originally to be called *The Return of Frankenstein.*

Son of Frankenstein (1939)—This is the last of the *Frankenstein* movies in which Boris Karloff is the

monster. Rowland V. Lee directed this story about the old Baron's son (Basil Rathbone) who comes home and begins to dabble in the dungeon, with the assistance of Ygor (Bela Lugosi). Lionel Atwill also stars.

The Ghost of Frankenstein (1942)—Lon Chaney, Jr. plays the creature who is rejuvenated when his neck bolts are accidentally struck by lightning. Director Erle C. Kenton tried hard, and so did Bela Lugosi, Cedric Hardwicke, and Lionel Atwill. But the story wasn't worthy of their talents.

Frankenstein Meets the Wolf Man (1943)—It was bound to happen. Lon Chaney, Jr. is the hairy creature, and Bela Lugosi plays the tall, dark, handsome monster. The movie is entertaining at times, but whether it entertains in the manner intended by those who made it is another question. Ilona Massey and Maria Ouspenskaya also appear. Roy William Neill directed.

House of Frankenstein (1945)—A mad doctor

thaws out the Wolf Man who was frozen at the end of *Frankenstein Meets the Wolf Man.* The Wolf Man then sniffs out Frankenstein, and even Dracula. This movie was to be called *Chamber of Horrors* and was Universal's first attempt to package lots of monsters in one movie. Boris Karloff plays the mad scientist Dr. Niemann, with Glenn Strange as the monster, John Carradine as Dracula, and Lon Chaney, Jr. as Wolf Man. Lionel Atwill and George Zucco also appear. Erle C. Kenton directed.

Abbott and Costello Meet Frankenstein (1948)—This was the last in Universal Studios' series of *Frankenstein* movies, and all the creatures show up to haunt the comedy duo. Charles Barton (who directed instead of the usual Abbott and Costello director Charles Lamont) deserves applause, as does the excellent cast: Glenn Strange as Frankenstein, Bela Lugosi as Dracula, and Lon Chaney, Jr. as the Wolf Man.

The Curse of Frankenstein (1957)—This Frank-

enstein movie is in color, and it's gory. It's the first in a series of episodes produced by Britain's Hammer Films and was directed by Terence Fisher, who also directed a number of Hammer's *Mummy* movies. Christopher Lee portrays the ugliest of all the creatures; Peter Cushing is the Baron.

The Revenge of Frankenstein (1958)—Get this one: The Baron evades the guillotine, and makes a new creature using the brain of a homicidal dwarf. Peter Cushing returns as the Baron and Michael Gwynn is the monster (not to be confused with Fred Gwynne, who played a creature look-alike on *The Munsters* TV series). Terence Fisher directed this one, too.

Frankenstein 1970 (1958)—Television filmmakers descend on the Baron's castle, and guess what they find—a futuristic creature. Boris Karloff gives a fine performance, but he would have been better off quitting while he was ahead. Howard Koch is the director.

THE MUMMY × 10

When the tomb of Tutankhamen was discovered and opened in the 1920s and stories began going the rounds about the curse of Tutankhamen, it was inevitable that moviemakers would develop a sudden fascination for the avenging mummy theme and its shock potential for audiences. Here are ten movie variations on that theme. They're listed chronologically.

The Mummy (1932)—This original film creation is the story of a 3000-year-old mummy that's brought back to life. The movie contains very little graphic horror, but the mood created by director Karl Freund and Boris Karloff as the creature makes this film as effective a shocker as any of the many sequels.

Mummie's Dummies (1938)—This is a classic Three Stooges short ... Larry, Moe, and Curly take on the mummy.

The Mummy's Hand (1940)—A high priest revives the Egyptian mummy, director Christy Cabanne borrows some tricks from the original *The Mummy* director, Karl Freund, and even adds a bit of comedy to break the ice. Then, just when you least expect it, guess who appears. Tom Tyler is the Mummy. Dick Foran, Wallace Ford, and George Zucco also star.

The Mummy's Tomb (1942)—This is a sequel to *The Mummy's Hand*,

Tom Tyler is the creature in *The Mummy's Hand*, in which a high priest revives the Egyptian mummy.

with the same stars, except that Lon Chaney, Jr. is now the Mummy. Only the Mummy survives. The rest of the stars are all killed off and never get to appear in another *Mummy* movie. Harold Young directed.

The Mummy's Ghost (1944)—How can a creature who's already dead and mummified turn into a ghost? This movie, directed by Reginald LeBorg, proves it can be done. Lon Chaney, Jr. is the creature; he's really scary in this one.

The Mummy's Curse (1944)—This next-to-last of the Universal series of *Mummy* motion pictures was directed by Leslie Goodwins. Lon Chaney, Jr. plays the Mummy one last time.

Abbott and Costello Meet the Mummy (1955)—A missing medallion leads to a lost tomb and, of course, the living mummy. This time Kurt Katch is the mummy. Marie Windsor also stars with the two comedians—who are showing their age by this movie. Charles Lamont directed.

The Mummy (1959)—Britain's Hammer studios produced this remake of the original. Christopher Lee is the monster (now in living color). Peter Cushing and Yvonne Furneaux also star. Terence Fisher directed this.

The Curse of the Mummy's Tomb (1964)—This one is supposed to be similar to *The Mummy's Hand*, the second original Mummy movie from Universal. This Hammer production doesn't bother with mood; it's quite graphically gory. Michael Carreras (son of Sir James Carreras, one of the cofounders of Hammer Films) directed Terence Morgan, Ronald Howard, and Fred Clark.

The Mummy's Shroud (1966)—The Mummy's last screen appearance, unfortunately, is far from his best, and does little to preserve his reputation in honor. This bloodiest of all Hammer's *Mummy* movies was directed by John Gilling and stars Andre Morell, John Phillips, David Buck, and Elizabeth Sellars.

TEN MOVIES TO SEND YOU BUGGY

Most people have some kind of bug-phobia—they can't stand creepy-crawlies of any kind, or there's one kind of creature that generates a fear singularly disproportionate to its size: they get hysterical at the sight of a hornet, or a spider in the bathtub sends them to a neighbor's house to take a shower. And the thought of keeping a tarantula as a *pet* .... Such is the stuff that bad dreams are made of, and filmmakers love to capitalize on such fears. Here are ten movies in which bees, bugs, spiders, and other such creatures really give the humans something to get upset about. If you don't like bugs, give these movies a miss:

The Swarm (1978)—African killer bees are brought into the United States by mistake and create all sorts of havoc in the lives of such top-name co-stars as Michael Caine, Richard Widmark, Fred MacMurray, Olivia de Havilland and Henry Fonda. Irwin Allen (*The Towering Inferno*) directs.

Empire of the Ants (1977)—Radioactivity causes regular ants to grow to an enormous size—800 pounds or so. Involved in this contest between regular-size people and monster ants are Joan Collins and Robert Lansing. Bert Gordon directs.

The Giant Spider Invasion (1975)—These

spiders emerge from a hole in the earth and go after everything they see. It takes a neutron bomb to stop them. In the cast are Barbara Hale and Steve Brodie. This one is directed by Bill Rebane.

Frogs (1972)—Frogs don't count as bugs, certainly, but here they're joined by co-stars that include scorpions, spiders, and (making a rare screen appearance) leeches. They all attack a family known to be cruel to animals. Frogs, directed by George McCowan, has a cast led by Ray Milland, Joan Van Ark, and Adam Roarke.

The Deadly Bees (1967)—A special potion transforms bees into killers. Unfortunately, the potion gets into the hands of unscrupulous humans. Freddie Francis directs. In combat with the killer bees, one way or another, are Catherine Finn, Guy Doleman, and Suzanna Leigh.

The Black Scorpion (1957)—Hidden for years inside a Mexican volcano, giant scorpions emerge and run amok in Mexico City. Direction is by Edward Ludwig. Involved in the escapade are Richard Denning and Mara Corday.

The Deadly Mantis (1957)—The moviemakers who thought this one up probably prided themselves on true originality. The protaganist is a praying mantis, which atomic testing causes to grow to enormous proportions— 100 feet long and 40 feet high. It runs riot over cities and towns and gets in the way of such human performers as Craig Ste-

vens, William Hopper, and Alix Talton. Nathan Juran directs.

Beginning of the End (1957)—Farmers use a special radioactive isotope to help their plants grow. The formula works fine on the crops but also, to everyone's dismay, on grasshoppers. The creatures grow to 15 feet long and are on their way to invade Chicago before the human cast (Peggy Castle and Peter Graves) gets the upper hand. Director is Bert I. Gordon.

Tarantula (1955)—A tarantula treated with a special serum escapes into the desert and goes on growing until it weighs 50 tons and develops an appetite to match its size. The creature devours entire cities, and the Air Force, armed with napalm bombs, is flown in to save the day. Jack Arnold directs a cast led by Leo G. Carroll, Mara Corday, and John Agar.

Them! (1954)—Radiation from an atomic explosion causes giant ants to breed in New Mexico and migrate to Los Angeles. Edmund Gwenn and James Whitmore are among those assigned to cope with the invasion. Gordon Douglas was the director assigned to cope with Them!

TEN BEASTLY CREATURE FEATURES

Creatures, some of them basically benign, that turn on the human populace have been sub-

ject matter for horror movies since the late, great King Kong (1933). Here are some beastly creatures—animals, birds, and sea creatures—that you may not have come across (and may not want to):

Alligator (1980)—This alligator makes its early screen appearance as a child's pet, but the kid's disgusted mother flushes the baby 'gator down the toilet and the creature survives in the sewers. The fun starts when the snapper eats a growth formula dumped into the sewer from an experimental laboratory. The formula works just fine on the 'gator. Among the human cast, directed by Lewis Teague, are Robert Forster and Robin Riker. The screenplay is by John Sayles (who directed The Return of the Secaucus 7 in 1980).

Piranha (1978)—A special hybrid breed of piranha fish are let loose in a California lake. The lake, thereafter, poses definite hazards for swimmers. Involved in this fishy tale are director Joe Dante and a cast headed by Bradford Dillman, Heather Menzies, and Keenan Wynn.

Day of the Animals (1976)—This one stars an assortment of creatures including bears, wolves, and birds of prey. They all become exceedingly ill-tempered and harass the population until an ozone layer kills them. William Girdler directs a cast headed by Christopher George, Linda Day George, and Leslie Nielsen.

Food of the Gods (1976)—A strange white

substance oozing from the ground is fed to farm animals and causes them to grow to abnormal size. The resulting giant roosters, rats the size of tigers, massive chickens, and the like then tire of their normal feed and turn to eating people instead. The offending growth substance also finds its way onto supermarket shelves, and the movie ends with a shot of a small boy drinking contaminated milk. This fable was written and directed by Bert Gordon, with a cast including Marjoe Gortner, Pamela Franklin, and Ida Lupino.

Jaws (1975)—The Great White shark in this film became much loved by the moviemakers who pocketed the profits—Jaws was a huge hit. Steven Spielberg directed from the Peter Benchley novel, with a cast led by Richard Dreyfuss, Roy Scheider, and Robert Shaw. The story, of course, has to do with a man-eating shark who shows up at a summer resort at Long Island, New York, and starts snacking on unsuspecting bathers. The movie won a best picture Academy Award nomination and spawned two sequels—by the second of which the novelty had definitely worn off.

Willard (1971)—An introverted man breeds some extroverted rats which he plans to have kill off people he doesn't like. His plan backfires when the rats turn on him and anyone else in their path. The movie, directed by Daniel Mann, starred Bruce Davison, Elsa Lanchester, Ernest Borgnine, and Sondra Locke. A sequel, Ben, directed by Phil

Karlson and starring Arthur O'Connell and Rosemary Murphy, came out the following year and showed the killer rats running amok. *Ben*, though, is best remembered for the title song, which was performed by Michael Jackson and was nominated for an Academy Award.

The Birds (1963)—Anyone who was spooked by the stuffed birds that adorned Anthony Perkins' infamous motel in Alfred Hitchcock's 1960 shocker *Psycho* is in for trouble with *The Birds*. Here a massive flock of live birds mysteriously attacks and kills inhabitants of a small coastal town in California. Hitchcock's cast for this one is led by Rod Taylor, Tippi Hedren, Jessica Tandy, and Suzanne Pleshette.

The Killer Shrews (1959)—These little creatures mind their own business on the remote island they inhabit until genetic tampering causes them to mutate. As they grow, so does their appetite for humans. The scientists who aren't devoured by the mutated shrews escape the island, leaving the creatures to turn on each other. Ray Kellog directs. James Best, Gordon McLendon, and Ingrid Goude head the cast.

It Came From Beneath the Sea (1955)—Where else would you expect a giant octopus to come from? Atomic radiation causes this octopus to grow all out of proportion to its fellows, and when its underwater food supply runs low it comes ashore and attacks San Francisco. Robert Gordon directs. Kenneth Tobey and Faith Domergue head the San

Franciscans who tangle with the octopus.

Attack of the Crab Monsters (1957)—This one offers another example of undesirable effects caused by atomic testing. Regular crabs grow enormous—about 8 feet high and 25 feet across. Their feeding habits change too, and they start lunching on people. Roger Corman directs, with Pamela Duncan, Russell Johnson, and Leslie Bradley heading the human cast.

TEN BEST BASEBALL MOVIES

Baseball and baseball players have always had a place in the affections of

In *The Stratton Story* James Stewart courageously pursues the national pastime—baseball.

moviemakers—and moviegoers. Here are ten of the film world's best baseball movies:

Casey at the Bat (1899)—This classic was also remade in 1927 starring Wallace Beery.

Speedy (1928)—Harold Lloyd plays a fast ball player who sometimes runs to third base before first base.

The Babe Ruth Story (1948)—The great Bambino's biopic starred William Bendix and Claire Trevor.

The Stratton Story (1949)—James Stewart is Monty Stratton, the courageous pitcher whose leg was amputated during his career. June Allyson, Frank Morgan, and Agnes Moorehead also star.

Take Me Out to the Ball Game (1949)—A woman takes over the ball team and the players aren't happy. Gene Kelly, Frank Sinatra, and Esther Williams sing their way around the bases.

The Winning Team (1952)—A telephone linesman becomes a great baseball player in this movie based on the life of flamethrower Grover Cleveland Alexander. Stars are Ronald Reagan and Doris Day.

The Pride of St. Louis (1952)—Dan Dailey stars as Dizzy Dean, the pitcher who was forced to end his career early. Joanne Dru and Richard Haydn also appear. Guy Trosper received an Academy Award nomination for best original story.

Fear Strikes Out (1957)—This one could have been titled *The Jim Piersall Story*. A father wants his son to become a big leaguer; the son has a nervous breakdown. Anthony Perkins, Karl Malden, and Norma Moore star.

Damn Yankees (1958)—The Devil interferes in the fortunes of a suffering baseball team. Gwen Verdon, Tab Hunter, and Ray Walston star. Ray Heindorf received an Academy Award nomination for his musical score.

The Natural (1984)—Robert Redford is a promising ball player shot down before he can become "the best there ever was." He tries again and comes back, making it to the big leagues and the World Series. Glenn Close and Robert Duvall co-star.

A
COLLECTION
OF
QUOTES

Who, and in which movie, said, 'It's not the men in your life that count. It's the life in your men'? Or, 'Fasten your seatbelts. It's going to be a bumpy night'? Or, 'Morals never bothered me too much but taste is so important'? Who described her movie character as 'a bagel on a plate of onion rolls'? Which playwright told which producer, 'The trouble . . . is that you are only interested in art, and I am only interested in money'? Quoting from the movies and the people who make them is one of the movie trivia fan's favorite pastimes. Here's a choice selection of quotes from and about movies to add to your own collection.

QUOTES ON LOVE IN ITS VARIOUS GUISES AND DISGUISES

Very few movies don't have a love interest of one kind or another. Here are some of the choicest movie quotes on the eternal enigma of love ... of one kind or another.

Well, who's asking you to be rational? Listen, when I was courting your grandmother, it took me two years to propose. Know why? The moment she'd walk into a room, my knees would buckle, blood'd rush up into my head and—and the walls'd start to dance. Why, twice I keeled over in a dead faint. . . . She finally dragged it out of me when I was in bed with a 104° fever—and in a state of hysteria. The moment she accepted, the fever went down to normal— and I hopped out of bed. Oh, the case was written up in all the medical journals as the phenomenon of the times. There was nothing phenomenal about it. I just had it bad, that's all, and I never got over it either.

—Lionel Barrymore to Jean Arthur in *You Can't Take It With You*

You don't know what love means. To you, it's just another four-letter word.

—Paul Newman to Burl Ives in *Cat on a Hot Tin Roof*

I remember every detail. The Germans wore gray. You wore blue.

—Humphrey Bogart to Ingrid Bergman in *Casablanca*

I don't want to be worshipped, I want to be loved.

—Katharine Hepburn to John Howard in *The Philadelphia Story*
—Also Grace Kelly to John Lund in the remake, *High Society*

In spite of everything, I still believe that people are really good at heart.

—Millie Perkins in *The Diary of Anne Frank*

Love means never having to say you're sorry.

—Ryan O'Neal quoting his late wife (played by Ali MacGraw) in the final scene of *Love Story*

Even as a kid, I always went for the wrong women. I feel that's my problem. When my mother took me to see Snow White, *everyone fell in love with Snow White. I immediately fell for the wicked queen.*

—Woody Allen in *Annie Hall*

Love is a miracle. It's like a birthmark. You can't hide it.

—George Segal in *Blume in Love*

Love isn't something you can put on or take off like an overcoat, you know.

—Arthur Kennedy to Ruth Roman in *Champion*

If you love a person, you can forgive anything.

—Herbert Marshall in *The Letter*

I was never to see her again. Nor was I ever to learn what became of her. We were different then. Kids were different. It took us longer to understand the things we felt. Life is made up of small comings and goings, and, for everything we take with us, there is something that we leave behind. In the summer of '42 we raided the Coast Guard station four times; we saw five movies and had nine days of rain; Benjie broke his watch; Oscy gave up the harmonica; and, in a very special way, I lost Hermie—forever.

—Narrator Robert Mulligan (as Gary Grimes, grown up) remembering his adolescent love for Jennifer O'Neill in *Summer of '42*

Scientists can write all the books they like about love being a trap of nature. I remember reading that—that it's biology and the chemistry inside of [a woman] that fools her. But all the scientists are going to convince are scientists, not women in love.

—Jean Arthur in *The Devil and Miss Jones*

Is that what love is? Using people? And maybe that's what hate is—not being able to use people.

—Elizabeth Taylor in *Suddenly, Last Summer*

If you had the choice . . . would you rather love a girl or have her love you?

—Jack Nicholson questioning Arthur Garfunkel in *Carnal Knowledge*

As for you, my galvanized friend, you want a heart. You don't know how lucky you are not to have one. Hearts will never be practical until they can be made unbreakable.

—Wizard Frank Morgan to Jack Haley (as the Tin Man) in *The Wizard of Oz*

You don't like her. My mother don't like her. She's a dog, and I'm a fat, ugly man. Well, all I know is I had a good time tonight. If we have enough good times together, I'm going to get down on my knees. I'm going to beg that girl to marry me. If we make a party New Year's, I got a date for that party. You don't like her? That's too bad.

—Ernest Borgnine in *Marty*

It's a mistake you always made, Doc, trying to love a wild thing. You were always lugging home wild things. Once, it was a hawk with a broken wing, and—and that time it was a full-grown wildcat with a broken leg. Remember? . . . You mustn't give your heart to a wild thing. The more you do, the stronger they get until they're strong enough to run into the woods or fly to a tree and then to a higher tree and then to the sky.

—Audrey Hepburn to Buddy Ebsen in *Breakfast at Tiffany's*

Even when I was making love to you, I had the feeling that you were wondering what time it was.

—Robert Montgomery to Bette Davis in *June Bride*

I'd almost forgotten about it, but, when I was in high school, I thought I was just one of those cold people who would never love anyone. I just—some people have the capacity, and I guess I didn't. It just wasn't in me. And, when I fell in love with this guy, it was just—I mean, it meant so much to me. It meant that I was a real person. I wasn't just a machine. I had really incredibly deep emotions, and I didn't know I could feel that strongly about anybody . . . . I'll never forget it. I was using a part of me —I still had a part of me that I'd never felt before, and the best part, too: my capacity to love somebody.

—"David," speaking about his first experience of falling in love with another man in the documentary *Word Is Out*

Greer Garson: *You're very puzzling, Mr. Darcy. At this moment, it's difficult to believe that you're so proud.*
Laurence Olivier: *At this moment, it's difficult to believe that you're so prejudiced. Shall we not call it quits and start again?*

—Exchange between Garson and Olivier in *Pride and Prejudice*

You know, there are three things that we could do right now: you could call a taxi and go home, or we could go on walking and I could lecture you on the real dilemma of modern art, or we could go to my place and we could thoroughly enjoy each other.

—Alan Bates to Jill Clayburgh in *An Unmarried Woman*

I used to—used to make obscene phone calls to her—collect—and she used to accept the charges all the time.

—Woody Allen, remembering past deeds in *Take the Money and Run*

There are no great men, buster. There's only men.

—Elaine Stewart in *The Bad and the Beautiful*

Used to have a boyfriend was a cowboy. Met him in Colorado. He was in love with me because I was a—an older woman and had some sense . . . . Took me up in the mountains one night and wanted to marry me, right there on the mountain top. He said the stars'd be our preacher and the moon our best man. Did you ever hear such talk?

—Rosalind Russell in *Picnic*

Fredric March: *I want this moment to last.*
Claudette Colbert: *How long?*
March: *At least until breakfast.*

—March tries to seduce Colbert in *Tonight Is Ours*

The only difference in men is the color of their neckties.

—Helen Broderick in *Top Hat*

That's the only good thing about divorce. You get to sleep with your mother.

—Virginia Weidler thinking about her parents' divorce in *The Women*

Helen Jerome Eddy: *Too many girls follow the line of least resistance.*
Mae West: *Yeah, but a good line is hard to resist.*

—Eddy and West discussing sex in *Klondike Annie*

Cloakroom girl: *Goodness, what beautiful diamonds!*
Mae West: *Goodness had nothing to do with it, dearie.*

—West disillusions a cloakroom girl in *Night After Night*

Well, it's not the men in your life that count. It's the life in your men.

—Mae West in *I'm No Angel*

Why don't you come up sometime and see me? I'm home every evening.

—Mae West to Cary Grant in *She Done Him Wrong*

Cameraman: *C'mon Carole, smile! Sex is fun!*
Carole Lombard: *I'd rather play tennis.*

—Cameraman trying to get Lombard to pose on the set

Funny thing is, you are sort of attractive—in a corn-fed sort of way. I can see some poor girl falling for you if—well, if you threw in a set of dishes.

—Bette Davis to Richard Travis in *The Man Who Came to Dinner*

That will be all, thank you.

—Norma Shearer's response to being kissed by Clark Gable in *A Free Soul*

Paris? No, not this city. It's too real and too beautiful. It never lets you forget anything. It reaches in and opens you wide, and you stay that way. I know. I came to Paris to study and to paint because Utrillo did and Lautrec did and Roualt did. I loved what they created, and I thought something would happen to me, too. Well, it happened all right. Now, what have I got left? Paris. Maybe that's enough for some, but it isn't for me anymore because the more beautiful everything is, the more it will hurt without you.

—Gene Kelly's response to Leslie Caron's assertion that "Paris has ways of making people forget" in *An American in Paris*

Melvyn Douglas: *It's midnight. Look at the clock. One hand has met the other hand. They kiss. Isn't that wonderful?*
Greta Garbo: *That's the way a clock works. What's wonderful about it?*
Douglas: *But, Ninotchka, it's midnight. One half of Paris is making love to the other half.*

—Midnight conversation between Douglas and Garbo in *Ninotchka*

Remember: you're fighting for this woman's honor, which is probably more than she ever did.

—Groucho Marx, insulting Margaret Dumont in *Duck Soup*

Why, you're one of the most beautiful women I've ever seen, and that's not saying much for you.

—Groucho Marx to Margaret Dumont in *Animal Crackers*

Oh, why can't we break away from all this, just you and I, and lodge with my fleas in the hills? I mean, flee to my lodge in the hills.

—Groucho Marx to Thelma Todd in *Monkey Business*

I could dance with you until the cows come home. On second thought, I'd rather dance with the cows until you came home.

—Groucho Marx insulting Raquel Torres in *Duck Soup*

It's the old story: Boy meets girl, Romeo and Juliet, Minneapolis and St. Paul

—Groucho Marx declaring himself in love in *A Day at the Races*

Oh, I—I'm not myself tonight. I don't know who I am. One false move, and I'm yours.

—Groucho Marx to Margaret Dumont in *The Cocoanuts*

Madge Kennedy: *What is it that makes you incompatible?*
Judy Holliday: *Being married to each other.*

—Exchange in which Holliday explains to the judge (Kennedy) why she wants a divorce in *The Marrying Kind*

QUOTES ON PHILOSOPHY, PSYCHOLOGY, MORALITY, AND OTHER SUCH MATTERS

The trouble, Mr. Goldwyn, is that you are only interested in art, and I am only interested in money.

—George Bernard Shaw to Sam Goldwyn

Morals never bothered me too much but taste is so important.

—Douglas Fairbanks, Jr. in *Scarlet Dawn*

Had I attempted only a fraction of the Clint Eastwood dirty tricks in my films, in my day, I would have been arrested or horse-whipped. Until I quit, most movie fans thought dancehall girls actually danced.

—Gene Autry

Today democracy, liberty, and equality are words to fool the people. No nation can progress with such ideas. They stand in the way of action. Therefore, we frankly abolish them.

—Henry Daniell in *The Great Dictator*

Those ain't lies. Those are campaign promises. They expect 'em.

—William Demarest in *Hail the Conquering Hero*

Let me tell you what stooling is. Stooling is when you rat on your friends, the guys you're with.

—Rod Steiger in *On the Waterfront*

The bottom's full of nice people; only cream and bastards rise.

—Paul Newman in *Harper*

In the twentieth century, the main product of all human endeavor is waste.

—Orson Welles in *I'll Never Forget Whatshisname*

My job is to teach these natives the meaning of democracy, and they're going to learn democracy if I have to shoot every one of them.

—Paul Ford in *The Teahouse of the August Moon*

I always get the fuzzy end of the lollipop.

—Marilyn Monroe to Tony Curtis in *Some Like It Hot*

I'm a bagel on a plate of onion rolls.

—Barbra Streisand in *Funny Girl*

Sidney Poitier: *Thanks for pulling me out.*
Tony Curtis: *Man, I didn't pull you out. I stopped you from pulling me in.*

—Exchange between Poitier and Curtis after Curtis has pulled Poitier out of a river in *The Defiant Ones*

The truth is something desperate, and Maggie's got it. Believe me, it is desperate, and she has got it.

—Paul Newman of the character played by Elizabeth Taylor in *Cat on a Hot Tin Roof*

"Most men lead lives of quiet desperation." I can't take "quiet desperation."

—Ray Milland in *The Lost Weekend*

You see, my dear, goodness is after all the greatest force in the world, and he's got it.

—Herbert Marshall of Tyrone Power in *The Razor's Edge*

Strange isn't it? Each man's life touches so many other lives—and when he isn't around he leaves an awful hole, doesn't he?

—Henry Travers in *It's a Wonderful Life*

What is there to fight for? Everything! Life itself! Isn't that enough? To be lived, suffered, enjoyed. What is there to fight for? Life is a beautiful, magnificent thing—even to a jellyfish.

—Charles Chaplin in *Limelight*

People here are funny. They work so hard at living they forget how to live. Last night, after I left you, I was walking along and—and looking at the tall buildings, and I got to thinking about what Thoreau said. "They created a lot of grand palaces here, but they forgot to create the noblemen to put in them." I'd rather have Mandrake Falls.

—Gary Cooper on New York City, in *Mr. Deeds Goes to Town*

Well, Pa, a woman can change better 'n a man. A man lives sorta—well, in jerks. Baby's born or somebody dies, an' that's a jerk. He gets a farm or loses it, an'—an' that's a jerk. With a woman, it's all in one flow, like a stream—little eddies and waterfalls—but the river, it goes right on. A woman looks at it thataway.

—Jane Darwell in *The Grapes of Wrath*

Now look, all I'm trying to say is that there are lots of things that a man can do, and in society's eyes it's all hunky-dory. A woman does the same things—the same, mind you—and she's an outcast. . . . All I'm saying is why let this deplorable system seep into our courts of law, where women are supposed to be equal?

—Katharine Hepburn in *Adam's Rib*

May it please the court, I submit that my entire line of defense is based upon the proposition that persons of the female sex should be dealt with, before the law, as the equals of persons of the male sex. I submit that I cannot hope to argue this line before minds hostile to and prejudiced against the female sex.

—Katharine Hepburn in *Adam's Rib*

I like you too much not to say it: you've got everything, except one thing—madness. A man needs a little madness, or else . . . he never dares cut the rope and be free.

—Anthony Quinn in *Zorba the Greek*

"Why"? Will no man ever do something without a "why"? Just like that, for the hell of it?

—Anthony Quinn in *Zorba the Greek*

Boss, life is trouble. Only death is not. To be alive is to undo your belt and look for trouble.

—Anthony Quinn in *Zorba the Greek*

I was suicidal, as a matter of fact, and would have killed myself, but I was in analysis with a strict Freudian, and if you kill yourself they make you pay for the sessions you miss.

—Woody Allen in *Annie Hall*

Killing is an excellent way of dealing with a hostility problem.

—James Coburn as a psychoanalyst in *The President's Analyst*

I can't get with any religion that advertises in Popular Mechanics.

—Woody Allen in *Annie Hall*

The Reverend Mother always says, when the Lord closes a door somewhere He opens a window.

—Julie Andrews in *The Sound of Music*

Oh, Christmas isn't just a day. It's a frame of mind.

—Edmund Gwenn as Kris Kringle in *Miracle on 34th Street*

Man is not made for defeat. Man can be destroyed but not defeated.

> —Spencer Tracy in *The Old Man and the Sea*

I feel that so much of contemporary life is a shocking matter, a really shocking matter. And one is obliged to catch the quality that prevails in contemporary life. If you just read the newspapers in America, you'll see that my plays are far from exaggerations.

> —Tennessee Williams, playwright, on the subject matter of his plays

I'm not interested in politics. The problems of the world are not in my department. I'm a saloon keeper.

> —Humphrey Bogart to Paul Henreid in *Casablanca*

Laurence Olivier: *Tell me, is Mrs. Van Hopper a friend of yours or just a relation?*
Joan Fontaine: *No, she's my employer. I'm what is known as a paid companion.*
Olivier: *I didn't know that companionship could be bought.*

> —Exchange between Olivier and Fontaine in *Rebecca*

Man came into this world to build, and not to destroy. Yet he's thrown into the necessity of destroying, and his one everlasting instinct is to try to save himself from having to destroy.

> —Sam Spiegel assessing the theme of *The Bridge on the River Kwai*

When it comes to dying for your country, it's better not to die at all.

> —Lew Ayres in *All Quiet on the Western Front*

You see, when you jumped in here, you were my enemy—and I was afraid of you. But you're just a man like me, and I killed you. . . . You're better off than I am—you're through—they can't do any more to you now. Oh, God! Why did they do this to us? We only wanted to live, you and I. Why should they send us out to fight each other? If they threw away these rifles and these uniforms, you could be my brother, just like Kat and Albert. You'll have to forgive me, comrade.

> —Lew Ayres in *All Quiet on the Western Front*

Trouble is, when men start taking the law into their own hands, they're just as apt to—in all the confusion and fun—to start hanging somebody who's not a murderer as somebody who is. Then, the next thing you know, they're hanging one another just for fun till it gets to a place a man can't pass a tree or look at a rope without feeling uneasy.

> —Henry Fonda in *Young Mr. Lincoln*

I was thrown out of N.Y.U. my freshman year for cheating on my metaphysics final, you know. I looked into the soul of the boy sitting next to me.

> —Woody Allen in *Annie Hall*

MORE QUOTES FROM MOVIES AND MOVIEMAKERS

Nothing happened, because I look like every other Italian on the street.

> —Rudolph Valentino, reporting to Bebe Daniels on his trip to Italy

Remember me? I'm the fellow you slept on last night.

> —Clark Gable to Claudette Colbert, his bus-seat companion in *It Happened One Night*

I spit in the sky and run under it.

> —A young Marlon Brando's response when asked whether he preferred a shower or a bath.

It has fifty-eight different functions. Fifty-nine if you want to light a cigarette.

> —James Coburn, displaying a cigarette lighter in *Our Man Flint*

I hate cold showers. They stimulate me, then I don't know what to do.

> —Oscar Levant in *Humoresque*

How did you get into that dress—with a spray gun?

> —Bob Hope to Dorothy Lamour in *Road to Rio*

Insanity runs in my family. It practically gallops.

> —Cary Grant in *Arsenic and Old Lace*

Little girls, I am in the business of putting old heads on young shoulders, and all my pupils are the crème de la crème. *Give me a girl of an impressionable age, and she is mine for life.*

> —Maggie Smith in *The Prime of Miss Jean Brodie*

I was a film critic for six years . . . if I didn't like the film I wouldn't write about it. That meant I couldn't write very often— and didn't get paid very often.

> —Paul Mayersberg

Waiter, will you serve the nuts—I mean, would you serve the guests the nuts?

> —Myrna Loy in *The Thin Man*

We mustn't underestimate American blundering. I was with them when they "blundered" into Berlin in 1918.

> —Claude Rains to Conrad Veidt in *Casablanca*

Damn the torpedoes! Full steam ahead!

> —Charles Coburn in *The More the Merrier*

You know me. I'm just like you. It's two in the morning, and I don't know nobody.

> —Robert Redford in *The Sting*

I don't want to live in a city where the only cultural advantage is that you can make a right turn on a red light.

> —Woody Allen on Los Angeles, in *Annie Hall*

What happened at the office? Well, I shot Mr. Brady in the head, made violent love to Miss Morris, and set fire to 300,000 copies of Little Women. *That's what happened at the office.*

—Tom Ewell in *The Seven Year Itch*

And now will you all leave quietly, or must I ask Miss Cutler to pass among you with a baseball bat?

—Monty Woolley in *The Man Who Came to Dinner*

No bar, no pinball machine. Just pool. This here is Ames, *son.*

—Jackie Gleason responding to Paul Newman's inquiry about whether the poolroom they are in has a bar in *The Hustler*

My check-out time in any hotel in the world is when I—is when I want to check out.

—Geraldine Page in *Sweet Bird of Youth*

[Rudolph Valentino is] the symbol of everything wild and wonderful and illicit in nature.

—*Life* magazine

Fasten your seatbelts. It's going to be a bumpy night.

—Bette Davis, preparing for a party in *All About Eve*

[He] uses words only to flog them. He makes them suffer.

—John Barrymore on Lionel Barrymore

It's a nice building. You get a—a better class of cockroaches.

—James Earl Jones to Diahann Carroll in *Claudine*

Some of us prefer Austrian voices raised in song to ugly German threats.

—Christopher Plummer in *The Sound of Music*

Fraulein, is it to be at every meal or merely at dinner time that you intend leading us all through this rare and wonderful new world of indigestion?

—Christopher Plummer to Julie Andrews in *The Sound of Music*

Strange? She's right out of The Hound of the Baskervilles.

—Monty Woolley in *The Man Who Came to Dinner*

There are two Hollywoods: the Hollywood where people live and work, and the Hollywood which lives in the mind of the public like a fabulous legend.

—Leo C. Rosten, screenwriter

A miserable newspaperwoman . . . wrote something implying that Rock Hudson, Julie [Andrews], and I were a sexual threesome. She also implied that Rock and I had spent a lot of time together in San Francisco leather bars . . . I walked up to Rock and repeated the story to him, and I loved his response: "How in the hell did she find out so quick?"

—Blake Edwards

To me, the imagination is a place all by itself. A separate country. Now, you've heard of the French nation, the British nation—well, this is the imagination. It's a wonderful place.

—Edmund Gwenn in *Miracle on 34th Street*

New York, skyscraper champion of the world, where the slickers and know-it-alls peddle gold bricks to each other, and truth, crushed to earth, rises more phony than a glass eye.

—Opening title of *Nothing Sacred*

He don't look so tough to me.
If he ain't tough, there's been an awful lot of sudden natural deaths in his vicinity.

—Exchange about Gregory Peck in *The Gunfighter*

I don't like to be alone at night. I guess everybody in the world's got a time they don't like. Me, it's right before I go to sleep. And now it's going to be for always. All the rest of my life.

—Bette Davis in *Watch on the Rhine*

Now you've done it! Now you've done it! . . . You tore off one of my chests.

—Jack Lemmon (in drag) in *Some Like It Hot*

Your Honor, we request an immediate ruling from this court: is there or is there not a Santa Claus?

—Jerome Cowan in *Miracle on 34th Street*

To get back my youth, I'd do anything in the world—except get up early, take exercise, or be respectable.

—George Sanders in *The Picture of Dorian Gray*

I'm trying to write good literature, but it always comes out nightingales and roses.

—Vanessa Redgrave in *The Loves of Isadora*

I believe in promotion with all my heart. We have never taken advantage of all the things that could be done in a promotional way for the movie business. Let's take 8½, which was a three-way co-production. Columbia Pictures took the whole world except for Italy. Italy was taken by producer Angelo Rizzoli. The picture did nothing in Italy. I was the co-producer in the United States and Canada. I never understood the picture, to tell you the truth, but we promoted the hell out of it.

—Joseph E. Levine

Groucho: *Gentlemen, Chicolini here may talk like an idiot and look like an idiot, but don't let that fool you. He really is an idiot. I implore you, send him back to his father and brothers who are waiting for him with open arms in the penitentiary. I suggest that we give him ten years in Leavenworth or eleven years in Twelveworth.*
Chico: *I tell you what I'll do. I'll take five and ten in Woolworth.*

—The Marx Brothers go to court in *Duck Soup*

You call this a party? The beer is warm, the women are cold, and I'm hot under the collar. In fact, a more poisonous little barbecue I've never attended.

—Groucho Marx being an ungracious guest in *Monkey Business*

Oh, I realize it's a penny here and a penny there, but look at me. I've worked myself up from nothing to a state of extreme poverty.

—Groucho Marx in *Monkey Business*

Jail is no place for a young fellow. There's no advancement.

—Groucho Marx in *The Cocoanuts*

You better beat it. I hear they're going to tear you down and put an office building where you're standing. You can leave in a taxi. If you can't get a taxi, you can leave in a huff. If that's too soon, you can leave in a minute and a huff. You know, you haven't stopped talking since I came here. You must have been vaccinated by a phonograph needle.

—Groucho Marx in *Duck Soup*

Clear? Huh! Why a four-year-old child could understand this report. Run out and find me a four-year-old child. I can't make head or tail out of it.

—Groucho Marx in *Duck Soup*

One morning I shot an elephant in my pajamas. How he got in my pajamas, I don't know.

—Groucho Marx lecturing on Africa in *Animal Crackers*

I now take great pleasure in presenting to you the well-preserved and partially pickled Mrs. Potter.

—Groucho Marx introducing Margaret Dumont in *The Cocoanuts*

Your eyes! Your eyes! They shine like the pants of a blue serge suit.

—Groucho Marx backhandedly complimenting Margaret Dumont in *The Cocoanuts*

You can have any kind of home you want to. You can even get stucco. Oh, how you can get stucco!

—Groucho Marx running an auction in *The Cocoanuts*

Margaret Dumont: *As chairwoman of the reception committee, I welcome you with open arms.*
Groucho Marx: *Is that so? How late do you stay open?*

—Exchange between Dumont and Groucho in *Duck Soup*

Take off your clothes, come in, and tell me all about it.

—Claudette Colbert inviting a maid to join her in a bath of asses' milk in *The Sign of the Cross*

One of the best reasons to do a film is when everybody tells you you shouldn't do it. Because if you stick to formulas, you're usually doomed to failure. You should go after material that is original and innovative. How many times did they tell me and my partner, Robert Chartoff, that films about fighters don't work, that women won't go to see them, that they have no overseas potential? And would you invest in a film with an unknown writer/actor named Sylvester Stallone? When everybody tells you there's not a chance in the world, that's the one you should go after.

—Irwin Winkler, producer

I became a good producer merely by not doing things I didn't think I should do. That's the trick of being good: to have the choice of saying no to something you're not wholeheartedly wed to.

—Sam Spiegel, producer

If you stop to analyze a picture, with all these guys sitting around at a board of directors' meeting and they don't want to make it because the wind is coming from the southeast—I mean, that's a lot of bunk. If you want to make it, make it.

—Joseph E. Levine, producer

When I write I keep Tolstoy around because I want great limits. I want big thinking.

—Mel Brooks

One thing I've discovered is that if a scene doesn't work one way, do the exact opposite of what you've been doing, no matter how insane it seems, and it'll sometimes work . . . . Sometimes doing just the opposite works . . . . Each of us has a vision of life, and part of the process of writing is not so much to explain your vision but to discover it.

—Robert Towne, screenwriter

I am not only walking out on this case, Mr. Whiteside, I am leaving the nursing profession. I became a nurse because all my life, ever since I was a little girl, I was filled with the idea of serving a suffering humanity. After one month with you, Mr. Whiteside, I am going to work in a munition factory. From now on, anything I can do to help exterminate the human race will fill me with the greatest of pleasure.

—Mary Wickes to her recent patient, played by Monty Woolley, in *The Man Who Came to Dinner*

I love you. Why don't you marry me? You take me and I'll take a vacation. I'll need to take a vacation if we're going to get married. I can see you right now in the kitchen bending over a hot stove. But I can't see the stove. I suppose you'll think me a sentimental old fluff, but would you mind giving me a lock of your hair? I'm letting you off easy, I was going to ask for the whole wig.

—Groucho Marx to Margaret Dumont in *Duck Soup*

THE
TRIVIA QUIZZES
TEST YOUR MOVIE KNOWLEDGE

Here it is—your opportunity to discover just how you rate in the movie trivia stakes. Here are nearly fifty question-and-answer and picture quizzes to get your memory working overtime. There are literally hundreds of questions here—a real challenge for the most dedicated movie expert. The question-and-answer quizzes cover an enormous range of trivia information and test your memory for words and music. And what about your visual memory? That's the key to the picture quizzes. Challenge yourself with this extensive store of fascinating trivia facts about movies since the days of the silents to the latest box office hits. The answers are at the end of the section—try not to look! Good luck.

Judy Garland

QUIZ #1
JUDY GARLAND TRIVIA

1. In 1936, when MGM was looking for a new singing ingenue, Judy Garland made a short film with a young soprano. Name the film and the soprano.
2. To whom did Garland sing "Have Yourself a Merry Little Christmas," and in which film?
3. Late in her life, Garland almost dropped "Over the Rainbow" as her theme song in favor of "Little Drops of Rain," a song from a film in which she starred yet never appeared. What was the film?
4. *A Star Is Born* was set in Hollywood; where did *I Could Go On Singing* take place?
5. Judy had already recorded the soundtrack for a 1949 western musical, and had started filming, when she was dropped from the production. What was the film, and who replaced her?
6. In 1950, Garland was asked to replace an actress in a Fred Astaire film, only to be dropped and replaced by another actress. What was the film, who was the original actress, and who was Garland's replacement?
7. Who played Garland's mother in *Meet Me in St. Louis*?
8. With whom did Garland run her farm in *Summer Stock*?
9. Who replaced Stanley Kramer as director of *A Child Is Waiting*?
10. What are the names of Garland's three children?
11. In 1961, Judy received her final Oscar nomination. What category was she nominated in and for which movie?
12. What popular World War II era dance was the subject of a musical number cut from the final print of *The Wizard of Oz*?
13. How many films did Judy make with Mickey Rooney, and what were their titles?
14. What makes Dorothy fall asleep on her way to see *The Wizard of Oz*?
15. Which movie marked Garland's development into a romantic leading lady, and who was her co-star?

Answers are on p. 352.

QUIZ #2
KATHARINE HEPBURN AND SPENCER TRACY TRIVIA

1. Who wrote *Adam's Rib* for Katharine Hepburn and Spencer Tracy?
2. In what movie did Spencer Tracy co-star with Ingrid Bergman?
3. What was the name of the computer that threatened to come between Hepburn and Tracy in *Desk Set*?
4. For the film version of *The Philadelphia Story*:
   A. Who did Hepburn want to play the roles of C. K. Dexter Haven and Macauley Connor?
   B. Who did play those roles in the movie?
5. Who played the real estate agent in *Without Love*?
6. Tracy starred in the film version of an Ernest Hemingway novel. Name it.
7. Why is *Woman of the Year* significant for the Hepburn and Tracy team?
8. What song did Hepburn sing to soothe 'Baby' in *Bringing Up Baby*?
9. Who played Hepburn's and Tracy's daughter in *Guess Who's Coming to Dinner?*
10. Spencer Tracy played the title role in *Father of the Bride*:
    A. Who played the bride?
    B. Who played the mother of the bride?
    C. Who directed the film?
11. What was the relationship between the characters played by Hepburn and Tracy in *Pat and Mike*?
12. Who played Katharine Hepburn's roommate in *Stage Door*?
13. Tracy played a reporter; Hepburn played the widow of a boys' club leader who was a covert fascist. What was the film?
14. In which movie did Tracy co-star with Loretta Young?
15. Who played "the other woman," a political benefactress, in *State of the Union*?
16. In which film did Katharine Hepburn have Fred MacMurray as a suitor and Hattie McDaniel as a maid?
17. What were Adam and Amanda Bonner's nicknames for each other in *Adam's Rib*?

Answers are on p. 352.

Spencer Tracy and Katharine Hepburn in *Adam's Rib*.

Joan Crawford with Michael Wilding in *Torch Song*.

Bette Davis in a classic scene from *Jezebel*.

QUIZ #3

JOAN CRAWFORD AND BETTE DAVIS TRIVIA

1. What does Mildred Pierce (Joan Crawford), in the film of that name, give daughter Veda for her birthday?

2. Who played Bette Davis' daughter in *Where Love Has Gone*?

3. When Joan Crawford threatens Sydney Greenstreet with a gun in *Flamingo Road*, what does he strike her with?

4. Bette Davis is best remembered by many movie buffs for her biting performance as Margo Channing in *All About Eve*. Which actress had originally been signed to play the role, and why didn't she?

5. Joan Crawford is credited with making three fashion accessories wildly popular; what were they?

6. Who played Joan Crawford's assistant, Woody, in *Goodbye My Fancy*?

7. What song did Bette Davis sing in one of her first feature films, *Cabin in the Cotton*?

8. Joan Crawford appeared in two films titled *Possessed*. In what years were they made and who were her co-stars?

9. In *Grand Hotel*, Wallace Beery asks his stenographer, Joan Crawford, what kind of job she really wants. What does Crawford reply?

10. In *All About Eve*, Bill Sampson is telling Eve Harrington about the time he looked into the wrong end of a camera in Hollywood. What line does Margo interrupt him with? And who played Bill Sampson and Eve Harrington?

11. Who was originally intended to play Joan Crawford in *Mommie Dearest*, only to be replaced by Faye Dunaway?

12. What condition is Bette Davis suffering from in *Dark Victory*?

13. In what film did Joan Crawford co-star with a prehistoric beast?

14. Who plays the daughter of Jane's and Blanche's next door neighbor in *Whatever Happened to Baby Jane*?

15. What was the name of Crawford's character in *Johnny Guitar*?

16. Bette Davis was reportedly upset over not being cast as Scarlett in *Gone With the Wind*. What movie did Jack Warner buy for her instead, and what benefit did Bette reap from it?

17. In *Above Suspicion*, Joan Crawford is shown an ancient instrument of torture that a Nazi describes as being used to tear fingernails from the victim's hand. What does she call the device?

18. What extraordinary cosmetic requirement did Bette Davis submit to for her role as Queen Elizabeth I in *The Private Life of Elizabeth and Essex*?

Answers are on p. 352.

QUIZ #4
SUSAN HAYWARD TRIVIA

1. Susan Hayward, though never known as a singer, played a singer in several movies. In one of them her own voice is heard on the soundtrack. Which is it?
2. In *My Foolish Heart* what '...funny old gentleman rabbit' does Walt (Dana Andrews) mention when Eloise (Hayward) cuts her finger?
3. What major radio/recording star did Hayward portray in *With a Song in My Heart*?
4. *Smash-Up* is loosely based on the story of a major singing star and his first wife. Do you know who they were?
5. What disease does Lillian Roth suffer from in *I'll Cry Tomorrow*?
6. Barbara Graham kept a good-luck keepsake with her through the harrowing ordeal recounted in *I Want To Live!* What was it?
7. In which movie does Susan Hayward appear as the wife of Gregory Peck?
8. Hayward replaced one of the screen's most famous musical stars in *Valley of the Dolls*. Who was that star?
9. In *With a Song in My Heart*, Hayward performs a nightclub number with a shell-shocked soldier. Who plays the soldier?
10. What movie co-starred Hayward with Veronica Lake?
11. One of Hayward's last professional engagements before her death was in a stage production of a musical that later became a successful movie. What was it?
12. In *Valley of the Dolls*, Hayward has a no-holds-barred fight with Patty Duke in a ladies' room. What possession of Hayward's does Duke try to flush down the toilet?
13. As Edythe Marrener, Hayward was a successful model in New York—what brought her to Hollywood?
14. Susan Hayward co-starred with John Gavin in a third remake of a film that originally starred Irene Dunne and was later remade with Margaret Sullavan. What was the film?

Answers are on p. 353.

Susan Hayward—close up, and in a classic pose.

Barbara Stanwyck

QUIZ #5
BARBARA STANWYCK TRIVIA

1. In which film did Barbara Stanwyck co-star with a telephone?
2. What is Barbara Stanwyck's real name?
3. Who played Stanwyck's not-so-gay sisters in *The Gay Sisters*?
4. Where has Charlie Pike (Henry Fonda) come from when he first meets Jean Harrington (Stanwyck) in *The Lady Eve*?
5. In *Double Indemnity*, where do Phyllis Dietrichson (Stanwyck) and Walter Neff (Fred MacMurray) meet surreptitiously to plot their deed?
6. In what film did Stanwyck give a birthday party, to which no one came, for her daughter?
7. Which early Stanwyck film was censured because of overtones of miscegeny involving the characters played by Stanwyck and Nils Asther?
8. What do Elizabeth Lane's readers continually send her as gifts in *Christmas in Connecticut*?
9. A. Which of Stanwyck's movies was based on a book by Gypsy Rose Lee?
   B. What was the title of Gypsy Rose Lee's book?
   C. In what other movie does Stanwyck play a stripper/showgirl?
10. What actor took his professional name from the character he played in *The Gay Sisters*?
11. In what early film did Stanwyck appear with newcomer Clark Gable?
12. Who were the two actors Stanwyck married?
13. Stanwyck made three movies with Robert Taylor. Can you name them?
14. In one of her movies Stanwyck played the madam of a New Orleans brothel. One of her 'girls' is now a superstar. Name the movie and the girl.
15. What is Stanwyck's on-set nickname?
16. Which screen legend vied for attention with Stanwyck in *Clash by Night*?
17. What is the first thing Walter Neff notices about Phyllis Dietrichson in *Double Indemnity*?

Answers are on p. 353.

Humphrey Bogart and Ingrid Bergman in *Casablanca*.

QUIZ #6

CASABLANCA TRIVIA

1. In *Casablanca*, Bogart never actually said, "Play it again, Sam." What *did* he say?
2. What year was *Casablanca* released?
3. Who were the two stars who were originally intended to play the roles of Victor Laszlo and Ilsa Lund?
4. Who directed *Casablanca*?
5. According to Rick, what color was Ilsa wearing when the Nazis occupied Paris?
6. Where does Rick hide the stolen letters of transit?
7. Ingrid Bergman was a glaring omission from the list of Oscar nominations that *Casablanca* received.
   A. For what other film was she nominated that year?
   B. How many Oscars did *Casablanca* win, and in which categories?
8. Who wrote the screenplay for *Casablanca*?
9. When Ilsa asks Sam to play "As Time Goes By," and he says he's forgotten the song, what does Ilsa do?
10. Apart from *Casablanca*, Humphrey Bogart made three other films in 1943; name them.
11. Who composed *Casablanca*'s memorable score?
12. According to Rick, what do "the problems of three little people" in this world not amount to ?

Answers are on p. 353.

QUIZ #7

KING KONG TRIVIA

1. Who produced the original *King Kong*?
2. In the movie, where did the film crew find Kong?
3. Which blonde actress did Kong have the hots for?
4. Give the years in which the original *King Kong* and the remake were released.
5. Who played the female lead in the remake?
6. Name the directors of the original *King Kong*.
7. Give the locations where Kong was killed in the original film and in the remake.
8. How did Ann Darrow (Fay Wray) first meet Kong?
9. The animation used in the 1933 version of *King Kong* set new standards for Hollywood special effects; who was responsible for the movie's special effects?
10. Joel McCrea was offered the role of Jack Driscoll in the original version of *King Kong*, but he turned it down. Who played the part?
11. Who produced the remake?
12. Who were Kong's discoverers working for in the remake?
13. In the original movie, what was the name of the ship that carried Kong to New York?
14. What does Kong do after letting Ann wash under a waterfall?
15. In the last line of the film, what is the cause given for King Kong's death?

Answers are on p. 353.

The original *King Kong*

QUIZ #8

GONE WITH THE WIND TRIVIA

1. How many directors worked on *Gone With the Wind*? And how many are credited on the final print?
2. Scarlett O'Hara's plantation was called, of course, Tara. What was the name of the Wilkes' plantation?
3. How much money—and in what currency—did Rhett Butler pay to dance with Scarlett at the Charity Ball?
4. Who played Scarlett's sisters, Careen and Suellen?
5. What ironical news does Melanie bring when she comes to console Rhett Butler over his wife's miscarriage?
6. What was the nickname of Scarlett's and Rhett's daughter, and how did she get that name?
7. How many times was Scarlett married during the course of *Gone With the Wind*, and how did the marriages end?
8. David O. Selznick decided to sign Vivien Leigh as Scarlett the night he filmed the "burning of Atlanta" scene. Who was the last leading contender for the role of Scarlett before Leigh was signed, and who was playing Scarlett in the "burning" scene?
9. Where did Scarlett and Rhett go on their honeymoon?
10. What are the key words in the opening and closing lines of *Gone With the Wind*?
11. Margaret Mitchell once told a reporter who she favored for the role of Rhett Butler . . . and it wasn't Clark Gable. Who was it?

12. When we first see her in the film, Scarlett's mother has been acting as midwife. To whom?
13. Of the four principal stars of *Gone With the Wind*, who got top billing?
14. Who saved Scarlett from certain death, or a fate worse than death, when she was attacked in Shanty Town?
15. How did Scarlett mask her secret drinking after the death of her second husband?
16. What does Scarlett say to prompt Rhett to respond, "Frankly, my dear, I don't give a damn"?
17. When Scarlett is "sittin' and waitin' " in Atlanta for Ashley to come home on leave how does Mammy describe her?
18. What is Ashley holding when he breaks down at Melanie's death?
19. Clark Gable did not win an Oscar for his portrayal of Rhett Butler. Who won the best actor award that year, and for which movie?
20. Who composed the score for *Gone With the Wind*?
21. Gerald O'Hara (Thomas Mitchell) dies when he is thrown from his horse. Why is this ironic?
22. A. Where was the premiere of *Gone With the Wind* held?
   B. Which of the stars of *Gone With the Wind* attended the premiere?
   C. Which of the leading performers in *Gone With the Wind* was excluded from the screening?

Answers are on p. 353.

Clark Gable and Vivien Leigh in *Gone With the Wind*.

QUIZ #9
HITCHCOCK TRIVIA

1. Alfred Hitchcock made one of his movies twice, in 1934 and 1956. What was it?
2. Which film marked Hitchcock's debut as a producer? Another clue: He also wrote the story.
3. Who was the controversial artist who designed the 'dream sequence' in *Spellbound*?
4. In *The Man Who Knew Too Much*, 1956, the prologue states that something would, in a moment's time, change the lives of an American family. What was it?
5. What was the name of Joan Fontaine's character in *Rebecca*?
6. Where does Marion Crane hide the money she's embezzled when she checks into the Bates Motel in *Psycho*?
7. In *Psycho*, who played Marion Crane, and who played her sister?
8. What were the thirty-nine steps in Hitchcock's 1935 movie of that name?
9. What did James Stewart use to stall his assailant in the climax of *Rear Window*?
10. Who plays Charles Laughton's wife in *The Paradine Case*?
11. Marnie (Tippi Hedren) committed a few felonies in *Marnie*. What were the crimes?
12. Who played both Cary Grant's mother in *North by Northwest* and Grace Kelly's mother in *To Catch a Thief*?
13. Ida Lupino's uncle starred in two of Hitchcock's earliest British silent films, *The Lodger* and *Downhill*. Name the uncle.
14. Hitchcock directed Charles Laughton and Maureen O'Hara in *Jamaica Inn* in 1939; who produced the movie?
15. An Oscar-winning actress played the role of Countess Kuchinski in *Torn Curtain*. Who was she?
16. *The Secret Agent* stars Peter Lorre, Lilli Palmer, Robert Young, and Madeleine Carroll. Name the young actor who plays Richard Ashendon.
17. Who plays Barbara Morton, Ruth Roman's sister, in *Strangers on a Train* and what other special connection does she have with the film?
18. In *Dial M for Murder*, Grace Kelly is attacked by a killer. What weapon does she use in self-defense?
19. *The Birds* opens with Tippi Hedren driving many miles to deliver a present to Rod Taylor. What was the gift?
20. *Rope* was Hitchcock's first film as an independent producer; his first film released by Warner Bros.; his first (and only) attempt to make a film appear as one single shot; and his first film with James Stewart. What other significant 'first' was it for him?
21. Aside from it being her second film with Hitchcock, why was Joan Fontaine glad she starred in *Suspicion*?

Answers are on p. 353.

Alfred Hitchcock with the cast of *Family Plot*: William DeVane, Karen Black, Barbara Harris, and Bruce Dern.

QUIZ #10
HITCHCOCK CAMEOS

One of the trademark characteristics of the late British director Alfred Hitchcock—the master of suspense—was that he liked to appear in cameo roles in his own films. By the peak of his career he was appearing in every film he made, sometimes making appearances so brief or unexpected that it became a viewers' game to spot him. Here are brief descriptions of the appearances Hitchcock made in 22 of his movies. Can you match the cameo to the film? Answers are on pp. 353–54.

Name the film in which Hitchcock appears as:
1. A man at a desk in a newsroom.
2. A man being annoyed by a little boy on a subway train.
3. A man walking down a street.
4. A man standing at a railway station.
5. The man in the phone booth next door to the one used by one of the movie's leading performers. (This scene appears in publicity stills but not in the finished film.)
6. A man reading a newspaper.
7. A man playing cards on a train (he has a full house).
8. A man pictured "before" and "after" in a weight reduction advertisement.
9. A man walking out of an elevator carrying a violin.
10. A man drinking champagne at a party.
11. A man carrying a cello.
12. A man crossing the street, after the credits.
13. As one character gets off the train, Hitchcock gets on carrying a bass fiddle.
14. A man in the photograph of a class reunion.
15. A man winding a clock.
16. A man walking in front of John Forsythe's outdoor exhibition.
17. The man watching acrobats in a marketplace.
18. A man crossing the street.
19. The man who misses a bus as the door slams in his face.
20. A man wearing a cowboy hat, outside a realty office.
21. A man walking out of a pet shop with two poodles.
22. A man walking down a hotel corridor.

QUIZ #11
FAMOUS ACTORS' CAMEOS

The following actors all had cameo roles in the movies listed. Can you name the parts they played or the scenes in which they appeared? Answers are on p. 354.

1. Ted Knight in *Psycho*
2. Harvey Korman in *Gypsy*
3. Audrey Hepburn in *The Lavender Hill Mob*
4. Jean Harlow in Laurel and Hardy's *Double Whoopee*
5. Sylvester Stallone in *Bananas*
6. Dustin Hoffman in *The Tiger Makes Out*
7. Robert Duvall in *Invasion of the Body Snatchers* (1978)
8. Jacqueline Bisset in *Casino Royale*
9. Gary Cooper in *Wings*
10. Jack Nicholson in *Head*
11. Lucille Ball in *Ziegfeld Follies*
12. Peter O'Toole in *Casino Royale*
13. Robert Blake in *The Treasure of the Sierra Madre*
14. Richard Dreyfuss in *The Graduate*
15. Shelly Hack in *Annie Hall*
16. Sigourney Weaver in *Annie Hall*
17. Jeff Goldblum in *Annie Hall*
18. Walter Huston in *The Maltese Falcon*
19. Rock Hudson in *Winchester '73*
20. John Huston in *The Treasure of the Sierra Madre*

QUIZ #12
ORIGINAL CASTING

In all the following movies, the star named was not the first to be considered for the role. Who was originally considered for the roles played by the following actors in these films? Answers are on p. 354.

1. Harrison Ford— *Raiders of the Lost Ark*
2. Kim Novak—*Vertigo*
3. Peter O'Toole— *Lawrence of Arabia*
4. Eddie Murphy— *Trading Places*
5. Marlon Brando— *Guys and Dolls*
6. W. C. Fields— *David Copperfield*
7. Dudley Moore— *Unfaithfully Yours*
8. Dudley Moore—*10*
9. Betty Hutton— *Annie Get Your Gun*
10. Clint Eastwood— *Dirty Harry*
11. Robert Redford— *Butch Cassidy and the Sundance Kid*
12. Bette Davis— *All About Eve*
13. Spencer Tracy— *Father of the Bride*
14. Elizabeth Taylor— *Cat on a Hot Tin Roof*
15. Don Ameche— *Trading Places*
16. Stanley Holloway— *My Fair Lady*
17. Elizabeth Taylor— *Cleopatra*
18. Peter O'Toole— *What's New, Pussycat?*
19. Jack Nicholson— *Five Easy Pieces*
20. Ron Moody— *Oliver!*
21. Richard Gere— *An Officer and a Gentleman*
22. James Mason— *A Star Is Born* (1954)

Name the actress pictured here with Fred Astaire and you'll have the answer to one of the questions in this quiz.

QUIZ #13
NAME THE WOMEN IN WOODY ALLEN'S LIFE

Woody Allen is a many-faceted talent, and in the course of his film career he has acted opposite or directed a select handful of actresses whose originality and talent are a perfect match for his own. Frequently he has worked repeatedly with the same actresses—notably, of course, Diane Keaton and Mia Farrow. How familiar are you with the women in Woody Allen's professional life? Name the actresses who starred with, or were directed by, Woody Allen in the following 12 movies. Remember that some of the answers call for more than one name. Answers are on p. 354.

1. *Take the Money and Run*, 1969
2. *Bananas*, 1971
3. *Everything You Always Wanted to Know About Sex (But Were Afraid to Ask)*, 1972
4. *Sleeper*, 1973
5. *Love and Death*, 1975
6. *Annie Hall*, 1977
7. *Interiors*, 1978
8. *Manhattan*, 1979
9. *Stardust Memories*, 1980
10. *A Midsummer Night's Sex Comedy*, 1982
11. *Zelig*, 1983
12. *Broadway Danny Rose*, 1984

QUIZ #14
FRED ASTAIRE'S OTHER WOMEN

Fred Astaire's most famous leading lady was, of course, Ginger Rogers, and together they made movie magic in ten wonderful musical films. In fact, though, there were many other women in Astaire's movie life. Can you name Astaire's partners in the following films? Answers are on p. 354.

1. *Broadway Melody of 1940*, 1940
2. *You'll Never Get Rich*, 1941
3. *Holiday Inn*, 1942
4. *The Sky's the Limit*, 1943
5. *Easter Parade*, 1948
6. *Royal Wedding*, 1951
7. *The Belle of New York*, 1952
8. *The Band Wagon*, 1953
9. *Daddy Long Legs*, 1955
10. *Funny Face*, 1957

Audrey Hepburn wears some stunning gowns in *My Fair Lady*. Who designed her costumes?

QUIZ #15
MOVIE SONG AND DANCE TRIVIA

1. In which movie did Clark Gable dance and sing "Puttin' on the Ritz"?
2. What was the title of Fred Astaire's debut movie, and who was its star?
3. Which English musical film was based on a Hans Christian Andersen story and starred Moira Shearer as a ballerina?
4. *High Society* is a musical remake of a famous movie. Name the original.
5. What is particularly memorable about Maurice Chevalier's 1929 movie *Innocents of Paris*?
6. Cyd Charisse was made up to look like a famous silent screen star in the "Gotta Dance" number in *Singin' in the Rain*. Who was that star?
7. *For Me and My Gal* introduced a musical star to the screen. Who was it?
8. Van Johnson and Judy Garland starred in *In the Good Old Summertime* for MGM.
   A. Who directed it?
   B. It was a musical remake of a movie. Name the movie.
   C. Which future singing star appeared for one minute in the last shot of the movie?
9. Who was Judy Holliday's romantic lead in *Bells Are Ringing*?
10. James Cagney portrayed a song-and-dance man in *Yankee Doodle Dandy*. Who was it?
11. In *Ziegfeld Follies*:
   A. What song provided the basis for the Oriental fantasy number?
   B. Who was Fred Astaire's partner in that number?
12. Who did Doris Day portray in *Love Me or Leave Me*?
13. Which musical featured Carmen Miranda and Benny Goodman?
14. Who designed Audrey Hepburn's costumes for *My Fair Lady*?
15. Elizabeth Taylor starred in the film version of a successful Broadway musical. Name the musical.
16. What song made popular by Mary Martin did Marilyn Monroe perform in *Let's Make Love*?

Answers are on p. 354.

QUIZ #16
SONGS FROM THE MOVIES

Some of the most popular songs of all time were first heard in movies. In which films were the following songs introduced? Answers are on p. 354.

1. "Black Magic"
2. "I've Got You Under My Skin"
3. "One for My Baby (and One More for the Road)"
4. "A Foggy Day (in London Town)"
5. "Thanks for the Memory"
6. "Tip Toe Through the Tulips"
7. "Chattanooga Choo Choo"
8. "Lullaby of Broadway"
9. "Singin' in the Rain"
10. "Louise"
11. "Beyond the Blue Horizon"
12. "Don't Fence Me In"
13. "Happiness Is a Thing Called Joe"
14. "I'm in the Mood for Love"
15. "Three Little Words"
16. "Heart and Soul"
17. "All I Do Is Dream of You (the Whole Night Through)"
18. "Call Me Irresponsible"
19. "You Must Have Been a Beautiful Baby"
20. "Cocktails for Two"
21. "Jeepers Creepers"

QUIZ #17
STAGE VS. SCREEN CASTING

PART 1
It usually happens that a star who is successful in a Broadway stage production is passed over when the movie version is cast. Here are some famous movies that originated as stage shows, along with the names of the actresses who played the leads in the film versions. Do you remember who originated the roles on Broadway?

1. *The Sound of Music*; Julie Andrews
2. *Mame*; Lucille Ball
3. *Annie Get Your Gun*; Betty Hutton
4. *Cabaret*; Liza Minnelli
5. *The Corn Is Green*; Bette Davis
6. *A Streetcar Named Desire*; Vivien Leigh
7. *Hello, Dolly!*; Barbra Streisand
8. *The Little Foxes*; Bette Davis
9. *Sweet Charity*; Shirley MacLaine
10. *My Fair Lady*; Audrey Hepburn

Anthony Quinn

PART 2
There have, however, been cases where stars have played the same role on the stage and on the screen. Name the shows the following performers appeared in both on the stage and on the screen.

1. Rex Harrison
2. Judy Holliday
3. Henry Fonda
4. Barbra Streisand
5. Yul Brynner
6. Katharine Hepburn
7. Anthony Quinn
8. Fred Astaire
9. Ethel Merman
10. Robert Preston

Answers are on p. 355.

You may recognize the actor and identify the movie, but do you remember the ad line with which the film was publicized? It's in the list of ad lines shown here.

QUIZ #18
AD LINES

Moviemakers spend an enormous amount of money on advertising campaigns, trusting in a catchy advertising slogan to capture the public imagination and draw the audiences into the movie houses. Can you identify the films that were heralded by these ad lines? Answers are on p. 355.

1. You must see it twice.
2. They had a date with fate in . . .
3. Nine men who came too late and stayed too long.
4. They'd never forget the day he drifted into town.
5. Where were you in '62?
6. It's more than a movie. It's a celebration! Boy do we need it now.
7. In 1959 a lot of people were killing time. Kit and Holly were killing people.
8. A long time ago in a galaxy far, far away . . .
9. Pathetic earthlings . . . who can save you now?
10. Thank God it's only a motion picture.
11. The seed is planted . . . terror grows.
12. In space no one can hear you scream.
13. They're young, they're in love and they kill people.
14. The movie with something to offend everyone.
15. Made in South America, where life is cheap.
16. Garbo laughs!
17. How did they ever make a movie out of . . .
18. You are cordially invited to George and Martha's for an evening of fun & games.
19. Crushed lips don't talk.
20. There never was a woman like . . .
21. Every father's daughter is a virgin.
22. The nearer they get to their treasure, the farther they get from the law.

QUIZ #19
OPENING LINES

Identify the films that open with the following lines. Answers are on p. 355.

1. The life of a playwright is tough. It's not as easy as some people seem to think.
2. Jones and Barry are doing a show.
3. Hello, Gorgeous.
4. Apaches, Captain! The hills are swarmin' with 'em.
5. Hey boy, what you doin' with my momma's car?
6. Senator Samuel Foley—dead, died a minute ago—here at St. Vincent's.
7. Last night I dreamt I went to Manderley again.
8. Hunger strike, eh? How long has this been going on?
9. What can you say about a 25-year-old girl who died?
10. Rosebud.
11. There was me, that is Alex, and my three droogs, that is Pete, Georgie and Dim . . .
12. If anyone moves, shoot 'em.
13. All right Curley, enough's enough. You can't eat the venetian blinds, I just had 'em installed on Wednesday.
14. Here you are, sir.
15. Excuse me . . . my name's Barrett, sir.
16. Joey, Joey Doyle!
17. When I stepped out into the bright sunlight from the darkness of the movie house, I had only two things on my mind . . .
18. Chapter One. He adored New York City. He idolized it all out of proportion.
19. Don't tell me, you didn't know it was loaded.
20. The dream is always the same.

QUIZ #20
CLOSING LINES

Identify the films that end with the following lines. Answers are on p. 355.

1. Alex, come in please, I wish to talk with you.
2. Where the devil are my slippers, Eliza?
3. I now pronounce you men and wives.
4. Hello, everybody. This is Mrs. Norman Maine.
5. Mother of Mercy, is this the end of Little Rico?
6. Well Tillie, when the hell are we going to get some dinner?
7. He used to be a big shot.
8. Louis, I think this is the beginning of a beautiful friendship.
9. All right Mr. De Mille, I'm ready for my close-up.
10. Why, she wouldn't even harm a fly.
11. They can't lick us. And we'll go on forever, Pa, 'cause we're the people.
12. Life is a state of mind.
13. Stand still, Godfrey, it'll all be over in a minute.
14. Except for a single, very powerful radio emission aimed at Jupiter the four million year old black monolith has re-

301

mained completely inert, its origin and purpose still a mystery.
15. We're sorry we were late, but we had to pick up our son Hank.
16. ...the stuff that dreams are made of.
17. It wasn't the airplanes. 'Twas beauty killed the beast.
18. Why Mr. Rusk, you're not wearing your tie.
19. After all, tomorrow is another day.
20. He who is secure within can say: Tomorrow do thy worst! For I have lived today.

In which movie did this "play within the play" appear?

QUIZ #21
PLAYS WITHIN PLAYS

Each one of the following plays, musicals, films, and operas takes place within a movie. Identify the film in which the following can be seen. Answers are on p. 355.

1. Broadway play: *Aged in Wood*, starring Margo Channing, directed by Bill Sampson, written by Lloyd Richards, produced by Max Fabian
2. Movie Musical: *The Dancing Cavalier*, starring Don Lockwood and Lina Lamont
3. Broadway Musical: *Pretty Lady*, starring Peggy Sawyer, directed by Julian Marsh
4. Broadway Musical: *Springtime for Hitler*, starring LSD, directed by Roger de Bris, written by Franz Liebkind
5. Broadway Musical: *Satan's Alley*, starring Tony Manero
6. Army Revue: *Jungle Jamboree*, starring Eric Young-Love, directed by Terri Dennis
7. Movie: *The Walls Are Closing In*
8. Opera: *Salammbô*, starring Susan Alexander
9. Movie Musical: *Hey Hey in the Hayloft*, directed by John L. Sullivan
10. TV Soap Opera: *Southwest General*

QUIZ #22
FICTITIOUS PLACES

Many movies are set in fictitious locations. Which movies take place in the following areas? Answers are on p. 355.

1. Concordia
2. Vulgaria
3. Tomania
4. Freedonia
5. Klopstokia
6. Arrakis
7. Brandrika
8. Missitucky
9. Ruritania
10. Grand Fenwick

Gary Cooper starred in *High Noon*. Who was his leading lady?

QUIZ #23
HOW WELL DO YOU KNOW YOUR WESTERNS?

1. What was the name of Tom Mix's horse?
2. *The Plainsman* was released in 1937:
   A. What character did Gary Cooper play?
   B. Who directed the film?
3. John Wayne specialized in playing tough cowboys with hearts of gold. Who was his love object in the following movies?
   A. *Hondo*
   B. *Pittsburgh*
   C. *Rooster Cogburn*
4. In *The Man Who Shot Liberty Valance*:
   A. Who played Liberty Valance?
   B. Who played "the man who shot Liberty Valance," and what profession did he attempt to follow?
5. Which actress starred with Gary Cooper in *High Noon*?
6. Who played the new arrival in town in *Bad Day at Black Rock*?
7. In *A Big Hand for the Little Lady*, Joanne Woodward is forced to play poker with several tough cowboys and has to ask the local bank for a loan. What does she offer as collateral?
8. Name the actors who portrayed *The Magnificent Seven*.
9. Which historical western figure did Burt Lancaster portray in *Gunfight at the OK Corral*?
10. In 1939, John Ford's classic western *Stagecoach* opened:
    A. Who played Ringo Kid?
    B. Who won an Oscar for best supporting actor for his performance as Doc Boone?
11. In 1969, George Roy Hill directed *Butch Cassidy and the Sundance Kid*:
    A. Who were the two stars, and which characters did they play?
    B. What was the name of their gang?
    C. When Butch, Sundance, and Etta (Katharine Ross) escaped from America, where did they go into hiding?

Answers are on p. 355.

Charlie Chaplin

QUIZ #24
GOLDEN SILENTS TRIVIA

1. Lillian Gish was one of the first actresses to direct a silent film. What was the name of the film that marked her directorial debut in 1920, and who starred in it?
2. A future cowboy star played Greta Garbo's brother in *The Single Standard*. Who was he?
3. Mary Pickford, Douglas Fairbanks, Charles Chaplin, and D. W. Griffith joined together to start an independent film company. What did they call it?
4. Mae Murray was one of the grandest of silent stars, and is credited with starting a craze for a certain fashion in make-up. What was it?
5. What famous boy did Betty Bronson first portray on the screen in a silent classic?
6. Mary Pickford was married, at different times, to three famous stars of the silent movies; name them.
7. Lillian Gish is usually associated with director D. W. Griffith, but he did not direct her in the hugely successful *The Wind*. Who did?
8. Their names don't necessarily provide clues to the original nationality of these silent movie stars. Can you name their homelands?
   A. Greta Garbo
   B. Natasha Rambova
   C. Pola Negri
   D. Norma Shearer
9. Garbo's *Anna Karenina* was the remake of one of her great silent movie hits—which one?
10. What was the title of Rudolph Valentino's last movie?
11. Comedians of the silent era relied on sight gags and generally had instantly recognizable individual characteristics. Each of the following silent clowns had his "trademark." What was it?
    A. Ben Turpin
    B. Buster Keaton
    C. Harold Lloyd
    D. Charlie Chaplin
12. Who was the director of the Keystone Studio?
13. D. W. Griffith made a movie with the working title of *The Mother and the Law*. It was released under another title and became a smash hit. What was the title?
14. One film has gone down in movie history as marking the end of the silent era and the beginning of the age of sound. What was the film, when was it made, and at which studio was it made?

Answers are on p. 355.

QUIZ #25

THE MAN WITH THE GOLDEN ARMS: OSCAR TRIVIA

1. The Oscar is actually the AMPAS award. What do the initials stand for?
2. Some years in Hollywood are best described as "banner years," and the 1950 awards represent a banner year. How much do you know about that year?
   A. Judy Holliday won the best actress award for *Born Yesterday*. Which four actresses, all nominated for now classic roles, lost to her?
   B. William Holden was nominated for best actor in *Sunset Boulevard*. He also starred in another film that was nominated for best picture that year. Which film was it?
   C. A director was among the losers in the best supporting actor category. Name him.
   D. Edith Head won two best costuming awards, one for a color film and the other for a black and white film. What were the two films?
   E. Who beat out William Holden, Louis Calhern, Spencer Tracy, and James Stewart for the best actor award?
3. For what film did George Cukor win his first Oscar, and when?
4. Janet Gaynor was the first recipient of the best actress Oscar. What was the movie?
5. Which four films have given Katharine Hepburn the best actress award-winning roles that make her the "most Oscared" actress in film history?
6. For 1931/32, nominees for the best actor Oscar were: Wallace Beery (*The Champ*), Alfred Lunt (*The Guardsman*), and Fredric March (*Dr. Jekyll and Mr. Hyde*). Who won?
7. Vivien Leigh won her second Oscar for her second Southern belle role, in *A Streetcar Named Desire* in 1951. Who accepted the award for her in her absence?

Katharine Hepburn has won four best actress Oscars. Can you name the movies for which she won those awards?

8. Luise Rainer became the first actress to win the best actress Oscar two years in a row (*The Great Ziegfeld*, 1935; *The Good Earth*, 1936). Both years she beat an actress who had been nominated for two of her most memorable comedy roles. Who was that actress?
9. In 1952, which actress beat Joan Crawford, Julie Harris, Bette Davis, and Susan Hayward for the best actress Oscar?
10. What was the significance of the best actor Oscar awarded to Henry Fonda in 1982?
11. 1934 saw the first "sweep" of the Oscars: *It Happened One Night* won awards for best picture, director, actress, actor, and writing. What movie, many years later, would equal this list of top honors?
12. What was the first musical to win a best picture Oscar?
13. Ingrid Bergman and Meryl Streep are in a unique Oscar class. What makes their awards so distinctive?
14. 1947 was an "upset" year: Rosalind Russell was the odds-on favorite to win the best actress award for *Mourning Becomes Electra*. She was competing against Joan Crawford for *Possessed*, Loretta Young for *The Farmer's Daughter*, Susan Hayward for *Smash-Up*, and Dorothy McGuire for *Gentleman's Agreement*. What was the upset?
15. Only one of Cecil B. de Mille's films won the Oscar for best picture; which film was it?

Clark Gable and Claudette Colbert in *It Happened One Night*.

Answers are on pp. 355–56.

QUIZ #26
ROMANTIC INTERLUDES

1. In what film did Irene Dunne co-star with two of Hollywood's most eligible bachelors?
2. Name Elizabeth Taylor's seven husbands . . . in order.
3. After his divorce from Louis B. Mayer's daughter, Irene, David O. Selznick married Phyllis Isley.
   A. By what name is Phyllis Isley more familiar to movie audiences?
   B. Phyllis Isley's first marriage also ended in divorce. Who was her husband before Selznick?
4. Spencer Tracy and Katharine Hepburn married after making a movie together. True or false?
5. Norma Shearer was the reigning queen of the MGM lot for years, thanks in part to the fact that her husband was a whiz-kid producer at that studio. Who was her husband?
6. What did both Peter Finch and Glenda Jackson covet in *Sunday Bloody Sunday*?
7. During the filming of *Gone With the Wind*, both Clark Gable and Vivien Leigh were involved in much publicized romances.
   A. Who were their respective partners?
   B. How did they resolve their situations?
8. Who were Marilyn Monroe's three husbands?
9. A star of *I Walked With a Zombie* and a star of *Bird of Paradise* have been married for many years. Name them.
10. Everybody knows that Snow White found her Prince, but can you name the seven dwarfs she encountered along the way?
11. Offscreen, he was married to Carole Lombard and later engaged to Jean Harlow. On-screen, he was "married" to Myrna Loy. Who was he?
12. Name *all* Judy Garland's husbands, in order.
13. Which two famous Hollywood couples have starred in film versions of *The Taming of the Shrew*?
14. In *A Letter to Three Wives*, Addie Ross is a woman who steals other women's husbands.
   A. Who played Addie Ross but got no screen credit?
   B. Why was the role uncredited?

Answers are on p. 356.

Norma Shearer, seen here in *Romeo and Juliet*, was married to a whiz-kid MGM producer. Who was he?

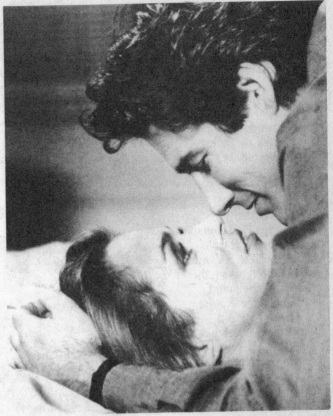

In this movie in which Richard Gere stars opposite Lauren Hutton, Gere plays a prostitute. Can you name the movie?

QUIZ #27
SAINTS AND SINNERS TRIVIA

The moral rectitude of the character a performer plays is immaterial when the acting awards are handed out. Academy Awards and nominations have gone to screen "sinners" and "saints" alike. Many performers have played both. Here are two lists. The first is a list of performers who have played prostitutes, and your job is to name a well-known film in which they played such a role. The second is a list of films in which one of the main protaganists is a nun. Name the actress who played the role. Answers are on p. 356.

The Sinners:
1. Vivien Leigh
2. Jane Fonda
3. Richard Gere
4. Greta Garbo
5. Shirley Jones
6. Jon Voight
7. Elizabeth Taylor
8. Jodie Foster
9. Lee Grant
10. Shirley MacLaine

The Saints:
1. *Black Narcissus*
2. *The Bells of St. Mary's*
3. *The White Sister* (1923)
4. *The Sound of Music*
5. *The Song of Bernadette*
6. *The Nun's Story*
7. *Come to the Stable*
8. *The Trouble With Angels*
9. *The Singing Nun*
10. *Two Mules for Sister Sara*

QUIZ #28
WHAT'S IN A NAME?

1. The following names are part of the Hollywood legend. Complete the names by telling what the initials stand for.
   A. C.B. de Mille
   B. D.W. Griffith
   C. L.B. Mayer
   D. Edward G. Robinson
   E. William S. Hart
2. In the earliest star rosters of Hollywood, the names of the silent screen's female stars often embodied descriptions of ladylike qualities. Here are the delicate surnames; can you supply the first names?
   A. Blythe
   B. Love
   C. Hope
   D. Joy
   E. Pretty
   F. Young
   G. Sweet
   H. Little
3. Into each trivia quiz must fall the inevitable "what's the real name?" question. But this question relates to movies: below is a list of movies as they were titled for British release. Can you give the American title? (If you know the movies, some of the British titles provide clues.)
   A. *The Murder in Thornton Square*
   B. *Pookie*
   C. *Zee and Co.*
   D. *The One-Piece Bathing Suit*
   E. *Bachelor Knight*
   F. *What Lola Wants*
   G. *Indiscretion*

Answers are on p. 356.

Joan Crawford and John Barrymore in *Grand Hotel*.

QUIZ #29
HOLLYWOOD DRINKERS TRIVIA

PART 1
The following actors and actresses have given memorable screen performances as alcoholics. Name the film in which each portrayed a character with a drinking problem.

1. Bing Crosby
2. Fredric March
3. James Mason
4. Ingrid Bergman
5. James Stewart
6. Susan Hayward
7. Jack Lemmon
8. Burt Lancaster
9. William Powell
10. Ray Milland

PART 2
Not every drinking scene in a movie depicts a problem drinker. There have been memorable scenes in which non-alcoholics tipple to dramatic or comic effect. Can you recognize some of them?

1. In what film did Charles Laughton fall down a coal chute while drunk?
2. With whom did Katharine Hepburn imbibe too much champagne in *Desk Set*?
3. In *Grand Hotel*,
   A. Who got drunk on "Louisiana Slips"?
   B. What did Joan Crawford order at the bar?
   C. Which of the film's stars was a notorious alcoholic in real life?

4. In *The Philadelphia Story*, Dexter (Cary Grant) reminds Tracy (Katharine Hepburn) of what she did the first time she got drunk on champagne. What did she do?
5. When Ray Milland is hunting for his last bottle of booze in *The Lost Weekend*, how does he eventually find it?
6. In *Gone With the Wind* Rhett Butler is drinking alone—and heavily—late one night, and Scarlett happens upon him in the dining room. Why has she come downstairs?
7. When Margo Channing has had too many drinks at her own party in *All About Eve*, what does she insist the piano player play over and over?

Answers are on p. 356.

QUIZ #30
MOVIE MISCELLANY TRIVIA

1. What was the name of Woody Allen's character in *Annie Hall*?
2. Which movie co-starred Marlon Brando and Jack Nicholson?
3. In which film did Barbra Streisand have a fantasy about Fidel Castro?
4. Who were James Dean's co-stars in *Rebel Without a Cause*?
5. Who wrote the original movie score for *Jaws*?
6. Jacqueline Bisset and Candice Bergen co-starred in a modern remake of a classic movie. Name the remake, the original, and the directors of each.
7. What was the title of Peter Sellers' next-to-last movie, and who wrote the book on which it was based?
8. Who played the woman in the lives of *Jules and Jim*?
9. What character did Peter O'Toole play opposite Richard Burton's *Becket*?
10. Who was the star of *Our Man Flint* and *In Like Flint*?
11. Which movie first co-starred Paul Newman and Joanne Woodward?
12. In which movie did Sidney Poitier appear with a sisterhood of nuns?
13. What was the Beatles' first movie, and when was it released?
14. Who was Elvis Presley's co-star in *Fun in Acapulco*?
15. *West Side Story* (1961) was a landmark production that changed the shape of movie musicals:
    A. Who was the choreographer?
    B. Who wrote the lyrics?
    C. Which cast members won Oscars?
16. Name the movie in which Meryl Streep made her film debut.
17. In *The Opposite Sex*, a '50s remake of *The Women*, Jeff Richards played Buck and Leslie Nielsen played Steven. Who played these roles in the 1939 original?

18. Which actress did Elizabeth Taylor replace in *Elephant Walk*?
19. In *Gaslight*, Charles Boyer was trying to drive Ingrid Bergman mad. Who, playing the maid, was trying to drive *him* mad with desire?
20. What profession did Montgomery Clift's character follow in *I Confess*?
21. Who played the two brothers who fought over Audrey Hepburn in *Sabrina*?
22. A scene was originally censored from *Modern Times*; it showed Charlie Chaplin, in jail, falling under the influence of an illicit substance hidden in a salt shaker. What was the substance?
23. She won an Oscar for bedding down with Warren Beatty, and she directed Melvyn Douglas' last film. Who is she?
24. Greta Garbo, as *Ninotchka*, finally gives in and buys an article typical of capitalist materialism. What is it?
25. In which movie did Ava Gardner play Venus?
26. When *Mr. Deeds Goes to Town*, what musical instrument does he take with him?
27. How do Cary Grant's 'aunts' refer to the basement in *Arsenic and Old Lace*?
28. Before she became a fast-food burger queen, what food did *Mildred Pierce* sell?
29. Cary Grant appeared with Mae West in two movies. Name them.
30. What was so interesting about James Stewart's clown makeup in *The Greatest Show on Earth*?
31. Preston Sturges had so many humorous lines in *The Palm Beach Story* that he needed four stars to say them all; who were the four?
32. What was the significance of the best supporting actress Academy Award for 1939?
33. Howard Hughes produced *The Outlaw* with Jane Russell. Who directed the film?
34. Which film co-starred James Fox and Mick Jagger?
35. For what film did posters proclaim "Garbo Talks!"?

Answers are on pp. 356–57.

Can you name the Beatles' first movie and the year of its release?

PICTURE QUIZ #1
WHO'S PLAYING WHO?

In the TV movie based on her autobiography, *Sophia—Living and Loving: Her Own Story*, Sophia Loren played both herself and her mother. On the big screen, however, it's unusual for a performer to play himself or herself in a movie—filmmakers usually favor the practice of casting stars to play *other* stars. The stars pictured below are portraying other stars, but which ones? The clues are the names in the accompanying list and part of your task is to match the performer to the star he or she is portraying. The second part of the task—for which we're not giving any clues—is to name the film in which each is pictured. Answers are on p. 357.

A. Pearl White
B. Al Jolson
C. Glenn Miller
D. Joan Crawford
E. Jean Harlow
F. W. C. Fields
G. Ruth Etting
H. Billie Holiday
I. Loretta Lynn
J. Gertrude Lawrence
K. Jenny Lind
L. Dorothy Stratten
M. Lillian Roth
N. Carole Lombard
O. Buddy Holly
P. Buster Keaton
Q. Grace Moore
R. Enrico Caruso
S. Woody Guthrie
T. Frances Farmer

1. Susan Hayward

2. Mario Lanza

3. Jessica Lange

4. Jill Clayburgh

5. Betty Hutton

6. Donald O'Connor

7. Julie Andrews

8. James Stewart

9. Kathryn Grayson

10. Larry Parks

11. Diana Ross

12. Grace Moore

13. Carroll Baker

14. Rod Steiger

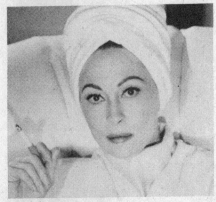
15. Faye Dunaway

16. Mariel Hemingway

17. Doris Day

18. David Carradine

19. Gary Busey

20. Sissy Spacek

PICTURE QUIZ #2
WHO SAID WHAT?

All the stars pictured appeared in comedy films. Some of the jokes they made (in many cases characteristic of the performer's comic style) are quoted here. Who said what? Answers are on p. 357.

A. "Either this guy's dead or my watch has stopped."

B. "Somebody put orange juice in my orange juice."

C. "I like two kinds of men, domestic and foreign."

D. "The trouble with you is you're just not couth."

E. "If we bring a little joy into your humdrum lives it makes us feel as if our hard work ain't been in vain for nothing."

F. "My great aunt Jennifer ate a whole box of candy every day of her life. She lived to be 102 and when she'd been dead three days she looked better than you do now."

G. "I fear I forgot myself and let her kiss me."

H. "I slid halfway down the mountain before I realized that Gustav didn't love me any more."

I. "Maybe alligators have the right idea. They eat their young."

J. "Call off your dog, I might bite him. I might bite you too if I knew who you were."

K. "That hat suits you, darling. It gives you a chin."

L. "She reminds me of an agent with one client."

1. Jack Lemmon

2. Jean Hagen

4. Peter Sellers

3. Jack Benny

5. Rosalind Russell

M. "So. They call me Concentration Camp Erhardt."

N. "I can't stand torture. It hurts."

O. "My darling, don't move, don't panic. All that has happened is that my hat has caught on one of your naughty little hairpins."

P. "What are you trying to do, crack the cement? Why don't you use your head?" "I did, but it hurts that way."

Q. "I'm beginning to think you're right." "You bet your life I'm right. You know I'm not as dumb as you look."

R. "These are my children. They were born in India, poor darlings. An awful place, what with the ahays and whatnot howling round the whatdoyoucall them. I don't know how they stood it, I know I couldn't have. Of course I've never been there myself."

S. "Of course he's upset. He's a lawyer. He's paid to be upset."

T. "This scandal will be forgotten in the morning. Remember what they said about what's-her-name before she jumped out of the window? See, I can't even remember her name—so why worry?"

6. Thelma Ritter

7. W. C. Fields

8. Laurel and Hardy

9. Eve Arden

10. Bob Hope

Picture Quiz #2 photos continued

11. Abbott and Costello

12. Claudette Colbert

13. Monty Woolley

14. Edward Everett Horton

15. Groucho Marx

16. Mae West

17. Judy Holliday

18. Billie Burke

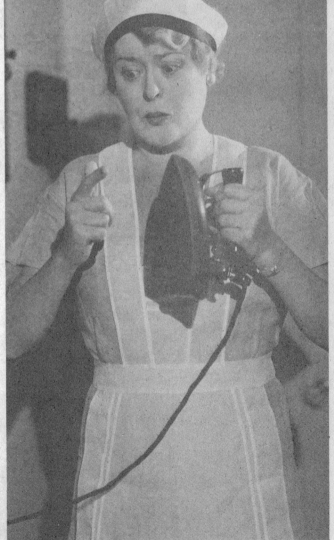

19. Lucille Ball

20. Mary Boland

PICTURE QUIZ #3
WHO FIGURED OUT WHODUNIT?

If the butler didn't do it, chances are Miss Marple, Philip Marlowe or Charlie Chan would have figured out who did by the end of a detective movie. But would you? If you're into whodunits you're into problem solving. Below are stills from famous and infamous detective movies; beneath each is a film title. It's the wrong title, but it's a clue to the correct one. Once you have identified the film, name the detective and the actor or actress who plays the role. Answers are on page 357.

1. *Through the Broken Looking Glass*

2. *Felonious Female Testimony*

3. *A Sphynx Drowns*

4. *An Anorexic Retires*

5. *A Bolt in the Blue*

6. *Introducing Caesar Loup*

7. *Twelve Stabs and No Stops in China*

8. *The Bird Is a Bully*

9. *Rough Rover's Retribution*

10. *Faaaaareweeeelllll*

11. *Corpses Prefer Paisley*

12. *Chopstick City*

13. *Stingy Dick*

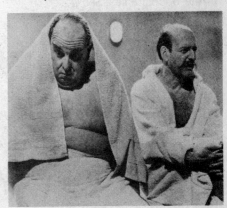

14. *A.B.C.D.E.A.T.H.*

15. *Dame in the Drink*

16. *Destroy My Dessert*

17. *China Cupboard*

18. *Trigger Happy*

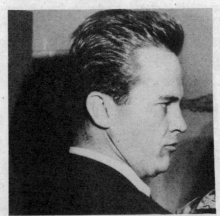

19. *Pucker Up and Kill Me*

20. *Cause by Effect*

PICTURE QUIZ #4
TOOTSIE AND HER (HIS?) KIND

Things are never quite what they seem, especially in the movies, and that holds true for the performers pictured here. All are masquerading as members of the opposite sex. See if you can identify each one—use the list of actors and actresses to help you—and then name the movie in which each appears in drag. Answers are on page 357.

Boris Karloff
Lou Costello
Jeff Bridges
Raquel Welch
Alec Guinness
Bing Crosby
Dick Shawn
Joanne Woodward
Rod Steiger
Anne Heywood
Jerry Lewis
James Coburn
Michael Palin
Louise Brooks
Julie Andrews
Paul Lynde
Marion Davies
Katharine Hepburn
George Sanders
Dennis O'Keefe

1.

2.

3.

4.

5.

6.

7.

8.

9.

10.

11.

12.

13.

14.

15.

16.

17.

18.

19.

20.

PICTURE QUIZ #5
ANY RESEMBLANCE ... IS PURELY COINCIDENTAL

What do you do if you want to tell a story that is basically true, but so scathing, scandalous, or shaky on facts that you might be sued for libel if you told it straight? When in Hollywood, you do what the moguls do: change the names to protect the guilty and throw in a red herring or two. The result: *"film à clef."* The pictures here are from films made daringly close to, but just this side of, the truth. Can you name who played who? For instance, in Blake Edwards' scathing satire, *S.O.B.*, his wife Julie Andrews played the actress she would have liked to have been and Robert Vaughn played ... who? Your clues are the movie titles under each still and the list of actors and the characters they portrayed. Your task is to match the character(s) portrayed and the actor(s) who portray them to the movie. Answers are on p. 358.

A. Robert Vaughn as Robert Evans
B. Patty Duke as Judy Garland
C. Roger Rees as Peter Bogdanovich
D. Janet Gaynor and Fredric March as Ruby Keeler and Al Jolson
E. Lee Bowman and Susan Hayward as Bing Crosby and Dixie Lee

1. *A Star Is Born* (1937)

2. *The Last of Sheila*

3. *The Miracle Woman*

4. *All About Eve*

5. *Citizen Kane*

6. *All the King's Men*

F. Anthony Quinn and Jacqueline Bisset as Aristotle Onassis and Jacqueline Kennedy
G. Ava Gardner as Rita Hayworth
H. Barbara Stanwyck (with David Manners) as Aimee Semple McPherson
I. Broderick Crawford as Huey Long
J. Bette Midler as Janis Joplin (with Alan Bates)
K. Dyan Cannon as Sue Mengers
L. Kim Stanley as Marilyn Monroe
M. Orson Welles as William Randolph Hearst
N. George Peppard and Carroll Baker as Howard Hughes and Jean Harlow
O. John Marley as Harry Cohn/Louis B. Mayer
P. Lauren Bacall as Libby Holman (with Robert Stack and Rock Hudson)
Q. Warren Beatty as Jon Peters
R. Peter O'Toole and Mark Linn-Baker as Errol Flynn and Mel Brooks
S. Marthe Keller as Greta Garbo (with William Holden)
T. Marsha Mason and James Caan as Marsha Mason and Neil Simon
U. Fred Astaire as himself (with Ava Gardner)
V. Bette Davis as Tallulah Bankhead/Elisabeth Bergner
W. Ann Sheridan as Gertrude Lawrence (with Bette Davis)
X. Liza Minnelli as Doris Day (with Lionel Stander)

7. *Shampoo*

8. *Chapter Two*

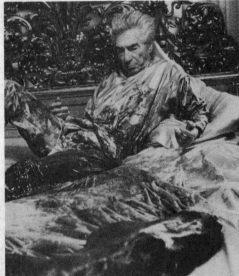

9. *The Godfather*

10. *Smash-Up: The Story of a Woman*

11. *My Favorite Year*

12. *S.O.B.*

Picture Quiz #5 photos continued

319

13. *The Goddess*

14. *New York, New York*

15. *The Band Wagon*

16. *Star 80*

17. *The Rose*

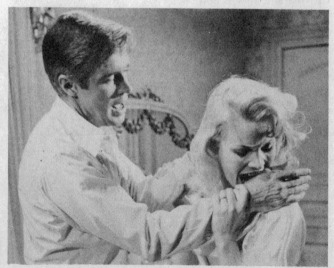

18. *The Carpetbaggers*

19. *The Barefoot Contessa*

20. *The Man Who Came to Dinner*

21. *Fedora*

22. *Valley of the Dolls*

23. *Written on the Wind*

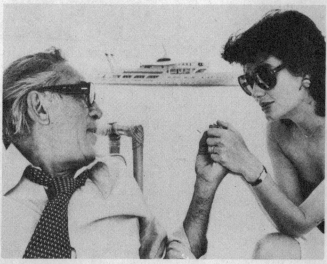

24. *The Greek Tycoon*

PICTURE QUIZ #6
A ROSE BY ANY OTHER NAME . . . ?

You probably recognize the actors and actresses here by the names under which they became famous—the names shown under the portraits. But would you know them by their *real* names? How many of these famous names can you match to the not-so-famous names listed here. The answers are on p. 358.

A. Roy Scherer, Jr.
B. James Stewart
C. Zelma Hedrick
D. Lucille Collier
E. Archibald Leach
F. Constance Ockelman
G. Lucille Langhanke
H. Maria Africa Vidal de Santo Silas
I. Natasha Gurdin
J. Issur Danielovitch Demsky
K. William Pratt
L. Lily Chauchoin
M. Simone Roussel
N. Edythe Marrener
O. Arthur Jefferson
P. Alfred Coccozza
Q. Sarah Fulks
R. Margarita Carmen Cansino
S. Ruby Stevens
T. Joe Yule, Jr.

1. Barbara Stanwyck

2. Mickey Rooney

3. Veronica Lake

4. Kirk Douglas

5. Cary Grant

6. Stan Laurel

7. Kathryn Grayson

8. Mario Lanza

9. Michèle Morgan

10. Maria Montez

11. Rock Hudson

12. Claudette Colbert

13. Jane Wyman

14. Ann Miller

15. Rita Hayworth

16. Susan Hayward

17. Stewart Granger

18. Natalie Wood

19. Boris Karloff

20. Mary Astor

PICTURE QUIZ #7

I COULD WRITE A BOOK . . .

In a famous publicity shot for *Gone With the Wind*, Scarlett and Melanie are waiting for Melanie's baby to be born and Melanie is reading a copy of *Gone With the Wind*. Hollywood has given us the play within the film and the film within the film—why not the book within the film? Better yet, how about a movie based on the life of an author? A number of such films have been made. How many do you remember? Here are stills from biographical movies about famous authors. Beneath each still is the name of the actor who played the author, and the title of one of the writer's best known books. Identify the film title, and the author or authors who are portrayed in the still. Answers are on p. 358.

1. Sydney Greenstreet; *Vanity Fair*. Olivia de Havilland; *Jane Eyre*

2. Danny Kaye; *The Red Shoes*

3. Michael O'Shea; *The Sea Wolf*

4. Beau Bridges; *The Front Page* (stage play)

5. Gregory Peck; *The Last Tycoon*

Picture Quiz #7 photos continued

6. Paul Muni; *Nana*

7. Herbert Marshall; *The Moon and Sixpence*

8. James Mason; *Salammbô*

9. John Heard; *On the Road*

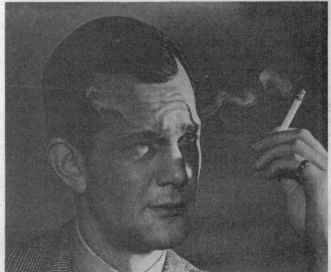

10. Daniel Massey; *Present Indicative*

11. Karl Boehm and Laurence Harvey; *Snow White*

12. Fredric March; *The Adventures of Huckleberry Finn*

13. John Shepperd; *The Fall of the House of Usher*

14. Pier Paolo Pasolini; *The Canterbury Tales*

15. Richard Chamberlain; *Childe Harold*

16. Elsa Lanchester; *Frankenstein*

17. Vanessa Redgrave; *The Mirror Crack'd*

18. Jane Fonda; *Pentimento*. Jason Robards; *The Thin Man*

19. Jack Nicholson; *The Iceman Cometh* (stage play)

20. Mary Steenburgen; *The Yearling*

PICTURE QUIZ #8
DIRECTORS TURNED ACTORS

What would you do if you were acting in a scene in a film and suddenly your fellow performer yelled "Cut!"? Presumably you'd stop acting; then you'd be smart to check if your fellow performer were not in fact your director . . . or somebody's director. It has happened —usually with great fanfare and often with some success—that a well-known director has assumed a role in a movie, playing either himself or herself or a character in the story. Pictured here are scenes from movies which featured directors as performers. Your clues: under each still is the title of the film pictured, followed by the title of a film the director is known for. Your task is to name the director. Answers are on p. 358.

1. *Margin for Error*; *Laura*

2. *All About Eve*; *The Heat's On*

3. *The Wedding March*; *Foolish Wives*

4. *Wild Strawberries*; *The Wind*

5. *The Story of Adele H.*; *Jules and Jim*

Picture Quiz #8 photos continued

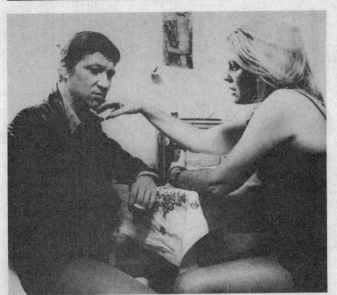

6. *Fox and His Friends*; *Querelle*

7. *The Day of the Locust*; *I Saw What You Did*

8. *The Cardinal*; *Annie*

9. *Passage Home*; *Séance on a Wet Afternoon*

10. *Tootsie*; *They Shoot Horses, Don't They?*

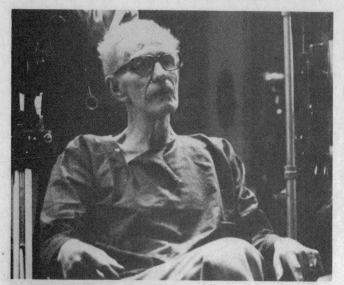

11. *Lightning Over Water*; *Johnny Guitar*

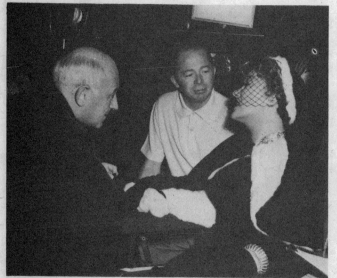

12. *Sunset Boulevard*; *The King of Kings*

13. *Contempt*; *Fury*

14. *The Tenant*; *Chinatown*

15. *Saint Jack*; *What's Up, Doc?*

17. *Bread, Love and Dreams*; *Yesterday, Today and Tomorrow*

18. *Never on Sunday*; *Phaedra*

16. *Damn Yankees*; *Star 80*

19. *A Wedding*; *Algiers*

20. *Play Misty for Me*; *Escape From Alcatraz*

PICTURE QUIZ #9
ACTORS TURNED DIRECTORS

The previous quiz indicated that many directors have aspirations to appear in front of the camera. Here we switch the situation and check out those actors who yearn to be—at least sometimes—behind the camera instead of in front of it. A few actors are also talented directors and can keep both irons in the fire: three very varied examples are Lillian Gish, Orson Welles, and Lee Grant. Others should stick to acting. We've selected a few of the more interesting instances in which performers have turned director, and we show here stills from films directed by noted actors. You are given two clues: the title of the film the actor directed, and the title of a film in which he or she starred. Your challenge is to name the actor. Answers are on p. 358.

1. *The Hunters*; *Murder My Sweet*

2. *Escape From the Planet of the Apes*; *Father of the Bride*

3. *Antony and Cleopatra*; *The Ten Commandments*

4. *Lumière*; *Jules and Jim*

5. *The Alamo*; *Fort Apache*

6. *My Six Loves*; *Give a Girl a Break*

7. *The Trouble With Angels*; *Devotion*

8. *The Man on the Eiffel Tower*; *The Story of G.I. Joe*

9. *The Night of the Hunter*; *Rembrandt*

10. *One-Eyed Jacks*; *Desirée*

11. *The Tunnel of Love*; *The Pirate*

12. *Kotch*; *The Apartment*

13. *The Heartbreak Kid*; *A New Leaf*

14. *The Kentuckian*;
Jim Thorpe, All-American

15. *Time Limit*; *On the Waterfront*

16. *Charlie Bubbles*;
Murder on the Orient Express

17. *The Lost One*; *The Maltese Falcon*

18. *Posse*; *Lust for Life*

19. *Reds*; *Shampoo*

20. *Young Winston*;
Séance on a Wet Afternoon

PICTURE QUIZ #10
MAKE IT AGAIN, SAM

They say that you can't get too much of a good thing, especially in Hollywood. Once onto a good movie, the tendency is to wait a while and make it again. Unfortunately, the remake doesn't always make it at the box office. Most remakes become as notorious for failing (*Cleopatra*, *King Kong*...) as their predecessors had been for succeeding. The movie stills shown here are all from remakes. Can you name the title of the original film and who originally played the roles that the actors pictured here played in the remake? (In some cases the latest remake is the third version of the story. If you can name *both* of the earlier versions, you're really doing well.) Answers are on p. 358.

1. *The Great Gatsby* (1974);
Robert Redford, Mia Farrow

2. *Victor/Victoria* (1982);
Julie Andrews, Robert Preston

3. *The Jazz Singer* (1980);
Neil Diamond

4. *The Blue Lagoon* (1980);
Brooke Shields, Christopher Atkins

5. *The Big Sleep* (1978);
Joan Collins, Robert Mitchum

6. *The Champ* (1979);
Jon Voight, Ricky Schroder

7. *Farewell, My Lovely* (1975);
Charlotte Rampling

8. *Little Miss Marker* (1980);
Julie Andrews, Sara Stimson, Walter Matthau

9. *Hurricane* (1979); Mia Farrow, Dayton Ka'ne

10. *The Lady Vanishes* (1979); Cybill Shepherd, Elliott Gould

11. *Rich and Famous* (1981); Jacqueline Bisset, Candice Bergen

12. *Young at Heart* (1954); Doris Day, Frank Sinatra

13. *The Thirty-Nine Steps* (1959); Taina Elg, Kenneth More

14. *The Postman Always Rings Twice* (1981); Jessica Lange

PICTURE QUIZ #11
THE SINGERS AND THE SONGS

The tunes listed here, all of which were to become standards, were first sung in movies by the pictured vocalists. Your task is to identify which singer (or singers) introduced each song. The answers are on p. 358.

A. "If I Had a Talking Picture of You"
B. "I Cover the Waterfront"
C. "Song of the Moulin Rouge"
D. "Everything I Have Is Yours"
E. "Temptation"
F. "Tumbling Tumbleweeds"
G. "I'm in the Mood for Love"
H. "Goodnight My Love"
I. "I've Got You Under My Skin"
J. "San Francisco"
K. "You Turned the Tables on Me"
L. "In the Still of the Night"
M. "Jeepers Creepers"
N. "Two Sleepy People"
O. "You Stepped Out of a Dream"
P. "All of a Sudden My Heart Sings"
Q. "One for My Baby (and One More for the Road)"
R. "Again"
S. "Paradise"
T. "Happy Days Are Here Again"

1. Tony Martin

2. Ida Lupino

3. Nelson Eddy

4. Alice Faye

5. Gene Autry

Picture Quiz #11 photos continued

6. Louis Armstrong

7. Fred Astaire

8. Shirley Temple

9. Joan Crawford

10. Charles Farrell and Janet Gaynor

11. Shirley Ross and Bob Hope

12. Bing Crosby

13. Jeanette MacDonald

14. Zsa Zsa Gabor

15. Claudette Colbert

16. Jack Benny

17. Pola Negri

18. Frances Langford

19. Kathryn Grayson

20. Virginia Bruce

PICTURE QUIZ #12
THE WAY TO THE OVAL OFFICE...

History has now made fact out of the fiction that any actor can be a president. Until Ronald Reagan forsook Hollywood for the White House, however, the actor's way to the presidency lay not on the campaign trail but via the casting department. Pictured here are actors who have played United States presidents. You are given a clue in the actor's name. Can you identify which president each one represented, and the name of the movie in which he played the presidential role? The answers are on pp. 358–59.

1. Walter Huston

2. Dan O'Herlihy (with Gregory Peck)

3. Stanley Hall

4. Brian Keith

5. Alexander Knox

6. Henry Fonda

7. Ralph Bellamy

8. Raymond Massey

9. Frank Forsyth

10. Henry Morgan

11. Burgess Meredith (with Ginger Rogers and David Niven)

12. Hugh Southern

13. Charlton Heston

14. Charles Edward Bull

PICTURE QUIZ #13
TARZAN'S IDENTITY CRISIS

If you've ever seen a *Tarzan* movie, you know that there is more than one way to corner Hollywood and Vine. If you've seen more than one *Tarzan* movie, you know there's more than one Tarzan, and MGM's Johnny Weissmuller, the actor most readily identifiable with the Englishman who got lost in the jungle in childhood and grew up among the apes, by no means holds the patent on the man of the jungle. In fact, he's one of a surprising numbers of Tarzans. Test your knowledge of *Tarzan* trivia—how many of the actors listed below can you match to the *Tarzan* movies in which they swing from the famous vine? Answers are on p. 359.

A. Glenn Morris
B. Gene Pollar
C. James H. Pierce
D. Buster Crabbe
E. Ron Ely
F. Elmo Lincoln
G. Dennis Miller
H. Miles O'Keeffe
I. Herman Brix
J. P. Dempsey Tabler
K. Jimmy Durante
L. Frank Merrill
M. Mike Henry
N. Gordon Scott
O. Jock Mahoney
P. Lex Barker
Q. Christopher Lambert

1. *The New Adventures of Tarzan*

2. *Greystoke: The Legend of Tarzan, Lord of the Apes*

3. *Tarzan's Revenge*

4. *Tarzan's Greatest Adventure*

5. *Tarzan and the Jungle Boy*

6. *Tarzan* (TV series)

7. *Tarzan's Savage Fury*

8. *The Return of Tarzan*

9. *Hollywood Party*

10. *Tarzan the Ape Man* (1959)

11. *Tarzan and the Golden Lion*

12. *The Son of Tarzan*

13. *Tarzan of the Apes*

14. *Tarzan the Mighty*

15. *Tarzan the Fearless*

16. *Tarzan Goes to India*

17. *Tarzan the Ape Man* (1981)

PICTURE QUIZ #14
MONSTERS OF THE MOVIES

If you're into horror movies, this quiz will be your idea of a good time. The monsters—human and otherwise—pictured here appeared in the movies listed. How many monsters can you match to the movies? Answers are on p. 359.

A. *Horror of Party Beach*
B. *Gorgo*
C. *The Beast From 20,000 Fathoms*
D. *It! The Terror From Beyond Space*
E. *Forbidden Planet*
F. *Jason and the Argonauts*
G. *The Day the Earth Stood Still*
H. *The Werewolf of London*
I. *London After Midnight*
J. *Mysterious Island*
K. *King Kong vs. Godzilla*
L. *King Kong Escapes*
M. *Son of Kong*
N. *Frankenstein*
O. *Munster, Go Home*
P. *The Bride of Frankenstein*
Q. *The Virgin of Nuremberg*
R. *The Creature From the Black Lagoon*
S. *The Wolf Man*
T. *It Came From Beneath the Sea*

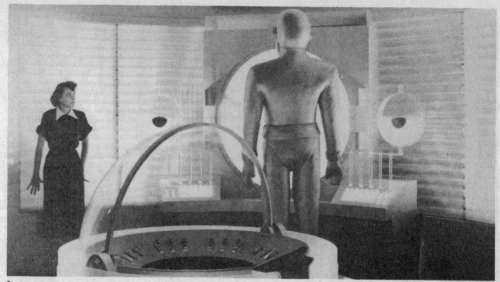

1.

2.

3.

4.

5.

Picture Quiz #14 photos continued

6.

7.

8.

9.

10.

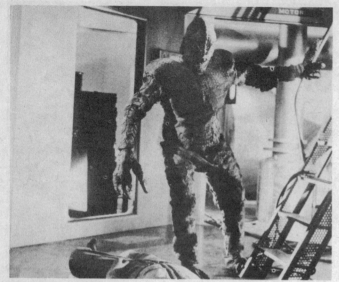

11.

12.

13.

14.

15.

16.

17.

18.

19.

20.

PICTURE QUIZ #15
COWBOYS AND INDIANS

Cowboys and Indians were the staple of western serials and B movies for years, way out west in wildest Hollywood. Here's a selection of familiar faces from those days. How familiar are they to you? All you have to do is match a name from the list to each face pictured here. Answers are on p. 359.

A. Roy Rogers
B. Ken Curtis
C. John War Eagle
D. Don Barry
E. Col. Tim McCoy
F. Rex Bell
G. Jack "The Lash" LaRue
H. Gene Autry
I. Wild Bill Elliott
J. Smiley Burnette
K. Jack Holt
L. Monte Hale
M. Buster Crabbe
N. Rod Cameron
O. William Boyd
P. Johnny Mack Brown
Q. Chief Dan George
R. Rex Allen
S. George "Gabby" Hayes
T. Tim Holt

1.

2.

3.

4.

5.

Picture Quiz #15 photos continued

6.

7.

8.

9.

10.

11.

12.

13.

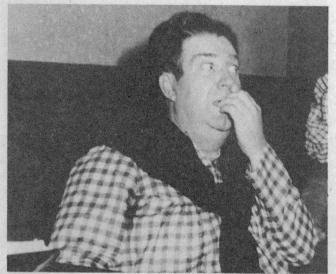

14.

15.

16.

17.

18.

19.

20.

TEN TOP MOVIE TEAMS: NAME THEIR MOVIES

Charles Farrell and Janet Gaynor made twelve movies together: *Seventh Heaven*, 1927; *Street Angel*, 1928; *Lucky Star*, 1929; *Sunny Side Up*, 1929; *High Society Blues*, 1930; *Happy Days* (duet in all-star revue), 1930; *The Man Who Came Back*, 1931; *Merely Mary Ann*, 1931; *Delicious*, 1931; *The First Year*, 1932; *Tess of the Storm Country*, 1932; *Change of Heart*, 1934.

Fred Astaire and Ginger Rogers made ten movies together: *Flying Down to Rio*, 1933; *The Gay Divorcee*, 1934; *Roberta*, 1935; *Top Hat*, 1935; *Swing Time*, 1936; *Follow the Fleet*, 1936; *Shall We Dance*, 1937; *Carefree*, 1938; *The Story of Vernon and Irene Castle*, 1939; *The Barkleys of Broadway*, 1949.

Nelson Eddy and Jeanette MacDonald made eight movies together: *Naughty Marietta*, 1935; *Rose Marie*, 1936; *Maytime*, 1937; *Girl of the Golden West*, 1938; *Sweethearts*, 1938; *New Moon*, 1940; *Bitter Sweet*, 1940; *I Married an Angel*, 1942.

Laurence Olivier and Vivien Leigh made three movies together: *Fire Over England*, 1937; *21 Days Together*, 1937 (released in 1940); *That Hamilton Woman*, 1941.

Mickey Rooney and Judy Garland made nine movies together: *Thoroughbreds Don't Cry*, 1937; *Love Finds Andy Hardy*, 1938; *Babes in Arms*, 1939; *Andy Hardy Meets Debutante*, 1940; *Strike Up the Band*, 1940; *Life Begins for Andy Hardy*, 1941; *Babes on Broadway*, 1941; *Girl Crazy*, 1943; *Words and Music*, 1948. Note: Both appeared in *Thousands Cheer* (1943) but not as a team.

Spencer Tracy and Katharine Hepburn made nine movies together: *Woman of the Year*, 1942; *Keeper of the Flame*, 1942; *Without Love*, 1945; *The Sea of Grass*, 1947; *State of the Union*, 1948; *Adam's Rib*, 1949; *Pat and Mike*, 1952; *Desk Set*, 1957; *Guess Who's Coming to Dinner?*, 1967.

Humphrey Bogart and Lauren Bacall made four movies together: *To Have and Have Not*, 1944; *The Big Sleep*, 1946; *Dark Passage*, 1947; *Key Largo*, 1948.

Bob Hope and Bing Crosby made seven movies together: *Road to Singapore*, 1940; *Road to Zanzibar*, 1941; *Road to Morocco*, 1942; *Road to Utopia*, 1945; *Road to Rio*, 1947; *Road to Bali*, 1952; *The Road to Hong Kong*, 1962.

Dean Martin and Jerry Lewis made sixteen movies together: *My Friend Irma*, 1949; *My Friend Irma Goes West*, 1950; *At War With the Army*, 1950; *That's My Boy*, 1951; *Sailor Beware*, 1951; *Jumping Jacks*, 1952; *The Stooge*, 1952; *Scared Stiff*, 1953; *The Caddy*, 1953; *Money From Home*, 1953; *Living It Up*, 1954; *Three Ring Circus*, 1954; *You're Never Too Young*, 1955; *Artists and Models*, 1955; *Pardners*, 1956; *Hollywood or Bust*, 1956.

Richard Burton and Elizabeth Taylor made ten movies together: *Cleopatra*, 1963; *The V.I.P.s*, 1963; *The Sandpiper*, 1965; *Who's Afraid of Virginia Woolf?*, 1966; *The Taming of the Shrew*, 1967; *Dr. Faustus*, 1967; *The Comedians*, 1967; *Boom!*, 1968; *Under Milk Wood*, 1971; *Hammersmith Is Out*, 1972. Note: Both appeared in *Divorce His—Divorce Hers* (1973), a made-for-TV film.

QUIZ #1
JUDY GARLAND TRIVIA

1. *Every Sunday*; Deanna Durbin
2. Margaret O'Brien; *Meet Me in St. Louis*
3. *Gay Purr-ee*, an animated feature in which Garland's voice only was used
4. London
5. *Annie Get Your Gun*; Betty Hutton
6. *Royal Wedding*; June Allyson; Jane Powell
7. Mary Astor
8. Marjorie Main
9. John Cassavetes
10. Liza Minnelli; Lorna and Joseph Luft
11. Best supporting actress; for *Judgment at Nuremburg*
12. The Jitterbug
13. Nine: *Thoroughbreds Don't Cry; Love Finds Andy Hardy; Babes in Arms; Andy Hardy Meets Debutante; Strike Up the Band; Life Begins for Andy Hardy; Babes on Broadway; Girl Crazy; Words and Music*
14. A field of poppies conjured up by the Wicked Witch of the West
15. *For Me and My Gal*; Gene Kelly

QUIZ #2
KATHARINE HEPBURN AND SPENCER TRACY TRIVIA

1. Garson Kanin and Ruth Gordon
2. *Dr. Jekyll and Mr. Hyde*
3. EMORAC
4. A. Clark Gable and Spencer Tracy
   B. Cary Grant and James Stewart
5. Lucille Ball
6. *The Old Man and the Sea*
7. They met for the first time on the set; and it was their first film together.
8. "I Can't Give You Anything But Love"
9. Katharine Houghton, Hepburn's niece
10. A. Elizabeth Taylor
    B. Joan Bennett
    C. Vincente Minnelli
11. Athlete and coach
12. Ginger Rogers
13. *Keeper of the Flame*
14. *A Man's Castle*
15. Angela Lansbury
16. *Alice Adams*
17. He was "Pinky"; she was "Pinkie"

QUIZ #3
JOAN CRAWFORD AND BETTE DAVIS TRIVIA

1. A convertible
2. Susan Hayward
3. A telephone
4. Claudette Colbert; she suffered a back injury before filming began
5. Shoulder pads; horn-rimmed glasses; open-toed strap sandals
6. Eve Arden
7. "Willie the Weeper"
8. 1931, Clark Gable; 1947, Van Heflin and Raymond Massey
9. "I want to be in movies."
10. "Remind me to tell you about the time I looked into the heart of an artichoke"; Gary Merrill and Anne Baxter
11. Anne Bancroft
12. Brain tumor
13. *Trog*
14. B. D. Davis, Bette's daughter
15. Vienna
16. *Jezebel*, for which she won an Oscar for best actress
17. "A totalitarian manicure"
18. She shaved part of her head

QUIZ #4
SUSAN HAYWARD TRIVIA

1. *I'll Cry Tomorrow*
2. Poor Uncle Wiggily
3. Jane Froman
4. Bing Crosby and Dixie Lee
5. Alcoholism
6. Her son's stuffed tiger
7. *The Snows of Kilimanjaro*
8. Judy Garland
9. Robert Wagner
10. *I Married a Witch*
11. *Mame*
12. Her wig
13. A screen test for the role of Scarlett in *Gone With the Wind*
14. *Back Street*

QUIZ #5
BARBARA STANWYCK TRIVIA

1. *Sorry, Wrong Number*
2. Ruby Stevens
3. Geraldine Fitzgerald and Nancy Coleman
4. Up the Amazon on a snake safari
5. In a supermarket
6. *Stella Dallas*
7. *The Bitter Tea of General Yen*, in which Asther played an Oriental
8. Rocking chairs
9. A. *Lady of Burlesque*
   B. *The G-String Murders*
   C. *Ball of Fire*
10. Gig Young
11. *Night Nurse*
12. Frank Fay and Robert Taylor
13. *His Brother's Wife*, 1936; *This Is My Affair*, 1937; *Night Walker*, 1965
14. *Walk on the Wild Side*; Jane Fonda
15. Missy
16. Marilyn Monroe
17. Her ankle bracelet

QUIZ #6
CASABLANCA TRIVIA

1. "You played it for her, you can play it for me . . . Play it."
2. 1943
3. Ronald Reagan and Ann Sheridan
4. Michael Curtiz
5. Blue; the Germans wore gray
6. In Sam's piano
7. A. *For Whom the Bell Tolls*
   B. Three: best picture, best director, best writing (screenplay)
8. Julius & Philip Epstein and Howard Koch
9. She reminds him of the tune by humming it.
10. *Sahara; Action in the North Atlantic; Thank Your Lucky Stars*
11. Max Steiner
12. ". . . a hill of beans"

QUIZ #7
KING KONG TRIVIA

1. Merian C. Cooper
2. Skull Island
3. Fay Wray
4. 1933; 1976
5. Jessica Lange
6. Merian C. Cooper and Ernest B. Schoedsack
7. The Empire State Building; the World Trade Center
8. She was offered as a sacrifice by Skull Island natives
9. Willis O'Brien
10. Bruce Cabot
11. Dino de Laurentiis
12. An oil conglomerate
13. The *Venture*
14. He blows her dry.
15. " 'Twas beauty killed the beast."

QUIZ #8
GONE WITH THE WIND TRIVIA

1. Four: George Cukor, Sam Wood, Victor Fleming, and William Cameron Menzies. Fleming is billed as director; Menzies was placated with the credit "Production designed by . . ." (Producer David O. Selznick also directed a scene or two.)
2. Twelve Oaks
3. $150, in gold
4. Ann Rutherford and Evelyn Keyes
5. Melanie tells Rhett that she is pregnant.
6. Bonnie Blue Butler: at Melanie Wilkes' suggestion the child was named for the Confederate flag.
7. Three: Charles Hamilton—died; Frank Kennedy—died; Rhett Butler—separated
8. Paulette Goddard; a stunt double was braving the flames
9. On the Mississippi to New Orleans
10. "War" and "Day" ("War, war, war . . ."; "After all, tomorrow is another day")
11. Basil Rathbone
12. Emmy Slattery, the "white trash" girl
13. Clark Gable, followed by Leslie Howard and Olivia de Havilland. Vivien Leigh was billed last with "and presenting . . ." until she won the Oscar; then "presenting" was changed to "starring."
14. Big Sam
15. Scarlett gargled with eau de cologne.
16. "Rhett, Rhett, what's to become of me? If you go, what shall I do? Where shall I go?"
17. ". . . just like a spider."
18. Melanie's glove
19. Robert Donat, for *Goodbye Mr. Chips*
20. Max Steiner
21. Mitchell was terrified of horses and had a clause in his contract stating that he didn't have to ride horseback.
22. A. In Atlanta
    B. Clark Gable, Vivien Leigh, Olivia de Havilland, Evelyn Keyes, Ona Munson
    C. Hattie McDaniel was present for the festivities, but was not allowed into the whites-only theatre.

QUIZ #9
HITCHCOCK TRIVIA

1. *The Man Who Knew Too Much*
2. *Notorious* in 1946
3. Salvador Dali
4. The clash of cymbals
5. The character had no name
6. In the folds of a Los Angeles newspaper
7. Janet Leigh; Vera Miles
8. Spies
9. He used the flash attachment from his camera to blind the attacker
10. Ethel Barrymore
11. Murder and compulsive theft
12. Jesse Royce Landis
13. Ivor Novello
14. Charles Laughton
15. Lila Kedrova
16. John Gielgud
17. Patricia Hitchcock, Alfred Hitchcock's daughter
18. A pair of scissors
19. A pair of lovebirds
20. *Rope* was Hitchcock's first movie in color
21. She won a best actress Oscar for her performance

QUIZ #10
HITCHCOCK CAMEOS

1. *The Lodger*, 1926
2. *Blackmail*, 1929
3. *The Thirty-Nine Steps*, 1935

4. *The Lady Vanishes*, 1938

5. *Rebecca*, 1940

6. *Foreign Correspondent*, 1940

7. *Shadow of a Doubt*, 1943

8. *Lifeboat*, 1944

9. *Spellbound*, 1945

10. *Notorious*, 1946

11. *The Paradine Case*, 1948

12. *Rope*, 1948

13. *Strangers on a Train*, 1951

14. *Dial M for Murder*, 1954

15. *Rear Window*, 1954

16. *The Trouble With Harry*, 1955

17. *The Man Who Knew Too Much*, 1956

18. *Vertigo*, 1958

19. *North by Northwest*, 1959

20. *Psycho*, 1960

21. *The Birds*, 1963

22. *Marnie*, 1964

QUIZ #11
FAMOUS ACTORS' CAMEOS

1. Ted Knight appears as the guard outside Norman Bates' cell in the closing minutes of *Psycho*.

2. Harvey Korman plays the agent on the telephone backstage in *Gypsy*.

3. Audrey Hepburn is the schoolgirl in the auditorium who spins around to watch Alec Guinness leave in *The Lavender Hill Mob*.

4. Jean Harlow plays the blonde in *Double Whoopee*.

5. Sylvester Stallone is seen as a thug on the subway in *Bananas*.

6. Dustin Hoffman is seen breaking up with his girlfriend in *The Tiger Makes Out*.

7. At the beginning of *Invasion of the Body Snatchers* Robert Duvall appears as the priest on the swing.

8. Jacqueline Bisset plays Miss Goodthighs in *Casino Royale*.

9. Gary Cooper in *Wings* is the aviator who crashes on his first flight.

10. Jack Nicholson plays Bob Rafelson's assistant in *Head*.

11. Lucille Ball is the "lion" tamer in *Ziegfeld Follies*.

12. Peter O'Toole plays a Scot in *Casino Royale*.

13. Robert Blake sells Humphrey Bogart a newspaper in *The Treasure of the Sierra Madre*.

14. In *The Graduate* Richard Dreyfuss can be spotted in the dormitory bathroom.

15. Shelly Hack is seen as one-half of one of the vacuous couples in *Annie Hall*.

16. Sigourney Weaver is Woody Allen's date at the end of *Annie Hall*.

17. Jeff Goldblum can be spotted as a party guest in *Annie Hall*.

18. In *The Maltese Falcon* Walter Huston is the man who delivers the Maltese Falcon.

19. In *Winchester '73* Rock Hudson plays an Indian.

20. In *The Treasure of the Sierra Madre* John Huston gives a coin to Humphrey Bogart.

QUIZ #12
ORIGINAL CASTING

1. Tom Selleck
2. Vera Miles
3. Marlon Brando
4. Richard Pryor
5. Gene Kelly
6. Charles Laughton
7. Peter Sellers
8. George Segal
9. Judy Garland
10. Frank Sinatra
11. Steve McQueen
12. Claudette Colbert
13. Jack Benny
14. Grace Kelly

15. Ray Milland
16. James Cagney
17. Susan Hayward
18. Warren Beatty
19. Dustin Hoffman
20. Laurence Harvey
21. John Travolta
22. Cary Grant

QUIZ #13
NAME THE WOMEN IN WOODY ALLEN'S LIFE

1. Janet Margolin
2. Louise Lasser
3. Lynn Redgrave, Louise Lasser
4. Diane Keaton
5. Diane Keaton
6. Diane Keaton
7. Diane Keaton, Geraldine Page, Kristin Griffith, Marybeth Hurt
8. Diane Keaton, Mariel Hemingway
9. Charlotte Rampling, Jessica Harper, Marie-Christine Barrault
10. Mia Farrow, Mary Steenburgen, Julie Hagerty
11. Mia Farrow
12. Mia Farrow

QUIZ #14
FRED ASTAIRE'S OTHER WOMEN

1. Eleanor Powell
2. Rita Hayworth
3. Virginia Dale, Marjorie Reynolds
4. Joan Leslie
5. Judy Garland, Ann Miller
6. Jane Powell, Sarah Churchill
7. Vera-Ellen
8. Cyd Charisse
9. Leslie Caron
10. Audrey Hepburn, Kay Thompson

QUIZ #15
MOVIE SONG AND DANCE TRIVIA

1. *Idiot's Delight*
2. *Dancing Lady*, with

Joan Crawford

3. *The Red Shoes*

4. *The Philadelphia Story*

5. It introduced his future theme song "(Every Little Breeze Seems to Whisper) Louise."

6. Louise Brooks

7. Gene Kelly

8. A. Robert Z. Leonard
   B. *The Shop Around the Corner*
   C. Liza Minnelli, as a small child

9. Dean Martin

10. George M. Cohan

11. A. "Limehouse Blues"
    B. Lucille Bremer

12. Twenties singer Ruth Etting

13. *The Gang's All Here*

14. Cecil Beaton

15. *A Little Night Music*

16. "My Heart Belongs to Daddy"

QUIZ #16
SONGS FROM THE MOVIES

1. *Star Spangled Rhythm*
2. *Born to Dance*
3. *The Sky's the Limit*
4. *A Damsel in Distress*
5. *The Big Broadcast of 1938*
6. *Gold Diggers of Broadway*
7. *Sun Valley Serenade*
8. *Gold Diggers of 1935*
9. *Hollywood Revue of 1929*
10. *Innocents of Paris*
11. *Monte Carlo*
12. *Stage Door Canteen*
13. *Cabin in the Sky*
14. *Every Night at Eight*
15. *Check and Double Check*
16. *Some Like It Hot* (1939)
17. *Sadie McKee*
18. *Papa's Delicate Condition*
19. *Hard to Get*
20. *Murder at the Vanities*
21. *Going Places*

QUIZ #17
STAGE VS. SCREEN CASTING

PART 1
1. Mary Martin
2. Angela Lansbury
3. Ethel Merman
4. Jill Haworth
5. Ethel Barrymore
6. Jessica Tandy
7. Carol Channing
8. Tallulah Bankhead
9. Gwen Verdon
10. Julie Andrews

PART 2
1. *My Fair Lady*
2. *Born Yesterday; Bells Are Ringing*
3. *Mister Roberts*
4. *Funny Girl*
5. *The King and I*
6. *The Philadelphia Story*
7. *Zorba the Greek* (stage title: *Zorba*)
8. *The Gay Divorcee* (stage title: *The Gay Divorce*)
9. *Call Me Madam*
10. *The Music Man*

QUIZ #18
AD LINES

1. *Family Plot*
2. *Casablanca*
3. *The Wild Bunch*
4. *High Plains Drifter*
5. *American Graffiti*
6. *That's Entertainment*
7. *Badlands*
8. *Star Wars*
9. *Flash Gordon*
10. *Airplane*
11. *Invasion of the Body Snatchers*
12. *Alien*
13. *Bonnie and Clyde*
14. *The Loved One*
15. *Snuff*
16. *Ninotchka*
17. *Lolita*
18. *Who's Afraid of Virginia Woolf?*
19. *I Confess*
20. *Gilda*
21. *Goodbye Columbus*
22. *The Treasure of the Sierra Madre*

QUIZ #19
OPENING LINES

1. *My Dinner With André*
2. *42nd Street*
3. *Funny Girl*
4. *Stagecoach*
5. *Bonnie and Clyde*
6. *Mr. Smith Goes to Washington*
7. *Rebecca*
8. *It Happened One Night*
9. *Love Story*
10. *Citizen Kane*
11. *A Clockwork Orange*
12. *The Wild Bunch*
13. *Chinatown*
14. *2001: A Space Odyssey*
15. *The Servant*
16. *On the Waterfront*
17. *The Outsiders*
18. *Manhattan*
19. *Charade*
20. *Risky Business*

QUIZ #20
CLOSING LINES

1. *Notorious*
2. *Pygmalion* (*My Fair Lady*)
3. *Seven Brides for Seven Brothers*
4. *A Star Is Born*
5. *Little Caesar*
6. *Guess Who's Coming to Dinner?*
7. *The Roaring Twenties*
8. *Casablanca*
9. *Sunset Boulevard*
10. *Psycho*
11. *The Grapes of Wrath*
12. *Being There*
13. *My Man Godfrey*
14. *2001: A Space Odyssey*
15. *The Man Who Knew Too Much*
16. *The Maltese Falcon*
17. *King Kong*
18. *Frenzy*
19. *Gone With the Wind*
20. *Tom Jones*

QUIZ #21
PLAYS WITHIN PLAYS

1. *All About Eve*
2. *Singin' in the Rain*
3. *42nd Street*
4. *The Producers*
5. *Staying Alive*
6. *Privates on Parade*
7. *Peeping Tom*
8. *Citizen Kane*
9. *Sullivan's Travels*
10. *Tootsie*

QUIZ #22
FICTITIOUS PLACES

1. *Romanoff and Juliet*
2. *Chitty Chitty Bang Bang*
3. *The Great Dictator*
4. *Duck Soup*
5. *Million Dollar Legs*
6. *Dune*
7. *The Lady Vanishes*
8. *Finian's Rainbow*
9. *The Prisoner of Zenda*
10. *The Mouse That Roared; The Mouse on the Moon*

QUIZ #23
HOW WELL DO YOU KNOW YOUR WESTERNS?

1. Tony
2. A. Wild Bill Hickok
   B. Cecil B. de Mille
3. A. Geraldine Page
   B. Marlene Dietrich
   C. Katharine Hepburn
4. A. Lee Marvin
   B. James Stewart; law
5. Grace Kelly
6. Spencer Tracy
7. The cards in her hand
8. Steve McQueen, Yul Brynner, Charles Bronson, Robert Vaughn, James Coburn, Horst Buchholz, and Brad Dexter
9. Wyatt Earp
10. A. John Wayne
    B. Thomas Mitchell
11. A. Paul Newman played Butch; Robert Redford played Sundance
    B. The Hole-in-the-Wall Gang
    C. Bolivia

QUIZ #24
GOLDEN SILENTS TRIVIA

1. *Remodeling Her Husband*; her sister, Dorothy Gish
2. Joel McCrea
3. United Artists
4. 'Bee-stung' lips
5. *Peter Pan*
6. Owen Moore, Douglas Fairbanks, Buddy Rogers
7. Victor Sjöström
8. A. Sweden
   B. America
   C. Poland
   D. Canada
9. *Love*
10. *Son of the Sheik*
11. A. Crossed eyes
    B. A dour, deadpan face
    C. Round, horn-rimmed glasses
    D. His "Tramp" character and his little mustache
12. Mack Sennett
13. *Intolerance* (1916); it was re-released in 1919 as two separate features titled *The Fall of Babylon* and *The Mother and the Law*
14. *The Jazz Singer*, 1927; Warner Brothers

QUIZ #25
THE MAN WITH THE GOLDEN ARMS: OSCAR TRIVIA

1. Academy of Motion Picture Arts and Sciences
2. A. Bette Davis, nominated for *All About Eve*; Anne Baxter, nominated for *All About Eve*; Gloria Swanson, nominated for *Sunset Boulevard*; Eleanor Parker, nominated for *Caged*

B. *Born Yesterday*
C. Erich von Stroheim, nominated for *Sunset Boulevard*
D. *Samson and Delilah* (color); *All About Eve* (b&w)
E. José Ferrer for *Cyrano de Bergerac*
3. *My Fair Lady*, 1964
4. Gaynor won for three films: *Sunrise, Seventh Heaven*, and *Street Angel*
5. *Morning Glory* (1933); *Guess Who's Coming to Dinner* (1967); *A Lion in Winter* (1968)—a tie with Barbra Streisand, who won for *Funny Girl*; and *On Golden Pond* (1981)
6. Beery and March tied for the award
7. Greer Garson
8. Irene Dunne, nominated for *Theodora Goes Wild* and *The Awful Truth*
9. Shirley Booth, for *Come Back, Little Sheba*
10. It was his first and only Oscar, awarded for his performance in *On Golden Pond* (1981); he died several weeks after the Awards ceremony
11. *One Flew Over the Cuckoo's Nest* (1975)
12. *The Broadway Melody* (1929)
13. Both have won in best actress *and* best supporting actress categories
14. Loretta Young won
15. *The Greatest Show on Earth* (1952)

QUIZ #26
ROMANTIC INTERLUDES

1. *My Favorite Wife*, with Cary Grant and Randolph Scott who were housemates, on and off, for ten years
2. Nick Hilton; Michael Wilding; Mike Todd; Eddie Fisher; Richard Burton; Richard Burton; John Warner

3. A. Jennifer Jones
   B. Robert Walker
4. False. The couple never married
5. Irving Thalberg
6. The affections of Murray Head
7. A. Carole Lombard; Laurence Olivier
   B. Gable and Lombard married in 1939; Olivier and Leigh married the following year
8. Jim Dougherty; Joe DiMaggio; Arthur Miller
9. Frances Dee and Joel McCrea
10. Doc, Sleepy, Sneezy, Bashful, Grumpy, Happy, and Dopey
11. William Powell
12. David Rose; Vincente Minnelli; Sid Luft; Mark Herron; Mickey Deans
13. Mary Pickford and Douglas Fairbanks; Elizabeth Taylor and Richard Burton
14. A. Celeste Holm
    B. The character of Addie Ross was heard but never seen

QUIZ #27
SAINTS AND SINNERS
TRIVIA

The Sinners:
1. *Waterloo Bridge*
2. *Klute*
3. *American Gigolo*
4. *Anna Christie*
5. *Elmer Gantry*
6. *Midnight Cowboy*
7. *Butterfield 8*
8. *Taxi Driver*
9. *Divorce American Style*
10. *Irma La Douce*

The Saints:
1. Deborah Kerr
2. Ingrid Bergman
3. Lillian Gish
4. Julie Andrews
5. Jennifer Jones
6. Audrey Hepburn

7. Loretta Young; Celeste Holm
8. Rosalind Russell
9. Debbie Reynolds
10. Shirley MacLaine

QUIZ #28
WHAT'S IN A NAME?

1. A. Cecil Blount
   B. David Wark
   C. Louis Burt
   D. Goldenberg (the Edward was originally Emmanuel)
   E. Shakespeare *or* Surrey—Hart went by either or both
2. A. Betty Blythe
   B. Bessie Love
   C. Gloria Hope
   D. Leatrice Joy
   E. Arline Pretty
   F. Clara Kimball Young
   G. Blanche Sweet
   H. Ann Little
3. A. *Gaslight*
   B. *The Sterile Cuckoo*
   C. *X, Y and Zee*
   D. *Million Dollar Mermaid*
   E. *The Bachelor and the Bobby Soxer*
   F. *Damn Yankees*
   G. Two films, a decade apart, were given this title: *Christmas in Connecticut*, and *Indiscretion of an American Wife*

QUIZ #29
HOLLYWOOD DRINKERS
TRIVIA

PART 1
1. *The Country Girl*
2. *A Star Is Born*
3. *A Star Is Born*
4. *Under Capricorn*
5. *Harvey*
6. *Smash-Up: The Story of a Woman*; *I'll Cry Tomorrow*
7. *Days of Wine and Roses*
8. *Come Back, Little Sheba*

9. *The Thin Man*
10. *The Lost Weekend*

PART 2
1. *Hobson's Choice*
2. Joan Blondell
3. A. Lionel Barrymore
   B. Absinthe
   C. John Barrymore
4. She stood naked on the roof, baying at the moon.
5. He turns on the ceiling lamp where the bottle is hidden and sees the shadow on the wall.
6. To get a drink of brandy
7. "Liebestraum"

QUIZ #30
MOVIE MISCELLANY
TRIVIA

1. Alvy Singer
2. *The Missouri Breaks*
3. *Up the Sandbox*
4. Natalie Wood and Sal Mineo
5. John Williams
6. *Rich and Famous*, George Cukor; *Old Acquaintance*, Vincent Sherman
7. *Being There*; Jerzy Kozinsky
8. Jeanne Moreau
9. Henry II
10. James Coburn
11. *The Long Hot Summer*
12. *Lilies of the Field*
13. *A Hard Day's Night*, 1964
14. Ursula Andress
15. A. Jerome Robbins
    B. Stephen Sondheim
    C. Rita Moreno, for best supporting actress; George Chakiris, for best supporting actor
16. *Julia*
17. No one. No men appeared on-screen in *The Women.*
18. Vivien Leigh, who became too ill to finish filming. However, Leigh can be seen, though not recognized, in several on-location distance shots.

19. Angela Lansbury
20. He was a priest.
21. William Holden and Humphrey Bogart
22. "Joy powder," probably referring to cocaine
23. Lee Grant
24. A Paris hat
25. *One Touch of Venus*
26. A tuba
27. They call it Panama.
28. Homemade pies
29. *She Done Him Wrong*; *I'm No Angel*
30. He never took it off.
31. Claudette Colbert, Joel McCrea, Mary Astor, Rudy Vallee
32. Hattie McDaniel won it, becoming the first black performer to win an Oscar.
33. Howard Hughes
34. *Performance*
35. *Anna Christie*

PICTURE QUIZ #1
WHO'S PLAYING WHO?

1. M; Susan Hayward as Lillian Roth in *I'll Cry Tomorrow*
2. R; Mario Lanza as Enrico Caruso in *The Great Caruso*
3. T; Jessica Lange as Frances Farmer in *Frances*
4. N; Jill Clayburgh as Carole Lombard in *Gable and Lombard*
5. A; Betty Hutton as Pearl White in *The Perils of Pauline*
6. P; Donald O'Connor as Buster Keaton in *The Buster Keaton Story*
7. J; Julie Andrews as Gertrude Lawrence in *Star!*
8. C; James Stewart as Glenn Miller in *The Glenn Miller Story*
9. Q; Kathryn Grayson as Grace Moore in *So This Is Love*
10. B; Larry Parks as Al Jolson in *The Jolson Story*
11. H; Diana Ross as Billie Holiday in *Lady Sings the Blues*
12. K; Grace Moore as Jenny Lind in *A Lady's Morals*
13. E; Carroll Baker as Jean Harlow in *Harlow*
14. F; Rod Steiger as W. C. Fields in *W. C. Fields and Me*
15. D; Faye Dunaway as Joan Crawford in *Mommie Dearest*
16. L; Mariel Hemingway as Dorothy Stratten in *Star 80*
17. G; Doris Day as Ruth Etting in *Love Me or Leave Me*
18. S; David Carradine as Woody Guthrie in *Bound for Glory*
19. O; Gary Busey as Buddy Holly in *The Buddy Holly Story*
20. I; Sissy Spacek as Loretta Lynn in *Coal Miner's Daughter*

PICTURE QUIZ #2
WHO SAID WHAT?

1. S		11. P
2. E		12. K
3. M		13. F
4. O		14. G
5. T		15. A
6. L		16. C
7. B		17. D
8. Q		18. R
9. I		19. J
10. N		20. H

PICTURE QUIZ #3
WHO FIGURED OUT WHODUNIT?

1. *The Mirror Crack'd*—Miss Marple played by Angela Lansbury
2. *Murder She Said*—Miss Marple played by Margaret Rutherford
3. *Death on the Nile*—Hercule Poirot played by Peter Ustinov
4. *The Thin Man Goes Home*—Nick Charles played by William Powell
5. *A Shot in the Dark*—Inspector Clouseau played by Peter Sellers
6. *Meet Nero Wolfe*—Nero Wolfe played by Edward Arnold (also shown, Rita Hayworth and John Qualen)
7. *Murder on the Orient Express*—Hercule Poirot played by Albert Finney
8. *The Falcon Takes Over*—The Falcon played by George Sanders (also shown, Helen Gilbert)
9. *Bulldog Drummond Strikes Back* (1934)—Bulldog Drummond played by Ronald Colman (also shown, Loretta Young)
10. *The Long Goodbye*—Philip Marlowe played by Elliott Gould
11. *Dead Men Don't Wear Plaid*—Rigby Reardon played by Steve Martin (also shown, Rachel Ward)
12. *Chinatown*—J. J. Gittes played by Jack Nicholson (also shown, Diane Ladd)
13. *The Cheap Detective*—Lou Peckinpaugh played by Peter Falk
14. *The Alphabet Murders*—Hercule Poirot played by Tony Randall (also shown, Robert Morley)
15. *Lady in the Lake*—Philip Marlowe played by Robert Montgomery
16. *Murder My Sweet*—Philip Marlowe played by Dick Powell
17. *Shanghai Chest*—Charlie Chan played by Roland Winters
18. *My Gun Is Quick*—Mike Hammer played by Robert Bray (also shown, Jan Chaney)
19. *Kiss Me Deadly*—Mike Hammer played by Ralph Meeker
20. *Murder by Death*—Jessica Marbles (a parody of Miss Marple) played by Elsa Lanchester

PICTURE QUIZ #4
TOOTSIE AND HER (HIS?) KIND

1. Rod Steiger in *No Way to Treat a Lady*
2. Dennis O'Keefe in *Sailors on Leave*
3. Bing Crosby in *High Time*
4. Anne Heywood in *I Want What I Want*
5. Dick Shawn (shown with Sergio Fantoni) in *What Did You Do in the War, Daddy?*
6. Jerry Lewis in *The Ladies' Man*
7. Joanne Woodward in *A New Kind of Love*
8. Katharine Hepburn in *Sylvia Scarlett*
9. James Coburn in *The Last of Sheila*
10. Boris Karloff in *The Girl From UNCLE*
11. Raquel Welch in *Myra Breckinridge*
12. Julie Andrews in *Victor/Victoria*
13. Alec Guinness in *The Comedians*
14. Michael Palin in *Monty Python's The Meaning of Life*
15. Jeff Bridges in *Thunderbolt and Lightfoot*
16. Lou Costello in *Buck Privates Come Home*
17. Louise Brooks in *Beggars of Life*
18. George Sanders in *The Kremlin Letters*
19. Paul Lynde in *The Glass Bottom Boat*
20. Marion Davies in *Beverley of Graustark*

PICTURE QUIZ #5
ANY RESEMBLANCE...IS PURELY COINCIDENTAL

1. D	13. L
2. K	14. X
3. H	15. U
4. V	16. C
5. M	17. J
6. I	18. N
7. Q	19. G
8. T	20. W
9. O	21. S
10. E	22. B
11. R	23. P
12. A	24. F

PICTURE QUIZ #6
A ROSE BY ANY OTHER NAME...?

1. S	11. A
2. T	12. L
3. F	13. Q
4. J	14. D
5. E	15. R
6. O	16. N
7. C	17. B
8. P	18. I
9. M	19. K
10. H	20. G

PICTURE QUIZ #7
I COULD WRITE A BOOK...

1. *Devotion*; William Makepeace Thackeray and Charlotte Brontë
2. *Hans Christian Andersen*; Hans Christian Andersen
3. *Jack London*; Jack London
4. *Gaily, Gaily*; Ben Hecht
5. *Beloved Infidel*; F. Scott Fitzgerald
6. *The Life of Emile Zola*; Emile Zola
7. *The Razor's Edge*; W. Somerset Maugham
8. *Madame Bovary*; Gustave Flaubert
9. *Heart Beat*; Jack Kerouac
10. *Star!*; Noel Coward
11. *The Wonderful World of the Brothers Grimm*;

Wilhelm and Jacob Grimm
12. *The Adventures of Mark Twain*; Mark Twain
13. *The Loves of Edgar Allan Poe*; Edgar Allan Poe
14. *The Canterbury Tales*; Geoffrey Chaucer
15. *Lady Caroline Lamb*; George Gordon, Lord Byron
16. *The Bride of Frankenstein*; Mary Shelley
17. *Agatha*; Agatha Christie
18. *Julia*; Lillian Hellman and Dashiell Hammett
19. *Reds*; Eugene O'Neill
20. *Cross Creek*; Marjorie Kinnan Rawlings

PICTURE QUIZ #8
DIRECTORS TURNED ACTORS

1. Otto Preminger
2. Gregory Ratoff
3. Erich von Stroheim
4. Victor Sjöström
5. François Truffaut
6. Rainer Werner Fassbinder
7. William Castle
8. John Huston
9. Bryan Forbes
10. Sydney Pollack
11. Nicholas Ray
12. Cecil B. de Mille
13. Fritz Lang
14. Roman Polanski
15. Peter Bogdanovich
16. Bob Fosse
17. Vittorio de Sica
18. Jules Dassin
19. John Cromwell
20. Don Siegel

PICTURE QUIZ #9
ACTORS TURNED DIRECTORS

1. Dick Powell
2. Don Taylor
3. Charlton Heston
4. Jeanne Moreau
5. John Wayne
6. Gower Champion
7. Ida Lupino
8. Burgess Meredith
9. Charles Laughton

10. Marlon Brando
11. Gene Kelly
12. Jack Lemmon
13. Elaine May
14. Burt Lancaster
15. Karl Malden
16. Albert Finney
17. Peter Lorre
18. Kirk Douglas
19. Warren Beatty
20. Richard Attenborough

PICTURE QUIZ #10
MAKE IT AGAIN, SAM

1. *The Great Gatsby* (1926); Warner Baxter, Lois Wilson. *The Great Gatsby* (1949); Alan Ladd, Betty Field
2. *Viktor und Viktoria* (1933); Renate Müller, Herman Thimig. *First a Girl* (1935); Jessie Matthews, Sonnie Hale
3. *The Jazz Singer* (1927); Al Jolson. *The Jazz Singer* (1953); Danny Thomas
4. *The Blue Lagoon* (1949); Jean Simmons, Donald Houston
5. *The Big Sleep* (1946); Sonia Darrin, Humphrey Bogart
6. *The Champ* (1931); Wallace Beery, Jackie Cooper. *The Clown* (1952); Red Skelton, Tim Considine
7. *The Falcon Takes Over* (1942); Lynn Bari. *Murder My Sweet* (1944); Claire Trevor
8. *Little Miss Marker* (1934); Dorothy Dell, Shirley Temple, Adolphe Menjou. *Sorrowful Jones* (1948); Lucille Ball, Mary Jane Saunders, Bob Hope
9. *Hurricane* (1937); Dorothy Lamour, Jon Hall
10. *The Lady Vanishes* (1938); Margaret Lockwood, Michael Redgrave
11. *Old Acquaintance* (1943); Bette Davis, Miriam Hopkins

12. *Four Daughters* (1938); Priscilla Lane, John Garfield
13. *The Thirty-Nine Steps* (1935); Madeleine Carroll, Robert Donat
14. *Ossessione* (1942); Clara Calamai. *The Postman Always Rings Twice* (1946); Lana Turner

PICTURE QUIZ #11
THE SINGERS AND THE SONGS

1. O	11. N
2. R	12. E
3. L	13. J
4. K	14. C
5. F	15. B
6. M	16. T
7. Q	17. S
8. H	18. G
9. D	19. P
10. A	20. I

PICTURE QUIZ #12
THE WAY TO THE OVAL OFFICE...

1. Walter Huston played Abraham Lincoln in *Abraham Lincoln*
2. Dan O'Herlihy played Franklin Delano Roosevelt in *MacArthur*
3. Stanley Hall played Abraham Lincoln in *Prince of Players*
4. Brian Keith played Teddy Roosevelt in *The Wind and the Lion*
5. Alexander Knox played Woodrow Wilson in *Wilson*
6. Henry Fonda played Abraham Lincoln in *Young Mr. Lincoln*
7. Ralph Bellamy played Franklin D. Roosevelt in *Sunrise at Campobello*
8. Raymond Massey played Abraham Lincoln in *Abe Lincoln in Illinois*
9. Frank Forsyth played Woodrow Wilson in *Oh! What a Lovely War*
10. Henry Morgan played Ulysses S. Grant in *How the West Was Won*

11. Burgess Meredith played James Madison in *Magnificent Doll*
12. Hugh Southern played Andrew Jackson in *The Buccaneer* (1938)
13. Charlton Heston played Andrew Jackson in *The Buccaneer* (1958)
14. Charles Edward Bull played Abraham Lincoln in *The Iron Horse*

PICTURE QUIZ #13
TARZAN'S IDENTITY CRISIS

1. I   10. G
2. Q   11. C
3. A   12. J
4. N   13. F
5. M   14. L
6. E   15. D
7. P   16. O
8. B   17. H
9. K

PICTURE QUIZ #14
MONSTERS OF THE MOVIES

1. G   11. D
2. K   12. H
3. R   13. N
4. O   14. T
5. C   15. M
6. S   16. B
7. J   17. E
8. F   18. L
9. I   19. P
10. A   20. Q

PICTURE QUIZ #15
COWBOYS AND INDIANS

1. Q   11. A
2. N   12. H
3. T   13. C
4. K   14. J
5. M   15. F
6. E   16. L
7. I   17. R
8. S   18. B
9. O   19. G
10. P   20. D

INDEX

A

The Body Snatcher

The Gay Divorcee

G

The Great Waldo Pepper

Wuthering Heights